Strategic and Competitive Analysis

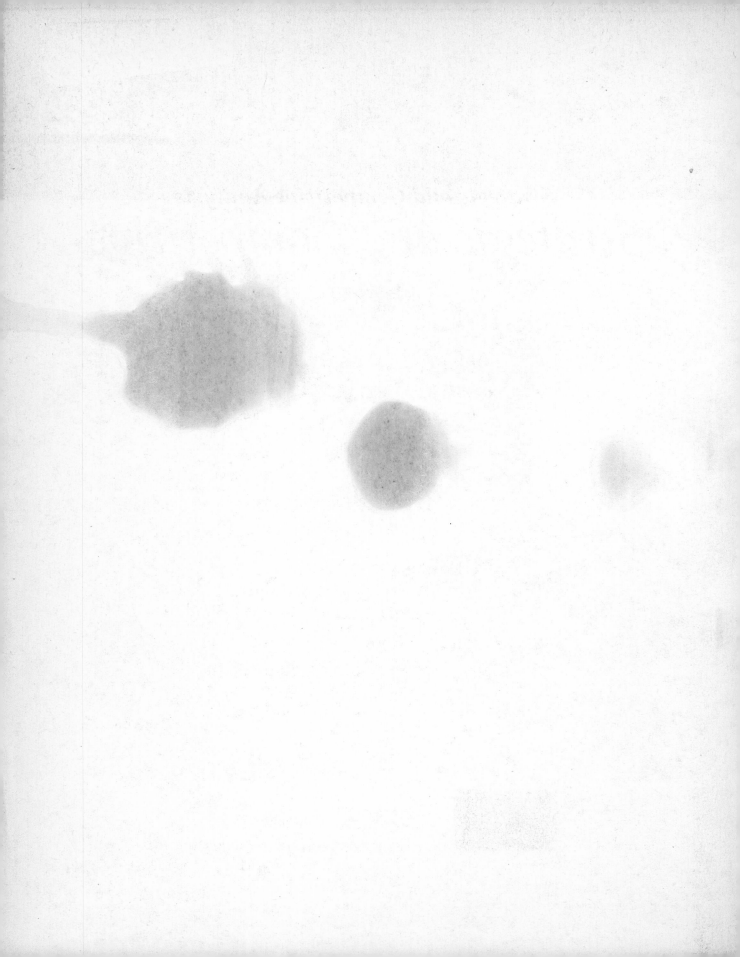

Strategic and Competitive Analysis

Methods and Techniques for Analyzing Business Competition

Craig S. Fleisher
University of Windsor

Babette E. Bensoussan
The MindShifts Group Pty. Ltd.

Prentice Hall

Upper Saddle River, New Jersey 07458

Library of Congress Cataloging-in-Publication Data

Fleisher, Craig S.
    Strategic and competitive analysis: methods and techniques for analyzing business
    competition/Craig S. Fleisher, Babette E. Bensoussan.
        p. cm.
    Includes bibliographical references and index.
    ISBN 0-13-088852-4
        1. Business intelligence. 2. Competition. 3. Strategic planning. I. Bensoussan, Babette
E. II. Title.

HD38.7.F58 2002
658.4'7–dc21   2002023104

Acquisitions Editor: David Shafer
Editor-in-Chief: Jeff Shelstad
Managing Editor (Editorial): Jennifer Glennon
Assistant Editor: Melanie Olsen
Editorial Assistant: Kevin Glynn
Media Project Manager: Michele Faranda
Marketing Manager: Shannon Moore
Marketing Assistant: Christine Genneken
Managing Editor (Production): John Roberts
Production Editor: Renata Butera
Production Assistant: Dianne Falcone
Permissions Coordinator: Suzanne Grappi
Associate Director, Manafacturing: Vincent Scelta
Production Manager: Arnold Vila
Manufacturing Buyer: Michelle Klein
Cover Design: Bruce Kenselaar
Cover Illustration/Photo: Photodisk, Inc.
Composition: Progressive Information Technologies
Full-Service Project Management: Progressive Publishing Alternatives
Printer/Binder: Victor Graphics

Credits and acknowledgments borrowed from other sources and reproduced,
with permission, in this textbook appear on appropriate page within text.

Pearson Education LTD.
Pearson Education Australia PTY, Limited
Pearson Education Singapore, Pte. Ltd.
Pearson Education North Asia Ltd
Pearson Education, Canada, Ltd
Pearson Educación de Mexico, S.A. de C.V.
Pearson Education–Japan
Pearson Eudcation Malaysia, Pte. Ltd

10 9 8 7 6 5 4 3 2
ISBN 0-13-088852-4

BRIEF CONTENTS

CONTENTS

Contents

PREFACE

Given the priority of competitiveness in modern companies, practitioners of competitive intelligence (CI) need to come to terms with what business and competitive analysis is and how it works. More importantly, they need to be able to convert the wealth of available data and information into a valuable form for decision making and action. Collected data must be converted into intelligence. This is accomplished through analysis.

Strategic and Competitive Analysis is a book about analysis. We know that using this term often makes the groups we advise and teach uncomfortable. People often conjure up images of the genius wearing glasses inputting oodles of data into arcane computer programs while simultaneously sifting through reams of paper containing differential equations and advanced statistics. This image does not meet the reality of today's effective analysts who know that analysis does not have to be complicated, complex, or convoluted to be valuable. As we try to remind our audiences, being a good analyst does not require ten years of postgraduate education, just some basic common sense, smarts, and a desire to learn. Nevertheless, analysis is one of the more difficult and critical roles a consultant, strategist, or intelligence specialist is called upon to perform. Although great strides have been made in recent years in terms of planning strategic and intelligence projects and collecting data, the same cannot be said for analysis.

The growth of competitive intelligence during the 1990s was fast paced. More and more conferences, workshops, and university courses in managing competitive intelligence than ever before were being offered around the world by individuals with strong CI research and practice backgrounds. Research in the field became more plentiful and mature as witnessed by the range of original articles appearing in places like *Competitive Intelligence Review, Competitive Intelligence Magazine, AGSI Journal*, and *Long Range Planning*. Popular books on the topic also increased in availability as an online search of Amazon.com or BarnesandNoble.com will quickly demonstrate.

Despite all of these advances and growth in CI, some areas of this burgeoning field have received more or less attention than others. The growth of digital communication and information technology, and especially the Internet, has led to much attention being given to processes and techniques of data collection. Planning competitive intelligence projects has also gotten a boost from the recent attention given more broadly to strategic planning. Despite these areas of popular interest, two areas that have received disproportionately less attention are analysis and its dissemination. In fact, survey research underlies the authors' contention that many practitioners have limited understanding of the breadth and depth of the challenge underlying these areas. It is our intention to begin remedying this situation by offering the first book devoted entirely to the management of competitive analysis.

This book comprehensively examines the wide spectrum of techniques involved in analyzing business and competitive data and information including strategic, competitive, customer, environmental, evolutionary, and temporal analysis models. It helps business analysts and decision makers to draw effective conclusions from limited data and to put together information that does not often fit together at first glance.

There are literally hundreds of strategic and competitive analysis techniques that we could have included in this book. It was not our intention to offer an exhaustive listing of the population of these techniques, assuming that it could be accurately done in the first place. Instead, we have extensively reviewed the literature in the field and considered survey research and our own experiences in determining those we view as potentially being the most applicable across a broad range of applications in the analysis process.

Although we have tried to include both classic and evolving techniques, we recognize that some techniques being used in consulting and industry may not be included here. Analysis is a process that requires both creativity and technical knowledge, and we have tried to provide a rigorous and sytematic contribution toward the latter with this book. We recognize and hope that analysts will creatively develop techniques not included in this book that will provide for better outcomes in their specific contexts.

The reader should also be alert to the fact that any listing of techniques is bound to run into a variety of problems of semantics and definitional confusion. Some of the techniques included in this book are known by multiple names. This may have occurred because the technique came to be associated with a particular originating organization (e.g., the BCG matrix), a particular company's use (e.g., the GE business screen), a particular author (e.g., Porter's Five Forces model), or has retained a generic nomenclature (e.g., environmental analysis). We also recognize that some of the techniques included in this book have seen modifications in use over the years or are derivatives of other closely related techniques. In all cases, we have tried to include and describe the most popularly known versions of the techniques as opposed to all of a technique's possible derivatives. We have also tried to alert the reader to where there is overlapping between techniques by referring the reader to the overlapping constructs elsewhere in the text.

We must also note to our readers that it was not our intention to "reinvent the wheel" when it comes to the analytical techniques. The techniques we have included herein all have a history. This book's techniques have been and are in use in real organizations; they do not exist just in theory.

Many of the included techniques were conceptualized by leading economists, financial and cost accountants, futurists, business professors, consultants, and other insightful practitioners or theoreticians. They often developed their ideas in an effort to solve pressing analytical problems that they faced. We are grateful to these individuals for enlightening our understanding of strategic and competitive analysis, and we make a sincere attempt to acknowledge the originators of these techniques in this book. Nevertheless, there are times when accurately making this acknowledgment can be difficult, such as when the technique (e.g., SWOT or TOWS) was quickly and widely accepted and now forms the commonly held body of knowledge underlying the domain.

Preface

How to Use This Book

To assist our readers, the majority of this book is self-contained, with the array of analytical techniques being supported by references for further reading for those individuals that want lengthier treatments. The book is organized into two main parts. Part I provides an introduction that establishes the context for the comprehensive selection of analytical tools. As such, it includes several chapters that describe and discuss the basic facts about analysis, and how analysis relates to strategy and competitive intelligence. The last chapter in Part I describes our unique FAROUT© method for understanding the application of the various tools. We strongly recommend that readers thoroughly review it before progressing into the remaining sections containing the analytical techniques themselves.

We have tried to make the book easy for the reader to use. The basic structure of the chapters containing the analytical techniques is common throughout Part II and contains the following format:

- **Short Description**   A brief definition of the purpose and objective of the analytical model to allow the analyst a quick and handy reference guide.
- **Background**   To place the model in the context of management, this section outlines a broad description of the history behind the development of the analytical technique.
- **Strategic Rationale and Implications**   Understanding the strategic thinking and implications associated with a particular analytical technique is important in order to evaluate the appropriateness of a particular tool. This section reviews the strategic issues inherent in each technique.
- **Strengths and Advantages**   Each model has its own strengths and advantages that need to be weighed in light of the purpose of the analysis. This section briefly reviews those strengths and advantages.
- **Weaknesses and Limitations**   Likewise, each model has its own inherent weaknesses and limitations. The weaknesses and limitations identified in this section need to be taken into account when performing the analysis.
- **Process for Applying the Technique**   Typically the most detailed section of each chapter, this is the "how to" of the analytical technique and identifies the necessary steps required to use this tool. Case studies, figures, and tables are also provided to guide the analyst through the strategic thinking required for each model.
- **FAROUT Summary**   Unique to this book, the FAROUT Summary allows analysts, at a quick glance, to identify the ease of use, practicality, and usefulness of each model.
- **Related Tools and Techniques**   Each model of analysis is related to or supported by several other techniques that may aid or enhance the analyst's task. This section provides a useful guide of related tools and techniques that support the objective and purpose of each analytical model.
- **References**   For those analysts wanting to delve further into a particular technique, references for additional readings are provided at the end of each chapter.

Readers will benefit themselves by becoming comfortable with this template. We did not design the book for the reader to complete in one sitting. Instead, we have designed it in order that it may be frequently used as a handy comparison and reference source. In this respect, it can be applied in a "just in time" fashion so as to proactively or concurrently meet analytical needs as they arise in the larger consulting, strategy, and CI processes.

The book features conceptual ideas about strategic and competitive analysis, along with a strong bias toward practical application. Among the unique aspects of this book that readers should find valuable are these:

- It provides in one easy location two dozen of the most common and popular models of analysis used in business. Normally, executives and students would have to go to multiple sources to locate each model. Here, for the first time, the most commonly used models are defined and explained in *one* book.
- Every model is also uniquely evaluated using FAROUT—an evaluation process for identifying the ease of use, practicality, and usefulness of each model. This is the first time that FAROUT will be introduced to the market. FAROUT allows analysts or decision makers to understand the strengths and weaknesses of the techniques.
- An easy-to-use, consistent format (i.e., template) is utilized to provide the reader with a faster understanding of how to apply the techniques.
- The book covers both the so-called classic strategy techniques (such as value chain analysis) along with some of the newer popular techniques (such as functional capability and resource analysis).
- It provides external techniques addressing the environments and industry that the organization competes in, along with the techniques for focusing internally on the organization.
- The book provides references to more comprehensive treatments of the techniques for those who want to investigate them in greater depth.

ACKNOWLEDGMENTS

Craig Fleisher wants to express his gratitude and thanks to several friends and colleagues without whose help this book could not have been written. In particular, special thanks go out to my very capable research assistants Jessica Smith at the University of Sydney, and Stuart Rutledge at Wilfrid Laurier University (WLU) who undertook the tasks of gathering background materials and assisted in compilation. My long-time research assistant and Laurier MBA grad Victor Knip deserves a huge thanks for his sustained helpfulness in uncovering and organizing the materials. Many classes of excellent MBA students in my various CI courses have offered me a wonderful sounding board for discussing many of the book's ideas, as has Dr. David L. Blenkhorn who taught CI courses at WLU with me. Additionally, several valuable workshops and conferences held under the auspices of the Society of Competitive Intelligence Professionals (SCIP) have also allowed Babette and me opportunities to hone these ideas. Also, my mentors in strategy through the decades such as Boston Consulting Group (BCG) founder Bruce Henderson, and former or present University of Pittsburgh professors John Prescott, Barry Mitnick, John Grant, Donna

Barry Mitnick, John Grant, Donna Wood, and John Camillus were so helpful. I'd also like to express my deep appreciation to my co-author, Babette Bensoussan, who has been a joy to work with and whose special experience, knowledge and talents in the CI field I keenly appreciated throughout this collaboration. This book is dedicated to my immediate family: my wife, Angela, and my children, Zachary, Austin, and Kieren. They have contributed love, patience, support, and understanding. Thanks again!

Babette Bensoussan notes that the path to this book was long and arduous but as with everything in life, you do it all with a little help from wonderful friends. Every person who knew about my efforts for this book added a dimension and fully supported me in my endeavors but there are several who stand out: my co-author Dr. Craig Fleisher who shared my vision and *really* made it happen; Dr. Chris Hall, for introducing me, many years ago, to the field of competitive intelligence. Diane Santucci who kept me sane in the office; Cyndi Allgaier who kept selling the book idea to colleagues; and of course the most important one—Garry Johnston—my husband and best friend. I dedicate this book to you.

The authors would also like to thank the following reviewers: Mary Coulter, Southwest Missouri State University; dt Ogilvie, Rutgers University; Helen Rothberg, Marist College; Conor Vibert, Acadia University; John Prescott, University of Pittsburgh; and Ruth Stanat, President and CEO of SIS International Research.

Without a doubt, a book like this does not come about without significant contributions from our colleagues at Prentice Hall. While many have worked to pull this book together we would like to thank in particular David Shafer, Renata Butera, and Donna King for all thier support and efforts. We could not have done in without your guidance.

ABOUT THE AUTHORS

Authors Craig S. Fleisher and Babette E. Bensoussan are uniquely placed as experts in the field of strategic and competitive analysis. They have extensive corporate consulting, research, and teaching experience in strategy and competitive intelligence and have both published and spoken internationally. Their collaboration also brings to this book a healthy balance of both theory and application.

Craig S. Fleisher is Odette Research Chair and Professor of Business (Strategy and Entrepreneurship), Odette School of Business, University of Windsor, Ontario, Canada. A member of the *Canadian Who's Who and Who's Who in Canadian Business*, he has also held positions on the faculties of the University of Pittsburgh (United States), Sydney (Australia), and Calgary and Wilfrid Laurier Universities (Canada). Elected as Canada's first Fellow of the Society of Competitive Intelligence Professionals (SCIP), Craig is an active author and researcher who has written 5 books and over 100 articles, has founded and/or served on the board of regional SCIP chapters, has facilitated workshops or guest lectured on CI around the globe, and serves on the editorial board of the *Competitive Intelligence Review*.

Babette E. Bensoussan is Director the MindShifts Group Pty. Ltd., a Sydney, Australia–based organization specializing in strategic planning, competitive intelligence, and strategic marketing projects in the Asia Pacific region. For over 10 years, she has undertaken major studies and consulted to Australian and Global Fortune 500 companies in strategic business and marketing planning, competitive intelligence, and strategic analysis in such industries and markets as aerospace, information technology, waste services, pharmaceuticals, utilities, mining, and manufacturing operations—to just name a few. Babette is Vice President of the Society of Competitive Intelligence Professionals in Australia (SCIP Aust), is a member of the NSW Board of Adult and Community Education, a member of the *Competitive Intelligence Review* editorial board, and was the first international recipient of the SCIP Fellows Award in 1996.

Analysis and Its Relationship to Strategy and Competitive Intelligence

Chapter

1

The Strategy and CI Process

THE STRATEGY PROCESS

Like a number of management terms, strategy is an overused word that means different things to different people. Even distinguished management scholars and senior executives can be hard pressed to agree on a clear definition. The main reason for their struggle is that strategy is a dynamic process. Times change, technology changes, markets change, and rules of competition and competitors change. Consequently, strategy can never stay the same.

Some basic tenets in strategy have, however, withstood the test of time. Winning strategies must be based on originality—being different from competitors in ways that customers value. For example, Michael Porter (1996) stated that a company can outperform rivals only if it can establish a difference of value to customers that can be preserved over time. The idea of these differences has been defined by economists to mean competencies, and, in strategy terms, *distinctive* competencies. The pursuit of distinctive competencies, defined as those resources and capabilities owned by the organization, which are unmatched by competitors and explain the origin of the economic value generated by a firm, has engaged executives' interest for decades.

A competitive advantage is the distinct way the organization is positioned in the market for it to obtain an advantage over competitors. This advantage is evidenced by the organization's ability to generate and maintain sustained levels of profitability above the industry average. Organizations that identify opportunities to create conditions of disequilibrium can legitimately allow the firm to claim economic rents beyond those resulting from perfect competition, and then to sustain and protect those conditions as long as possible. Sustainability of a competitive advantage refers to the organization's ability to maintain the economic value generated by the distinctive competencies of an organization, from either imitation or substitution by competitors.

The process that is primarily associated with helping an organization to attain competitive advantage is strategic planning. The *strategic planning process* is defined here as a disciplined and well-defined effort aimed at the complete specification of an organization's strategy and the assignment of responsibilities for its execution. It is graphically portrayed in Figure 1-1.

Strategic planning is also part of a larger process that has demonstrated staying power. *Strategic management* is a way of conducting the organization that has as its

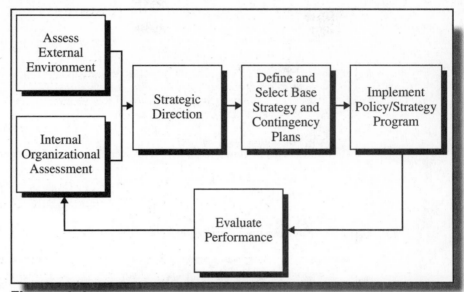

Figure 1-1
A Generic Strategic Planning Process

ultimate objective the development of values, managerial capabilities, organizational responsibilities, and administrative systems that link strategic and operational decision making, at all hierarchical levels, and across all lines of authority. An illustration of this concept is presented in Figure 1-2.

The double-headed arrows suggest that any given element can constrain or drive a strategy. Each element affects every other element. Each element is important individually, but strategy looks more critically at the interrelationships (also called fit or alignment) between the elements over space and time. The strategic management framework is supposed to help decision makers understand the elements that must "fit" together in order to make effective strategic decisions. See Table 1-1.

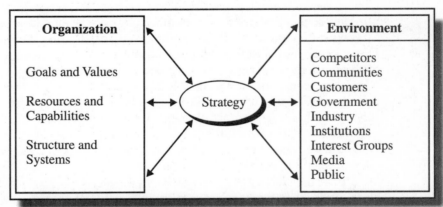

Figure 1-2
A Generic Strategic
Management
Framework

Table 1-1

Elements of a Strategic Decision

Strategic decisions are concerned with

1. The *scope* of the organization's activities: Where (geography, product/service markets, value chain, etc.) are we going to operate?
2. The matching of an organization's activities to its environment: This is usually captured by the idea of "fit" between these items.
3. The matching of the activities of an organization to its resource capability: This means doing within the organization's means.
4. Implications for change throughout the organization: These are likely to be complex in nature.
5. The allocation and reallocation of significant resources of an organization: This means optimizing resources.
6. The values, expectations, and goals of those influencing strategy: The decision makers.
7. The direction the organization will move in the long run: This can be over 10 years or even several decades.

Finding the means for achieving this fit or congruence between an organization and its (business or competitive) environment is a critical task of the strategic and competitive analyst. The analyst will always attempt to understand how to position the organization so that it can achieve the tightest fit. The process for generating this form of understanding underlies the competitive intelligence "process": Competitive intelligence should help the organization make more effective strategic decisions. Strategic decisions are far more rare, have larger implications for the ongoing competitiveness of the firm, impact more subsequent decisions, and are more difficult to reverse than decisions of a more operational or tactical nature.

The Need for Strategic Thinking

Many experts, including such luminaries as Henry Mintzberg and Tom Peters, have claimed that strategic planning, as it has been practiced, needs to be replaced with a capacity for strategic thinking. What is the difference between these concepts and why should decision makers care about strategic thinking?

The focus of most strategic plans is on process, an extension of the work done by early-twentieth-century management theorists to systematize the workplace. This process was helpful during the industrial period when industry and competitive conditions were slow changing and slow paced. In today's fast-changing, fast-paced, and competitive world, step-by-step, lock-step strategic planning impedes dynamic and innovative executive decision making and required marketplace action. While many organizations are developing their strategic plans, their competitors are out executing their strategies designed to win in the marketplace.

Mintzberg observes that planning defines and preserves categories. Managers have frequently been separated from their plans, often because some strategic planning expert, isolated from the company's everyday doings, has done most of the work for them. In this case, thinking gets disassociated from acting. This leads to less than successful performance over the long run. It also suggests the need for strategic

Table 1-2
Strategic Thinking

Strategic thinking:

- is a synthesis of intuition and creativity (Mintzberg, 1994).
- is a marriage of information and insight (that is, intelligence) that allows a clear understanding of how to reorder elements to maximize results within an emerging and often discontinuous context (Ohmae, 1982).
- offers an integrated perspective on the organization.
- concentrates on interrelationships as opposed to individual components.
- sees the environment as a "motion picture" as opposed to a "snapshot."
- responds to competition, the environment, and stakeholders with a comprehensive set of initiatives.
- dissects situations into constituent parts and reassembles them into patterns based on their significance and relationship to desired outcomes.
- consists of pragmatic dreaming—combining left- (i.e., linear, logical, rational) and right-brain (i.e., holistic, spatial, synthesizing, timeless) thinking "patterns."

thinking by management. What, then, is strategic thinking? Table 1-2 provides a useful overview.

Strategic thinking is necessary today because our organizations compete in an increasingly global, postindustrial, knowledge- and information-based competitive environment as opposed to the slower paced, domestic, industrial competitive environment of only a few decades ago. The hierarchical, linear models that dominated management thinking, and in some cases still do, have given way to newer, more flexible, perpetually self-reorganizing, network-based arrangements. No senior executive can reasonably be expected to know the entire competitive terrain well enough to correctly strategize in the same way as the great industrial and military leaders of the past. This pressing need for strategic thinking is why organizations need to improve and enhance their competitive intelligence.

THE CI PROCESS

While strategy and planning can tell an organization in which direction to head and where the journey should end, intelligence identifies and illuminates the storms on the horizon and allows the pilot to benefit from the best airways. Making the right choice hinges upon the quality of the information available. Intelligence often spells the difference between success and failure.

Competitive intelligence (CI) is often viewed as a relatively new discipline, coming into prominence about 1980. It grew out of developments in economics, marketing, military theory, and strategic management and continues to evolve from these roots into a separate function within organizations. CI has enough conceptual development and practical, historical, and empirical support to stand on its own. Although there still remains some doubt as to whether competitive intelligence has achieved the status of a profession such as accounting, it is certainly progressing in that direction.

Intelligence may be defined as the valued-added product resulting from the collection, evaluation, analysis, integration, and interpretation of all available information that pertains to one or more aspects of an executive's needs, and that is immediately or potentially significant to decision making. This definition of intelligence serves three useful purposes:

1. it distinguishes intelligence from information (unevaluated material);
2. it captures the dynamic, cyclical nature of intelligence; and
3. it highlights the partnership between senior managers and intelligence staffers.

Intelligence is necessary to reduce uncertainty and risk in decision making. Often, the options available to an organization will depend upon how early problems are identified. Choosing the most appropriate option, in turn, depends upon knowing what are the likely consequences. Once a course of action is chosen, it becomes important to know what the effects of the decision have been so that any necessary midstream adjustments may be made.

CI encompasses the potential effects (i.e., threats and opportunities) created by *all* external elements of the business environment that impact on the current competitiveness and future competitive ability of an organization. It is a systematic process or cycle (see Figure 1-3) for collecting and analyzing information about competitors' activities, one's business environment and business trends to further one's own organizational goals. In summary, CI is an ethical and legal multistep process that ultimately can make an organization a dominant player or break it.

The driving purpose of performing competitive analysis is to better understand one's industry and competitors in order to make decisions and to develop a strategy that provides a competitive advantage that achieves continuing performance results superior to one's competitors. The analysis outputs produced should be actionable, meaning that they are future oriented, help decision makers to develop better competitive strategies, facilitate a better understanding than that of competitors, and identify current and future competitors, their plans, and strategies. The ultimate aim

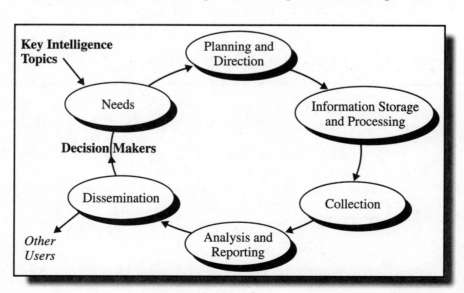

Figure 1-3
Intelligence Cycle

Part I   Analysis, Strategy, and Competitive Intelligence

of analysis is to produce better business *results*. Extracting these results from competitive analysis has become a more important facet of competitiveness in recent years because of the following important reasons.

Increased Level of Competition

First, globalization has increased the absolute level of competition present in most marketplaces. In the past, a competitor could sustain marketplace advantages by being in the right place at the right time. Geographic, physical, and sociopolitical barriers served to keep competitors at bay and out of many marketplaces. Most of these barriers are falling or have fallen in light of vast progress made in communication, trade policy, technology, and transportation. New competitors quickly appear when and where these marketplace barriers fall.

These new competitors may compete very differently from existing competitors. They learned in different contexts and often faced differing customer demands, and so now utilize unique resources and understand competition based on their unique contexts and experiences. No longer can organizations expect competitors to compete by outmoded rules or means of competing. Sometimes, the form of competition may not even appear logical, insightful, or even ethical, yet still remain legal. Because of this new global competition, the need to thoroughly understand competitors and business contexts grows in importance.

The Global Economy Is a Knowledge Economy

Second, the global economy is increasingly being characterized as a knowledge economy. A paradigm shift (whereby a large proportion of individuals *have* changed their way of seeing the world and now see it from a new shared perspective) has occurred as we move farther away from the industrial economy paradigm that dominated most of the last two centuries. As opposed to tangible things, services and related intangibles now constitute the largest part of GDP in most of the leading economies, and services are more knowledge-based than material-based.

Companies amass data and information, but they don't generally recognize that knowledge is not the same thing as information. Because of improvements in communication channels, information is available in quantities heretofore unseen. Information has become increasingly meaningless. It is a product in what economists call a "state of oversupply" in most developed economies, and this is also becoming true in the lesser-developed economies. Sustaining a competitive advantage requires companies to uniquely apply data and information, to create order out of chaos and complexity, and to leverage and transfer knowledge while striving towards acquiring expertise.

Knowledge is a capacity to act and it is mostly tacit—that is, individuals typically know more than they can tell about it. The conversion of knowledge to intelligence and action, a critical task underlying competitive intelligence processes, requires competence. Competence embraces such things as experience, factual understanding about industry and organizational conditions, decision-making and managerial skills, human networks, and insightful value judgments. Competence is developed through making mistakes, practice, reflection, repetition, and training. More than ever before, the knowledge economy means that organizations will need to develop further their resources, abilities, competence, and ultimately expertise if they intend to sustain a competitive advantage.

Increased Imitation

Third, the new economy is characterized by increasing imitability, whereby corporations have a greater ability than ever to quickly replicate most facets of a competitor's new product or service offering. Fending off imitators is increasingly difficult because of market complexity and the subsequent need to involve other organizations in alliances, multipoint collaborations with competitors, expanding social and physical networks, spin-offs, and ever-changing outsourcing and staffing arrangements between organizations. It is easy for a competitor to manufacture around a new offering because so much information is required to provide public protection for a product or service through legally recognized vehicles such as copyrights, patents, and trademarks. Finding this information has also gotten easier in an age where governments and international agencies must share this information with one another in order to establish the legal viability of a new offering. Some companies succeed by being "quick seconds" into the marketplace and stressing their competitive abilities at providing an improved product or service on the heels of the originator.

Increased Complexity and Speed

Fourth, there is increasing complexity and speed. Underlying the changing marketplace is communication and information technology that allows for the transfer of data at rates faster than ever before. However, human ability to process data remains essentially stable. Computations can be made in most offices in sizes and rates that a decade ago could only have been achieved using supercomputers. Whereas years ago a company could establish a formidable lead of several years for product or service introductions, today a company's time at the top market position has shrunk to a never-before-seen short-term duration. The cycle time underlying new product or service introductions is shorter, and companies must continue shrinking it while at the same time increasing the number of introductions they make in order to stay ahead of competitors.

Intelligence and analysis must be user driven to be of enduring value. By user driven, we mean that the process must be first focused on identifying and understanding the user's decision or policy-making needs. Refer to Figure 1-4. This is central to knowing your customer. However, this is not always an easy task, as users may not be able to accurately express their own needs or even know or understand clearly what it is they really need. Because of this difficulty, it is critical that the competitive analyst establishes and sustains an ongoing dialogue with key organizational policy makers.

In order for CI to retain credibility in the eyes of an organization's senior decision makers, analysis must be closely tied into the strategic and operational needs of the organization. This occurs most frequently when line managers are involved in the process. Most time-constrained senior decision makers do not want more data, facts,

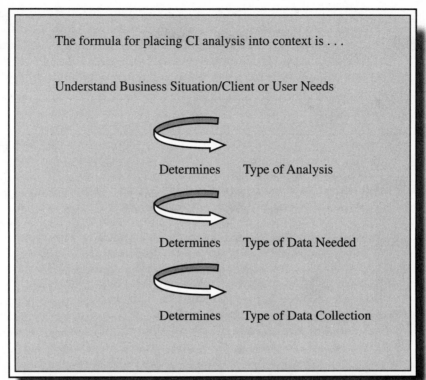

The formula for placing CI analysis into context is . . .

Understand Business Situation/Client or User Needs

Determines   Type of Analysis

Determines   Type of Data Needed

Determines   Type of Data Collection

Figure 1-4
Where Does
Analysis Fit into the
CI Process?

and information, especially if these are unfiltered and unanalyzed. Instead, they need timely flows of accurate and complete analyses to assist them in formulating and guiding the implementation of strategy.

Herring (1996, pp. 70–73) suggests there are five basic types of intelligence analysis:

1. Preventing surprises to the organization by providing *early warning*.
2. Supporting the *decision-making* process.
3. *Competitor* assessment and monitoring.
4. Intelligence assessments for *planning and strategy* development.
5. Comprising a key part of *collection and reporting*.

During the last few years we have witnessed a vast increase in the speed, capacity, and comprehensiveness of intelligence analysis because of advanced modeling, computational, display, and interaction tools. *Speed* has increased by administrative gains such as wider acceptance of CI in companies, better training of analysts, and by new computer-based analytical tools, databases, and communication methods. *Capacity* has improved because more participants from diverse locations can be involved in CI; consequently, the number of analysts, tools, or data sources that can be linked has increased. *Comprehensiveness* has improved because we have better ability to integrate a broader range of perspectives or viewpoints on the input data.

Good competitive and strategic intelligence requires effective analysis. Successful business and competitive analysis requires in-depth understanding of environments, industries, and organizations. This comes from, among other things, experience, solid data and information, the proper choice and utilization of analytical techniques, and organizationally institutionalized models of competition and how to compete.

REFERENCES

Herring, J. (1996). "Creating the intelligence system that produces analytical intelligence." In B. Gilad & J. Herring (Eds.), *The art and science of business intelligence analysis* (pp. 53–81). Greenwich, CT: JAI Press.

Mintzberg, H. (1994). *The rise and fall of strategic planning.* New York, NY: Free Press.

Ohmae, K. (1982). *The mind of the strategist—The art of Japanese business.* New York: McGraw-Hill.

Porter, M. (1996). "What is strategy?" *Harvard Business Review*, November–December. Vol. 96, Issue 6, pp. 61–78.

Chapter

2

Analysis and Its Pitfalls

ANALYSIS

Today's global competitive climate is *faster paced* than any other in recorded history. Companies are constantly repositioning themselves to stay ahead of or to make up ground on their competition. Companies must now have better tools of strategic and competitive analysis at their disposal. *Strategic and Competitive Analysis* intends to help analysts, strategists, managers, and decision makers to effectively and efficiently make sense of the environment and of their organizations' evolving and dynamic position within it. This is the primary objective underlying the process of managing strategic and competitive analysis.

Since the origination of the principles of scientific management in the early 1900s, few management scholars or experienced practitioners have recommended the making of arbitrary decisions. Instead, business decision makers have been encouraged to make decisions supported by a healthy dose of systematic study and reflection. As time passes, a slew of management fads, fashions, or formulas become outmoded and are replaced by new ones, but the underlying message is often the same: Formal analysis—the systematic study of important managerial concerns—can help organizations make better decisions. This seemingly plausible hypothesis is supported by extensive literature in cognitive psychology that shows convincingly that unaided human judgment is frequently flawed. For example, research has demonstrated that people seem to be unduly influenced by recent or vivid events (i.e., known as the recency bias), consistently underestimate the role of chance, and are often guilty of overly optimistic thinking (i.e., the rose-colored glasses bias). The successful application of formal analytical techniques like the ones we describe in this book are an effective way to avoid or to minimize the deleterious impact of such problems.

In *Competitive Strategy*, Michael Porter asserted the need for sophisticated competitor analysis in the modern organization, and subsequently the "need for an organized mechanism—some sort of competitor intelligence system—to insure that the process is efficient" (Porter, 1980; p. 72). Most managers in the competitive environments faced by contemporary organizations recognize the need for more systematic analysis of their competition. However, recognizing there is a need for the capability, and organizing the systems, structures, and skills needed to exploit the capability are entirely different things. Indeed, research for many years has identified the enduring gap between what is viewed as being needed for decision making in organizations (i.e., expectations) and what is actually being delivered by organizational competitor analysis systems (i.e., performance) (Ghoshal & Westney, 1991; p. 19).

As identified previously, strategic management involves all aspects of a business and requires a knowledge and understanding of the environmental impacts on an organization to ensure that correct decisions are made. It is not just about looking at best fit but also of taking into account the needs of different stakeholders and diagnosing the factors required to formulate a good strategy.

So how do you formulate strategies and ensure they are the right ones? It is only through the careful collection, examination, and evaluation of the facts that appropriate strategic alternatives can be weighed in light of organizational resources and requirements.

In today's world of information overload, collection of data or information is not, in our opinion, the key issue. Instead, it is the examination and evaluation of the information through analysis that are key to defining appropriate strategies. This process requires skill, time, and effort. While most organizations gather some forms of competitive information, surprisingly few formally analyze it and integrate the results into their business strategy.

When we use the word *analysis* we mean the separation of the whole into its constituent parts to understand each part's value, kind, quantity, or quality. It is not just about reasoning from the universal or general to the particular nor is it about summarizing the information collected. It is about breaking down an issue into its parts. Today's strategic mindset says that every organization needs to have at least some professionals who are actively engaged in evaluating and examining each part.

Analysis is a multifaceted, multidisciplinary combination of scientific and non-scientific processes by which an individual interprets the data or information to provide meaningful insights. It is used to derive correlations, evaluate trends and patterns, identify performance gaps, and above all to identify and evaluate opportunities available to organizations. Analysis answers that critical "So what?" question about the gathered data and brings insight to bear directly on the decision maker's needs. (See Figure 2-1).

Effective analysis requires experience, good inputs, intuition and models, and, some would argue, even a dash of serendipity. It requires constantly varying combinations of art and science, common sense and informed models, and intuition and instruction. Effective analysis is a valuable resource that is not in as ample supply as some observers would think.

Figure 2-1
Generic Approach to Analysis

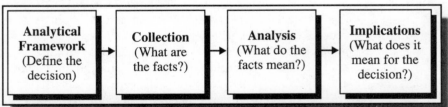

Part I   Analysis, Strategy, and Competitive Intelligence

The reason we do analysis is that, although there may be plenty of information around, the issues being analyzed are often quite complex and the overall reality of the situation may not be obvious at first glance.

The Scope and Focus of Analysis

In the field of business and competitive analysis, it is critical to have a clear understanding of the target or scope of the analysis effort. In our understanding of analytical scope, we would suggest that the following six categories would encompass the focus of the vast majority of analytical efforts.

1. *Decision Scope.* This is the level of the organization at which the analysis is intended to impact. Management decisions differ depending on what level they are made, who makes them, how long term are the effects, how frequently the decision is made, and how structured are the decisions. Decision scope is frequently classified as strategic, tactical, or operational.

    A. *Strategic* decision analysis is intended to impact decisions that are generally rare in the organization's life, have significant resource allocation impacts, set the precedents or tone for decisions further down the organizational ladder and have a potentially material effect on the organization's competitiveness within its marketplace. They are made by top managers and involve determining long-term organizational goals and objectives. Strategic decisions affect the business direction of an organization and help determine what markets to compete in. Because of the long-term affects, these types of decisions are infrequently made. Strategic decisions are generally unstructured.

    B. *Tactical* decision analysis is done to support decisions that are less pervasive than strategic ones. They involve formulating and implementing organization policies. Policy decisions have more lasting affects in the organization than operational decisions. Tactical decisions are usually made by mid-level managers. They often materially affect one function (e.g., marketing, accounting, human resource management, etc.), business unit, or product as opposed to the entire organization. Tactical decisions generally have lower resource implications than strategic decisions, are usually semistructured, and the procedure for making these decisions is not well defined.

    C. *Operational* decisional analysis is done to support the day-to-day decisions needed to operate the organization. These decisions affect the organization for short periods of time, perhaps for a few days or weeks. This type of decision is typically made by a lower-level manager. Operational decisions are distinct from tactical and strategic decisions in that they are made frequently. Operational decisions tend to be highly structured and there are well-defined procedures and mathematical formulas to help make these decisions.

2. *Geographic Scope.* Whereas in the past the key focus of analysis tended to be constrained within national or nation-state boundaries (e.g., the U.S. chemicals market), today's organizations increasingly compete in global environments. Contemporary

strategic and competitive analysis requires the analyst to consider various forms of geographical competition and organization including national, multinational, and global formats. Multipoint competition, in which a diversified company might compete with another company across a variety of different market sectors, is increasingly commonplace. This may mean that an analyst needs to consider how a business must prepare to simultaneously compete against dozens of other businesses. Companies compete in multiple markets and often in multiple countries, each of which has its own competitive rules, customers, and policy contexts. If a firm operates in markets across 15 different countries, there may be 15 separate sets of competitive contexts and rules to which it must conform.

3. *Environmental sectors.* Although we provide a chapter on macroenvironmental (STEEP) analysis (See Chapter 17), Montgomery and Weinberg (1998) suggest competitive intelligence systems should ideally focus on the following six environmental sectors: (a) competitive—this suggests the analyst should assess both current and prospective competitors; (b) technological—the analyst needs to consider current and emerging technologies, product and process innovations, and basic R&D conditions; (c) customer—this would include the firm's current customers, its competitor's customers (also known as noncustomers), and potential customers (i.e., those who are not currently purchasing products and services from the focal firm or its competitors but who may do so in the future); (d) economic—the analyst needs to assess issues such as GDP/GNP, inflation, the money market, and interest rates along with prices of product inputs, fiscal and monetary policy, and exchange rate volatility; (e) political and regulatory—this would include issues, institutions, and stakeholders that establish the "rules of the competitive game"; and (f) social—the analyst must assess demographics, wealth distributions, attitudes, and other cultural characteristics that shape the context within which competition occurs.

4. *Temporal.* This suggests that a key focus of the analysis should be in assessing how the chain of activities and events has evolved over time. In particular, the analyst would try and determine whether events of the past and present were correlated and what variables would retain positive associations. The analyst would also need to assess to what degree the variables and context of the past and present would potentially carry over into the future.

5. *Decision-Maker Position.* Intelligence analysts must always remain focused on the critical intelligence needs (CINs) of the internal clients or customers for whom they are providing the analysis. These individuals tend to be from among the following groups, each of which has different needs for the outputs the analysts provides: senior or top executives who make the lion's share of strategic choices for the firm over time, middle managers, functional area (e.g., marketing, accounting, human resource management, etc.) heads, supervisory, and front-line decision makers. The FAROUT system we describe in this book can assist the decision maker in thinking through how the analysis methodology chosen can best meet each of these decision maker's differing needs for analytical outputs.

6. *Product Technological Scope.* The analyst needs to consider what critical activities are involved in bringing products and services to the customer. This can include concepts such as the demand, supply, and or value chain (See Chapter 9), and also the

technological base of the process, product, or service in terms of new or emerging technological capacity.

The Importance of Good Data Inputs to Analysis

As a process, analysis depends upon inputs in the form of raw data. However, not just any data will lead to effective analysis. The data set collected in order to respond to the user's requirements needs to be assessed against several criteria before one can draw helpful conclusions. A key criterion is accuracy. Understanding accuracy means recognizing that not all data are of equal quality. Some data may be excellent, some marginal, some may be bad, and some might even be intended to deceive. Data sources must be identified and assessed in order to know whether input data are accurate and reliable. When all else is equal, the analyst prefers to receive accurate information from reliable sources. The well-known phrase of "garbage in, garbage out" applies well to data sources.

Sources often have different reasons for supplying data, and data collection can be used for many purposes. Knowing the source of an individual or group's data is important in establishing the fit of these data for analysis. For example, many data sets are derived from other data sources and they could all be inaccurate if an original set of data was flawed. Also, much data generated by a group over time may be tracked back to a single individual, whose methods may have been flawed from the outset.

Some data sources can be notorious for projecting biases onto data sets. For example, advocacy groups having policy agendas often skew the data they provide to policy makers to support their positions. Business competitors, through disinformation, outright fraud, or false confirmations, may also purposefully attempt to send out blurry, contradictory, or false signals as a means for confounding their competitors. Disinformation is incomplete or inaccurate data that is purposefully designed to mislead others. Fraud involves distributing erroneous or false information with the intent to mislead or exploit. A false confirmation occurs when a second source of data appears to but does not actually confirm data originating from a particular source.

Reliability is another important criterion for assessing data inputs. As with the process for assessing accuracy, the analyst must identify the data's originator in order to assess reliability.

It is important when conducting the analysis itself to carefully study the data inputs and outputs. One way of doing this is to follow the "AID" anagram:

Anomalies. Data that do not seem to fit well with the others or do not seem quite right typically warrant further inspection. Anomalous data often indicate problems with one's assumptions or that some unexpected phenomenon is occurring. These data are often the most powerful items at the analyst's disposal.

Indicators. It is always important to look for the most direct and specific (as opposed to secondary and indirect) indications of the phenomenon being sought. For example, if you are analyzing a high-tech business, it would be worthwhile to know whether a competitor has changed its policy relating to the formula underlying what percentage of revenues it devotes to basic research, the turnover of key skilled professional employees, whether it has been developing patents around particular processes or products, or whether it has recently built or sold research facilities.

Disaggregation. Often it can be difficult to find the proverbial needle in a competitor's haystack. Sometimes, as opposed to looking just for the needle, it is useful to take a step back and to look at the haystack itself. A review of the haystack can allow the analyst to subsequently cull away all data associated with matters in which the analyst is not interested. What is left after this culling process may provide the outlines of what information is really desired. For example, if you cannot determine what a competitor is spending on new Management Information Systems (MIS), you can examine its total financial picture, and then eliminate all expenditures for all non-MIS. What is left should set the bounds of its expenditures on MIS.

Effective analysis relies upon effective data collection, and vice versa. When data are incomplete or missing, as is almost always the case, the analyst must rely upon one of the following five basic types of problem solving (Belkine, 1996):

1. *Analogy.* This occurs when the analyst reasons from the evidence found in parallel cases. This approach is one that particularly demonstrates the "art" of analysis as opposed to its "disciplinary aspects." It is often most helpful when figures and formulas generated by interpolation do not provide the missing data.

2. *Deduction.* This most common form of analysis entails the ability to identify patterns from a reasonably complete set of data (i.e., from the general to the particular). The analyst can draw conclusions despite the absence of some facts or informational elements. The lower the proportion of available to missing data, the lower the probability that the conclusions will be valid. Deduction is particularly useful for forecasting techniques.

3. *Extrapolation.* Similar to interpolation, extrapolation is a forecasting process whereby data are extended beyond a series. One particularly popular form of extrapolative analysis is known as trend extrapolation, in which the analyst identifies and projects historical trends into the future. Extrapolation is used frequently in actuarial and demographic research (e.g., accident rates, birthrates, and mortality trends); however, it is vulnerable to events that "shock the system."

4. *Induction.* This is the ability to identify patterns from a limited set of data (i.e., general inferences made from particular instances). It is the reasoning process by which we pass from the perception of particular phenomena, such as events or things, to the knowledge of more general truths.

5. *Interpolation.* A way of providing the missing link in a set of data, interpolation happens when data are inserted into a series. It is similar to finding the missing letter in a crossword puzzle. A common competitive intelligence application of this discipline is when the analyst disaggregates financial data of a corporate entity in order to figure out the financial performance of a particular business unit (company).

There is no single best way to perform competitive analysis. The authors have met their share of individuals who have wanted to drink from the mythical "analysis spring." The mythical spring, more popularly known as intelligence or analysis software, does not exist and we strongly doubt that it ever will. Despite this, we do believe it is possible to improve one's expertise in several tasks, such as knowing the following: How to select and sort data and informational inputs (i.e., the "need to know" from the "nice to know" or "who cares about knowing" items); what analytical technique to apply to a particular need; and what must be understood in effectively informing organizational actions and decisions.

What does it take for an analyst to successfully perform analysis? There are several "competencies" that the analyst should demonstrate. One of the better summaries of these competencies comes from the Society of Competitive Intelligence Professionals (SCIP) who suggests the following:

- Recognize the interaction between the collection and analysis stages.
- Use creativity.
- Employ both deductive and inductive reasoning.
- Use alternative thinking.
- Understand the basic analytical models.
- Introduce exciting and attractive models to elicit the discovery notion of analysis rather than the dry, research approach.
- Know when and why to use the various analysis tools.
- Recognize the inevitable existence of gaps and blind spots.
- Know when to stop analyzing so as to avoid "analysis paralysis".

THE PITFALLS OF ANALYSIS

In spite of the presence of the broad range of analytical techniques we describe in this book, some organizations may still adopt poor strategies if their decision-making processes are vulnerable to any of the following common individual cognitive biases: escalating commitment, groupthink, illusion of control, prior hypothesis bias, reasoning by analogy, and representativeness.

Escalating Commitment. This is where individuals commit more and more resources to a project even when they receive evidence that it is failing. Rationality is often overcome in these cases by feelings of personal responsibility, an inability to admit one's error, or a failure to acknowledge changes in the assumptions that supported the initial decision.

Groupthink. This occurs when a group of decision makers (e.g., a senior management team) embark on a poorly determined course of action without thoroughly questioning the underlying assumptions of the decision. It is often based on an emotional, rather than an objective assessment of the appropriate course of action and is most prevalent in organizations with strong leadership and cultures. This bias partially explains why so many organizations make bad decisions, despite the fact that they have sophisticated CI systems.

Illusion of Control. This is an individual's tendency to overestimate her ability to control events. For example, someone who has had an ongoing string of picking winning lottery numbers may come to think that they are better "pickers" than they truly are. This often is the result of overconfidence, and senior executives have been shown to be particularly prone to this bias.

Prior Hypothesis Bias. Individuals who have strong beliefs about the relationships between variables tend to make decisions on the basis of these beliefs even when presented with analytical evidence that contradicts them. Additionally, these individuals often seek and use data only when it confirms their beliefs and ignore data that contradicts them. In strategic terms, this may happen when the top executive has a strong belief that the organization's extant strategy makes sense and continues to pursue it despite evidence that shows it is inappropriate.

Reasoning by Analogy. This is where individuals use simple analogies to make sense out of complex problems. Oversimplifying complex problems is dangerous and can lead an organization into bad decisions. This is one of the key cautions we make in applying the techniques contained in this book.

Representativeness. This is a bias that violates the statistical law of large numbers in that individuals often display a tendency to generalize from small samples (such as their experience) to explain a larger phenomenon or population.

Within the task of analysis, these biases show up commonly in one of four forms (Bernhardt, 1996; Katz & Vardi, 1991):

1. *Ambiguity.* This is the difficulty the analyst faces when confronted by overlapping variables that make definition difficult. This can happen when one is trying to surmise the reasons or motivators for a foreign competitor's new advertising program. Is this driven by a long-term strategy to build sales? Is it a tactical response to flagging sales? Could it be a test for a new marketing campaign? Or could it be an attempt to warn competitors that it is willing to fight their promotional forays?

2. *Contextual Evaluation.* A given object or event is perceived differently when viewed on different backgrounds. For example, think about how the analyst might respond differently to the advertising campaign scenario described under "Ambiguity" if she knew it was being conducted by automobile manufacturer Lexus or Kia?

3. *Parameter Validity.* Parameters provide points of reference for the analyst and often serve as a good starting framework from which the analysis will proceed. These parameters will be closely associated with their subjective and personal values, attitudes, opinions, and past experiences. This raises the point that the analyst must adopt a critical approach to analysis and generation of alternatives by being clear from the outset about the analytical setting in which data collection and analysis will take place.

4. *Tacit Knowledge.* This is the difficulty that individuals often have in explaining objectively the intuitive side of their opinions or recommendations. A good way to understand this is to think about how you would explain to your five year old how you know how to ride the bicycle you just gave her as a gift. This often has a negative influence on objectivity or teamwork.

The existence of cognitive biases and groupthink raises issues of how to bring critical intelligence to bear on organizational decisions so that they are realistic and based on the best inputs and analysis. To examine the use of formal analysis, it is important to understand the range of motives behind it. March and Feldman (1981) point out that people in organizations often tend to collect more information than is strictly necessary for decision making, partly to influence others and partly to be seen as rational. In other words, analysis is often used not just for objective decision making but also for political purposes.

Langley (1995) defined four broad categories of purpose behind analysis: (1) information, (2) communication, (3) direction and control, and (4) symbolism. Similar categories have emerged in other discussions in the literature.

1. *Information.* Decision makers often seek information to support their decisions as opposed to making decisions "in the dark" or on a "best guess" basis. The acquisition of additional relevant information can alleviate a decision maker's uncertainty. Information gathering may be proactive as people use analysis to help them reflect on an issue. At other times, it is reactive, whereby it is done to support one's preconceived ideas.

2. *Communication.* Individuals frequently initiate formal analysis when they are not confident or certain about matters they have been asked to respond to. In these situations, analysis is used as a means for making their views known or to persuade others that a particular decision can be viewed more reliably.

3. *Direction and Control.* Managers sometimes initiate analysis to solve problems or implement decisions. They may ask subordinates, a staff person, consultant, or task force to produce analytical reports, often by specific deadlines.

4. *Symbolism.* Formal analysis may symbolically convey rationality, concern, and willingness to act, even when, in reality the initiator of the analysis is either impotent or indifferent to the issue. Analysis can also be used to delay decisions, consume energy that needs to be redirected, or occupy otherwise idle people.

Thus, formal analysis would be less necessary if people could execute their decisions themselves and nobody had to convince anybody of anything. In fact, the more strategic decision making power is shared among people who cannot quite trust each other, the more formal analysis may become important. Langley (1995) does not imply that formal analysis is a purely political tool and should therefore be categorically and cynically ignored but rather focuses on its two roles in decision making. When used for gathering information, it may help determine and improve the substance of decisions directly, as most of the literature indicates. But it can also help bind individuals' decisions together to create organizational decisions through communication, direction and control, and symbolism. The second, political, role can be equally as important as the first. Formal analysis helps to improve decisions indirectly by ensuring that ideas are thoroughly debated and verified, and that errors in proposals are detected before implementation. This is particularly important in contexts in which different organization members may not necessarily have the same goals or the same information sources. In summary, nearly all well-done formal analysis has the potential to be useful.

WARNINGS IN PERFORMING ANALYSIS

Whether the application of analytical methods can achieve their potential usefulness depends on several factors. Based on our experience and understanding of the application of these techniques, there are several warnings to be heeded in performing formal analysis.

First, many organizations have utilized formal methods as a means of taking "superficial shortcuts" to management decision making. The methods we describe in this book are all based on empirical research and are supported by solid theory developed across a range of managerial disciplines. By presenting the methods individually and in a simplified fashion as we have here, we do not mean to suggest that their application can lead to "magic bullet" answers.

There is no one right analytical tool for every situation, or as the saying goes, "if one has only a hammer then everything will begin looking like nails." The depth and complexity of analysis is dependent upon the business situation and user's needs. It is the analyst's responsibility to determine the situation and critical intelligence needs (CINs). This may be difficult as the client may not always know or be able to adequately communicate their own needs. No method by itself will provide all the answers needed by decision makers intent on improving their competitiveness. Methods nearly always have to be used for specific purposes and in various combinations to obtain the optimal decision-making results.

Second, individuals often will become overly reliant on a small number of techniques. This is especially prevalent with inexperienced analysts. This can happen for several reasons, including generating positive results from the application of a particular technique, developing a level of comfort with using the technique, or having convenient data that supports the application of a particular technique.

Decision makers are cautioned to remain vigilant about a natural human tendency to revert back to the use of a limited number of tools. The FAROUT system is designed to help combat this tendency by requiring the analyst to consider the application of each technique every time it is required to perform analysis.

Third, some decision makers will become concerned that the application of these techniques by one's company and its competitors may lead to a "me-too" set of decisions, thus reducing the likelihood that good strategy leading to improved competitiveness will result. In other words, a competitor that knows you are commonly relying upon a particular technique can accurately anticipate your strategic moves. Here again, we strongly encourage analysts and decision makers to thoroughly think through why they apply certain combinations of techniques in any particular strategic decision making situation. In reality, the use of this book should help combat "me-too-ism" by sensitizing analysts and decision makers to the broad range of techniques available.

The other caution we offer is that the use of these techniques can compel analysts and decision makers to circumvent the quality or quantity of analysis necessary for formulating and implementing effective competitive strategy. For example, our experience suggests that it is far too easy to draw incorrect conclusions from incomplete or defective data with a number of these techniques. Because of this and related problems, these techniques should never be used to circumvent the strategic thinking necessary to gain a thorough understanding of a company's business and competitive environment today or in the future.

REFERENCES

Belkine, M. (1996). "Intelligence analysis as part of collection and reporting." In B. Gilad, J. Herring (Eds.), *The art and science of business intelligence analysis* (pp. 151–164 of Part B). Greenwich, CT: JAI Press.

Bernhardt, D. (1993). *Perfectly legal competitor intelligence: How to get it, use it and profit from it*. London: Financial Times/Pitman Publishing.

Feldman, M. S., & March, J. G. (1981). "Information in organizations as signal and symbol." *Administrative Science Quarterly*, (26), 171–186.

Ghoshal, S., & Westney, D. E. (1991). "Organizing competitor analysis systems." *Strategic Management Journal, 12*(1), 17–31.

Katz, Y., & Vardi, Y. (1991). "Strategies for data gathering and evaluation in the intelligence community." *International Journal of Intelligence and Counterintelligence, 5*(3), 313–328.

Langley, A. (1995). "Between 'paralysis by analysis' and 'extinction by instinct'." *Sloan Management Review, 36*(3), 63–76.

Montgomery, D. B., & Weinberg, C. B. (1998). "Toward strategic intelligence systems." *Marketing Management, 6*(4), 44–52.

Porter, M. (1980). *Competitive strategy*. New York: Free Press.

Chapter 3

The FAROUT System

Few people write about analysis, fewer discuss it, and even fewer still claim to be expert at it. Just compare the commercial availability and visibility of data analysis with data collection. Data collectors are seemingly found everywhere, collection methods are common and available to most data takers, and data collection agencies abound.

Why then has analysis gotten a bad rap? We think there are several reasons that explain why analysis is not among the most popular topic at strategy or competitive intelligence discussions:

1. Analysis is difficult for most people. People tend to take the path of least resistance when it comes to putting forth effort or expending energy. In today's supercharged digital world, it is far easier to collect a lot of data than it is to figure out what to do with them.
2. Few people have publicly recognized or established analysis expertise. Even those who do may not necessarily be able to teach or disseminate how to do it. Analysis skills can be developed over time as one grows in experience and knowledge, but some analysis expertise will require a degree of tacit skill or inherent creativity.
3. There are few frameworks for understanding how the analysis component can be managed as part of the strategy and competitive intelligence (CI) process. Few individuals can thoughtfully explain how analysis can be successfully managed according to the "three Es" of efficiency, effectiveness, and efficacy.

It is our view and the output of several large-scale CI surveys that data collection is managed far more successfully than is analysis. In our experience, we see several prevalent symptoms that suggest why analysis is not managed properly:

1. *Tool rut.* Like the man with a hammer who sees everything as a nail, people keep using the same tools over and over no matter the project. We describe this tendency to overuse the same tools as being in a "tool rut." This is counter to the principle that in addressing the complexity of this ever-changing world, the analyst needs to look at numerous models to provide value.

2. *B-school recipe.* Many individuals charged with doing analysis have completed MBA programs whose instructors have financial and management accounting backgrounds and can offer only standardized blueprints or "recipes" to follow. Competitive

analysis is as far different from accounting analysis, as strategy is from accounting. This may help explain why few accountants lead CI functions and vice versa.

3. *Ratio blinders.* Most businesspeople do analysis based on historical data and financial ratios. This can at best provide only comparison and tell the analyst the size of the gap (the *what*) between two organizations on a particular data point or data set. It does not help the analyst explain the reasons for *why* the gap exists or *how* to close it. It is akin to driving forward by using the rear-view mirror.

4. *Convenience shopping.* Individuals frequently do analysis on the basis of the data they happen to have, as opposed to the data they *should* have. Because the analyst has certain data at her disposal, she uses the analytical technique that suits the data rather than focusing the analysis on the user's question or the intelligence actually required. This is especially true when accountants are asked to do analysis and they provide outputs that reflect only financial manipulations.

Having recognized some of the reasons why analysis has been problematic in strategy and competitive intelligence undertakings, we would like to offer a system for considering how best to manage the analysis process.

A FAROUT SOLUTION TO MANAGING ANALYSIS

Over the years of doing and supervising strategic and competitive analysis, we realized that there was a limited number of key features common to all high-value analytical output. These features deal with both the content and process of the analysis, as opposed to any particular analytical method itself.

It is our intention in this chapter to provide an easy-to-use framework that will help analysts determine the optimal methods or techniques for managing their particular analytical challenges: the FAROUT system. The FAROUT system for managing strategic and competitive analysis is designed to assist analysts in discovering what analytical techniques are appropriate for any situation.

The FAROUT system is based on the premise that for analytical output to be intelligent, and therefore valuable to business decision makers, it needs to have several common characteristics. The output needs to be future oriented, accurate, resource efficient, objective, useful, and timely. Failure to meet all these criteria to a satisfactory level will result in the analytical output being of less value to business decision makers. Let us briefly describe each of the six elements.

Future Orientation. The past can be a dangerous and notoriously inaccurate predictor of the future. This is especially important if the present or the future has little in common with the past, as is increasingly the case in today's marketplace. Intelligence must be prospective oriented, looking both deeply and broadly at an indeterminate and uncertain future, and willing to take risks by being both predictive and inventive. Foresight is not gained by looking in the rearview mirror or by using data that point toward the past. The better analytical methods for strategy and CI will be future, as opposed to historically, oriented.

Accuracy. The analyst should develop analytical outputs that aim for high levels of accuracy. High levels of accuracy are difficult to attain under several common conditions, such as when the data underlying the analysis

- have come from only one source;
- have not been cross-validated against both hard and soft information;
- need to be converted from sources in ways for which they were not originally designed; and
- come from sources filled with high levels of bias.

Although achieving perfect accuracy is desirable in theory, it is often less desirable in practice and requires that the analyst make trade-offs against other conceptual and pragmatic considerations, including the other five FAROUT elements. In particular, some authors have suggested that accuracy or precision often may be less important than understanding or perspective, especially in strategy and CI decision making applications that most analysts are regularly faced with.

Resource efficiency. In order for analysis to be done efficiently, data needs to come from sources that not only cost less than the resultant output is worth, but also should not take so long to gather that they are stale by the time the decision actually needs to be made. When data being used in analysis come from primary sources (i.e., most human intelligence or HUM-int), it impacts the probable level of analytical accuracy. It also requires greater skill and understanding to elicit what is actually required from the primary sources. Nevertheless, many secondary databases may give great accuracy and timeliness but little in the way of a future-orientation, and may cost a lot as well.

Objectivity. This relates to the presence of biases held by the analyst or organization (refer to Chapter 2 and Pitfalls of Analysis for a greater discussion on this issue). Too many good analyses are clouded by cognitive or social biases, ranging from prior hypothesis bias to recency of availability, or groupthink to comfort in dealing with risk or uncertainty. To minimize the potentially destructive nature of these common biases, the data or information should be viewed and analyzed using a rational and systematic approach. In other words, successful analysis minimizes the destructive potential of analytical and decision-oriented biases.

Usefulness. Almost by definition, valuable outputs must meet the critical intelligence needs (CINs) of a decision maker in a particular decision-making context. Valuable analytical output must be appropriate to the decision maker's responsibilities, organizational context and style of communication. It is key for the analyst to develop outputs that are "need to know" and not "nice to know" and that meet or surpass the client's critical intelligence needs.

Timeliness. How long it takes the analyst to undertake the analysis will either hinder or assist the organization's use of intelligence. Much business information or competitive data have limited shelf lives especially where those decisions are being made in dynamic, hypercompetitive, or turbulent contexts. Information loses its value the longer it remains excluded from decisions underlying organizational action. Certain methods of analysis may provide the intelligence required but take far too long to develop. On the other hand, other methods of analysis may require little time but do not deliver the required features of objectivity, accuracy, utility, and resource efficiencies. Valuable analysis will allow enough time for the organization to implement the course of action recommended by the analysis.

USING THE FAROUT RATING SYSTEM

Managing the analysis of business and competitive data is a difficult task and we are not aware of any "10-minute analyst" books or software that can replace a good balance of both science and creativity. We do know that it is highly unlikely that good data analysis will be based on just one analytical method or tool. Rather, a combination of several techniques will normally be required.

Each analytical method has unique limitations, and these limitations multiply when placed in specific organizational contexts. Using the FAROUT system will enable the analyst to mix the appropriate tools to be applied in analysis tasks to maximize the intelligence value. It is our view that good analysts recognize and are sensitive to the limitations associated with any particular analytical method or technique. The sensitized analyst can address these issues throughout the whole of the competitive intelligence process to overcome the recognized limitations.

In this book we use a five-point rating scale to assess each analytical technique contained in Part II. The five-point scale ranges from low (1) to high (5). Refer to Table 3-1. Every technique in this book is assessed against the six FAROUT elements. Optimally, the best analysis will be oriented from the present to the future, and be

Table 3-1

The FAROUT Scale

Future orientation	A score of 1 identifies that the model's output provides a low level of future orientation, whereas a 5 indicates that the model is highly future focused.
Accuracy	A 1 indicates a low level of accuracy for this model, taking into account the probable sources of data. A score of 5 indicates that the level of accuracy has been greatly increased, based on the requirements of the model.
Resource efficiency	A score of 1 would identify that this model requires a large volume of resources (financial, human, data, etc.) and is probably low in efficacy. A 5 indicates that this analytical technique is highly efficient in its use of resources and in deriving outputs.
Objectivity	A 1 rating indicates that a particular tool was not highly objective, often due to the presence of biases and mindsets. On the other hand, a score of 5 means that the potential for biases could be minimized.
Usefulness	Usefulness of a particular tool is based on the strategic output that a particular tool can deliver. A model that scores a 5 delivers a high level of valued output, and one that scores a 1 delivers a low level of valued output.
Timeliness	A score of 5 indicates that a particular model takes little time to do as compared with a score of 1, which indicates that this method of analysis requires a great deal of time to complete effectively.

accurate, resource efficient, objective, useful, and timely. Of course, in the real world trying to achieve optimal analysis will require some trade-offs among the six FAROUT elements. Our objective in offering the FAROUT framework is to assist analysts in assessing the outputs of different analytical methods to ensure high intelligence value. If the analysis output delivers on all six characteristics, analysts and decisions makers can be confident that the intelligence will make a difference. All the techniques and their ratings are summarized for easy reference in Table 3-2.

Consumers of intelligence want insightful and relevant outputs that provide a guide to decisions and actions that enable them to increase their organization's competitiveness. Actionable outputs of strategic and competitive analysis are future oriented, help managers to develop superior competitive strategies, identify the plans and strategies of present and prospective competitors, and help an organization's decision makers to better understand their business and competitor environment than their peers employed by competitors.

Table 3-2
FAROUT Summary of Methods

Chapter	Analysis Method	Future Orientation	Accuracy	Resource Efficiency	Objectivity	Usefulness	Timeliness
	Section 1 — Strategic Analytical Techniques						
4	BCG growth/share portfolio matrix	3	2	4	3	3	4
5	GE Business screen matrix	2	3	3	3	3	4
6	Industry analysis	3	3	4	3	4	3
7	Strategic group analysis	5	2	3	3	5	3
8	SWOT analysis	2	3	4	3	4	4
9	Value chain analysis	2	3	2	4	5	1
	Section 2 — Competitive and Customer Analysis						
10	Blindspot analysis	3	4	5	3	5	5
11	Competitor analysis	4	4	1	5	5	2
12	Customer segmentation analysis	2	3	2	3	5	1
13	Customer value analysis	5	3	1	5	5	1
14	Functional capability and resource analysis	4	2	5	5	4	5
15	Management profiling	4	2	5	3	5	2
	Section 3 — Environmental Analysis						
16	Issue analysis	4	3	2	3	4	2
17	Macroenvironmental (STEEP) analysis	4	2	3	2	3	2
18	Scenario analysis	5	4	2	3	4	2
19	Stakeholder analysis	2	2	3	1	3	3
	Section 4 — Evolutionary Analysis						
20	Experience curve analysis	3	1	3	3	4	3
21	Growth vector analysis	3	3	3	3	4	3
22	Patent analysis	5	4	2	4	5	1
23	Product life cycle analysis	2	2	3	3	3	4
24	S-Curve analysis	5	3	1	2	5	1
	Section 5 — Financial Analysis						
25	Financial ratio and statement analysis	1	3	5	5	2	5
26	Strategic funds programming	5	3	3	3	4	2
27	Sustainable growth rate analysis	4	4	5	4	4	5

Part II

The Techniques of Strategic and Competitive Analysis

Strategic Analytical Techniques

Chapter 4

BCG Growth/Share Portfolio Matrix

SHORT DESCRIPTION

The Boston Consulting Group (BCG) growth/share portfolio matrix was designed to help managers of diversified multiproduct, multimarket, and multinational businesses diagnose corporate level strategy by providing an analytical framework to determine the optimal product or business portfolio; prescribing a set of generic strategies to guide resource allocation across the optimal product or business portfolio; and providing a framework for analyzing competitive business portfolios.

The BCG matrix allows a multibusiness firm to compare the merits of its individual business units in order to determine appropriate market strategies for each business. The business units are evaluated based on the attractiveness of the industry in which they compete and their relative competitive position. Generic strategies are then recommended depending on the position of the individual business unit in the portfolio matrix.

BACKGROUND

At the core of strategic planning is the necessity of crafting a fit between the organization's goals, capabilities, and the environment in which it operates. The tactical manifestation of this imperative of strategy is the allocation of resources to competing internal opportunities. This is a challenging enough task for focused companies, but it can quickly spiral into unmanageable complexity for a diversified firm. Nonetheless, during the 1950s and 1960s, the compelling logic of diversification was that it spread risk and offered a wider universe of opportunity for the firm. The most important justification, however, was an enduring faith in professional management skills fostered by the management process school of thought that asserted professional business skills could be universally applied across different types of businesses (Gould & Luchs, 1993).

Many M.B.A. programs began to see management as a science that could systematically apply fundamental principles to a broad spectrum of businesses. Backed by academic support, the new business environment favored optimistic acquisition sprees. Confident that this background would justify increasingly complex and diverse corporate level strategy, graduates of these M.B.A. programs began to build conglomerates composed of many unrelated businesses across different industries. Management skill was thought to be the driving force behind the generally held conviction that the sum of a conglomerate's business units was more valuable under the direction of corporate-level strategy than if its individual composite enterprises were operated under another type of ownership structure. Under this strategy, decades of empire building attracted few empirical, theoretical, or anecdotal challenges.

In the late 1960s, however, many of these conglomerate corporations began to experience protracted periods of profitless growth. When the stock market crashed in early 1969, the accepted mode of management theory was forced into question. The increasing complexity of crafting fit between the diversified conglomerate's goals, capabilities, and the competitive environment was beginning to challenge even the abilities of widely esteemed professional managers. What was needed was a practical framework to guide resource allocation among the many widely divergent businesses in the typical portfolio that then comprised corporate strategy. There remained great demand in the market for management theories to reaffirm the management process school—that despite increasing complexity and environmental turbulence, managers could still manage diversified corporations by quantitative analysis and the systematic application of universal management principles. The BCG growth matrix filled this demand by providing a practical model designed to simplify the corporate-level strategy of increasingly diversified and complex corporations.

Other factors leading to the development of the BCG matrix included economic matters. The rapid growth of the 1950s and 1960s increased the demand for funds. This was followed by inflationary pressures in the 1970s, which severely impinged on the relative attractiveness of outside capitalization. As a result, firms began to look for ways to grow through internal financing.

Interestingly, portfolio planning models developed from two areas: the planning department at General Electric and the Boston Consulting Group. However, General Electric is generally credited with being the first to articulate a comprehensive portfolio matrix. In the early 1960s, GE's management consultants McKinsey & Co. developed the concept of independent strategic business units (SBUs). This new approach viewed the firm as a portfolio of SBUs that individually contributed toward the firm's profitability and growth. The SBU's underlying rationale was that a diversified firm could be divided into the different product/service markets that it served. Each SBU was then placed into a 3 × 3 matrix based on its competitive position and market strength. Resource allocation strategy was then directed based on the SBU's position in the matrix. (See Chapter 5 for a detailed treatment of the GE business screen.)

Shortly after these pioneering developments at GE, the Boston Consulting Group (BCG) took the business world by storm with the introduction of the growth/share matrix. The first commercial application of the concept occurred in 1969 during a client engagement with Mead Corporation. Its intuitive appeal and vivid imagery combined with the appearance of robust quantitative analysis caught the interest of many strategic planners searching for a legitimate tool to manage diversified multiunit corporate strategy.

STRATEGIC RATIONALE AND IMPLICATIONS

The BCG matrix integrated two previously established management theories: the Experience Curve (covered in Chapter 20) and the Product Life Cycle (see Chapter 23).

Link to the Experience Curve

The Boston Consulting Group in their research found that per unit costs often decrease as cumulative output increases due to the impact of the experience curve. Experience is principally composed of three functions: learning, specialization, and scale. The *learning function* shows how anyone doing a job learns to do it better over time. Labor costs should decline by about 10–15 percent each time cumulative experience doubles. The *specialization function* shows that by dividing jobs into individual tasks, each employee's experience with the task increases and costs decline because of the increased learning. The *scale function* suggests that capital costs required to finance additional capacity diminish as that capacity grows.

The sequential impact of these three functions on profitability is shown schematically in Figure 4-1.

Based on this logical sequence, a major strategic implication was drawn from experience curve theory: the firm capturing the largest market share will achieve the highest accumulated volume bestowing a superior competitive position by cost reductions from the experience curve effect. BCG used this logic as the basis for using market share as the dependent variable in the matrix. In essence, relative market share is used as a proxy for unit costs.

Link to the Product Life Cycle

The other building block of the BCG growth matrix was the well-established concept of the product life cycle (PLC). The product life cycle was selected as the natural complement to the experience curve based on the following chain of logic:

1. If market share is the surest road to higher accumulated volumes and subsequent lower costs/higher profitability, then the firm's resources are best spent pursuing high growth markets.

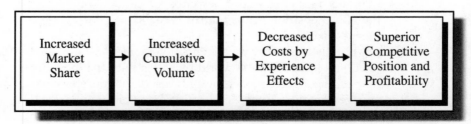

Figure 4-1
Experience Curve
Sequence

2. The surest route to maximize total firm profitability is to maximize market share across the SBU portfolio. The best way to accomplish this is to manipulate the product life cycle by transferring profits away from the mature and declining products to support products in the introductory and growth stages of the PLC. The relevant underlying presumptions of the PLC are twofold:

- Market share is easiest to secure in high growth markets because competitive retaliation is less severe when the firm's market share is secured through new growth instead of being wrestled away from the existing customer base of rivals. It is also easier because new users have a low branding preference.
- Products in the maturity stage will generate excess cash, while products in the growth stage will absorb cash.

Hence, the underlying logic for selecting market growth rate as the independent variable in the portfolio matrix as prescribed by PLC theory. Essentially, market growth is used as a proxy for stages in the product life cycle.

Combining the Experience Curve and the PLC

The BCG matrix shown in Figure 4-2 is the manifestation of this integration of experience curve logic and PLC theory. The BCG matrix plots market attractiveness (as measured by market growth as derived from PLC theory) and competitive position (as measured by market share as derived from experience curve theory) to compare the situation of different products and/or SBUs. Market attractiveness is measured by the industry's growth rate, while competitive position is measured by the business unit's market share relative to that of its largest competitor in the industry (as opposed to the market as a whole). For example, if a business unit has a market share of 20 percent and its largest competitor has a market share of 40 percent, then the business unit's relative market share is 0.5. The purpose of this comparison is to understand and define an appropriate market strategy for each business unit.

The overall strategy of the multibusiness firm as postulated by the BCG matrix is to maximize market share in as many high growth markets for as many SBUs as is possible. The upper limit of this possibility is limited by cash flow because the model assumes a requirement of internal cash balance between cash uses and cash generation. Hence, the strategic goal for senior executives is to allocate limited cash resources across the SBUs to maximize firm profitability. Each quadrant in the BCG matrix offers generic strategies to achieve maximum profitability under this constraint of limited cash resources.

Stars—High Growth Rate, High Market Share
The high growth rate of stars requires a heavy cash investment. An offsetting factor is their strong market share position that infers that stars will have moved along the experience curve the farthest. Therefore, stars should soon develop high margins resulting in potentially strong cash flow in the near future. The balance of these two effects will generally be a sustainable cash position. Application of the model presumes that stars will eventually become cash cows. The BCG matrix application

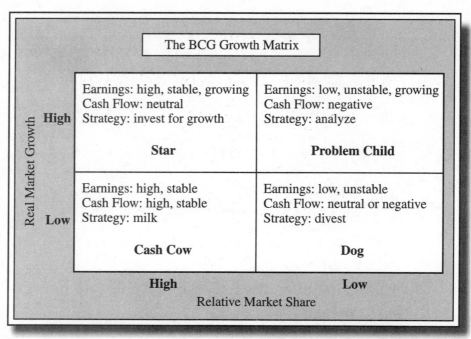

Figure 4-2

recommends that stars are cash deficient; they should be supported with a level of cash investment necessary to maintain their market share. If they are cash providers, the surplus should be reinvested.

Cash Cows—Low Growth Rate, High Market Share

The low growth rate of cash cows results in a higher generation of cash flow. Products or SBUs in mature markets require lower cash investments and therefore will be a source of cash flow from which to finance businesses in other more promising quadrants. The BCG matrix suggests that cash cows be "milked" by a strategy that only invests to maintain their present position. Excess cash flow should be reinvested in either stars or selected problem children.

Dogs—Low Growth Rate, Low Market Share

The low growth rate of dogs infers that increasing market share will be a costly proposition. Additionally, the low market share of dogs implies an uncompetitive cost structure by virtue of their inferior position on the experience curve. Hence, dogs are unprofitable and usually require heavy cash investments just to maintain their low market share. An application of the BCG matrix recommends three options for dogs: First, dogs can become profitable with a focus strategy on a specific desirable niche or segment. Second, any further investment can be withheld while "milking" them for any cash that they generate. Third, dogs can be divested or slowly put to sleep.

Problem Children—High Growth Rate, Low Market Share

The high growth rate of problem children requires a heavy cash investment. An intensifying factor is their low market share that also implies an uncompetitive cost structure by virtue of their inferior position on the experience curve. As the maturity stage sets in, the problem child will follow one of two paths on the matrix. If market share cannot be grown, the problem child will become a dog. Alternately, if market share can be increased by a high enough amount, the problem child will be exalted into star status and, eventually, a cash cow. The BCG matrix recommends that the most promising problem children should receive cash investment to increase market share. Those problem children with dismal prospects should not receive further cash investment.

Overall Strategic Sequence

The integration of these classifications and their requisite strategies can be shown in Figure 4-3 (the numbers indicate strategic priority).

Figure 4-3
Overall Strategic Sequence

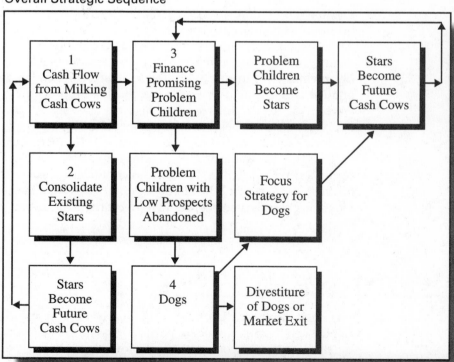

STRENGTHS AND ADVANTAGES

Overall Picture of the Firm's Portfolio

The BCG matrix presents a great deal of information in one diagram. The complexities of multibusiness strategy are seemingly captured in an intuitively accessible format. Many other management tools cannot match the depth and breadth of information that the growth/share matrix offers in one concise document. This simplicity allows the portfolio matrix to be used easily and quickly to identify areas for further in-depth analysis.

Fosters a Mindset Focus on Future Demand.   The BCG matrix challenged the status quo that internal investment should be directed on the basis of past performance or to reward managers for past performance. In some respects, the portfolio approach invited firms to begin framing investment decisions around future considerations of market demand.

Trend Analysis.   Changes in the relative SBU markets can be detected easily through the use of multiperiod matrices.

Competitive Analysis.   Determining the strategic progress of rival firms can be easily facilitated by plotting a time series of rival matrices.

Easy to Communicate.   The matrix and the resultant recommendations from its use are inherently easy for decision makers to understand.

Challenged Incumbent Managerialism Philosophy.   One of the main strengths of portfolio analysis is the change in perspective that it induces in the minds of its users. At the core of portfolio planning lies the recognition that corporate strategy must be an integration of individual business strategy at the business unit level. This was an improvement from the preceding mindset that tended to use blanket strategies applied indiscriminately across the entire multiunit firm that neglected the differences across the various product markets in which it operated. The BCG portfolio approach serves to heighten management sensitivity to this necessity by combining corporate level and business level strategy. In this respect, the BCG matrix challenged the incumbent management philosophy that general management skills, combined with scientific tools and techniques constituted a universal solution to business management. While the operational model is used less frequently today, many of the underlying conceptual precepts still influence management thought.

WEAKNESSES AND LIMITATIONS

The belated recognition of several theoretical and application issues has greatly diminished the prominence of portfolio planning since its heyday in the 1970s. While the BCG matrix is a conceptual tool allowing one to easily and quickly identify areas for further comprehensive analysis, it has several limitations.

Part II   The Techniques of Strategic and Competitive Analysis

Conceptual Flaws/Incorrect Assumptions

1. *Questionable Relevance of the Experience Curve.* The experience curve link to the BCG matrix may not be relevant to the competitive parameters of a particular product market. Relative market share is not necessarily a good proxy for competitive position (i.e., there is not a clear and definitive relationship between market share and profitability in all industries).

Examples include industries with a low value-added production function, experience curve shifts due to technological innovation or new product introductions, secular cost variables more influential than accumulated volume, and capacity utilization.

High market share is not necessarily more profitable than low market share. Many profitable firms have demonstrated that competition in low growth mature markets should not be categorically ruled out as a strategic option. Similarly, the emphasis on market dominance is being constantly challenged by successful niche players premised on differentiation.

2. *Questionable Validity of the Product Life Cycle.* The theoretical validity of the PLC, one of the main tenets of the BCG matrix, is dubious. Additionally, the assumption that high growth markets offer lower costs for securing market share has not been consistently demonstrated by empirical research.

Industry growth is not necessarily a good proxy for industry attractiveness. There is not a clear relationship between growth and profitability in all industries. The assumption that high growth markets offer firms the easiest and most cost-effective route to market share is also tenuous. Aaker and Day (1986) identify several challenges to the successful penetration of high growth markets, including competitive overcrowding, risk of shakeout, distribution constraints, resource constraints, changing key success factors, changing technology, superior competitive entry, and disappointing market growth.

3. *Determinism versus Strategic Choice.* Market share is assumed to be an endogenous or dependent variable, while market growth is assumed to be an exogenous or independent variable. This dichotomy is tantamount to internal inconsistency. The inherent assumption that market growth rate is an exogenous variable beyond the control of management confuses the cause-and-effect sequence of effective strategy. Strategy should lead to growth rather than growth leading to strategy.

4. *Flawed Assumption of Diversification.* The BCG matrix assumes that investment opportunities inside a firm are inherently superior to the universe of investment opportunities outside the firm. That is, portfolio approaches assume that a firm's management is more adept at maximizing investment returns than their shareholders. The emergence of advanced capital markets coupled with the great difficulty of managing diversity in the absence of specific market knowledge suggests that portfolio management has become less useful. It is quite possible that increasing dividends or investing surplus cash cow funds in money markets offers a higher rate of return than internally investing in stars and problem children.

5. *No Recognition of SBU Synergy.* Strategic business units cannot be unambiguously defined. The BCG model assumes that the firm's production function is additive when in reality it is probably nonadditive. The hierarchical nature of

SBUs with regards to their interrelatedness (i.e., joint costs, synergy demand inter-dependencies, etc.) makes the positioning on the matrix at best meaningless and at worst misleading. In some cases, the most fundamental unit of analysis, the independent strategic business unit (SBU) can be a misnomer and a fruitless exercise in taxonomy.

6. *The Concept of Marginality Is Ignored.* Lumping investment prospects into quad-rant categories may yield suboptimal returns at the margin. The first dollar invested in a dog may potentially yield higher returns than the last dollar invested in a star.

Dependency on Market Definition

The definition of the product market heavily influences the strategic recommenda-tions offered by this model. There is significant room for error in applying the trade-off between operational breadth to include competitive experience effects and depth to allow for meaningful segmentation.

Erosion of Strategic Posturing Around Vulnerability

Often it is valuable for a firm to retain dogs to maintain a portfolio of strategic options such as supply security, a source of competitive intelligence, escape the onset of entry barriers in certain industries, and so on. Often the benefits from strategic flexibility supercedes profitability. For example, strict application of portfolio theory would suggest that most car dealerships would be wise to divest their new car busi-ness. However, new car sales are an important market maker for the highly lucrative profitable service segment.

Practical Implementation Problems

Several of the input variables cannot be objectively determined (e.g., precise defini-tion of the strategic business unit or product market). The resulting introduction of judgment may bias the analysis into suboptimal strategic prescriptions. A further source of bias may be the selectivity of data and definition choice by managers seek-ing to achieve a star label for their particular management domain. The unintended consequences of the BCG matrix may be "politics" and game playing around the subjective analytical parameters.

Lulled into Complacency

Since the BCG growth matrix only incorporates the competitive threat to market share from the most dominant rival, a significant opportunity exists to be blindsided. A rapidly rising competitor will not show up on the BCG radar screen until it is almost too late—when the rival has become a dominant player in the market.

There are significant areas of strategic analysis that are not even broached by portfolio analysis, most notably supply side dynamics of the market. While the BCG matrix remains an impressive conceptual framework, it should be primarily used as a rough approximation or starting point in conjunction with other tools and techniques in a holistic approach to strategy development.

PROCESS FOR APPLYING THE TECHNIQUE

True to its systematic nature, the process for utilizing the BCG growth/product matrix is very sequential and can be generalized into the following steps:

Step 1: Divide the Firm into Strategic Business Units (SBUs)

Divide the firm into its economically distinct or unique product market segments. Great care must be taken in this first step because the SBU's position on the matrix and hence the strategic recommendations of the model depend in large part on this initial definition of the SBU. Common segmentation criteria include similar strategically relevant situational or behavioral characteristics, a discontinuity in growth rates, share patterns, distribution patterns, cross elasticity of substitute products, geography, interdependent prices, similar competition, similar customers served, and/or a potential for shared experience (Day, 1977; Coate, 1983). A general rule of thumb suggests that a management team can only realistically manage strategies for approximately 30 different SBUs. Anything beyond this number becomes unmanageable and counterproductive. A great deal of judgment is thus required to determine the extent of segmentation within the product market definition. Substantial iterative analysis will be required to find the right balance between short- and long-term strategies and their requisite narrow and broad SBU definitions. A wide enough scope must be maintained to correctly incorporate competitive opportunities and threats from areas outside of the traditional or intuitive boundaries. Conversely, the definition of an SBU must be narrow enough to allow for distinctions fine enough to make the analysis operational. Despite the difficulty of properly defining the individual SBUs, often this process of analysis offers important strategic insights of its own accord.

Step 2: Measure the Growth Rate of Each SBU Market

A useful percentage growth formula for measuring the market growth rate is

$$\text{Market Growth Rate, year}_x = \frac{[\text{Market Size, year}_x] - [\text{Market Size, year}_{x-1}]}{\text{Market Size, year}_{x-1}} \times 100$$

Step 3: Measure the Relative Market Share of Each SBU

Contrary to the formula in step 2, relative market share is not measured in percentage terms. Rather, it is measured as a ratio of the SBU's market share versus that of its largest competitor. The formula is

$$\text{SBU Relative Market Share, year}_x = \frac{\text{SBU Sales, year}_x}{\text{Largest Competitor's Sales, year}_x}$$

For example, a market share ratio of 2 reflects that the SBU has a relative market share twice that of its leading rival. Alternately, a ratio of 0.5 indicates that the SBU has a relative market share half of that of its leading rival. Normally, the SBU will have more than one product making the use of a weighted average of the individual product growth rates a suitable technique. Either nominal or real sales data may be used.

Step 4: Position Each SBU Along the Matrix Dimensions

Plotting on the Vertical Axis—Market Growth Rate

Simply plot the percentages on the vertical axis. Next, a threshold point must be drawn to distinguish SBUs that are experiencing fast growth from those that are slowly gaining market share. The BCG matrix uses the average growth rate for the market as this horizontal line of demarcation. Alternately, a corporate target may be used to define this threshold. Consistent with the product life cycle, SBUs that lie above this line are currently considered to be in the growth stage. SBUs below this line are classified as being in either the maturity or decline stage of the product life cycle. Yet another method is to use an arbitrary rule of thumb that classifies a market growth rate of 10 percent as a high growth market. Regardless of which method is used, it is important to incorporate the same level of inflation adjustment (real or nominal) in the cutoff point as was used in determining the market growth rate.

Plotting on the Horizontal Axis—Relative Market Share

The experience curve theory asserts that market share is related to total accumulated volume, which is the major factor driving down costs through the experience curve effect. Theoretical consistency, then, dictates that the relative market share be plotted on a semi-log scale. A cutoff point also needs to be established on the horizontal axis with regard to high market share and low market share. The BCG matrix recommends this vertical line of demarcation to be a relative market share of 1.0. Any relative market share to the right of 1.0 indicates the threshold of competitive strength in that market. Often, as a hedge, analysts will use a cutoff point of 1.5 in order to solidify the classifications to the right of this line of SBUs occupying a position of significant market strength.

Plot Contribution Bubbles

The two cutoff points established (high vs. low growth; high vs. low market share) allow the graph to be divided into the characteristic four quadrants of the BCG matrix. Plotting the growth rate vs. relative market share will only give pinpoint locations on the matrix. A helpful technique is to plot bubbles around these points to indicate the relative size of each SBU in terms of its contribution to total firm sales or profitability.

$$\text{Relative Size of Bubble} = \frac{\text{(SBU Sales or Profitability)}}{\text{Total Firm Sales or Profitability}}$$

Sales is generally a preferred basis for determining the size of the bubbles for several reasons: It is easier to make a comparison to competition (see step 5), competitor profit figures by SBU are difficult to obtain, and internal profit figures are often distorted by arbitrary allocations. Each bubble should also be labeled using a common convention like numerical or alphabetical order for further referencing.

Upon determining each business unit's placement within the matrix, the following inferences can be made: The size, stability, and growth potential of the future earnings of each business unit may be predicted; and the cash flow that each business unit should provide may be predicted.

The intermediate analytical product of steps 1 through 4 should look similar to the graph displayed in Figure 4-4.

Step 5: Construct a Matrix for All SBU Competitors

Repeat steps 1 through 4 to construct matrices for competitor SBUs. This will help to give the analysis an external focus on the competitive environment.

Step 6: Assign Optimal Generic Strategies to Each SBU

Table 4-1 summarizes the appropriate strategies recommended by an application of the BCG matrix after the SBUs have been positioned in the matrix. Boiled down to the basics, the strategies can be summarized by the following modes of action: Divest the dogs; milk the cash cows; invest in the stars; and analyze the problem child to determine whether it can be grown into a star or will degenerate into a dog.

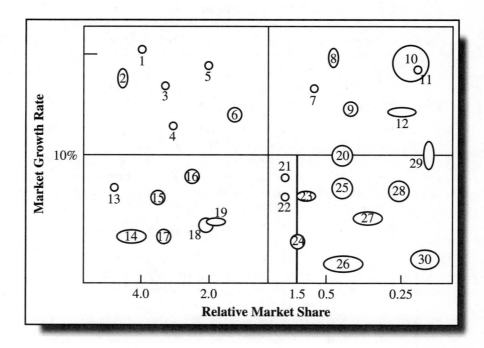

Figure 4-4

Table 4-1
Normative Strategies

BUSINESS CATEGORY	MARKET SHARE THRUST	BUSINESS PROFITABILITY	INVESTMENT REQUIRED	NET CASH FLOW
Stars	Hold/Increase	High	High	Around zero or slightly negative
Cash Cows	Hold	High	Low	Highly positive
Problem Child (a)	Increase	None or negative	Very high	Highly negative
Problem Child (b)	Harvest/Divest	Low or negative	Divest	Positive
Dogs	Harvest/Divest	Low or negative	Divest	Positive

Source: Adapted from "The Use of the Growth Share Matrix in Strategic Planning," by A. Hax and N. S. Majluf, 1983, *Interfaces, 13*(1), p. 51.

Step 7: Further Disaggregate the Analysis

The matrix approach can be further defined to map out the relative positions of the composite products within each SBU. This may help with the tactical implementation of step 6.

Step 8: Introduce Analytical Dynamics

Steps 1 through 7 result in a static analysis. Two analytical tools can be introduced at this stage to incorporate (a) historical market evolution and (b) sustainable growth rate.

Construct a Share Momentum Graph (Lewis, 1977). The purpose of a share momentum graph is to alert the analyst to the blinding effects of simultaneously gaining sales while eroding relative market share. This tool plots long-term market growth versus long-term sales to detect which SBUs are losing market share despite growing sales. This tool is easy to apply because it uses the same data as the matrix. Nonetheless, it serves to highlight important distinctions that may be overlooked by only using the matrix. (See Figure 4-5.)

Sustainable Growth Rate Analysis. Introduced during the high inflationary era of the 1970s, the BCG model assumes that the firm's growth will be internally financed. In today's lower inflation environment, the sustainable growth rate formula (see Chapter 27 for a detailed treatment of this formula) can be used to determine the maximum rate of growth without increasing equity. It is a helpful way to integrate financial strategy with the BCG matrix.

$$g = p \times [ROA = D/E(ROA - i)] \text{ where}$$

$$g = \text{upper limit on sustainable growth}$$
$$p = \text{percentage of earnings retained}$$
$$ROA = \text{tax adjusted return on assets}$$
$$D = \text{total debt}$$
$$E = \text{total equity}$$
$$i = \text{tax adjusted cost of debt}$$

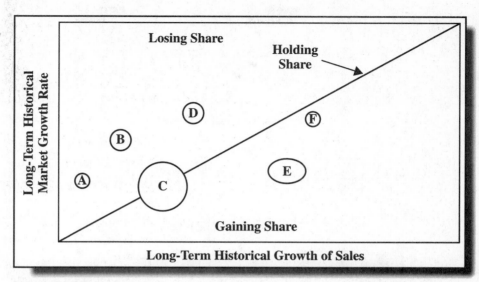

Figure 4-5
Share Momentum Graph

SOURCE: Adapted from "The Use of the Growth Share Matrix in Strategic Planning," by A. Hax and N. S. Majluf, 1983, *Interfaces, 13*(1) p. 52.

Step 9: Iteration

Repeating steps 1 through 8 serves several dynamic strategic purpose:

Strategic Evaluation. The success of the chosen strategies over time can be graphically displayed by overlaying a time series matrix chart to determine if SBUs are moving into their desired positions on the matrix. An optimal result would show that problem children increase in both market share and market growth rate to become stars; stars decrease in market growth rate but sustain market share to become cash cows; dogs are either divested or moved into the problem child or star quadrants; and cash cows exhibit stable positions.

Competitive Analysis. The progress of rival firms can be monitored by (a) repeating this process with a time series of matrix graphs compiled of rivals and (b) constructing an updated share momentum graph for competitors. Competitive threats and opportunities may reveal themselves with these tools. Hax and Majluf (1983) suggest that the best competitive analysis within a matrix format is the share momentum graphs, for two reasons: Temporary aberrations will not distort the analysis, and cutoff points may change over time.

The dual conceptual support underlying the BCG matrix, the product life cycle, and the experience curve often form dangerous strategic blindspots around technology strategy. Consider the following strategic blunders caused in large part by the portfolio mindset.

1. Complacent Technology Strategy
   a. Premature Standardization

      - *Oxirane Corporation*: In a race to be the first along the ethylene glycol industry's experience curve, Oxirane decided to forgo staged technological learning by jumping into full production. Standardizing early by cutting back on R&D resulted in bankruptcy.
      - *Bowmar Calculators*: Attempting to achieve experience-based competitive superiority on an inferior technological platform (discrete components) left the firm vulnerable to integrated circuit technology. Resulting obsolescence ceded the market to Texas Instruments and Fairchild.

   b. Cash Cows Slaughtered by Competitive Innovation

      - *Baldwin Locomotive*: Once the market leader, Baldwin was too slow to adopt the new diesel electric technology, forcing it to yield the product market to GM.
      - *Swiss watchmakers*: Employing innovative quartz and LCD technology, Seiko and Texas Instruments were able to favorably restructure the watch industry, allowing them to steal significant market share from the Swiss.

   c. Self-Fulfilling Decline

      - *Fiat*: Building "turnkey" automotive assembly factories in Poland and the former U.S.S.R. backfired into a failed milking/decline strategy. Both countries now export into Fiat's home markets
      - *Westinghouse and General Electric*: Prematurely labeling their heavy electrical equip-

ment technology as mature, both firms decided to license to firms in France, Switzerland, Germany, and Japan. Shortly thereafter, neither GE nor Westinghouse were able to win major contracts to build generating plants in any of these countries.

2. Myopic Focus on Cash Flow

The disproportionate importance that the BCG matrix ascribes to cash flow causes firms to underestimate the strategic value of other equally important competitive parameters.

   - *General Electric, Siemens, Philips, and Honeywell*: Lured by the high profits and growth potential that IBM was enjoying in the 1960s macrocomputer market, these firms entered the market. High profit potential and market growth blinded their entry strategy to necessary key success factors exogenous to the BCG model such as relevant technological expertise, a compatible organizational culture and industry-specific marketing and financial management. They placed blind faith in the universality of growth/share strategies regardless of contextual supply-side market dynamics or the importance of other internal competencies. Several unprofitable years later, all four firms were forced to divest and exit the industry.

3. One Firm's Dog Is Another Firm's Star

   - *The U.S. Television Industry*: During the mid-1970s, an almost unanimous strategic conclusion in the U.S. television industry labeled itself as mature teetering on decline. Consistent with the growth/share model, incumbent firms actively engaged in harvesting strategies. The resulting dearth of technological innovation and marketing support made the industry vulnerable to properly oriented Japanese competitors. Optimistically regarding the TV market as holding profitable long-term potential, the Japanese industry invested heavily in marketing and

(continued on following page)

product improvement (e.g., quadraphonic stereo sound, inexpensive portable models, modular design, big screens, remote control, etc.). Today, the Japanese dominate the global television industry, and seem destined to continue given the potential resurgence of market growth through high definition television (HDTV) and the "500 channel universe."

SOURCE FOR NO. 1: Adapted from "Rejuvenating the Life Cycle Concept," by Robert U. Ayrees and W. A. Steger, 1985, *The Journal of Business Strategy, 6*(1), pp. 66–76.
SOURCE FOR NO. 2: Adapted from "Pitfalls in Using Portfolio Techniques—Assessing Risk and Potential," by Frans, Derkinderen, G. J. and R. L. Crum, 1984. *Long Range Planning, 17*(2), pp. 129–136.

FAROUT SUMMARY

	1	2	3	4	5
F	■	■	■		
A	■	■			
R	■	■	■	■	
O	■	■	■		
U	■	■	■		
T	■	■	■	■	

Future orientation   Present to medium term future. The application of the BCG matrix suggests market strategies to be pursued by strategic business units in the future.

Accuracy   Low to medium degree. Market growth and relative market share are narrow measures of future profitability.

Resource efficiency   Medium to high degree. Simple to perform if market growth and relative market share are known.

Objectivity   Medium degree. Depends on the information source employed to obtain market growth and relative market share. Subjective estimates reduce objectivity.

Usefulness   Medium degree. A relatively simple way of performing organizational portfolio planning. Typically requires application of additional and more precise tools to increase usefulness.

Timeliness   Medium to high degree. Possible to perform quickly if market growth and relative market share are known or can be easily estimated.

RELATED TOOLS AND TECHNIQUES

- experience curve analysis
- market segmentation
- product life cycle
- sustainable growth rate analysis

REFERENCES

Aaker, D. A., & Day, G. S. (1986). "The perils of high growth markets." *Strategic Management Journal, 7*(5), 409–421.

Bettis, R. A., & Hall, W. K. (1983). "The business portfolio approach—where it falls down in practice." *Long Range Planning, 16*(2), 95–104.

Coate, M. B. (1983). "Pitfalls in portfolio planning." *Long Range Planning, 16*(3), 47–56.

Day, G. S. (1977). "Diagnosing the product portfolio." *Journal of Marketing, 41*(2), 29–38.

Davidson, K. (1985). "Strategic investment theories." *The Journal of Business Strategies, 6*(1), 16–28.

Derkinderen, F., Crum, G. J., & Crum, R. L. (1984). "Pitfalls in using portfolio techniques—assessing risk and potential." *Long Range Planning, 17*(2), 129–136.

Gould, M., & Luchs, K. (1993). "Why diversify? Four decades of management thinking." *Academy of Management Executive, 7*(3), 7–26.

Grant, R. M., "Contemporary Strategic Analysis," 2nd edition, 1995, Malden, Mass: Blachwell Publishers.

Hammermesh, R. G., & Silk, S. B. (1979). "How to compete in stagnant industries." *Harvard Business Review, 57*(5), 161–168.

Hammermesh, R. G., Anderson, M. J., & Harris, J. E. (1978). "Strategies for low market share businesses." *Harvard Business Review, 56*(3).

Haspeslagh, P. (1982). "Portfolio planning: Uses and limits." *Harvard Business Review, 60*(1), 58–73.

Hax, A. C., & Majluf, S. N. (1983). "The use of the growth share in strategic planning." *Interfaces, 13*(1), 46–60.

Hedley, B. (1977). "Strategy and the business portfolio." *Long Range Planning, 10*(1), 9–15.

Kiechel, W., III. (1981). "Oh where, oh where has my little dog gone? Or my cash cow? Or my star?" *Fortune, 104*(9), 148–154.

MacMillan, K. (1986). "Strategy: Portfolio analysis." *Journal of General Management, 11*(4), 94–112.

Porter, M. "From competitive advantage to corporate strategy." *Harvard Business Review,* 1987, May/June, Vol 65, 3, pp. 43–59.

Seeger, J. A. (1984). "Reversing the images of BCG's growth/share matrix." *Strategic Management Journal, 5*(1), 93–97.

Varadarajan, R. P. (1999). "Strategy content and process perspectives revisited." *Academy of Marketing Science, 27*(1), 88–100.

Walker, R. F. (1984). "Portfolio analysis in practice." *Long Range Planning, 17*(3), 63–71.

Wensley, R. (1981). "Strategic marketing: Betas, boxes or basics." *Journal of Marketing, 45,* 173–182.

Wensley, R. (1982). "PIMS and BCG: New horizons or false dawn?" *Strategic Management Journal, 3*(2), 147–158.

Wind, Y., & Mahajan, V. (1981). "Designing product and business portfolios." *Harvard Business Review, 59*(1), 155–165.

Woo, C. Y., & Cooper, A. C. (1982). "The surprising case for low market share." *Harvard Business Review, 60*(6), 106–113.

Yelle, L. E. (1983). "Adding life cycles to learning curves." *Long Range Planning, 16*(6), 82–87.

Chapter 5

GE Business Screen Matrix

SHORT DESCRIPTION

The GE business screen matrix is a descriptive device with evaluative and normative strategy implications. It consists of a matrix that combines internal analysis of business strength with external industry analysis to describe the competitive situation of various strategic business units (SBUs) and to help guide resource allocation across SBUs.

BACKGROUND

The rationale for the business screen matrix begins as far back as the 1930s, when the diversified conglomerate was becoming a dominant business model. Large organizations composed of many unrelated businesses were organized as holding companies to maximize tax benefits. This model worked suitably well until the 1950s when General Electric and other conglomerates began to encounter difficulty in managing multibusiness concerns in general. More specifically, they were having trouble in determining a rational method of resource allocation across divisions. Traditional theory offered no help because it dealt in a generalized go–no go capital budgeting decision focused only on the single business model. A framework was needed that offered advice on resource allocation for the increasingly complex task of managing diversified firms.

A second impetus for change came from the external competitive environment. The high growth economies of the 1950s and 1960s generated significant cash requirements to fund fast growing, cash draining business divisions. In the 1970s, rising inflation dimmed the prospects of raising funds in capital markets. These external conditions focused the corporate mindset on finding strategic frameworks that incorporated internal funding sources for resource allocation.

A third impetus for change was given by the growing inaccuracy of forecasting in increasingly turbulent competitive environments. Incorrect predictions and forecasts were starting to seriously undermine the capital allocation process at widely diversified conglomerates. Most notable were the disappointing results in the computer, nuclear power, and aircraft divisions at GE. During the 1960s, profitless growth began to manifest itself in GE's financial performance. Despite the fact that GE increased sales by the equivalent of the total sales of Westinghouse over the course of this decade, return on investment (ROI) decreased and earnings per share (EPS) remained flat (Thackery, 1978). Put another way, GE's era of profitless growth can best be described by the dismal financial performance from 1965–1970 when sales increased by 40 percent but profits plunged (Goold & Luchs, 1993). A problem identified was that investing in hopeful opportunities only rarely realized the expected returns because of poor forecasting.

The fourth factor contributing to the development of the business screen was the erosion of the power of the incumbent managerial philosophy. As companies grew more diversified, it became increasingly difficult for corporate-level strategists and their strategies to assert control over wide-ranging divisions. Portfolio management was seen as a way to bridle the trend toward decentralization by refocusing resource allocations across the entire firm, rather than allowing division management to reinvest profits independent of other, perhaps more profitable, divisions.

The fifth factor was also related to the incumbent managerial philosophy. Two separate research initiatives served to reinforce the enduring belief that "natural laws" existed in the business realm that could be universally applied through scientific management. Research on the impact of the experience curve on costs by the Boston Consulting Group (BCG) as well as research on the impact of market share on profitability by the Strategic Planning Institute (the PIMS project) combined to suggest that business strategy could be viewed as more of a science than an art. This found great resonance with managers who embraced the scientific portfolio approach; it offered them a way forward to increase strategic success while simultaneously reclaiming lost power at the head office.

The culmination of these agents for change set off a chain of events leading to the development of the business screen. During the late 1960s, GE began to work closely with consultants McKinsey & Co. to determine why some of their businesses were performing better than others. The result was the conceptualization of a fundamental new tenet of strategy—the SBU. The concept of the SBU asserted that a multibusiness corporation should be divided into the distinct product markets that it serves. Many divisions were created or redefined by this new criterion. By 1970, GE also decided to build a formal strategic planning structure that replaced inaccurate forecasting with robust competitive analysis of each division's external environment. That same year, GE flirted with the idea of permanently incorporating the BCG portfolio matrix but only implemented the growth matrix in their SBU strategy plans for one year. The reliance of the BCG model on only two variables, market growth and market share, seemed at once too limiting and too vulnerable to incorrect judgment and forecasts. Instead, GE asked McKinsey & Co. to develop a more comprehensive matrix that incorporated their goal of introducing rigorous competitive and internal analysis into the strategic planning process. By 1971, Mike Allen, one of McKinsey's consultants, developed the business screen while conducting an analysis of GE's components and materials divisions. General Electric immediately implemented the business screen on a companywide basis to manage their 43 SBUs. Financial performance soon improved as GE's return on equity increased from 13.4 percent in 1970 to 19.4 percent in 1977 (Thackery, 1978). Soon, many other diversified conglomerates recognized GE's success and used the business screen matrix. By 1979, the GE business screen had become the most popular of the portfolio approaches. Fully 45 percent and 36 percent of the Fortune 1000 and the Fortune 500 industrial companies, respectively, had implemented some form of portfolio planning (Haspeslagh, 1982).

STRATEGIC RATIONALE AND IMPLICATIONS

A multibusiness company can use the business screen on a regular basis to track the evolving nature of its portfolio of businesses as well as use it in developing simple financial strategies to improve the performance of the portfolio. To facilitate these objectives, the centerpiece of the business screen compares industry attractiveness against business strength within a 3×3 matrix as shown in Figure 5-1.

Industry Attractiveness

The analyst needs to locate an industry in one of three vertical rows according to the industry's relative attractiveness. The labels usually ascribed to the rows are high, medium, and low attractiveness. Attractiveness is determined by considering a wide range of factors, including such elements as absolute market size, market potential, competitive structure, financial factors, economic factors, technological factors, and social and political factors.

Business Strength

The analyst also needs to place the business unit's position in terms of strength in one of three horizontal columns. These columns are typically labeled strong, medium, and weak. This positioning typically requires the analyst to look at the business unit's size, market share, positioning, and comparative advantages using a variety of analytical methods discussed throughout this book.

The three areas of the matrix are labeled low, medium, and high overall attractiveness, to reflect the evaluative aspects of the completed assessment. Business units placed in the lower right three cells (hatched cells) have low overall attractiveness because they have relatively weak positions in unattractive industries. Those units positioned in the upper left have high overall attractiveness (gray cells) because they have relatively strong positions in relatively attractive industries. The diagonal cells across the matrix (clear cells) are labeled as medium overall attractiveness.

Note that the variables on both axes are a mixture of both qualitative and quantitative factors. Further, the two axes can be compared on the basis of controllability by the firm. The horizontal axis, business strength, represents internal factors over which the firm has greater ability to influence. In contrast, the vertical axis, industry attractiveness, is generally composed of external factors that are far less controllable by the firm. The model assumes that the combination of these variables will provide the raw analytical material necessary to conduct robust strategic analysis and subsequent choice of action.

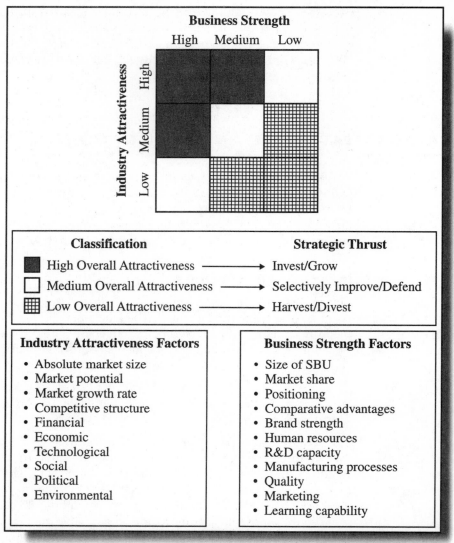

Figure 5-1
The GE Business Screen

Once the SBU is positioned on the matrix, six general normative strategies are suggested by the business screen:

1. *Invest to Hold.* Incrementally increase investment in the SBU by the marginal amount necessary to offset any erosion of competitive position by external factors.
2. *Invest to Penetrate.* Intensify investment to increase the business strength of the SBU.
3. *Invest to Rebuild.* Attempt to reposition the SBU to its formerly more attractive status and restore damage done by other strategies that are no longer optimal.

4. *Selective Investment.* Invest in SBUs that offer marginal return through a predicted positive cost/benefit ratio. Allow SBUs that pose a negative or unattractive cost/benefit ratio to decline.

5. *Low Investment.* Pursue a harvesting strategy by minimizing investment in the SBU in order to free up cash.

6. *Divestiture.* Exit the market by divesting the SBU.

In general the strategies prescribed by the business screen increase investment to those SBUs with high business strength and high industry attractiveness. Those SBUs with low business strength and low industry attractiveness will receive less investment. Selective investment is applied to those SBUs falling in between these two extremes reflecting various tradeoffs between industry attractiveness and business strengths. An example of potential applications of these six general strategies across the nine cells of the business screen are summarized in Table 5-1.

The McKinsey/GE business screen approach shares some similarities with the BCG portfolio matrix: They are both based on the idea of managing a conglomerate business by selectively apportioning surplus resources from successful current businesses to finance promising future opportunities that will, it is hoped, become future successes. They both use the concept of the independent strategic business unit as the fundamental unit of analysis. Also, they both use the basic parameters of business strength and market attractiveness.

The similarity stops here, however, as there are several significant differences in the two approaches: The business screen incorporates many more variables into the definition of business strength (vs. the singular variable of market share incorporated in the BCG matrix) and in the definition of market attractiveness (vs. the singular variable of market growth incorporated in the BCG matrix). The business screen matrix is composed of nine cells as opposed to the four cells offered by the BCG matrix. Accordingly, the business screen offers the analyst sharper positioning options and strategic choices than those offered by the BCG matrix. The business screen focuses on ROI as compared to the cash flow focus of the BCG matrix. The conceptual foundation of the business screen is the general theory of competitive advantage. The precepts underlying the BCG matrix are more closely related to the experience curve and the product life cycle.

STRENGTHS AND ADVANTAGES

Richer Set of Analytical Variables

This richer mix of variables in the definitions of business strength and market attractiveness makes the business screen both more elegant and precise. This allows the analyst to consider more of the relevant variables, making it a more effective diagnostic tool. As such, it supports a wider set of potential applications in contrast to the BCG model, which is much more attuned to high-volume industries due to its conceptual link with the experience curve. This comprehensive appeal of the business screen is much more amenable to matching business strength with industry attractiveness and vulnerability of competitors—an important part of the environment/resources link in the strategic process.

Table 5-1

Specific Strategies for Each Cell of the Business Screen

INDUSTRY ATTRACTIVENESS	BUSINESS STRENGTH		
	HIGH	MEDIUM	LOW
HIGH	• **Premium**: Invest for growth • Provide maximum investment • Diversify worldwide • Consolidate position • Accept moderate near-term profits	• **Selective:** Invest for growth • Invest heavily in selected segments • Share ceiling • Seek attractive new segments to apply strength • Selectively invest for earnings	• **Protect/Refocus:** Selectively invest for earnings • Defend strengths • Refocus to attractive segments • Evaluate industry revitalization • Monitor for harvest or divestment timing
MEDIUM	• **Challenge:** Invest for growth • Build selectively on strengths • Define implications of leadership challenge • Avoid vulnerability–fill weaknesses	• **Prime:** Segment market • Make contingency plans for vulnerability	• **Restructure:** Harvest or divest • Provide no unessential commitment • Position for divestment • Shift to more attractive segment
LOW	• **Opportunistic:** Selectively invest for earnings • Ride market • Seek niches, specialization • Seek opportunity to increase strength by acquisition	• **Opportunistic:** Preserve for harvest • Act to preserve or boost cash flow out • Seek opportunistic sale • Seek opportunistic rationalization to increase strengths	• **Harvest or divest:** • Exit market or prune product line • Determine timing so as to maximize present value

Source: "An Overview of Marketing Planning," by D. D. Monieson, 1978, in *Executive Bulletin* no. 8, Ottawa: The Conference Board of Canada, p. 5. Used with permission of the Conference Board of Canada.

Flexibility

The business screen model allows the analyst increased flexibility over the BCG matrix for two reasons: (1) Different variables can be included in the definition of business strength and industry attractiveness, allowing for a more tailored analysis. (2) Different weights can be assigned to the chosen variables, making the business screen more adaptable to the unique situation of each SBU.

Intuitive Appeal

The business screen gives the analyst a valuable comprehensive view of the corporate portfolio. Although it doesn't share the vivid imagery of the BCG matrix, the business screen still holds high intuitive appeal, making it relatively simple to implement and communicate.

WEAKNESSES AND LIMITATIONS

Questionable Assumptions

1. *Definition of the SBU.* Like the BCG matrix, the idea of an independent strategic business unit may be a misnomer. If many of the SBUs under analysis are interrelated (e.g., joint costs, supporting strategic options), the analytical outputs will also be flawed.

2. *Choice of Variables.* The business screen assumes that the variables chosen to define business strength and industry attractiveness will be accurately comprehensive. Further, the choice of weightings to assign each variable is subject to bias and error.

3. *Risk Is Ignored.* Using ROI as its sole focus does not explicitly addresses the variability of returns associated with SBUs competing for firm resources.

Dangers of Misapplication

The business screen is subject to several potential misapplications:

1. *Static Analysis.* It is important to remember that the business screen gives only a static snapshot at one point in time of the SBU's competitive situation. Continuous monitoring for any changes in the variables is required for a dynamic analysis.

2. *Relying on Normative Strategies.* The business screen should be regarded only as a descriptive model to aid strategic analysis. The normative strategies are provided only as a guide to aid in strategic decision making.

3. *Defining the SBU or Industry Incorrectly.* Even small errors in defining the SBU or the boundaries of the industry could conceivably position the SBU incorrectly on the nine-cell matrix. Given the difficulties in finding a robust definition of either variable, the chance of flawed analytical output and misleading strategy rises.

4. *Simplistic Strategies.* The three generic strategies offered by the business screen might prevent lateral "out of the box" thinking. Insightful analysis, unbridled by the straightjacket of formal models, may, for example, recommend investing instead of harvesting in the pursuit of innovation or securing strategic flexibility. In particular, the probability of misapplication in new markets is high because it is difficult to accurately gauge the attractiveness of embryonic industries.

Ambiguity

Ironically, one of the main strengths of the business screen, the inclusion of many analytical variables, is also a source of weakness. The related subjectivity introduces ambiguity, sometimes making it difficult for a team of analysts to agree on selection, weighting, and positioning. Further, each SBU will likely be evaluated using different variables. While this will ensure that the unique situation of each SBU is considered, it presents an obstacle to uniform comparison of like to like when contrasting the investment prospects of the firm's SBUs.

PROCESS FOR APPLYING THE TECHNIQUE

The business screen in Figure 5-1 reflects the results of a process conducted at the business unit level. The process involves two primary tasks. The first requires the analyst to identify the factors that are relevant in determining industry attractiveness and strength of the business unit position. The second task requires the analyst to determine the nature of the overall relationship of these factors.

Business managers may be surveyed to determine an industry's most important market, competitive, financial, technological, social, and political characteristics. This step is often supplemented with a rigorous environmental scan. Once this judgment is made, assessments can be combined, using either a subjective basis or a weighting ratings scheme, into an overall ranking.

As shown in the scenario in Figure 5-2a, managers decided upon six factors that comprised an industry's attractiveness. For each factor, the analyst surveys knowledgeable managers or external experts to gauge an attractiveness score and an importance rating. Attractiveness can be rated between 0 and 1, 0 being "unattractive" and 1 being "attractive."

Column A indicates the score assigned by a consensus of managerial opinion to each of the six factors, on a 0 to 1 scale. The importance weight, also determined through managerial consensus techniques, is shown in column B. The last column indicates the product of column A multiplied by column B. In this case, the total score equals 47 in the current state, but a less attractive 45.5 in the future. This score becomes meaningful when compared with similarly derived rankings of other industries using similar factors. It may be used as a basis for locating an industry in one of the three rows of Figure 5-1. This process would be replicated to determine the positioning of the SBU in terms of business strength on the three columns of the screen in Figure 5-1.

Even more graphical acuity may be garnered through the use of bubbles or pie charts to represent the relative positions and contribution of each SBU. Another supplement to the business screen analysis recommended by Hax and Majluf (1983) is the use of profile charts. Separate charts are constructed for the business strength and the industry attractiveness ascribed to each SBU. Each profile chart positions the SBU on a five-point scale with the symbols − − denoting extremely unattractive, − denoting mildly unattractive, E denoting even or neutral, + denoting mildly attractive, and + + denoting extremely attractive. Figure 5-2b displays the corresponding profile chart of the earlier example. Profile charts are particularly illuminating when they are conducted for several years and overlaid to give a concise visual depiction of dynamic changes in SBUs performance on the variables.

The normative implications of the business screen are evidenced by considering the changes in business unit positioning that might be caused by environmental

Industry Factors	A. Attractiveness Score		B. Importance Weight		A. × B. Overall Score	
Year	Current	Future	Current	Future	Current	Future
Market Size	.5	.7	25	20	12.5	14
Growth Rate	.2	.4	10	15	2	6
Intensity of Competition	.9	.5	15	20	13.5	10
Financial	.3	.3	20	15	6	4.5
Technology	.7	.5	10	20	7	10
Sociopolitical	.3	.1	20	10	6	1
Total			100	100	47	45.5

Figure 5-2a
Assigning Weights to the Analytical Variables

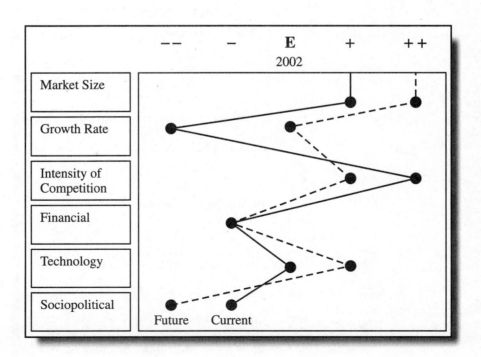

Figure 5-2b
Profile Chart.

changes or accomplished by proactive strategy changes. For example, some of these have been depicted in Figure 5-3.

This requires the same procedure described so far for the static analysis of the current situation, except forecasting is the analytical technique used instead of analysis based on extrapolations from historical data and experiential knowledge. Trend analysis and other forecasting techniques are applied to each variable of the industry attractiveness composite to determine an approximation of its relative future attractiveness. Next, the ideal, desired, or forecasted position of each variable of the business strength composite is determined in light of the predicted industry attractiveness. Then, the analyst positions these new values in the nine-cell matrix and compares it to the current situation. To provide additional insight, a new set of profile charts may be constructed based on these new values for both the industry attractiveness and business strength. The forecast profile chart is superimposed over the current charts. This is indicated in Figure 5-2b by the dashed line.

At this stage the essence of the business screen is materialized. The analyst and management team must determine the appropriate strategies to achieve competitive advantage by matching internal resources and capabilities to the strategic challenges imposed by the dynamic marketplace—a reactive strategy; or matching internal resources and capabilities to impact the industry structure to the firm's benefit—a proactive strategy. Figure 5-3 displays a conceivable strategic plan based on a business screen analysis.

Figure 5-3
Strategic
Maneuvering
Around the
Business Screen

Source: Figure 5-3 adapted from "The Use of the Industry Attractiveness-Business Strength Matrix in Strategic Planning," by C. A. Hax and N. S. Majluf, 1983, *Interfaces,* 13(2) pp. 54–71.

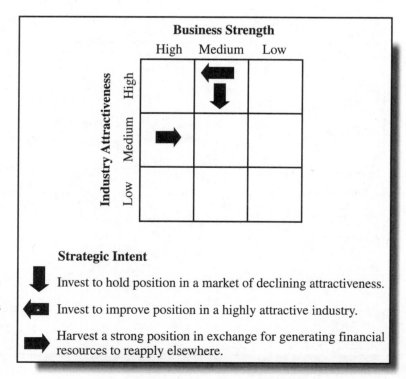

Part II   The Techniques of Strategic and Competitive Analysis

No organization epitomized the portfolio approach to formal strategic planning more intensely than General Electric in the 1970s. At its peak, GE employed more than 200 planners. When asked to comment on GE's selection of the McKinsey business screen over the BCG matrix, then vice president Mike Allen replied, "We feel it is more important to understand the profit anatomy of an industry and how it is changing rather than use a simplified yardstick. There's something conceptually different here. This is not a decision formula that makes decisions for management. It only claims to help management use its judgmental expertise better."

And so the business screen was implemented with great fervor at GE's 43 strategic business units (SBUs). The size of these SBUs ranged from US$50 million to $1.5 billion in sales. Each SBU's strategic plan differed in form as well. Allen defended this diversity: "You can't plan the same way for an aircraft engine business and a coffee brewer business."

Initially, GE used 40 different variables to define industry attractiveness and business strength at its SBUs. Shortly thereafter, the number of factors was reduced to 15. Industry attractiveness was measured by overall size, market growth, market diversity, competitive structure, overall industry profitability, technology, social factors, environmental factors, legal factors, and human resources. Business strength was measured by relative market share, product quality, technological strength, vertical integration, and distribution, among others.

General Electric would subsequently add and remove factors as warranted by industry and firm change. For instance, in the mid- to late 1970s, inflation, business cycles, and the energy crisis were added to the list of composite variables.

Most of GE's 200 strategic planners operated out of the SBU sites, with only a handful located at GE's Fairfield, Connecticut, headquarters. The following illustrates the planning process at GE under the business screen:

- Top management would hand down "planning challenges" to the planners at the SBUs on various socioeconomic themes, such as the spate of United States – foreign direct investment.

- The SBUs would respond with both proactive and reactive strategies geared toward these planning challenges to an intermediary planning unit called a sector.

- These sectors fulfilled three roles: (1) to work with top management to create and control growth amid the complexity of the world's largest conglomerate corporation; (2) work with the SBU planners to communicate to headquarters the ongoing strategies of their divisions; and (3) work on strategic planning projects outside of the scope of the SBU planners.

- These planning projects manifested in sector plans that provided the primary impetus for the continually evolving corporate master strategy. A significant portion of each sector plan also included strategic plans regarding the optimal number of growing and mature businesses in order to maintain a balanced portfolio while still encouraging growth.

GE was very satisfied with this organizational structure based on the business screen because it made the planning more homogenous and gave them more control due to its integration.

Application of the controls imparted by the discipline of the business screen resulted in many radical strategies. Large investments were made in service industries such as computer network services, financial services, and broadcasting and cable television. International diversification spawned growth in international sales, which rose from 13 percent of total revenues in 1966 to 40 percent in 1976. In keeping with the rationale of the business screen, resources from poorly performing businesses with weak business strengths and low industry attractiveness were transferred to more promising SBUs. This strategic imperative resulted in the divestment of a wide array of businesses, ranging from computers, educational equipment and materials, medical operations in Belgium, and European retail outlets. In addition to these

(Continued on following page)

efforts, GE initiated major changes to increase their control over the so-called uncontrollable factors of the business screen: for example, they established a lobby in Washington, D.C., to strengthen their sociopolitical strategy and results.

All was well with GE and the business screen until 1983 when CEO Jack Welch radically downsized the once-heralded planning department. Instead of focusing on creating and sustaining competitive advantage, Welch asserted that the small army of GE planners was too involved with the minutiae of operations and finance, despite their growing isolation from the daily problems of managers on the corporate front line. Many companies followed suit, paving the way for a new paradigm of strategy, Total Quality Management, followed by a massive wave of corporate divestiture, business process reengineering, and a reversion to core competencies.

SOURCE: Adapted from "GE's Planned Prognosis," by John Thackaray, 1978 *Management Today*, pp. 66–69.

FAROUT SUMMARY

	1	2	3	4	5
F	■	■			
A	■	■	■		
R	■	■	■		
O	■	■	■		
U	■	■	■		
T	■	■	■	■	

Future orientation Present to short term future. Needs to be tracked over time to be more helpful.
Accuracy Medium degree. Can be subjectively generated or done through consensus methods. Consensus methods increase accuracy levels.
Resource efficiency Medium degree. Higher accuracy requires generation of some quantitative data about industry factors and business position. Can be highly resource efficient if only subjective considerations are made.
Objectivity Medium degree. Depends on data used. Subjective data reduce objectivity; consensus methods and the use of expert inputs increases it.

Usefulness Medium. A relatively simple way of doing an overall strategic position assessment. Typically requires application of additional and more precise tools to increase usefulness. Generates overly simplistic strategy alternatives around growing, defending, harvesting, or exiting business units.
Timeliness Medium to high. Can be done quickly if analyst uses subjective methods, less quickly if consensus methods used or quantitative data generated to support consensus decision making.

RELATED TOOLS AND TECHNIQUES

- BCG matrix
- competitor analysis
- environmental scanning
- industry analysis
- portfolio theory

REFERENCES

Anonymous. (1975, April 28). "General Electric's stop-light strategy for planning." *Business Week*, 49.

Borgeois, L. J. (1988). *Note on portfolio techniques for corporate strategic planning*. Charlottesville, VA: University of Virginia Darden School Foundation.

Goold, M, & Luchs, K. (1993). "Why diversify? Four decades of management thinking." *Academy of Management Executive*, 7(3), 7–25.

Haspeslagh, P. (1982). "Portfolio planning: Uses and usefulness, uses and limits." *Harvard Business Review*, 60(1), 58–73.

Hax, A. C., & Majluf, N. S. (1983). "The use of the industry attractiveness—business strength matrix in strategic planning." *Interfaces*, 13(2), 54–71.

MacMillan, K. (1986). "Strategy: Portfolio analysis." *Journal of General Management*, 11(4), 94–112.

Monieson, D. D. (1978). "An overview of marketing planning." (Executive Bulletin no. 8). Ottawa: The Conference Board of Canada.

Rothschild, W. E. (1976). *Putting it all together: A guide to strategic thinking*. New York: AMACOM.

Segev, E. (1995). *Corporate strategy: Portfolio models*. London: International Thompson.

Thackaray, J. (1978). "GE's planned prognosis." *Management Today*, 66–69.

Chapter 6

Industry Analysis

SHORT DESCRIPTION

Industry analysis provides a structural analysis and outline of an industry—its participants and characteristics. The objective of this process is to identify the profit potential of an industry; uncover the forces that would harm profitability; driving the profit potential; protect competitive advantage by defending against the forces that would harm profitability; extend competitive advantage by favorably influencing these forces; and proactively anticipate changes in industry structure.

BACKGROUND

Industry analysis is formed from a cross between industrial economics and the field of strategy. The impetus for this innovative new analysis came from the dissatisfaction with the theory of industrial organization as an applicable framework for strategic industry analysis. This theory assumed industry homogeneity—that the economic characteristics of firms are alike in all ways except size. Since the mid-1950s, a growing body of research challenged this assumption. Most notable were the pioneering works of Joe S. Bain of Harvard University, who disputed the theory of industrial organization by suggesting that industry structure is not limited to size but is also determined by mobility barriers. Bain concluded that above-average industry profits were driven by the existence of market power created through mobility barriers. He asserted that these mobility barriers serve to prevent market entry, thus protecting the profits of the concentrated firms through imperfect competition. However, he still retained the idea of a homogeneous rate of profit that accrued equally across an industry proportionate to firm size through what he called the "shared asset" of market power.

In the early 1970s, empirical research and anecdotal evidence began to accumulate that challenged the established concept of profit homogeneity through market power. A nascent theory of industry structure started to evolve based on the premise that *different* rates of firm profitability are a function of market power driven by interindustry *and* intraindustry structures. In 1972, Michael Hunt, also of Harvard University, extended the concept of market power by introducing the concept of strategic groups while studying the major home appliance industry. Strategic groups can be generically defined as a group of firms that follow essentially the same strategies (see Chapter 7 for a detailed treatment of strategic groups). Strategic groups impact the distribution of industry profits by either differentiating barriers to entry or influencing rivalry.

In 1980, Hunt's colleague at Harvard, Michael Porter, significantly advanced the theory of strategy in two ways by adding to the established concepts of mobility barriers and strategic groups with the addition of several new variables that explain industry structure and profitability. Thus, he combined this new knowledge of industrial economics and applied it to the study of business strategy to yield several useful insights and analytical approaches to industry analysis.

In his 1980 book, *Competitive Strategy: Techniques for Analyzing Industries and Competitors*, Michael Porter integrated three key areas of analysis—industry structural analysis, competitor analysis, and industry evolution analysis—to form a comprehensive new model of competitive industry analysis. This integrated model has become widely known as the Porter's Five Forces model and was widely regarded as an excellent complement to the SWOT (strengths, weaknesses, opportunities, threats) model developed by Ken Andrews in the early 1970s.

STRATEGIC RATIONALE AND IMPLICATIONS

The purpose of the Five Forces model is to analyze major economic and technological forces that will ultimately influence an industry's profit potential. Identifying the profit potential (i.e., attractiveness) of an industry provides the foundation for bridging the strategic gap between the firm's external environment and its resources. Porter classifies five forces or "rules of competition" as follows:

1. Threat of new entrants.
2. Bargaining power of suppliers.
3. Bargaining power of buyers.
4. Threat of substitute products or services.
5. Rivalry among existing competitors.

Porter states that competitive strategy must grow out of a sophisticated understanding of these rules of competition with the ultimate aim of developing competitive strategies to cope with and, ideally, influence or change these forces in favor of a firm. The scope of each of the five forces is as follows:

1. *Threat of New Entrants.* Entry barriers define the level of difficulty facing those firms considering competitive entry into the industry. If these barriers are low, new competition will add capacity to the industry and increase demand and prices for inputs, resulting in lower industry profitability. The threat of new entrants is defined by several entry barriers:

- *Entry Deterring Price.* If the forecasted marginal costs of entry exceed the forecasted marginal revenues, new firms will not be enticed to enter the industry.

Often, incumbents will lower prices under this threshold to thwart competitive entry.

- *Incumbent Retaliation.* Several factors will influence the perceived or signalled intensity of response of existing firms to competitive entry such as control of substantial resources to finance a fight or the growth rate of the industry.
- *High Costs.* The level of capital required to enter an industry may deter competitive entry, especially if a high proportion of the start-up costs are unrecoverable. Additionally, new entrants will generally have a higher risk premium built into their capital cost structure.
- *Experience Effects.* Scale and learning economies may allow incumbent firms with cost structures dictated by an advanced location down the industry experience curve to price at or below the entry deterring price.
- *Other Cost Advantages.* Incumbent firms may enjoy cost advantages independent of experience effects such as access to valuable inputs, proprietary technology, or control of the best locations.
- *Product Differentiation.* Many advantages are available to incumbents through branding identity, including established customer loyalty and the flexibility to co-brand other products. The high expense and the unrecoverability of most marketing efforts pose significant entry barriers.
- *Distribution Access.* To make inroads into a new market, the entrant may encounter significant barriers to market access posed by having to surmount the incumbent's established relations with distributors. Even when this can be done, costly incentives often have to be offered to persuade distributors to carry the new product.
- *Government.* Subsidies to incumbents, regulations that increase capital costs, or entry restrictions are some of the entry barriers introduced by interventionist government policy.
- *Switching Costs.* It is often costly for consumers to switch to a new product, heavily favoring the incumbents' competitive position.

2. *Bargaining Power of Suppliers.* This force refers to the ability of the suppliers to influence the cost, availability, and quality of input materials to firms in the industry. Bargaining power has several causal factors:

- *Concentration.* If the supplier industry is concentrated and dominated by fewer firms than the industry it sells to, supplier power will be high. The availability of substitute inputs will offset this influence.
- *Diversification.* The proportion of total supplier sales that an industry represents will vary inversely with supplier power. This influence is offset by the importance of the industry to the supplier's business model and the resulting symbiotic motivations for stability.
- *Switching Costs.* An industry's ability to switch suppliers cost effectively will decrease supplier influence. Availability to forward integrate will increase supplier influence; open options for the industry to backward integrate will decrease supplier power.
- *Organization.* Supplier organization (e.g., cartels, unions, patents, copyright) will increase supplier power through increased collective bargaining strength.

- *Government.* In mixed economies, the government often functions as a supplier and can exert substantive bargaining force.

3. ***Bargaining Power of Buyers.*** The influence of the firm's customers plays an important role in defining industry structure by virtue of their ability to force prices down by comparison shopping, or by raising quality expectations. Several factors impact buyers bargaining power:

- *Differentiation.* A rich and unique set of product attributes will decrease buyer power. Conversely, a commodity product will increase buyer power.
- *Concentration.* If the buyer represents a high proportion of the firm's sales, buyer power will be high.
- *Importance.* The proportion of total buyer's purchases sold by an industry will vary directly with buyer power. A high proportion will provide an incentive for the buyer to focus cost control on the price of the industry's product.
- *Profitability.* A buyer earning low profits will be much more price sensitive.
- *Importance of Quality.* If product quality is vital to the buyer's business model, buyers will be less price sensitive.
- *Access to Information.* Buyer power will vary directly with knowledge about the industry structure.
- *Switching Costs.* Open options to backward integrate will enhance buyer power.

4. ***Threat of Substitute Products or Services.*** The risk of market displacement by existing or potential substitutes is determined by:

- *Relative Price/Performance Trade-Off.* If existing or potential competitive products or services offer a more favorable combination of product attributes or low cost, the threat of substitutes is high.
- *Switching Costs.* Threat of substitution varies inversely with switching costs.
- *Profitability.* A highly profitable provider of a credible substitute product or service poses a high threat of substitution.

5. ***Rivalry Among Existing Competitors.*** Intensity of competition within an industry which has been empirically demonstrated in a number of instances to be the most influential of the five forces, is determined by several factors:

- *Market Growth.* High market growth will reduce rivalry because one firm's sales increases will not displace the sales growth of competitors, thus reducing the probability of retaliation.
- *Cost Structure.* A high fixed cost structure usually precipitates overcapacity during demand troughs and the requisite fight for market share to secure feasible volume ranges.
- *Barriers to Exit.* Often, low-profit firms are induced to remain in the industry for several reasons, including asset specialization, fixed costs of exit, emotional attachment, government restrictions, or product market importance in the firm's platform of strategic options.
- *Switching Costs.* Commodity products will encourage switching based on price leading to competition on market share/volume. Conversely, product

differentiation will protect the firm from unwanted switching by existing customers.

- *Experience Effects.* If ramping down the industry experience curve can be achieved only by large increases in volume, the risk of overcapacity and price competition is high.
- *Diversity.* Rivalry will increase if the industry is composed of many firms of equal size and competitive position. Entry by firms from distant geographic locales, such as could easily occur via the Web, will also increase the intensity of competition. Additionally, diverse strategies among rivals will also increase competition when strategic intents clash.

With the objective of identifying the individual and collective strength of each of the five forces, the analyst ultimately needs to answer the questions: How attractive is the industry? How best can we compete? The Five Forces model is useful in answering these questions.

STRENGTHS AND ADVANTAGES

Static Analysis

Static analysis will help the analyst craft a reactive positioning strategy that matches the firm's strength and weaknesses with the current industry structure. The analysis of competitive forces is used to identify the main sources of competitive forces and the corresponding strength of these pressures. Competitive forces matter because to be successful, strategy must be designed to cope effectively with competitive pressures. The ultimate objective of the Five Forces model, then, is to build a strong market position based on competitive advantage.

The competitive environment is unattractive when rivalry is very strong, entry barriers are low, competition from substitutes is strong, and suppliers and customers have considerable bargaining power.

The competitive environment is attractive when rivalry is only moderate, entry barriers are relatively high, there are no good substitutes, and suppliers and customers are in a weak bargaining position.

The weaker the competitive forces, the greater an industry's profits. A company whose strategy and market position provide a good defense against the five forces can earn above-average profits even when some or all of the five forces are strong. The Five Forces model provides the analyst with the raw analysis necessary to craft a strategy that will insulate the company from competitive forces, provide a strong position from which "to play the game" of competition, and help create competitive advantage.

Dynamic Analysis

The Five Forces model is also very amenable to dynamic analysis of industry evolution. Dynamic analysis allows the analyst to craft a proactive strategy designed to influence industry's competitive rules in a company's favor. Industry evolution is an important component of the Five Forces model because it allows the analyst to identify strategic windows of opportunity to capitalize on changes in any of the five forces of industry structure.

The theory of industry evolution was first formulated in 1943 by Harvard economist Joseph Schumpeter, who developed the concept of creative destruction. His essential argument was that the strength of capitalist economies lies in the constant change introduced by technological and conceptual innovation. The root of progress is driven by constant innovation in which current business models are replaced by new and better business models. The theory of destructive innovation was supplemented in the early 1960s by the product life cycle (PLC) concept (see Chapter 23 for a detailed treatment of PLC analysis). When the PLC concept was combined with experience curve theory, an early model for strategically managing industry evolution was developed. However, given the questionable validity of the PLC, the fact that there cannot be one universal evolutionary process, and the limited relevance of experience curve logic, Porter asserts that the Five Forces model is a superior analytical framework to analyze industry evolution.

Central to industry evolution analysis is the explicit recognition that the five forces are mutually dependent—a change in one force will impact the other forces resulting in malleable industry structure and boundaries. The essential analytical task in industry evolution analysis is to:

- forecast future changes in each of the five competitive forces
- discover how these changes will impact the other forces
- discover how the culmination of these interrelated changes will impact the future profitability of the industry
- discover the predicted strength of the firm's position in this future scenario employing the current strategy
- discover how the strategy might be changed to exploit this changing industry structure by either reacting to competitor actions or by proactively seeking to secure competitive advantage through strategic change

Important Extension of Environmental Analysis

The Five Forces model was an important extension of SWOT analysis and the "resource-environment" construct of strategy theory. It introduced an interdisciplinary application of industrial economics to the purview of strategy. Use of the Five Forces model will greatly improve the analysis of the environmental component of strategy formulation and implementation. A higher probability of achieving a tight strategic fit is one of the lasting contributions of this model.

Precursor of Formal Scenario Theory

The emphasis that the Five Forces model places on industry evolution created a strong foundation for scenario analysis. Examining the five forces places the analyst in the proper mindset for long-range planning by giving prominence to the concept of mutual dependency between the forces; the idea that these forces change over time; and the assertion that a business strategy can and should both reactively defend against *and* proactively manage these forces to improve competitive position.

WEAKNESSES AND LIMITATIONS

The main weakness of the Five Forces model is the converse of its main strength—the assumption that the economic structure of industries drives competition. Critics of the five forces framework claim that this emphasis underestimates the core competencies of a firm that may serve as its competitive advantage in the long term, while focusing on shorter-term market positions. Further, the framework is designed for analyzing individual business unit strategies, as it does not account for synergies and interdependencies within a corporation's overall portfolio.

Another weakness of the Five Forces model is its lack of explicit recognition of the importance of sociopolitical (SP) factors. The model only implicitly incorporates the influence of SP factors within each of the five forces. However, the increasing importance of SP strategy likely warrants treating government and other social factors as a separate sixth force. Without this distinct inclusion, the analyst is at risk of overlooking the impact of SP factors that lie outside of the purview of the five forces but nonetheless directly impinge on the competitive parameters of the industry.

Initially, Porter was criticized for ignoring the difficult task of developing a robust industry analysis and for failing to provide a methodology for choosing and implementing one of the three generic strategies of low cost, differentiation, or scope. In response, in 1985 Porter offered the value chain model to address this implementation gap. (See Chapter 9 for a detailed treatment of the value chain.)

The framework also can be tautological, that is, it posits that firms in attractive industries are successful. They are successful because they are in attractive industries (Black & Boal, 1994). The question of which comes first, organizational or industry success, remains problematic.

Another important limitation of this framework is pointed out by Porter himself. The framework is concerned with cross-sectional problems and not longitudinal ones. The cross-sectional problem focuses on what makes some industries, and some positions within them, more attractive. It does not directly address *why* or *how* some firms are able to get into advantageous positions in the first place, and why some firms are able to sustain these positions over time and others are not (Black & Boal, 1994).

Other limitations stem from the implicit advice it gives to managers for formulating strategy. McWilliams and Smart (1993) note that the framework misdirects managers to focus on industry-level characteristics, encouraging them to allocate resources on influencing the industry's structure even though their firm may not uniquely benefit from the changes, thus allowing competitors to benefit from and take a free ride on the coattails of another firm's resources. This course of action may be justifiable if industry structure was the dominant determinant of firm performance. Recent evidence from several researchers suggests it is not (Rumelt, 1991; Roquebert, Phillips, & Dean, 1993). They note that, at best, industry structure accounts for 8 to 15 percent of variance in firm performance. Furthermore, market power-based strategies can be harmful to the firm. For example, Carr (1993) in his analysis of the vehicle components industry found that firms utilizing a market power based strategy significantly underperformed, on multiple performance measures, their competitors who followed a resource-based strategy.

PROCESS FOR APPLYING THE TECHNIQUE

The process of utilizing the Five Forces model essentially involves two major steps and several substeps. The first is to collect information to identify the characteristics of each force (see Figure 6-1) and to examine and assess their impact on the industry. Figure 6-2 suggests factors that can be used to determine the degree of impact of each force. While much of the information required in this step can be obtained from secondary sources, primary sources should be consulted to improve the objectivity of this analysis.

The procedure for analyzing the five competitive forces starts with identifying the main sources of competitive pressures: rivalry among competitors, substitute products, potential entry, bargaining power of suppliers, and bargaining power of buyers.

Next, the relative strength of each factor is determined by ascribing a value to each factor indicating if it is strong, moderate, or weak. One way to facilitate this ranking is to use a scale of 1 to 5, with 5 indicating a strong force and 1 indicating a weak force. An important analytical input into this process is determining a logical explanation of how each competitive force works and its role in the overall competitive picture.

The second step involves collectively assessing and evaluating the five forces in light of your organization's competitive ability. The ultimate goal is to identify the ability of your firm to successfully compete within this industry, given the collective strength of the five forces. A comparison of the firm's resource strength with regards to the size of the "fit" gap with the five forces will shed valuable insight on strategic opportunities and threats.

The third step requires the analyst to focus on proactive strategy by reiterating the first two steps in light of industry evolution. To improve the usefulness of this analysis, long-term industry trends should be analyzed to determine whether the profitability of the industry is sustainable, and their affect on your firm's competitive position. These trends include, among other things, proposed government legislation and regulations, social and consumer trends, international trends, economic trends, and technological trends.

Next, the analyst must integrate the environmental analysis within the broader context of corporate strategy—finding the tightest fit between the firm's resources

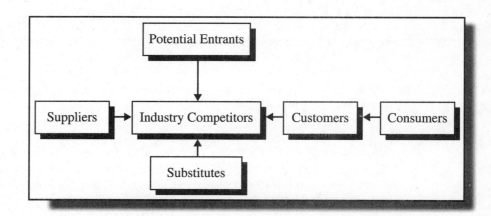

Figure 6-1
Generic Process for Applying the Technique

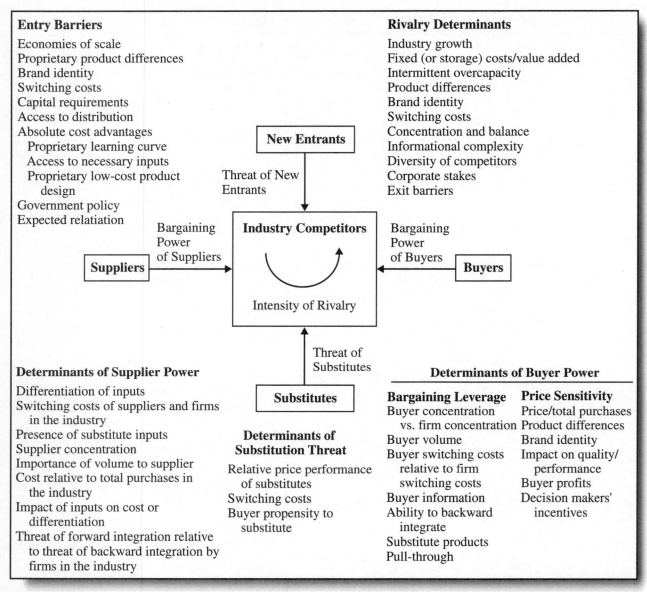

Entry Barriers

Economies of scale
Proprietary product differences
Brand identity
Switching costs
Capital requirements
Access to distribution
Absolute cost advantages
  Proprietary learning curve
  Access to necessary inputs
  Proprietary low-cost product
    design
Government policy
Expected relatiation

Rivalry Determinants

Industry growth
Fixed (or storage) costs/value added
Intermittent overcapacity
Product differences
Brand identity
Switching costs
Concentration and balance
Informational complexity
Diversity of competitors
Corporate stakes
Exit barriers

New Entrants

Threat of New
Entrants

Bargaining
Power
of Suppliers

Industry Competitors

Suppliers

Intensity of Rivalry

Bargaining
Power
of Buyers

Buyers

Threat of
Substitutes

Substitutes

Determinants of Supplier Power

Differentiation of inputs
Switching costs of suppliers and firms
  in the industry
Presence of substitute inputs
Supplier concentration
Importance of volume to supplier
Cost relative to total purchases in
  the industry
Impact of inputs on cost or
  differentiation
Threat of forward integration relative
  to threat of backward integration by
  firms in the industry

**Determinants of
Substitution Threat**

Relative price performance
  of substitutes
Switching costs
Buyer propensity to
  substitute

Determinants of Buyer Power

Bargaining Leverage	**Price Sensitivity**
Buyer concentration vs. firm concentration	Price/total purchases
	Product differences
Buyer volume	Brand identity
Buyer switching costs relative to firm switching costs	Impact on quality/ performance
Buyer information	Buyer profits
Ability to backward integrate	Decision makers' incentives
Substitute products	
Pull-through	

Figure 6-2
Porter's Model

Reprinted with the permission of The Free Press, a Division of Simon & Schuster, Inc., from *Competitive Advantage: Creating and Sustaining Superior Performance* by Michael E. Porter. Copyright © 1985, 1998 by Michael E. Porter.

and capabilities, and the external environment. This involves three types of strategic analysis: reactive strategy against likely competitor moves; proactive strategy to manipulate changing forces already in motion; and proactive strategy to explicitly force change in one or all of the five forces.

STATIC ANALYSIS—TWO INDUSTRY EXTREMES

1. Rating the Five Forces of the Airline Industry (5 = strong, 1 = weak)
   a. Barriers to Entry—Weighting 5
      - Massive deregulation in the 1980s reduced legislative barriers
      - Capital intensity offset by ability to lease aircraft and hire ground crews on contract
      - Limited availability of terminal slots offset by use of secondary airports
   b. Bargaining Power of Buyers—Weighting 5
      - Hypercompetition has made air travel a commodity resulting in overcapacity
      - Price sensitivity of consumers has not been significantly offset by loyalty programs
      - Market share warfare is the industry norm
   c. Bargaining Power of Suppliers—Weighting 5
      - Militant pilot and machinist unions have eroded economic rent associated with producer surplus
   d. Market Growth—Weighting 3
      - Total growth is relatively high but only in price-sensitive travel class
      - Growth in travel class offset by larger planes and competitive entry, resulting in overcapacity and lower margins
      - Market growth of profitable business class is slowing due to the impact of information technology reducing the need for face-to-face communication
   e. Cost Structure—Weighting 5
      - Majority of costs are fixed regardless of load
      - Resulting variable cost pricing through heavy discounting to maximize contribution margin from excess capacity
   f. Barriers to Exit—Weighting 5
      - Lax bankruptcy legislation allows airlines to essentially tear up union contracts and continue operations
      - Government ownership of international airlines makes exit or capacity reduction unlikely due to conflicting sociopolitical considerations

Conclusion: Competitive forces are strong, profitability of the airline industry is low

2. Rating the Five Forces of the Pharmaceutical Drug Industry (5 = strong, 1 = weak)
   a. Barriers to Entry—Weighting 1
      - High capital requirements (average drug requires $200 million in R&D and substantial unrecoverable marketing expenditures)
      - Hence, niche strategies are the only feasible basis of competition for new entrants that, if successful, are frequently subject to aggressive takeover overtures
   b. Bargaining Power of Buyers—Weighting 1
      - Doctors, not patients, usually make the purchase decision based on product attributes and efficacy, not price
      - When consumers do make the purchase decision, they show a high brand loyalty that works against private-label drugs
      - Patent protection promotes and protects innovation
   c. Bargaining Power of Suppliers—Weighting 3
      - Many of the raw inputs to pharmaceuticals are commodities
      - Few substitutes for pharmaceutical drug therapy, and it is often much cheaper than surgical interventions
      - Biotechnology and gene therapy are still in the developmental stage
      - Many of the promising new biotech firms have or will be acquired by established drug firms
   d. Market Growth—Weighting 1
      - Continual product innovation creates demand
      - Aging baby boomers will foster growth
      - Increased longevity of humans

(Continued on following page)

e. Barriers to Exit—Weighting 2
  - A high percentage of unrecoverable costs such as R&D and marketing/distribution increase barriers to exit
  - Offsetting effect of high premiums offered by incumbents for acquisitions of smaller firms

Conclusion: Competitive forces are weak; profitability of the drug industry is high

SOURCE: Adapted from "Understanding Industry Structure," by R. Suutari, 2000, *CMA Management, 73*(10), pp. 34–37.

Crafting Strategy with the Five Forces Model

DYNAMIC ANALYSIS—THE U.S. MEMORIES PROJECT

In the 1970s, the U.S. semiconductor industry enjoyed seemingly secure first mover advantages. The interventionist industrial policy of the Japanese government had designs to change this to support aspirations of global dominance in electronics. Soon the Japanese were investing much more heavily than the Americans in semiconductor random access memory chips (DRAM) technology, product development, and manufacturing capacity. The results were astounding. By 1985, the Japanese had captured 15 percent of the 1K DRAM market. Further, by 1984, they controlled 40 percent of the global market for 64K DRAM. In 1989, Price Waterhouse completed a competitive analysis for U.S. Memories, a consortium of American manufacturers (IBM, ADM, Digital, Intel, LSI Logic, and National Semiconductor). The goal was to displace Japanese global dominance and reclaim the industry. Dominant Japanese producers were planning to produce 4 MB chips in early 1990. U.S. Memories was looking for strategy to surpass the Japanese in market share by the mid-1990s. To do this, in 1993 Price Waterhouse had to develop a scenario regarding the future competitive structure of the industry.

The approach taken by Price Waterhouse sheds insight into how to integrate industry analysis with other conceptual tools. The use of industry analysis helped to determine the current competitive position of the industry as well as why and how to improve this position in order to meet strategic goals. Price Waterhouse engaged in a sequential analytical process as follows:

Step 1—Investigate the Strategic Issues

The value chain was analyzed to understand the internal business model. Further, scenario analysis was performed around the possibility of the competitive response of the Japanese (increasing scale, technological innovation, next generation 64 MB chips, etc.).

Step 2—Industry Analysis

Out of necessity, the industry analysis was decidedly forward looking, as timing was a critical issue. As such, the industry analysis focused on

- What type of DRAM to produce
- Which technology would bestow competitive advantage
- Which manufacturing processes would support the lowest costs
- Competitive analysis of the industry experience curve to forecast future pricing policy of competitors and the position of the U.S. Memories on the curve upon market entry

Much inside information was available by virtue of the consortium's membership in the Semiconductor Industry Association. Other sources of information for the industry analysis came first from secondary sources

(Continued on following page)

such as the Aerospace Industries Association of America, Society of Automotive Engineers, and the Office for the Study of Automotive Transport at the University of Michigan. Next, the consultants developed a hypothesis based on the secondary information and tested them on line mangers at U.S. Memories. The analytical product of this process was a tentative industry boundary to limit the scope of the analysis to a manageable and meaningful product market definition.

Step 3—Value Chain Analysis

With the product market defined, customer value became the focus of investigating the corresponding value chain. Once the competitive parameters were identified, strategic differences between the Japanese and U.S. Memories were identified. Internal benchmarking analysis revealed that the most important process variable was yield rate (i.e., the ratio of quality product to scrap). The most important economic variable as an important driver of the yield rate was identified as economies of scale. Other important variables were wafer size, yield of manufacturing operations, design complexity, materials, and overhead. External benchmarking revealed that the Japanese industry was more highly leveraged, focused, incremental, and lower cost than the American industry. The famous "team approach" was also discovered to be a major competitive advantage.

Experience curve analysis also revealed a key insight—increasing production volume correlated to major cost reductions. In fact, the price of 1 MB DRAMs declined by 25 to 30 percent each year during the 1980s. Strategic implications of this analysis served to refute a faulty assumption of the U.S. Memories project. At the onset of the project, it was assumed that the Japanese would have only single production lines in their semiconductor plants. This supported the initial strategy to license technology from several U.S. companies in order to save the costs of development. The strategic implications of rivals operating multiple production lines rendered invalid the assumption that licensing would provide a sustainable competitive advantage.

Step 4—Design Strategy

Scenario analysis around the five forces was used to contemplate the strategic ramifications of contingent changes in the industry structure such as

- the impact of Japanese FDI and production on American soil
- the impact of U.S. Memories forming joint ventures
- product innovation
- Japanese outsourcing of links in its value chain

The final strategic recommendations for U.S. Memories were the following:

- Disregarding the longer-term technology costs by using IBM expertise would only achieve competitive parity instead of supremacy.
- Utilizing only one production line would significantly raise manufacturing costs per unit above the Japanese.
- Competitive design and process improvement would surpass the American cost advantage by 1994.
- The flat technology licensing fee and the absence of process cost reductions would prevent the achievement of sustainable competitive advantage.
- Volume and technological improvements would have to be significantly ramped up from the original assumptions.

The U.S. Memories project failed largely because the organizational complexity of the consortium prevented the implementation of these recommendations. The DRAM market collapse of 1990, the failure to revise licensing agreements, the casual disregard of the importance of the experience curve on the long-term costs of technology, and superior innovation of rivals all played a role. Nonetheless, the use of evolutionary industry analysis was pivotal in correctly identifying the strategic implications of industry evolution and the requisite strategy.

SOURCE: Adapted from "U.S. Memories: The Secrets of Successful Competitive Analysis," by S. J. Berman, 1991, *Planning Review*, 19(6), pp. 28–35.

These strategies are formulated under the overarching framework of sustainable competitive advantage delivered through value chain analysis. That is choosing a differentiated, low-cost, or scope strategy that meets the three criteria of sustainable competitive advantage for a resource based strategy: inimitability, demand, and scarcity.

Industry structure fundamentally impacts strategic choices. Important direction for initially selecting and subsequently managing the strategy around these criteria comes from the industry evolution analysis. Each competitive force should be constantly monitored for their impact on the current strategy and the opportunities they represent for extending sustainable competitive advantage.

Finally, not all industries are alike. Therefore, for companies with product portfolios across numerous industries, this model must be repeated for each unique industry served.

FAROUT Summary

	1	2	3	4	5
F	■	■	■		
A	■	■	■		
R	■	■	■	■	
O	■	■	■		
U	■	■	■	■	
T	■	■	■		

Future orientation   Present to medium term. Needs to be reviewed regularly as industry forces change.

Accuracy   Medium degree. Accuracy will be dependent upon sources of information used. Cross validation with industry experts will increase accuracy of the analysis.

Resource efficiency   Medium to high degree. Much of the information required should already be available to the firm. Cost of analysis will depend on the number and positions of analysts employed.

Objectivity   Medium degree. Depends on information used as subjective data reduces objectivity. There is a high emphasis placed on qualitative analysis.

Usefulness   Medium to high degree. Provides an overall picture of an industry, highlighting key competitive factors and elements that require close monitoring for strategies to be successfully implemented.

Timeliness   Medium degree. Time is required to undertake a close analysis of the five forces, particularly if primary sources are addressed.

Related Tools and Techniques

- competitor analysis
- environmental analysis
- experience curve analysis
- industry evolution analysis
- product life cycle analysis
- strategic group analysis
- SWOT analysis
- value chain analysis

REFERENCES

Bain, J. S. (1956). *Barriers to new competition*. Cambridge, MA: Harvard University Press.

Berman, S. J. (1991). "U.S. memories: The secrets of successful competitive analysis." *Planning Review, 19*(6), 28–35.

Black, J. A., & Boal, K. B. (1994). "Strategic resources: Traits, configurations and paths to sustainable competitive advantage." *Strategic Management Journal*, [Special summer issue], *15*, 131–148.

Black and Boal (1994) paraphrasing Porter, M. E. (1991). "Towards a dynamic theory of strategy." *Strategic Management Journal* [Special summer issue], *12*, 95–117.

Carr, C. (1993). "Global, national, and resource-based strategies: An examination of strategic choice and performance in the vehicle components industry." *Strategic Management Journal, 14*(7), 551–568.

McWilliams, A., & Smart, D. L. (1993). "Efficiency v. structure conduct performance: Implications for strategy and practice." *Journal of Management, 19*, 63–79.

Porter, M. E. (1979). "How competitive forces shape strategy." *Harvard Business Review, 57*(2), 137–145.

———. (1979). "The Structure within Industries and Companies Performance," *The Review of Economics and Statistics, 61*(2), 214–227.

———. (1980). *Competitive strategy: Techniques for analyzing industries and competitors*. London: Collier Macmillan Publishers.

———. (1980). "Industry structure and competitive strategy: Keys to profitability." *Financial Analysts Journal, 36*(4), 30–41.

———. (1985). *Competitive advantage: Creating and sustaining superior performance*. London: Collier Macmillan Publishers.

Roquebert, J., Phillips, R., & Duran, C. (1995). "How much does strategic management matter?" Presentation at the meeting of the National Academy of Management, Atlanta, GA.

Rumelt, R. P. (1991). "How much does industry matter?" *Strategic Management Journal, 12*(3), 167–185.

Scherer, F. M. (1970). *Industrial market structure and economic performance*. Chicago, IL: Rand McNally.

Schumpeter, J. A. (1943). *Capitalism, socialism and democracy*. London: Gorge Allen and Unwin Ltd.

Suutari, R. (2000). "Understanding industry structure." *CMA Management, 73*(10), 34–37.

Chapter 7

Strategic Group Analysis

SHORT DESCRIPTION

Strategic group analysis is a subset of industry analysis that studies different groups of rival firms clustered on the premise of similar competitive approach and strategic position. A *strategic group* consists of those rival firms with similar competitive approaches and positions in an industry. A *strategic group map* displays different competitive positions that rival firms occupy. Strategic group analysis is used to determine

- Different competitive positions that rival firms occupy
- Intensity of competitive rivalry within and between industry groups
- Profit potential of the various strategic groups in an industry
- Static and dynamic strategic implications for the competitive position of the firm under analysis.

BACKGROUND

The concept of strategic groups was first articulated by Michael Hunt in his 1972 doctoral thesis at Harvard University to explain the performance of companies within the major home appliance industry in the 1960s. He postulated that three factors explained the differences in economic performance of the industry's firms: vertical integration, degree of product diversification, and differences in product diversification. Using these factors, he divided the industry into four strategic groups. For a firm planning to enter the major home appliance industry, this analysis could be used to determine the different barriers to entry of each strategic group.

Soon after this, Hunt's colleagues at Harvard, Newman (1973) and Porter (1973) both explored this new concept for different applications in their doctoral dissertations. Since then, many researchers have applied the strategic groups concept to a wide variety of different industries. Their work is well documented (e.g., see McGee & Thomas, 1986) and constitutes one of the better developed empirical areas of strategy studies.

Prior to these developments, the standard approach in strategic analysis was to draw industry borders and consequent strategic prescriptions based on markets (i.e., cross-elasticity of demand, product life cycle) or technological and manufacturing processes (i.e., experience curve). The familiar portfolio approaches of the 1970s incorporated both of these definitions. In contrast, industry analysis sought to embrace a wider swath of competitive variables to both define industry boundaries and to explain competition within those boundaries. This nascent theory of industry structure analysis was being developed during the era when portfolio approaches had reached the peak of their popularity.

It wasn't until 1980, with the publication of Porter's seminal work, *Competitive Strategy: Techniques for Analyzing Industries and Competitors,* that industry structure analysis began to surpass in popularity portfolio approaches such as the BCG matrix and the GE business screen. Porter's book also broke new ground because it was the first comprehensive foray into using industrial economic theory as an explicit framework for strategic analysis. Strategic group analysis figured prominently in this theoretical evolution and has become an important component of modern strategy theory and practice.

STRATEGIC RATIONALE AND IMPLICATIONS

A strategic group can be defined as a group or cluster of firms in an industry that are similar to each other but distinct from other industry groups because they differ in one or more key aspects of their competitive strategy. Different competitive strategies are a function of the historical evolution of the industry, different resources and capabilities across firms, unique goals, different chronological points of entry, segmentation, varying risk profiles, and so on. This far-from-exclusive list of strategically relevant competitive variables will distinguish differences between groups and similarities within groups. Strategic groups are important because the five forces of competitive pressure have an asymmetric influence on the profitability of each strategic group in the industry. This will have important strategic implications for the analyst studying the profitability of the individual firm within a particular group.

As described in Chapter 6, Porter's Five Forces model stipulates that industry structure is the result of five interacting competitive forces: (1) threat of new entrants, (2) bargaining power of suppliers, (3) bargaining power of buyers, (4) threat of substitute products and services, and (5) rivalry among existing firms. Strategic group analysis explicitly addresses the fifth component, competitive rivalry and how it both impacts and is impacted by the other four forces. It forms the analytical link between industry structure and the individual firm. The five competitive forces will have disproportionate impacts on the profitability across strategic groups and, by association, on firms within each strategic group. By analyzing the structure of strategic groups and their impact on the five competitive forces, the analyst gains a perceptive insight into the strategic options facing the firm within a context of industry evolution.

Impact of the Threat of Entry on Strategic Groups

By forming mobility barriers that protect their competitive position from erosion through competitor imitation, individual firms wield a powerful weapon to protect their profitability by thwarting entry. Similarly, mobility barriers also intensify the competitive structure between strategic groups, making it difficult for firms to change strategy to move into another strategic group. These mobility barriers, in effect, define both the boundaries and structure of a strategic group. Common mobility barriers include superior cost structures, economies of scale or learning, product/service attribute differentiation, switching costs, distribution access, vertical or horizontal diversification, capital intensity, proprietary technology, and favorable sociopolitical factors, to name but a few.

It is important for the analyst to note that mobility barriers change over time. Waves of creative destruction in market economies will radically change established competitive parameters in an industry. Innovation is a key to dislodging established mobility barriers because it radically changes the industry structure. Very seldom is superior operational excellence an effective strategy to combat mobility barriers because it attempts only to imitate strategy rather than to employ a creative and different strategy. The chances of running headlong into an established mobility barrier are much higher for an imitation strategy than for a uniquely innovative strategy. Therefore, the optimal strategic focus for a firm attempting to redefine competition inside of its existing strategic group, to jump to another strategic group, or to define a new strategic group, is to precipitate creative destruction through innovation or at least to be "ahead of the curve."

Impact of Internal Rivalry on Strategic Groups

Three factors determine the intensity of rivalry between strategic groups: (1) *number of groups in the industry and market share distribution among the groups*; (2) *strategic distance between groups* (i.e., the magnitude of strategic differences between groups); and (3) *Market interdependence of groups* (i.e., the overlap of market segmentation and product/service differentiation between groups).

A directly proportional relationship exists between each of these three factors and rivalry. First, the higher the number of firms within a strategic group and the more similar their market share distribution, the greater the rivalry. Second, the greater the strategic distance, the greater the rivalry. Third, the greater the market interdependence, the greater the rivalry.

For example, strategic groups, who by definition are pursuing different strategies, may nonetheless target the same customer segment. The resulting clash for customer share will increase rivalry between strategic groups. Alternately, if strategic groups within an industry are targeting different market segments, the different strategies will not impinge on each other's competitive parameters, thus avoiding the intense rivalry of the first scenario.

Impact of Bargaining Power of Buyers and Suppliers on Strategic Groups

There are two separate ways that strategic groups can influence the bargaining power of suppliers and buyers:

1. *Common Suppliers and Buyers.* All of the strategic groups within an industry may source from the same set or type of suppliers and may sell to the same customer segment. Therefore, the only differentiating feature will be the different strategies between groups. As a result, some groups will be more susceptible to bargaining power than others.

2. *Different Suppliers and Buyers.* When strategic groups source from different types of suppliers and sell to different customer segments, another dimension is added to the balance of power. In this scenario, bargaining strength could be a factor of different strategies among strategic groups, different types of buyers and suppliers, or a combination of both.

Impact of the Threat of Substitution on Strategic Groups

Different strategic groups, by their nature, will focus on different strategic dimensions or competitive variables. That is, the distinct strategies between strategic groups will necessarily place emphasis on different parts of the industry value chain. If the link(s) in the value chain that are the source of a competitive advantage of a strategic group are threatened by substitutes, the group is at risk of lower profitability or worse, displacement. As such, some groups will be more susceptible to substitution; others will be less susceptible depending on which link of the value chain they compete on and upon which link which the threat of substitution bears.

The competitive position of a firm within a strategic group will also impact the profitability of its composite firms. Porter suggests four factors that influence the competitive structure within strategic groups:

1. *Intensity of Internal Rivalry Between Firms in the Same Group.* The same three factors that determine the intensity of rivalry between strategic groups also apply at the interfirm level of abstraction. Similarly, the same directly proportional relationship between each factor and firm profitability holds.
   - *Number of firms in the strategic group and market share distribution across the firms*
   - *Strategic distance between groups* (i.e., the magnitude of strategic differences between firms in the strategic group)
   - *Market interdependence of groups* (i.e., the overlap of market segmentation and product/service differentiation between firms in the strategic group)

2. *Scale Effects.* If the potential for economies of scale still exist in the strategic group's market, then the firms with the highest market share will enjoy superior cost structures.

3. *Cost of Entry into the Strategic Group.* The costs for entering a strategic group are determined by several factors:
   - Superior resources available to the entering firm perhaps secured by leveraging core competencies earned in other strategic groups or industries
   - Timing of entry

4. *Organizational Capabilities to Implement the Firm's Chosen Strategy.* Even if every other competitive variable were held constant, some firms would still be more profitable than others due to superior organizational skill and capabilities, which manifest themselves in better implementation and higher profitability.

Porter (1980) suggests a "cascading array" of the five forces that will jointly determine the profitability of the industry, the profitability of the strategic groups in the industry, and the profitability of individual firms within the strategic groups. The essential task of the analyst is to best position the firm's resources and capabilities to capitalize on opportunities and defend against or move away from threats in the competitive environment. Selecting the most attractive industry group in which to compete is an essential component of this process. The selection of the appropriate low cost, differentiation, or focus strategy in the strategic group that will bestow upon the firm the highest probability of competitive advantage is the strategic purpose of this conceptual model. (See Figure 7-1.)

The value of strategic group analysis can be extended from consideration of current strategic issues to address the challenges of industry evolution. Porter (1980) suggests that there are several strategic opportunities facing the firm in times of change.

1. Improve the existing competitive structure of the firm's existing strategic group or the firm's relative position in this group.
2. Move to a better strategic group in search of a tighter strategic fit.
3. Move to another group and improve the competitive structure of this new group.
4. Creating an entirely new strategic group.

Notice that the proactive intensity of these strategies increases with (1) being the least proactive and (4) being the most proactive. Herein lies the core value of strategic group analysis. There is little room for reactive strategy in this model. By employing strategic group analysis, the analyst is forced into a mind-set of tradeoffs between intensity of proactive strategy. Compare this to the traditional tradeoff between proactive and reactive strategies that many other models encourage.

Some of the strategic risks posed by industry evolution include (Porter, 1980):

1. Threat of entry from other strategic groups.
2. Weakening mobility barriers.
3. Weakening bargaining power.
4. Risks of investing to increase the strength of existing mobility barriers.
5. Risks of investing to overcome mobility barriers to support moving to other strategic groups or to support creating an entirely new strategic group.

The bottom box of Figure 7-1 indicates the versatility of this model not only to guide current strategy but also to address the critical issue of industry evolution. The development of the current strategy discussed above is very helpful in determining the relative profitability of the various strategic groups, the root causes of this profitability, and how these five forces interact to create various intensities of mobility factors within the strategic groups. Through this analytical process, the analyst will build a thorough knowledge of the competitive environment facing the firm within its established or chosen strategic group. This specialized knowledge can then be applied to analyzing the impact of industry evolution on the competitive structure of the strategic groups within an industry.

By forecasting expected impacts of endogenous competitive innovation or exogenous evolution on mobility barriers between strategic groups, the analyst can anticipate the consequent threat of entry or increased internal rivalry both within its strategic group and between strategic groups. From this analysis, the analyst can

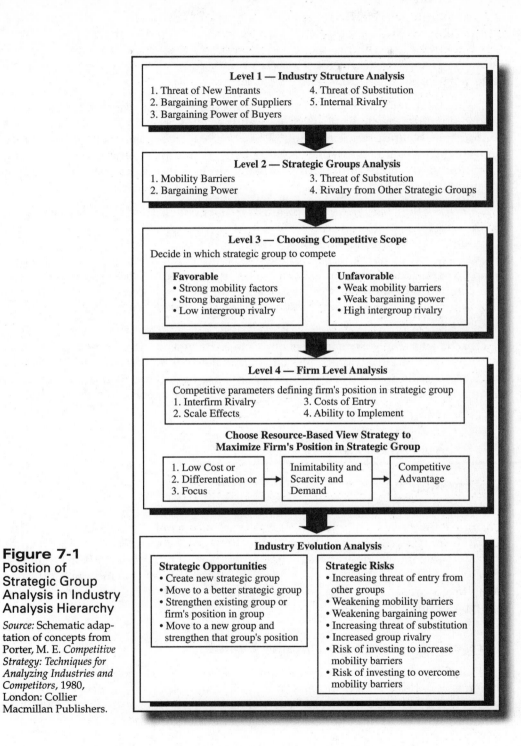

Figure 7-1
Position of
Strategic Group
Analysis in Industry
Analysis Hierarchy

Source: Schematic adaptation of concepts from Porter, M. E. *Competitive Strategy: Techniques for Analyzing Industries and Competitors*, 1980, London: Collier Macmillan Publishers.

Level 1 — Industry Structure Analysis
1. Threat of New Entrants   4. Threat of Substitution
2. Bargaining Power of Suppliers   5. Internal Rivalry
3. Bargaining Power of Buyers

Level 2 — Strategic Groups Analysis
1. Mobility Barriers   3. Threat of Substitution
2. Bargaining Power   4. Rivalry from Other Strategic Groups

Level 3 — Choosing Competitive Scope
Decide in which strategic group to compete

Favorable
• Strong mobility factors
• Strong bargaining power
• Low intergroup rivalry

Unfavorable
• Weak mobility barriers
• Weak bargaining power
• High intergroup rivalry

Level 4 — Firm Level Analysis

Competitive parameters defining firm's position in strategic group
1. Interfirm Rivalry   3. Costs of Entry
2. Scale Effects   4. Ability to Implement

**Choose Resource-Based View Strategy to
Maximize Firm's Position in Strategic Group**

1. Low Cost or
2. Differentiation or
3. Focus

→

Inimitability and
Scarcity and
Demand

→

Competitive
Advantage

Industry Evolution Analysis

Strategic Opportunities
• Create new strategic group
• Move to a better strategic group
• Strengthen existing group or firm's position in group
• Move to a new group and strengthen that group's position

Strategic Risks
• Increasing threat of entry from other groups
• Weakening mobility barriers
• Weakening bargaining power
• Increasing threat of substitution
• Increased group rivalry
• Risk of investing to increase mobility barriers
• Risk of investing to overcome mobility barriers

determine the relative future competitive position of the firm's strategic group within the industry structure under different scenarios. This analysis will in turn provide further insight into the future competitive position of the firm within the strategic group. Strategic group analysis offers the analyst two primary strategic directions for dealing with industry evolution:

1. *Mildly Proactive Strategy.* Strategy here would focus on securing the resources and capabilities needed best cope with the redefined competitive parameters introduced by industry evolution. The primary coping mechanism would be investing to strengthen existing mobility barriers in order to improve the existing competitive structure of the firm's existing strategic group or the firm's relative position in this group.

2. *Intensely Proactive Strategy.* In contrast, an intensely proactive strategy for coping with industry evolution would be to refuse to cope with change. Rather, the firm would become what some colloquially refer to as a "shape-shifter." That is, the firm would explicitly choose to precipitate industry change though innovation rather than be impacted by innovation. At its extreme, this type of strategy would redefine the competitive parameters of competition on the firm's own terms rather than attempting to cope with change induced primarily for the benefit of the instigating competitor.

Each increasingly more intensely proactive strategy requires increasing amounts of investment in the resources and capabilities needed to overcome, or ideally skirt around, existing mobility barriers in order to move into more attractive strategic groups or to create a new group. The corresponding reward risk is higher as well.

STRENGTHS AND ADVANTAGES

Comprehensive

One of the main strengths of strategic group analysis is its comprehensiveness. It encompasses a wide array of conceivable variables when conducting an environmental analysis. More importantly, the linkages between the environmental variables are much tighter than that offered by standardized SWOT models. Strategic group analysis offers the analysts several layers of increasingly finer analytical procedures for making the link from broad industry structure to firm-specific strategic implications.

Strategic Guidance for Industry Evolution

The identification of strategic opportunities and risks associated with industry evolution is very helpful for dealing with change. Further, this holistic perspective from which to analyze industry evolution provides a realistic tool for making the transition from current strategy to future strategy. Strategic group analysis can help firms to apply the "judo" principle of competitive strategy, that is, to resist the traditional approach of a boxer and avoid direct confrontation with the five forces of competitive pressure. Rather, this model encourages the analyst to look further afield, across the entire spectrum of groups to find innovative pathways of least resistance or, ideally, to build new pathways through innovation.

Supply Side Orientation

Strategic group analysis fills the analytical vacuum left by many other types of strategic analysis. Its supply side orientation makes a nice complement to the other predominantly demand side models that preceded its genesis.

Delineates Homogenous from Heterogeneous Industries

Without first distinguishing the differences between industry structure as evidenced by the existence of strategic groups, average comparisons across the industry are meaningless at best and misleading at worst. Strategic group analysis often results in much more accurate strategic analysis as opposed to more traditional approaches to product/market segmentation and stereotypical definitions of strategic business units.

Positive Effects of Strong Group Identity

Peteraf and Shanley (1997) identify three types of positive effects from firms associating strongly as part of a strategic group:

• *Coordination Effects.* The explicit recognition of interrelated linkages and mutual dependence between the various parameters that comprise the competitive dimension of an industry provides a positive incentive for co-opetition. This can manifest itself in a myriad of ways, including joint ventures, alliances, and cooperation, in order to jointly increase mobility barriers and bargaining strength to enhance the profitability of the strategic group as a whole with secondary reference to individual firm benefit.

• *Efficiency Effects.* Firms in strongly recognized strategic groups tend to share information more readily which decreases the costs of innovation and increases efficiency generally.

• *Reputation Effects.* Customers will recognize strong group identities which will reduce their information search costs thereby increasing the relative value proposition offered by group firms.

WEAKNESSES AND LIMITATIONS

Limited Guidance on Capabilities Needed for Successful Implementation

Strategic group analysis gives little guidance on implementation and gives short shrift to the internal organizational capabilities needed for successful implementation of the chosen strategies. Supplementation with value chain analysis will compensate for this weakness, and in fact was one of the reasons Porter subsequently developed value chain analysis.

No Explicit Recognition of the Impact of Sociopolitical Strategy

Strategic group analysis does not explicitly incorporate the importance of government and social issues as a separate variable on the competitive dimension. Sociopolitical effects are only given implicit recognition by including its impact through the other competitive variables and mobility barriers.

Presumption That Firms Have Cognitive and Learning Abilities

Peteraf and Shanley (1997) suggest that it is erroneous to "anthropomorphize" strategic groups. The larger firms in a strategic group become, the more tenuous this assumption becomes due to such effects as group normalization and agency theory. Unless the majority of firms have truly become learning organizations, strategic group theory is subject to question.

Negative Effects of Strong Group Identity

Peteraf and Shanley (1997) identify three types of negative effects from firms associating strongly as part of a strategic group:

• *Reduced Flexibility.* If cooperation becomes too strong in a strategic group, the development of group norms may function to reduce the ability of the group to respond to changes in the group's external environment. A group with strong identity may become more focused on issues within the group rather than adopting an industrywide perspective. Given the new economics of information, threats often appear "out of nowhere like a thief in the night" through innovation. This permits migration from other strategic groups or industries, allowing firms with newly secured capabilities and resources to break links in the existing value chain that the strategic group competes on. Even more damaging is the increasing prevalence of industry immigration premised on entirely new value chains.

• *Strategic Myopia.* Preoccupation with a strong group identity may concentrate the minds of management to the neglect of casting an outward strategic vision. Predisposal to reducing intergroup competition may make the firm particularly vulnerable to blindspots from intragroup competition or from entirely different industries.

• *Suboptimizing Behavior.* Preoccupation with group-level strategy and goals that might accompany a strong group identity may lead to goal-incongruent behavior at the firm level. Examples of this phenomenon include decision bias, risk pooling, and agency problems. An example of decision bias would be incorrect perceptions of sunk costs in order to preserve prior investments in strengthening group identity. An example of risk pooling induced by strong group identity may be the perverse incentives to imitate rather that innovate in order to preserve affiliation with the established group identity. Agency problems could occur if managers copycat the strategies of prestigious members of her or his strategic group according psychological benefits that don't flow to shareholders or that don't improve the profitability of the firm.

Measurement Problems

The correct application of strategic group analysis depends on correct identification of the strategically important dimensions of competition. Inaccurate identification and inappropriate weighting of these variables could lead to the incorrect identification of strategic groups, leading to ineffective strategic recommendations. Thus, the model is dependent on achieving accuracy from this admittedly subjective input.

Lack of Empirical Support

Even though the model is advocated as a dynamic analytical tool to deal with industry evolution, most of the empirical research to date has focused on a descriptive static analysis rather than testing the normative validity of the model.

While most every research study starts with similar theoretical definitions, the study's authors invariably used a different operational definition to define strategic groups ranging from size and market share to various performance indicators to vague descriptive catchalls to define different strategies (e.g., vertical integration, diversification, mobility barriers, etc.).

PROCESS FOR APPLYING THE TECHNIQUE

Step 1: Complete a Five Forces Industry Analysis Based on the Methodology Outlined in Chapter 6

Determine the overall competitive structure of the industry by analyzing the five forces that apply the same intensity of competitive pressure to all of the firms in the industry.

1. Threat of entry
2. Threat of substitutes
3. Bargaining power of suppliers
4. Bargaining power of buyers
5. Internal rivalry

After this initial step, the process of strategic group analysis is initiated to further refine the analysis by determining the unique impacts of membership in a certain strategic group on the competitive position of its composite member firms.

Step 2: Identify All of the Major Competitors in the Industry Based on Competitive Variables

All of the significant participants within an industry must be identified based on the various strategic variables in the industry. Porter (1980) suggests the following list:

- Specialization
- Brand identification
- Push vs. pull
- Channel selection
- Product quality
- Technological leadership
- Vertical integration

- Cost position
- Service
- Price policy
- Leverage
- Relationship with parent company
- Relationship to home and host government

Rumelt (1981) suggests the framework in Figure 7-2 for determining elements of the competitive dimension. Alternatively, Gailbraith and Schendel (1983), Ackoff (1970), Dill (1958), and Aldrich (1979) suggest the elements listed in Figure 7-3 for determining the elements of the competitive dimension. These lists are by no means inclusive but may serve as a useful launch pad for brainstorming.

Step 3: Map the Strategic Groups

Separate the list of significant competitors from step 2 into strategic groups, that is those firms with similar strategies and competitive positions.

Sudharshan et al. (1991) found that grouping variables by functional strategy (e.g., production strategy, marketing strategy) was an effective method of selecting the criteria for separate strategic groups.

The best sources of information are top managers and functional experts in the firm. Indeed, Mascaranhas and Aaker (1989) found that in-depth interviews with top management is an effective methodology because top management is one of the best sources of information about alternative strategies, key success factors, assets and skills, and mobility barriers.

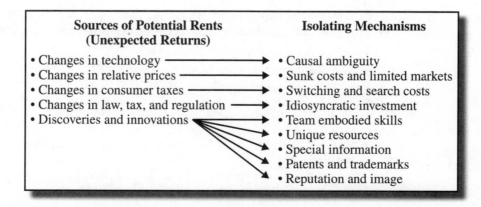

Figure 7-2

Sources of Potential Rents (Unexpected Returns)	Isolating Mechanisms
• Changes in technology	• Causal ambiguity
• Changes in relative prices	• Sunk costs and limited markets
• Changes in consumer taxes	• Switching and search costs
• Changes in law, tax, and regulation	• Idiosyncratic investment
• Discoveries and innovations	• Team embodied skills
	• Unique resources
	• Special information
	• Patents and trademarks
	• Reputation and image

Part II   The Techniques of Strategic and Competitive Analysis

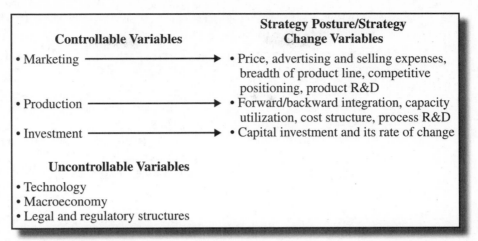

Controllable Variables	Strategy Posture/Strategy Change Variables
• Marketing ⟶	• Price, advertising and selling expenses, breadth of product line, competitive positioning, product R&D
• Production ⟶	• Forward/backward integration, capacity utilization, cost structure, process R&D
• Investment ⟶	• Capital investment and its rate of change

Uncontrollable Variables
• Technology
• Macroeconomy
• Legal and regulatory structures

Figure 7-3

One problem the analyst will encounter is accessing profitability data for the companies composing the strategic groups. Another that might be encountered are the issues of nonpublic firms. Even if industry firms are publicly traded, often the financial information is aggregated for diversified firms. The best solution for this challenge is to access public sources of profitability data and then supplement this with comparative cost analysis and disaggregated financial ratio analysis.

Next, map the different groups on a graph that incorporates the two strongest strategic variables that differentiate them. This map will look similar to the strategic group map illustrated in the last exhibit on page 89. Often, the sizes of the bubbles are drawn proportional to the market share of each strategic group. In-depth knowledge about the industry and iterative learning are the two most important ingredients needed to choose the best two dimensions for each axis of the strategic group map. Often, more than one map is constructed if more than two competitive variables are deemed significant. Additionally, the analyst may discover that some groups overlap while other groups cannot be defined by the model because they do not exhibit any type of coherent strategy or they radically oscillate between strategic extremes.

Step 4: Gauge the Strength of Mobility Barriers Between Groups

The factors that prevent firms in one strategic group from competing with firms in another strategic group must then be identified. Porter (1980) offers several types of mobility barriers that might be strategically relevant, depending on the competitive structure of the industry under analysis:

• Economies of scale
• Product differentiation
• Switching costs
• Cost advantages
• Distribution access

• Benefits from relationship with parent company
• Capital intensity
• Government policy

Alternately, McGee and Howard (1986) suggest the following three classifications of mobility barriers:

MARKET-RELATED STRATEGIES	INDUSTRY SUPPLY CHARACTERISTICS	FIRM CHARACTERISTICS
• Product line • User technologies • Market segmentation • Distribution channels • Brand names • Geographic coverage • Selling systems	• Economies of scale in production, marketing, administration • Manufacturing processes • R&D capability • Marketing and distribution systems	• Ownership • Organizational structure • Control systems • Management skills • Diversification • Vertical integration • Firm size • Relationship with influence groups

These lists are by no means inclusive. The analyst will normally discover some mobility barriers that are unique to the industry under analysis.

Step 5: Gauge the Strength of Bargaining Power Between Groups and Industry Buyers and Suppliers

Identify the relative importance of the two sources of bargaining power between strategic groups: common suppliers and buyers and different suppliers and buyers.

Step 6: Gauge the Threat of Substitutes Between Groups

Analyze the different links in the value chain that the different strategic groups compete around to determine the vulnerability of each group to the threat of substitutes.

Step 7: Gauge the Intensity of Internal Rivalry Between Groups

Determine the relative impact of the four factors that determine group rivalry:

- *Intensity of internal rivalry between firms in the same group*, including the number of firms in the strategic group and market share distribution across the firms, the strategic distance between groups, and the market interdependence of groups
- *Scale effects*
- *Costs of entry into the strategic group*, including both superior resources and timing
- *Organizational capabilities to implement the firm's chosen strategy*

Step 8: Five Forces Analysis of Strategic Groups

Integrate the analysis of steps 4 through 6 to determine the relative competitive positions of each strategic group, the intensity of mutual dependence between each group, and the potential for industry volatility based on

- Strength of mobility barriers between groups
- Strength of bargaining power between groups and industry buyers and suppliers
- Threat of substitutes between groups
- Intensity of internal rivalry between groups

Porter (1980) suggests constructing another strategic group map at this stage similar to the one made in step 3 but changing it to include only one competitive variable on the vertical axis and placing the different market segments in the industry that the strategic groups are competing for on the horizontal axis. Figure 7-4 depicts such a graph. This graph will function as an effective visual aid to reinforce which groups are experiencing a collision of strategies. By definition, the strategic groups will employ different strategies but will collide if their target customers are the same.

Step 9: Select Membership in the Optimal Strategic Group

Mentally overlay the Five Forces model of the strategic groups on top of the firm's strengths and weaknesses. Identify the strategic group that presents the greatest opportunity to exploit the firm's strengths and minimize the firm's weaknesses, given the firm's existing strategy, by analyzing

- Group mobility barriers
- Group bargaining power
- Threat of substitution to the group
- Threat of rivalry from other groups

Figure 7-4
Rivalry Between Strategic Groups

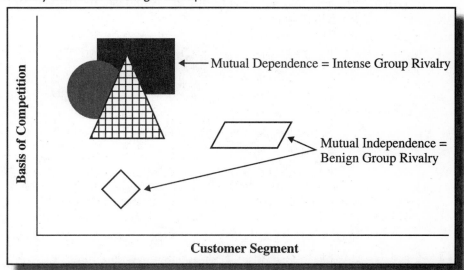

Source: Adapted from *Competitive Strategy: Techniques for Analyzing Industries and Competitors,* by M. E. Porter, 1980. London: Collier Macmillan Publishers.

In addition to listing these group-specific factors, Porter (1980) also suggests that several firm-specific factors should permeate the selection decision:

- Economies of scale opportunities for the firm relative to the group
- Costs of entry relative to other firms within the group
- Internal capabilities to implement the chosen strategy within the group
- Strong enough resources to surpass mobility barriers to more attractive groups in the future

Step 10: Industry Evolution Analysis

Analyze strategic opportunities and threats that accompany radical industry change.

- *Strategic opportunities of industry change*:
    1. Improve the existing competitive structure of the firm's existing strategic group or the firm's relative position in this group.
    2. Move to a better strategic group in search of a tighter strategic fit.
    3. Move to another group and improve the competitive structure of this new group.
    4. Create an entirely new strategic group.
- *Strategic threats of industry change*
    1. Threat of entry from other strategic groups
    2. Weakening mobility barriers
    3. Weakening bargaining power
    4. Risks of investing to increase the strength of existing mobility barriers
    5. Risks of investing to overcome mobility barriers to support moving to other strategic groups or to support creating an entirely new strategic group

Depending on the resources available to the firm, organizational capabilities, and the risk preferences of the firm, two different types of strategic intent can be pursued in order to meet the challenge of industry evolution:

- *Mildly proactive—coping strategy*
    a. focus on strategic opportunities 1 and 2
    b. focus on strategic opportunities 1, 2, 3, and 4
- *Intensely proactive—shape-shifter strategy*
    a. focus on strategic opportunities 3 and 4
    b. focus on strategic threats 1, 2, 3, and 5

It is helpful at this stage to revisit the original strategic group map, turning it into a dynamic visual tool. The insertion of arrows can be used to indicate where group strategies will collide in light of industry evolution.

Step 11: Keep a Cautious Eye on Group Identity Dysfunction

It is important for the analyst to be watchful for any signs of common dangers resulting from strong identity with a strategic group, such as reduced flexibility, strategic myopia, and suboptimizing behavior.

Application of Strategic Group Analysis in the Pharmaceutical Drug Industry

Indicative of the existence of strategic groups, profits in the pharmaceutical drug industry are not symmetrically distributed across the industry. A strategic group analysis will reveal three distinct strategic groups: patented prescription (ethical pharmaceutical companies), over-the-counter, and generic brand manufacturers.

Strategic Dimension	Ethical Drug Makers	Over-The-Counter	Generic Brands
Proprietary technology	Yes	Some licensing	None
Capital intensity	Highest	Moderate	Moderate/Low
Level of innovation	High	Moderate	Low
R&D capability	Advanced	Low	Very Low
% Products needing prescription	High	Low	Moderate
Consumer advertising	Low	High	Low
Distribution	Doctor-Direct medical channels/Pharmacies	Drug stores/Discount retailers	Pharmacies
Timing of entry	First	Second	Third
Cost structure	High	Moderate	Low

As the chart shows, each group differs significantly in their strategies and consequently in the way that each group is influenced by each of the five forces of competitive pressure:

Strategic Group Map

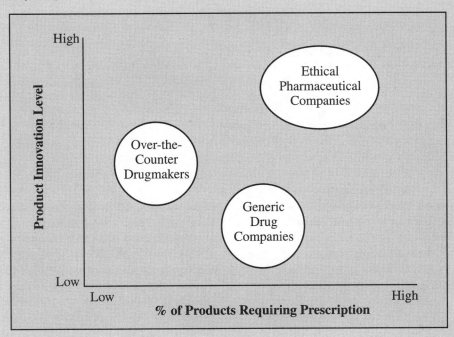

SOURCE: Adapted from *Strategic Management* (pp. 95–96), 3rd ed., by A. Miller, 1998, New York, NY: Irwin/McGraw Hill.

FAROUT Summary

	1	2	3	4	5
F	■	■	■	■	■
A	■	■			
R	■	■	■		
O	■	■	■		
U	■	■	■	■	■
T	■	■	■		

Future orientation High. An excellent tool for scenario analysis and industry evolution analysis.

Accuracy Low to medium. Highly qualitative inputs, statistically nonverifiable, accuracy will decline if the analysis isn't part of a broader industry analysis.

Resource efficiency Medium. Input from various data sources both primary and secondary may be necessary to achieve correct identification of multiple variables.

Objectivity Medium. Significant inputs are subjective and rely on the analyst's judgment, objectivity can be reduced by iteration, group identity effects can drastically reduce objectivity if left unchecked.

Usefulness High. Can be used for both current and dynamic strategy formulation.

Timeliness Medium. Strategic group analysis can be conducted in a relatively short period of time.

RELATED TOOLS AND TECHNIQUES

- blindspot analysis
- comparative cost analysis
- competitor analysis
- customer segmentation and needs analysis
- Five Forces industry analysis
- industry evolution analysis
- SERVO analysis
- scenario analysis
- sustainable growth rate analysis
- SWOT analysis

REFERENCES

Ackoff, R. L. (1970). *A concept of corporate planning.* New York, NY: John Wiley.

Aldrich, H. (1979). *Organizations and environments.* Englewood Cliffs, NJ: Prentice Hall.

Barney, J. B., & Hoskisson, R. E. (1990). "Strategic groups: Untested assertions and research proposals." *Managerial and Decision Economics, 11,* 187–198.

Kim, W. C., & Mauborgne, R. (1999). "Creating new market space." *Harvard Business Review, 77*(1), 83–93.

Dill, W. R. (1958). "Environment as influence on managerial autonomy." *Administrative Science Quarterly, 2,* 409–443.

Dranove, D., Peteraf, M., & Shanley, M. (1998). "Do strategic groups exist? An economic framework for analysis." *Strategic Management Journal, 19*(11), 1029–1044.

Fiegenbaum, A., & Thomas, H. (1995). "Strategic groups as reference groups: Theory, modeling, and empirical examination of industry and competitive strategy." *Strategic Management Journal, 16*(9), 461–476.

Galbraith, C., & Schendel, D. E. (1983). "An empirical analysis of strategy types." *Strategic Management Journal, 4*(2), 153–173.

Harrigan, K. R. (1985). "An application of clustering for strategic group analysis." *Strategic Management Journal, 6*(1), 55–73.

Hunt, M. S. (1972). *Competition in the major home appliance industry 1960–1970*. Unpublished doctoral dissertation, Harvard University.

Mascarenhas, B., & Aaker, D. A. (1989). "Mobility barriers and strategic groups." *Strategic Management Journal, 10*(5), 475–485.

McGee, J., & Thomas, H. (1986). "Strategic groups: Theory, research and taxonomy." *Strategic Management Journal, 7*(2), 141–160.

Miller, Alex. (1998). *Strategic management* (3rd ed.). New York, NY: Irwin/McGraw Hill.

Nayyar, P. (1989). "Research notes and communications, strategic groups: A comment." *Strategic Management Journal, 10*(1), 101–103.

Newman, H. H. (1973). *Strategic groups and the structure/performance relationship: A study with respect to the chemical process industries*. Unpublished doctoral dissertation, Harvard University.

Olusoga, S. A., Mokwa, M. P., & Noble, C. H. (1995). "Strategic groups, mobility barriers, and competitive advantage." *Journal of Business Research, 33*(2), 153–164.

Peteraf, M., & Shanley, M. (1997). "Getting to know you: A theory of strategic group identity." *Strategic Management Journal, 18* (Special Issue), 165–186.

Porter, M. E. (1973). *Consumer behavior, retailer power, and manufacturer strategy in consumer goods industries*. Unpublished doctoral dissertation, Harvard University.

————. (1979). "The Structure of industries and companies performance." *The Review of Economics and Statistics, 61*(2), 214–227.

————. (1980). *Competitive strategy: Techniques for analyzing industries and competitors*. London: Collier Macmillan Publishers.

Reger, R. K., & Huff, A. S. (1993). "Strategic groups: A cognitive perspective." *Strategic Management Journal, 14*(2), 103–124.

Rumelt, R. P. (1984). "Towards a strategic theory of the firm." In R. B. Lamb (ed.). *Competitive Strategic Management* (pp. 556–570). Englewood Cliffs, N.J: Prentice Hall.

Sudharshan, D., Thomas, H., & Fiegenbaum, A. (1991). "Assessing mobility barriers in dynamic strategic group analysis." *The Journal of Management Strategies, 28*(5), 429–438.

Thomas, H., & Venkatraman, N. (1988). "Research on strategic groups: Progress and prognosis." *Journal of Management Studies, 25*, 537–555.

Chapter 8

SWOT *Analysis*

SHORT DESCRIPTION

SWOT (or TOWS) is an acronym for strengths, weaknesses, opportunities, and threats. A SWOT analysis, a subset of the broader situation analysis, is used to assess the fit between an organization's strategy, its internal capabilities (i.e., its strengths and weaknesses), and external possibilities (i.e., its opportunities and threats).

BACKGROUND

Ken Andrews is generally regarded as the pioneer of SWOT analysis. In 1971, he was one of the first strategy theorists to formally articulate the concept of strategic fit between the firm's resources and capabilities with the external environment. He argued that this methodology was a sound approach to determine a niche strategy—the best way for a firm to use its strengths to exploit opportunities and to defend both the firm's weaknesses and strengths against threats.

Figure 8-1 is a depiction of Andrews' strategy model that was the precursor to SWOT analysis. The essential thrust of the model asks four questions (Andrews, 1971):

1. What can we do (i.e., strengths and weaknesses)?
2. What do we want to do (i.e., organizational and individual values)?
3. What might we do (i.e., external opportunities and threats)?
4. What do others expect us to do (i.e., stakeholder expectancies)?

The answers to these strategic choices are the raw material of strategic management. As Figure 8-1 also shows, Andrews' initial SWOT model can be supplemented with four additional corresponding questions that further refined the strategic analysis of his first SWOT model:

1. What resources and capabilities do we want to develop?
2. What should we be caring about?

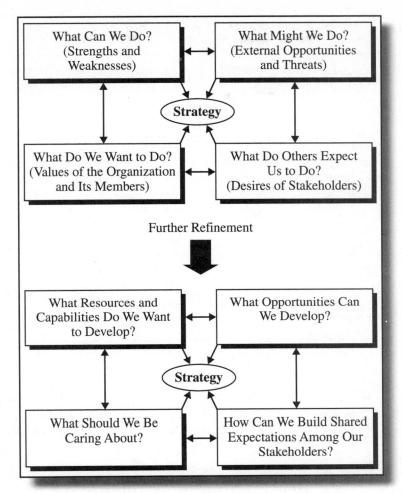

Figure 8-1
The Roots of SWOT: Key Questions That Guide Strategic Choice

Source: Adapted from *Strategic Thinking* (UVA-BP-0391) (pp. 4–5), by J. G. Clawson, Charlottesville, VA: University of Virginia Graduate School of Management, Darden Graduate Business School Foundation.

The diagram contains the following boxes:

Top section:
- What Can We Do? (Strengths and Weaknesses)
- What Might We Do? (External Opportunities and Threats)
- What Do We Want to Do? (Values of the Organization and Its Members)
- What Do Others Expect Us to Do? (Desires of Stakeholders)
- **Strategy**

Further Refinement

Bottom section:
- What Resources and Capabilities Do We Want to Develop?
- What Opportunities Can We Develop?
- What Should We Be Caring About?
- How Can We Build Shared Expectations Among Our Stakeholders?
- **Strategy**

3. What opportunities can we develop?
4. How can we build shared expectations among other stakeholders?

Today, many of the SWOT analysis models are diagrammed as shown in Figure 8-2. It has been significantly simplified from Andrews' original, partly to make it a cleaner conceptual tool for rough, first-cut, environmental analysis and partly because some of the areas of the original model less relevant to pure SWOT analysis have been relegated to more advanced management techniques and tools developed since its inception. Nonetheless, Andrews' model provided the bedrock foundation of modern environmental analysis.

A SWOT analysis is conceptually simple and comprehensive; it can be applied to many facets of an organization. These factors have made it one of the most popular models, particularly for determining an organization's ability to deal with its environment. As well, it has been taught in undergraduate and M.B.A. strategy courses for over 25 years and is frequently used by consultants.

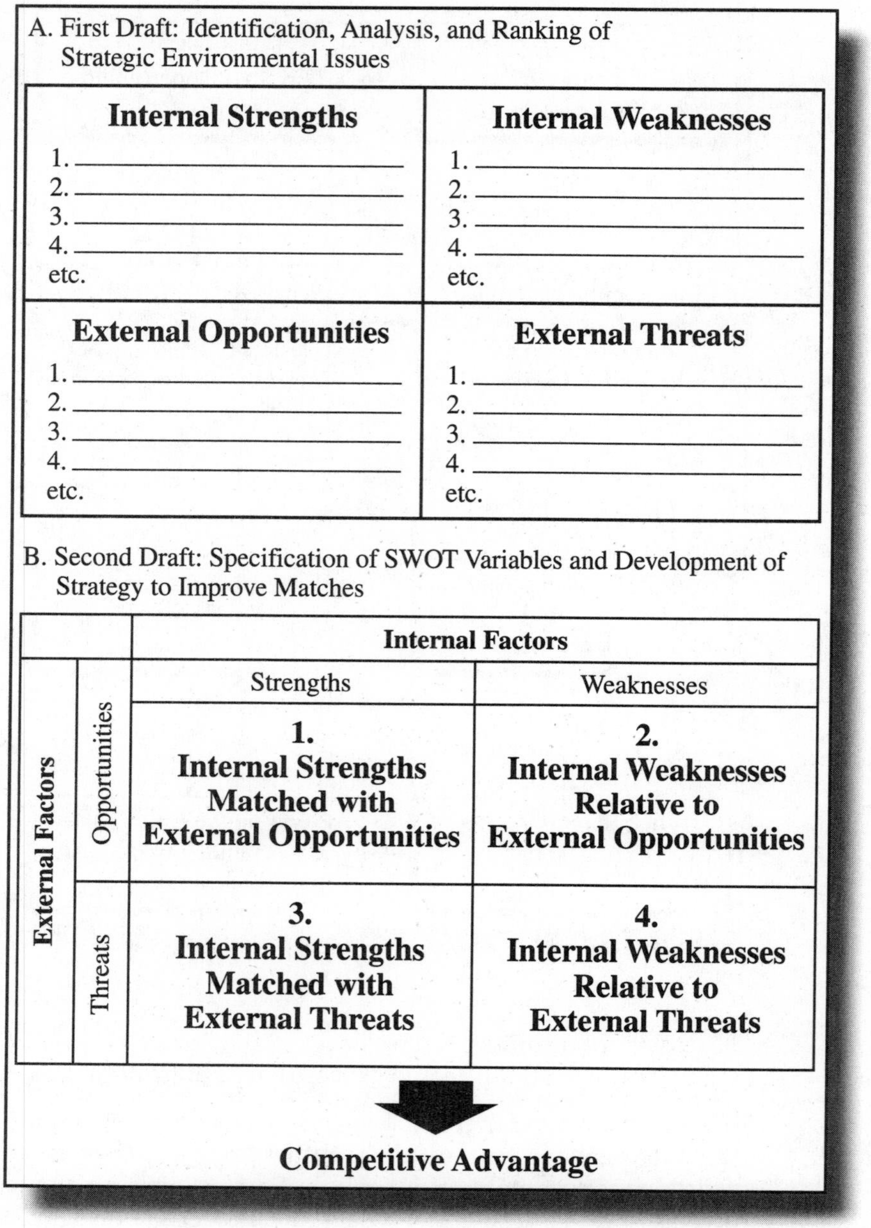

```
┌─────────────────────────────────────────────────────────────┐
│ A. First Draft: Identification, Analysis, and Ranking of      │
│    Strategic Environmental Issues                             │
│ ┌─────────────────────────┬─────────────────────────────┐   │
│ │   Internal Strengths     │   Internal Weaknesses        │   │
│ │  1. _____    │  1. _____        │   │
│ │  2. _____    │  2. _____        │   │
│ │  3. _____    │  3. _____        │   │
│ │  4. _____    │  4. _____        │   │
│ │  etc.                    │  etc.                        │   │
│ ├─────────────────────────┼─────────────────────────────┤   │
│ │   External Opportunities │   External Threats           │   │
│ │  1. _____    │  1. _____        │   │
│ │  2. _____    │  2. _____        │   │
│ │  3. _____    │  3. _____        │   │
│ │  4. _____    │  4. _____        │   │
│ │  etc.                    │  etc.                        │   │
│ └─────────────────────────┴─────────────────────────────┘   │
└─────────────────────────────────────────────────────────────┘
```

B. Second Draft: Specification of SWOT Variables and Development of
   Strategy to Improve Matches

		Internal Factors	
		Strengths	Weaknesses
External Factors	Opportunities	**1.** **Internal Strengths Matched with External Opportunities**	**2.** **Internal Weaknesses Relative to External Opportunities**
	Threats	**3.** **Internal Strengths Matched with External Threats**	**4.** **Internal Weaknesses Relative to External Threats**

Competitive Advantage

Figure 8-2
The Common SWOT Model
a. First Draft: Identification, Analysis and Ranking of Issues
b. Second Draft: Specification of SWOT variables and development of strategy to improve matches.

STRATEGIC RATIONALE AND IMPLICATIONS

SWOT is part of the more encompassing analysis of an organization's situation. Situation analysis is viewed as one of the fundamental elements of strategy formulation. Broadly speaking, situation analysis is undertaken to provide an organization with an overview of the best possible data, information, and understanding of the forces, trends, and root causes of a defined context in which it intends to intervene in the competitive marketplace. These insights are then used to make informed choices about broad action areas that utilize the organization's comparative advantage and increase its likelihood of fulfilling its mission and achieving its goals and objectives.

Situation analysis typically consists of both an external (i.e., macroenvironment) and an internal (i.e., microenvironment) component. Environmental analysis is the process of scanning and monitoring the environment to identify both present and future positive (i.e., opportunities) and negative trends (i.e., threats) that may influence the firm's ability to reach its performance goals.

For purposes of analysis, a firm's macroenvironment can be divided into two main segments or levels: (1) the operating or task environment that generally constitutes an industry such as its supplier, competition, customer, labor, and international components, and (2) the general environment that entails the social, technological, economic, environmental, and political/legal (STEEP) components within which the industry and organization is situated (see Chapter 17 for more detail).

Environmental analysis will help the decision maker to answer critical questions such as:

- What are the industry's main economic traits?
- What are the competitive forces and how powerfully will they affect the organization?
- What factors are creating changes in the dynamics affecting competition?
- What are our competitors' assumptions about the changing environment?
- What are the environmental factors that are key to the organization's competitive success?
- Is the industry's environment attractive or unattractive both now and in the future?

The firm's microenvironment is an equally important facet of situation analysis. The analyst assesses the microenvironment in order to better understand the company's internal situation. As such, the analyst reviews the company's current situation, studies its costs, its resources and capabilities, and its internal organizational issues. One particularly powerful way of studying the organization is to do so through the application of the McKinsey 7S framework (Waterman, 1982). This suggests studying the organization's strategy, structure, skills, systems, shared values, style, and staff. Two other chapters in this book provide additional techniques that help the analyst assess the organizational environment including functional capability and resource analysis (see Chapter 14) and management profiling (see Chapter 15).

Environmental analysis must thoroughly understand and meet the critical information needs (i.e., CINs) of senior decision makers. Analysts must recognize that executives' information needs often change over time and so must adjust their environmental analysis to reflect such changes. Top managers will continuously support effective environmental analysis because it will regularly assist them to make better decisions.

Environmental analysts should focus on identifying existing and potential strengths, weaknesses, opportunities, and threats suggested by components of the firm's environment. Strategists must interpret the results of environmental analysis in light of their in-depth understanding of company operations. The analyst must share the strategist's skill to contribute to an effective strategy.

SWOT analysis applies a general framework for understanding and managing the environment in which an organization operates. The model seeks to help the analyst isolate the major issues facing an organization through careful analysis of the four individual SWOT elements. Managers can then formulate strategies to address key issues. Although these questions may help direct a SWOT analysis, much insightful work is required to answer them properly and to place them in perspective. For example, the analyst must assess the relative importance of each issue and the issue's potential impact on the firm and its strategy. Furthermore, the priority or relative importance of each issue may vary for strategies formulated at the different corporate, business or functional levels.

SWOT analysis forces managers to better understand and respond to those factors that have the greatest actual and potential importance for the organization's performance. These factors are called the organization's strategic issues. A strategic issue is a factor that exists either inside or outside the organization and that is likely to have a prominent and long-term impact on the ability of the enterprise to meet its competitive objectives. Strategic issues, unlike their tactical or operational counterparts, occur less frequently, typically impact across the entire organization, and require greater allocations of organizational resources to effectively address.

It should be emphasized that strategic issues do not just arrive neatly labeled on top of a decision makers' desk. Instead, information derived from SWOT analysis assists in the identification of new technologies, market trends, new competitors, and customer satisfaction trends. These require interpretation and translation, that is, analysis, before they are labeled as strategic issues. Often, managers draw upon their experience to categorize issues as controllable or uncontrollable, as threats or opportunities. The categories then determine how an issue appears to an individual manager, how well it can be sold to other managers, and what action, if any, the firm subsequently takes.

The value of SWOT analysis is that it is an intuitively appealing method of organizing voluminous amounts of information and data. After the initial analysis is conducted and the relevant strategic issues have been identified, the analyst places the issues onto the four-quadrant grid like that shown in Figure 8-2. This grid is the intermediate analytical output of the SWOT analysis and provides a concise visual depiction of the prior analysis. Some analysts prefer to emphasize the internal strengths and weaknesses of the company by putting the company at the top of the matrix. Other analysts prefer to place the opportunities and threats on the top of the matrix in order to underscore the environmental aspect of SWOT analysis.

STRENGTHS AND ADVANTAGES

Traditional SWOT analysis is possibly the most widely known and among the most utilized means of situation analysis. Over many years it has achieved almost universal status and has contributed to the achievement of competitive advantage not only in organizational settings, but also at the personal and team performance level.

A huge advantage of SWOT analysis is its wide applicability. It can be used for analyzing a variety of units, including but not limited to individual managers or decision makers, teams, projects, products/services, function areas of the organizations (i.e., accounting, marketing, productions, and sales), business units, corporations, conglomerates, and product markets. It works equally well for profit or not-for-profit organizations. It is arguably among the most extensively taught analytical tools in business education. Its simplicity makes it an excellent method for quickly ordering organizational thinking around key factors that underlie the organization's fit with its external environment.

SWOT analysis does not require a great deal of financial or computational resources and can be done both quickly and with some degree of efficacy without the necessity of extensive information acquisition. When dealing with complex situations in a limited amount of time, trying to address all the strategic issues involved often does not pay off. Rather, strategists should aim to limit their efforts to those issues that have the most impact on the situation and can be effectively dealt with by the organization's stock of capabilities and resources. SWOT analysis provides an effective framework for identifying these critical issues.

It can provide the impetus to analyze a situation. It can also offer an enhanced way of thinking through the range of viable tactics or strategies for responding to an organization's competitive environmental dynamics. In addition, it can also serve as an effective means for assessing the organization's core capabilities, competences, and resources.

SWOT analysis can be an effective team-building method when performed jointly by functional specialists from marketing, production, finance, and so on. These experts review the environments closest to their specialties, and bring issues they see as critical to the attention of their peers from other functions, as well as general managers who have responsibilities for overall or integrated SWOT analysis. When developed within such a larger group context, SWOT can sometimes provide the needed evidence to stimulate organizational change. It is effective for helping groups arrive at consensus understandings around changes that need to be stimulated and for the need to catalyze organizational activity.

SWOT analysis can provide insight into why a particular organization has been successful or unsuccessful in carrying out its strategy. The process of gathering, interpreting, and organizing the many sources of data onto the SWOT grid also provides an excellent foundation from which to guide further strategic analysis. An appropriate analogy would be that the SWOT analysis only identifies the chess pieces on the board and the opponent's possible moves. It is up to the analyst to calculate the series of moves leading to the ultimate winning chess move in the business world—that of achieving competitive advantage.

WEAKNESSES AND LIMITATIONS

The SWOT model is a purely descriptive model in that it does not offer the analyst explicit or formulaic strategic recommendations. SWOT analysis will not give the decision maker specific answers. Instead, it is a way to organize information and assign probabilities to potential events—both good and bad—as the basis for developing business strategy and operational plans. Only very generalized self-evident, common-sensical recommendations are typically offered: Move the company away from threats; match the company's strengths with opportunities; or defend against the weaknesses through divestment or bolstering.

The inherent simplicity of SWOT masks a great deal of complexity. The primary concerns for the analyst who must complete a situation analysis are gathering and interpreting massive quantities of data about the most significant environmental forces, and then deciding what to do in response to them. Interpretation represents a form of judgment and will likely differ between individual managers. For example, one manager may see an environmental factor, say, loosening of government-imposed trade barriers between nations, as a market expansion opportunity, while another may view this as a threat because of increasing competition from new rivals.

Detractors of this model suggest that a SWOT analysis is limited in its ability to help prescribe specific actions to be followed by a faltering organization. Due to the individual complexities of business, the general recommendations are necessarily calibrated to a very high level of abstraction.

Further, if an organization attempts to implement only those strategies that build on its strengths and mitigate its weaknesses, it may miss out on the most attractive opportunities that are possible only if the firm stretches itself. Other critics of SWOT analysis stress its reliance on qualitative rather than quantitative data, its focus on creating reactive rather than proactive strategies, and its inherent simplification in distinguishing between strengths and weaknesses, and opportunities and threats. Last, weaknesses are often broader than anticipated and strengths are usually more narrow than expected—without testing and experience, analysts are often overly optimistic in their assessment of a firm's strengths and opportunities versus their weaknesses and threats.

To overcome many of these weaknesses, an analyst must adhere to the facts and must not be overly influenced by the dominant "beliefs" held within the organization. This model often fails due to the blindspots held by management about the firm's capabilities (see Chapter 10 for a detailed treatment of blindspots). Therefore, it is often appropriate that an unbiased outsider be brought in to assist in the analysis to ensure biases are kept at a minimum.

Another important factor that will guide the successful application of this model is the application of rigorous, disciplined, yet creative analysis. There are several warning signs that this crucial ingredient is missing:

- Extremely long lists indicate that the screening criteria used to separate data and information from strategic issues is not tight enough.
- The absence of weighting factors indicates a lack of prioritization.
- Short and ambiguously phrased descriptions of each SWOT factor indicate that the strategic implications have not been considered.

PROCESS FOR APPLYING THE TECHNIQUE

The first step in utilizing a SWOT analysis to evaluate existing and possible future strategies involves listing and evaluating the firm's strengths, weaknesses, opportunities, and threats. Each of these elements is described in detail here.

Part II   The Techniques of Strategic and Competitive Analysis

1. *Strengths.* Strengths are those factors that make an organization more competitive than its marketplace peers. Strengths are what the company has a distinctive advantage at doing or what resources it has that are superior to the competition. Strengths are, in effect, resources or capabilities that the organization holds that can be used effectively to achieve its performance objectives.

2. *Weaknesses.* A weakness is a limitation, fault, or defect within the organization that will keep it from achieving its objectives. It is what an organization does poorly or where it has inferior capabilities or resources as compared to the competition.

3. *Opportunities.* Opportunities include any favorable current or prospective situation in the organization's environment, such as a trend, change, or overlooked need, that supports the demand for a product or service and permits the organization to enhance its competitive position.

4. *Threats.* A threat includes any unfavorable situation, trend or impending change in an organization's environment that is currently or potentially damaging or threatening to its ability to compete. It may be a barrier, constraint, or anything that might inflict problems, damages, harm or injury to the organization.

A firm's strengths and weaknesses (i.e., its internal environment) are made up of factors over which it has greater relative control. These factors include the firm's resources; culture; systems; staffing practices; and the personal values of the firm's managers. Meanwhile, an organization's opportunities and threats (i.e., its external environment) are made up of those factors over which the organization has lesser relative control. These factors include, among others, overall demand; the degree of market saturation; government policies; economic conditions; social, cultural, and ethical developments; technological developments; ecological developments; and the factors making up Porter's Five Forces (i.e., intensity of rivalry, threat of new entrants, threat of substitute products, bargaining power of buyers, and bargaining power of suppliers.) Refer to Chapter 6 for a detailed treatment of the Five Forces model, also known as Industry Analysis.

The methodology used to gather and interpret this information should be an interrelated, iterative, and reinforcing process of consultation with executives and functional experts, team discussions, and competitive intelligence.

The intermediate analytical product will look similar to Figure 8-2a—a ranked list of strategic issues classified as internal strengths, internal weaknesses, external opportunities, and external threats. It is most important that the analyst clearly share their criteria for ranking so that decision makers can better understand the foundation upon which these issues were prioritized.

The next step for the analyst is to identify the firm's strategic fit given its internal capabilities and external environment. This fit or misfit should help indicate the degree of strategic change necessary. Four scenarios will become evident as the analyst fills up the quadrants in Figure 8-2b with the identified strategic issues:

- Quadrant 1—Internal strengths matched with external opportunities
- Quadrant 2—Internal weaknesses relative to external opportunities
- Quadrant 3—Internal strengths matched with external threats
- Quadrant 4—Internal weaknesses relative to external threats

Winnebago Industries Inc. is the largest manufacturer of recreational vehicles in the world, based in Forest City, Iowa. The application of SWOT analysis to their competitive environment in the early 1970s exemplifies the strategic insights afforded by this model.

The final analytical product is depicted in the SWOT chart. Bear in mind that significant analysis would precede this diagram. Similarly, the individual analysis of each strategic issue would be significantly supplemented in the complete analysis. Nonetheless, the SWOT matrix here exemplifies how this analytical approach can identify relevant issues and provide a framework for further strategic analysis and selection. The numbers behind each possible strategy reflect the interrelationships between the issues.

Internal / External	Strengths	Weaknesses
Internal / **External**	1. Identifiable corporate name with a good reputation 2. Good service and warranty 3. Established dealer network with good dealer relations 4. Extensive R&D capabilities 5. Automated economical plant 6. Manufacturing of most parts for the RV	1. Vulnerability because of its one-product focus 2. Concentration on higher-priced units 3. Heavy investment in tool-making will raise cost of model changes 4. One plant location 5. No preparation for transition from family to corporate management
Opportunities 1. Demand for smaller RVs 2. Development of international market 3. Demand for low-cost modular housing (FHA subsidy for mortgage loans)	**Possible Strategies** 1. Emphasize smaller, more efficient RV (O_1, S_1, S_2, S_3, S_4, S_5, S_6) 2. Expand into foreign markets (O_2, S_1, S_4) 3. Diversity into modular housing (O_3, S_1, S_4, S_6)	**Possible Strategies** 1. Develop and produce smaller RVs (O_1, O_2, W_1, W_2) 2. Build smaller plants in different parts of the country and abroad (O_1, O_2, W_4)
Threats 1. Gasoline shortage and higher prices of gasoline 2. Slackening demand for RVs 3. Trade up creates secondary market 4. Increased competition (GM, Ford, International Harvester, VW, Toyota) 5. Impending safety regulations	**Possible Strategies** 1. Diversify into farm equipment, railroad cars (T_1, T_2, T_3, S_1, S_3, S_4, S_5) 2. Consider diesel engines for motor homes (T_1, S_4) 3. Make RVs safer in anticipation of safety regulations (e.g., visibility, flame retardant, crash resistant, brakes) (T_5, T_4, S_6)	**Possible Strategies** 1. Sell the company (T_1, T_2, T_4, W_1, W_3, W_4, W_5)

SOURCE: Adapted from "The TOWS Matrix—A Tool for Situational Analysis," by H. Weihrich, 1982, *Long Range Planning*, 15(2), pp. 54–66.

Figure 8-2b will be helpful as a guide to both determine the existing strategic fit and also devise effective strategies in response to forecasted environmental issues. To determine the strategic fit, the analyst should predict the firm's performance going forward (i.e., articulate the firm's performance several years in the future if no changes are made to its strategy, and its internal and external environments do not change).

Finally, the analyst should evaluate alternative strategies in a similar manner in search of one that provides a competitive advantage. While no strategy may become evident that produces a competitive advantage, a SWOT analysis, at a minimum, provides a prognostic tool to allow the firm to evaluate its current and alternative strategies:

- *Quadrant 1: Internal strengths matched with external opportunities.* This location is the ideal match as it represents the tightest fit between the firm's resources and competitive opportunities in the external environment. The strategy would be to protect these internal strengths by either finding the unique combination of resources needed to achieve competitive advantage or to bolster these resources to extend an already established competitive advantage. Further opportunities to leverage these strengths to bolster weaknesses in other areas (most notably those in Quadrant 2) should be explored.

- *Quadrant 2: Internal weaknesses relative to external opportunities.* The general strategic thrust in this quadrant would be to choose the optimal trade-off between investing to turn the weaknesses into the strengths necessary to exploit the opportunity, or abdicating to rivals.

- *Quadrant 3: Internal strengths matched with external threats.* Transforming the external threats into opportunities by reconfiguring the competitive position of the firm's resources is one strategic option indicated by this quadrant. Alternately, the firm may choose to maintain a defensive strategy in order to focus on more promising opportunities in other quadrants.

- *Quadrant 4: Internal weaknesses relative to external threats.* This is the worst position for the firm and obviously one to be avoided. Nonetheless, the vagaries of competition are such that there will inevitably be several strategic issues located in this quadrant. If the firm's survival is at stake, a proactive strategy may be the only option. If the strategic implications are ancillary, one possible strategy is to divest in order to focus on other, more promising opportunities in other quadrants. It is important, however, to avoid immediately dismissing the possibility of moving an issue out of this quadrant. This might not be as secondary as it may seem. Rather, consider the potential to provide a significant strategic option to the firm or to support other more profitable activities in other quadrants. The technique of blindspot analysis is gainfully employed in this quadrant to reduce this counterproductivity.

Once a strategy is decided upon for each issue, constant monitoring and periodic iteration is required to revisit established issues, and to proactively conceive strategies to address developing issues. Consider this iteration as a sweep over the environmental radar screen to monitor movement of identified blips and to benefit from the early warning capabilities afforded by the SWOT technique.

A helpful method to manage the complexity introduced by a large number of strategic issues is the use of an interaction matrix. Weihrich (1982) suggests that such a matrix as presented in Figure 8-3 may help the analyst manage the different combinations of interrelationships between the different quadrants and actually use the matrix as one of the bases for evaluating strategic options across the quadrant range. Each issue is assigned either a " + " (indicating a strong match between strengths and opportunities) or a "0" (indicating a weak or nonexistent match between

Figure 8-3
Interaction Matrix

Source: Reprinted from *Long Range Planning,* Vol. 15, No. 2, H. Weihrich, "The TOWS Matrix—A Tool for Situational Analysis," pages 54–66, Copyright 1982, with permission of Elsevir Science.

Strength \ Opportunity	1	2	3	4	5	6	7	8	9	10
1	+	0	0	+	+	0	0	+	0	1
2	0	+	0	0	+	+	0	0	+	1
3	+	+	+	0	0	0	0	+	+	0
4	0	0	0	0	+	0	0	+	+	0
5	+	+	+	0	0	0	0	+	+	0
6	0	0	0	0	0	0	0	0	0	0
7	+	+	+	+	+	+	+	+	0	0
8	0	0	0	0	+	0	0	+	+	0

Opportunity 7 would appear to offer several favorable matches.
Opportunity 6 would appear to offer no favorable matches.

strengths and opportunities). Reading across the matrix will help to identify strategic issues where the firm's strengths could potentially be matched with opportunities in the external environment (i.e., the " + "s). A matrix is built to compare the match optimality for each quadrant.

It is important here not to ascribe unfounded accuracy to this matrix. The analyst must remain aware of the risk of quantitatively ranking qualitative data and information. A binomial ranking doesn't properly capture the subtle and often intangible mutual dependencies between issues and their interrelated impact on the firm's competitive position. Nonetheless, it can serve as a useful tool to concisely visualize a rough approximation of the set of opportunities within the theoretical construct of the SWOT model.

Finally, a separate SWOT analysis is typically required for each business or product market. These analyses should then be conducted regularly over time.

FAROUT Summary

	1	2	3	4	5
F	■	■			
A	■	■	■		
R	■	■	■	■	
O	■	■	■		
U	■	■	■	■	
T	■	■	■	■	

Future orientation Present to short term future. Needs to be reviewed regularly as industry issues change and organizational improvements are made.

Accuracy   Medium degree. Accuracy will be dependent upon biases held. Cross-validation with outside experts will increase accuracy of the analysis.

Resource efficiency   Medium to high degree. This will vary depending on the degree of outside consultation employed and the availability of internal and external information. Generally, SWOT is among the most resource efficient analytical techniques available.

Objectivity   Medium degree. Support from outside experts will increase objectivity. Blindspots and cognitive bias corresponding to the position of the executives and functional experts sourced for input will be introduced.

Usefulness   Medium to high degree. Provides a quick picture of the current position of the firm and its competitive capabilities.

Timeliness   Medium to high degree. A SWOT analysis can be done fairly quickly.

RELATED TOOLS AND TECHNIQUES

- blindspot analysis
- competitor profiling
- country and political risk analysis
- Five Forces industry analysis
- issue analysis
- SERVO analysis
- scenario analysis
- stakeholder analysis
- STEEP analysis
- strategic group analysis
- value chain analysis

REFERENCES

Andrews, K. (1971). *The concept of corporate strategy.* Homewood, III: R. D. Irwin.

Clawson, J. G. (1998). *Strategic thinking* (UVA-BP-0391). Charlottesville, VA: University of Virginia Graduate School of Management, Darden Graduate Business School Foundation.

Grant, R. (1995). *Contemporary strategy analysis.* Cambridge, MA: Blackwell Publishers.

Hill, T., & Westbrook, R. (1997). "SWOT analysis: It's time for a product recall." *Long Range Planning, 30*(1), 46–52.

Rowe, A. J., Mason, R. O., & Dickel, K. E. (1986). *WOTS-UP analysis, strategic management — A methodological approach.* Reading, MA: Addison-Wesley.

Stevenson, H. H. (1976). "Defining corporate strengths and weaknesses." *Sloan Management Review, 17*(3), 51–68.

Waterman, R. H. Jr. (1982). "The seven elements of strategic fit." *Journal of Business Strategy, 2*(3), 69–73.

Weihrich, H. (1982). "The TOWS matrix — A tool for situational analysis." *Long Range Planning, 15*(2), 54–66.

Chapter 9

Value Chain Analysis

SHORT DESCRIPTION

Value chain analysis (VCA) is a method used to identify potential sources of economic advantage by suggesting how the firm's internal core competencies can be integrated with its external competitive environment to direct optimal resource allocation. The value chain of the firm is regarded as part of a larger industry value system that includes the value-creating activities of all of the industry participants, from raw materials suppliers through to the final consumer. Value chain analysis disaggregates the firm into the strategically relevant value-creating activities within a holistic industry context. This deconstructive analysis provides extremely rich insights into industry profit pools and the consequent strategies needed to generate competitive advantage.

BACKGROUND

Harvard University business school professor Michael Porter popularized the value chain concept in his 1985 book, *Competitive Advantage*, and is shown in Figure 9-1. Porter's pioneering work extended the area of strategy analysis known as systems analysis that was first developed by Jay Forrester at the Massachusetts Institute of Technology. As far back as 1961, Forrester was developing his *industrial dynamics* approach to industry disaggregation by activity (see Forrester, 1961). Further evolution of this type of competitive analysis continued in the 1970s, when consulting firm McKinsey & Co. developed its *Business System*, a not-so-distant cousin of VCA.

Porter envisioned his model as a clinical approach to identifying and closing the strategic gaps between the firm's internal capabilities and the external competitive environment. The unique strength of value chain analysis is that it can be used as an analytical tool to help firms bridge the strategic gaps between the firm's capabilities and opportunities and threats in its competitive environment. Hence, the two main purposes of value chain analysis are to identify (1) opportunities to secure cost advantages and (2) opportunities to create product/service attribute differentiation. Companies gain competitive advantage by performing some or all of these activities at lower cost or with a greater degree of customer-valued differentiation than its competitors.

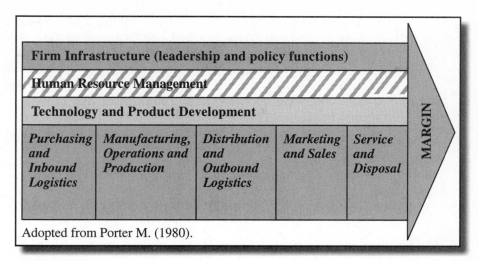

Firm Infrastructure (leadership and policy functions)

Human Resource Management

Technology and Product Development

| Purchasing and Inbound Logistics | Manufacturing, Operations and Production | Distribution and Outbound Logistics | Marketing and Sales | Service and Disposal |

MARGIN

Adopted from Porter M. (1980).

Figure 9-1
The Value Chain

Source: Porter, M. (1985): *Competitive Advantage*. The Free Press, New York.

Value chain analysis starts with the goal of competitive strategy, which is to create customer value in excess of the costs of delivering that value—this is the source of a firm's profit. Customer value is derived from the interlinked sets of value-creating activities that a firm performs. Porter (1985) views the firm's value chain as composed of all of the activities and processes that a company performs to design, produce, market, deliver, and support its product or services. A firm's value chain and the way it performs individual activities reflect its unique history, strategy, implementation approaches, and the underlying economic behaviors of the activities themselves. He classifies all of these activities into two main categories:

1. Primary Activities
   - Inbound logistics—inventory warehousing and handling
   - Operations—transformation of inputs into the final product or service
   - Outbound logistics—distribution
   - Marketing and sales—marketing communications, pricing and channel management, etc.
   - Service—post-sale support

2. Support Activities
   - Technology development—engineering, R&D, information technology, etc.
   - Human resource development—hiring, incentive systems, motivation, training, promotion, labor relations, etc.
   - Firm infrastructure—administrative support activities such as accounting, legal, planning, and all forms of stakeholder relations (i.e., government and public affairs, community investment, investor relations, etc.)

The price charged to the firm's customers less the costs of all of these activities determines the firm's profit. All of the suppliers of the firm's inputs and buyers of the firm's products or services will also have value chains composed of their own primary and support activities. Collectively, all of these value chains comprise the industry value system shown in Figure 9-2.

The totality of activities in the industry's entire value system determines the total customer value created. It is the customer who pays for the margins earned by all of the participants of the industry value system. The share of industry profit earned by each participant is determined by Porter's five market forces that powerfully shape the industry's structure (see Chapter 6): threat of new entrants, bargaining power of suppliers, threat of substitutes, bargaining power of buyers, and internal rivalry. The relative power of each force will determine the profitability of the industry. The relative power of the firm in the value system will determine the firm's share of overall industry profits. Value chain analysis is used to determine the current power of the firm and suggests how to increase that power in order to gain a higher share of industry profits by securing competitive advantages.

Figure 9-2
Value Chains Within Industry Value System

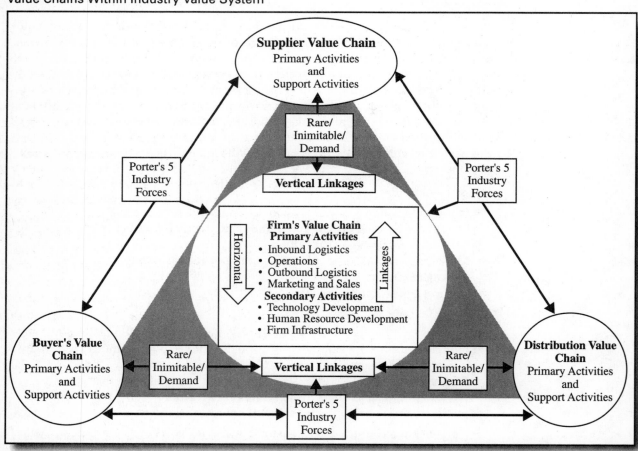

While most of the individual types of activities in the value chain are discrete, they are not independent—in fact, most of the activities are interlinked with the other types of activities. Competitive advantage may be achieved by the individual activities themselves, but generally the most intense sources of competitive advantage derive from higher-order linkages in and among the value chain. Generally, the more intangible and complex the linkage, the more difficult it will be for competitors to replicate and usurp the rents generated by the firm's strategy. The following list points out this relationship by ranking various types of value chain linkages by increasing capability of generating competitive advantage:

- *Separate individual activities within the firm's value chain*—(e.g., being an industry leader in inbound logistics)
- *Interlinked primary activities in the firm's value chain*—(e.g., increasing quality inspection which reduces rework, scrap and customer returns and increases customer value)
- *Interlinked secondary activities in the firm's value chain*—(e.g., an organizational structure that fosters learning in all of the relevant activity areas of the firm)
- *Vertical linkages within the industry value system*—(e.g., developing close relationships with suppliers and customers to co-develop low cost or differentiation strategies for mutual but usually disproportionate benefit that is dependent on each party's bargaining strength in the value system)

Combinations of these linkages within the firm's own value chain or within the industry's value system will allow the firm to increase its power in the industry structure and command a greater share of industry profits. In some cases, value chain analysis will pinpoint opportunities to radically reconfigure industry value systems by eliminating or bypassing entire value chains within an industry's value system. A well-known example of this is Amazon.com's innovative use of technology and relationship management to bypass the traditional book retailer channel through developing close ties with publishing houses and selling solely over the Internet.

There are also many different secondary applications or subsets of value chain analysis used in the pursuit of competitive strategy:

- *Competitor analysis.* Analyzing competitor's cost structures and sources of differentiation are intrinsic to crafting strategy by providing a holistic frame of reference validated through robust economic discipline.

- *Customer value analysis.* Stitching the common thread of customer value-creating activities into the strategy formulation process provides insight that keeps the analysis relevant to this lowest common denominator of profit. Guidance on determining the drivers of customer value and the concept of life cycle costing are some of the greatest contributions of the value chain analysis model.

- *Determining company scope.* Value chain analysis helps answer the core strategy question, What business activities and which competitive areas the firm's strategies will be implemented in? Expanding the limiting idea of the traditional concept of product–market scope to a much broader expanse of all of the value-creating activities of the value chain allows for the exploration of a corporate strategy comprised of unique business unit strategies. Porter (1985) specifies four different types of scope that affect competitive advantage: segment, vertical, geographic, and industry. Focus strategies can be used in conjunction with either low cost or differentiation strategies.

• *Strategic cost management.* Expanding the parameters of cost management from traditional approaches of universal cost containment and reduction across the firm to recognition of the unique cost drivers for each value activity allows for better management of costs. For example, VCA allows the firm to exploit vertical linkages with suppliers and customers. Expanding the cost horizon will also orient the firm to the feasibility of investing in some activities (e.g., quality management) in order to save in other activities in the value chain (e.g., rework), thereby increasing customer value.

• *Integration.* Value chain analysis helps firms invest wisely in vertical or horizontal integration strategies or, conversely, to divest by framing the investment/divestment decision on the impact of the firm's value chain and the resulting impact on the firm's strategic position in the industry's value system.

• *Supply chain management.* Determining the bargaining power of suppliers as well as recognizing their position in the same industry value system potentially generates opportunities for mutually beneficial cooperation.

• *Strategic outsourcing.* Requires knowledge of core competencies that is provided by VCA. With a firm grasp of the firm's core competencies and the relative importance of various activities in the value chain, strategic outsourcing decisions can be made that reduce cost or improve differentiation and flexibility without harming the firm's competitive advantage.

• *Acquisition, mergers, alliances, or joint ventures.* Synergy or strategic fit can be advantageously framed by VCA. Target firms can be selected on the basis of how the acquisition would enhance the firm's strength in the industry's value system.

• *Organizational structure.* Drawing the boundaries of organizational units based on discrete value creating activities and the vertical linkages of the value chain will put the firm more in tune with the sources of its competitive advantage.

• *Global strategy.* Value chain analysis can help multinational corporations detangle the often confusing distinctions between competitive advantage and comparative advantage. This will allow the firm to effectively optimize the relative trade-offs between nation-specific strategy based on comparative advantage and firm-specific strategy based on competitive advantage.

STRATEGIC RATIONALE AND IMPLICATIONS

Michael Porter developed value chain analysis because of general dissatisfaction with the unacceptable performance of the predominant strategic management systems of the time. During the 1970s and early 1980s, portfolio theory concepts reigned supreme with their requisite bottom-up planning systems and decentralized

Part II   The Techniques of Strategic and Competitive Analysis

organizational structures. As a result, most corporations at the time were linearly focused on separately managing distinct and diversified strategic business units (SBUs) through portfolio analysis. Portfolio theory was increasingly being called into question by wildly successful corporate raiders who bought larger firms in order to profit by selling off the pieces, and by practicing conglomerates themselves who began to experience extended periods of profitless growth. The underlying dysfunction of portfolio theory manifested itself in little or no cooperation between SBUs and a dearth of synergy between business- and corporate-level strategy. Portfolio theory led managers to make the false assumption that corporate strategy could be successfully crafted by managing only two of the *symptoms* of business strategy success—market share and market growth.

Porter argued that managers must encompass a comprehensive analysis of the root *causes* that drive business success—how customer value is created in an industry. Value chain analysis was proposed to encourage firms to exploit the often-ignored potential vertical synergies that exist between a firm's SBUs, and between SBUs, overall corporate strategy, and other participants in the industry value system. The overriding logic driving VCA is that most sources of competitive advantage lie in these (often intangible) synapses. Porter challenged conventional management theory with the argument that a superior method of exploiting these sources of competitive advantage was to employ value chain analysis.

Porter also developed the value chain concept as a direct response to criticisms of his earlier work as depicted in his 1980 book, *Competitive Strategy*. In this book, Porter proposed a three-stage process for achieving competitive advantage. Stage 1 recommended that the analyst use his now-famous Five Forces model of industry structure, which asserted that industry profitability is determined by the five competitive forces. Stage 2 draws on this analysis to decide on a generic competitive strategy that will generate a sustainable competitive advantage as evidenced by earning returns greater than normal economic rents for a protracted period of time. The firm can pursue either a low-cost or a differentiation strategy to achieve a sustainable competitive advantage. Within each generic strategy, the firm may pursue a focused or nonfocused strategy. It was Porter's third stage—implementing the firm's chosen strategy—that drew practical criticism for its lack of specific methodological guidance. Previous models, including Porter's, did not offer guidance to fill the analytical vacuum between identifying and closing the strategic gaps between the firm's internal capabilities and the external competitive environment. In response, Porter offered VCA to implement competitive strategy.

STRENGTHS AND ADVANTAGES

Value chain analysis addressed several critical deficiencies with the inward-looking focus of previous management tools. It provided a major leap ahead during the mid-1980s that allowed strategists to move away from obscure generalizations and qualitative conjecture about where sources of competitive advantage existed within the organization and among its industry competitors.

From the firm's perspective, VCA is a useful tool for better understanding what the strengths and weaknesses of a firm are; from the industry perspective, VCA supports a better understanding of competitive positioning relative to key customers and suppliers.

VCA provides the analyst with better understanding of the nature of advantages the firm's resources and capabilities potentially and actually generate, how sustainable that advantage is, and what new resources and capabilities the firm might require to be competitive in the future. As such, it augments the benefits of traditional SWOT analysis (see Chapter 8) and functional capability and resource analysis (see Chapter 14) in detailed ways that better illustrate how competitive advantage can be achieved and sustained.

Traditional strategic planning frameworks, especially management accounting, focused on limited definitions of value added which deducted input costs from revenue generated. Conventional cost analysis like this was criticized for starting too late and stopping too soon (Shank & Govindarajan, 1992). Traditionally, management accounting started the cost analysis process with purchases and ended with the customer sale. This narrow fixation excluded consideration of the horizontal and vertical linkages of value-creating activities between the firm and other industry participants. For example, management accounting traditionally started with purchase price and ignored any opportunities for capitalizing on opportunities to create value through vertical linkages with suppliers. Similarly, excluding the total costs of ownership of its product or service from competitive analysis robs the firm of exploiting many potential sources of competitive advantage and customer value generation. Value chain analysis encourages the firm to adopt a strategic cost analysis that allows for a comprehensive treatment of all of the value-creating activities that deliver value to the customer. It is also much more inclusive of the complex economic cost drivers that impact the customer's value equation such as structural drivers (e.g., scale, scope, experience, technology, complexity) and executional drivers (e.g., management style, total quality management, plant layout, capacity utilization, product configuration, vertical linkages with suppliers and customers). Compare this to traditional costing systems that focus internally by reducing cost drivers to a single driver, usually volume. In this way, VCA builds much more realistic cost/value analysis that more closely models economic reality because of its external customer and industry focus. Think of value chain analysis as changing the Cost/Volume/Profit (CVP) acronym for the popular management accounting tool to a more appropriate Cost/*Value*/Profit relationship.

WEAKNESSES AND LIMITATIONS

Despite all of the unique strengths of VCA, several weaknesses have been associated with this innovative management tool. The efficacy of VCA is being challenged by the radical changes that information technologies have wrought. The resulting obliteration of the traditional trade-off between the breadth and depth of information poses a direct threat to many established value systems. A growing school of thought asserts that the traditional VCA oriented around vertical linkages cannot constantly reinvent value at the speed required for successful strategy in this new paradigm. Information technology is threatening value chains everywhere. Consequently, it is argued, the tools required for this new paradigm have become obsolete or at least in need of some upgrading. Traditional VCA was developed for physical assets and may not be as appropriate for competition based around intellectual assets. The concepts of virtual value chain (VVC) are offered as more comprehensive approaches that add a fourth dimension to VCA. The guiding principles of e-commerce are rewriting some established laws of economics and may need to be incorporated into any management tool in use today. Rayport and Sviolka (1995) suggest five new principles that are rewriting the laws of economics that underlie traditional management theories and tools such as VCA:

1. *The law of digital assets.* The marginal variable costs of creating customer value with digital assets are zero or very near zero.

2. *New economies of scale.* No longer do only large companies have proprietary access to low unit costs. Small firms can now achieve the same cost efficiencies at small volumes.

3. *New economies of scope.* One digital asset may simultaneously provide depth and breadth of market focus.

4. *Reduction of transaction costs.* Transaction costs are much lower on the virtual value chain than on the traditional physical value chain. This presents new opportunities for infomediaries and lessens the traditional potency of switching costs.

5. *Rebalancing supply and demand.* Rather than viewing markets as composed of aggregated segments, focus strategies can be disaggregated to a market of one. This new reality confers more importance to demand side strategy than supply side strategy.

Couched in a similar context, Andrew and Hahn (1998) offer value web management (VWM) to supplement value chain analysis. This concept views strategy not in terms of a few layers of relatively linear linkages between value chains but rather, VWM imagines the value web as multiple layers of webs in which each node is a virtual partner with a dizzying array of multidimensional linkages between nodes in each web and between webs. They suggest that two new principles are driving these complex web matrices:

1. *Synchronization.* Value can be created in virtual value chains only when complete information is available in real time simultaneously to each member of the value web. This allows participants in the value web to craft strategy functionally as one unit rather than as a collection of value chains.

2. *The guiding principles of the value web.* Disintermediation, reintermediation, infomediation, role transformation, dematerialization, and digitization are affecting the rules of competition.

This discussion of theoretical enhancements to Porter's value chain model is by no means exhaustive. While still in their infancy and not yet fully articulated, these theoretical developments serve to highlight the need to constantly reevaluate accepted practices in dynamic competitive environments. The conclusions, however, of most of these concepts such as VVC and VWM are similar. Managing value chains in the context of information communication and technology requires the analyst to broaden his or her scope to include new and challenging economic realities that are not explicitly addressed by Porter's VCA model. The value chain treats information as a supporting element in the firm's strategy, at best only part of a secondary activity. Alternatively, new models such as VVC and VWM treat information as a separate and distinct value-creating factor that must be explicitly managed, alongside and intertwined, separate but together, with the physical value chain.

Porter developed his VCA by framing anecdotal cases that were predominantly manufacturing focused. Since then, critics who asserted that value chain analysis could not be operationalized for service companies have been refuted. Perhaps the same will be concluded of those who point toward VCA as lacking robustness for Internet e-commerce applications—the proverbial jury is still out. Nonetheless, it is entirely appropriate for the analyst to scan the academic horizon for new and innovative refinements in current management tools and techniques to incorporate the pervasive impacts of information technology.

Porter has also been criticized for being too simplistic because many of his qualitative prescriptions are very difficult to quantitatively operationalize. As such, the most prominent shortcoming is that it requires significant amounts of resources. Effective VCA requires a large investment in customer research, competitive analysis, and industry structure analysis, often using data that is not either freely or easily available. Conducting a VCA might be straightforward in theory, but it is relatively difficult and time-consuming to apply in practice.

Much of the difficulty stems from the extensive data requirements that underlie comprehensive VCA. Large portions of these data, both internal to the organization and external into its industry and competitors, are difficult to acquire. Most of the firm's internal accounting data are incompatible with the analytical dimensions of VCA for several reasons:

- Traditional management accounting systems rarely, if ever, collect data around SBUs.
- Traditional management accounting systems rarely, if ever, collect data around value-creating activities; instead, they collect data around product/service and period costs.
- Traditional management accounting systems rarely, if ever, collect period costs by product or service making it difficult to accurately assign overhead costs to value-creating processes.
- Transfer prices and arbitrary cost allocation of traditional management accounting systems do not appropriately encapsulate the synergies created by horizontal linkages in the firm's value chain or the vertical linkages in the industry's value system.
- Traditional management accounting systems rarely, if ever, collect data around cost drivers; departmental budgets will rarely be an accurate source for determining the actual cost of value-creating activities.

If the firm has adopted activity-based accounting (ABC), then the process of VCA will be easier, as ABC eliminates many of the distortions of traditional management accounting. However, this is a non sequitur because the theoretical rationale of ABC is value chain analysis. Therefore, when considering the adoption of ABC, it is probably wise to first conduct a value chain analysis to determine the types of data collection that will be required of the ABC system in its support of value chain analysis. In fact, activity-based management (ABM) shares many similarities with value chain analysis.

Hence, conducting a successful VCA requires equal parts judgment, attention to detail, competitive knowledge, and quantitative analysis. Nonetheless, this difficulty is well endured because it is directly proportional to the strategic value of this type of analysis. Understanding the firm's industry structure and, more importantly, meshing this knowledge with the firm's capabilities are intrinsic to crafting successful strategy. Furthermore, the development of such a comprehensive competitive intelligence system may itself become a sustainable source of competitive advantage that can be extremely difficult for competitors to replicate.

PROCESS FOR APPLYING THE TECHNIQUE

The process of VCA begins with an internal analysis of the firm's value chain and then radiates outward with an external competitive analysis of the industry value system. It concludes by integrating these two analyses to identify, create and potentially sustain competitive advantage.

Step 1: Define the Firm's Strategic Business Units

The first level of disaggregation entails drawing boundaries around the various analytical segments of the business. Porter rationalizes that this is necessary because the different segments of the business will have different sources of competitive advantage requiring different strategies. Usually, the firm's organizational structure or accounting system will not classify business units in a manner consistent with strategic business units. Here, the analyst must divorce him- or herself from the usual classifications such as departments, functions or cost, revenue, and investment centers. This leaves the analyst with two conflicting criteria: (1) Define SBUs by autonomy (i.e., where managerial decisions about one SBU will have little or no impact on the other SBUs). (2) Define SBUs by the ability of the resulting disaggregation to support value chain analysis (i.e., shared linkages within the firm and between value chains in the value system).

Much judgment is required to proceed where these two criteria conflict. Where the two criteria collide, it is probably best to choose the latter as the whole focus of value chain analysis is to leverage shared linkages—a high potential source of competitive advantage.

Step 2: Identifying the Firm's Critical Value-Creating Activities

Unless the firm has adopted activity-based costing, traditional management accounting data will be of little help for the analyst in this regard. Instead Porter offers several helpful distinctions that define value-creating activities—those which:

- Have different economic structures.
- Contribute to a large or growing percentage of total costs.
- Contribute or stand a high probability of contributing to product/service differentiation.

Step 3: Conduct an Internal Cost Analysis

An internal cost analysis is composed of several substeps:

•   Assign costs to each critical value-creating activity identified in step 2. It is recommended to use full costing/product life cycle costing approach that incorporates full capacity utilization.

•   Find the cost drivers for each critical value-creating activity using multiple cost drivers. Structural cost drivers are long term in nature that impact the economic cost structure of the firm's products and services. Examples of structural cost drivers that the analyst should consider include scale, scope, learning curves, technology, and complexity. Executional cost drivers are more operational in nature (management style, total quality management, plant layout, capacity utilization, product configuration, and vertical linkages with suppliers and customers).

•   Diagnose the firm's current strategy for areas of potential low cost advantage. Search for horizontal linkages in the firm's value chain in the form of interlinked value creating activities that reduce costs by virtue of their symbiosis. This is the point in the analysis to explore opportunities for strategic cost management. It is important at this point to be externally focused by comparing the firm's cost structure to its competition through benchmarking and associated practice comparisons. Then, business process design and reengineering approaches can be utilized to secure any potential low cost advantages.

Step 4: Conduct an Internal Differentiation Analysis

Similar to the internal cost analysis, the internal differentiation analysis starts with an identification of the firm's value-creating activities and cost drivers. Next, the analyst must meld customer knowledge with the appropriate strategy through a series of substeps:

•   Conduct customer research to determine a precise definition of customer value. Helpful ways to secure this knowledge is (1) to engage in a dialogue with the customer and (2) to analyze the customer's own value chain to gain insights into how the firm's products and services may provide additional value.

•   Several differentiation strategies are available to differentiate the firm's product or service, including product or service attributes, channel management, customer support, pre- and post-sale support, branding, and price.

- Choose the best differentiation strategy based on the firm's core competencies that will achieve competitive advantage by offering a product or service that is rare, in demand, and difficult for competitors to imitate.

Step 5: Map Out the Industry Profit Pool

a. Define the Parameters of the Industry Profit Pool

The parameters of the industry profit pool are contingent on the value-chain processes that impinge on the firm's current and future ability to earn profit. The analyst must cut a broad-enough swath to incorporate the potential of migrating competitive scope from other industries. This must be tempered by a need to constrain the deconstruction to a manageable level of detail. It is helpful here to assume the perspective of the firm, competitors, and customers in order to capture all of the relevant value-creating activities into the analysis, starting with the raw material inputs and ending with the total cost of ownership for the final consumer.

b. Estimate the Total Size of the Industry Profit Pool

Several different estimation methodologies should be employed here to gauge accuracy. For example, the total size of the profit pool can be determined by companies, products, channels, or regions. Usually, accounting profit will suffice as the denomination of profit. However, when mapping the profit pool of an industry with international participants, one of the most effective denominations of profit is economic value added (EVA), because it eliminates many of the distortions caused by differing national generally accepted accounting principles (GAAP) regimes. Some sources of information for these estimates are analyst reports, financial statements, security commission reports, and by engaging industry experts.

c. Estimate the Distribution of the Profit Pool

A good starting point is to leverage the firm's own profit structure by activity (step 1–4) into the external analysis of rival firms in the industry. A few general rules of thumb at this stage are

- Use your knowledge of the underlying economics of your own firm to outline each activity's profit. Take care to rationally segregate allocated costs. This information can be used as a relative gauge to estimate the activity profits of rival firms in the industry.

- Sources of competitive information include financial statements, analyst reports, security exchange commission filings, trade journals, the business press, industry associations, and government regulators.

- A helpful hint is to use the market value or replacement costs of assets that support value-creating activities and the full costing approach under full capacity for costing the same value-creating activities.

- Use the 80/20 rule. This suggests that 20 percent of the industry's firms will generate 80 percent of the industry profit; therefore, concentrate on the largest companies first.

- The level of the analytical disaggregation will depend on the degree of vertical integration present in the industry. Start with the focused firms first. Then estimate the relevant activity profits of diversified firms by adjusting your knowledge of your own firm's economics and that of the focused firms in the industry. Follow this with inclusion of the smaller firms (the 80 percent responsible for 20 percent of industry profit) by transposing, based on sampling.

- For accuracy, sum the activity profits determined in this step and compare to the total industry profit pool determined in step b. If the two estimates are wildly divergent, change the assumptions and tweak the methodology through iteration until the two estimates are reasonably similar.

A graphical representation of an industry profit pool should look similar to Figure 9-3. The results may be surprising in that the activities that command the largest industry revenue share may garner a disproportionately low share of industry profits.

Step 6: Vertical Linkage Analysis

It is now time to drill down into the essence of VCA. At this stage, the opportunities to achieve cost and differentiation advantages within the firm's value chain have been exhausted in steps 1 through 4. Vertical linkage analysis allows the analyst to seek out opportunities to exploit the most intense sources of competitive advantage in the industry's value system. Step 5 will have allowed the analyst to determine whether the firm is strategically positioned in the shallow or deep end of the industry's profit pool. Vertical linkage analysis allows the analyst to combine his or her intimate knowledge of the firm's economic structure, customer value, and external competitive analysis to

Figure 9-3
Stylistic Industry Profit Pool Graphic

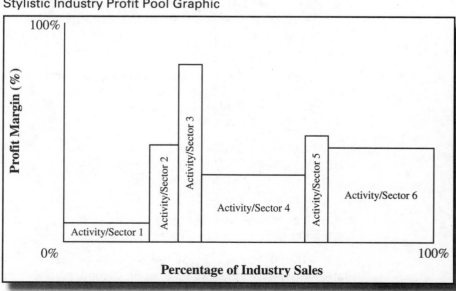

Part II   The Techniques of Strategic and Competitive Analysis

determine how to reposition the firm into the deep end of the industry profit pool and how to keep the firm in the deep end in a dynamic competitive environment.

The methodology to accomplish these objectives is the crux of vertical linkage analysis. It is also the most difficult stage, because many of the vertical linkages in the industry's value chain are less tangible and extremely difficult to root out. Nonetheless, it is because of this difficulty that VCA often offers a direct route to competitive advantage. The methodology consists of several substeps:

• Use Porter's Five Forces analysis to determine the industry's economic structure.

• Determine the cost drivers and core competencies driving the low cost or differentiation for each of the value creating activities of competitors.

• Evaluate the firm's existing core competencies. Core competencies are those capabilities, skills, and technologies that create low cost or differentiated customer value. Usually, core competencies are acquired through collective learning and relationships. Identify any opportunities to surpass the competing customer offerings by securing missing competencies or to supplement existing competencies needed to successfully craft, maintain, and strengthen a low cost or differentiation strategy.

• Based on the relative bargaining strength of other value chains in the value system, determine opportunities to acquire or strengthen the required competencies through vertical linkages with suppliers, channels, or buyers in the value system.

• Avoid the temptation to cop out for a mixed strategy—part differentiation and part low cost. This is the easy way out and will not generate competitive advantage for the average firm. Rather, it will leave a firm wading aimlessly in the shallow end of the industry profit pool trying in vain to get past the agressive swimmers in the deep end. A large and growing body of academic work validated by practice asserts that crafting successful strategy is highly valuable because of the difficulties it forces executives to make in the form of often painful trade-offs. Dual approaches offer a feasible chance of success only for firms that are pushing the production possibilities frontier or for firms that have a truly integrated global strategy.

• Identify any potential opportunities for competitive advantage in the vertical linkages between the firm's own value chain and the value chains of suppliers, channels, and customers. By co-opting or cooperating with other value chains in the industry's value system, the firm can often craft a low-cost or differentiation strategy that is impossible for competitors to replicate.

• Complex and less or intangible vertical linkages offer the most impenetrable combinations of rarity, demand, and inimitability—the triad underlying competitive advantage.

Step 7: Iteration

Repeat steps 1 through 6 periodically by making VCA a central component of your firm's competitive intelligence and strategy development system in order to proactively manage evolutionary and revolutionary industry change.

Sweden's IKEA Furniture presents an excellent example of how firms can use the concept of VCA to reconfigure industry value chains to their benefit. Value chain analysis played a prominent role in IKEA's growth from a small, domestic, mail-order furniture company into a multinational chain of more than 100 stores with 1992 revenues of $4.3 billion and a global customer base of 96 million. More importantly, IKEA has profitably managed this growth as witnessed by an estimated 8 to 10 percent profit margin in a notoriously low-margin discount furniture industry. An initial analysis of IKEA's business model would suggest that it was able to achieve this through efficient and effective management of its internal value chain: low-cost components, efficient warehousing, and customer self-service have allowed IKEA to offer discounts from 25 to 50 percent lower than competitors. IKEA's true source of success goes much deeper than this, however, and can be shown by its skillful management of the industry value system.

IKEA has successfully reconfigured its industry value system by redefining almost every aspect of its industry by leveraging vertical links in its value system. The premise of this reconfiguration lies in managing many of the individual value chains within the value systems to increase its power in the furniture industry.

SUPPLIER'S VALUE CHAIN

A major source of IKEA's low cost is derived from extensive outsourcing. IKEA works closely with its suppliers in a cooperative relationship to mutually exploit synergies. Thirty IKEA buying offices pre-evaluated its 1,800 suppliers in 50 countries for low cost and high quality. Furniture designers in the home office in Almhut, Sweden, then work two to three years ahead of the current product life cycle to determine which supplier will provide parts. Once accepted, IKEA's suppliers gain economies associated with global markets and receive technical assistance and leased equipment from IKEA. Suppliers even receive quality advice from IKEA engineers. IKEA's business service department deepens the supplier relationships with a computer database that assists in sourcing raw materials and matches suppliers with each other.

DISTRIBUTION VALUE CHAIN

To manage this global network of suppliers, IKEA operates fourteen warehouses worldwide. Direct links from every cash register in every store to these warehouses are an integral part of the cost reduction strategy by supporting lean inventory management. They also function to support customer value by allowing IKEA to tightly integrate supply with demand.

CUSTOMER VALUE CHAIN

The cornerstone of IKEA's strategy is to convince customers that it is in their best interests to assume more responsibility in creating value by performing more activities in the industry value system themselves: choosing, ordering, delivering, and assembling furniture themselves in exchange for low-cost, high-quality furniture. To encourage this radical and voluntary redesign of the value system, IKEA employs its core competence—its knowledge of how to make this restructure easy, enjoyable, and valuable for its customers:

- IKEA produces more than 45 million catalogues in 10 different languages. Each catalogue carries only 30 to 40 percent of the entire 10,000-item product line and instead transcends the traditional role of the catalogue as a simple ordering tool. Rather, the catalogue functions as a role-playing guide, essentially explaining to the customer what is expected of him or her in exchange for exceptional discounts on high-quality furniture.

- Shopping at IKEA is fun. IKEA provides shoppers with many value-creating amenities that increase the value of the shopping experience—an important component of the total benefits of ownership. Strollers, supervised day care, playgrounds, cafes, restaurants, and wheelchairs for the disabled are provided, some of which are free of charge.

(Continued on following page)

Value Chain Analysis at IKEA Furniture (Continued)

- Shopping at IKEA is easy, quick, and productive. IKEA provides several tools to assist customers to create their own value in partnership with IKEA. Items such as catalogues, tape measures, and pens and paper are handed out free of charge. Design ideas are created through IKEA's store displays. Each item in these displays is tagged with only the necessary details—product name, price, available dimensions, materials, and color, care instructions, order, and pickup location. If the chosen merchandise doesn't fit in the customer's vehicle, IKEA will lend a roof rack. Value chain analysis has allowed IKEA to offer its customers what no one else can: a large selection of high-quality furniture at low cost. This combination obliterates many of the traditional trade-offs long held sacrosanct in the industry. By leveraging the vertical linkages in its value system, IKEA's strategy is rare, in demand, and inimitable. Small wonder that IKEA is a shark swimming in the deep end of the industry profit pool.

Adapted from "From Value Chain to Value Constellation: Designing Interactive Strategy," by R. Normann and R. Ramirez, 1993, *Harvard Business Review, 71*(4), pp. 65–77.

Value Chain Analysis at U-Haul

Traditional competitive analysis of the U.S. consumer truck rental industry in the 1990s would get it wrong. U-Haul's strategy appeared to be faltering. A woeful combination of old trucks, higher maintenance costs, and lower prices had manifested into break-even performance far behind its competitors Ryder, Hertz-Penske, and Budget. Surprisingly, however, U-Haul enjoyed the highest profitability in the group. The conventional lens of business analysis would yield an incorrect spectrum of insight that would leave the analyst blind to the real picture. Why? Because the industry includes much more than just consumer truck rental.

U-Haul earns a 10 percent margin far above the industry average of 3 percent because it effectively employs a value chain approach to craft strategy. By exploiting vertical linkages in the industry value system, U-Haul was able to bury its competition without its industry peers even realizing it.

CONSUMER VALUE CHAIN

U-Haul analyzed its consumer value chain to reveal several innovative opportunities to increase the total benefits of ownership of its products and services. Renting trucks at below-average margins attracted customers into U-Haul's real profit stream—the high-margin accessories business. This highly profitable segment includes boxes, hitches, insurance storage space, and anything else that enhances the consumer's moving experience. In effect, U-Haul increased the scope of its competitive premise by packaging and selling the U-Haul moving experience rather than just renting trucks. To further entrench its competitive advantage, U-Haul was able to lower costs by securing cheap storage property that is of limited availability in most cities. Thus, a virtual cycle was created:

- Cheap truck rentals subsidize high margin accessories sales.

- Low-cost trucks and storage space further amplify profitability.

- Relative customer value is further enhanced by the pricing differential from competitors forced to cover their costs of capital through high truck rental rates.

- Customers return to U-Haul time after time after comparison shopping only on the basis of lowest-price truck rentals.

(Continued on following page)

Value Chain Analysis at U-Haul (Continued)

Herein lies the power of value chain analysis. In many industries, the profit pool is structured to grant innovative companies a disproportionate share of industry profit for performing certain value-creating activities regardless of the share of industry revenue associated with that activity. Many examples abound. Leasing and postsale maintenance service is the most profitable portion of the automobile industry. Gas stations make the highest margins selling snacks and drinks. Credit card companies lust after that sliver of the market that consistently makes only minimum monthly payments. In each case, value chain analysis is an excellent analytical vehicle for rooting out these hidden gems that make corporate strategy sparkle.

Adapted from "Profit Pools: A Fresh Look at Strategy," by O. Gadiesh and J. L. Gilbert, 1998, *Harvard Business Review, 76*(3), pp. 140–147.

FAROUT SUMMARY

	1	2	3	4	5
F	■	■			
A	■	■	■		
R	■	■			
O	■	■	■	■	
U	■	■	■	■	■
T	■				

Future orientation Present focused. A value chain analysis provides a snapshot in time of the firm's competitive position. It is important to conduct periodic iterations to ensure the relevancy of the analytical conclusions. Scenario building, the strategic challenge of assumptions, and the incorporation of the new economics of information should build expectational analysis into the process that approximates reality through staged dynamism.

Accuracy Medium. Value chain analysis is littered with assumptions, estimates, incomplete, inappropriate, or missing information sources, and qualitative judgments.

Resource efficiency Low to medium. From a cost perspective, VCA is very resource intensive. Ironically enough, from a value perspective, VCA is very cost effective because of its high probability of delivering competitive advantage.

Objectivity Medium to high. The application of microeconomic theory interspersed throughout the analysis provides reinforcing reality checks that force the analyst to reevaluate key assumptions made throughout the analysis.

Usefulness High. The process of VCA provides a depth of insight into competitive strategy that few other strategic management techniques can rival. Unraveling the firm by reducing it to its lowest common denominator of strategy provides the structural support upon which to build the learning organization.

Timeliness Low. The comprehensive nature of VCA is time-consuming. Dynamic adjustments to incorporate industry change will consume considerably less time as the analyst ramps up the learning curve.

RELATED TOOLS AND TECHNIQUES

- activity-based costing
- activity-based management
- benchmarking
- business process reengineering
- customer value analysis
- competitive intelligence
- competitor profiling
- core competency analysis
- disaggregated financial analysis
- shareholder value-based management
- strategic cost management
- supply chain management
- total quality management
- scenario analysis
- SWOT analysis

REFERENCES

Andrews, P. P., & Hahn, J. (1998). "Transforming supply chains into value webs." *Strategy and Leadership, 26*(3), 7–11.

Cartwright, S. D., & Oliver, R. W. (2000). "Untangling the value web." *Journal of Business Strategy, 21*(1) 22–27.

Clarke, C. J. (1987). "Acquisitions: Techniques for measuring strategic fit." *Long Range Planning, 20*(3), 12–18.

Forrester, J. (1961). *Industrial dynamics*, Cambridge, MA: MIT Press.

Gadiesh, Orit, & Gilbert, J. L. (1998). "Profit pools: A fresh look at strategy." *Harvard Business Review, 76*(2), 139–147.

———. (1998). "How to map your industry's profit pool." *Harvard Business Review, 76*(2), 149–162.

Hergert, Michael, & Morris, D. (1989). "Accounting data for value chain analysis." *Strategic Management Journal, 10*, 175–188.

Heskett, J. L., Jones, T. O., Loveman, G. W., Sasser, W. E., & Schlesinger, L. A. (1994). "Putting the service-profit chain to work." *Harvard Business Review, 72*(1), 164–174.

Kogut, B. (1985). "Designing global strategies: Comparative and competitive value-added chains." *Sloan Management Review, 26*(4), 15–28.

Magretta, J. (1998). "The power of virtual integration: An interview with Dell Computer's Michael Dell." *Harvard Business Review, 76*(1), 73–84.

McTavish, R. (1995). "One more time: What business are you in?" *Long Range Planning, 28*(2), 49–59.

Normann, R., & Ramirez, R. (1993). "From value chain to value constellation: Designing interactive strategy." *Harvard Business Review, 71*(4), 165–177.

Porter, M. E. (1980). "Industry structure and competitive strategy: Keys to profitability." *Financial Analysts Journal, 36*(4), 30–41.

———. (1985). *Competitive Advantage*. New York: The Free Press.

Prahalad, C. K., & Hamel, G. (1990). "The core competence of the corporation." *Harvard Business Review, 68*(3), 79–91.

Quinn, J. B., & Hilmer, F. G. (1994). "Strategic outsourcing." *Sloan Management Review, 35*(4), 43–55.

Rayport, J. F., & Sviokla, J. F. (1995). "Exploiting the virtual value chain." *Harvard Business Review, 76*(2), 75–85.

Reimann, B. C. (1989). "Sustaining the competitive advantage." *Planning Review, 17*(2), 30–39.

Shank, J. K., & Govindarajan, V. (1992). "Strategic cost management and the value chain." In B. J. Brinker, (ed.), *Handbook of cost management* (pp. D1-1–D1-37). Boston: Warren Gorham Lamont.

Society of Management Accountants of Canada, (1997). *Value chain analysis for assessing competitive advantage.* Management Accounting Guideline 41.

Chapter

10

Blindspot Analysis

SHORT DESCRIPTION

Blindspot analysis examines the underlying reasons for inaccuracies or flaws in the strategic decision-making process. It combines cognitive psychology, strategy theory, and organizational behavior dynamics to explain why analysts often misread the competitive environment and why internal scrutiny can lead to overestimates of a firm's competitive capability. This knowledge sensitizes the firm to potentially critical flaws in the organization's decision-making process with the aim of improving strategic decisions.

BACKGROUND

Contemporary strategy theory is replete with analytical techniques and management tools designed to guide industry and competitive analysis. A great number of these are rooted in classic economic theory and focus on the end result of strategic decision making—securing and maintaining competitive advantage. At the other end of the realm of strategy lies the behaviorist school that focuses on the actual strategic decision-making process from a psychological perspective. For many decades, significant contributions were made in each of these streams but they were seldom integrated. That is, competitive and industry analysis virtually ignored the individual and organizational psychological filters through which strategic analysis and decision making pass. This is understandable given that industry analysis was often based on classical economic theory that assumes rational and optimal decisions. Conversely, behaviorists often overlooked the very important distinction that strategic decisions are made within a competitive economic and financial context.

Blindspot analysis evolved to directly address this lack of integration. It focuses on the process of strategic decision making *within* a competitive context by loosening the "optimal rationality" assumption. It is surprising that growing recognition of the importance of blindspots in strategic decisions developed at the same time from both the industrial economists and the behaviorist schools of strategy.

Michael Porter (1980) was one of the first strategists from the industry organization/economics (i.e., I/O economist) school to formally address the problem of blindspots. He couched the issue into two main categories: (1) the firm's own assumptions about itself and (2) the firm's assumptions about its competitors and the industry in which they compete. When these assumptions are faulty, as they commonly are, perceptual biases or blindspots develop.

The manifestation of these blindspots is threefold. First, the firm may not be aware of strategically important developments. Second, the firm may inaccurately perceive strategically important developments. Third, even in the event that the firm correctly perceives strategically important developments, it may do so at too slow a pace to allow for timely responses. Porter suggested that the removal of blindspots is an important precursor to successfully negotiating potential competitive reaction to the firm's planned strategies within an industry analysis scenario. It is also a key to correctly assessing the firm's own competitive strength against any contingent competitive reaction once the firm's strategy is implemented.

It is this idea of contingent competitive reaction that lies at the heart of blindspot analysis. In the late 1970s and early 1980s, organizational behaviorists began to emulate I/O economists by borrowing game theory from mathematics in order to reduce the complexity of decision making to a manageable level for analysis. One of the important strengths of game theory is its explicit incorporation of this contingency concept—the idea that decisions of one rational player should not be independent of the reaction of the other player(s) in the game. Blindspot analysis zones in on the fact that competitive strategic decision making often strays from the contingency concept of game theory. In actual practice, firms and their decision makers typically do not fully incorporate the contingent competitive responses to their planned strategies.

While the contingency assumption is applicable, the rationality assumption limits the application of game theory to the study of strategic decision making. Any manager will tell you that competitors in the "game" of business often do not appear or do not in practice exhibit rational decision making. Similarly, that same manager will also suffer from the same fate without being fully cognizant of her or his own deviation from rational decision making! Pioneering research, most notably the work of Kahneman and Tversky in the late 1970s and early 1980s, formally challenged this central tenet of classical economic theory—that economic actor always exhibit rational behavior. In reality, many strategic decisions suffer from several psychological deficiencies that result in irrational behavior, incorrect analysis, failed strategy, and, ultimately, uncompetitive and poor business performance.

Blindspot analysis is based on the premise that strategic success depends on conducting the correct analysis and making the right decisions that will allow the firm to do the right things well. A necessary precursor to this ideal scenario, however, is knowledge of how and why firms conduct flawed analysis and make incorrect strategic decisions. Blindspot analysis provides this knowledge.

The Seven Common Sources of Blindspots

All types of blindspots commonly have the reaction of fundamental human nature to complex, ambiguous, and unstructured decisions. Human beings simplify the decision process through a trial-and-error process in order to ease the psychological pain and cognitive dissonance associated with uncertainty. While this mental coping mechanism reduces the complexity and ambiguity to a manageable level of structure and perceived certainty, it also introduces serious perception bias. Decision makers are more susceptible to this phenomenon than others because strategic competitive analysis brings with it a large number of these instigating conditions—complexity, ambiguity, and a decided lack of analytical structure. As such, the sources of blindspots within a firm can be many and varied. Flawed internal scrutiny, incorrect competitive analysis, and the poor strategic decisions that they conspire to produce may be the result of one or any combination of the following blindspot sources.

1. Invalid Assumptions

Gilad (1994) expanded on Porter's original assertion that blindspots are caused by faulty assumptions. He suggests three types of dangerous assumptions often take root inside of firms, with disastrous effects on competitive position.

The first type is termed an *unchallenged assumption* that is basically an incorrect assumption about diverse elements in the firm's competitive environment. Unchallenged assumptions may include invalid assumptions that the firm holds about its competitors, customers, suppliers, or any other member of the firm's value chain. They are presumed to be valid by default because no one in the firm challenges them. Gilad (1994) cites the example of Schwinn Bicycle Company, which assumed that serious competition would only come from its larger rivals. As a consequence, small and seemingly insignificant rivals were able to capture the lucrative and burgeoning mountain bike market.

The second type of flawed assumption is referred to as a *corporate myth*, which is an incorrect assumption about the firm's competitive capabilities. Often, these types of assumptions cloud internal scrutiny by completely disengaging internal analysis from any relevance to the realities of the firm's competitive environment. Gilad (1994) cites the reaction in the early 1990s of Compaq Computer Corp. to changing market demand. Given that Compaq was founded by engineers, technological supremacy was assumed to be the dominant reason for their past and current success. Consumers, however, were rapidly becoming price sensitive and opting for cheaper PC clones offered by Dell, AST, and Gateway 2000. The corporate myth that technology was far more important than price was incredibly strong. Even as sales dipped by 17 percent in 1991, Compaq was attributing their lackluster performance to economic recession. The company's solution was to change its CEO. This action precipitated a revised strategy to shatter the entrenched corporate myths by becoming a low-cost competitor.

The third type of invalid assumption is the *corporate taboo*. Corporate taboos are those untouchable assumptions that are regarded as sacred cows within the firm's organizational culture. These flawed assumptions manage to escape most challenges. Often, this type of blindspot is rooted in the strongly held convictions of senior management. Gilad uses the experiences of Apple Computer, Inc. to illustrate the negative impact of corporate taboos. In 1983, Apple recruited a former top executive from Pepsi who immediately transferred his tried-and-true strategy of premium pricing to Apple's strategy. The expected high margins were planned for reinvestment into R&D and advertising. Unfortunately, these high margins never materialized, as customers preferred lower-cost IBM and PC-based machines. It wasn't until IBM developed a low-cost alternative that exceeded Apple's technological superiority that the new CEO decided to abandon his pet strategy of premium pricing that had worked so well at Pepsi. Despite persistent challenges by Apple sales staff to reduce prices, this corporate taboo of premium pricing was not relinquished until severe damage to Apple's competitive position forced a strategic change.

2. Winner's Curse/Hubris Hypothesis

Often, the winner in a bidding auction will unwittingly pay too much. Sellers know the true economic value of the item and, in the absence of duress, generally won't sell below this amount. In their zest to acquire, the winning bidders will be the ones who have ascribed an unrealistically optimistic value to the bid item. The strategic implications of the winner's curse do much to explain the persistence of unprofitable acquisitions. Without foreknowledge and explicit recognition of the winner's curse, decision makers will tend to overpay for things such as patents, companies, or personnel, resulting in profitless acquisitions that fail to yield expected returns.

Several factors explain the ungrounded optimism that drives this adverse selection process. Certainly, the presence of multiple bidders and uncertainty of the real economic value of the bid item will exacerbate adverse selection during the heat of the bidding process. Also, several analytical flaws are often committed even before the bidding begins. In the market for corporate control, the concept of synergy is commonly overestimated. Legitimate strategic relatedness is more rare than perceived by most managers. Even when genuine synergy is identified, two obstacles prevent its capture in most instances. First, many unexpected events postacquisition, most notably culture clash, militate against the full realization of expected synergies. Second, many firms fail to properly consider the potential synergy between other bidders and the target firm. The failure to consider that competing bidders may ascribe a higher relative value to potential synergies may unknowingly engage the firm in a bidding war that it cannot win. Either the firm will not acquire the target or, even worse, it will get caught up in a bidding war that will bargain away any potential synergies, resulting in negative returns to the "successful" firm—the proverbial winner's curse. Unrealistic assessment of perceived synergies between both the firm and the target and between competing bidders and the target are often sources of blindspots in the strategic decision-making process around acquisition opportunities.

The winner's curse has been extended to the common scenario where firms also "overpay" for other strategic goals such as capacity expansion, market share, and new business entry. In these contexts, the winner's curse often shadows successful firms by eventually causing their downfall. That is, it is more common to see firms in the top tier of their industry lose competitive position rather than maintain it for long periods of time.

3. Escalating Commitment

Resource investments will yield negative return either because the initial analysis was flawed, the competitive environment has changed, or internal capabilities have eroded. Three rational responses to this common scenario would dictate retrenchment, a change in strategy, or intensified resource allocation. The observed result, however, shows a disproportionate bias for the latter—strategic decision makers exhibit a strong tendency to intensify resource investment in the hopes of averting strategic disaster. Ironically, this behavior of throwing good money after bad often precipitates further losses and eventual policy failure. This phenomenon is termed the escalating commitment to a losing course of action and is one of the leading causes of blindspots in competitive analysis and strategic decision making. While this blindspot may appear tantamount to throwing pearls to swine, there are several logical reasons for its disturbing frequency. Several underlying factors explain this rather counterintuitive deviation from rational behavior.

The traditional explanation is twofold. First, it proffers that individual decision makers bearing a full load of personal accountability will escalate their commitment to a losing course of action in order to achieve internal and external justification of past decisions. Unduly optimistic perception bias is a coping mechanism that managers use to perceive negative consequences of past decisions more favorably than they actually are. This is a misguided attempt to appear rational, protect their ego, and to maintain the esteem of their peers. By escalating commitment, the manager appears to know what she or he is doing, is seen as bravely pursuing a superior strategic vision in the face of adversity, and is perceived as exhibiting the consistency norm of the corporation's culture. In reality, the manager may not know what she or he is doing and increases investment by default in the vain hope that fortuitous circumstances will work in his or her favor to vindicate the original investment. Thus, the traditional explanation asserts that serious blindspots develop when economic rationality becomes entwined with personal accountability and the psychological need of the decision maker to maintain internal and external justification of managerial competence.

4. Constrained Perspective/Limited Frame of Reference

In contrast, prospect theory challenges the traditional explanation of escalating commitment to a course of action. Prospect theory suggests two reasons why decision makers often display irrational behavior toward risk, often leading to an escalating commitment to a course of action (Kahneman & Tversky, 1979, 1982a, b, 1984; Whyte, 1986). The first reason is that people often gauge the relative risk of a decision relative to a neutral reference point instead of the wealth effect on the firm. The second reason relates to the "certainty effect," which suggests that a decline in the estimated probability of a decision outcome will be more influential when the decision outcome was originally thought to be inevitable rather than somewhat possible.

Figure 10-1 illustrates prospect theory by assigning a generic value function that regards many strategic decisions under uncertainty as options. Notice that the curve is concave above the origin and convex below the origin. The value function is also steeper for losses relative to gains. These properties reflect an important distinction

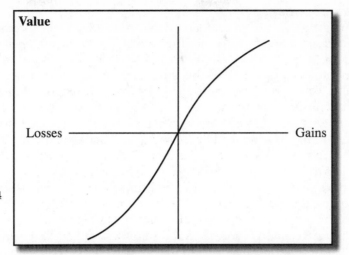

Figure 10-1
Prospect Theory
Value Function

Source: Copyright © 1984
by the American
Psychological
Association. Reprinted
with permission.

made by prospect theory that people are generally more risk averse to losses than they are attracted to gains.

The implication for strategic decisions is that the actual decision made depends on the position of the decision maker's frame of reference on the value function. Consider a manager who has made an original resource allocation decision of $100,000, subsequently lost due to unforeseen competitive factors. The opportunity to invest another $50,000 is estimated to have a 10 : 1 chance of payoff. The decision that the manager makes will depend on his point of reference on the value curve. The manager may view the incremental investment as a potential loss of $50,000 or a potential gain of $500,000. This decision frame places higher weighting on the more recent decisions surrounding the incremental investment. Alternately, the manager may view the investment decision in terms of its total impact on the wealth of the firm since the project's inception. In this case, the decision outcome will be viewed as an option between the original loss of $100,000 or a cumulative loss of $150,000. In this decision frame, the temptation to succumb to the escalating commitment to a losing course of action is much greater because of the "certainty effect" associated with the chosen frame of reference. That is, managers will deviate from rational risk avoidance when the decision is framed as an option between two losses rather than as an option between a loss and a gain.

Another common source of the limited frame problem concerns the fact that decision makers, quite naturally, will often look at a strategic challenge only from the firm's perspective. That is, they may operate from a limited frame of reference that only considers the strategic implications for their firm. Innovative strategies, however, often require an explicit consideration of the strategies of rivals. This has always been true of traditional competitive analysis. It is also becoming increasingly vital in the era of co-opetition and alliance building that requires an explicit knowledge and perspective of competitor strategies. Without broadening the frame of reference, the firm is at risk of being usurped by rivals in the race to secure competitive advantage through cooperation with other firms in the industry value chain.

5. Overconfidence

Many managers are overconfident of the knowledge and expertise that they bring to the decision-making process. The flip side of this overconfidence is the common phenomenon that managers are quite unaware of what they don't know—often an equally important parameter in a strategic decision. Russo and Schoemaker (1992) call this awareness of the limits of one's own knowledge *metaknowledge*. They assert that the failure of decision makers to accurately measure the confidence range of their analysis and decisions reflects their ignorance of what they don't know. The result is another potentially lethal blindspot—underestimating risk.

The root causes of overconfidence lie in the fundamental psychological responses to complexity and uncertainty associated with many strategic decisions. In order to cope with this complexity and uncertainty, cognitive simplification is used as a coping mechanism. Strategic decision makers often engage in this process on a subconscious level and eventually believe their simplified depictions of reality to be accurate. Hence, they are lulled into overconfidence regarding their abilities to successfully conduct analysis and the strategic decisions it supports. Several causes of overconfidence have been identified in the literature namely, availability, anchoring, confirmation bias, illusion of control, hindsight, and information volume (Langer, 1983; Schwenk, 1984, 1986; Russo & Schoemaker, 1992).

• *Anchoring* pertains to the pervasive influence of "guesstimates," a slang term for initial and often informal estimates or forecasts. Managers unknowingly cling to these guesstimates and frame their formal analysis around them. In effect, guesstimates become the implicit reference point controlling the range of the formal and explicit analysis and subsequent decision. As a result, strategic vision becomes artificially limited to a range around the guesstimate base point.

• *Availability* refers to the tendency of people to limit the universe of possibilities and options in order to reduce the number of potential decisions to be made. Often, only the possibilities thought to be likely are considered. As a result, overconfidence in judgment will be based in large part on only considering a small fraction of the possible decision options and event outcomes. Blindspots will develop because the decision options and event outcomes that were initially thought improbable may actually occur.

• *Confirmation bias* relates to the way people weigh evidence. Evidence that supports the decision maker's initial views and beliefs, or their gut instinct, is often given greater analytical weight than evidence that challenges preconceived notions. Thus, an incorrect gut instinct will be perceived as correct due to selective internalization of evidence.

• *Hindsight* concerns the distortions caused by the apparent predictability of past successful decisions. The phenomenon of 20/20 hindsight acuity lulls managers into believing that the competitive environment is more predictable than it actually is. As a result, managers often fail to develop contingency plans to deal with the unexpected.

• *Illusion of control* is the firm belief of managers in their ability to control organizational and competitive reality born out of an enduring faith in their competence and skill. It is closely related to confirmation bias in that information is often selectively chosen to confirm a prior hypothesis that has confirmed management control in the past.

- *Information volume* refers to the phenomenon in which managers infer that the quantity of information is directly related to the quality of the analysis upon which decisions are based. Additionally, each item in a high volume of information may be regarded as a reason or pillar of support for a management decision. These inferences may not be correct, however, rendering invalid the decision inputs.

6. Representativeness Heuristic/Reasoning by Analogy

Coined by Tversky and Kahneman (1974), the *representativeness heuristic* causes managers to make rash generalizations from limited samples or incomplete information. This blindspot can manifest itself in several ways, including the assumption that past strategic challenges are similar to present decisions confronting the firm, confusing correlation with causality, and the assumption that the firm is able to predict future outcomes with reasonable accuracy. This belief in "the law of small numbers" lures decision makers into making invalid inferences based on sample sizes that are too small to support such analytical demands. An important contributing factor to the representativeness heuristic is the pronounced tendency for managers to be much more influenced by colorful anecdotal stories than by strictly quantitative statistical analysis, thus limiting the sample size and type of their analytical inputs. In this respect, the related concept of reasoning by analogy (Steinbruner, 1974) is an operational mode of the representativeness heuristic because it allows managers to simplify reality and add color to anecdotal stories. Unfortunately, the analogies used to support a strategic decision may not be analogous or representative of the strategic parameters of the decision at hand. The results are blindspots rooted in oversimplification of the complexities and uncertainties of the firm's competitive environment.

7. Information Filtering

Top management often receives their decision support analysis from lower levels of management in the firm's hierarchy. As such, the impact of the previous six sources of blindspots will also filter back up to distort the decision-making process of top management. To the extent that information filtering will impact blindspots in the executive suite, Gilad (1994) identified four conditions that will encourage the growth of blindspots in an organization.

The first condition concerns the organizational structure of the firm. Strategic challenge, shared responsibility, and opinion diversity fostered by decentralized structures may counter blindspots. However, this tendency comes with the trade-off that exceptionally lateral organizational structures may slow strategic decision making down to a snail's pace. The trick is to find the right balance. The second growth factor of blindspots relates to how firms handle strategic failure. If the firm openly regards failure as a learning opportunity, blindspots are far less likely to develop. The third characteristic impacting the virility of blindspots is the volatility of the competitive environment facing the firm. Firms competing in political, economic, social, or technological turbulence will recognize blindspots much more quickly than their counterparts in more staid industries because radical change will impact bottom-line performance much more quickly. The fourth growing condition for blindspots is associated with the level of organizational slack that exists in the firm. Often, successful firms will have accumulated resources that serve to protect against times of adversity. For these incumbents, blindspots will become readily apparent only when deteriorating performance has eaten through this organizational slack.

STRATEGIC RATIONALE AND IMPLICATIONS

The previous discussion has focused on the psychological and organizational causes of blindspots. This represents only half of the equation of blindspot analysis. The other half relates to how these blindspots impinge on analysis and strategic decision making within a competitive context. Organizational behaviorists (e.g., Zajac & Bazerman, 1991) have extended the original insights of industrial economists (e.g., Porter, 1980) into how blindspots impinge on three of the most significant strategic decisions made within a competitive context: capacity expansion, new business entry through internal development, and new business entry through acquisition.

Capacity Expansion

Overcapacity is a common feature of many industry structures because many firms attempt to preempt one another in the race to meet growing demand. Rational competitive analysis should predict that only the fastest preemptors will succeed and that rivals who cannot expand capacity as quickly will recognize this and halt any plans to increase capacity. Yet this is often not the case. In many instances in the capacity expansion scenario, too many firms believe themselves to be legitimate preemptors based on incorrect competitive analysis and internal scrutiny. Many blindspots in industry and competitive analysis can be attributed to insufficiently considering contingent competitive action or reaction. Incorrect capacity expansion decisions relate directly to several types of blindspots:

- *Overconfidence.* Firms often suffer from overconfidence, they believe themselves to be preemptors, when in reality rivals are surpassing them. The increased capacity only adds to the supersaturated market demand conditions.

- *Limited Frame of Reference.* Firms that incorrectly predict competitive reaction to their own capacity expansion plans or market growth opportunities also suffer from a limited frame of reference. They will frame the strategic decision only within the context of gain (e.g., sales growth, capacity utilization, and lower unit costs) and will fail to adequately incorporate the very real possibility of losses accruing from capacity expansion decisions of rivals. The root of the problem usually lies in underestimating contingent competitive reaction or overestimating the power of the firm's internal strengths to counter these contingencies.

- *Escalating Commitment to a Course of Action.* Once managers commit resources to capacity expansion, they may become entrapped in escalating commitment despite obvious signs that their firm is not a legitimate preemptor. In order to achieve internal justification in light of personal responsibility for the capacity expansion decision, managers will allocate more resources to expansion. Hope that this intensified commitment will reaffirm the firm's preemptive status in the future usually reflects irrational psychology more than economic rationality.

- *Winner's Curse.* Firms often incorrectly map their rivals' intentions when considering the capacity expansion decision. Competitive analysis may miss the fact that rivals place a greater relative strategic value on capacity expansion and will pursue this goal regardless of competitive preemption. The faulty assumption that rivals will relent in the race for preemption often blindsides firms who are aggressively attempting to achieve preemptive growth. Contrary to their expectations, rivals will not relent in their expansion plans. As a result, much, if not all of the spoils of victory will have been bargained away due to the resulting industry overcapacity resulting in profitless growth—the proverbial winner's curse.

New Business Entry Through Internal Development

As with industry capacity decisions, considerations around new business entry through internal development are also often rife with blindspots:

- *Overconfidence.* Managers are often overconfident of their ability to successfully enter a new market because they underestimate contingent competitive reaction.

- *Limited Frame of Reference.* Analysis supporting new business entry decisions often assumes that the industry's attractiveness will remain the same after the firm enters. In reality, basing the justifying financial analysis on industry structure that exists prior to the firm's entry is not an accurate portrayal of competitive reality. Instead, the financial analysis should explicitly incorporate how the firm's entry will instigate competitive and customer reactions and change the industry's attractiveness.

- *Escalating Commitment to a Course of Action.* Once the firm enters the market, managers often fall prey to escalating their commitment to their original course of action despite being blindsided by unexpected competitive retaliation or customer reluctance.

- *Winner's Curse.* Strategic decision makers often underestimate the willingness of rival firms in a new industry to retaliate. For example, rivals may have invested in unrecoverable assets, creating barriers to exit that force them to aggressively protect their existing market shares by lowering their prices below the prospective firm's profitability pricing point. As a result, when the firm enters the market, the expected profitability does not flow from market share gains.

New Business Entry Through Acquisition

Similar to new business entry by internal development, acquisitions are also not immune to blindspots:

- *Overconfidence.* As indicated by persistent overpayment relative to market value, many managers are overconfident in their abilities to achieve synergies postacquisition.

- *Limited Frame of Reference.* When analyzing potential acquisitions, managers often suffer from a limited decision frame because their point of reference is based on fully

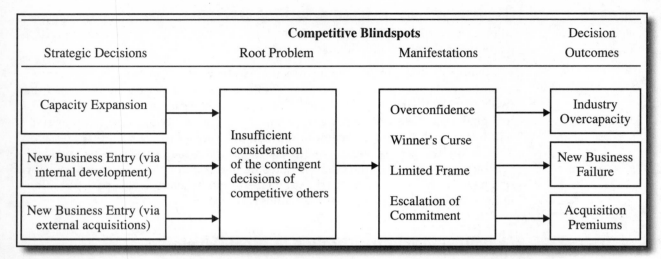

Figure 10-2
Strategic Implications of Blindspots

Source: Academy of Management Review by E. J. Zajac and M. H. Bazerman. Copyright 1991 by Acad of Mgmt. Reproduced with permission of Acad of Mgmt in the format Textbook via Copyright Clearance Center.

exploiting expected synergy gains. The reality that these gains are usually bargained away to the target firm's shareholders via the bidding process is usually ignored.

- *Escalating Commitment to a Course of Action.* Overconfidence in the firm's ability to realize expected synergies may lead the firm to ignore the possibility that rival bidders may also expect to achieve similar synergies. As a result, managers get caught in a trap of escalating commitment where multiple bidders exist in the market for corporate control.

- *Winner's Curse.* As a result of the preceding blindspots, the acquiring firm often enjoys dubious success, as most of the expected synergies will have been eroded by overpayment.

Through these three strategic decisions, Zajav and Bazerman assert that the source of many blindspots lies in the absence of adequate consideration of contingent competitor reaction to planned strategies. Figure 10-2 provides a schematic overview of the strategic implications of blindspots on the three strategic decisions discussed above.

STRENGTHS AND ADVANTAGES

An Early Warning System for the Firm's Early Warning System

The firm's competitive intelligence system functions as an early warning system for detecting eroding competitiveness. As such, blindspot analysis can be seen as added insurance for the firm's early warning system. That is, the real power of blindspot analysis is its proactive stance toward detecting flaws in the firm's competitive intelligence (CI) system before they manifest into deteriorating performance. In this respect, blindspot analysis can be regarded as a fundamental building block of the learning organization.

Comprehensive

Simply put, blindspot analysis is essential to effective analysis and decision making. Its strength as a strategic analysis concept cannot be overstated. Blindspot analysis is comprehensive and permeates every corner of the firm. Similarly, blindspot analysis should act not as a stand-alone analytical tool but rather as an overarching philosophy guiding the use of all other strategic analysis tools in the firm's employ.

Flexibility

Blindspot analysis can function to analyze flaws inherent in the firm's current decision processes. It is also amenable to being used on an ongoing basis to monitor any developing blindspots and potential weaknesses in the firm's competitive intelligence system or among its decision makers.

Cost Effective and Easy to Implement

On its own, blindspot analysis is inexpensive and relatively easy to implement. In the context of the high probability of strategic failure in its absence, the benefit/cost ratio of this analytical technique is high.

WEAKNESSES AND LIMITATIONS

Deceptively simple in theory, blindspot analysis is notoriously difficult to achieve because strategic analysis and decision making are extremely complex processes that incorporate great amounts of uncertainty and ambiguity. Most decision makers have trouble with accounting for uncertainty and complexity, and this is compounded when these factors enter into often politicized or fast-paced decision making and planning processes.

Although recognition of one's own blindspots is important, doing something about them can be difficult. Many decision makers and organizations that recognize their own blindspots are incapable of deciding or unwilling to determine how to respond to them. Organizational politics, history, culture, power structures and organizational design, among other things, can all contribute to this situation.

To be effective, blindspot analysis must also become part of the philosophical fabric of the organization's decision making. This is far easier to do in theory than in practice. Few firms have managed to diffuse blindspot awareness through their ranks, and even fewer have organized or institutionalized processes to utilize blindspot analysis on an ongoing basis.

Last but not least, most decision makers have a blindspot for blindspot analysis. This technique is not always on the radar screen of practicing managers and is rarely covered in the formal business education of managers. There are very few systematic or empirical studies of the application of blindspot analysis and its impact on a firm's decision making or competitiveness. This doesn't negate its importance; if anything, it enhances it, but requires analysts and managers to become educated about its benefits and applicability.

PROCESS FOR APPLYING THE TECHNIQUE

The process of applying blindspot analysis is significantly different from other management tools and techniques. Blindspot analysis is not applied in a systematic procedure. Rather, it is more of a philosophical approach that permeates all areas of competitive analysis and strategic decision making. In short, blindspot analysis should be woven across the other management tools and techniques that the firm employs in its pursuit of strategy. Even though the breadth of blindspot analysis defies a rigorous implementation procedure, several helpful core principles provide an overarching framework for this integration. The process we describe here for developing blindspot analysis is the one promoted by Gilad (1994).

By definition, blindspots are difficult to expose. Many firms suffer from blindspots without even being aware of their existence. Thus, the first step in introducing blindspot analysis is to identify possible sources of blindspots within the firm. Three useful tests exist to help a firm diagnose how susceptible the firm is to blindspots and whether they might be impinging on competitive analysis, internal scrutiny, and strategic decision making within the firm:

1. *The Visceral Test.* This test refers to how knowledgeable the firm is about all aspects of both its competitive environment and its internal capabilities. This may sound like a generic standard, but in the context of blindspot analysis, it is very rigorous. It involves knowledge about where *and* how rival firms compete, industry boundaries, tactical details, strategic overviews, and everything in between. An active competitive intelligence (CI) program and benchmarking initiatives are two indications that the firm has a visceral knowledge of itself, its markets, and its competitors. Firms will often fail the visceral test because long periods of success will lull the firm into the complacency of assuming that it knows everything. Quite simply, this is impossible, especially considering the fast pace of change and structural ambiguity present in many of today's global markets.

2. *The Reaction Test.* This test refers to whether the firm explicitly considers contingent competitive reaction to planned strategies. Often, companies mistakenly assume that market research is a surrogate for CI. They are very different.

3. *The Mute, Blind, and Deaf Test.* Essentially, this test asks whether the firm is capable of competitor analysis. That is, is the firm a genuine learning organization?

Each of these tests may seem simplistic and rhetorical. Many managers would cursorily award passing grades to their firms for each test. However, the apparent simplicity of each test reflects the insidious nature of blindspots. In answering the visceral test, for example, a firm may consider itself protected from competitive blindspots even though an unknown competitor may be planning an imminent entry from an entirely different industry. Within the context of blindspot analysis, ignorance is not bliss: It is dangerous. Often, blindspots do not become apparent until the damage is done. Hence, the purpose of blindspot analysis is to identify them early and eliminate them before they manifest into negative impacts on the firm's competitive position. Aside from the intuitive logic of blindspot analysis, ample anecdotal evidence exists to highlight this danger. Chief among them is the fact that few, very few, firms remain in business for longer than 30 years. The unkind reality is that in the vast majority of firms, blindspots will cripple and ultimately kill if they are not identified and eradicated.

Next, a four-step process for implementing the blindspot susceptibility test is conducted:

Step 1. Establish strong top management support for the blindspot analysis initiative and symbolically communicate this commitment to all decision makers in the firm.

Step 2. Appoint a "china breaker" who will function as a strategic challenger within the firm. Often, this individual is an outsider and is someone who embodies nontraditional lateral thinking processes. Alternately, the position can be shared by one insider and one outsider.

Step 3. Grant unconditional access to the strategic challenger to investigate potential infestation of blindspots within the firm. She or he is given the important role of questioning every aspect of the firm and so should be present, at a minimum, as an observer at all strategy meetings. Additionally, the strategic challenger should be witness to all facets of strategic analysis within the firm.

Step 4. Encourage the strategic challenger to perform all three susceptibility tests on the firm's internal scrutiny process, competitive analysis process, and, finally, its strategic decision-making process.

After step 4 is completed, the strategic challenger will report her or his findings to the senior executive group. If the firm is found to be susceptible to blindspots, the next phase of blindspot analysis requires an explicit attempt to identify and eradicate blindspots. This can be accomplished through the following four-stage process:

Stage 1. Select a specific strategic decision to be studied. For example, the firm's new product development or market entry decision processes are good places to start.

Stage 2. Determine the analytical parameters and informational needs relevant to the decision. This analysis is often secured by interviewing various functional experts both internal and external to the firm.

Stage 3. Identify the key decision makers and implementers for the selected strategic decision under study.

Stage 4. Ask each key decision maker to rank each analytical parameter or key item involved in the strategic decision on the basis of both importance and availability. The rankings are then averaged to isolate only those areas where CI is deemed highly

Table 10-1
CI Importance/
Availability Matrix

	Participant 1	Participant 2	Participation 3
Intelligence item 1	Importance and Availability	Importance and Availability	Importance and Availability
Intelligence item 2	Importance and Availability	Importance and Availability	Importance and Availability
Intelligence item 3	Importance and Availability	Importance and Availability	Importance and Availability

Source: "Identifying Gaps and Blindspots in Competitive Intelligence," by B. Gilad, G. Gordon, and E. Sudit, 1993, *Long Range Planning, 26*(6), pp. 107–113; *Business Blindspots,* by B. Gilad, 1994, Danvers, MA: Probus Publishing Company.

important but is only marginally available. Then, summarize the responses in a chart similar to the one depicted in Table 10-1.

This importance/availability response matrix will reveal serious gaps between available CI (i.e., internal scrutiny, competitive analysis) and that which is required for effective strategic decision making. It is in these gaps that blindspots lurk.

Based on Table 10-1, the most efficient route is to first concentrate on those CI items that are experiencing the largest gaps. More insights can be garnered by separating each participant in the importance/availability interview by functional area. Similarly, separate each CI item by type. Next, build a matrix comparing functional area to information type such as shown in Table 10-2. It will summarize the CI areas ranked to be important by users that are actually being adequately supplied CI and highlight those areas that are not achieving this critical task. Table 10-2 will also allow the firm to gauge how effectively the firm is sharing CI across the functional areas. This knowledge will offer opportunities to increase the learning capability of the firm by isolating areas where cross-functional CI sharing is poor.

The strategic value of the blindspot analysis process is the identification of blindspots within the firm's strategic and CI process. By following these steps, three

Table 10-2
Availability of CI
Type by Functional
Area

TEAM MEMBER FUNCTION	INFORMATION TYPE			
	MARKETING	TECHNOLOGY	COMPETITOR STRATEGY	TOTAL ($N = 14$)
General mgmt	63%	76%	91%	73%
Marketing	48%	43%	42%	45%
Technical	47%	54%	45%	49%
Total ($n = 11$)	51%	57%	58%	

Note: N = Number of items rated important or critical
n = Number of respondents classified by function

Source: "Identifying Gaps and Blindspots in Competitive Intelligence," by B. Gilad, G. Gordon, and E. Sudit, 1993, *Long Range Planning, 26*(6), pp. 107–113; *Business Blindspots,* by B. Gilad, 1994, Danvers, MA: Probus Publishing Company.

critical dimensions of CI and its impact on eradicating blindspots from the firm's strategic decision-making process will be identified: the specific CI required for various strategic decisions; the individuals in the functional areas who will be using this CI; and the opportunities to increase the sharing of CI to increase the learning capability of the firm.

At this point in blindspot analysis, the firm will have a good idea whether its current CI infrastructure and strategies are adequate to ensure competitiveness. If it is found deficient, the next phase involves overhauling both the CI capability as well as the organizational strategy developmental pathways. Many resources are available to the analyst regarding the general design of a solid CI program. The insights gleaned from the previous analysis will provide direction for individualizing the CI function for firm specific requirements.

Even if the firm's CI function is found to be adequate, several blindspots will also exist inside individual executives' decision making processes. That is, even though the decision maker is being supplied with adequate CI on important strategic parameters, the mental process of translating this analysis into action may be flawed. In this regard, the knowledge of the various sources of blindspots can be used to permeate a philosophy of strategic challenge throughout the firm.

A case in point is shown by leveraging knowledge of the psychological aspects of overconfidence in order to root out this particular type of blindspot. Russo and Schoemaker (1992) identify five techniques for treating the overconfidence blindspot:

- *Accelerated Feedback.* Ideally applicable to young managers, this treatment quizzes future decision makers about their knowledge of the firm and their responsibility areas. Immediate feedback is given to drive home the point of how limited their knowledge really is and, in the process, to reduce any chance of overconfidence.
- *Counterargumentation.* Challenging the premises underlying current and planned strategies will identify both explicit and implicit assumptions. This process often discovers flawed assumptions upon which overconfidence is built.
- *Paths to Trouble.* These are fault tree diagrams that attempt to list all of the potential pathways to strategic failure. Asking managers to add to this diagram will heighten their sensitivity to how susceptible the firm is to strategic failure.
- *Paths to the Future.* Rather than listing separate paths to trouble, scenario analysis attempts to analyze how these separate paths might be linked together in the future.
- *Awareness Alone.* Knowledge of the frequency of overconfidence blindspots is often incentive enough for managers to find their own internal control and treatment mechanisms.

Blindspot analysis can be conceived as a composite of three guiding philosophical approaches. First, the firm must strategically challenge itself through objective internal examination of the effectiveness of its CI and strategy functions. Usually found lacking, the next principle is to determine where and how a deficient CI and strategy infrastructure can be improved. Third, managers in the firm must be made aware of the psychological distortions through which they may unwittingly be filtering their internal scrutiny, competitive analysis, and strategic decision making. These three principles are mutually reinforcing and do much to ensuring that decision

SEARS

Between 1971 and 1990, Sears, Roebuck & Co. did not keep abreast of a radically changing U.S. retail marketplace. As the following table shows, Sears' management was bound by several blindspots related to unchallenged assumptions and entrenched corporate myths.

CORPORATE MYTH	COMPETITIVE CHALLENGE
Founding strategy based on domestic sourcing, high pricing, and periodic sales	Market entry by discounters such as Wal-Mart, Kmart, and Target premised on everyday low pricing, international sourcing, and efficient supply chain management
Status quo offering of a full line of merchandise regardless of competitive conditions or profitability per item	Market entry by niche chains such as Home Depot, which focused on narrow product lines and low prices premised on volume and specialization
Traditional strategy of relying on the same catalogue design format and outdated ordering system that had built the company	Market entry by savvy specialty catalogues such as L.L. Bean and Land's End premised on 365/24/7 service through toll-free numbers

The strength of corporate myths lurking in the organizational culture at Sears prevented management from reacting to these competitive challenges. In fact, blindspots essentially prevented management from even recognizing these competitive challenges as a direct threat to their franchise. Sears executives, having been successful for so long, became isolated from reality and were operating on competitive assumptions that were over a century old! Similarly, Sears promoted management personnel from within. Not surprisingly, strategic challengers, or "china breakers," were silenced by the pressuring mass of corporate yes-men. It is not inconceivable that some of them probably left to pursue well-paid careers at Wal-Mart, Home Depot, or L.L. Bean!

The damage caused by the blindspots afflicting Sears' management attest to the critical necessity of conducting blindspot analysis:

- Between 1971 and 1990, market share fell by 15 percent.

- Between 1984 and 1989, earnings fell annually by 7.7 percent.

- In 1991, Sears lost $1.3 billion on operations.

- CEOs needed replacement.

- Sears was forced to liquidate its insurance company and its real estate company, then the largest in America.

WAL-MART

The story of Wal-Mart's success was almost the mirror opposite of Sears' failure. Instead of being blindsided by competitive developments, Wal-Mart founder Sam Walton used knowledge of competitor's blindspots as a competitive weapon. The following table summarizes the strategy used so effectively by Wal-Mart against its rivals:

RIVAL BLINDSPOTS	WAL-MART STRATEGY
Traditional retailers such as Kmart and Sears located in large cities premised on attracting large crowds	Wal-Mart initially located in small towns with an average population of 15,000, premised on the fact that it was much easier to grow by eliminating mom-and-pop stores in small towns than by trying to steal market share from established large retailers
Large retailers started to invest heavily in diversification	Wal-Mart "stuck to its knitting" by investing heavily in its stores, making them much more attractive relative to the facilities of large, established retailers

(Continued on following page)

Blindspots: A Tale of Two Retailers (Continued)

Established stores were relatively neglected and lost their luster	Used profits of smaller town locations to finance penetration in larger cities
The distribution system at Sears was one of the weak links in its value chain, resulting in common stock outs and long order lag times	Wal-Mart invested intensely in distribution and logistics, making it a core competence of the firm and a strong source of competitive advantage
Blindspots made management at established retailers extremely hesitant to recognize that their store staff were demoralized due to low wages, little training, etc.	Wal-Mart symbolically "promoted" clerks to "associates," initiated profit sharing plans and invested heavily in merchandising training.
Over the years, Chinese walls were erected between management and line staff built out of the bricks of tradition and the mortar of outdated management philosophies	Wal-Mart treated all employees as partners as symbolically communicated by many and frequent on-site visits by the CEO

SOURCE: Adapted from Gilad, Benjamin, *Business Blindspots*, by B. Gilad, 1994. Danvers, MA: Probus Publishing Company; "Reversing the Downward Spiral: Lessons from W. T. Grant and Sears Roebuck," by W. Weitzel and E. Jonnson, 1991, *Academy of Management Executive*, 5(3), pp. 7–22.

makers have the right information and analysis at the right time and that the right people are using it to make the right decisions. Easier said than done, but much easier with blindspot analysis than without.

Blindspot Analysis in Action—A Process Example

A large pharmaceutical firm was considering the development of a new diet nutrient product. It conducted blindspot analysis to determine why the initiative had to be terminated soon after the initial production run was completed.

To initiate the analysis, analysis from within and outside of the firm drew up a list of 15 competitive intelligence parameters bearing on the new product development decision. These CI items were then divided into two main functional areas:

MARKETING	TECHNICAL
• Identify competitors	• The cost of production and distribution of close substitutes and competing products
• Current market size	• Raw materials availability
• Future market size	• R&D efforts by competitors in this product category
• Competitor's prices	• How costly would it be for competitors to add similar value
Market entrants	• The state of technology
Supply/capacity conditions of close substitutes	UNCLASSIFIED
Competitors' experience with their existing products	Relationship of competitors with their parent companies (if applicable)
Relationship of competitors with firm's clients	
Consumers' perception of product and close substitutes	

(Continued on following page)

In developing this list, the items that include bullets were deemed to be important CI parameters impacting on the new product development decision. Next, the key decision makers were identified as general managers, marketing managers, and technical managers. The following table was then derived comparing the functional decision makers on how they ranked the availability of each type of important CI information.

	INFORMATION TYPE AVAILABILITY SCORE		
Functional Area	Marketing (%)	Technology (%)	Total ($N = 14$) (%)
General mgmt.	71	25	54
Marketing	75	42	60
Technical	78	50	65
Total ($n = 10$)	75	40	

Note: N = Number of item rated important or critical
n = Number of respondents classified by function

As a result of this procedure, many blindspots were identified in the gaps between the assumptions held by the decision makers, the CI support that they received, and competitive reality:

ASSUMPTION/BLINDSPOT	CI SUPPORT	IMPACT
Technological superiority	A lack of CI on competitive market offerings especially of potential Japanese rivals despite awareness of lack of CI on the Japanese Research director declined to meet with Japanese researchers who visited the plant	Susceptibility to Japanese market entry
Similar costs across industry Flawed perception of how rivals compete	CI on parent company of European rival revealed knowledge of low cost process technology Managers ignored this information because of flawed assumptions and a lack of a CI dissemination mechanism Japanese price reduction dismissed as temporary dumping	European rival introduced competing product based on lower cost process technology Japanese price cut below the firm's pricing point
Low threat of North American–based competition Flawed perception of where rivals compete	Technical manager possessed valuable CI on the plans of a North American firm to introduce similar product using different technology Managers ignored this CI, despite the fact that the marketing manager belatedly lamented the fact that he would have significantly changed his forecasts had this CI been available a priori	Top management surprised by market entry of North American rival

(Continued on following page)

Stable sociopolitical environment	SBU manager in retrospect admitted that his anticipation of this CI parameter was poor Other managers dismissed this development to "politics as usual" Technical manager had prior knowledge of this development from lawyers but chose not to follow up with contacts at the FDA	Severe regulations introduced by the FDA on the new diet product category

Had blindspot analysis been conducted before the product launch, many of these faulty assumptions would have been eliminated. For example, the low availability scores on technical CI would have alerted management to increase CI efforts in this area. Further, the disparity between functional areas and CI availability would have alerted the firm to debilitating deficiencies in its CI dissemination process. Together, these insights would have lifted the strategic blinders that caused the pharmaceutical firm to misread the competitive arena so thoroughly. Absence of blindspot analysis played a large role in the strategic failure of the firm's new product launch.

SOURCE: Adapted from "Identifying Gaps and Blindspots in Competitive Intelligence," by B. Gilad, C. Gordon, and E. Sudit, 1993, *Long Range Planning, 26*(6), pp. 107–113.

FAROUT SUMMARY

	1	2	3	4	5
F	■	■	■		
A	■	■	■	■	
R	■	■	■	■	■
O	■	■	■		■
U	■	■	■		■
T	■	■	■	■	■

Future orientation   Medium. Blindspot analysis is forward looking mainly by virtue of its function as an early warning system for the CI function. Detection of flaws in the firm's internal scrutiny, competitive analysis, and strategic decision-making processes provide a solid foundation for present and future success, but the technique itself isn't necessarily focussed on elucidating specific future decisions, just improving them.

Accuracy   Medium to high degree. Requires lateral thinking and strategic challenge of entrenched assumptions. Accuracy declines to the extent that the analysis is reliant on insiders or on analysts poorly versed in this multidisciplinary approach of strategy theory, cognitive psychology, CI, and organizational dynamics.

Resource efficiency   High degree. The actual process of blindspot analysis is very cost effective. To the extent that blindspot analysis leads to an overhaul of the firm's CI infrastructure, its cost impact will be heavier. This is mitigated by the fact that undetected blindspots often lead to strategic failure and, very possibly, firm failure. Viewed as an option, then, blindspot analysis' gain potential is high, the probability of net loss is minimal.

Objectivity   Medium. The absence of outside strategic challengers may result in groupthink and overwhelming conviction of long-held assumptions. The objectivity of the analysis depends in part on the amount of organizational slack protecting the firm from crisis and deteriorating performance.

Usefulness   High. Blindspot analysis is critical to future strategic success and in many instances, the very survival of the firm. Usefulness is also enhanced by its diverse application as a broad set of principles to enhance many other management tools and techniques.

Timeliness   High. The detection of blindspots can usually be performed in a short period of time. The subsequent eradication of blindspots, however, can often involve protracted issues of organizational change, CI program overhaul, and so on.

RELATED TOOLS AND TECHNIQUES

- comparative cost analysis
- competitor profiling
- country and political risk analysis
- customer segmentation analysis
- customer value analysis
- functional capability and resource analysis
- industry analysis
- issue analysis
- management profiling
- scenario analysis
- S-Curve analysis
- stakeholder analysis
- STEEP analysis
- strategic groups analysis
- SWOT analysis
- value chain analysis

REFERENCES

Barnes, J. H. Jr. (1984). "Cognitive biases and their impact on strategic planning." *Strategic Management Journal, 5*(2), 129–137.

Barney, J. B. (1988). "Returns to bidding firms in mergers and acquisitions: Reconsidering the relatedness hypothesis." *Strategic Management Journal, 9* (Special issue), 71–78.

Bateman, T. S., & Zeithaml, C. P. (1989). "The psychological context of strategic decisions: A model and convergent experimental findings." *Strategic Management Journal, 10*(1), 59–74.

Duhaime, I. M., & Schwenk, C. R. (1985). "Conjectures on cognitive simplification in acquisition and divestment decision making." *Academy of Management Journal, 10*(2), 287–295.

Dowie, M. (1977). "How Ford put two million firetraps on wheels." *Business and Society Review, 23*, 46–55.

Elkington, J. & Trisoglio, A. (1996). "Developing realistic scenarios for the environment: Lessons from Brent Spar." *Long Range Planning, 29*(6), 762–769.

Gilad, B., Gordon, G., & Sudit, E. (1993). "Identifying gaps and blindspots in competitive intelligence." *Long Range Planning, 26*(6), 107–113.

———. (1994). *Business Blindspots.* Danvers, MA: Probus Publishing Company.

Kahneman, D., & Tversky, A. (1979). "Prospect theory: An analysis of decisions under risk." *Econometrica, 47*, 263–291.

———. (1982a). "The framing of decisions and the psychology of choice." *Science, 211*, 453–458.

———. (1982b). "The psychology of preferences." *Scientific American, 246*, 160–173.

———. (1984). "Choice, values, and frames." *American Psychologist, 39*, 341–350.

Langer, E. J. (1983). *The Psychology of Control.* Beverly Hills, CA: Sage.

Mintzberg, H., Raisinghani, D., & Theoret, A. (1976). "The structure of unstructured decision processes." *Administrative Sciences Quarterly, 21*(2), 246–275.

Porter, M. (1980). *Competitive Strategy.* New York: Free Press.

Prescott, J. E., & Smith, D. C. (1987). "A project-based approach to competitive analysis." *Strategic Management Journal, 8*(5), 411–423.

Roll, R. (1986). "The hubris hypothesis of corporate takeovers." *Journal of Business, 59*(2), 197–216.

Russo, J. E., & Schoemaker, P. J. H. (1990). *Decision Traps.* New York: Simon and Schuster.

———. (1992). "Managing overconfidence." *Sloan Management Review, 33*(2), 7–17.

Schwenk, C. R. (1984). "Cognitive simplification processes in strategic decision making." *5*(2), 111–128.

———. (1986). "Information, cognitive bias and commitment to a course of action." *Academy of Management Review, 11*(2), 298–310.

Staw, B. M. (1976). "Knee-deep in the muddy: A study of escalating commitment to a chosen course of action." *Organizational Behavior and Human Performance, 16*(1), 27–44.

———. (1981). "The escalation of commitment to a course of action." *Academy of Management Review, 6*(4), 577–587.

Steinbruner, J. D. (1974). *The cybernetic theory of decision.* Cambridge, MA: MIT Press.

Tang, M.-J. (1988). "An economic perspective on escalating commitment." *Strategic Management Journal, 9* (Special issue), 79–92.

Tversky, A., & Kahneman, D. (1974). "Judgement under uncertainty: Heuristics and biases." *Science, 185,* 1124–1131.

Utal, B. (1979). "Texas Instruments wrestles with the consumer market." *Fortune, 100*(11), 50–57.

Weitzel, W., & Jonnson, E. (1991). "Reversing the downward spiral: Lessons from W. T. Grant and Sears Roebuck." *Academy of Management Executive, 5*(3), 7–22.

Weigalt, K., and Camerer, C. (1988). "Reputation and corporate strategy: A review of recent theory and applications." *Strategic Management Journal, 9*(5), 443–454.

Whyte, G. (1986). "Escalating commitment to a course of action: A reinterpretation." *Academy of Management Review, 11*(2), 311–321.

Zajac, E. J., and Bazerman, M. H. (1991). "Blindspots in industry and competitor analysis: Implications of interfirm (mis)perceptions for strategic decisions." *Academy of Management Review, 16*(1), 37–56.

Chapter 11

Competitor Analysis

SHORT DESCRIPTION

Competitor profiling provides a comprehensive picture of the strengths and weaknesses of current and potential rivals. This analysis provides both an offensive and defensive strategic context through which to identify opportunities and threats. Competitor profiling coalesces all of the relevant sources of competitor analysis into one framework in the support of efficient and effective strategy.

Competitor profiling has four major purposes: to identify competitors' future strategies and plans; to predict competitors' likely reactions to competitive initiatives; to determine how well matched a competitor's strategy actually is to its capabilities; and to understand a competitor's weaknesses.

BACKGROUND

The concept of competitor profiling was borrowed by the corporate sector from military strategists who have long used profiling techniques as an effective and efficient way to manage military intelligence. Generals engaged in the heat of battle were furnished with incredible volumes of information about the enemy from all points in the theater of engagement and from many levels of the military hierarchy. Somehow, all of these data and analyses have to be formulated into a battle plan. From this necessity, the concept of the war room was born.

The critical feature of the war room is the inclusion of only relevant intelligence. The support activities of data gathering, information accumulation, and analysis take place outside of the war room. In this way, the war room functions as an extremely effective and efficient method of dealing with information overload. Ensconced within the walls of the war room, generals and their staff are able to concentrate only on analysis strictly relevant to the battle plan. The war room concept has been successfully applied within the context of business strategy and competitive intelligence (Shaker & Gembicki, 1999).

For many years, corporate strategists enjoyed the luxury of operating in "theaters of engagement" far less hostile than the battlefields of war. The use of war room profiling of competitors was not a necessity. Economic growth after World War II provided rich sources of demand relatively free from international competition. However, the energy crisis of the 1970s radically disrupted this ideal scenario, acting as a harbinger of permanent environmental turbulence and change. The liberalization of trade and globalization in the 1980s furthered this new competitive era. Finally, the strategic implication of the furious pace of technological change has cemented this new competitive environment. Attanasio (1988) suggests that corporate strategy has passed through four phases during the 200 years of its existence as a separate body of principles and practice:

Phase 1. Companies operated explicitly on financial planning premised on functional efficiency in order to meet annual budget goals.

Phase 2. Companies used forecast-based planning through which they extrapolate the past to make inferences about the future. This new technique allowed the development of longer budget periods and resource gap analysis.

Phase 3. Firms began to pursue strategic management based on externally oriented analysis. During this phase, the predominance of tactical management yielded to the concept of strategic analysis of trade-offs.

Phase 4. Rather than waiting to react to future challenges when and if they occur, firms are now beginning to position themselves in order to "create the future."

During this competitive evolution, the necessity of competitor intelligence became increasingly apparent. Michael Porter rang the clarion call of change for competitor analysis in two of his very influential works, one on competitive strategy in 1980 and the other on competitive advantage in 1985. His essential premise was that since strategy is concerned with finding a unique and differentiated customer value relative to rivals, competitor analysis is quite properly a central component of strategy.

Since Porter's pioneering work in the area of competitor analysis, many others have contributed to this important area of strategy. Today, as more and more firms enter phase 4, competitor profiling has become an integral component of the strategic process needed to "create the future."

STRATEGIC RATIONALE AND IMPLICATIONS

Given that competitor analysis is an essential component of corporate strategy, Porter (1980) argued that most firms do not conduct this type of analysis systematically enough. Rather, a lot of firms operate on what he calls "informal impressions, conjectures, and intuition gained through the tidbits of information about competitors every manager continually receives." As a result, traditional environmental scanning places many firms at risk of dangerous competitive blindspots due to a lack of robust competitor analysis.

To rectify this situation, Porter was one of the first writers to propose a formal and systematic process through which to gather information about competitors. His models as depicted in Figure 11-1 and Table 11-1 has a decided proactive orientation. The forward-looking stance of competitor profiling is intentional, as its primary design is to predict the future strategic actions of rivals. That is, the models encourage the analyst to use current and past information about rivals in order to predict the future strategic moves that a competitor may pursue in response to the firm's own strategies, the strategies of other firms in the industry, or changes in the competitive environment exogenous to business strategies. Armed with this knowledge, the analyst is in a superior position to craft both defensive and offensive strategies.

Figure 11-1
The Components of Competitor Analysis

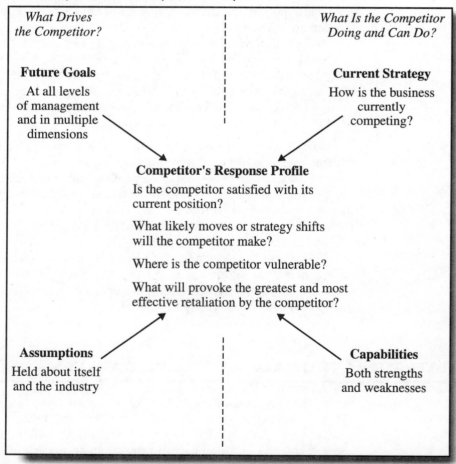

Source: Reprinted with the permission of The Free Press, a Division of Simon & Schuster, Inc., from *Competitive Strategy: Techniques for Analyzing Industries and Competitors,* by Michael E. Porter. Copyright © 1980, 1988 by The Free Press.

Table 11-1

Typical Categories and Types of Competitor Profile Information

BACKGROUND INFORMATION	PRODUCTS/SERVICES	MARKETING
• Name • Location • Short description • History • Key events • Major transactions • Ownership structure	• Number of products/services • Diversity or breadth of product lines • Quality, embedded customer value • Projected new products/services • Current market shares by product and product line • Projected market shares	• Segmentation strategies • Branding and Image • Probable growth vectors • Advertising/promotions • Market research capability • Customer service emphasis • 4 P parameters—product, price, promotion, place • Key customers
HUMAN RESOURCES	**OPERATIONS**	**MANAGEMENT PROFILES**
• Quality and skill of personnel • Turnover rates • Labor costs • Level of training • Flexibility • Union relations	• Manufacturing capacity • Ability to mass customize • Cycle time, manufacturing agility, and flexibility • TQM implementation • Overhead costs • Lean production methods	• Personality • Background • Motivations, aspirations • Style • Past successes and failures • Depth of managerial talent
SOCIOPOLITICAL	**TECHNOLOGY**	**ORGANIZATIONAL STRUCTURE**
• Government contacts • Stakeholder reputation • Breadth and depth of portfolio of sociopolitical assets • Public affairs experience • Nature of government contracts • Connections of board members • Issue and crisis management capacity	• Process technology • R&D expertise • Proprietary technology, patents, copyrights • Information and communication infrastructure • Ability to internally innovate • Access to outside expertise through licensing, alliances, joint ventures	• Nature of hierarchy • Team building • Cross functionality • Major ownership • Cultural alignment
CI CAPACITY	**STRATEGY**	**CUSTOMER VALUE ANALYSIS**
• Evidence of formal CI capacity • Reporting relationships • Profile • CEO and top management level of support • Vulnerability • Integration • Data gathering and analysis assets	• Positioning • Future plans • Mission and vision • Goals, objectives • Corporate portfolio • Synergies • Resources/capabilities • Core competencies • Strengths and weaknesses	• Quality attributes • Service attributes • Customer goals and motivations • Customer types and numbers • Net worth (benefits minus costs) of ownership

(Continued on following page)

Table 11-1 (Continued)

FINANCIAL
• Financial statements
• Securities filings
• Absolute and comparative ratio analysis
• Disaggregated ratio analysis
• Cash flow analysis
• Sustainable growth rate
• Stock performance
• Costs

Despite the elegance and theoretical legitimacy of competitor profiling models, a disturbingly large number of firms do not formally profile their rivals with the systematic rigor required of competitor profiling analysis. In a recent survey of nine major studies investigating current practices of competitor profiling within U.S. companies, Ram and Samir (1998) came to a promising conclusion. A 1988 Conference Board Study found that only 3 percent of firms surveyed had fully developed systematic competitor profiling systems in place. Their 1998 survey, however, indicated that 24 percent of those firms surveyed had a fully functional, advanced competitor profiling program. It seems that Western firms are slowly starting to learn some valuable lessons from their East Asian counterparts who have benefited from advanced competitor profiling for at least a decade if not longer.

The strategic rationale of competitor profiling is powerfully simple. Superior knowledge of rivals offers a legitimate source of competitive advantage. The raw material of competitive advantage consists of offering superior customer value in the firm's chosen market. The definitive characteristic of customer value is the adjective *superior*. Customer value is defined relative to rival offerings, making competitor knowledge an intrinsic component of corporate strategy. Profiling facilitates this strategic objective in three important ways. First, profiling can reveal strategic weaknesses in rivals that the firm may exploit. Second, the proactive stance of competitor profiling will allow the firm to anticipate the strategic response of their rivals to the firm's planned strategies, the strategies of other competing firms, and changes in the environment. Third, this proactive knowledge will give the firms strategic agility. Offensive strategy can be implemented more quickly in order to exploit opportunities and capitalize on strengths. Similarly, defensive strategy can be employed more deftly in order to counter the threat of rival firms from exploiting the firm's own weaknesses.

Clearly, those firms practicing systematic and advanced competitor profiling have a significant advantage. As such, a comprehensive profiling capability is rapidly becoming a core competence required for successful competition. An appropriate analogy is to consider this advantage akin to having a good idea of the next move that your chess match opponent will make. By staying one move ahead, checkmate is one step closer. Indeed, as in chess, a good offense is the best defense in the game of business as well.

STRENGTHS AND ADVANTAGES

Given the close relationship between competitor profiling and competitive advantage, many of the strengths of this tool are self-evident. However, several unique benefits arise. First, profiling encourages the firm to adopt a confident, aggressive, and proactive stance toward competitive strategy. The knowledge of rivals that profiling grants allows firms to define the parameters of strategy rather than react to unexpected competitive sideswipes. Done well, competitor profiling will become one of the firm's core competencies, contributing to competitive advantage.

From an organizational performance standpoint, the inclusive nature of profiling greatly facilitates sharing insights and perspectives across traditional functional boundaries of the firm. As such, many unique opportunities are often articulated that would have remained hidden in the absence of a formal profiling approach. Often, the process of profiling acts as a rallying point for many of the firm's employees.

The tactical implementation of profiling also creates an efficient and effective approach to strategy formulation. The analytical product of profiling in the form of relevant, timely, concise, and visually accessible presentation formats is an excellent vehicle to communicate the relevant factors of strategy. Compare this to the traditional vinyl-bound tomes produced by traditional environmental scanning that are probably gathering dust on many shelves as you read this.

WEAKNESSES AND LIMITATIONS

The primary criticism of competitor profiling relates to the temptation for firms to make it the all-encompassing cornerstone of competitive strategy. The irony of this is that in attempting to become an industry leader, the firm will eventually become a follower if it defines leadership too closely related to current rivals. Several reasons are responsible for this apparent oxymoron. Comparisons to rivals must always relate to the notion of customer value. Constantly referencing the firm's strategy to rivals based on the idea of strategic groups or interindustry competition will eventually blind the firm to innovative approaches of potential rivals in delivering superior customer value from outside the industry. This underscores the importance of keeping one eye on potential rivals from seemingly unrelated sectors and industries in order to root out complacency and blindspots that seem to grow unimpeded.

Another related weakness of competitive profiling refers to the copycat nature of outpacing the competition. Critics suggest that such a strategy prevents any competitive advantage from becoming sustainable. Rather, they insist that firms should focus solely on customer value in search of innovation, not imitation.

PROCESS FOR APPLYING THE TECHNIQUE

The process of competitor profiling is composed of nine stages:

1. Determine who your competitors are.
2. Determine who your potential competitors may be.
3. Decide upon the information that is required about these rivals.
4. Build a competitor analysis capability in order to secure this information.
5. Conduct a strategic analysis of the gathered information.
6. Present the information in an accessible format.
7. Ensure that the right decision makers get the right information on a timely basis.
8. Develop strategy based on the analysis.
9. Continually monitor rivals and continually scan for potential rivals.

Steps 1 and 2: Determine Who Your Competitors Are and Who They May Be in the Future

The first two steps are very closely related. Determining your current competitors is usually quite obvious upon cursory observation. A typical criterion includes those firms that serve the same customer base. However, upon deeper analysis this distinction will probably become blurred. What exactly is the customer base? Is it customers of the same product? The same product category? Ultimately, all firms are rivals in the perspective that they are all trying to attract the same discretionary income. Although this last delineation is extreme, it underscores the importance of cutting a broad-enough swath to effectively include potential rivals on the firm's radar screen at the beginning of the analysis. Given the industry migration and value chain erosion that is commonplace these days, it is important to cement this critical assumption at the onset in order to prevent the analysis from becoming too narrowly focused.

There are two very distinctive ways to define competitors. The traditional method has taken a supply side perspective centered on defining strategic groups. Strategic groups are closely related firms that are usually premised on relatively similar strategies, occupy similar links on the industry's value chain, and share similar resource capabilities. As such, this method is more adept at identifying current competitors within strategic groups or within industries. Operationally, strategic groups can be plotted on a graph with two axes into which all of the traditional rivals are initially plotted in the graph space relative to some set of distinctions along each axis. Next, the rivals occupying niches within the market are plotted. The final plot locates those potential rivals that are currently operating on the fringe of the industry's conventional parameters such as firms employing a substitutable technology, suppliers who may choose to forward integrate, and customers who may eventually choose to reverse integrate. At a minimum, every member of the industry value chain should be included when the strategic map is finished, starting with the most intense current rivals and extending outward to potential rivals lurking on the industry's periphery. It is important to be as creative as possible at this point, because often potential rivals are not obvious.

The other method of defining markets explicitly addresses the fact that potential rivals are rarely obvious. Usually they are hidden, developing entirely new ways of delivering customer value on completely new competitive platforms totally oblivious to current companies that they will soon supplant. By focusing on customer value and the simple question, Which competitors do *your* customers see to be *your* major competition? firms can define potential rivals according to their provision of comparable customer value but through different platforms. Here, the focus of the analysis is on defining potential rivals based on changing customer tastes and preferences, motivations, product or service deployment, or technological innovation.

Generally, the most valuable sources of information regarding the identification of both current and potential competitors will be the firm's customers, sales staff, marketers, and operations managers. Other, less valuable sources may be found in industry directories, trade association materials, and other such secondary resources.

Step 3: Decide Upon the Information That Is Required About These Rivals

The first place to start this step is to go to the internal end user of the intelligence—the strategic decision makers within the firm. They will be in the best position to itemize exactly what types of competitor information would be most beneficial. It is important to ensure that the competitive intelligence (CI) efforts around competitor profiling are user oriented. To facilitate this objective, the information gathering efforts should be demand oriented from the start.

Related to this requirement to stay closely attuned to internal demand for CI is the necessity to keep the information gathering activities closely relevant to external demand—those competitive parameters that impact customer value. Although far from exclusive, Table 11-1 depicts the types and categories of information that may be considered during this stage.

Aside from this main requirement, helpful ideas can be garnered from the various CI surveys and benchmarking initiatives that have been conducted. An excellent summary of nine major studies can be found in the Ram and Samir (1998) study cited previously. For example, one study conducted by the Conference Board asked 308 responding companies to rate the most useful types of information (see Tables 11-2 and 11-3). This may give the analyst some ideas regarding potentially useful types of information. Bear in mind, however, that information needs will be largely industry specific or even firm specific and will change over time.

Step 4: Build a Competitor Analysis Capability in Order to Secure This Information

Although this step is beyond the scope of this chapter, some fundamentals are pertinent. First is the concept of the intelligence cycle as it applies to CI capability. The infrastructure of the CI system should include competencies based on four distinct organizational skills of collection, processing, analysis, and dissemination. Second, an important item to keep in mind is the fact that, contrary to intuition, most of the information required already exists inside of the firm. That is,

Table 11–2
Most Useful Type of Information (by type of market)

	Total (%)	Industrial Products (%)	Consumer Products (%)	Both Consumer and Industrial (%)
Pricing	23	26	20	19
Strategy	19	20	15	22
Sales data	13	11	18	12
New products, product mix	11	13	8	10
Advertising/marketing activities	7	3	19	4
Costs	6	8	3	5
Key customers/markets	3	3	6	1
R&D	2	2	1	3
Management style	2	1	3	1
Other	4	4	—	8
No answer	10	9	7	15
	100%	100%	100%	100%
Number of responding companies	308	158	72	78

Source: Competitive Intelligence. (1988). Conference Board Report No. 913. New York: The Conference Board.

Table 11–3
Types of Information About Competitors Rated Useful or Fairly Useful

Present Status	Total (%)	Prospects	Total (%)	Costs	Total (%)	Organization & Operations	Total (%)
Pricing	97	Strategic plans	93	Manufacturing costs	83	Company operating style	76
Sales statistics	94	New product plans	91	Marketing costs	71	Service capabilities	76
Market share changes	93	Expansion plans	91	Advertising costs	48	Manufacturing processes	75
Key customers	91	Acquisition/ merger prospects or activities	83			Company organization structure	62
Advertising/ marketing activities	81						
Company reputation	77	R&D activities	80			Executive changes	58
		Product design	79			Financing practices	47
Distributors	63	Patents	56			Legal actions	46
Suppliers	50					Executive compensation	20

Source: Adapted from Competitive Intelligence. (1988). Conference Board Report No. 913. New York: The Conference Board.

salespeople, marketing staff, operations—in fact, everyone in the firm—are probably in possession of valuable nuggets of competitive information. Figuring prominently in these primary sources of information are the customers and suppliers related to the firm. This has been confirmed by the Conference Board report on competitive intelligence that cited internal sources as the most valuable. Table 11-4 and Table 11-5 ranks the common sources of competitor information.

Step 5: Conduct a Strategic Analysis of the Gathered Information

Porter's framework depicted in Figure 11-1 can be used as a helpful guide for performing the analysis of the gathered information.

- *Future Goals.* Determining the future goals of rivals will help to forecast their strategies with other rivals, and planned strategies of the analyst's firm. To understand where a competitor is headed, it is crucial to identify the direction intended with regard to market share, profitability, and organizational performance, to name a few. What has been stated with regard to their future direction? How do they see themselves operating in the future?

- *Current Strategy.* First, determine which of the three generic strategies (low cost, differentiation, or focus) the firm is pursuing. Next, the analysis can be delineated into the strategic implications for each functional area of the rival's business. A competi-

Table 11-4
Most Useful Sources of Information

	TOTAL (%)	INDUSTRIAL PRODUCTS (%)	CONSUMER PRODUCTS (%)	BOTH CONSUMER AND INDUSTRIAL (%)
Salesforce	27	35	18	23
Publications, databases	16	13	15	22
Customers	14	13	11	17
Marketing research, tracking services	9	3	24	9
Financial reports	5	7	3	1
Distributors	3	4	1	1
Employees (unspecified)	2	2	6	—
Analysis of products	2	1	3	3
Other	8	6	8	13
No answer	14	16	11	11
	100%	100%	100%	100%
Number of responding companies	308	158	72	78

Source: Competitive Intelligence. (1988). Conference Board Report No. 913. New York: The Conference Board.

Table 11-5
Information Sources Rated Very or Fairly Important

Sources Within the Company	Total (%)	Contact Within the Trade	Total (%)	Published Information	Total (%)	Other Sources	Total (%)
Sales force	96	Customers	92	Industry periodicals	89	Security analysts	40
Marketing research staff	83	Meetings, trade shows	74	Companies' promotional materials	84	Tracking services	38
Analysis of competitors' products	81	Distributors	70			Electronic databases	35
		Suppliers	65	Companies' 10K reports	77		
Planning staff	63	Trade associations	59	Security analysts' reports	74	Investment banks	22
Engineering staff	53	Consultants	43			Court records	16
		Retailers	37	Financial periodicals	64	Want ads	15
Former employees of competitors	49	Competitors' employees	37	Speeches by managers	55	Commercial banks	11
		Ad agencies	24				
Purchasing staff	42			General business periodicals	54		
				National newspapers	43		
				Newspapers in cities where competitors have facilities	42		
				Directories (Standard & Poor's, etc.)	31		
				Government publications	26		

Source: Adapted from Competitive Intelligence. (1988). Conference Board Report No. 913. New York: The Conference Board.

tor's current strategy may be identified on the basis of what the firm says and what it does currently. What are its stated short-term goals? Start by identifying the differences between future goals and what it is currently doing. Is there synergy and sense or will it require a major shift if it is to achieve its long-term goals? Are its short-term activities in line with its future goals? Remember, in the absence of particular forces for change, it can be assumed that a company will continue to compete in the future in the same way it has competed in the past.

• *Capabilities.* Use the information gathered in step 2 to conduct a SWOT analysis (strengths, weaknesses, opportunities, and threats) of each rival. The objective here is to identify what the competitor is doing and what it can really do. This is about capacity, skills, and resources. Although a competitor may have announced its strategic intentions, these may be quite different to its current capabilities and as such poses questions about the internal thinking of the company.

• *Assumptions.* A rival's competitive assumptions about itself, the industry, and other rivals will yield many useful insights regarding any potential incorrect assumptions or blindspots. Often, these blindspots offer competitive opportunities. This is the crux of the analysis. What assumptions does the competitor hold about its world and are these reflected in its strategies, both current and future? Assumptions can be identified by the mismatch between capabilities, current strategies, and future goals. On the other hand, a company that has all three areas in sync may be a formidable competitor. However, all companies hold assumptions and tenets about the world and the future and it is these assumptions that need to be uncovered.

The critical issue underlying competitor analysis is understanding what are the key assumptions made by the management team of competitors. This identifies fundamental weaknesses in how they compete and provides a framework of how they see their marketplace. Answering questions such as, Are they satisfied with this position? What are their plans? What are their vulnerabilities? can provide the necessary strategic input and understanding to take competitors on.

All four of the analyses are then integrated into a competitor profile. The purpose of this integration is to forecast with reasonable accuracy how a rival will precipitate or respond to various competitive pressures. First, the offensive stature of rivals is determined to predict any proactive moves they may initiate. Second, the defensive stature of rivals is determined to forecast how a rival will react to various competitive pressures. In making these determinations, qualitative factors often predominate over the more traditional quantitative approach of business analysis.

Step 6: Present the Information in an Accessible Format

Many different formats exist through which to communicate the analysis. Most effective are visual depictions as opposed to written reports. Figures 11-2 to 11-4 depicts three of many different types of formatting schemes available.

• *Comparison Grids.* Plot rival positions (performance, capabilities, key success factor, etc.) on high/low dependent and independent variable cross-hair axes. Depending on the application, the analyst's firm's performance or industry averages are used as the point of reference. Comparison grids provide nice snapshots of the relative performance across two competitive parameters. (See Figure 11-2.)

• *Radar Charts.* Simple to comprehend yet dense with information, radar charts are often used to communicate profiling analysis. Radar charts are composed of an underlying circle with several points on the circumference representing industry averages around relative competitive parameters. Superimposed over these circles are geometric shapes representing the performance of the firm or rival under analysis. Depending on superior or inferior performance, the resulting geometric shape of the overlay will depict a concise visual of relative performance. (See Figure 11-3.)

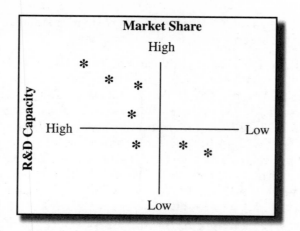

Figure 11-2
Presentation Tools
Comparison Grids

- *Color-Coded Competitor Strength Grid*. Developed by Aaker (1998), competitor strength grids are a simple but powerful way of depicting the relative superiority between rival firms along any number of competitive parameters. By assigning a spectrum of colors to represent relative competitive inferiority, parity, and superiority, the graph effectively and efficiently depicts the spectrum of relative competitive advantage among rivals. (See Figure 11-4.)

These charts and similar visual depictions should be used as wallpaper for the war room wall. Being surrounded by many concise summaries of relevant strategic parameters will greatly facilitate the brainstorming sessions during the strategy development process.

Figure 11-3
Radar Charts

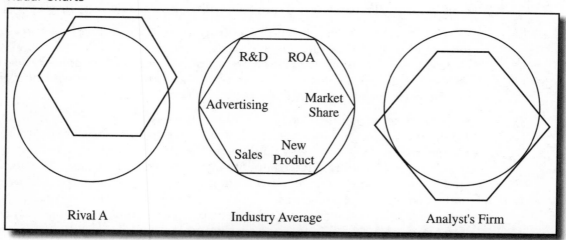

Assets and Competencies	Ralston Purina	Nestlé	Mars	Heinz	Hill's	Iams	Doane
Name recognition	Strong	Strong	Above average	Above average	Below average	Below average	Weak
Breadth of product line	Strong	Strong	Average	Average	Weak	Weak	Weak
Breadth of channel coverage	Strong	Above average	Above average	Above average	Weak	Strong	Average
Specialty/veterinarian coverage	Average	Weak	Weak	Weak	Strong	Weak	Weak
Financial resources	Strong	Strong	Strong	Strong	Strong	Weak	Weak
Cost structure	Strong	Average	Average	Average	Weak	Weak	Strong
Geographical coverage: United States	Strong	Strong	Average	Average	Below average	Below average	Weak
Geographical coverage: International	Strong	Strong	Strong	Average	Weak	Weak	Weak

■ Strong   ■ Above average   ■ Average   ▨ Below average   □ Weak

Figure 11-4
Competitor Strength Grid
Pet Food Competitors in the U.S. Market

Source: Strategic Market Management 2e by D. A. Aaker, Copyright © 1988 John Wiley and Sons, Inc. This material is used by permission of John Wiley & Sons, Inc.

Step 7: Ensure That the Right Decision Makers Get the Right Information on a Timely Basis

Given the rapidity of environmental and competitive change, competitor intelligence has value only if it is received in a timely fashion by the relevant strategic decision maker. In this respect, timeliness and relevance supercede complete accuracy.

Step 8: Develop Strategy Based on the Analysis

At this point in the analysis, the proverbial rubber hits the road. Competitor profiles are used to develop strategy around several relevant competitive considerations such as determining the probable rules of engagement within that strategic position; and choosing the arena of engagement—where, how, and against whom the firm will compete—by developing a strategy that leverages the firm's strengths, exploits rivals' weaknesses, neutralizes competitive threats, and defends against weaknesses.

In answering these questions, knowledge of how competitors are likely to react is used to compromise their ability to respond in a strategically optimal fashion. Strategies are chosen that will force rivals to make costly strategic trade-offs should they decide to impinge on the firm's strategy.

Step 9: Continually Monitor Rivals and Continually Scan for Potential Rivals

The analyst should always assume that rivals are simultaneously performing similar profiles for their own firm. This is reason enough to engage in continuous monitoring to counter competitive moves. Volatile markets, hypercompetition, industry migration, and decoupling value chains give ample rationale for continuous monitoring of current *and* potential rivals.

Letting Customers Do the Competitor Profiling

A study was conducted to determine a competitive profile of U.S. banks, savings and loans, and credit unions to analyze the impact of image and reputation as a possible source of competitor profiling distinction. Specifically, the answers to two questions were sought through a telephone survey of 1,016 randomly selected homes:

1. What are the competitive strengths and weaknesses of banks, savings and loans, and credit unions as perceived by their customers?

2. What image characteristic variables differentiate consumers' perceptions of their major financial institution from their perceptions of their minor financial institution from the perspective of their minor financial institution?

The image profile variables used were:

1. Having tellers who always call you by name.
2. Having well-trained tellers.
3. Leading most other financial institutions in offering new services.
4. Having lower-than-average service charges on checking accounts.

5. Having drive-up tellers who give faster-than-average service.
6. Having higher-than-average interest rates on savings.
7. Having officers with an above-average level of concern about you as a customer.
8. Having tellers in the bank who give faster-than-average service.
9. Having lower-than-average interest rates on loans.
10. Having operating hours that meet your needs.
11. Having above-average drive-up window convenience.
12. Making it easier to obtain a loan.
13. The friendliness of tellers in helping you manage your financial affairs.
14. Showing an interest in helping you manage your financial affairs.
15. Above-average friendliness of officers.
16. Having offices that are very easy to get to.

As a result of the survey around the above image variables, the following competitor profile was developed:

(Continued on following page)

Letting Customers Do the Competitor Profiling (Continued)

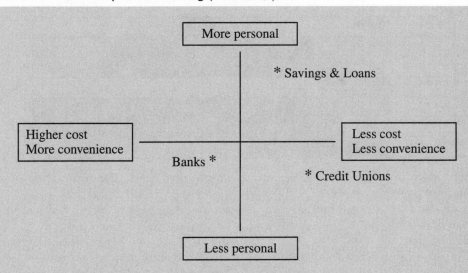

CONCLUSIONS

Significant differences exist between consumers' perceptions of the strengths and weaknesses between banks, credit unions, and savings and loans.

- Banks: high cost, high convenience
- Credit unions: lower cost, lower convenience
- Savings and loans: occupies the mental space between banks and credit unions

STRATEGIC IMPLICATIONS

The authors of the survey were able to surmise several significant strategic implications as a result of the competitor profile:

- Banks have a strong competitive advantage and credit unions have a weak competitive advantage with regard to targeting affluent customers who are attracted to convenience and are willing to pay for it. The source of this competitive advantage for banking convenience was found to be location and quick service. The flip side of these conveniences was found to be higher service costs and interest rates on loans.

- Credit unions have a competitive advantage over banks in targeting consumers attracted to no-frills service in exchange for reduced costs.

- Despite scoring well on personalized service (a relatively small impact on image perception compared to convenience and price), savings and loans are in the classic "stuck in the middle" position, having no competitive advantage with regard to banks or credit unions.

To achieve greater customer share, banks would presumably pursue growth by cross-selling to existing customers and attempting to convince credit union customers to switch based on a relatively diversified service and product offering. Credit unions and savings and loans would probably emphasize relationship marketing in order to develop the image of a "major" financial institution in the eyes of their customers.

SOURCE: Adapted from "The Competitive Marketing Profile of Banks, Savings and Loans, and Credit Unions," by T. R. Kenneth and J. P. Wong, 1988, *Journal of Professional Services Marketing*, 3(3,4), pp. 107–121.

FAROUT Summary

	1	2	3	4	5
F	▪	▪	▪	▪	
A	▪	▪	▪	▪	
R	▪				
O	▪	▪	▪	▪	
U	▪	▪	▪	▪	
T	▪	▪			

Future orientation   Medium to high. The forward-looking orientation of focusing on potential rivals as defined by customers is mitigated by the emphasis on current rivals as defined by strategic groups and industry analysis.

Accuracy   Medium to high. Accuracy is increased by including the notion of customer value in defining competitors. Also the multitude of sources and analytical approaches allows for substantial cross-referencing.

Resource efficiency   Low. Building a robust competitor profiling capability requires significant investment in human resources and intelligence infrastructure.

Objectivity   High. The comprehensiveness of competitor profiling analysis increases the accuracy through internal checks for consistency.

Usefulness   High. Used correctly, this tool is one of the most pervasive in contributing to the achievement of competitive advantage.

Timeliness   Low to medium. Starting from the ground up will require a significant time lag until actionable intelligence is produced. Operating CI systems are quite timely in collecting, organizing, digesting, analyzing, and disseminating actionable intelligence on both current and potential rivals.

RELATED TOOLS AND TECHNIQUES

- blindspot analysis
- comparative cost analysis
- customer segmentation analysis
- customer value analysis
- functional capability and resource analysis
- industry analysis
- management profiling
- ratio and statement analysis
- sustainable growth rate analysis
- scenario analysis
- structural groups analysis
- SWOT analysis
- value chain analysis

REFERENCES

Aaker, D. A. (1998). *Strategic market management*. New York: John Wiley and Sons.

Attansio, D. B. (1988). "The multiple benefits of competitor intelligence." *The Journal of Business Strategy*, 9(3), 16–19.

Cvitkovic, E. (1989). "Profiling your competitors." *Planning Review*, 17(3), 28–30.

Conference Board, *Competitive Intelligence*, 1988, Conference Board Report No. 913. New York: The Conference Board.

Kenneth, T. R., & Wong, J. P. (1988). "The competitive marketing profile of banks, savings and loans, and credit unions." *Journal of Professional Services Marketing*, 3(3,4), 107–121.

Porter, M. (1980). *Competitive strategy: Techniques for analyzing industries and competitors*. New York: Free Press.

———. (1985). *Competitive advantage: Creating and sustaining competitive advantage*. New York: Free Press.

Ram, S., & Samir, I. T. (1998). "Competitor analysis practices of U.S. companies: An empirical investigation." *Management International Review, 38*(1), 7–23.

Shaker, S., & Gembicki, M. (1999). *The war-room guide to competitive intelligence*. New York: McGraw Hill.

Chapter 12

Customer Segmentation Analysis

SHORT DESCRIPTION

Customer segmentation analysis comprises a first step in external analysis that divides markets into groups based on distinct heterogeneous customer needs between groups and relatively homogeneous customer needs within groups. This model maps a path to potential competitive advantage by matching the value embedded in the firm's products and services with customer groups most attracted to that value.

BACKGROUND

During much of the early twentieth century, classical economic theory held sway over corporate strategy. The theory of perfect competition dominated with its assumption of homogeneous demand and supply. As such, the fundamental unit of analysis became the aggregate supply and demand functions. Any observed instances of price differentials were attributed solely to informational asymmetry and other market imperfections. The idea that these price differences might be attributed to heterogeneous supply and demand was rejected because of its contradiction with the orthodoxy of homogeneous aggregation of these market forces.

The manifestation of this perspective within corporate strategy resulted in a focus on achieving economies of scale and mass production. Extending from the principle of homogeneous supply and demand, firms were considered similar, producing basically the same products. Similarly, consumers were regarded as one large group with similar needs. This left cost as the only relevant competitive parameter. As such, conventional business wisdom held that the route to optimal profitability was to produce massive volumes of standardized products in order to achieve the lowest possible cost.

This status quo persisted for many years, despite the work of several preeminent contrarian thinkers. A case in point was the publication in 1933 of *The Theory of Monopolistic Competition* by economist Edward Chamberlain. His main thesis challenged the concept of aggregate demand and supply by suggesting that multiple demand curves exist within markets as a result of differentiation strategies designed to meet different needs of consumers. The important distinction that he made was that if product differentiation achieves a tight fit with the taste and preferences driving selected multiple demand curves, those affected demand curves will undergo a secular shift to the right and become less price elastic because customers in those segments will become less price sensitive. Despite the prescience of Chamberlain's work, it was generally regarded as an academic foray not applicable to corporate strategy. It lay dormant for several decades.

Wendell Smith reawakened interest with his 1956 article in *The Journal of Marketing*, "Product Differentiation and Market Segmentation as Alternative Marketing Strategies." Where traditional economic theory defined demand as a function of price and rivalry, Smith extended this notion to include differences in customer perceptions of value as one of the central determinants of demand. As such, he challenged managers to attend to differences in customer needs, tastes, and preferences through its explicit recognition in marketing strategy. Smith's main argument was the existence of heterogeneity among both supply and demand within imperfect markets.

This view, like Chamberlain's, also contrasted directly with the traditional economic model that was premised on the assumption of supply and aggregate demand within perfect competition. Smith argued that characteristics of modern markets were becoming increasingly unexplainable by traditional economic theory. Instead of recognizing only one aggregate demand curve, Smith's theory envisioned markets as a disaggregation of multiple demand schedules. Similarly, he also observed that firms within a market operate on a diversity of supply functions. The important strategic implication of Smith's work was the challenge for firms to revisit and extend their views of marketing strategy. During the era of mass production, marketing strategy generally attempted to "bend" the aggregate demand curves to fit standardized product offerings. Smith turned this convention on its head by suggesting that, with increasingly sophisticated production technology and wealthier markets, another strategic option existed for firms: to "bend" marketing and production strategy (i.e., the firm's individual supply function) to fit increasingly divergent consumer demand within imperfect markets (i.e., multiple demand functions that comprise the aggregate demand function).

The widespread adoption of Smith's theory did not occur until several environmental developments confirmed its validity. The competitive pressures introduced by increasing globalization, coupled with the increasing wealth of consumers, resulted in a transition from push economies to pull economies. Firms now faced the discipline of excess supply and intense competition. The efficacy of mass production predicated on economies of scale became increasingly untenable. Segmentation theory slowly evolved to replace it.

Today, customer segmentation analysis has become one of the most important contributions of the marketing discipline to modern strategy theory. Firms regularly use this technique as a first step in environmental analysis because of its close relationship to the ultimate goal of competitive advantage.

Strategic Rationale and Implications

Customer segmentation analysis offers the analyst a rational method in which to frame the scope of corporate strategy, that is, the product or service market focus of the firm. Scope must be limited for two reasons. The first and most obvious reason is that it is impossible for the firm to serve all customers. The second reason is more subtle and strategically relevant as it speaks directly to the essence of dynamic competition: Even if it were possible to serve all customers, this would not be the most profitable strategy for the firm to pursue.

Customer segmentation is an integral source of competitive advantage. This strategic relationship is premised on the heterogeneity of both customers and competitors within a market. Customers have different concepts of value, the difference between the total benefits and total costs of ownership of the firm's product or service. Similarly, competitors have different capabilities and resources available to satisfy customer value. The individual firm simply does not have the diversity of resources to satisfy the entire diversity of customer value. Attempts to do so are misguided because an attempt to please all customers will inevitably please only some or none of them.

If all firms within a market or industry attempted to sell to all customers, the industry's attractiveness would eventually erode, as product differentiation would converge. Consumers would become extremely price sensitive and the competitive position of individual firms would decline in the ensuing price wars. Only the lowest cost firm would be profitable, but the majority of consumers would remain unsatisfied.

Contrast this situation to a more enlightened scenario involving customer segmentation analysis. Here, the firm targets only those customer groups whose perception of value can be best satisfied by their unique resources. Customers in these segments are willing to pay higher prices for the satisfaction of their tastes and preferences. As a result, the firm will enjoy a much stronger competitive position and higher profitability. This provides the underlying rationale for segmentation.

Segmentation theory incorporates this demand orientation because the customer is in fact the raison d'etre of the firm. However, it explicitly challenges managers to recognize that satisfying customers is not enough to ensure competitive advantage. Rather, satisfying *profitable* customers is the cornerstone of superior financial performance and is quite properly the frame of segmentation theory.

The segmentation process involves drilling down the analysis to identify those assets, capabilities, and competencies driving the firm's superior customer value proposition. Any growth strategies should be premised on leveraging these resources. Appropriate growth and diversification strategies may offer different value propositions to the chosen customer segment(s) but should be based on the same fundamental business strengths of the firm. Exploiting this synergy is intrinsic to achieving competitive advantage.

Many of the firm's potential customers will not be profitable if their perceptions of value are not closely matched with the value proposition that the firm's resources and capabilities can provide. These marginally satisfied customers will not be willing to pay as high a price as completely satisfied customers. Similarly, they will be much more likely to defect. Given the limited resources of the firm, it is better to focus all of its energies on only those segments that are the most profitable.

Segmentation analysis provides a holistic framework to combine both the demand and supply perspectives of strategy in the pursuit of competitive advantage. Demand considerations are expressly entertained by the focus on finding and satisfying the needs, tastes, and preferences of particular customer segments. Supply strategy is also attended to by leveraging the firm's resources to those segments best satisfied by the firm's value proposition. If segmentation analysis is conducted properly, these targeted segments will pay higher prices for the superior value propositions provided by the firm. They will also become very loyal because rivals, operating from a different set of resources, will not be able to usurp that level of customer value. Thus, the two conditions of competitive advantage are satisfied by segmentation theory: protracted and superior financial performance. Figure 12-1 indicates how this tight weave between the firm's resources and customer value offers promise of securing a competitive advantage.

Two caveats impinge on this optimal scenario. First, the firm must remain alert to the existence of legitimate loss leaders. That is, some unprofitable activities will be part of a larger system of activities that provide value to the firm's target segments. For example, marginally profitable new car sales at auto dealerships effectively support the highly profitable service, maintenance, and repair that inevitably follow from future car sales. Second, segmentation strategy must be set in a dynamic context. Customer value analysis must be continually monitored to ensure the sustainability of the initial competitive advantage secured by segmentation strategy. That is, the firm must remain ever vigilant to the possibilities of changing customer value, erosion in the value of the firm's resources, or an increase in the relative value of rival offerings.

Of course, this general case of why segmentation makes strategic sense requires a more robust analysis to determine the market conditions that will foster a greater chance of achieving competitive advantage through segmentation. Valid growth and diversification strategies are predicated on economies of scope. As such, Davis and Devinney (1997) provide an insightful analysis in this regard, which is summarized in Figure 12-2.

As Figure 12-2 implies, segmentation strategy is viable in markets where customer value is premised more on tastes and preferences than on price, where different groups of customers exist in a market, and where the economies of scope and focus predominate the economies of scale within the market. In these types of markets, growth and diversification strategies based on customer segmentation offer feasible opportunities to deliver profitable growth through a strong and differentiated competitive position.

This search for profitable customers should direct the firm's growth and diversification aspirations. From Ansoff (1957), the firm has four basic strategies through which to pursue growth:

1. Market penetration
2. Product development
3. Market extension
4. Diversification

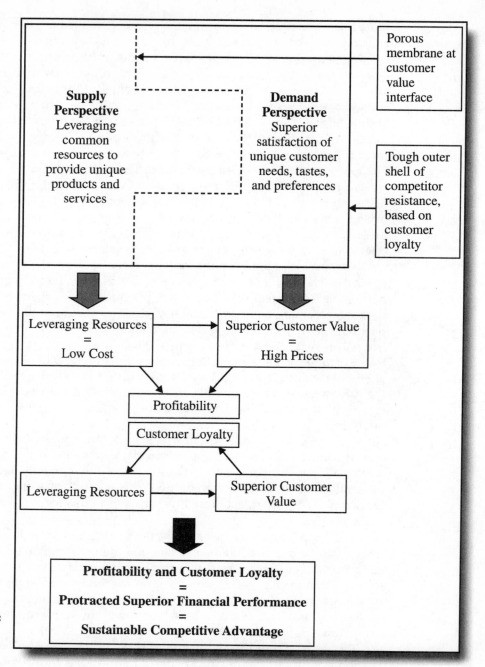

Figure 12-1
The Strategic Logic
of Segmentation
Analysis

Segmentation provides an excellent analytical tool for determining which of these strategies will lead to profitable growth. The most profitable strategies will be those that target customer segments that ascribe the highest relative value to the firm's unique products and services. These customer groups will be willing to pay the highest prices and will be the least susceptible to migrating to rival offerings.

Figure 12-2
The Economic
Logic of Market
Segmentation
Analysis

Source: Adapted from *The
Essence of Corporate
Strategy: Theory for
Modern Decision Making,*
by J. Davis and T.
Devinney, 1997, St.
Leonards, Australia:
Allen & Unwin.

Condition 1

Premise: Segmentation makes strategic sense when
- **consumers in the market exhibit heterogeneous needs, tastes, and preferences that override their price sensitivity.**

Firm's customer value offering: Customer value $= V_A(X) - P_X$ where A = customer group X = characteristics of the firm's product P_X = price firm's product	**VS.**	**Rival's customer value offering:** Customer value $= V_A(Y) - P_Y$ where A = customer group Y = characteristics of rival's products P_X = price of rival's product

Given that $Y < X$ and $P_y < P_x$, (i.e., product Y is inferior but also cheaper), consumers will buy product Y when the rival customer value offering exceeds the firm's customer value offering, or more formally: when $V_A(Y) - P_Y > V_A(X) - P_X$.

Conversely, under the same conditions, consumers will buy product X when the value of its superior product characteristics exceeds the value of the lower price of product Y, or more formally: when $V_A(X) - P_X > V_A(Y) - P_Y$.

Condition 2

Premise: Segmentation makes strategic sense when
- **customer groups exist based on different tastes and preferences;**
- **economies of scope and focus dominate the market more than economies of scale.**

Logic:
Assume: Customer Group A prefers Product X
Customer Group B prefers Product Y

However, the preferences of each customer group will be impacted by relative prices of each product. More formally, segmentation strategy makes sense when:

$$V_A(X) - V_A(Y) > P_x - P_y \text{ and } V_B(Y) - V_B(X) > P_Y - P_x$$

In this scenario, the firm would price at $P_X = V_A(X)$ capturing Customer Group A and the rival would price at $P_Y = V_B(Y)$ capturing Customer Group B. This will only be feasible in two types of market conditions:
- Economies of focus prevail: Due to efficiencies associated with narrower range, the specialized firm can offer a high value customer offering below the customer's threshold switching price (i.e., $V_A(X) - V_A(Y) > P_x - P_y$)
- Economies of scope prevail: Due to synergies associated with targeting multiple segments, the firm can offer a high value customer offering below the customer's threshold switching price (i.e., $V_A(X) - V_A(Y) > P_x - P_y$)

In markets where economies of scale predominate, some producers may be able to feasibly lower costs below consumer's threshold of differentiation value. For example, if the rival firm is able to lower costs (by virtue of economies of scale) so that $V_A(X) - V_A(Y) < P_x - P_y$. Customer Group A will migrate toward product Y. In these markets, segmentation is a losing proposition.

As the integrated Ansoff matrix in Figure 12-3 shows, even though the selected segments targeted by each strategy will have different perceptions of customer value, this unique value should be driven by the same set of core resources unique to the firm. Growth and diversification based on any other premise will fail to deliver profitable growth and will not secure competitive advantage. In short, it is equally important for the firm to say no as it is to say yes to growth and diversification options. Segmentation provides structure to this decision by making deliberate the

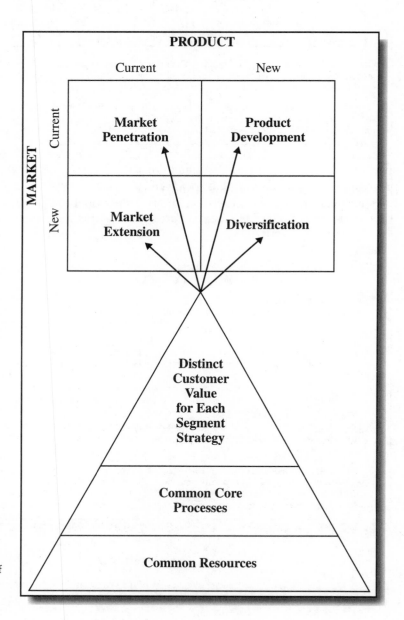

Figure 12-3
Strategic Growth through Segmentation

(Matrix in upper half of figure is adapted from Ansoff, 1957)

Part II   The Techniques of Strategic and Competitive Analysis

strategic trade-offs between targeting profitable segments and ignoring all others. The result is a much higher probability of profitable growth.

During the late 1980s, market segmentation developed into niche marketing through which customer segments became divided into ever-finer distinctions. The ultimate realization of this evolution is the concept of mass customization that is currently challenging many of the premises underlying traditional market segmentation strategy.

Mass customization is one of the most innovative developments of the information revolution. New technologies such as computer-aided design and manufacturing (CAD/CAM) are blurring the traditional trade-off between the economics of scale and the economics of scope. These flexible production processes are allowing companies to produce large quantities yet customize each unit to the specifications of individual consumers. Similarly, information technology is allowing services to be individually tailored to each specific customer. Differentiation, volume, quality, and low cost can now be achieved simultaneously where previously definite trade-offs existed between each of these production functions.

An example of mass customization is the Japanese modular housing industry (Davis, 1989). Within hours, home buyers can design their own home. With each specification, computer programs automatically change all of the plans regarding process scheduling and material requirements. The plans are then sent electronically to the factory. Within 30 to 60 days, a totally customized two-story, three-bedroom house, complete with deck and greenhouse, can be built for a very reasonable amount plus the cost of the plot. This is a truly remarkable achievement that was previously considered impossible. This type of mass customization is becoming increasingly pervasive in all facets of our economy.

Interestingly, mass customization can be seen not as a linear progression of development but rather as a circular evolution that has brought the concepts of marketing back to square one. Before the industrial revolution, small businesses offered individualized sales and services to each customer. Consider the farrier who fitted each customer's horse with a unique set of horseshoes. Then, during the industrial revolution, mass production premised on the economics of scale precipitated a corollary theory of mass marketing. The concepts of segmentation challenged the theoretical shackles induced by limited technology by rejecting the notion of homogeneous markets. Ironically, technology is now challenging the established marketing theory of segmentation. Instead of viewing the market as composed of heterogeneous groups of customers, the market can now be viewed as the individual. That is, in a lot of markets today, the level of segmentation has been delineated to a market of one. Instead of share of market, or share of segment, the appropriate measurement today is the individual consumer—a market of one.

The strategic implications of these developments for segmentation theory are enormous. The traditional imperative of segmentation sought to target profitable segments within a market. Instead of targeting relatively distinct segments, mass customizers are now able to tailor their offerings to the unique differences between each individual customer. Recall that segmentation analysis was developed to fill the gaps between the average offerings of mass marketing to a more refined average offering for various segments. The opportunities for providing customer value through mass customization now lie in the gaps produced by segmentation

Figure 12-4
Mass
Customization

Source: Reprinted by permission of *Harvard Business Review,* (The Four Approaches to Customization). From "The Four Faces of Customization," by J. H. Gilmore and J. Pine: II, Jan./Feb. 1997. Copyright 1997 by the President and Fellows of Harvard College; all rights reserved.

Strategy	Description	When to Use	Example
Collaborative	Explicit input from customer to design exact specifications	Customers are not able or cannot be bothered to accurately describe needs when presented with many options	Custom Foot uses digital foot imager, hand measurements, and customer conversation to create guarateed exact fit of custom-made Italian shoes
Adaptive	Standardized product that is customizable by the consumer	Customers who will use product differently depending on its application	Lutron Electronics Company produces programmable lighting systems
Cosmetic	Standardized product but customized delivery	Customer applications are similar but perceive benefits differently	Planters Company is able to customize packaging of peanut products for different retail applications
Transparent	Customized products, the uniqueness of which customers are not completely aware	Customers with repeated similar needs but who prefer not to stipulate this unchanging need each time they use the product	Ritz Carlton hotel chain maintains database on guests in order to offer increasing customization with each subsequent stay

approaches and what each individual customer within that segment really needs or wants. Gilmore and Pine (1997) refer to these gaps as "customer sacrifice gaps" and suggest four strategies through which to pursue mass customization strategy based on an intimate knowledge of the nature of these gaps. The top portion of Figure 12-4 depicts their schematic of four approaches to mass customization. The chart below this matrix summarizes their guidelines as to when to use each strategy.

A more generous view would assert that mass customization doesn't so much challenge the validity of segmentation theory, but rather that it doesn't go far enough. In this light, mass customization can be seen as the ultimate conclusion of

Part II   The Techniques of Strategic and Competitive Analysis

segmentation. However, just as segmentation was seen as the final fruition of marketing strategy theory, technology is once again extending even the concept of mass customization. Multiple segments are now thought to exist within each customer. That is, individual customers exist in different markets at different times and different places (Gilmore & Pine, 1997). They cite the example of an airline traveler who prefers soda on the trip to a business meeting and a refreshing alcoholic beverage on the return trip. The next challenge, then, for marketers will be to successfully target the multiple segments that exist in each individual customer.

STRENGTHS/ADVANTAGES

Efficient and Effective Route to Competitive Advantage

A common analogy is to compare segmentation analysis as an accurate rifle shot to the heart of the target as opposed to the hit-and-miss approach of the shot gun blast of traditional mass marketing. By correctly matching the firm's resources with those segments most attracted to the value produced by those resources, the firm can achieve effective marketing strategies with minimum investment in both resource acquisition/upgrading and promotional expenditure. Segmentation analysis stands a high probability of developing competitive advantage through profitable growth. Further, this new growth will be protected from competitive encroachment by virtue of being composed of the tightest relative satisfaction of customer value.

Tool for Achieving a Marketing Orientation

Segmentation analysis puts the firm in a legitimate market orientation. Instead of producing a product and then trying to sell it, or targeting a heterogeneous market with a homogeneous marketing strategy, segmentation analysis encourages the firm to first identify customer value and then formulate an optimal marketing and production strategy to satisfy customer needs.

Effective Complement to Competitive Intelligence Processes

An important component of segmentation analysis includes competitive analysis through an exploration of how the firm's products or services stack up against the competition. Similarly, segmentation often detects market changes in the process, thus strengthening the firm's early warning systems.

Impetus for New Product Development

The identification of unmet needs through the needs analysis component of segmentation often uncovers opportunities to develop new products. The identification of lead users often provides design information infinitely more valuable than what could be generated internally.

Flexibility

The flexibility of segmentation analysis is underscored by its equally relevant application to evaluation of current strategies as well as appraisal of future growth strategies under consideration. Additionally, segmentation analysis offers excellent guidance for the tactical management of the product, price, place, promotion, and people components of marketing strategy.

WEAKNESSES AND LIMITATIONS

Segmentation Provides Only Aggregate Profiles of Segments

Despite the apparent robustness of the analysis, it must be remembered that segmentation is limited by its composite nature. For example, predictions based on customer characteristics may fail to materialize in sales due to the impact of more influential behavioral factors that were not identified during the segmentation analysis.

Adaptability to Mass Customization

The increasing complexity of today's markets and the proliferation of customer segments is making segmentation increasingly difficult. Additionally, the prospects of widespread mass customization will continue to challenge the relevance of segmentation. Strong proponents of mass customization assert that this development has rendered segmentation obsolete.

Segmentation Is Only One Piece of the Strategic Puzzle

A firm may have the most brilliantly conceived and executed segmentation analysis but still fail to secure any strategic benefit from its implementation. An appropriate overall strategy, along with support from the 5 Ps of marketing strategy, is still necessary. Additionally, top management buy in to the concept of legitimate marketing orientation is crucial to effective implementation.

PROCESS FOR APPLYING THE TECHNIQUE

While the process of customer segmentation may appear to be quite systematic, it does require significant amounts of creativity at each step. Lateral thinking should be encouraged throughout the development and implementation of a customer segmentation analysis. The following process is advocated only as a disciplined approach to what essentially is a combination of art and science.

Customer segmentation analysis can be viewed as an analytical framework involving the following three fundamental stages: (1) segmentation, (2) targeting, and (3) strategic positioning.

Step 1: Segmentation

The myriad of different ways to segment a market can appear perplexing. An overview of the purpose of segmentation is helpful to keep the analysis in perspective. The purpose of the segmentation analysis will be to identify customer groups that are both similar within segments as well as different between segments. To this end, it is helpful to select from the following list several different types of variables within each segmentation category. These lists are by no means exhaustive and are only suggested as a general guide and starting point.

Segmentation Criteria for Consumer Markets

Customer Characteristics—A user-based approach that asks, "Who purchases what?"	
Demographic Age Family size Marital status Sex	Socioeconomic Income Class Vocation Education Religion Ethnicity
Geographic Global, hemispheric, national, state, city, postal code Climate Rural vs. urban	Lifestyle/Personality Attitudes/opinions Interests Avocations Tastes and preferences

Product Related Approaches—A behavioral approach that asks, "Why do they purchase?"	
User types Regular Non-users First-time Potential	Price Sensitivity Low-cost orientation Higher-cost quality/differentiation focus
Consumption Patterns/Usage Frequency Low Medium Strong	Perceived benefits Performance Quality Image enhancement Service
Brand Loyalty Loyal/satisfied Experimenters Unsatisfied/Defectors Unaware	Application Purchase Occasion/Buying Situation Media Exposure

It is important to distinguish between consumer and industrial markets. Industrial markets are significantly different in many respects from consumer markets. Some of these differences include a much larger geographic area, larger but fewer individual purchases, complex organizational versus individual purchase decisions, and the importance of personal promotion. Because of these differences, industrial market segmentation requires different segmentation variables.

Segmentation Criteria for Industrial Markets

Customer Characteristics — A user-based approach that asks, "Who purchases what?"	
Industry type: e.g., SIC codes	Company size
Geographic	Technology employed
Industry position	

Product Related Approaches — A behavioral approach that asks, "Why do they purchase?"	
Consumption patterns/usage frequency	Relationship between seller/purchaser
End use application	Psychodemographics of purchaser
Perceived Benefits	Purchasing policies
Size of purchase	

In general, segmentation criteria for consumer markets focuses more on product-related behavioral approaches while industrial market segmentation is often premised more closely on the user-based customer characteristics approach. As a general rule, user-based analysis is more accessible, less costly to conduct, but also less insightful. Conversely, product-based analysis is often more difficult and costly to conduct but is also more insightful. Given the inconclusive nature of the relative merits of each approach, it is probably best to selectively use both approaches as they both offer unique insights.

After selecting the key criteria upon which to base the segmentation analysis, the search begins for identifying segments that are relatively homogeneous within segments and heterogeneous between segments. There are many tools and techniques available to identify segments that meet these criteria including statistical analysis and more qualitative methods:

- *Quantitative Methods.* Many statistical analysis tools are available, including regression analysis, factor analysis, cluster analysis, etc.
- *Qualitative Methods.* Consumer surveys, transaction analysis, lead user analysis, dialogue with current customers, fishbone diagrams, brainstorming, segment trees, etc.

The narrowing down process is exceptionally iterative as the multiplicity of possible combinations can easily explode given the number of criteria upon which to base segmentation. Any number of market research texts will give the analyst a more extensive treatment of these techniques.

Step 2: Targeting

Once a reduced number of promising segments has been identified, specific segments need to be selected for further analysis. The 4 R test poses four questions to determine if segmentation is viable (Weinstein, 1987):

a. *R1 — Rating the Market:* Is the segment amenable to both quantitative and qualitative valuation?
b. *R2 — Realistic in Size:* Is the segment large enough to support a viable segmentation strategy?

c. *R3—Reach:* Is the segment reachable by a feasible communications strategy?

d. *R4—Responsiveness:* Will the segment be responsive to the marketing communications strategy and product offering?

The 4 R test is only a rough first draft that will eliminate obvious segments that are not viable. However, several segments will pass the 4 R test. At this point, each segment will have to be passed through more detailed analyses, many of which are described in more detail in other chapters of this book. One type of analysis is *competitive analysis*, which includes tools and techniques such as competitor profiling, strategic groups analysis, and so on. Another type of analysis is *external analysis*, which includes tools and techniques to analyze the general market condition in which each segment is located, including STEEP analysis, SWOT analysis, industry structure analysis, and so on.

After each segment has been filtered through a competitive and external analysis viewpoint, a robust internal scrutiny is required. This is probably the most important phase of the process because it deals directly with the strategic purpose of segmentation—matching the firm's resources with the segments' perception of customer value. The process of finding the tightest fit between the needs, wants, and desires of each segment with the firm's business strength can be achieved through several techniques, such as *customer value analysis.* This analysis determines an extremely refined definition of exactly what customers in each segment value. Chapter 13 provides tools and techniques for conducting an in-depth analysis such as quality and price profiles, value maps, and so on. Another technique is *internal resource analysis*, which determines the resources requirements necessary to support the customer value in each segment. Here, functional capability and resource analysis and value chain analysis will be helpful tools to conduct this internal scrutiny.

Select those segments that offer the tightest fit between customer value analysis and the internal resource analysis. This selection must be set against a backdrop of the competitor and external analysis in order to determine that the firm will be able to offer a superior value position. Another approach is to organize the analysis by comparing each segment on a matrix comparing segment attractiveness against business strength.

The final stage in the targeting process involves passing each selected segment(s) through a rigorous financial test to determine the profitability of targeting each segment. The mere existence of a market opportunity or the ability of the firm to competitively meet that opportunity does not guarantee profitability. Profitability will ensue only if the lifetime value of each segment will exceed the costs of marketing to that segment. Profitability is also a direct reality test of whether the tightness of fit between the firm's resources and customer value really exists. The format of this approach is as follows:

Cost of Customer Acquisition

- Estimate the cost of making the first sale to the selected segments
- Estimate the projected profit margin that will be earned on the initial sale

Lifetime Value Calculation

Estimated Annual Marketing Cost × Estimated Annual Response Rate × Gross Margin
× Present Value Factor − Acquisition Cost = Lifetime Value

The so-called gray market, those individuals aged 50 and over, is becoming an increasingly attractive market segment. Do you recognize the oxymoron in this sentence? Referring to this market as one segment reflects years of stereotyping by marketers at their own peril. In fact, the gray market is composed of many distinct segments, each offering unique opportunities to those marketers able to spot them. Segmentation analysis provides a useful tool to achieve this. A 1999 British study segmenting the gray market in relation to a marketing strategy for a sports center complex reveals this usefulness.

The first tier of segmentation rejected the assumption that this market could be segmented by age. Given the longevity and health of seniors today, more appropriate segmentation variables are health and social independence. This initial segmentation resulted in four roughly defined segments:

Young Old	• Preretired, no health restrictions • Independent, restricted leisure time
New Old	• Newly retired, few health restrictions • Independent, substantial leisure time
Middle Old	• Some health restrictions • Requires limited assistance, substantial leisure time
Very Old	• Extensive health restrictions • Requires extensive assistance, substantial leisure time

The New Old was selected as representing the greatest segment at which to target a sports complex. As such, it was further explored introducing the variable of disposable income to reveal further insights:

Consumer A	• High level of disposable income; good health • High need for social support/market interaction from sports activity
Consumer B	• Low level of disposable income; good health • High need for social support/market interaction from sports activity
Consumer C	• High level of disposable income; good health • Low need for social interaction from sports activity
Consumer D	• Low level of disposable income; good health • Low need for social support/market interaction from sports activity

It can be seen at this point in the segmentation analysis that regarding the gray market as homogeneous would have blinded the firm to a very promising market positioning strategy. Specifically, Consumers A and B were honed in on as providing the most profitable market niches within the New Old segment. Both groups have similar profiles; namely, health, leisure time, independence, and a predisposition for a high level of social interaction. The only difference between the two groups is relative affluence that might offer a basis for differentiated value offerings. Consumer A would be a prime candidate for an exclusive private membership club. Alternately, Consumer B would be amenable to a user-pay, public facility similar to a YMCA.

Given that relationship marketing is becoming a critical competitive premise, the analysis was filtered through yet another round of segmentation based on the motivational aspects of the gray market:

	Motivation	
	Intrinsic	Extrinsic
Finance high/social support needs low	"Good Timers" Fun-centered Group activity Staff directed Strong customer care/relations High-quality facilities	"Health Seekers" Health promotion Health maintenance Physician referral Staff directed Strong customer care/relations Volunteer coaching High-quality facilities

(Continued on following page)

	Motivation	
	Intrinsic	Extrinsic
Finance high/social support needs low	"Affluents" Individual activities Autonomous Low staff involvement High quality facilities	"Affluent Health Seekers" Health promotion Physician referral Autonomous Low staff involvement High quality facilities
Finance low/social support needs high	"Companionables" Discounts Staff Directed Fun-centered Group activities Strong customer care/relations	"Directeds" Discounts Health promotion Health maintenance Physician referral Group activities Staff directed Strong customer care/relations Volunteer coaching
Finance low/social support needs low	"Independents" Discounts Autonomous Low staff involvement Fun-centered	"Indirected Directeds" Discounts Health promotion Health maintenance G.P. referral Autonomous Low staff involvement

This last round of segmentation revealed further insights into possible product marketing strategies. For example, activities that are fun, sociable, high quality, and healthy (e.g., line dancing) would appeal to several groups with different motivational influences such as Good Timers, Health Seekers, Companionables, and Directeds. Similarly, expensive independent activities (e.g., fly fishing) would appeal to Affluents and Health Seekers.

More important, within the context of a relationship marketing strategy, the motivational influences of each segment is of invaluable strategic importance. Given the importance of social interaction and staff involvement, a key success factor in these markets would be human resources and training. The staff of the sports center is the most primary component of the customer value offering.

A real life example was then analyzed to test the validity of the segmentation analysis. The Moor Hall Health Club in Britain has experienced much success with targeting the gray market. The health club market is notorious for incidences of clubs opening and closing overnight, yet Moor Hall has a waiting list for membership and a customer retention rate of 76 percent. Effective segmentation explains much of their success:

Segmentation Aspect	Moor Hall Value Offering
Many members belong to the Good Timers and Health Seekers motivational segments	Many group sports activities Members involved planning both sports and social activities
Many members belong to Affluents and Affluent Health Seeker motivational segments	Many individual activities also available
Staff interaction	Staff selected and trained heavily in customer service, psychological needs of various segments First-name basis Warm, friendly, flexible staff

(Continued on following page)

Segmentation Aspect	Moor Hall Value Offering
Physician referral	Staff trained in therapeutic sports therapy for health conditions such as osteoporosis
Quality facilities	High-quality equipment Located in very attractive forested, rustic setting

Despite the fact that this segmentation was an emergent strategy for Moor Hall, the benefits of their approach are clearly evident. Consider their competition, struggling blindly in the absence of segmentation strategy. When interviewed if they explicitly targeted the gray market, most immediately dismissed the notion as folly. Instead, they responded that they were actively trying to target the status quo youth market and felt that too many old members would tarnish their image with their target segment. Given that the local population contains a gold mine of 38 percent seniors, small wonder that Moor Hall has a long waiting list.

SOURCE: Reprinted from *Long Range Planning*, Vol. 32, No. 2, M. Carrigan, "'Old Spice'—Developing Successful Relationships with the Grey Market," pages 253–262, Copyright 1999, with permission of Elsevir Science.

Step 3: Strategic Positioning

This step involves how to strategically position the product or service with regard to competitive offerings. This analysis will offer many insights into how best to manage the 4 Ps of the marketing mix. Chapter 13 offers several techniques to analyze strategic positioning including conjoint analysis, competitor maps, and performance matrices.

The 4 Ps are essentially the tactical manifestation of the strategic positioning:

1. Product: embedded customer value
2. Price: high, low, parity
3. Promotion: advertising, personal sales
4. Place: distribution channel management

Often, a fifth P, "people," is added especially if service is an important component of the customer value.

The financial parameters surrounding each of these 4 Ps should be consistent with those used to estimate lifetime value.

FAROUT SUMMARY

	1	2	3	4	5
F	■	■	■		
A	■	■			
R	■	■			
O	■	■	■		
U	■	■	■	■	■
T	■				

Perhaps the strongest argument supporting the logic of customer value is the fact that customer retention is much more profitable than continually targeting new customers. Traditional marketing effort is often heavily biased toward acquiring new customers through discount pricing and other promotional efforts designed to woo customers from rivals. Not only are these customers expensive to attract, they are inherently predisposed to disloyalty. In addition, such programs often attract customers whose definition of value is not closely aligned to what the resources of the firm are able to provide. As such, many of these new customers will be unprofitable in the long term. Eventually, trying to satisfy these new customers involves trade-offs that will dilute the customer value that attracted the firm's original customer base. Traditional marketing that ignores the CVA concept poses two threats to the firm's profitability. New customers it attracts are rarely profitable, and serving these new customers often alienates the firm's existing base of profitable customers. This may lead to the all-too-common occurrence of profitless growth.

Contrast the drawbacks of this approach to the enhanced profitability associated with a customer value focus on marketing toward existing customers. Figure 13-1 provides the results of a 1990 study showing the remarkable impact of customer retention on profitability.

The impact of customer loyalty on profitability is multifaceted, having a positive effect on the price, cost, and sales dimensions of profitability. Specifically, several impacts have been identified empirically (Reichheld & Sasser, 1990; Birch, 1990; Naumann, 1995):

1. Cost Impacts of Customer Retention. Customer acquisition incurs significant marketing costs (advertising, promotion, etc.). Loyal customers incur lower direct operating costs (less overhead and variable costs associated with a more efficient customer service function), and also incur lower direct costs associated with

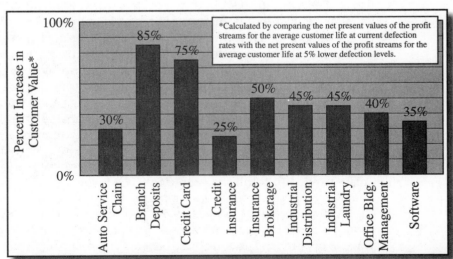

Figure 13-1
Reducing Defections 5 Percent Boosts Profits by 25 to 85 Percent

Source: Reprinted by permission of *Harvard Business Review, (Reducing Defections 5%, Boost Profits 25% to 85%).* From "Zero Defections: Quality Comes to Services," by F. F. Reichheld and W. E. Sasser Jr., Sept./Oct. 1990. Copyright 1990 by the President and Fellows of Harvard College; all rights reserved.

warranties, product returns, and replacement. Loyal customers incur lower indirect costs associated with lost sales and also offset advertising costs through positive word of mouth advertising.

2. Price Impacts of Customer Retention.   Loyal customers will pay more for superior value that they feel they can rely on by virtue of their experience with the firm.

3. Sales Impacts of Customer Retention.   Loyal customers tend to purchase higher volumes over time as their confidence in the firm grows. Loyal customers also increase sales through word-of-mouth advertising, often to individuals that share similar profiles thus growing the firm's base of profitable customer segmentation.

The combinations of these cost, price, and sales impacts of customer loyalty on profitability lend strong support for the concept of CVA. Rather than view embedded product quality and service as costs, CVA encourages managers to more properly regard them as investments that will generate handsome returns.

The case for customer value is solid. First, it is used to guide customer segmentation to ensure that the firm's resources are properly aligned with those customers most attracted to the value offering those resources can support. Second, CVA is used to build customer loyalty in order to maximize customer retention and to pursue profitable growth. In both applications, CVA ensures optimal profitability and competitive position.

The more difficult issue remains regarding how to specifically define customer value so that it may be managed strategically. This dimension of CVA distinguishes it from the familiar customer satisfaction axiom of TQM. Rather than being an exercise in academic semantics, the differences between customer value and customer satisfaction are real and pose significant implications for the firm's bottom line. Simply put, customer satisfaction entails doing things well from an internal process perspective. Customer value is of a higher order of magnitude in that it entails doing the *right* things well. In the parlance of CVA, *right* is defined as providing value as defined by the customer in terms of both quality and cost attributes. This difference explains the often high rate of customer defection experienced by firms, despite high levels of customer satisfaction. Where customer satisfaction often singularly pursues quality as a limitless source of improvement from the customer's current experience with the firm's products and services, customer value pursues quality and cost attributes relative to rival offerings and firm profitability. Perhaps Reichheld (1996) stipulates this difference most elegantly when he states: "Companies can avoid the satisfaction trap if they remember that what matters is not how satisfied you keep your customers but how many satisfied and profitable customers you keep." From this perspective, CVA can be seen as the bridging mechanism needed to fulfill the promise of TQM elevating it from a tactical tool to an integral component of corporate strategy.

Customer value is defined as the total benefits of ownership of the product or service less the total costs of ownership. There are two different but complimentary ways to operationally define these benefits and costs—attribute cost models and the goal/motivation models.

Attribute/Cost Models of Customer Value

One of the most useful formal attribute models of customer value has been developed by Naumann (1995). As Figure 13-2 indicates, this model views customer value as a combination of expected benefits and expected costs.

Expected Benefits

Expected benefits are composed of product and service attributes, which can be further broken down into three categories of attributes that customers use to define benefits:

• Presale attributes include all of the tangible product and search attributes that the customer can evaluate before the purchase. For example, before buying a personal computer, the customer may evaluate its features and capacity and may operate it for several minutes in order to weigh the benefits of ownership against the costs of ownership.

• Postsale attributes include the often intangible product and service attributes that can only be evaluated postsale after using the product or service for some time. For example, the taste and texture of a new brand of chocolate bar cannot be fully determined until after the first few bites. Most services are even more heavily reliant on experienced-based usage attributes. A case in point is the value of a hairstylist that cannot be surmised until after the service has been experienced. For

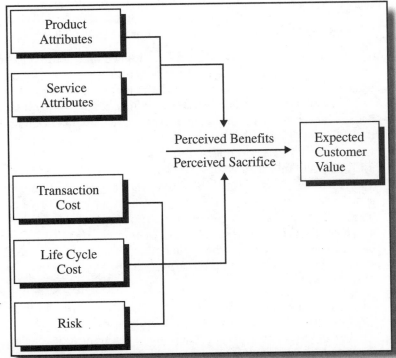

Figure 13-2
Attribute-Cost
Model of Customer
Value

Source: Creating Customer
Value: The Path to
Competitive Advantage, by
E. Naumann, 1995,
Cincinnati, OH:
Thompson Executive
Press.

markets premised on postsale attributes, it is paramount that firms attend to ensuring that they provide superior product and service experiences.

• Extended postsale attributes include those products and services for which an evaluation of value can only be determined after extended usage. For example, the value of brokerage services cannot be determined until after the returns over an extended period have been realized. Similarly, the value of a chiropractor cannot be evaluated until a few days after the visit to determine the absence of back pain.

Markets premised on presale attributes will generally experience a high degree of price competition as many tangible attributes are easily imitated, eroding any source of competitive advantage through attribute differentiation. Conversely, markets based on postsale and extended postsale experience attributes offer a high chance of competitive advantage to those firms who successfully deliver superior experiences.

Expected Costs

Included in the Figure 13-2 schematic depicting customer value is the concept of expected costs which comprise three different types of cost:

• *Transaction costs* are the up-front cash costs or "sticker price" for the product or service
• *Life cycle costs* are the additional costs incurred by the customer over the total span of ownership of the product or service such as delivery, installation, learning curves associated with initial usage, maintenance, repair, disposal, etc.
• *Risk* is the costs incurred by the customer when actual costs are higher than expected costs. Risk is usually higher when the total span of ownership is long.

Transaction costs have the most influence on the purchase decision in commodity markets in which products have short life spans, For products and services with longer life spans, life cycle costs and risk are more important.

Since TQM methods adequately address issues of product attribute quality and because services are becoming an increasingly valuable point of both product differentiation and the larger economy, it is important to attend equally to the quality of services. One of the premiere models of service quality is the Service Quality (SERVQUAL) model developed by Parasuraman et al. (1985) as shown in Figure 13-3.

The developers of the SERVQUAL model propose that perceived service quality is dependent on the size and positive or negative direction of GAP 5 in Figure 13-3. In turn, GAP 5 can be managed by decomposition into GAPS 1–4. Due to the nature of services, customer purchase behavior is most heavily influenced by experience-based attributes on both a postsale and extended postsale basis. Ten determinants of service quality can then be used by management to close the various gaps in the SERVQUAL model:

1. *Reliability*: consistency of performance and dependability.
2. *Responsiveness*: employees' availability to provide service.
3. *Competence*: employees' possession of the required skills and knowledge to capably perform the service.

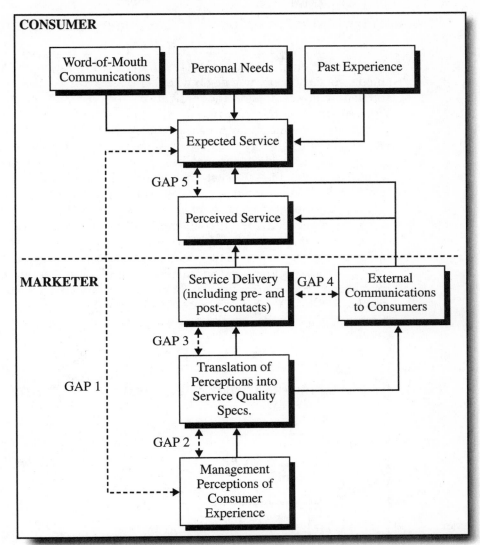

Figure 13-3
Service Quality
Model

Source: Reprinted with permission from the *Journal of Marketing*, published by the American Marketing Association, A. Parasuraman, V. A. Zeithaml & L. L. Berry, Fall 1985, 49(4), pp. 41–50.

4. *Access*: approachability and ease of customer contact with employees.
5. *Courtesy*: attitudes such as politeness, respect, consideration, and friendliness of contact personnel.
6. *Communication*: two-way, symmetric dialogue that keeps customers informed in a language they can understand and employees listening to the customers.
7. *Credibility*: traits and attitudes such as trustworthiness, believability, and honesty.
8. *Security*: customers' freedom from danger, risk, or doubt.
9. *Understanding/Knowing the Customer*: the range and nature by which employees make the effort to understand customers' needs.
10. *Tangibles*: physical evidence of the service.

Goal/Motivation Models of Customer Value

The most definitive goal/motivation model to date is the customer value hierarchy model developed by Woodruff (1997), depicted in Figure 13-4. Goal/motivation models of customer value begin where attribute/cost models end. This higher level of abstraction centers on the motivations for customer purchases as opposed to attribute models that analyze only the manifestation of these motivations. In addition, it is a dynamic model because it incorporates the fact that as the customer's use situation changes, every other aspect of the model changes as well. Viewed from this perspective, customer value can be seen as constantly changing. This model also explains why achieving customer satisfaction around product attributes is not enough. Customers that are satisfied around product attributes will defect if their goals and motivations are more closely met by rival offerings. Similarly, if a customer's unmet needs are suddenly met by a competitive product or service, previous standards of customer value become meaningless. For these reasons, customer intimacy is an essential part of the process of customer value analysis.

The most important strategic implications of CVA are the interrelationships among price, product quality, service quality, and customer value. To encapsulate the strategic implications of CVA in one phrase: Customer value can be achieved only when the firm meets or exceeds the customer's expectations regarding product quality, service

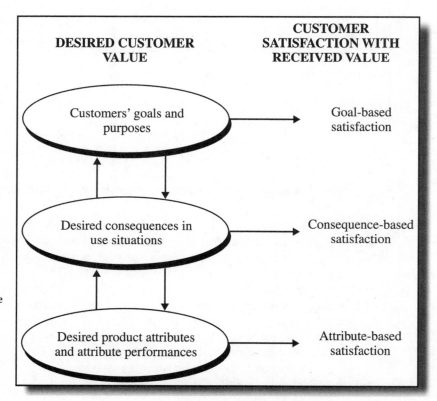

Figure 13-4
Customer Value Hierarchy Model

Source: Journal of the Academy of Marketing Science, by R. B. Woodruff. Copyright 1997 by Sage Pubns Inc. (J). Reproduced with permission of Sage Pubns Inc. (J) in the format Textbook via Copyright Clearance Center.

quality, and price. This is a rigorous test in that if any one of these conditions is absent, the firm will fail to deliver customer value. This implies that, depending on the situation, the firm will realize limits to the pursuit of product and service quality if its customers do not value additional quality. Alternately, the concept of CVA will present significant stretch goals in order to win over and retain targeted customers.

Naumann (1995) identifies five very useful strategic implications that should guide the implementation of CVA:

1. Customer value (product quality, service quality, and price) is defined by the customer.
2. Customer value is defined relative to rival offerings.
3. Customer value will change over time.
4. Customer value is created throughout the entire value chain.
5. Customer value is a cooperative effort involving everyone in the firm.

These five guidelines are equally rigorous because each one is only a necessary condition. All five must be pursued simultaneously to effectively deliver customer value.

STRENGTHS AND ADVANTAGES

Customer value analysis is an extremely useful strategic framework for achieving competitive advantage. The close link to the customer and competitors at all stages of the analysis keeps the strategic recommendations very realistic. It is one of the few tools that can provide a robust quantifiable approach to customer and competitive analysis as opposed to qualitative platitudes offered by many other models. CVA is also very comprehensive, making it possible to leverage this tool with many other management techniques, such as TQM, supply chain management, competitor analysis, and resource analysis.

Another strength of this model is its improvement upon the TQM approach by including the concepts of cost and customer determined value—two fundamental concepts previously missing from quality-oriented approaches. The most valuable contribution of CVA, however, is its forward-looking orientation. In today's turbulent competitive environments, premising a strategic management system on a leading indicator of change, the customer, is sound strategy.

WEAKNESSES AND LIMITATIONS

The main weakness of CVA is its resource and time intensity. Conducting a customer value analysis requires the gathering of much complex data from a wide array of *individual* sources. Similarly, designing the appropriate research techniques and analyzing the data requires significant skill levels and expertise. The most resource-intensive aspect of CVA, however, comes with the continuous or frequent monitoring of customer value after the initial segmentation has been achieved. This high cost is substantially mitigated when compared to the associated benefits that CVA has been well documented in delivering.

Another potential weakness of CVA is the rigorous necessary and sufficient conditions qualifying its successful implementation. As noted above, formulating a superior value proposition requires superior product quality, service quality, and price. Similarly, implementing CVA requires constant attention to the five guidelines discussed previously. Without significant organizational change toward a market orientation, CVA will be a waste of time and effort and contain few ancillary benefits.

Customer value analysis is also highly dependent on the GIGO principle. Almost all of the input data come from outside sources. This reality places tremendous importance on first devising the appropriate research methodology and, second, interpreting it correctly. For example, if the proper scaling techniques are not used in plotting customer value maps, the whole exercise becomes arbitrary with little real strategic significance. Without proper care and expertise, the proven principles of CVA can be easily sabotaged by unwitting procedural errors.

PROCESS FOR APPLYING THE TECHNIQUE

The process for conducting customer value analysis consists of three major stages: (1) customer intimacy through conversation; (2) formal customer value analysis; and (3) strategic management of customer value.

Stage 1: Customer Intimacy

The traditional modes of customer conversation consist of occasions when the customer instigates contact with the firm to voice positive and negative feedback. The conduits for this communication usually consist of the firm's customer service department or via the front line sales staff. The problem with relying exclusively on this form of feedback is that defecting customers rarely voice their intentions—they just leave. Further, loyal customers rarely voluntarily discuss their goals and motivation; typically, their conversations are limited to product or service attributes.

Although much of this traditional customer conversation is of extreme value to the firm and should be encouraged, it pales in comparison to the insights generated from the more useful and more proactive methods, such as the following:

• *Customer Surveys.* This tool involves mail or telephone interviews of current or potential customers to gauge the firm's effectiveness in delivering value at key product and service quality attributes. It is important to reduce the number of attributes to a minimum in order to increase the response.

• *Focus Panel Groups.* This tool presents a prototype of a planned product or service to a group of target customers and asks for their feedback. Their verbal responses are supplemented by body language feedback observed by hidden evaluators through one-way mirrors or panels. The important procedural point to attend to is the potential for the dominant member of the panel to create a group-think phenomenon.

- *Conjoint Analysis.* This tool presents focus groups with several different options, each incorporating a different set of quality attributes. By analyzing their choices, the attributes that create the most customer value can be determined.

- *Price Sensitivity Analysis.* This tool is similar to conjoint analysis, except that quality attributes and features are compared to price and vice versa. Price elasticity of sample customers is determined by asking them to explicitly state their price trade-off threshold for various quality attributes. Conversely, they are also asked to state their quality attribute or feature trade-off threshold for various price points. Essentially, this tool quantifies the limits of profitably pursuing higher quality.

- *Motivation Analysis.* Best performed through one-on-one interviews, motivation analysis seeks to uncover the underlying psychological reasons driving customer purchase criteria. Essentially, motivation analysis is the natural precursor to product and service attribute analysis.

- *Unmet Needs Analysis.* Also best performed through in-depth personal interviews, unmet needs analysis seeks to define motivations, needs, or attributes not currently satisfied by existing offerings. Often, customers aren't even aware of unmet needs and are delighted when a firm assists in articulating them. As such, providing unmet needs by becoming a solutions provider is often a rich source of customer loyalty.

- *Lead User Interviews.* Lead users are customers who are "ahead of the curve" in terms of product or service application. They are often excellent partners in new product development and most receptive to a mutual search for solutions.

- *Defection Analysis.* Often there is more to be learned in failure than in success. Borrowing from this maxim, defection analysis attempts to glean reasons from defecting customers regarding exactly why they have left the firm. Isolating the root causes of alienated customers is difficult, time-consuming, and often requires asking, Why? an average of five times before this reductionist iteration yields results (Reichheld, 1996).

The many, varied sources of customer information can make it difficult for a firm to establish priorities or an organizing framework from which to conduct the analysis. To this end, Parasuraman (1997) has developed a very useful framework for deciding what information to collect from whom:

- Attribute information from first-time customers and lost customers is especially relevant for strategies designed to attract new customers.
- Consequence information from short-term customers and lost customers is especially relevant for strategies designed to strengthen an existing base of customers.
- Motivational information from long-term customers and lost customers is especially relevant for strategies designed to strengthen customer intimacy.

- Changing perceptions of customer value from cohorts (i.e., customers moving into an increasingly deeper level of customer intimacy with the firm such as first-time users moving to short-tem customers to long-term customers) is especially relevant for developing future competitive strategies.

Stage 2: Formal Customer Value Analysis

Several tools and techniques have been developed through which to conduct customer value analysis. Many of the tools will incorporate much of the information gathered in stage 1. Eight of the more common techniques are discussed here.

Market Perceived Quality Profile

This tool examines the key purchase criteria of customers for the product or service under analysis. Customers of both the firm and rivals are asked to rank their purchase criteria on a weighted basis out of a possible 100 points. They are then asked to rank the performance of the firm and its rivals in delivering on each key purchase criteria on a 10-point scale. Then each firm's score on each purchase criteria is multiplied by the weight assigned to each criterion. Adding up each firm's total score will yield the market perceived quality profile. Instead of using this constant sum approach, many firms use conjoint or regression analysis to determine performance rankings because the results are more amenable to further statistical analysis. Similarly, the use of ratio scales is recommended instead of interval scales to reduce arbitrary mapping (Higgins, 1998).

Figure 13-5a depicts such a profile for Burgers R Us within the fast-food hamburger market. The market perceived profile provides several valuable insights into how successfully they are fulfilling customer value. Overall, Burgers R Us outranks its competition by a margin of 9.25 percent. Additionally, this tool breaks down this overall performance figure into relative strengths and weaknesses.

Market Perceived Price Profile

Relative price profiles are very similar to market perceived quality profiles except that customer perception of total cost of ownership is used instead of perceived quality parameters. The construction of relative price profiles shares the same methodology as market perceived quality profiles. Figure 13-5b depicts a relative price profile for luxury cars.

Customer Value Map

A customer value map combines both of the market perceived profiles discussed above into a four-cell matrix. Market perceived quality is plotted on the horizontal axis and market perceived price is plotted on the vertical axis as shown in Figure 13-5c. For this market, a 45-degree diagonal is then superimposed over the grid depicting a fair value line. Along this line, quality is balanced against price in a 1 : 1 ratio. However, for other markets, a different angle might be chosen,

	Market Perceived Quality Profile for Hamburger Fast Food				
		Performance Scores			
Quality Attributes 1	**Weight** 2	**Burgers R Us** 3	**Avg. comp.** 4	**Ratio** 5 = 3/4	**Weight times ratio** 6 = 2 × 5
Taste	20	9.5	7.4	1.28	25.6
TV ads	20	7.1	8.5	0.835	16.7
Appeal to kids	10	8.8	6.5	1.35	13.5
Convenient location	20	7.5	7	1.07	21.4
Cleanliness	15	7.6	8.2	0.93	13.9
Promotional (movie tie-ins, prizes, toys, etc.)	15	8.2	6.8	1.21	18.15
	100				109.25
Customer satisfaction		8.1	7.4		
	Market-perceived quality ratio				

Figure 13-5a
Tools of Customer Value Analysis

Source: Adapted from *Managing Customer Value,* by B. T. Gale, 1994, New York: Free Press.

Implications:

- Burgers R Us quality ranks better overall by a margin of 1.09 : 1
- Relative strength in taste, appeal to kids, location, and in-store promotions
- Relative weakness in TV ads and cleanliness

reflecting a weighting ratio of quality versus price other than 50 percent as the case may be.

At any rate, the firms with positions below and to the right of this fair value line will be in the best position to increase market share at their current price level. Firms with positions above and to the left of the fair value line will probably lose market share. Further, these firms will probably have to lower price in order to grow market share. These conclusions are driven by the key strategic implications of the customer value map. For a premium quality product to earn a price premium, it is crucial that customers perceive the quality premium to be worth more than the price premium. Only then will premium quality translate into superior customer value and strong competitive position.

Market Perceived Price Profile for Luxury Cars

Price Satisfaction Attributes 1	Importance Weights 2	Satisfaction Scores		Ratio 5 = 3/4
		Acura 3	Others 4	
Purchase price	60	9	7	1.29
Trade-in allowance	20	6	6	1.00
Resale price	10	9	8	1.13
Finance rates	10	7	7	1.00
	100			
Price satisfaction score		8.2	6.9	
Price competitiveness score				1.18
Relative price score				0.85

Figure 13-5b

Figure 13-5c

Note: Data for relative performance based on *Consumer Reports* ratings, April 1993, p. 228.

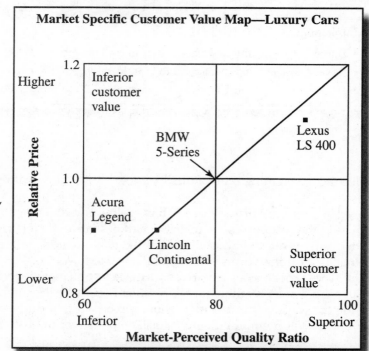

Market Specific Customer Value Map—Luxury Cars

Customer value maps can also be used to analyze the customer value that each strategic business unit, division, or product is delivering relative to rival offerings. Figure 13-5d depicts such an application.

Both applications of customer value analysis can fulfill two functions. One, they provide a static snapshot of the firm's competitive position in terms of relative customer value. Two, knowledge of the slope of the fair value line can determine the improvements in price and quality that the firm needs to pursue in order to capture more customer value.

Win/Loss Analysis

This simple yet powerful technique analyzes the core reasons for recent gains or losses in market share. Specifically, win/loss analysis focuses on the quality and price attributes that were responsible for recent market share gains and losses. Win/loss analysis is where an organization systematically studies important aspects of its operations with respect to customer experiences and perceptions. Analysts seek to identify customer segments at risk and areas requiring improvement in order to develop and implement cost-effective corrective actions to prevent further erosion of its market share. This requires the organization to have a keen understanding of the primary drivers and the justification for customers' decisions. This understanding helps organizations learn from their market wins and losses. Based upon this actionable information, the organization can inform its sales and marketing personnel about the most effective positioning

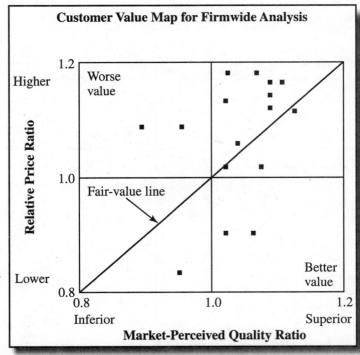

Figure 13-5d
Source: Reprinted with the permission of The Free Press, a Division of Simon & Schuster, Inc., from *Managing Customer Value: Creating Quality and Services That Customers Can See* by Bradley T. Gale. Copyright © 1994 by Bradley T. Gale.

toward competitors and monitor the impact of its market positioning strategies over time.

Head-to-Head Area Chart of Customer Value

This customer value tool is especially applicable to markets in which there are only two main competitors because in these instances it will yield more useful analysis than a customer value map. Figure 13-5e depicts a head-to-head area chart of customer value comparing Mercedes and Lexus automobiles. In this tool, the relative competitive parameters revolve around the firm's primary competitor rather than a composite of every firm in the market. Hence, on the horizontal axis, several key quality attributes are listed and the thickness of the related bar reflects that attribute's relative importance in defining total quality. The length of the each horizontal bar is determined by the ratio of Lexus's ranking out of 10 divided by the same ranking for Mercedes. For Lexus, trouble-free operation was ranked to be the quality attribute in which Lexus most exceeds Mercedes. Conceivably, if Mercedes were to compile a similar chart, safety, brand image, and prestige would rank relatively higher than Lexus. In terms of price competitiveness, Lexus achieves parity with Mercedes. The important conclusion to be drawn from head-to-head charts is

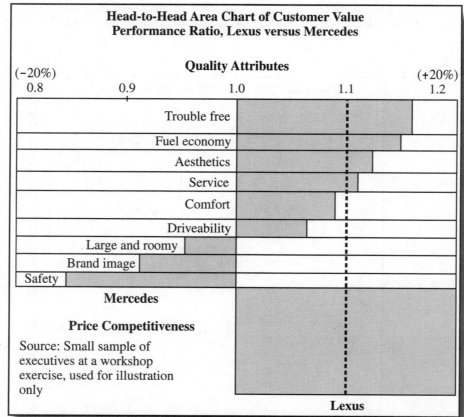

Figure 13-5e

Source: Reprinted with the permission of The Free Press, a Division of Simon & Schuster, Inc., from *Managing Customer Value: Creating Quality and Services That Customers Can See* by Bradley T. Gale. Copyright © 1994 by Bradley T. Gale.

a clear delineation of where and how well the firm is competing with its main rival around key quality and price attributes. In other words, this tool provides an unambiguous identification of the firm's competitive advantage and competitive weaknesses calibrated on its main rival.

Key Events Time Line

A key events time line outlines significant events in a product or service market. The qualifying criteria for what constitutes a key event are twofold: how strategies of the firm and its rivals impact perceptions of customer value, and how dynamic perceptions of customer value impact both the type and weighting of attributes over time.

Figure 13-5f depicts a key events time line in the luxury automobile market.

Key Events Time Line in the Luxury Auto Market

- October 20, 1993 — *Wall Street Journal* report entitled "Mercedes Benz Tries to Compete on Value," including the following telling commentary ". . . this year's model, the C-Class are symbols of a new phase for Mercedes-Benz as it tries to shed its old and arrogant ways."
- September 29, 1993 — Mercedes reaffirms its commitment to value pricing by running another two-page ad in the *Wall Street Journal* on the theme "It will send the competition running back to our drawing board. . . . The new E-Class."
- September 24, 1993 — Mercedes signals its commitment to value pricing by running two-page ads in the *Wall Street Journal* on the theme " To all those that think a sensible Mercedes-Benz is an oxymoron. Introducing the new E-Class."
- September 23, 1993 — Mercedes announces price cuts by as much as 14.8% in an attempt to reposition closer to Lexus and Acura around customer value.
- Summer 1992 — German media critics assail Mercedes for misreading the market by building a car that was too big, too heavy.
- 1991–1992 — Customer migration to Japanese offerings combined with recessions in most of Europe and the United States leads to declining sales, losses, and layoffs at Mercedes.
- 1991 — Mercedes introduces the S Class, choosing to compete even more intensely around its traditional competitive advantage in superior quality. The S Class is 17 feet long, weighs 5,000 pounds, costs $60,000–$135,000.
- 1989 to 1991 — BMW attempts to improve around its trouble-free performance and driveability attributes. Cadillac retools its design and new product introduction process.
- 1988 — Toyota enters the "top-quality" segment of the luxury car market with the Lexus but competes in the high quality/average price quadrant of the customer value map.
- 1986 — Honda creates a new luxury division, Acura, transferring its competitive advantage around trouble-free operation to the luxury car market, which quickly captures the "economy" segment of that market.
- Pre-1986 — Luxury car market dominated by German and American firms (e.g., Mercedes, BMW, Cadillac, Lincoln).
- Post-1980 — In the economy and intermediate segments, Japanese automakers consistently outperform European and American rivals on the key attribute of trouble-free operation.

Figure 13-5f

Source: Adapted from *Managing Customer Value*, by B. T. Gale, 1994, New York: Free Press.

What/Who Matrix

The what/who matrix is a tactical implementation tool designed to track progress toward meeting the firm's customer value improvement objectives. It is a tool that assigns *who* (processes and functional areas) in the firm will be responsible for delivering on *what* key product attributes embedded into the firm's value offering. When building a what/who matrix it is important to distinguish between perceived and actual customer value. For example, if the firm's relative competitive position is impaired because of customer value that is perceived to be inferior, then clearly the responsibility rests with the marketing and sales functions. If in fact the inferiority is actual, then it is important to ferret out its root causes. For example, if goods are damaged in transit, then it is apparent to assign responsibility to distribution rather than manufacturing or product design. Figure 13-5g shows a typical what/who matrix. Highlighted categories indicate those functions and processes with the most direct influence on the relevant key attribute.

Root Cause Analysis: Price and Value Trees

This tool is commonly used after the customer value map has been developed. Price and value trees can then be used to determine which actions will lead to improvement in price and quality performance in order for the firm to improve on its customer value. By disaggregating the firm's processes into its most primary components, actionable opportunities can be identified that isolate areas of improvement that will have the most impact on customer value. Figure 13-5h provides an example of both a price and value tree that identify areas with the most leverage by assigning percentage impacts for each process. The analysis is then further refined into the constituent components of each process that provides customer value.

Figure 13-5g

Source: Reprinted with the permission of The Free Press, a Division of Simon & Schuster, Inc., from *Managing Customer Value: Creating Quality and Services That Customers Can See* by Bradley T. Gale. Copyright © 1994 by Bradley T. Gale.

			What/Who Matrix			
Quality Attributes	**Designing**	**Assuring Conformance**	**Manufacturing**	**Selling and Servicing**	**Distributing**	**Manufacturing**
Trouble free	X	X	☐X☐	X	X	
Comfort	☐X☐	X				
Safety	☐X☐	X	X	X		
Drivability	☐X☐	X				
Service				☐X☐	X	
Aesthetics	X					☐X☐
Brand image	X			X		☐X☐

Root Cause Analysis

Quality Trees

	Business Process	Customer Need	Internal Metric
Overall Quality	Product (30%)	Reliability (40%)	% Repair call
		Easy to use (20%)	% Calls for help
		Features/functions (40%)	Function performance test
	Sales (30%)	Knowledge (30%)	Supervisor observations
		Response (25%)	% Proposal made on time
		Follow-up (10%)	% Follow-up made
	Installation (10%)	Delivery interval (30%)	Average order interval
		Does not break (25%)	% Repair reports
		Installed when promised (10%)	% Installed on due date
	Repair (15%)	No repeat trouble (30%)	% Repeat reports
		Fixed fast (25%)	Average speed of repair
		Kept informed (10%)	% Customers informed
	Billing (15%)	Accuracy, no suprise (45%)	% Billing inquiries
		Resolve on first call (35%)	% Resolved first call
		Easy to understand (10%)	% Billing inquiries

Figure 13-5h

Source: Copyright © 1993, by The Regents of the University of California. Reprinted from the *California Management Review,* Vol. 35, No. 3. By permission of The Regents.

Stage 3: Strategic Management of Customer Value

Armed with the knowledge from stage 1 and stage 2, the firm will be in a good position to start implementing CVA. After having completed the customer value analysis, the firm will know which product and service attributes provide superior customer value. The first step is to protect those activities, processes, and resources that provide this value and seek to strengthen them in the future. For attributes around which the firm is slipping, the relevant levers will have been identified for strategic action. Improving on these levers should produce measurable results because

(a) CVA has identified them as closely linked to superior value creation and (b) CVA has identified them as having a disproportionate impact on customer value relative to other levers identified in (a). Finally, processes that are not linked to customer value in any way may be considered for streamlining. In the final analysis for optimal profitability, the firm should be operating at the point of maximum difference between the value price and the cost of product and service quality.

Figure 13-6 depicts a generalized process map for conducting CVA. The essence of CVA is to match customer value with the firm's resources by providing a superior combination of product quality, service quality and price. This requires two sets of parallel disaggregations. First, the customer's value must be delineated into product

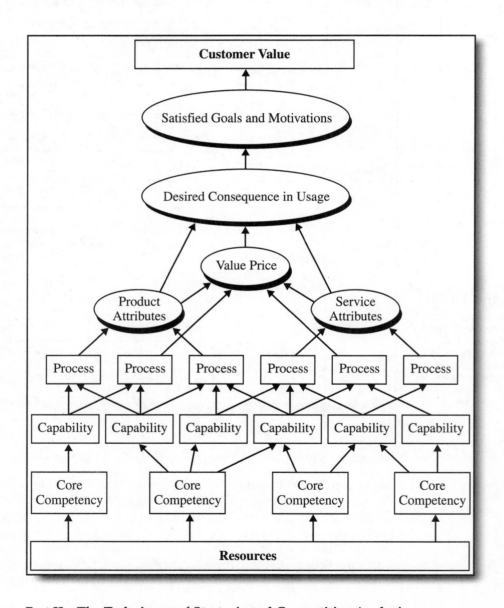

Figure 13-6
Strategic
Management of
Customer Value

Part II   The Techniques of Strategic and Competitive Analysis

As an increasing number of firms adopt CVA, the notion of exceeding rather than just meeting customer expectations is becoming an important competitive parameter. This strategy is yielding handsome dividends for the Old San Francisco chain of four restaurants based out of San Antonio, Texas. In the notoriously competitive restaurant industry, volatility is a common market condition. A case in point is the recent study conducted jointly by Cornell University and Michigan State University that found that 60 percent of restaurants go bankrupt inside of five years, while 25 percent of all start-ups fail in under one year of operation. It is difficult to envision an industry where customer value is more decisive in culling the winners from the losers.

The Old San Francisco chain is definitely one of the winners with a record of 28 years of profitable operation. The owner of the firm attributed most of this success to an unswerving commitment to exceeding the expectations of his diners. Here are a few of the creative ways they achieve this goal:

THEME

Way back in 1968, Old San Francisco was one of the first restaurants to offer casual dining themes—a market segment that is now very popular. The 1890s theme includes period antiques, dueling pianos, 35-foot ceilings, and the famous "red girl on a swing"—the hostess rides a red velvet swing every half hour. This unique theme has allowed Old San Francisco to successfully compete with steakhouses and other theme restaurants such as Planet Hollywood.

RESTAURANT MANAGERS

Contrary to the consistency norm of most restaurant chains, managers are given free reign to offer unique and creative menus. For example, the San Antonio locations offer emu and ostrich, the Austin and Houston locations offer desserts on hand-painted plates, while the Dallas location offers bleu-cheese burgers. These different menus are the result of head office encouragement of local managers to be innovative in their search to exceed their diners' expectations. Bucking the industry trend, Old San Francisco wants to ensure that their "products and services are consistently excellent, not necessarily consistently the same." They choose not to compete with the standard roadhouse fare that disappoints so many diners. Besides, Old San Francisco couldn't compete on price with the standard roadhouses anyway. In addition to their creative license, managers are encouraged to spend their time on only the "high pay-off" activities. This allows for more time to spend dreaming up ways to profitably exceed customer expectations.

EMPLOYEES

Valets are instructed to immediately retrieve any items that customers leave in their car. For sensitive personal items such as wallets and purses, the car is brought to the customer to placate fears of the item having been touched.

FOOD

Old San Franciso uses only 100 percent certified Angus beef for their steaks. When the chain decided to add duck to the menu, it took years to find a suitable supplier. The qualifying criterion for new menu items is premised on adding only unique items unavailable elsewhere.

VALUE

The price point for most of the meals at the restaurant locations is about $30. Old San Francisco strives to provide a dining experience equivalent to a $100-a-meal establishment.

THE DINING EXPERIENCE

The mission of Old San Francisco is to provide "the most memorable dining experience in the world." Guests who have to wait during busy periods are offered free drinks, appetizers, party hats, and blowers. This unexpected gesture of attention often delights guests, who immediately dispense any negative feelings about waiting.

(Continued on following page)

OUTSMARTING INSTEAD OF COPYING THE COMPETITION

Hosting wine-tasting nights has become a popular traffic generator for restaurants in many U.S. cities—so popular, that similar events were being hosted by five restaurants in the same city on the same night. In response, Old San Francisco partnered with a local wine store that sent out invitations to each customer in its extensive database. The result was a draw of 100 wine aficionados to the restaurant.

As the experience of the Old San Francisco restaurant chain exemplifies, customer value is not the exclusive purview of large corporations. Nor is customer value usually attributable to one particular activity. Rather, it is the combination of many small activities, the whole of which is larger than its parts. At Old San Francisco, a focus on constantly exceeding customer expectations has fostered the core of their client base: repeat customers based on exceptional previous dining experiences and new customers attracted by positive word-of-mouth advertising. It has also been the core of their success for almost 30 years—an uncommon feat in one of the world's most competitive industries.

Source: Adapted from "The 'WOW' Effect: How One Restaurateur Continues to Delight Customers," by B. Cohen, 1997, *Cornell Hotel and Restaurant Administration Quarterly, 38*(2), pp. 74–81.

quality, service quality, and consequent value prices that will provide desired consequences in usage and ultimately satisfaction of goals and motivations. Second, the firm's resources have to be strategically managed to support a hierarchy of core competencies, capabilities, and ultimately business processes and activity sets. Profit is created at the point of intersection between these two levels of internal and external disaggregation. Competitive advantage may be created if this locus is the tightest in the market. Sustainable competitive advantage may be created if the linkages between the firm's resources, core competencies, capabilities, and processes are weaved together so intricately to customer value that competitors find it virtually impossible to replicate.

These two fundamental processes of CVA must be done ideally on a continuous basis but at least on a frequent basis because of three sources of internal or external dynamic change:

- Customer's goals and motivation change
- Customers defect to rivals for a superior value offering
- Internal resources, core competencies, capabilities, and processes may erode over time or be rendered obsolete by the above two factors.

FAROUT Summary

	1	2	3	4	5
F	■	■	■	■	■
A	■	■	■		
R	■				
O	■			■	■
U	■	■	■	■	■
T	■				

Future orientation High degree. The emphasis on continuous improvement focuses the firm intently on environmental change. Additionally, changing customer value is very often a leading indicator of changing market dynamics.

Accuracy Medium. Obtaining and correctly interpreting the necessary information on customer value components is difficult. Failure to do so will impact accuracy.

Resource efficiency Low. CVA is very resource intensive as it necessarily involves everyone and most business processes of the firm. Additionally, the information requirements are varied and complex, making it costly to obtain. This high resource intensity is offset by the many ways CVA can be leveraged into other management tools and techniques including TQM, supply chain management, pricing strategy, competitor analysis, and resource analysis.

Objectivity High. The premise of CVA that customers determine value makes the analysis inherently objective. Bias might be introduced in analysis through weaknesses in the quantitative methodology.

Usefulness High. Probably one of the most useful management tools and techniques because of its close link to competitive advantage.

Timeliness Low. Depending on the complexity of the firm, developing a CVA monitoring system could take several years.

Related Tools and Techniques

- comparative cost analysis
- competitive benchmarking
- functional capability and resource analysis
- value chain analysis

References

Andreasen, A. R. (1985). "'Backward' market research." *Harvard Business Review, 63*(3), 176–182.

Birch, E. N. (1990). "Focus on value." *Creating Customer Satisfaction.* (Research Report No. 944, pp. 2–39). New York, NY: The Conference Board.

Cohen, B. (1997). "The WOW effect: How one restaurant continues to delight customers." *Cornell Hotel and Restaurant Quarterly, 38*(2), pp. 74–81.

Gale, B. T., & Buzzell, R. D. (1989). "Market perceived quality." *Planning Review, 17*(2), 6–15.

Gale, B. T. (1994). *Managing customer value.* New York: Free Press.

Griffin, J. (1995). *Customer loyalty: How to earn it, how to keep it.* New York, NY: Lexington Books.

Heskett, J. L., Jones, T. O., Loveman, G. W., Sasser, E. E. Jr., & Schlesinger, L. A. (1994). "Putting the service profit chain to work." *Harvard Business Review, 72*(2), 164–174.

Higgins, T. (1998). "The value of customer value analysis." *Marketing Research, 10*(4), 38–44.

Ho, D. C. K., Cheng, E. W. L., & Fong, P. S. W. (2000). "Integration of value analysis and total quality management." *Total Quality Management, 11*(2), 179–186.

Jaworski, B., & Kohli, A. (1993). "Market orientation: Antecedents and consequences." *Journal of Marketing, 57,* 53–70.

Jones, T., & Sasser Jr., W. E. (1995). "Why satisfied customers defect." *Harvard Business Review,* November/December, Vol. 73, No. 6, 88–99.

Kohli, A. K., & Jaworski, B. J. (1990). "Market orientation: The construct, research propositions, and managerial implications." *Journal of Marketing, 54,* 1–18.

Kordupleski, R. E., Rust, R. T., & Zahorik, A. J. (1993). "Why improving quality doesn't improve quality (or whatever happened to marketing?)." *California Management Review, 35*(3), 82–95.

Kordupleski, R. E., & Laitamaki, J. (1997). "Building and deploying profitable growth strategies based on the waterfall of customer value added." *European Management Journal,* April, 158.

Miles, L. D. (1972). *Techniques in value analysis and engineering.* New York: McGraw-Hill.

Narver, J. C., & Slater, S. F. (1990). "The effect of a market orientation on business profitability." *Journal of Marketing, 54,* 20–35.

Naumann, E. (1995). *Creating customer value: The path to competitive advantage.* Cincinnati, OH: Thompson Executive Press.

Parasuraman, A., Zeithaml, V. A., & Berry, L. L. (1985). "A conceptual model of service quality and its implications for future research." *Journal of Marketing, 49*(4), 41–50.

Parasuraman, A. (1997). "Reflections on gaining competitive advantage through customer value." *Journal of the Academy of Marketing Science, 25*(2), 154–161.

Reichheld, F. F. (1996). "Learning from customer defections." *Harvard Business Review, 74*(2), 56–69.

Reichheld, F. F. & Sasser, W. E. Jr., (1990). "Zero defections: Quality comes to services." *Harvard Business Review, 68*(5), 105–111.

Society of Management Accountants of Canada (1997). *Monitoring customer value.* (Management Accounting Guideline 36) Toronto, Ontario, Canada.

Sprague, D. A. (1996). "Adding value and value analysis to TQM." *Journal for Quality and Participation,* January/February, 70–73.

Treacy, M., & Wiersema, F. (1993). "Customer intimacy and other value disciplines." *Harvard Business Review, 71*(1), 84–93.

Woodruff, R. B. (1997). "Customer value: The next Source of competitive advantage." *Journal of the Academy of Marketing Science, 25*(2), 139–153.

Chapter 14

Functional Capability and Resource Analysis

SHORT DESCRIPTION

Functional capability and resource analysis views the firm as a collection of resources comprised of tangible and intangible assets and core capabilities. It combines internal organizational scrutiny with external competitive analysis to determine if these assets are valuable resources that may drive the firm's competitive advantage.

BACKGROUND

The origins of functional capability and resource analysis evolved from several significant developments in the history of economic thought and contemporary strategy theory. Its conceptual foundations were first developed by several influential economists (most notably Ricardo, 1891; Schumpeter, 1934; Penrose, 1959) who were the first to regard the firm as a collection of heterogeneous resources. They variously asserted that differentiated characteristics of resources owned or controlled by firms partially explained why only some firms were able to capture economic rent.

The next major development was the critical success factor (CSF) concept (Daniel, 1961). This idea that profitability was directly related to certain internal factors gave further impetus to the development of internal organizational scrutiny. Further, it laid the groundwork for an expanded definition of *resource* to include the concept that capabilities, the activities and processes applied to resources, should also be considered as important factors in achieving profitability.

Functional capability and resource analysis then continued to evolve from gradual developments in contemporary strategy theory. Figuring prominently was the pervasive strengths, weaknesses, opportunities, and threats (SWOT) paradigm developed by Kenneth Andrews in 1971. One of the central tenets of the SWOT model encouraged managers to find the best fit or congruence between the firm's strengths and weaknesses and opportunities and threats in the competitive environment. This model built on the idea of resource heterogeneity as holding the key to competitive advantage by asserting that strategic success depends on matching strengths (i.e., a conceivable proxy for superior resources) against competitive opportunities.

The first developments in strategy theory to build upon SWOT analysis, however, focused on the external half of the SWOT paradigm—opportunities and threats. For example, portfolio models of the 1970s focused almost exclusively on the external marketing aspects of products and the management on individual strategic business units. Then in the 1980s, Porter's Five Forces model of industry structure analysis also significantly elaborated on the external realm of corporate strategy. The Five Forces model was reflective of the industry structure school of strategy theory in its assertion that roots of competitive advantage lay in finding optimal positions in attractive industries, based on a careful examination and manipulation of mobility barriers.

It wasn't until the mid-1980s that the internal half of the SWOT equation, internal strengths and weaknesses, began to receive more attention. This development responded to the dissatisfaction with the disproportionate focus of strategy theory on the external threats and opportunities facing the firm. Four main weaknesses of the industry structure school of strategy theory became increasingly apparent (Black & Boal, 1994). First, the Five Forces model suffers from circular logic because it argues that firms in attractive industries are successful and firms are successful because they are in attractive industries. Second, it gave no strategic guidance with regard to how to locate the firm into an optimal position within an attractive industry. Third, the benefits of successfully manipulating industry structure did not accrue solely to the instigating firm but was also frequently enjoyed by rival firms, thus diluting any competitive benefits. Fourth, research was beginning to question the impact of industry structure on firm profitability. These criticisms were more of a function of the incomplete nature of industry structure analysis rather than a function of its validity. Nonetheless, strategic decision makers were becoming aware that the roots of competitive advantage were to be found inside as well as outside of the firm.

In the early 1990s, the concept of core competencies came to the fore as a promising new theory to address this lack of internal scrutiny (Prahalad & Hamel, 1990). Where industry analysis only described the external sources of competitive advantage that lay outside the firm, core competency analysis provided internal insights into how firms actually achieve competitive advantage. Similarly, where portfolio theory regarded the firm as a portfolio of products and services, core competency analysis viewed the firm as a collection of five or six skills that allowed it to perform the critical success factors necessary for competitive advantage. The ability of the firm to learn these skills and coordinate them with technology through various production capabilities was offered as the route to superior customer value and competitive advantage.

Similar to the shortcomings of industry analysis, the problem with core competency analysis was its singular focus on only the other half of the SWOT equation—internal strengths and weaknesses. Its high level of abstraction also made it very difficult to operationalize. Functional capability and resource analysis provided an integrating mechanism to greatly expand the definition of the resources available to the firm. The traditional categorization of economics defined resources as capital, land and plant, and labor. The critical success factor concept expanded this definition to include activities and processes. Functional capability and resource analysis further expanded the domain of resources within strategy theory to include the intangible assets related to core competencies, that is, individual human skill, and collective organizational learning capability under the purview of resource analysis.

While still in its infancy, functional capability analysis and resource analysis provided one important way to integrate a rigorous analysis of intangible assets and core competencies. Previous to this, analysis of these "soft" competitive parameters was often relegated to poor cousin status by default because no operational analytical framework was available.

To address this problem, functional capability and resource analysis provided a more exact definition of exactly what constitutes a firm's strength. Prior experience with the critical success factor concept, the SW portion of the SWOT model, and core competency analysis left strategic decision makers with a feeling that identifying strengths and weaknesses was an exercise in obscurity. Where industry analysis provided them with a methodology to determine opportunities and threats, functional capability and resource analysis offered an equally robust analytical framework to identify strengths and weaknesses.

Over time, all of the various components of functional capabilities and resource analysis have been grouped under one umbrella classification known as the Resource Base View (RBV) of the firm. Included in the RBV of the firm are the strategic analyses of tangible assets, intangible assets, critical success factors, capabilities, and core competencies. RBV theory integrates the components of internal scrutiny with external competitive analysis by passing them through a series of robust market tests to determine their competitive value. Because it is so comprehensive and integrative, RBV theory has become a major paradigm in strategy theory. Currently, many academics are further exploring this promising new theory as an overarching framework to both operationalize internal scrutiny and integrate it with environmental analysis in support of securing and maintaining competitive advantage.

STRATEGIC RATIONALE AND IMPLICATIONS

The fundamental premise underlying RBV theory is the recognition that firms own or control sets of resources that support unique strengths, allowing the firm to perform activities better or at lower cost than rivals. RBV theory defines a hierarchy of four broad categories of resources as potential sources of competitive advantage:

1. *Tangible Assets.* Physical factors of production consumed in the delivery of customer value. Examples include plant, equipment, land, inventory, and buildings.
2. *Intangible Assets.* Factors of production that cannot be seen or touched that contribute to the delivery of customer value without being consumed. Examples include brand names, customer goodwill, patents, corporate reputation, and copyright.
3. *Organizational Capabilities.* Processes and activities that transform tangible and intangible assets into goods and services.

4. *Core Competencies.* Individual human skill and talent, collective organizational capacity, and learning that allow the firm to act on critical processes and activities to transform its tangible and intangible assets into competitively superior customer value.

The source of competitive advantage within a firm is often multifactorial in that it usually cannot be attributed to only one type of resource. Rather, it is the interaction between these four different types of resources within a competitive context that drives a firm's competitive advantage.

Another way of looking at the relationships between resources is to consider the link between the economist's concept of rent and the strategist's concept of competitive advantage. Sustained and superior financial performance, the hallmark of competitive advantage, is derived from four different types of economic rent, the returns generated over the firm's opportunity cost (Mahoney & Pandian, 1992):

1. *Ricardian Rent.* Returns from owning scarce valuable resources
2. *Monopoly Rent.* Returns from legal, collusive mechanisms, or market power (e.g., patents, entry barriers, etc.)
3. *Entrepreneurial Rent.* Returns from risk and innovation
4. *Quasi Rent.* Returns from firm-specific heterogeneous resources

The last category of rent is critical to understanding RBV theory. For a firm to earn above normal economic rents it must earn quasi rent. That is, in order to increase Ricardian, monopoly, and entrepreneurial rents to an order of magnitude higher than normal profits, the firm must own or control resources which have several unique characteristics that make them competitively superior. Only then can the firm capture the disproportionate share of the generated economic rents over and above the competitive level that fuel sustained and superior financial performance.

Figure 14-1 integrates these two perspectives of the same fundamental concept in a schematic of the resource-based view of the firm. RBV theory does not exclude the possibility that competitive advantage may be attributable to individual resources. Rather, it asserts that more often the roots of competitive advantage lie in the product of a combination of some or all of four types of resources as indicated by the equation shown in Figure 14-1. The product of capabilities applied on the firm's tangible and intangible assets generates competencies. Most often competencies represent the highest order of resources that are frequently also the most valuable. However, not all resources are competitively valuable in that they will not necessarily generate competitive advantage by securing quasi rent. The crucial distinction of RBV theory is therefore the rigorous testing of assets, capabilities, and competencies to determine their competitive value.

The Five Market Test Approach

Resources must pass through a series of five external market tests to determine if they are capable of capturing quasi rents and delivering competitive advantage. These tests are a staple of RBV analysis and can be commonly found in management literature (e.g., Collis & Montgomery, 1995).

Part II   The Techniques of Strategic and Competitive Analysis

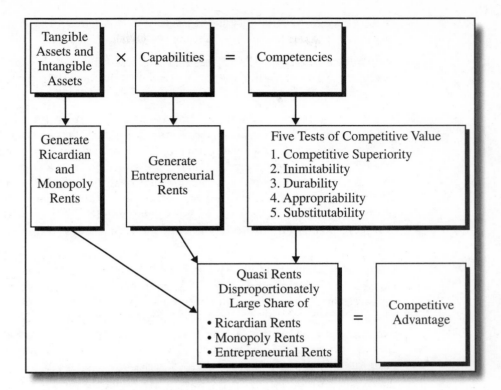

Figure 14-1
The Resource-Based View of the Firm

Test 1: Competitive Superiority

The test of competitive superiority contains three facets. First, the necessary condition for a resource to be valuable is, of course, customer demand. A resource must support absolute customer value. The asset, capability, competence must support the provision of a product or service that meets minimum customer needs, tastes, preferences, and price.

Second, correctly determining the competitive value of the firm's resources is also contingent on a relative competitive comparison—the necessary and sufficient condition for competitive superiority. Often, the temptation exists to adopt an intuitive inward focus when analyzing core competencies premised on answering the wrong question: "What activities do we do best?" Instead, RBV theory asks the more insightful question: "What activities do we do better than competitors?" This second question incorporates a more thorough analytical frame in which the test of competitive superiority should be couched.

Third, competitive superiority is often secured through the combination of resources. The firm may achieve competitive superiority through a combination of resources, which by themselves may not be competitively superior, but their product in creative combination achieves a superior effect to competitive offerings.

Test 2: Inimitability

Inimitability refers to how difficult it is for rivals to secure or imitate the same resource. If rivals can copy a resource, then the profits generated by that resource will be short-lived. Inimitability is very rarely permanent, but several isolating mechanisms will prolong the inimitability of resources:

- *Physical Uniqueness.* Resources that are physically unique cannot by definition be easily copied. Copyrights, patents or prime facility locations are examples of physical uniqueness.

- *Path Dependency.* Resources may be protected from imitation because of the unique historical process and conditions through which the resource was developed. It is very difficult for rivals to mimic path dependency because they cannot be purchased or developed internally. Often, the exact processes and conditions that created the resource cannot be replicated. For example, the Coca-Cola brand name is very path dependent. It has become an American cultural icon by virtue of the length of time it has been on the market. Pepsi, realizing this path dependency, has instead chosen to position their product toward the younger, less sentimental generation.

- *Causal Ambiguity.* As discussed above and shown in Figure 14-1, resources are often the product of many complex combinations of tangible assets, intangible assets, capabilities, and competencies. These interrelationships often make the firm's resources appear to rivals as an enigma wrapped in a riddle that further isolates the resource's inimitability. The innovative product technology at 3M is often cited as an example because the underlying resource supporting these products is the organizational culture of 3M—a product of many intertwined resources that has proven exceptionally difficult to replicate.

- *Economic Scale Deterrence.* Preemptive investments in capacity expansion or new market entry often thwart rivals who may otherwise have entertained similar plans. Limited market demand may not be able to absorb the total supply if rivals choose to follow the preemptor. Rather than initiate a price war, or fail to achieve the scale required for success in capital intensive and scale dependent industries, rivals often back off, thus securing a source of inimitability through entry barriers for the preemptor. The preemptive investment of a North American car manufacturer into building huge plants in post–Cold War Poland is an example of scale deterrence. Rival manufacturers realizing the limited market demand in Poland for autos would probably hesitate to make the same massive expenditure. As the middle class develops in Poland, the preemptive manufacturer will reap the rewards of scale deterrence.

Test 3: Durability

Durability refers to the speed at which a resource depreciates. Due to constant innovation and hypercompetition in many market environments, previously valuable resources often lose their ability to secure competitive advantage. The ability of a resource to withstand external challenges to its durability acts as an isolating mechanism to protect the firm's competitive advantage. The hypercompetitive computer industry provides an excellent example. The relative ease of cloning PC platforms has stripped IBM of what was once a potent competitive resource. Conversely, Microsoft has been able to maintain the durability of its Windows operating system through a combination of patents and aggressive efforts to ensure that Windows technology stays in the center of product innovation or is at least compatible with the latest innovations.

Test 4: Appropriability

Appropriability refers to who captures the profits generated by a resource. If competitively valuable resources are immobile, the firm stands a much higher chance of capturing the quasi rents that flow from them. Conversely, if these resources are not closely linked to the firm, that is, if they can be easily purchased or developed, the profits that flow from them may be easily bargained away by other suppliers, customers, rival firms, or employees. For instance, the skills of professional athletes and film stars are not closely integrated with the business models of the teams and studios that they represent. As such, they represent extremely mobile resources and often use this mobility as leverage in bargaining for the lion's share of the profit they generate.

Test 5: Substitutability

Substitutability refers to the availability of alternative resources that can meet or exceed the value of the firm's incumbent competitive resources. Rival firms may secure access to substitute resources that enable them to offer a lower cost or a more differentiated value offering. History is replete with examples of substitution. Consider, for example, the replacement of aluminum cans for glass and the impact of this on glass manufacturers. More recently, the substitutability of plastic for aluminum posed significant ramifications to aluminum can manufacturers. Substitutability can impact not only products and services, but can also affect the underlying capabilities and competencies upon which products and services are built. Indeed, it is often the availability of substitute capabilities and competencies that allow rivals to offer superior customer value rather than a radical change in the nature of the product itself.

The VRIO Framework—Another Useful Approach

Although the task of analyzing the external environment and marketplace has received the lion's share of academic attention in the business world, few would argue that the task of analyzing the internal market had received as much attention or achieved such clarity. The "SW" aspect of SWOT analysis of the firm's strengths and weaknesses remains a more ambiguous and subjective process relative to its external counterparts. For example, the definition of what constitutes a strength or a weakness can be easily manipulated by the individuals performing the analysis, leaving open the concerns of empire building and politics as a subjective basis for decision making. Management scholars recognized about a decade ago that one way to remove some degree of this subjectivity was to develop a model for analyzing the internal environment that had the advantages of models that were tried-and-true for assessing the external environment. Out of this search for improved analysis and decision making arose the value, rarity, inimitability, and organization (VRIO) model.

Originally described by Barney (1991), the VRIO model is a simple four-question framework that allows managers to analyze individual resources as being catalysts of competitive advantage. Using the resource is relatively easy. The analyst selects the resource to be assessed and sequentially asks each of the four key questions. If the answer to a question is yes, they move on to the next question. If the answer is no, the analysis stops and the analyst concludes that the resource will not lead to a competitive advantage.

The Value Question

Traditional strategic management definitions of value match internal resources to the external environment. The key to their application is to assess the alignment, congruence, or fit of the match. In that context, a resource adds value to a firm if it helps in the exploitation of an opportunity or in the reduction of a threat. The VRIO model argues that for a resource to be valuable, it must provide a net increase in revenues or a net decrease in costs to the organization. Another adaptation suggests that these net effects may also be indirectly related through the reduction of risk and time effects on costs and revenues.

The Rareness Question

Valuable resources must also be rare for them to lead to competitive advantage. Organizational resources are rare when they are not currently possessed by many other organizations. The difficulty in applying this criterion is to objectively set a standard for rarity. Is it rare if only two organizations have the valuable resource? Four firms? Twelve firms? For our purposes here, a resource is rare if the number of firms that have the resource is small enough to allow for oligopolistic or monopolistic economic returns.

The Inimitability Question

Inimitability refers to the ability of other organizations to copy the nature or implementation of rare resources. Rarity deals with the present nature of the resources; inimitability deals with the evolution of these resources. Inimitability is related to sustainability of the competitive advantage in that the valuable and rare resources must remain that way over time if they are to be a source of competitive advantage. Easily copied, substituted, or trumped resources will not suffice for an organization to sustain competitive advantage. Barney (1991) suggests that three factors may be closely associated with inimitability including unique historical conditions, causal ambiguity, and social complexity.

Unique organizational histories have space and time dependencies and can endow a firm with valuable resources that are out of control of competitors and are difficult to imitate. These resources can be developed from a firm's unique path through history.

Causal ambiguity occurs when the relationship between the organization's resources and competitive advantage is not understood, or understood only ambiguously, by competitors. It exists where cause and effect relationships cannot be easily understood. This can occur in the way that a visionary leader is able to infuse the workforce with energy and vision or in the way that a grassroots effort among industry players grows in importance over time.

Social complexity refers to resources that revolve around "very complex social phenomena, beyond the ability of firms to systematically manage and influence"

(Barney, 1991, p. 110). Examples of socially complex phenomena include 3M's innovation-driven culture, GE's leader-driven style, or the internal power dynamics that occur at tightly held, family controlled firms like Mars.

The Organization Question

This criterion forces managers to ask whether the organization actually has the capability to take advantage of a valuable, rare, and inimitable resource. To assess this, the analyst usually needs to take into account such things as human resource policies, technology, organization culture, values of the dominant coalition, or laws that impact the use of a particular resource. The McKinsey 7S and SERVO approaches provide helpful means for assessing the organization question.

Few resources will pass the five tests or VRIO assessments, testament to the analytical rigor of RBV analysis. Only those resources that pass each test are deemed competitively valuable resources, capable of driving the firm's competitive advantage. As depicted in Figure 14-2, the true source of competitive advantage exists at the intersection of all of the market tests of resource value.

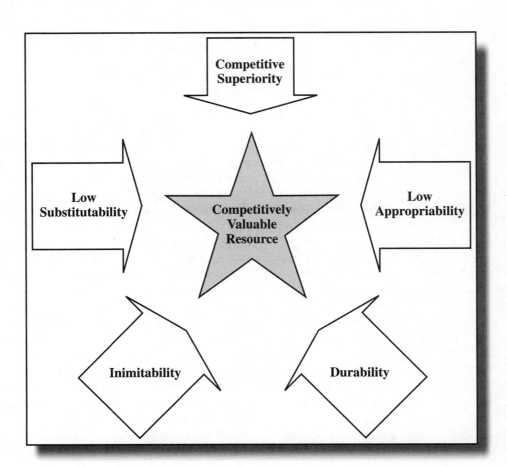

Figure 14-2
The Locus of Competitively Valuable Resources

The fact that many resources fail the RBV test is consistent with the observation that very few firms possess a sustainable or even strong competitive advantage. Nonetheless, given the immense benefit of achieving competitive advantage, RBV analysis is well worth pursuing. It speaks directly to the essence of strategic management in at least four very important ways.

First, while industry structure analysis remains a necessary and valuable complement to RBV analysis, much research has shown that characteristics within industries are much more influential on profitability than characteristics between industries (e.g., Buzzell & Gale, 1987; Schmalensee, 1988; Rumelt, 1991; Rocquebert, Phillips, & Duran, 1993). Globalization and value chain migration via the transformational capabilities of information technology have made interfirm rivalry much more intense that interindustry rivalry. This development has refocused attention back onto the question of why firms enjoy different levels of profitability and, by extension, competitive advantage. The answer increasingly being proffered in response has been observed differences between the competitive value of rival resources.

Second, RBV theory offers managers an actionable framework to operationalize the three generic strategies of low cost, differentiation, or scope. The selection of these strategies, however, requires an a priori consideration of the availability of competitively valuable resources to support each strategy. Hence, RBV can serve three important roles in the formulation of generic strategies:

- Test the strength of the firm's current strategy
- Test the viability of the firm's planned strategy
- Assist in setting stretch goals

Third, the differences between industry analysis and RBV theory may be purely taxonomical in nature. That is, mobility barriers, the central lever in the Five Forces model, can really be seen as the ownership of competitively valuable resources. That is, each mobility barrier at its core can be reduced to the ownership of specific resources. For example, entry barriers such as patents, brand equity, scale effects, and so forth can all be traced to the ownership of competitively valuable resources that differ among firms in terms of their competitive superiority, inimitability, durability, appropriability, and substitutability.

Fourth, a singular analysis of core competencies may lead the firm to pursue suboptimal diversification and growth strategies. Core competencies analysis assumes that the roots of competitive advantage are inherent inside of the firm. As such, growth and diversification strategies may be limited by an incorrect assumption that the firm's current stock of resources are static and limited. RBV analysis counteracts this faulty logic by gauging the value of internal resources relative to market forces that validate their value. Because market forces continually change, RBV analysis will help management keep its finger on the pulse of these changes. Similarly, this knowledge will allow the firm to correctly pursue strategic growth and diversification strategy by investing in, upgrading, or leveraging competitively valuable resources. In this way, growth and diversification stand a much higher chance of resulting in profitable growth associated with competitive advantage. The process of implementing RBV analysis discusses how to invest, upgrade, or leverage competitively valuable resources in the support of dynamic strategy.

STRENGTHS AND ADVANTAGES

Integrative.   The greatest strength of RBV theory is its ability to cohesively integrate many previously disparate threads of strategy theory into one robust analytical framework. It is one of very few strategic management systems that effectively combines competitive analysis, industry structure, and internal scrutiny.

Disciplined, Realistic, Objective, and Actionable.   The strong grounding of RBV theory in economic theory coupled with its incorporation of market validation results in an extremely useful analytical tool.

A New Theory of Growth and Diversification.   RBV offers important insights into the strategic challenges of growth and diversification as a function of the limits of resource support. Given the massive failure of previous theories of growth and diversification, RBV theory is very promising.

New Strategic Language.   RBV theory greatly increases the strategic vocabulary for which to describe strategic analysis. Managers and scholars alike, well versed in RBV theory, will be able to articulate strategy theory to a much finer degree. This represents a significant improvement from other approaches plagued by a high level of abstraction.

WEAKNESSES AND LIMITATIONS

Little Empirical Support.   As intuitive and logically appealing as RBV theory is, it remains theoretical conjecture. This is probably more a function of its relative newness as opposed to questionable validity. Others are less generous, claiming that anecdotal evidence is selectively cited to bolster RBV theory. In many studies successful strategy is attributed to RBV variables with a casual disregard for a consideration of experimental control. Unsuccessful companies are ignored, leaving unanswered the question of whether their lack of RBV strategy contributed to their fate.

Research to date has focused only on generic conceptual overviews of RBV theory. Scant research has been conducted on the impact of different contexts on the competitive value of resources. Expect much empirical research regarding the validation of RBV theory to start flowing in to address these unresolved issues.

Tautological.   Critics of RBV theory assert that it incorporates circular logic. Porter (1991) argues this potential flaw by pointing out that, according to RBV theory, strategic success is achieved through the ownership of valuable resources but that firms need to acquire these resources to achieve strategic success. To be fair, critics respond to this criticism by stating that the independent variable in RBV analysis (resources) is located at a lower level of functional aggregation than the dependent variable (competitive advantage), which is located at the higher functional level of business or corporate aggregation (Black & Boal, 1994). Accordingly, RBV theory may not be a tautology.

Complex and Ambiguous Taxonomy. The taxonomy used in RBV analysis tends to be ambiguous, leaving the strategist with the perception of inconsistent and interchangeable classifications with some conceptual overlap. Definitional distinction between the terms used (e.g., intangible asset, capability, competence, resource) may appear blurred, thus blunting the initial accessibility of RBV theory. This complex and somewhat unclear terminology is probably a temporary function of the relative newness of RBV theory. This problem is also related to the broad integration of many theories and concepts of RBV theory. As a result, the instances of apparent inconsistency are caused by the diversity of contributors, each introducing their own peculiar taxonomy.

RBV Theory Adds Nothing New. Critics claim that calling RBV theory a new paradigm of strategic management is premature and possibly untruthful given that it is steeped in many concepts of classical economic theory. Similarly, some view RBV theory as just a rehash of the well-worn SWOT paradigm developed in 1971. Still others argue that RBV theory just explicitly articulates strategy that managers implicitly pursue in the normal course of rational analysis.

PROCESS FOR APPLYING THE TECHNIQUE

Step 1: Determine the Firm's Critical Success Factors

Critical success factors (CSFs) are the relatively few factors that are necessary to secure and sustain competitive advantage. They can be composed of a special skill or talent, a competitive capability, or something the firm must do to satisfy customers. Telltale qualifying criteria of CSFs are their direct link to organizational performance. Excellent execution around CSFs will ensure the firm's competitiveness and requisite excellent financial performance. Conversely, poor execution around CSFs will manifest in declining competitiveness and, ultimately, poor financial performance. Other qualifying criteria of CSFs are that they usually revolve around one of the firm's most significant business areas, involve large dollar amounts, and directly impact the customer in some way.

Rockart (1979) identified four major sources of CSFs:

- *Macroenvironmental Characteristics.* Changes in the firm's political, environmental, social, or technological environment may impinge on the firm's critical success factors.
- *Industry Characteristics.* CSFs are not generic but are extremely industry specific. For example, key success factors in the auto industry may be design engineering, strong dealer distribution networks, cost control, and pollution abatement processes and technologies. Additionally, it is important to note that CSFs are a function of industry structure and will change as industries evolve.
- *Competitive Position.* CSFs are also a function of the firm's position with its rivals. Innovation by rivals may warrant assessment of a potentially new set of critical success factors.

- *Firm Specific.* These are success factors critical to the successful functioning of the firm's internal organization. The firm must ensure that these CSFs are being executed well before considering the other types of CSFs listed here.

Leidecker and Bruno (1984) suggest several helpful methods and sources that may be used to identify CSFs, including environmental analysis, industry structure analysis, industry and business experts, analysis of how rivals compete, and internal analysis. Another excellent source to initiate the search for CSFs is best-practice benchmarking studies, which are often published by industry trade associations.

Step 2: Identify the Firm's Resources

This step requires the identification of tangible resources, intangible resources, capabilities, and competencies that the firm controls or owns. Tangible assets will be the easiest to identify but generally hold little analytical value because they are easily imitated, therefore, they hold less promise of supporting competitive advantage. The larger challenge will come from identifying the other types of resources that don't show up on the firm's financial statements, namely, intangible assets, capabilities, and competencies. One way to gauge the magnitude of the value of intangible assets to the firm is to compare the difference between the firm's book value of its assets with the capitalized value. If the firm practices activity based costing or total quality management, much information can be gleaned from the management accounting and operations functions regarding the firm's capabilities, activities, and processes. Identifying core competencies is the most difficult task in step 2. Prahalad and Hamel (1990) developed three criteria to identify core competencies:

- A core competence provides potential access to a wide variety of markets.
- A core competence will make a major contribution to customer value.
- A core competence is difficult to imitate because it is often a complex combination of production skills and technology.

Further, these authors assert that most firms will not possess more than five or six core competencies. It is extremely important in this step to properly disaggregate the resource analysis as much as possible. To accomplish this, the analyst needs to drill down to get as close as possible to the lowest common denominator of competitive advantage. Without achieving this vital step, RBV analysis will remain the limited intuitive approach it was designed to replace. Instead, a robust analysis premised on objective market tests requires high-quality inputs. The most important of these high-quality inputs is disaggregated resource identification.

Step 3: Evaluate the Firm's Resources

Run the identified resources through the five tests or VRIO to determine if they are indeed competitively valuable resources. Don't forget to consider the possibility that groups of resources working in concert will probably form some of the firm's competitively valuable resources. Additionally, the analyst will find that most of the firm's valuable resources are in the form of intangible assets, capabilities, and competencies.

Step 4: Identify Gaps Between the Firm's Resources and CSFs

Once the firm's resources have been identified and evaluated, they should be compared to the CSFs identified in step 1. If the firm has been successfully performing in the recent past, chances are that many of the CSFs will match with the firm's competitively valuable assets. If not, this step provides a unique diagnostic tool for determining where gaps exist between the CSFs and the firm's stock of competitive resources. This information is vital in formulating RBV strategy and provides a foundation for a robust analytical framework to correctly match the various components of the SWOT paradigm.

Step 5: Diagnose Current Strategy

Based on the analysis of step 4, the analyst is now in an ideal position to test the competitive strength of the firm's current strategy. With an intimate knowledge of the firm's CSFs and the competitive value of its resources, two options will present themselves:

• If the firm's current strategy is operating successfully, knowledge of the firm's competitively valuable resources (i.e., competitive superiority, inimitability, durability, appropriability, substitutability) will in turn give the analyst a rich source of analysis from which to devise strategies to protect these core assets in order to extend the firm's competitive advantage.

• If the firm's current strategy is running into difficulty, knowledge of the firm's competitively valuable resources (i.e., competitive superiority, inimitability, durability, appropriability, substitutability) will highlight the strategic gaps that currently exist between the firm's resources, its strategy, and the competitive environment.

Step 6: Formulate Rational Future Strategies

This step incorporates perhaps the most valuable aspect of RBV analysis. Given that the competitive environment is constantly changing, the firm's stock of competitively valuable resources is at constant risk of becoming obsolete, bargained away, or surpassed by rivals. Similarly, the firm will be presented with a host of potential directions to pursue growth and diversification. RBV analysis provides guidance for both of these strategic challenges through investing in, upgrading, or leveraging its competitively valuable resources (Collis & Montgomery, 1997):

• *Investing in Resources.* A simplistic interpretation of RBV theory would suggest that only competitively valuable resources should receive substantial investment because these are the only resources that will earn quasi rents through competitive advantage. However, this decision is significantly more complex within a dynamic competitive context and involves difficult trade-offs between continuity versus adaptability and between commitment and flexibility:

1. *Continuity vs. adaptability.* The firm has essentially three options regarding where and how to invest in times of environmental change. One, it may invest in the firm's current stock of resources that support its current source of competitive advantage. Two, it may choose to support a new strategy by investing in new resources premised on its vision of future CSFs. Three, the firm may refrain from investing until the uncertainty clears. Each option carries significant risk. The first option may move the firm toward a worsening competitive position. The second option carries the risk of either not being able to develop the required valuable resources or misreading environmental change. The third option might freeze the firm from acting until crisis.

2. *Commitment vs. flexibility.* Related to the trade-off in (1), commitment versus flexibility refers to the common decision of firms to avoid commitments to either current or future strategy. Since many resource investments are irreversible and unrecoverable, strategic commitment carries the risk of either locking into an unsuccessful strategy or being locked out of what would have been a successful strategy. As a result, many firms try to maintain flexibility by straddling the sidelines with dual contingency strategies ready to employ either one depending on the outcome of environmental change.

Interestingly, it is this uncertainty that lies at the root of competitive advantage. Without it, all firms would pursue similar strategies, eliminating all chance of quasi rents.

- *Upgrading Resources.* The resource stocks of most firms will fail the strict market-based tests of competitive value. One option, then, is to upgrade its resources in the hope that they will become competitively valuable in the future. For firms that do own or control competitively valuable resources, the strategic imperative to upgrade resources is similar. Upgrading resources for these firms offers a rational strategy to keep its resources valuable against the continuous threat that environmental change and competition will usurp that value. There are three ways in which firms, for whatever reason, may upgrade their resources (Collis & Montgomery, 1997):

   a. *Strengthening existing resources.* Increasing the quality of the resources currently in place through development, education, experience sharing, or a variety of other improvement techniques

   b. *Adding complementary resources.* Enhancing the firm's position in its existing markets through alliances, networks or strategic outsourcing arrangements

   c. *Developing new resources.* Allowing the firm to enter new, more attractive markets

- *Leveraging Resources.* This option involves extending the reach of the firm's competitive resources into markets where strategic success is premised on similar

A 1996 study tested the resource-based view of the firm among the major Hollywood studios during the period 1936 to 1965. Included in the sample were competitors MGM, Twentieth-Century-Fox, Warner Brothers, Paramount, United Artists, Universal, and Columbia. The study's purpose was to explore the differential impact of property-based and knowledge-based resources on the competitive advantage of these Hollywood film studios.

The widescale adoption of television in the early 1950s catalyzed much external dynamism and uncertainty for the studios. Hence, the period from 1936 to 1950 was classified as a stable competitive environment, while the period from 1951 to 1965 was classified as an unstable competitive environment. The table summarizes the very different industry structures and sources of competitive advantage that existed within these two time periods:

Stability: 1936–1950	Turbulence: 1951–1965
a. Oligopolistic studio system	a. Direct competition from television: By 1950, 25 percent of homes had a TV set, a penetration that doubled to 50 percent by 1952
b. Stable demand: 80–90 million admissions per week, with demand slowly rising	b. Declining demand: 40–50 million admissions per week by 1953
c. Stable consumer preferences, virtually no box office failures	c. Studios began differentiating films to reclaim lost audiences; moviegoers became much more fickle; increasing frequency of box office failures
d. Studio stars, directors, and film genres had a long shelf life; high volume of films based on same concept of moviemaking	d. Films became much grander and lavish, incorporating innovations such as color film, wide screens, and stereophonic sound
e. Routine production processes, with the same crew working under the same producer for many different movie productions	e. Technical and creative skills of studios became a competitively valuable resource
f. Low-risk, exclusive long-term contracts for many popular stars	f. High-risk, short-term contracts for relatively smaller numbers of stars, directors, and producers whom the studios perceived as having a limited time period of popularity
g. Ownership or control of theaters would guarantee audiences for studios	g. U.S. Justice Department forces theaters to divest their theater holdings; however, most of the downtown theaters had already lost market share to competing suburban locations
h. Studios controlled many stars and majority of distribution securing competitive advantage	h. Stars, producers, and directors become independent from studios, controlling much of the industry's bargaining power. Competitive advantage for studios changed to focus on coordinative skills required to assemble and direct nonpermanent cast members in very complex and diverse productions

The following conceptual framework was used to distinguish between property-based and knowledge-based resources in the Hollywood studio industry in these two different eras:

(Continued on following page)

Resource Type and Example	Value From	Created or Protected by	Suitable Environment
Property-Based			
Discrete: Patents and exclusive contracts	Control of factor	Law, preemption, intrinsic scarcity	Stable or predictable
Systemic: Integrated production or distribution systems	Control of an entire system	Property rights, first-mover advantages, complimentarity of system parts	Stable or predictable
Knowledge-Based			
Discrete: Functional and creative skills	Adaptation and renewal	Uncertain inimitability Flexibility	Uncertain
Systemic: Coordinative and team skills	Adaptation and renewal	Asset specificity, Uncertain inimitability Robustness	Uncertain

Based on these two different environments, rigorous statistical analysis was then conducted on over 30 years of industry data to determine if property-based and knowledge-based resources could explain the differences in financial performance of movie theaters in each era. RBV theory was essentially validated as the following statistically significant relationships were borne out from the analysis:

1. Discrete property-based resources will secure competitive advantage in stable environments but not in unstable environments.
   - Long-term contracts for stars significantly impacted return on sales, profits, and market shares during the stable era but not in the turbulent era.

2. Systematic property-based resources will secure competitive advantage in stable environments but not in unstable environments.
   - Ownership and control of theaters significantly impacted return on sales and market share (but not profitability) during the stable era but not in the turbulent era.

3. Discrete knowledge-based resources will secure competitive advantage in unstable environments but not in stable environments.

- Academy Awards won by the studios (a proxy for technical and creative skills) significantly impacted return on sales, market share, and profitability during the turbulent era but not in the stable era.

4. Systematic knowledge-based resources will secure competitive advantage in unstable environments but not in stable environments.
   - Average production budgets per film (a proxy for coordinative and collaborative skills) significantly impacted return on sales and profitability (but not market share) during the turbulent era but not in the stable era.

While studies such as these validate RBV theory, they also push the theoretical envelope by determining the context in which a particular resource is valuable. The distinction between the competitive value of property and knowledge-based resources within different types of competitive environments offers a promising pathway to integrate the work of the industrial economic school of strategy with that of RBV enthusiasts. Proper RBV analysis must be dynamic. The ability of a resource to secure competitive advantage will be just as much a function of the environmental context in which the resource is employed as it is on the inherent resource characteristics. Similarly, it is important to

(Continued on following page)

note that, while valuable resources can secure competitive advantage within a firm's environment, environmental change can also turn that valuable resource into a commodity in a relatively short period of time. This offers further affirmation for the necessity of dynamic RBV analysis.

SOURCE: Adapted from "The Resource-Based View of the Firm in Two Environments: The Hollywood Film Studios from 1936–1965," by D. Miller and J. Shamsie, 1996, *Academy of Management Journal,* June, *39*(3), pp. 519–543.

sources of competitive advantage. Here, the five tests of competitive value are invaluable in determining if this is possible.

The unique strategic value of RBV analysis is highlighted by a consideration of the strategic imperatives of investing in, upgrading, and leveraging resources. Just as the five market tests of competitive value can be effectively used to analyze resources within the firm's current strategy, they can also be used as effective screens for any planned growth or diversification strategies. This provides a useful and very realistic methodology for testing whether the existing or planned resources are capable of securing competitive advantage in different environmental contexts and markets. This type of proactive market-based appraisal of future strategy is perhaps the most valuable contribution of RBV analysis.

FAROUT Summary

	1	2	3	4	5
F	███	███	███	███	
A	███	███			
R	███	███	███	███	███
O	███	███	███	███	███
U	███	███	███	███	
T	███	███	███	███	

Future orientation   Medium to High. RBV analysis addresses the need to continuously monitor changes in the environment that impinge on the competitive value of resources.

Accuracy   Low to medium. Often, the criteria for competitively valuable resources are applied too liberally. Like the sustainable competitive advantage that they support, competitively valuable resources are extremely rare.

Resource efficiency   High degree. Can be conducted with minimal costs, as much of the informational input is already in place. Most of the resource expenditure involves analysis.

Objectivity   High. The market validation of the resource value tests introduce a high level of objectivity into the analysis.

Usefulness   Medium to high. The focus on only competitively valuable resources reduces the analysis from a high volume of "nice to know" to a manageable amount of strategically relevant "need to know" analysis. The ambiguous taxonomy of RBV theory reduces its usefulness.

Timeliness   High. RBV analysis can be performed in a relatively short period of time.

RELATED TOOLS AND TECHNIQUES

- comparative cost analysis
- competitive benchmarking
- competitor profiling
- customer segmentation analysis
- customer value analysis
- industry analysis
- SERVO analysis
- STEEP analysis
- strategic group analysis
- SWOT analysis
- value chain analysis

REFERENCES

Aaker, D. A. (1980). "Managing assets and skills." *California Management Review, 31*(2), 91–106.

Anonymous. (1998). "Strategic management: Which way to competitive advantage?" *Management Accounting, 76*(1), 32–37.

Barney, J. (1989). "Asset stocks and sustained competitive advantage." *Management Science, 35*, 1511–1513.

Barney, J. (1991). "Firm resources and sustained competitive advantage." *Journal of Management, 17*(1), 99–120.

Black, J. A., & Boal, K. B. (1994). "Strategic resources: Traits, configurations and paths to sustainable competitive advantage." *Strategic Management Journal*, (Summer special issue) 15, 131–148.

Buzzell, R. D., & Gale, B. T. (1987). *The PIMS Principles.* New York: Free Press.

Collis, D. J., & Montgomery, C. A. (1995). "Competing on resources: Strategy in the 1990s." *Harvard Business Review, 73*(4), 118–128.

Collis, D. J. & Montgomery, C. A. (1997). *Corporate strategy: Resources and the scope of the firm.* Chicago, IL: McGraw Hill/Irwin.

Daniel, R. D. (1961). "Management information crisis." *Harvard Business Review*, September/October, Vol. 39, No. 5, 111–121.

Diereckx, I., & Cool, K. (1989). "Asset stock accumulation and sustainability of competitive advantage." *Management Science, 35*, 1504–1511.

Garvin, D. A. (1993). "Building a learning organization." *Harvard Business Review, 71*(4), 78–91.

Grant, R. M. (1991). "The resource-based theory of competitive advantage: Implications for strategy formulation." *California Management Review, 33*(3), 114–135.

Hamel, G., & Prahalad, C. K. (1993). "Strategy as stretch and leverage." *Harvard Business Review, 71*(2), 75–84.

Hall, R. (1992). "The strategic analysis of intangible resources." *Strategic Management Journal, 13*(2), 135–144.

Leidecker, J. K., & Bruno, A. V. (1984). "Identifying and using critical success factors." *Long Range Planning, 17*(1), 23–32.

Mahoney, J. T., & Pandian, J. R. (1992). "The resource-based view within the conversation of strategic management." *Strategic Management Journal, 13*(5), 363–380.

Miller, D., & Shamsie, J. (1996). "The resource-based view of the firm in two environments: The hollywood film studios from 1936 to 1965." *Academy of Management Journal, 39*(3), 519–543.

Penrose, E. (1959). *The theory of the growth of the firm.* New York: John Wiley & Sons.

Peteraf, M. (1993). "The cornerstones of competitive advantage: A resource-based view." *Strategic Management Journal, 14*(3), 179–191.

Porter, M. E. (1991). "Towards a dynamic theory of strategy." *Strategic Management Journal*, (Summer special issue), 12, 95–117.

Prahalad, C. K., & Hamel, G. (1990). "The core competence of the corporation." *Harvard Business Review, 68*(3), 79–91.

Ricardo, D. (1891). *Principles of political economy and taxation.* London: G. Bell.

Rockart, J. F. (1979). "Chief executives define their own data needs." *Harvard Business Review, 57*(2), 81–93.

Rocquebert, J., Phillips, R., & Duran, C. (1993). "How much does industry matter?" Presentation at the National Academy of Management Meeting, Atlanta, GA.

Rumelt, R. P. (1991). "How much does industry matter?" *Strategic Management Journal, 12*(3), 167–185.

Schoemaker, P. J. H. (1992). "How to link strategic vision to core capabilities." *Sloan Management Review, 34*(1), 67–81.

Schmalensee, R. (1988). "Industrial economics: An overview." *Economic Journal, 98*, 643–681.

Shumpeter, J. A. (1934). *The theory of economic development*. Cambridge, MA: Harvard University Press.

Wernerfelt, B. (1984). "A resource-based view of the firm." *Strategic Management Journal, 5*(2), 171–180.

Chapter 15

Management Profiling

SHORT DESCRIPTION

Management personality profiling is an analytical tool that provides organization's decision makers with an understanding of the backgrounds, goals, personalities, and psychological characteristics of rival decision makers. Based on the assertion that personalities remain stable over time and that people repeat patterns, this information is used to predict management's future strategic decision making at competing firms and provides a unique insight into how competitors think, operate, and manage.

Management profiling can allow analysts to assess competitors' leadership, managerial and decision making styles; anticipate competitors' likely reaction or market initiatives; provide useful strategies for understanding players in mergers, acquisitions, and strategic alliances; and evaluate the strengths and weaknesses of multiple leadership teams across a range of competitors.

BACKGROUND

Personality profiling has long been a primary component of both military and political intelligence. Military strategists have successfully used personality profiling to complement the other forms of intelligence analysis. That is, conventional intelligence provided insights into the enemy's logistics, fighting capability, infrastructure, and so forth. Essentially, it answered the question about capability; "What can our enemy do?" Personality profiling, on the other hand, of opposing generals, commanders, and politicians was used to supplement this valuable information with the extremely relevant corollary "What will our enemy do?" This strategy has an analogy in the business community as well. Where traditional strategic analysis initially focused on the resources and capabilities of rivals, personality profiling was subsequently added to include consideration of how the decision makers at competing firms will marshal those resources in the pursuit of competitive strategy.

The eminent psychologist Carl Jung was the first to explore the concept of personality as a set of preferences or traits that drives a person's motivation and behavior. An integral part of his theory suggested that personality is formed at a very young age and remains essentially the same over the course of an individual's life.

One of the first to develop a comprehensive framework of personality was German philosopher Eduard Spranger. In 1928 he devised six broad classifications of personal values: theoretical, economic, aesthetic, social, political, and religious. Over time, many other value classification systems were developed; the majority of which, however, were premised on a theoretical exploration of this branch of psychology. The most famous of these systems was the Myers-Briggs Type Indicator (aka, MBTI) in the 1930s. The MBTI is primarily concerned with the differences in people that result from where people like to focus their attention, the way they like to take in information, the way they like to decide, and the kind of lifestyle they adopt.

Their framework was based on Jung's preferences and they developed 16 different personality classifications based on combinations of the 8 fundamental personality groups, as shown in Figure 15-1(a).

Every individual lies somewhere on each of these four scales or groups, and combining the four scales provides an understanding of the ways human personalities interact with the environment to satisfy their needs.

The 16 types (that is, the four scales in all possible combinations) are

INFP	ISFP	INTP	ISTP
ENFP	ESFP	ENTP	ESTP
INFJ	ISFJ	INTJ	ISTJ
ENFJ	ESFJ	ENTJ	ESTJ

This new knowledge of personality theory was initially applied not to competitive analysis but to internal hiring processes. Employment testing using various personality profiling techniques became extremely popular after World War II. Many of these tests were developed in the military and were later adopted and adapted to become a routine part of the corporate hiring process. Civil rights activists during the 1960s began to question the ethics of intrusive personality testing as a screen for potential job applicants. As a result, in the early 1970s, corporate use of profiling in the hiring process was placed under significant regulation as the result of several legal precedents. The interest in applying personality profiling in the hiring process has recently been revived, however, by the high costs resulting from poor hiring decisions.

It wasn't until 1965 that an applied perspective was brought to bear on the impact of values and personality traits on strategic decision making. Fittingly, the work of Guth and Tagiuri (1965) was based on Spranger's original classification of personal values. They asserted that values define a significant component of a per-

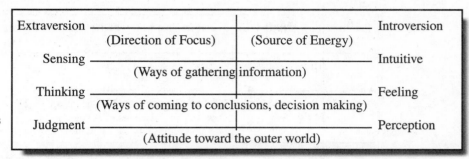

Figure 15-1a
Scales of the Myers
Briggs Type
Indicator (MBTI)

Extraversion ————————————————————— Introversion
(Direction of Focus)   (Source of Energy)

Sensing ———————————————————————— Intuitive
(Ways of gathering information)

Thinking ———————————————————————— Feeling
(Ways of coming to conclusions, decision making)

Judgment ———————————————————————— Perception
(Attitude toward the outer world)

son's personality and are a powerful force driving an individual's behavior. In their study of 988 business executives, scientists, and research managers, they attempted to classify each individual into one of Spranger's value categories. The results indicated the value orientation of business executives were predominantly economic, theoretical, and political. The reader should bear in mind that these conclusions were based on averages and so significant variation exists among individual executives. Nonetheless, this study was one of the first to explicitly propose that, when framing strategy, executives use their predominant values and personality traits to apply judgment as to how to best rally the firm's resources to exploit opportunities in the competitive environment.

Personality profiling was then increasingly applied to the issue of internal promotion as a guide to match an individual's personality to the requirements of various positions. One of the more common applications was as an input into assigning managers to various SBUs, depending on the tightness of fit between the managerial requirements of the SBU in terms of its position on portfolio grids. Often managers were promoted in part on the assertion that different personalities and styles were required to successfully manage through different stages of the product life cycle. See Figure 15-1(b).

Traditionally, management personality profiling has been relegated to second-tier status in favor of more quantitatively oriented strategic tools and techniques. This is not surprising, given the predominant values of most executives. Within the last decade, however, the competitive intelligence discipline has renewed interest in some of the "softer," more qualitative tools available for strategic analysis. Principal among these is management personality profiling.

STRATEGIC RATIONALE AND IMPLICATIONS

Companies do not make strategic decisions; individuals do. Despite the self-evident nature of this truism, it is has been a critical oversight of traditional strategic analysis. Barndt (1991) cites the decided lack of formal analysis around personality profiling

Figure 15-1b
Myers Briggs Type
Indicator (MBTI)

*Source: Production and
Inventory Management
Journal,* by D. W.
Krumiede, C. Sheu, and
J. Lavelle. Copyright
1998 by AM Production
& Inventory Co.
Reproduced with per-
mission of AM
Production & Inventory
Co. in the format
Textbook via Copyright
Clearance Center.

Group A	Extraversion (E)	Is comfortable with people and things; expresses emotions easily, and is friendly, talkative, and easy to know.
	Introversion (I)	Is comfortable with ideas and thoughts; does not express emotions easily and is reserved, quiet, and hard to know.
Group B	Sensing (S)	Uses the five senses to become aware of things, likes precise and routine work, is not comfortable with solving new problems, and takes pleasure in the current moment.
	Intuitive (N)	Uses unconscious ideas or associations to become aware of things and likes solving problems, planning for the future, and forging ahead in new areas.
Group C	Thinking (T)	Uses logic, makes decisions based on facts, likes to analyze and organize, doesn't like to confront or express emotions, and is skeptical when approaching problems.
	Feeling (F)	Likes relationships to work well, enjoys people, is sensitive to others, makes decisions based on values and impact upon people, and is trusting when approaching problems.
Group D	Judging (J)	Is orderly and organized, likes to finish tasks, likes to make quick decisions, and likes to make plans.
	Perceiving (P)	Is curious, adapts well to change, likes to start many projects but may have trouble finishing them, and may have difficulty making decisions.

in the competitive intelligence tool kit. Rigby's (1997) study under the auspices of Bain & Company revealed that personality profiling was not among the 25 most popular management tools and techniques that Bain tracks on a regular basis. It ranked as a far less-utilized tool relative to more traditional information around activity-based costing, benchmarking, customer retention, and mass customization, for example. This low utilization creates a gap or blindspot in strategic decision making.

Management personality profiling fills this critical gap. It provides insights about the goals and motivations driving rival decision makers. It is precisely this type of information that provides valuable qualitative insights into what competitors will do. This provides a complementary approach to the more traditional quantitative purview of traditional strategic analysis around the concept of what the competition can do.

Knowledge of the personalities of rival decision makers will offer very valuable competitive intelligence. Specifically, it addresses how the individual's decision-making process is affected under stress. Under normal circumstances, most individuals are flexible when it comes to making decisions. Strategic decisions, however, involve trade-offs that often induce uncertainty, ambiguity, and stress. When under stress, individuals will resort to their primary drivers as dictated by their personality traits. It is this distinction that lies at the heart of personality profiling and is the source of the richest competitive intelligence derived from the application of this analysis. Personality profiling provides the analyst with inferences and clues as to how competitive management makes decisions and, more importantly, what decisions they are likely to make.

STRENGTHS AND ADVANTAGES

The primary benefit of incorporating personality profiling into the firm's analytical tool kit is the cost-effective development of a more complete strategic analysis. Knowledge of personality profiles offers unique insights into competitor strategy that few other analytical tools can provide. As a result, more effective decisions will be made based on a solid prediction of competitive response. Instead of regarding rival firms as faceless entities, personality profiling adds a human dimension to rivals that attunes managers more closely to competitive reality. Personality profiling provides analysis regarding what strategy rivals will probably pursue that nicely complements the firm's disproportionate amount of CI regarding what strategies rivals are capable of pursuing. Profiling offers the practicing firm several sources of competitive advantage including support for successful preemptive industry expansion or internal product development; removal of the common blindspot that often results from not adequately considering the contingent decisions of competitors; and identification of opportunities and threats by virtue of knowing where the decision-making priorities of rival firms lie.

WEAKNESSES AND LIMITATIONS

The primary weakness of personality profiling lies in its potentially invalid assumptions. First, rival executives are assumed to have stable personalities that remain constant over time. In reality, personalities may change as a result of learning. Further, many executives are capable of managing their personalities in order to provide contingent leadership as the situation demands. This chameleon capability introduces several discontinuities into the analysis. The rapid pace of technological change creates one of these discontinuities. This condition challenges the methodology of profiling analysis that attempts to transfer tangible observations about previous behavior into predictions of future action. In a turbulent environment, the past may no longer transmit information about the future if future competitive premises are based on novel paradigms. Additionally, the increasing prevalence of alliances and joint ventures introduces a great deal of complexity. Failure to properly adjust the analysis for the impact of co–decision making between firms or groups of firms may result in incorrect analysis. The decreasing popularity of hierarchical decision structures in favor of empowerment and one time decision teams weakens the predictive capacity of personality profiling analysis. Finally, the existence of irrational decision making is not uncommon in many firms. As such, another discontinuity is introduced into the analysis.

PROCESS FOR APPLYING THE TECHNIQUE

The process of management personality can be divided into three main areas that are pursued in a simultaneous rather than sequential fashion: analyzing backgrounds, analyzing management personality, and environment/culture.

1. Analyzing Backgrounds

A good place to start building a management personality profile of rivals is the background of individual executives. Often, this analysis will offer clues to the person's history of experience and functional expertise that will impinge on future decision making. Some examples of such information include

- *Career History and Positions.* Managers with marketing backgrounds tend to focus more on innovation, differentiation; managers with accounting backgrounds tend to focus on cost control; managers with financial or legal backgrounds tend to emphasize growth through acquisition and merger; managers with scientific or technical backgrounds tend to focus on new product development through internal R&D.
- *Educational Background.* Executives may tend to emphasize the areas in which they specialized during school.
- *Age.* Younger executives tend to be less risk averse than older executives.
- *Length of Tenure (i.e., experience).* New management teams can be more adept at restructuring and turnaround strategies.
- *Internal Development versus Outside Hiring.* Managers hired from outside the firm tend to more aggressively pursue change management.
- *Past Decisions.* Managers who have experienced major failures with certain types of strategies may be hesitant to reemploy them in the future. Alternatively, they are likely to repeat successful strategies.
- *Hobbies, Affiliations, Circle of Social Friends, Social Memberships, Interests.*

Information secured from the above points will serve as a useful backdrop against which to set the analysis of executive behavior and personality in the following section.

2. Analyzing Management Personality

Again using a combination of both secondary and primary information collection, an analyst can obtain the necessary information to undertake a personality assessment. Combining a leader's background, psychological profile and previous actions and inactions can provide analysts with considerable insight into the ways rivals think, operate, process information and lead their organizations.

With the development over time of the MBTI, analysts can now use this tool without direct access to the executives being profiled. It can be managed simply by speaking to a number of primary sources who know and have interacted with that person. Further, analysts can review press interviews and other public speaking forums to see how executives have handled themselves, their use of words to communicate, the ease with which they communicate, and so on. Combined with their background and past actions, what behaviour did they exhibit? The breadth of this technique provides an invaluable insight.

When using the MBTI as a tool, the place to start, however, is understanding in greater depth the four scales and the combination of personalities and temperaments.

Extraverts (E) Versus Introverts (I)

People who prefer extraversion focus on the outer world of people and the external environment. Extraverts usually prefer to communicate more by talking than by writing. Introverts focus more on their own inner world, being comfortable when their work requires a good deal of activity to take place quietly inside their heads. Example of descriptors include

Extraversion	Introversion
Attention focused outward: people, things, action	Attention focused inward: concepts, ideas, feelings
Energized by being with others	Energized by being alone
External	Internal
Breadth	Depth
Interaction	Concentration
Multiple relationships	Close relationships
Sociable	Territorial
Extensive	Intensive
Action	Reflection
Interest in external events	Interest in internal reactions
Easy to know	Hard to know

Sensing (S) Versus Intuition (N)

Information comes to us in two ways, through our five senses and through our intuition. Sensing people consistently prefer to use their five senses when collecting information. They focus on the "what is." Intuitive people look at the big picture, attempting to find meanings, relationships and possibilities. Intuitive types value imagination and inspirations.

Sensing	Intuition
Facts	Meaning
Details	Big picture
Reality	Possibilities
Experience	Hunches
Specifics	Patterns
Here and now	Future
Practical	Ingenious
Literal	Figurative
Concrete	Abstract
Sequential	Random
Perspiration	Inspiration
Down to earth	Head in clouds

Thinking (T) Versus Feeling (F)

There are two different ways of arriving at a decision or conclusion. One is an objective and logical process, the other is a subjective valuing process. *Thinking* is the word used to describe decisions that are impersonal, objective, and logical. They focus on the what of a decision, not on the who. People with a preference for thinking seek an objective standard of truth. Feeling describes decisions that are subjective and are made in terms of values. Decisions are made on the basis of person-centered values. They look at the who in the decision-making process. (Note: The word *feeling*

Thinking	Feeling
Objective	Subjective
Principles	Personal values
Policy	Circumstances
Justice	Mercy
Categorize	Harmonize
Critique	Appreciate
Analyze	Sympathize
Firmness	Persuasion
Logic	Impact on people
Why	Who

here means making decisions based on values; it does *not* refer to your feelings or emotions.)

Judgment (J) Versus Perception (P)

This scale relates to the way we deal with our external world. Those with a judging attitude want to live in a planned, orderly way, wanting to regulate life and control it. They prefer a lifestyle that is organized, where they can settle things and make plans and follow them through. Those who prefer a perceptive process like to live in a flexible, spontaneous way, often "going with the flow." They want to understand things and be open to take advantage of things as they come up. (Note: Judgment here does not mean judgmental—any of the types can be judgmental.)

By identifying and combining each preference in each of the scales above, analysts can identify specific profiles—each one providing a brief picture in our attempt to understand observable human behavior. A brief summary of MBTI profiles is provided in Table 15-1.

Judgment	Perception
Closure	Options
Decided	Open minded
Plan ahead	Adapt as you go
Scheduled	Spontaneous
Planned	Open ended
Settled	Pending
Fixed	Flexible
Completed	Emergent
Punctual	Leisurely
Purposeful	Adaptable
Control events	Respond to moment

Another element within the MBTI is the identification of temperament. Behaviors cluster into activity patterns that appear to be organized around core themes or values specific to a temperament. One's temperament is... "given, not acquired: it is the inborn form of the living being" (Keirsey & Bates, 1984, p. 27). Temperament looks at the themes and core values of a personality and its configuration as a whole. These patterns can in fact be observed over and over again. Table 15-2 provides an overview of temperaments with regards to the world of work while Figure 15-2 describes the temperaments or behavior clusters.

The process throughout is that of converting observable information sourced from both primary and secondary sources to identify behavior patterns about how a particular personality operates with regard to the world at large.

By understanding the profile of a competitor's management team and combining it with their personal professional history, an analyst can deliver some predictions as to likely decision-making styles, actions, and the likely success of companywide strategies.

(*Text continued on page 240*)

Table 15-1
Myers Briggs Type Indicator (MBTI) Profiles

INTJ	INFJ	ISTJ	ISTP
Independent, innovative, logical, usually have original minds and great drive for their own ideas and purposes. Introspective, place their trust in logical analysis and intuition to guide their thoughts and decisions. Can organize a job and carry it through with or without help. Skeptical, critical, determined, attracted to theoretical and analytical areas of inquiry.	Intuitive, caring, quiet and peace-loving, succeed by perseverance, originality, and desire to do whatever is needed or wanted. Articulate, empathic, and idealistic. Likely to be honored and followed for their clear convictions as to how best to serve the common good. Enjoy being of service to others.	Quiet, serious, responsible, sensible, patient and steadfast. Achieve success through concentration and thoroughness—decide what needs to be accomplished and work toward it regardless of distrac-tions. Practical, orderly, matter-of-fact. See to it that everything is well organized. Logical, realistic, and dependable.	Factual, sensible, logical and reflective. Curious, practical and often mechanically adept, interested in cause and effect, and how and why things work. Coolly rational, and objective, observe and analyze life with detached curiosity and unexpected flashes of humor. Organize facts using logical principles.

INTP	INFP	ISFJ	ISFP
Private, intellectual, analytical, logical and reflective. Value ideas, principles, abstract thinking and solving problems with logic and analysis. Tend to have clearly defined interests. Independent thinker. Strength lies in patiently and thoroughly working out the fundamental principles of a system, operation, or problem.	Quiet, creative, sensitive and perceptive. Care about learning, ideas, language and independent projects of their own. Capacity for deep caring and commitment to both people and causes they idealize. Behavior guided by strong inner sense of values. Strongly philosophical, spiritual or religious, with little concern for possessions or physical surroundings.	Private, faithful, sensible, conscientious, and sensitive. Work to meet obligations and provide stability to projects or groups. Concerned with how other people feel, considerate and compassionate. Thorough and accurate, interests are not usually technical but rather human related.	Quiet, retiring, practical, sensitive, kind, modest about their abilities. Do not force opinions or values on others, shun disagreements or situations which become unpleasant, confining or demanding. Enjoy the present moment and do not want to spoil it with undue haste or exertion. Usually are often loyal followers.

ENTP	ENFP	ESTJ	ESFP
Enthusiastic, quick, ingenious, outgoing, multitalented. Stimulating company, alert and outspoken. Independent, non-conforming, may argue for fun on either side a of a question. Resourceful in solving new and challenging problems, will retreat from detail work and hum-drum routine. Will seek new interests, one after another.	Open-minded, imaginative, caring and outgoing. Multitalented, able to do almost anything that interests them. Ready to help others. Warmly enthusiastic, high-spirited, ingenious. Often rely on their ability to improvise rather than preparing in advance. Usually find compelling reasons for whatever they want.	Assertive, practical, realistic, matter-of-fact, opinionated. Natural no-nonsense, take-charge approach. Like to organize and run activities. Prefer to enforce existing policies and procedures, and linear channels of communications. Brings others into line, rational, traditional, and conservative. Need to consider others' feelings and points of view.	Warm, cheerful, outgoing, optimistic, easygoing, caring, always ready for a good time. Life, work and relationships should be fun and rewarding. Find remembering facts easier than mastering theories. Charming, clever, and open-minded, are best in situations that need some common sense and practical ability.

(Continued on the following page)

Table 15-1 (*Continued*)

ENTJ	ENFJ	ESFJ	ESTP
Outgoing, frank, logical, decisive. Intuition fuels vision and defines goals. Natural leaders, use their reasoning ability to control. Assertive, analytical and objective. Usually well informed and enjoy learning. May ignore the personal element in accomplishing their purpose. Struggle between creative spontaneity and desire for order.	Sociable, intuitive, sensitive, and organized. Feel real concern for what others think or want and will address matters with due regard for other peoples' feelings. Responsible, tenacious, idealistic. Will honor commitments. Able to present or lead group discussions with ease and tact. Warm personal interactions important.	Warm-hearted, outgoing, sociable, conscientious born cooperators, active committee members. Harmonize, entertain, and nurture others. Traditional, conservative, and loyal, work hard devoting time and energy to family and friends. Work best with encouragement and praise. Main interest is in working with others and organizing people and events.	Adaptable, tolerant, outgoing, practical thinkers—masters of observations and analysis of cause-effect relationships. Good on-the-spot problem solving, free from the biasing influence of tradition and emotion. Resourceful, spontaneous, and team spirited, enjoy whatever comes along.

235

Table 15-2
Temperaments in the World of Work

NAME	VISIONARIES (NT)	CATALYSTS (NF)	TROUBLE-SHOOTER / NEGOTIATOR (SP)	TRADITIONAL / STABILIZERS (SJ)
Look at the world and see:	Possibilities, meanings and relationships.	Possibilities, meanings and relationships.	Facts and realities.	Facts and realities.
And want to:	Examine their consequences analytically, impersonally.	Judge their value to people and for people.	Collect more, manipulate them.	Organize them.
They have a lifelong drive for:	Competence and knowledge.	Meaning, authenticity, identity.	Action, excitement, competition.	Contributing to meaningful social institutions.
And thus they are effective:	As architects of change, as organizational entrepreneurs.	In getting people to work effectively together to achieve organizational goals.	In crisis situations, in pulling "the fat out of the fire," producing results.	As stabilizers of organizations, as maintainers of tradition.
Their strengths include:	Looking ahead, seeing new possibilities. Conceptualizing, designing especially with regard to organizational change. Setting high standards, particularly intellectually. Seeing right to the heart of complex issues or problems. Seeing the large picture, the larger context. Grasping the underlying principles, dynamics, laws. At their best when someone says "it can't be done."	Drawing out the best in people. Working with and through people—participative leadership. Good verbal and listening skills. Being sensitive to the organizational climate. Expressing empathy. Being creative. Getting people to work effectively and harmoniously together. Learning new things, particularly about self and others.	Handling crisis situations. Seeing what's negotiable. Being ingenious and resourceful getting things done. Knowing how to expediate things. Being honest and straightforward — "telling it like it is." Having a practical approach to concrete problems. Being adaptable, flexible. Taking risks.	Being realistic and practical. Being decisive. Paying attention to rules, policies, and regulations. Bringing a planned, organized approach to work. Being dependable, steady workers, good at following through. Being thorough, systematic and precise, especially with details.
Their potential weaknesses:	Do not easily show sensitivity and appreciation to others. Not following through on details—getting bored with routine.	Being too generous in giving of time and self to others. Deciding on the basis of personal likes and dislikes. Giving too much autonomy and freedom.	Disliking, being impatient with the theoretical, the abstract, the conceptual. Being unpredictable. Becoming bored when there are no crises to solve.	Not always being responsive to the need for change. Being a "rule is a rule is a rule/if I made an exception for you I'd have to make an exception for everybody" person.

(Continued on the following page)

236

Table 15-2 *(Continued)*

NAME	VISIONARIES (NT)	CATALYSTS (NF)	TROUBLE-SHOOTER/ NEGOTIATOR (SP)	TRADITIONAL/ STABILIZERS (SJ)
	Can lose people with their fascination for complexity. Elitist. Impatient with those whom they don't see as competent.	Being too easily hurt—personalizing criticism. Placing too much focus on people—not enough on organizational goals. Having trouble "biting the bullet," especially when it may mean hurting people.	Creating crises to have something exciting to do. Producing written documents. Not taking a stand, seeming indecisive. Being impulsive—not looking before they leap.	Deciding things too quickly. Being impatient with delays and complications. Having an excessive concern for crises that may never occur.
Their contributions in a work team include:	Tracking thought processes. Problem solving. Providing theoretical input. Contagious enthusiasm for ideas.	Adding the personal dimension. Selling the organization or cause they believe in. Bringing out the contributions of others.	Making things happen. Spotting practical problems. Negotiating agreements or plans of action.	Focusing on what needs to be done. Focusing on follow through. Focusing on important details.
They like to be appreciated for:	The quality of their ideas and their intellectual competency.	Themselves as people who make important contributions.	The clever way they make things happen or get things done.	Their careful, thorough, accurate work.
They provide:	Idea charisma	People charisma	Crisis charisma	Relief from charisma!
Their motto might be:	"Some men see things as they are and say why, I dream things that never were and say, why not?" Robert F. Kennedy	"This above all: to thine own self be true And it must follow, as night the day, Thou canst not then be false to any man." William Shakespeare, *Hamlet*	"Damn the torpedoes, full speed ahead." David Farragut, Battle of Mobile Bay, 1863"	"Neither rain, nor snow, nor sleet, nor dark of night shall stay the courier from the swift completion of his appointed rounds." Post Office motto

Source: Reprinted by permission of The Human Resources Management Press, Inc.

Figure 15-2
Behavior Clusters

IDEALISTS—INTUITIVE FEELING

(NF—includes ENFJ, INFJ, ENFP, and INFP)

The Idealists want to be authentic, benevolent, and empathic. They search for identity, meaning, and significance. In fact, life is one constant search for identity. They are relationship oriented and they must have meaningful relationships for their life to be worth living. They devote a lot of time to nurturing those relationships. They tend to be romantic and idealistic and want to make the world a better place. They are future oriented. NFs trust their intuition, their imagination, and their fantasy. These are as real and significant to them as an actual tree or a chair. Their focus tends to be on developing potential, fostering and facilitating growth through coaching, teaching, counseling, and communicating. They will add these dimensions to whatever job they hold. If a job description does not call for these inclinations, they will do these things on their own, often providing a greater value to the organization by virtue of greasing the wheels and diffusing tension than the contribution they make doing their prescribed job. Generally, they are enthusiastic, especially about the ideas or causes that interest them. Their natural thinking style is one of integrating and seeing similarities. They look for universal principles and usually hold a global view. NFs are usually gifted in the use of language, both oral and written. Metaphors abound in their language and they use this gift to bridge different perspectives and create harmony. Idealists are usually diplomatic; they put their many people and communication talents to work in the service of their ideals and morale.

RATIONALS—INTUITIVE THINKING

(NT—includes ENTJ, INTJ, ENTP, and INTP)

The Rationals seek knowledge, competence, and achievement. They strive to understand what makes the world run and people tick. Rationals are fascinated by and drawn to theories. Everything is conditional and relative to the context in which it is found or expressed. Like the Idealists, they are future oriented. They trust logic and reason. Everything must be logical and proceed from carefully defined premises. Rationals want to have a rationale for everything and are natural skeptics. They think in terms of differences, delineating categories, definitions, structures, and functions. If their job is too routine, they formulate hypotheses and theories to make it interesting. They hunger for precision, especially in thought and language. Long-range planning, inventing, designing, and defining are their areas of strength and they bring these gifts to any job, even if these qualities are not called for. Their mood is generally calm and they prefer a peaceful environment. They foster individualism rather than conformity. Frequently, they gravitate toward technology and the sciences and are well suited for engineering and devising strategy.

(Continued on following page)

Figure 15-2 *(Continued)*

GUARDIANS—SENSING JUDGING

(SJ—includes ESTJ, ISTJ, ESFJ, and ISFJ)

The Guardians want to belong, to have membership in whatever group is theirs. They hunger for responsibility and accountability. Frequently, they take on too much responsibility and become overworked. They expect others to work hard and be accountable. They favor generosity, service, and duty. They establish and maintain institutions and standard operating procedures. SJs want to preserve the world and protect their charges, so they stand guard, so to speak. They can be found to fire warnings when someone or something is going off course or varying too much from the prescribed norm. They look to the past and tradition for security and standards. Frequently, they foster enculturation with ceremonies, rules, and rituals. Guardians trust contracts and authority and distrust chance. They want security and stability. SJs think in terms of convention, association, and discrete elements, and thus emphasize memory and drill as paths to mastery. Generally, they are serious and concerned, with a fatalistic stance. Guardians are skilled at ensuring that things and people are in the right place, in the right amounts, the right quality, and at the right time. Frequently, they gravitate toward business and commerce, especially in the areas where safekeeping and logistics are required.

ARTISANS—SENSING PERCEIVING

(SP—includes ESTP, ISTP, ESFP, and ISFP)

Artisans want the freedom to choose the next act. They must experience and act on impulses. They want to be graceful, bold and impressive and to have impact on their audience. They are generally excited and optimistic, expecting luck to be on their side. SPs may become so absorbed in the action of the moment that they lose sight of distant goals. However, they see opportunities that others miss (which they seize if at all possible). Artisans are oriented toward the present and they seek adventure and experiences. They hunger for spontaneity. SPs trust their impulses, luck, and their ability to solve any problem they run into. Thus, they frequently rush in when others hold back with fear and hesitation. Artisans are natural negotiators and enjoy getting others to concede even some small part. They think in terms of variation, thus the name Artisan. The capacity for producing variations on a theme shows up in all that they do, not just in the limited sense of arts and crafts. No matter what their job, they will find some way to vary it. They have a keen ability to notice and describe detail. They like the freedom to move, festivities, and games. They are gifted tacticians, figuring out the best move to make at the instant. Artisans do the expedient thing, not the acceptable, friendly, or logical thing. Frequently they are drawn to the manual, visual, and performing arts as well as entrepreneurial aspects of business.

Source: Adapted from "Working Together," by O. Isachsen and L. V. Berens, 1988, San Juan Capestrano CA, Institute for Management Development, pp. 48–51.

Other models have been developed to assist in structuring this area of strategic analysis. Another useful model, the Personality and Organizational Impact Model, developed by Barndt (1994) leverages several models developed in the field of psychology. The value of Barndt's tool lies in its applicability to the task of strategic analysis.

Essentially, this process involves manipulating observable information into psychological inferences based on the fact that human personalities and behavior usually remain stable over time. The model acts like a "black box" that translates observable information into actionable intelligence about the values, goals, risk aversion, and many other relevant aspects of personality that will impinge on the future strategic decisions made by executives at rival firms. It is a valuable mechanism to convert tangible information about a rival decision maker's actions and behavior into intangible information about how his or her mind really works.

The second main benefit of the personality and organizational impact model is its relative simplicity. Anyone who has taken a course in psychology knows that the purview of that discipline is immense, encompassing all facets of life and human behavior. This broad scope results in models that are cumbersome, complex, and burdened with too much detail for practical application to management profiling. Brandt's model has cut through the clutter by reducing the analysis to only three operational styles and three psychological adaptations impacting nine core behavior patterns. With these 12 components, the analyst will be well equipped with the adequate methodology required to conduct a management personality profile.

As shown in Table 15-3, in the center of the model are nine separate behavior patterns called cores: supporter, performer, follower idealist, organizer, controller, independent, leader/aid, and rule keeper. Running across the top of the nine-cell matrix of cores are three adaptations: right brain, balanced and left brain. Running down the left side of the nine-cell matrix of cores are three styles: polyactive, proactive, and reactive.

The key to applying this model is to understand that the three adaptations and the three styles will impact each of the nine types of behaviors. In Table 15-3, the three cells above the matrix and the three cells on the left margin of the matrix help to define each of the nine behavior patterns inside the matrix. Therefore, knowledge of the adaptations and styles is a necessary precursor to elucidating this model.

Adaptations

- *Left*. Adaptations referenced to the left side of brain functionality center on intellectualizing, logic seeking, analyzing, and thinking. Thinkers tend to engage in cerebral deliberation before deciding to act and often appear aloof and emotionally detached.
- *Right*. Adaptations referenced to the right side of brain functionality center on responsiveness, emotions, expression, reaction, and feeling. Feelers tend to react spontaneously to circumstances and analyze their decisions later.
- *Balanced*. Adaptations referenced to an equal combination of both right and left brain functionality.

Table 15-3
Extended
Framework of the
Personality and
Organizational
Impact Model

ADAPTATIONS →	RIGHT	BALANCED	LEFT
	INTERACTIVE	ORGANIZATIONAL	INDIVIDUALISTIC
↓	Emotional	Determined	Intellectualizing
	Expressive	Committed	Deliberate
	Spontaneous	Entrepreneurial	Insulated
STYLES	Feeling		Detached
Outer-Directed			
Idealistic, dedicated			
Mission oriented			
Conscientious			
Planners, Givers	Supporter	Idealist	Independent
Build for future			
"Be prepared"			
Can panic if overextended			
Inner-Directed			
Self-focused			
Independent			
Individualistic	Performer	Organizer	Leader/Aid
Self-serving			
Complacent			
Live now/takers			
"Project" stress			
Outer-Directed (Controlled)			
Controlling/need for control	Follower	Controller	Rule Keeper
Overwhelmed			
Passive (inhibiting)			
Can be precipitous or			
immobilized by stress			

Source: Barndt, W. D. Jr. *User-Directed Competitive Intelligence: Closing the Gap Between Supply and Demand,* 1994, Westport, CT: Quorum Books.

Styles

• *Proactive or Inner-Directed.* People who are incessant planners, predisposed to making lists in order to effectively cope with the challenges of life. Proactives tend to be optimistic about their realm of influence but often become overwhelmed in times of crisis.

• *Polyactive or Outer-Directed.* People who can manage several different activities or mental processes simultaneously. Multitasking comes naturally to them so they are often very self-confident, can manage stress very well, and are able to balance many different demands on their time. Polyactives are very self-directed and can easily persuade others to share their interests through delegation—the qualities of born leaders.

• *Reactive or Outer-Directed (Controlled).* People who are often fatalistic if not pessimistic about their personal influence. Reactives tend to view any attempts to plan or influence as hopeless and tend to take events as they come. They depend on rules, regulations, and externally imposed order to control what they essentially view as an unwieldy and hostile environment.

There is one key difference between adaptations and styles. In general, adaptations refer to the differences between the functionality of the right and left hemispheres of the brain. In contrast, styles refer to how well the individual's right and left hemispheric functions can integrate with each other.

Behaviors

The impact of each adaptation and style can be used to define each of the nine behavior patterns.

SUPPORTERS

• *Impact of Right-Brain Adaptation*. When push comes to shove, supporters will ascribe primary importance to relationships as opposed to tradition, rules, or regulations. Decisions will tend to be spontaneous and predicated on feelings and reactions. Analysis is usually conducted after the decision is made. Supporters will tend to provide for everyone's needs but will not relinquish individual responsibility through delegation. They become too wrapped up in tactical and interpersonal issues at the expense of attending to broader strategic decisions. Subjective bias often clouds their judgment.

• *Impact of Proactive/Outer-Directed Style*. Supporters are, by nature, nurturing individuals who require recognition and appreciation in return for their selflessness. Leadership roles, however, often are isolated environments that don't provide adequate amounts of positive feedback that supporters crave. As a result, supporters can become uncertain and indecisive.

PERFORMERS

• *Impact of Right-Brain Adaptation*. Concern for others by supporters is essentially selfish. When push comes to shove, performers will put their own needs and goals ahead of those of their firm.

• *Impact of Polyactive/Inner-Directed Style*. To secure recognition and credit for their efforts in order to increase their importance, performers often exhibit very expressive and theatrical behavior. It is this behavior that results in a large, influential presence wherever they are, reinforcing their quest for recognition.

FOLLOWERS

• *Impact of Right-Brain Adaptation*. Manifestation of their tendency to be loyal, committed, and self-sacrificing requires structure sharply defined through rules, traditional culture, or external leadership from others. In the absence of these precipitating conditions, followers in positions of leadership will become uncertain and indecisive. Occasionally, driven by their need to establish structure, they will act out of character and be impulsive or precipitous.

- *Impact of Reactive/Outer-Directed (Controlled).* Followers need rules, procedures, and external leadership in order to function well. Without these conditions, they will have trouble defining and achieving the firm's goals and purposes. Rather, they regard success as meeting the wishes of their leaders and organizational routine. In positions of leadership themselves, they become heavily dependent on their close circle of advisers and support staff. Without effective advisers, followers become indecisive because of their inability to internally generate goals and objectives.

IDEALISTS

- *Impact of Balanced Adaptation.* Idealists have a strong affinity to a core set of values and ideals. They view the firms and organizations to which they belong as embracing those ideals. Hence, this happy balance makes their actions consistent with the goals of the firm. In addition, they are generally quite optimistic and encouraging.

- *Impact of Proactive/Outer-Directed Style.* Due to their close affinity to the goals of the firm, idealists will easily sacrifice short-term objectives in the pursuit of longer-term organizational goals.

ORGANIZERS

- *Impact of Balanced Adaptation.* Organizers view their firms as part of themselves and view themselves as part of the firm. As such, they tend to be very entrepreneurial as they seek to make the firm the best that it can be and, by extension, bolster their own self-image. Often, organizers are predisposed to empire building and are generally very energetic, determined, and hard-nosed.

- *Impact of Polyactive/Inner-Directed Style.* The organizers' entrepreneurial zest gives them a need for growth. Because the firm is viewed as an extension of themselves, they equate business growth with personal growth. In order to support growth, they are quite willing to assume risk. Organizers will readily delegate so that they can pursue more growth. Further, they are not afraid to fire personnel unfit for the mantle of delegated responsibility if those personnel fail to maintain the firm's progress.

CONTROLLERS

- *Impact of Balanced Adaptation.* Controllers feel a need to control every aspect of their firms. Their pessimistic outlook motivates them to dominate the firm in an attempt to prevent what their fatalism perceives as entropy from destroying the firm. Their predisposition to control and resistance to delegation often stifles innovation, risk, and growth.

- *Impact of Reactive/Outer-Directed (Controlled) Style.* Firms led by controllers are often inhibited from achieving real potential by a strict, rule-oriented and procedurally based organizational culture.

INDEPENDENTS

• *Impact of Left-Brain Adaptation.* Independents tend to be technocrats whose primary interest is their own area of expertise. As such, they tend to ignore the broader strategies of their firms outside of their purview of skill or experience. Often, executives of scientifically oriented firms such as biotech, pharmaceutical, computer, or engineering firms are led by "independents."

• *Impact of Proactive/Outer-Directed Style.* Often, independents will focus their strategies only on their particular area of expertise. Growth strategies or innovation foci can usually be predicted with a fair degree of accuracy for firms led by independents. Further, independents tend to relate only to those who share similar interests or possess similar skills.

LEADER/AIDES

• *Impact of Left-Brain Adaptation.* As opposed to independents, leader/aides tend to have much broader aspirations for leadership. Their quest for leadership, however, is related to personal power and influence, as opposed to pursuing their area of expertise. In general, they are quite mercenary and can easily transplant both their loyalty and commitment.

• *Impact of Polyactive/Inner-Directed Style.* Leader/aides prefer to occupy positions of leadership but will settle for positions that allow them to exert a large influence on those who wield power. Much of their attraction to power is self-centered.

RULE KEEPERS

• *Impact of Left-Brain Adaptation.* Rule keepers are more interested in enforcing rules than in devising them. They prefer to work as specialists within well-defined structure. As such, in positions of leadership they often exhibit a lack of imagination or breadth of focus and become obsessed with detail.

• *Impact of Reactive/Outer-Directed (Controlled) Style.* Often promoted to functional leadership, rule keepers are very effective at establishing order. However, in positions of broad leadership, they tend to become very controlling, leading to risk averse strategies that seek to protect existing businesses rather than pursue growth through innovation.

The nine-cell matrix can now be filled out with fairly precise definitions of these management personalities as depicted in the dynamics model and dynamics table in Figure 15-3 and Table 15-4. Combining information from the background analysis as well as from observed behavior will allow the analyst to develop reasonably accurate profiles of targeted executives. From this initial classification, this framework can then be used to make inferences about strategic decisions that competitive decision makers may make in the future.

3. Environment/Culture

While everyone knows that organizations differ in size, structure, and purpose, they also differ in character. Organizational character varies greatly and subtly as

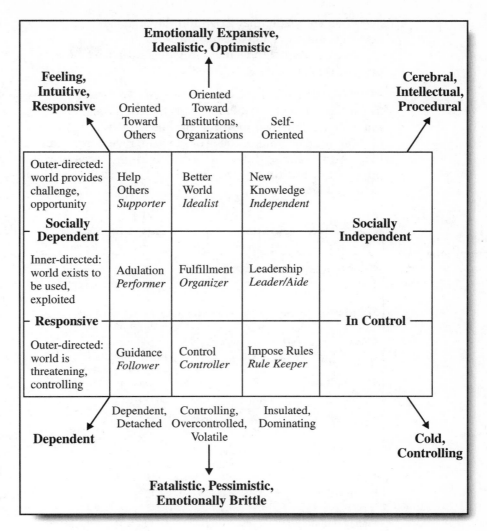

Figure 15-3
Dynamics Model

Source: User-Directed Competitive Intelligence: Closing the Gap Between Supply and Demand, by W. D. Brandt Jr., 1994, Westport, CT: Quorum Books.

well as by departments and subdivisions. Innovative work by William Bridges in 1992 identified organizational types or groups along the 16 MBTI profiles. Using the same processes identified previously, analysts can also identify the organizational character. While it is interesting to note that the organization's character is largely set by its leader or founder, the organization's ability to react or enact strategies will be defined by its character and provides insight for analysts about an organization's resistance or acceptance of particular strategic and tactical behaviors.

Although the personality of the CEO will be of paramount importance to the analysis, it is also worthwhile not only to develop profiles of the executive suite, functional managers, and SBU executives but also to review the framework in which decisions are made, that is, within the organization's character. Generally, strategic decisions are not made in isolation.

Two additional tools may provide assistance in analyzing the impact of the corporate decision-making culture that exists at rival firms (Ball, 1987).

- *Comparison Chart of Executive's Support for Strategic Issues.* This tool superimposes the background and personality profiles of targeted rival decision makers to determine their relative support for various key strategic issues. Often this will provide hints about the strategic focus of the firm, revealing potential threats to the analyst's firm. Additionally, this chart may highlight areas of relative neglect, signifying potential opportunities for the analyst's firm. Figure 15-4 depicts a hypothetical example of such a chart.

Table 15-4
Dynamics Table

	SUPPORTER	IDEALIST	INDEPENDENT
General Style	Supportive	Idealistic	Dedicated, committed
Focus	Other people	Core values, goals	Parochial: "Community of interest"
Priorities	People, service	Preserve values, improve institutions	"Push" special goals
Management Style	Supportive, "Happy ship"	Supportive, encouraging, calculated risk	Aggressive, narrow
Vulnerability	Overinvolvement	Disillusionment	Narrow perspective
	PERFORMER	ORGANIZER	LEADER/AIDE
General Style	Dramatic, self promoting	Optimistic, challenging	Aggressive, dominating
Focus	Own needs, recognition	Organization, resources, personnel	Leadership, influence, advancement
Priorities	Personal acclaim	Growth	Take charge, exert influence
Management Style	Press own interests	Encourage, challenge, delegate; "fair"	Aggressive, self-confident
Vulnerability	Ignore broad obligations	Overextend resources, underassess risks	Exceed mission, overreach
	FOLLOWER	CONTROLLER	RULE KEEPER
General Style	Get along	Fearful, mistrustful	Controlling, enforcing
Focus	Do the job	Maintain control	Procedures, rules
Priorities	Narrow	Avoid risk and chaos	Impose rules
Management Style	Limited vision, indecisive	Controlling, inhibiting	Petty, narrow
Vulnerability	Immobilized, miss opportunity	Strangle innovation, impede growth	Inhibit creativity, ignore broader needs

Source: User-Directed Competitive Intelligence: Closing the Gap Between Supply and Demand, by W. D. Brandt Jr., 1994, Westport, CT: Quorum Books.

Figure 15-4
Comparison Chart of Executives' Support for Strategic Issues

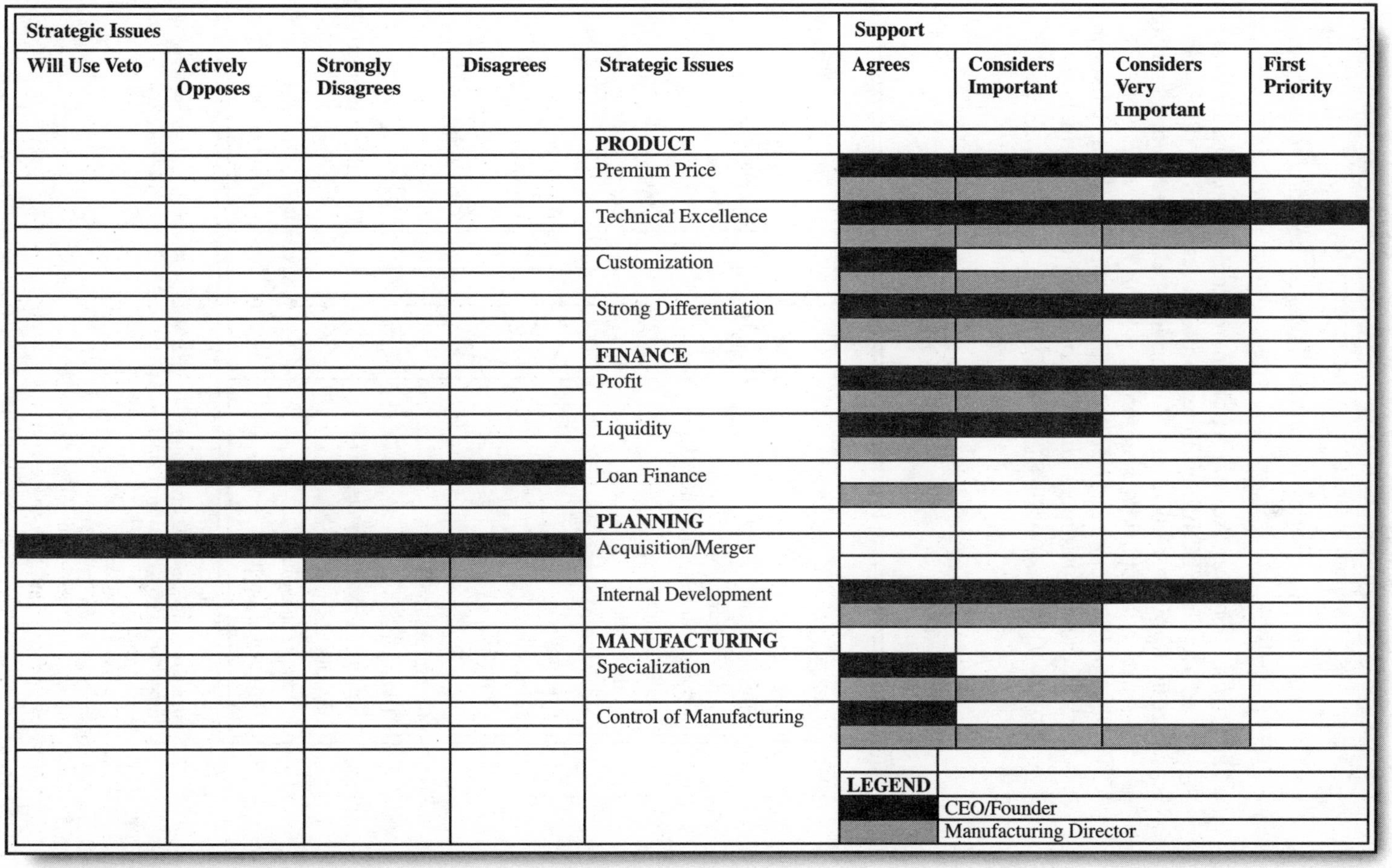

Strategic Issues	Will Use Veto	Actively Opposes	Strongly Disagrees	Disagrees	Strategic Issues	Agrees	Considers Important	Considers Very Important	First Priority
					PRODUCT				
					Premium Price			■	
					Technical Excellence		▨		■
				▨	Customization	■			
					Strong Differentiation	▨	■		
					FINANCE				
					Profit	▨	■		
					Liquidity	▨	■		
	■	■			Loan Finance	▨			
					PLANNING				
	■	■	▨		Acquisition/Merger				
					Internal Development	■	▨		
					MANUFACTURING				
					Specialization	■	▨		
					Control of Manufacturing	■	▨		

LEGEND: ■ CEO/Founder, ▨ Manufacturing Director

Source: Reprinted from Long Range Planning, Vol. 20, No. 2, R. Ball, "Assessing Your Competitor's People and Organization," pages 32–41, Copyright 1987, with permission of Elsevir Science.

- *Cultural Profile.* Compiling the cultural profile of a rival firm will help to determine the latitude individual decision makers have to make strategic decisions. Figure 15-5 shows how such a profile may be constructed.

Sources of information for all the stages of the management personality profiling process include:

- *Published Sources.* Annual report (management, discussion and analysis, chairman's letter), SEC filings, biographies, career history directories and indexes, press clippings, radio and TV interviews, database searches, consultant reports, security analyst briefs, academic cases, and the Internet.
- *Non-published Sources.* Industry experts, suppliers, journalists, industry trade associations, customers, distribution channels, personnel department gossip, and marketing and sales personnel.

Figure 15-5
Cultural Profile

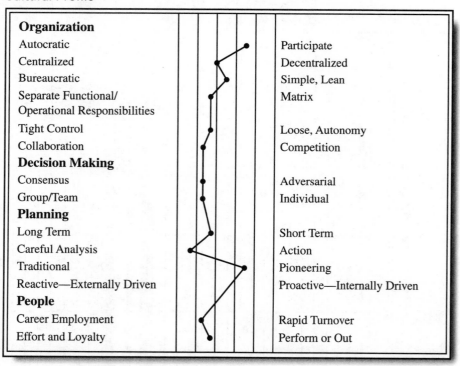

Source: Reprinted from Long Range Planning, Vol. 20, No. 2, R. Ball, "Assessing Your Competitor's People and Organization," pages 32–41, Copyright 1987, with permission of Elsevir Science.

In one of the pioneering articles exploring the impact that personal values can have on strategic decision making, the authors analyzed the values of several companies using Spranger's framework.

NATIONAL DUPLICATING PRODUCTS (NDP)

NDP was a small manufacturer of office equipment. The primary core values of its management in order of priority were found to be social followed by aesthetic value. The importance of social values translated into several tangible effects on strategy. The firm's current strategy reflects many of these values:

- slow to moderate growth
- emphasis on a single product
- an independent agent form of sales organization
- very high-quality products with aesthetic appeal
- refusal to compete on a price basis

The personal values of the president were paramount, as he owned the majority of stock. As such, the president refused to implement any productivity standards or growth strategies for fear of alienating his staff. His concern for their welfare superceded any economic ramifications. Another manifestation of both the president's social and aesthetic values were the elaborate facilities built primarily for the enjoyment of his staff.

ACOUSTIC RESEARCH INC.

High on the values priority list for management at Acoustic, a manufacturer of loudspeakers, were theoretical and social values. Again, these values were plainly evident in the firm's strategy:

- scientific truth and integrity in advertising
- lower margins to dealers than competitors were paying
- maintenance of "truth and honesty" in relation to suppliers, dealers, and employees
- high-quality at the lowest possible price to the consumer

Despite appeals by many members in the firm's value chain to expand sales in a growth market, Acoustic refused, as this would jeopardize product quality, value pricing, and truthful advertising. Indirectly, all of these impacts would have contradicted its theoretical and social values.

SOURCE: Adapted from "Personal values and Corporate Strategy, by W. D. Guth and R. Tagiuri, 1965, *Harvard Business Review,* 1965, 43(5), pp. 123–132.

FAROUT SUMMARY

	1	2	3	4	5
F	■	■	■	■	
A	■	■			
R	■	■	■	■	■
O	■	■			
U	■	■			
T	■	■			

Future orientation Medium to high. By definition, the purpose of profiling is to predict future decision-making behavior. However, profiling is based on the assumption that personalities are basically fixed and that past behavior is a good indication of future action. To the extent that both of these concessions are absent, the tool becomes less future oriented. Additionally, profiling does not handle discontinuity very well.

Accuracy Low to medium. The initial classification of personality traits is highly subjective and drives all downstream analysis. If this stage is done incorrectly, the analysis will not be accurate.

Resource efficiency High. Many of the inputs are readily available from publicly accessible materials, interviews, and cursory CI techniques.

Objectivity Medium. It should be noted that personal bias is introduced because the analysis is based on a psychological theory requiring testing of the individual under observation.

The process of transferring observable actions and behaviors into intangible and unobservable personality traits may be based on subjective judgment.

Usefulness High. Understanding the underlying psychology of rival decision makers is extremely useful, especially in ambiguous contexts. It is a unique tool in that it fills an analytical void left by most other tools and techniques.

Timeliness Low to medium. A profile based on recent information can be done very quickly. More extended profiles that reach back farther into a target background requires significant amounts of time because it is a composite of many different sources of information over long time periods.

RELATED TOOLS AND TECHNIQUES

- blindspot analysis
- competitor profiling
- industry structure analysis
- scenario analysis
- SWOT analysis

REFERENCES

Ball, R., (1987). "Assessing your competitor's people and organization." *Long Range Planning, 20*(2), 32–41.

Barndt, W. D. Jr. (1991). "Profiling rival decision makers." *The Journal of Business Strategy, 12*(1), 8–11.

Barndt, W. D. Jr. (1994). *User-directed competitive intelligence: Closing the gap between supply and demand.* Westport, CT: Quorum Books.

Bridges, W. (1992). *The character of organizations.* Palo Alto, CA: Davies-Black Publishing.

Briggs Myers, I. (1991). "Introduction to Type". Palo Alto, CA: Consulting Psychologists Press, Inc.

Brownsword, A. W. (1988). "Psychological Type: An Introduction", Human Resources Management Press, Inc. San Anselmo, California.

Giovannoni, L. C., Berens, L. V., & Cooper, S. A. (1990). "Introduction to Temperament." Huntington Beach, CA: Telcos Publications.

Guth, W. D., & Tagiuri, R. (1965). "Personal values and corporate strategy." *Harvard Business Review, 43*(5), 123–132.

Hirsh, S. K., & Kummerow, J. M. (1990). "Introduction to Type in Organisations—Individual Interpretative Guide," 2nd ed. Palo Alto, CA: Consulting Psychologists Press, Inc.

Isachsen, O., & Berens, L. V. (1988). "Working Together" San Juan Capistrano, CA: Institute for Management Development.

Keirsey, D., & Bates, M. (1984). "Please Understand Me—Character & Temperament Types." Del Mar, CA: Prometheus Nemesis Book Company.

Krumiede, D. W., Sheu, C., & Lavelle, J. (1998). "Understanding the relationship of top management personality to TQM implementation." *Production and Inventory Management Journal, 39*(2), 6–10.

Myers, K. D., & Kirby, L. K. (1994). "Introduction to type® dynamics and development—Exploring the next level of type." Palo Alto, CA: Consulting Psychologists Press, Inc.

Poirer, C. A. (1993). "Personality intelligence: Anticipating your competitor's next move." *Manage, 44*(4), 22–24.

Rigby, D. (1997). *Management tools and techniques: An executive's guide.* Boston, MA: Bain and Company.

Spranger, E. (1928). *Types of men.* Halle, Germany: Niemeyer.

Chapter 16

Issue Analysis

SHORT DESCRIPTION

Issue analysis helps strategic and competitive intelligence efforts by giving managers insights that enable their organizations to better anticipate changes in their external environment and to become a more active or proactive participant in shaping its external environment by influencing public policy developments.

BACKGROUND

Most strategic management prescriptions suggest that a firm must carefully monitor its social and political (i.e., sociopolitical) environments for opportunities and threats. These opportunities and threats often take the form of strategic issues. Heath (1997, p. 84) defines an issue as a "contestable point, a difference of opinion regarding fact, value or policy the resolution of which has consequences for the organization's strategic plan." Dutton and Ashford (1993) state that an issue becomes strategic when top management believes that it has relevance for organizational performance. Another common way of viewing a strategic issue is a difference (or gap) of beliefs, facts, or values between a company and stakeholders that could significantly impact the organization's performance; that the organization must respond to in an orderly and timely fashion; and over which the organization may reasonably expect to exert some influence.

Issues arise from the convergence of trends and events. A trend is the trajectory an issue takes because of the discussion it receives and the sociopolitical forces that impinge on it (Heath, 1997, p. 84). This convergence usually manifests itself in one of the following ways:

1. *Unfavorable Current Policies.* Groups develop issues in order to change policies believed to be unfavorable to their interests. The pharmaceutical industry has seen several battles fought over these issues between the ethical and generic manufacturers.

2. *Unanticipated Events.* People often become interested in an issue because of events they had not expected, such as tanker oil spills, the possible linkage by

researchers of products such as asbestos or silicon to health ailments, or train or truck accidents that lead to tighter governmental restrictions on goods transport.

3. *Public Interest Causes.* Some groups and individuals promote interests that they think are in the broader public interest, such as environmental clean-up, smoking restrictions in public places, or the reduction of unemployment in the inner-city.

4. *Developments Abroad.* Issues often float onto national agendas because they loom large in other countries. They become more important because of increasing activity on trade conditions negotiated within and between trade blocs (e.g., NAFTA or APEC) or by larger trade organizations such as the World Trade Organization.

5. *Political Entrepreneurialism.* Politicians and political parties frequently introduce issues into the public agenda as a means for getting electoral attention and votes.

Issue analysis remains a widely utilized technique in most large organizations—particularly in industry and trade associations—that have strategic exposure to trends and events occurring in the social and political environment surrounding their firms. The technique is used heavily within organizational areas dealing with external policy such as community relations, government relations, and public affairs. It is not used as frequently within competitive intelligence functions, although competitive and strategy analysts should have this helpful technique within their analytic toolboxes.

STRATEGIC RATIONALE AND IMPLICATIONS

Some business leaders and academics believe that the very survival of business and the business system is at stake and that business must develop better and more constructive responses to public issues (Buchholz, 1995). Many observers have believed that most business organizations have done a less-than-adequate job at responding to STEEP factors (see Chapter 17) through the years and that business has lost some credibility in its ability to address its stakeholders. If this observation is true, it should mean that there are competitive advantages to be gained by some organizations that can effectively address public issues.

Issue analysis is an important technique in the arsenal of the competitive and strategy analyst because it helps companies position themselves to deal with change. It seeks to help decision makers know what facts, premises, and values key stakeholders or the public use and what conclusions they draw from them (Heath, 1997). Opinions of key stakeholders can affect corporate decisions related to consumer protection, environmental protection, financing options, health and safety, marketing, operating standards, product packaging and placement, and site location, among others.

Even though many firms recognize the importance of public policy (hereafter referred to as PP) decisions, a varied range of attitudes and opinions exist about the importance of systematic intelligence efforts for actually gathering, analyzing, and using PP information. For many firms, these considerations have a major impact on performance. Nevertheless, the empirical evidence generated by broad-based surveys in the CI literature has not provided a strong indication of an active management of the organization–public policy interface (Prescott & Bhardwaj, 1995; Prescott & Fleisher, 1991; Prescott & Gibbons, 1991; Stanat, 1993). Only infrequently does one find more than passing mention to PP issues in the mainstream strategy or CI literature as taught in universities or found in the texts on bookstore shelves (Goldsmith, 1996).

Broadly speaking, issue analysis and issue management are a subset of the larger process of public policy competitive intelligence (PPCI). PPCI provides early warning of threats and opportunities emerging from the global public policy environment that affects the achievement of a company's strategy (Fleisher, 1999). PPCI can be used in a variety of decision-making areas, including

- Engaging in actions to create, change or defeat legislation or regulation— examples include enabling Sunday retail sales, modifying tariff regimes, and compliance scheduling timetables.

- Changing operating standards to adapt to evolving PP—several media companies now broadcast violent or sexually explicit shows only in late hours.

- Altering employee performance criteria/procedures or labor practices to adapt to PP issues—examples include providing benefits to same-sex couples, not using underage contract employees in less-developed countries, and providing equal opportunity to employment or advancement regardless of one's demographic background.

- Changing the organizational mission or taking a leadership role in PP issues— a prime example is what chemical companies did with their Responsible Care initiative, voluntarily phasing out controversial practices ahead of legal standard setting such as dolphin-free tuna.

- Taking a public communication stance on key policy issues—several large Internet firms have been vocally addressing privacy and free speech issues.

- Changing vendors/suppliers as a result of PP—U.S. retailer Wal-Mart established a preference policy of purchasing from U.S. suppliers when it could be done competitively.

- Entering or exiting product or service lines to adapt to PP issues and standards of liability or public expectations—examples include the refusals by Internet service providers to host so-called "hate sites," former defense-related companies moving into commercial areas related to their former contracts, and the sale of products banned in one country to others where the bans were not similarly legislated (Heath, 1997).

Issue analysis is also part of the larger issue management process. According to Weller (1982, p. 4) issue management is "...a strategic management and planning process... its central focus is identifying current or emerging issues and trends that will affect organizational goals, developing and analyzing information on these issues and trends, and undertaking intelligent management strategies in response to these identified issues and their anticipated impacts." Bartha (1990) says it is the application of the tools of strategic management to the conduct of corporate external relations. Like many of the other environmental analysis methods reviewed in this book, it is based on the familiar saying, "To be forewarned is to be forearmed." Bartha (1990, p. 7) put it in perspective when he suggested: "By systematically following and evaluating information about events, players and relationships in the company's public environment, managers can learn to recognize in today's [STEEP] pressures the harbingers of tomorrow's government policies."

The strategic purpose of issue analysis is to assist decision makers in identifying, monitoring, and selecting issues for organizational action. Many environmental developments can impact the organization's bottom line and competitiveness. Organizations cannot and should not be responding to every issue that exists in their broader environment. Also, issue analysis helps strategic decision makers avoid surprises that emanate from change in the STEEP environments, and also helps organizations to better address STEEP issues, regardless of whether they are opportunities or threats.

Many issues could have adverse or favorable consequences for the organization, but no organization has the resources in place to respond to every issue that it confronts. Some issues are likely to produce better or worse consequences for the organization in terms of the resources expended to see a favorable outcome versus the value of the outcome itself. Therefore, it is always important that analysts help decision makers understand those issues in which an organizational response can have the greatest expected benefits-to-costs ratio. These calculations also have to be made under a cloud of uncertainty that makes these analyses and calculations difficult for the uninitiated. This uncertainty can be a major factor in tilting the balance of competition within or across industries and makes the need to analyze issues more acute.

STRENGTHS AND ADVANTAGES

Issue analysis is not meant to be a static process. It can offer several advantages to increase the competitiveness of companies that can effectively utilize the process:

1. It injects research performed on the public policy and STEEP environments into the strategic decision-making process. It gives management an advantage in selecting the highest impact issues that the organization should respond to as opposed to getting distracted by lower impact issues.

2. It allows for the early identification of emerging issues in order to provide additional lead time to help coordinate both internal organizational and external environmental responses. It allows for management of instead of reaction to issues.

3. The active monitoring and addressing of issues can allow the organization the chance to deflect issues before they become major problems and the ability to transform emerging trends into corporate opportunities. In other words, it can allow the organization to accommodate change with minimal disruption.

4. It provides for a corporatewide process for anticipating and dealing with STEEP-emanating issues. This allows the organization to be in tune with societal expectations and avoid serious public mistakes that could harm its credibility with critical stakeholders.

5. It can reduce the perceived levels of risk or uncertainty felt by decision makers in moving corporate initiatives in a changing environment.

WEAKNESSES AND LIMITATIONS

Although issue analysis can be beneficial to organizations in several ways, its applicability and usefulness is constrained by several factors. The most common of these are listed here.

1. Issue analysis is a helpful tool in the arsenal of organizations facing public policy challenges, but it may not always assist organizations in achieving a competitive or strategic advantage.

2. Issue analysis must be done on an ongoing basis. For this to happen, it must be fed by inputs generated out of a regular scanning of the organization's environment. Most firms have great difficulty in doing environmental scanning today due to the overwhelming amount of data available in the environment and difficulties in filtering out the important facets from the unimportant ones.

3. Many issues defy logical or rigorous systematic assessment. This is because many issues contain an emotional or attitudinal factor, often emblazoned through the media's attention, that can make their evolution difficult to predict.

4. There are few yardsticks by which to evaluate the effectiveness or success of the issue analysis process (Fleisher, 1995). This can lead to the underallocation of resources even though many executives recognize that it simply must be done regardless of the unreliability of the results.

5. Many executives do not understand the language and methods associated with doing issue analysis and therefore will be uncomfortable discussing it with analysts (Chase, 1984).

6. The ability to provide for direct correlations between issues and financial or market measures can be tenuous.

PROCESS FOR APPLYING THE TECHNIQUE

The task of issue analysis is to take all the environmental data gathered during scanning and monitoring and to sort it into informational categories, ranking the information, evaluating it according to selected criteria, and drawing conclusions for managerial decisions. Former Imperial Oil public affairs manager Peter Bartha (1982) suggests that there are three tasks that are precursors to issue analysis, including (1) identifying issue categories, (2) identifying their source, and (3) assessing their evolutionary development.

Before an issue can be analyzed, it has to be identified. The techniques listed here are some of the more popular ones for identifying issues:

• *Content Analysis.* In practice, this technique involves scanning communication vehicles such as newspapers, journals, books, articles, newsletters, speeches, and so forth. The approach and the results can be either quantitative or qualitative.

- *Scenario Development.* Scenarios are written descriptions of a variety of plausible, alternative futures based on specified assumptions about relevant environmental forces (frequently categorized as social, technological, economic, ecological, and political—STEEP) and their interactions.

- *Survey Techniques.* The major techniques in this category include public and stakeholder opinion polling, attitudinal surveys, and delphi panels. Delphi panels use a sequence of questionnaires distributed to experts in which the responses to one questionnaire are used to produce the next and successive questionnaires. Any set of information available to some experts and not others is then passed along to the others, which allows each person on the panel to have all of the information available within the panel in producing their forecasts. Delphi panels improve the use of expert opinion through polling based on anonymity, statistical display, and feedback of reasoning.

Stanbury (1993) suggests that the issue analysis process consists of three components: (1) forecasting, (2) assessment, and (3) selection of issues to allow decision makers to determine the nature of potential responses by the organization.

Step 1: Issue Forecasting

In this step, the analyst attempts to anticipate the sequence and nature of development of the issue that the organization monitors. One particularly helpful tool for achieving this is known as the issue life cycle. It is based on the premise that issues tend to evolve through a fairly logical progression from when they first appear on an organization's radar screen until they are no longer prevalent in the firm's environment.

Two caveats should be noted in using the issue life cycle: (1) Issues can be derailed at almost any stage of the life cycle by other issues, as other issues grow in attention, as political or social attention shifts, as media coverage of them declines, or when interest and stakeholder groups take effective actions that either accelerate or impede its progress. (2) The amount of time between issue stages can vary a great deal from country to country, government to government, and issue to issue.

As issues evolve over time, public attention increases until a peak point while managerial discretion steadily decreases. The four common stages that public policy issues progress through include:

1. *Formative.* Developments usually signal structural changes, and give rise to recognition of an issue. It is often difficult to identify the subtle often imperceptible, changes that occur in societal expectations that underlie this stage. It has been suggested by Graham Molitor (1975) that the observation of certain stakeholders can be helpful in identifying expectation shifts, including academics, authors, government-sponsored researchers, media commentators, public crusaders, public policy researchers, and think tanks. It is usually best for an organization to attempt to affect the evolution of an issue at this early stage as it is easiest to set the boundaries and nature of the debate.

2. *Politicization.* This gives rise to the creation of ad hoc or formal organizations that have a significant interest in seeing the issue ultimately resolved. These groups frequently try and get the matter placed on the public policy agenda, whereby items are actively considered by public bodies. Some specific remedies to address the matter will start to make their presence felt in debate. The organization will have decreasing discretion in affecting the evolution of the issue in this stage as compared to the previous one, but can still have an effect if it is willing to take an active role in the shaping of the issue.

3. *Legislative Formalization.* This signals a peak in public attention wherein the issue is defined in more concrete terms (operational, legal), which frequently end up in the form of laws and legislation. These laws are enforceable through governmental agencies and ultimately legal systems. This is usually the last chance an organization has to influence the development of the issue, although influence at this stage in an issue's evolution is usually a very costly matter that requires heavy lobbying, grassroots activity, and public communications.

4. *Regulation/Litigation.* This represents a plateau in public attention when enforcement procedures become routine and penalties apply to those who ignore or violate the law. At this point, it is very difficult for an organization to affect change in the issue and the cost to do so is often the highest in terms of such resources as dollars and time.

Figure 16-1 (Bucholz, 1995) provides a visual view of the issue life cycle and shows how the four-stage model evolves. The figure also shows the nature of the discretion given to the organization as it determines when it will respond to the issue depending on where the issue has evolved in the cycle.

The generic four-stage model just described is not the only one that analysts can use to understand the evolution of issues. Corrado (1984) suggests that issues develop through seven stages:

1. *The Problem.* The public generally feels some state of dissatisfaction over events in the STEEP environment, although they may not yet have achieved consensus as to what the problem actually is.
2. *The Label.* This is where a stakeholder, usually an interest group, starts addressing the issue and is able to attach a label to it.
3. *Crystallization.* The media gets wind of the issue and gives it further impetus into the public's understanding. The reason for the problem is now clear.
4. *Solutions.* Numerous answers to resolving the problem emerge as the media continues to fan the issue. If the issue is one impacting a business organization, it had better be involved in shaping the agenda by this point or it will have little opportunity to shape it later.
5. *Legislation.* Political leaders get involved. They put forward bills and laws to address the issue and the issue now goes in directions called for by the public policy makers' constituencies.
6. *Implementation.* The newly passed laws are implemented by government agencies or departments. Sometimes court action will crop up as some stakeholder

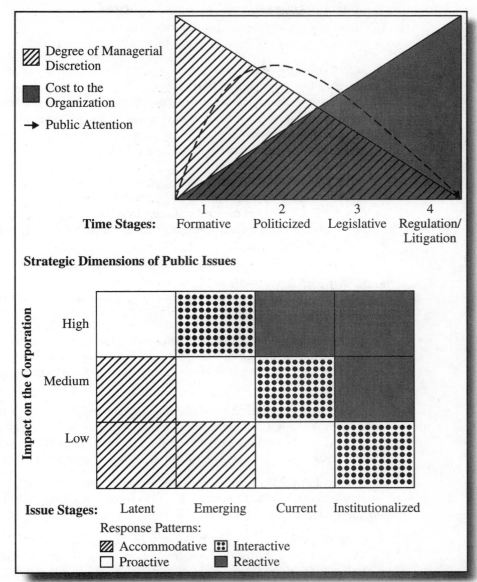

Figure 16-1
Decision-Oriented Applications of the Issues Life Cycle Model

Source: Business Environment and Public Policy: Implications for Management (5th ed.), by R. A. Bucholz © Reprinted by permission of Pearson Education, Inc., Upper Saddle River, NJ.

groups perceive the implementation of the regulation is not up to snuff with the spirit of the legislation.

7. *New Problems Arise.* Issues often grow out of the solutions to older issues. This can often start the cycle over again. Over- and underregulation are examples of where issues can come around and go around through the cycle again.

Issue Expansion Map Approach

An issue expansion map (Mahon, 1989) explains how an issue expands and how various stakeholders get involved. It consists of four groups:

1. *Identification Groups.* These are the first to become involved as the dispute expands beyond original participants. They are relatively powerless, unless they begin to bind in interlocking networks with other groups.
2. *Attention Groups.* They tend to be organized around a small set of issues important to their membership (and easily mobilized) and they have resources and access to the media, giving them power to expand the issue beyond their own limited membership.
3. *Attentive Public.* This is the well-educated and well-read members of the population in which you find society's opinion leaders.
4. *General Public.* Issues expand to this group because either the organization did not contain the issue at the attention group level and/or because the issue is highly generalizable and symbolic.

Issue Timing Approach

Another useful way to classify issues is according to timing. In this case, there are four major categories of issues:

1. *Latent Issues.* These are issues that are still not widely discussed in the media or by activist groups and other stakeholders. Scanning these issues should be focused on detecting whether pressure is building that might make this issue more important in the future.

2. *Emerging Issues.* These are public policy questions that have three underlying characteristics: (a) The issue's definition is still evolving as are the positions of the contending parties; (b) the issue is likely to be the subject of formal government action in the next few years; and (c) the issue can still be acted upon and affected by companies.

3. *Current Issue.* This is being debated or otherwise acted on within governmental institutions at any level. Specific policies to resolve the issue are being legislated and debated by elected or appointed officials.

4. *Institutionalized Issue.* Public policy has been formulated and adopted as an attempt to resolve the issue. Whatever policies were approved are being implemented, most likely within a government agency or bureaucracy

Stanbury (1993) notes there are several key lessons to be learned for analysts that utilize the issue life cycle approach to analysis:

1. The duration of time over which an issue develops can vary enormously; sometimes it can develop in days or weeks, sometimes over decades.
2. All issues will not move through the entire cycle as some will flame out before any political decision making and action occurs.
3. Many issues will get transformed as they evolve through the life cycle. There are many twists and turns in public policy making that can shift the expected trajectory of an issue.

4. There is much uncertainty surrounding which issues will actually make it to the public policy making institutions' agenda for decision making.

Step 2: Issue Assessment

Some of the techniques described in the issues identification section can also be used in assessing issues, especially delphi panels and scenario development. There are several other techniques frequently used for analyzing issues, the most popular of which are discussed here.

Issues Distance Approach

Frank Corrado (1984) has suggested an approach for analyzing issues based on the "distance" between the organization and the issues under consideration. His three categories include:

1. *Current Issues.* These are already under consideration by public policy makers (i.e., in stage 3 of the issue life cycle) and organizations are basically forced to react to them.

2. *Emerging Issues.* These are still forming (i.e., moving from stage 1 to stage 2 of the issue life cycle) and are likely to be coming onto the formal public policy making agenda in the form of legislation in the near future. These issues can still be influenced by proactive and preemptive organizational public affairs actions.

3. *Societal Issues.* These are vague and frequently remote concerns that may or may not affect business interests in the future. For the time being and until these issues become better delineated, they are not issues over which the organization should be actively concerned.

Issue Impact Approach

Another helpful approach to classifying issues is offered by Bartha (1982). His approach for analysis and subsequent decision making is to base the classification on the number of persons affected, the severity of the issue's impact, immediacy of the issue's impact, and the costs of solving the problems underlying the issue. The use of these four criteria results in the following scheme:

1. *Universal Issues.* These issues affect a large number of people, have a direct and personal impact on these individuals, and are viewed as being serious and of imminent concern. These issues are usually not of a permanent nature. An energy and inflationary crisis or a regional uprising by smaller groups tends to characterize the typical nature of these issues. The public generally looks to government in these cases to provide a quick response and solution.

2. *Advocacy Issues.* These are issues for which the public again seeks governmental action to resolve, although these tend not to be as spontaneous or as omnipresent as universal issues. These issues are generally complex and usually build steadily over time. Issues such as the de- or re-regulation of certain industries, the provision of day care, or foreign investment guidelines commonly fit into this category.

3. *Selective Issues.* These issues typically concern only specific stakeholder groups. These issues usually generate costs to the public at large but the benefits tend to be received by those heavily committed interests who promoted the issue. These stakeholders promoting these issues tend to be identifiable by certain characteristics such as demography (i.e., the unique job and retirement concerns held by baby busters), geography (e.g., urban dwellers concerned about the provision of satisfactory schools in run-down downtown areas), occupation (e.g., the provision of benefits to migrant laborers), or sector (e.g., the protection of certain forests from logging activity).

4. *Technical issues.* These issues generally are not well known by or a concern to most members of the general public. Experts are most concerned about these issues and they usually end up being settled within regulatory arenas.

Issues Priority, Leveraging, and Scoring Matrixes

Given the large number of issues that exist in an organization's environment at any point in time, an assessment must be made by analysts in order to recommend to decision makers which issues should be selected for action and resource allocation by the organization. Because all organizations have limited resources, efforts should be made to determine where the organization's actions produce the greatest net-positive effects.

There are several important questions that need to be answered in this process, including some of the following (Bartha, 1993):

- Where is the issue in its stage of development?
- How probable is it that the issue will evolve so that some governmental body will take it on through legislation and cause the issue to have a material impact on the organization?
- What is the estimated magnitude of the expected new public policy likely to be on the organization's bottom line?
- Does the organization have the capabilities to influence the issue evolution process or to influence the range or nature of possible governmental responses?

This requires the analyst to take the list of issues generated within the identification phase and place them in the cells of a matrix bounded by the selection of two variables. Among the variables used most frequently are *probability* (or the likelihood that the issue will indeed occur and affect the organization) and *impact* (the severity of the possible effect of the issue on the organization). These are often combined into a 3 × 3 matrix, with the variables ranging from high to medium to low, resulting in nine cells, each of which suggests a different priority for subsequent action on behalf of the organization. Common versions of this matrix are presented as Figure 16-2.

Several companies utilize definitional schemes for ranking issues in terms of their organizational importance or impact. A few of these are described in the boxes that appear in this chapter.

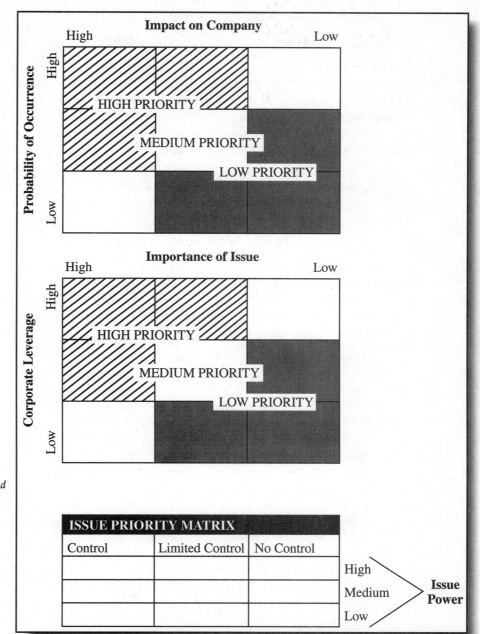

Figure 16-2
Issues Priority,
Leveraging, and
Scoring Matrixes

*Sources: Social Change and
Corporate Strategy: The
Expanding Role of Public
Affairs, by A. B. Gollner,
1983, Stamford, CT:*
Issue Action
Publications. *The
Critical Issues Audit, by
E. Sopow, 1994, in The
Issue Management
Workbook Collection,*
Leesburg, VA: Issues
Action Publications.

Step 3: Selection of Issue Response Patterns and Types

A firm's response to an issue needs to be a coordinated and planned set of actions, some of which may be internal to the firm, some of which will occur in the external or public policy environmental context encompassing the firm. It is helpful for the analyst to consider these response patterns in making an action recommendation to the organization's decision makers. There are several ways that an issue may be responded to by an organization, including (Cochran & Nigh, 1987):

1. The organization could alter its behavior, that is, its policies or its activities, in such a way to reduce or eliminate the stakeholder pressures being felt. Johnson & Johnson did this with its pain medication Tylenol after it was discovered that the medication had been tampered with. One side benefit of "proactive" behavior such as this was that the company may have forestalled government's taking very costly steps such as changing the packaging requirements for its products.

2. The organization might try and alter the expectations of its stakeholders in order to close the gap by bringing their expectations of corporate behavior closer to their perceptions of the organization's performance.

3. Communication and education of stakeholder groups as to what the organization was actually trying and was really doing in the public arena.

4. The firm may contest the issue in the public opinion arena. This could be done through lobbying public decision makers, using the court system and legal challenges, applying grassroots pressure to the issue, or through advocacy ads and editorializing.

5. The organization can ignore the issue and hope it goes away or that time will resolve the matter in its favor.

Another option is shown in Table 16-1 that presents Mahon's (1989) political issues alternative matrix. It suggests that there are two dimensions to consider when planning a response to an issue. The first dimension is whether a direct or indirect mode of attack should be launched, while the second dimension looks at whether the focal unit of analysis should be an issue or organization.

Four different tactics arise from these two dimensions as follows:

1. *Defuse the Issue.* This is a symbolic action that lacks real substance, for example, set up a special committee to look into the issue, fire the leader, say you will change amidst publicity but don't.
2. *Blur the Issue.* Bring in other stakeholders, add issues, refine the current issue, postpone action to await more study, discuss all the reasons (constraints) why the organization cannot possibly comply or respond.
3. *Attack the Group.* This is a risky tactic where an organization raises questions about the individual's or group's legitimacy in an attempt to discredit them.
4. *Undermine the Group.* Co-opt stakeholders, direct appeals to memberships bypassing the leadership, and use secondary sources of influence.

		ORIENTATION	
		ISSUE	GROUP
MODE OF ATTACK	DIRECT	Defuse the Issue	Attack the Group
	INDIRECT	Blur the Issue	Undermine the Group

Adapted from Mahon (1989).

Table 16-1
Political Issues
Alternatives Matrix

Part II   The Techniques of Strategic and Competitive Analysis

We rate the external forces that can impact our success with factors such as the credibility of the groups initiating the proposal, the opposition's strengths and weaknesses, the impact on the state's budget, the positions of the governor and state agencies, and our ability (or lack thereof) to get coalitions to work with us.

We then compile an average score for each legislative initiative. That score is weighed against the degree of financial impact to the company, the likelihood for success, and any other public affairs impacts.

We also look at the impact the initiative will have on our public affairs relationships. We ask ourselves; Are we going to harm legislative relationships, or are we going to improve them with this effort? How are other utilities in the industry going to react? How are our customers going to react? What other coalition actions are we going to have to deal with?

These three elements—chance for success, financial impact, and public affairs impact—are taken together and averaged.

Adapted from "Using the Tools of Quality to Assess State Government Relations," by K. Sundberg, 1994, in P. Shafer [Ed.], *Adding Value to the Public Affairs Function*, p. 195, Washington, DC: Public Affairs Council.

Another alternative classification scheme for preparing responses to public issues is also presented in Mahon (1989). This model suggests that the organization can totally resist, bargain, capitulate, terminate, or cessate its activity that underlie the issue. Actual examples of where each of these strategies and tactics are used can be seen in Table 16-2.

Table 16-2
Strategies and Tactics for Political Response

STRATEGIES	TACTICS	EXAMPLES
Resistance	Persuade and propagandize	Ford and Pinto
	Deny responsibility	Nestle and Infant Formula Ford Explorer roll-overs
	Question other stakeholders' legitimacy	Tobacco industry
	Countercharge and diversionary tactics	Discrimination against smokers
Bargaining	Positive inducements	Union Carbide and the town of Institute, West Virginia
	Negative inducements	Medical practitioners withholding their services in order to force policy changes
Capitulation	Concede; seek best solution or exoneration	J&J and Tylenol P&G and Rely Tampon
Termination	Cease relationships with external stakeholders	GD Searle & IUD Levis staying out of China
Cessation	Dissolve the organization	File bankruptcy

Adapted from Mahon (1989).

ISSUE/TOPIC DEFINITION

- *Issues*: A public policy requiring action for which a planned program can be developed with an identified completion point.
- *Topic*: An area of interest where Xerox wishes to maintain a degree of activity or awareness.

PRIORITY RATING

1 = Issue has high potential impact on Xerox and will require a high level of Government Affairs Office activity; may be longer term; high impact potential requires priority treatment.

2 = Less Xerox-specific impact but important enough to require active monitoring; adequately covered by third party organization, but should include Government Affairs Office involvement in third party activity.

3 = Low potential impact for Xerox or very long-term issue with little or no current activity; Government Affairs Office will attempt to monitor but will rely on third parties for active monitoring and input.

Adapted from "Quality in the Washington Office," by R. Scheerschmidt, 1994, in P. Shafer [Ed.], *Adding Value to the Public Affairs Function*, p. 256, Washington, DC: Public Affairs Council.

1. *Total Resistance.* The organization refuses to change, repulses all challenges, or forces the environment to change or adapt to the organization's goals.
2. *Bargaining.* The organization bargains or compromises so that adjustments on all sides are required.
3. *Capitulation.* The organization ends the bargaining with external actors, seeks a replacement, or changes its environment, all the while seeking the best solution for the organization and exoneration.
4. *Termination.* The organization ends the relationship with the external group, and seeks a replacement.
5. *Cessation of Activity.* The organization, unwilling or unable to adapt or respond to changes demanded, disbands.

The eventual outcome of issue analysis is the determination of a handful of issues that would be most important for the organization to be acting upon. Although we have provided several helpful ways of identifying, classifying, and prioritizing issues, we do not want to suggest that the process does not contain a good degree of subjectivity. This is largely due to the analyst's perceptions of uncertainty and risk that are always prevalent in the issue environment.

In reality, the issue identification, analysis, and response process rarely unfolds in the linear, sequential fashion we have described in this chapter. In the chaotic STEEP environment in which organizations operate, issue analysis and management are multilayered, iterative, trial-and-error processes that must continuously adapt to the evolving conditions. Uncertainty is ever present. While it is difficult to determine whether the issue analyst has optimized recommendations for response, it is clearly possible to do better than competitors by learning and applying some of the tools discussed in this chapter.

FAROUT Summary

	1	2	3	4	5
F	■	■	■	■	
A	■	■	■		
R	■	■			
O	■	■	■		
U	■	■	■	■	
T	■	■			

Future orientation   Medium to high. Has the potential to be one of the most anticipatory methods, especially when combined with forecasts and scenarios.

Accuracy   Medium degree. Requires sophisticated skills in tracking and understanding sociopolitics. To the extent that issues track historical patterns, accuracy increases.

Resource efficiency   Low to medium degree. Much issue information has to be gleaned from primary sources. Requires comprehensive coverage of what can be broad areas.

Objectivity   Medium. Concrete categories for issue classification and prioritization increases objectivity when combined with expert or consensus approaches.

Usefulness   Medium to high. This is one of the most valuable techniques for covering matters in the social and political environments.

Timeliness   Low to medium. Can be done more quickly if the organization has an issue tracking system in place. In its absence, this analysis can take substantial time to perform.

Related Tools and Techniques

- macro-environmental (STEEP) analysis
- scenario analysis
- stakeholder analysis
- SWOT analysis

References

Bartha, P. (1982). "Managing corporate external issues: An Analytical Framework." *Business Quarterly,* Autumn, 47(3), 78–90.

Bucholz, R. A. (1995). *Business environment and public policy: Implications for management* (5th ed.). Englewood Cliffs, NJ: Prentice-Hall.

Chase, H. (1984). *Issue management: Origins of the future.* Stamford, CT: Issue Action Publications.

Cochran, P., & Nigh, D. (1987). "Issues management and the multinational enterprise." *Management International Review, 27*(1), 4–12.

Corrado, F. (1984). *Media for managers.* Englewood Cliffs, NJ: Prentice-Hall.

Dutton, J., & Ashford, S. (1993). "Selling issues to top management." *Academy of Management Review, 18,* 397–428.

Fleisher, C. (1999). "Public policy competitive intelligence." *Competitive Intelligence Review, 10*(2), 23–36.

Fleisher, C. (1995). *Public affairs benchmarking: A comprehensive guide.* Washington, DC: Public Affairs Council.

Goldsmith, A. (1996). *Business, government, society: The global political economy.* Chicago: Irwin.

Gollner, A. B. (1983). *Social change and corporate strategy: The expanding role of public affairs.* Stamford, CT: Issue Action Publications.

Heath, R. (1997). *Strategic issues management.* Thousand Oaks, CA: Sage.

Mahon, J. (1989). "Corporate political strategy." *Business in the Contemporary World.* Autumn, 50–62.

Prescott, J., & Bhardwaj, G. (1995). "Competitive intelligence practices: A survey." *Competitive Intelligence Review, 2,* 4–14.

Prescott, J., & Fleisher, C. (1991). "SCIP: Who we are, what we do." *Competitive Intelligence Review, 2*(1), 22–26.

Prescott, J., & Gibbons, P. (1991). "Europe '92 provides new impetus for competitive intelligence." *Journal of Business Strategy,* November-December, *12*(6), 20–26.

Scheerschmidt, R. (1994). "Quality in the Washington office." In P. Shafer [Ed.], *Adding value to the public affairs function* (p. 256). Washington, DC: Public Affairs Council.

Sopow, E. (1994). *The critical issues audit.* Leesburg, VA: Issues Action Publications.

Stanat, R. (1993). "A survey of global CI practices." *Competitive Intelligence Review, 2*(3), 20–24.

Stanbury, W. (1993). *Business-government relations in Canada: Influencing public policy* (2nd ed.). Toronto: Nelson.

Sundberg, K. (1995). "Using the tools of quality to assess state government relations." In P. Shafer [Ed.], *Adding value to the public affairs function* (p. 195). Washington, DC: Public Affairs Council.

Weller, B. C. (1982). "The process of issues management: Some emerging perspectives," (p. 4). Boulder, CO: TrendTRACK Company.

Chapter 17

Macroenvironmental (STEEP) Analysis

SHORT DESCRIPTION

Industries are embedded in a wider macroenvironment that can significantly impact the competitiveness of industries and the companies within industries. The starting point of any strategic analysis is some form of environmental analysis. This chapter focuses particularly upon the STEEP sector of the environments, covering the social, technological, economic, ecological, and political or legal aspects that impact competitiveness. These are generally considered to be beyond the direct influence of an individual organization.

BACKGROUND

Environmental analysis has been a part of the business landscape from very early on. Indeed, even the first merchants recognized the importance of understanding their trading environment, defined broadly, and how this understanding could often spell the difference between commercial success and defeat. Environmental analysis has, of course, gotten more systematic and rigorous in modern times, so much so that we now have several university degree programs and professional associations devoted in part or in whole to its study. Studies of the environment were conducted by business and management researchers from the late 1950s when it first became popular and continues in the present. The reader may want to review Dill (1958), Thompson (1967), Starbuck (1976), and Lenz and Engledow (1986) for a scan of the organization environment research through these four decades.

Although the word *environment* can conjure up images of natural scenery and visual aesthetics, this is not the way the term is used in the business strategy literature. In this chapter, we define *organizational environment* generally as the broad set of forces emanating or operating from outside the organization that can affect its competitive performance. If an organization were a closed system with no inputs from outside, its environment would be of no consequence; as an open system, it is subject to a broad range of outside inputs and influences. All organizations, like all living things, "import" from the external environment items such as resources in the form of finances, people, raw materials, and most will then "export" products or services back out into the environment. The environment is a prime determinant of the form and behavior of an organization; therefore, any competitively successful organization must rely upon an effective evaluation of the environment.

Various types of environmental changes occurring in isolation or combination help to define and drive industry factors and forces. Most environmental analysis is premised on the assumption that industry forces are *not* the sole explanation of all that occurs within the industry. The environment beyond an industry's boundaries can either be a primary determinant or may almost always influence what actually takes place within an industry's competitive environs. External factors for change can be among the primary determinants of competition and competitiveness in a global trading marketplace economy.

Although many organizations outwardly recognize the importance of the environment, all too often this analysis ends up making a small or minimal contribution to strategy analysis and formulation. This can occur because the organization views the environment as containing too much uncertainty to do anything about or something that the organization can just respond to as events, issues, or trends unfold. Also, because many environmental factors have delayed or indirect effects on the organization, it often escapes the insights or notice of managerial members who are more concerned with day-to-day operations.

Management research on environments has been done from several different perspectives. Lenz and Engledow (1986) suggest five popular models:

1. *Industry Structure Model.* The dominant aspects of an organization's environment are assumed to exist in and around the industry or industries in which the firm competes. An industry environment would consist of a particular set of competitive forces that create both threats and opportunities. Porter's Five Forces model (described in Chapter 6) would be representative of this perspective.

2. *Cognitive Model.* This model looks at senior management's collective understanding of the environment that is embodied within a cognitive structure. These cognitive structures serve as a context for formulating corporate strategies and are fashioned and sustained by those with requisite power and influence. Strategies are assumed to be ways in which organizations interact with reality.

3. *Organization Field Model.* This includes both hierarchical and nonhierarchical conceptions of how interdependent organizations pursue their goals and resources from the perspective of a focal organization. Hierarchical conceptions (such as the three-tiered approach we use in this chapter) divide the environment into categories or levels. Nonhierarchical conceptions look at exchanges, organizational fields/sets, or stakeholders and look at relative exchanges (power, resources, etc.) that take place between organizations in the set.

4. *Ecological and Resource Dependence Model.* Organizations are assumed to be the most important part of their environments. Organizations compete for resources over a number of hierarchically structured levels in a continually evolving manner.

5. *Era Model.* An era is a time period marked with a distinctive character. These models describe environments as periods of stability, change, and restability in unique orders. This is based on an assumption that patterns of institutional arrangements and values in a society are dependent on certain underlying structural features.

As the astute reader might suspect by now, there remains no consensus on how to view the organization's environment. The definition of the organization's environment and the approach by which it may be strategically and competitively analyzed will often differ depending on the perspective the organization's members choose to pursue. Here, we have chosen to make some suggestions about the process based on our experiences with environmental analysis, at the same time recognizing that there is no one best way to perform this process.

Basic Structures of Environments

In order to perform an environmental analysis, a manager must understand the basic structures of organizational environments. Analysts commonly divide the organization into three distinct levels: the general environment, the operating environment, and the internal environment. Figure 17-1 illustrates the relationship of each of these levels with each other and with the organization at large.

Managers must be aware of these environmental levels, know what factors they include, and try to understand how each factor and the relationships among the factors affect organizational performance. They can manage organizational operations in light of this understanding. We will focus here on the general environment, and look only briefly at the operating and internal environments. Several other chapters in this book will cover techniques associated with analyzing the operating and internal environments.

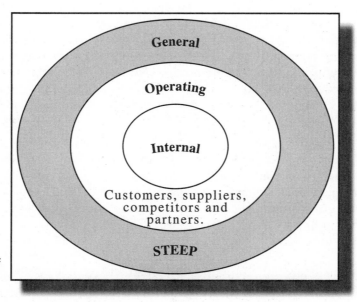

Figure 17-1
The Three Levels of
the Environment

General Environment

The general environment is that level of an organization's environment that is broad in scope and has long-term implications for managers, firms, and strategies. These are usually understood to be beyond the direct influence or primary control of any single organization.

In order to make the task of environmental analysis more meaningful, the general environment has to be broken down into more homogeneous and manageable subcategories. One effective subcategorization is known as the STEEP categorization scheme. The acronym STEEP stands for *s*ocial, *t*echnological, *e*conomic, *e*cological, and *p*olitical/legal sectors. Each sector operates over a large geographic swath (e.g., global, international, multinational, regional, national, provincial/state, and local) and over time (i.e., past, present, and future).

The STEEP domains are not meant to be nor should they be thought of as mutually exclusive—the lines between the categories remain fluid. We should note that the primary purpose of the breakdown is to avoid overlooking major aspects of the general environment in the analysis. The absence of rigid boundaries between the STEEP sectors normally will not cause any major problems in using this approach.

The five STEEP sectors are described in greater detail below.

1. *Social.* The social component of the general environment describes characteristics of the societal context in which the organization exists. Demographics, cultural attitudes, literacy rates, education levels, customs, beliefs, values, lifestyles, the age distribution, the geographic distribution, and the mobility of the population all contribute to the social component of the general environment. The pace of change in this sector can often be slow, but its effects are commonly both inexorable and profound. Therefore, it is important that the analyst monitor and evaluate this sector's impact in terms of strategic directions and also take a proactive role in helping to develop competitive strategy that builds the company's reputation among its key stakeholders.

Ethical norms of a society are elements of its culture that specify in more general ways the behavior that individuals and organizations expect of one another, but that are not prescribed by law. As the list of laws implies, many ethical norms (e.g. consumer and worker safety and environmental protection) that are important to a society's long-term future, but are seen as receiving inadequate attention, often become translated into laws. For example, in the 1950s, a manager who allowed the nearby river to be polluted by runoff from a manufacturing plant was violating an ethical norm. In the 2000s that same manager would be commonly violating environmental protection laws.

2. *Technological.* Digital communication, biotechnology, chemicals, energy, and medicine are only a few of the fields in which major technological changes have opened new areas to commercial competition. The technological component of the general environment is compounded by the impact of science and technology in product and process innovation as well. This includes new approaches to producing goods and services; new procedures as well as new equipment. The effects of technology and technological change can be felt by an organization from the acquisition of raw materials right through to the repair and recovery of the product after its use by consumers.

The major task of the analyst is to identify and monitor the effects of technological change as it affects competitive strategy. This can be seen in the final goods and services market as well as in new product and process innovation, and even communication, human resource attraction, and marketing methods. Interfacing with the organization's R&D functions is another obvious requirement for competitive and strategy analysts intent on effectively assessing this sector.

3. *Economic.* The economic component of the general environment indicates the distribution and uses of resources within an entire society. It is important because consumption patterns are largely influenced by economic trends such as balance of payment issues, employment rates, exchange rates, interest rates, inflation rates, credit availability, fiscal and monetary policies, debt, spending patterns, and levels of disposable income. Of prime importance to the analytical task are the identification, monitoring, and forecasting of those economic variables to which the company's strategic competitive efforts are most sensitive.

The relationship between strategy and the economic sector is not simply that when the economy improves, all firms will do better. Although many firms may indeed do better, some will also see conditions worsen. Changes in macroeconomic variables can often have broad impacts, yet can affect some economic sectors in ways very different from others. Urgent economic issues can require analysis through the development of custom-designed and expensive economic market research. This makes it even more critical that organizations remain vigilant to both aggregate and more microlevel economic factors and adjust their decisions and policies accordingly so as to maximize their competitiveness.

4. *Ecological.* The ecological environment encompasses both the physical and biological environments within which organizations interact. The so-called "greening" of the environment points to the power that this sector can now exert on organizational performance. Aspects of the ecological environment covered in a STEEP analysis would include such things as the global climate (e.g., effects of greenhouse gases), sustainable development (e.g., forest practices and production), cradle-to-grave product life cycles, recycling, pollution, and biotechnological advances (e.g., genetic advances in agricultural products), among others.

5. *Political/Legal.* The political component of the general environment relates to government and public attitudes toward various industries, lobbying efforts by interest groups, the regulatory climate, platforms of political parties, and (sometimes) the predisposition of politicians. The legal component of the general environment consists of laws that members of society are expected to follow. In most nation-states, many legal constraints in the form of public policies and regulations affect an organization's discretionary ability to act. Besides being a large consumer and producer in their own right, governments can actually legislate greater or lesser competition and therefore become a critical focus of the competitive and strategy analyst's efforts in this sector. For many companies, such as defense contractors, educational institutions, health care organizations, and not-for-profits, the action and mood of public policy makers are absolutely vital inputs to the competitive strategy development process.

Naturally, over time many new laws are passed and old ones rescinded. The nature of competition changes because of both procedural and structural changes from this sector. Analysts must commonly assess and recommend organizational actions such as advocacy advertising, community contributions, legal tactics, lobbying and government relation strategies, and public and stakeholder communications. These are also assessed using techniques such as issue and stakeholder analysis that are covered in other chapters within this section.

Table 17-1 shows several key variables that would be present under each individual STEEP factor.

Operating Environment

The operating environment, sometimes termed the competitive or market environment (see Chapter 6), is that level of the organization's external environment with components that normally have relatively specific and immediate implications for managing the organization. The major components of the operating environment are customers, suppliers (such as capital providers or labor), competitors, partners, and global/international issues surrounding these stakeholder groups. The operating environment, unlike the general environment, can be controlled or influenced, at least to some extent, by individual organizations. Also unlike the general environment, analysis at this level is organization specific.

The customer component of the operating environment reflects the characteristics and behavior of those who buy or could potentially purchase the organization's goods and services. Describing in detail those who buy the firm's products is

Table 17-1
Key STEEP Variables

SOCIAL	TECHNOLOGICAL	ECOLOGICAL	ECONOMIC	POLITICAL/LEGAL
Ideological characteristics	Patents held	Air and water quality	GDP growth rates	Policies of political parties
Types of union organizations	R&D budgets	Recycling capacity	Exchange reserves	Activism of regulatory agencies
Income gaps among social segments	Number of colleges and universities in region	Sources of power	Rate of inflation	Presence of property protection laws
Percentage of population in economic and social segments	Pace of technological change	Stage of evolution in product life cycle	Income distribution levels and bands	Ability to influence political decision making
Value systems for social classes	Presence of technology clusters	Pollution levels	Interest rates	Voting rates and trends
Cultural background of citizens	Pace of process or product improvements	Substitutability of raw materials	Small business lending levels	Nature of power and decision-making structures
Birth and death rates	Bandwidth capacity	Level of environmental regulation	Balance of payments	Public opinion

a common business practice. Such profiles help management generate ideas about how to improve customer satisfaction.

The competitor component of the operating environment consists of rivals, present and prospective, that an organization must overcome in order to reach its objectives. Understanding competitors is a key factor in developing an effective strategy, so analyzing the competition is a fundamental challenge to management. Basically, competitor analysis is intended to help management appreciate the strengths, weaknesses, and capabilities of existing and potential competitors and predict their responses to strategic initiatives.

The labor component of the operating environment is made up of influences on the supply of workers available to perform needed organizational tasks. Issues such as the skill levels, union membership, wage rates, and average ages of potential workers are important to the operation of the organization. Managers often overlook another important issue: the attractiveness of working for a particular organization, as perceived by potential workers.

The supplier component of the operating environment includes the influences of nonlabor resources on the organization. The firm purchases and transforms these resources during the production process into final goods and services. How many vendors offer specialized resources for sale, the relative quality of material they offer, the reliability of their deliveries, the credit terms they offer, and the potential for strategic linkages—all these issues affect managing this element in the operating environment.

The global/international component of the operating environment comprises all factors related to global issues. Though not all organizations must deal directly with international issues, the number that do is increasing dramatically. Significant aspects of the international component include the laws, political practices, cultures, and economic climates that prevail in the countries in which the firm does business.

Taken as a group, the five components of the operating environment define the territory or domain in which an organization resides. The structure of key relationships within this operating environment (or environments if the firm operates in multiple industries) will determine the profit potential as well its prospects for achieving competitive advantage.

Internal Environment

The organization's internal environment includes forces that operate inside the organization with specific implications for managing organizational performance. Unlike components of the general and operating environments, which act from outside the organization, components of the internal environment come from the organization itself. Several chapters in this book look at the analysis of particular facets of the internal environment, particularly Chapters 14 and 15.

The aspects of an organization's internal environment (production, marketing, etc.) collectively define both trouble spots that need strengthening and core competencies that the firm can nurture and build. By systematically examining its internal activities a firm can better appreciate how each activity might add value or contribute significantly to shaping an effective strategy. Michael Porter has proposed a method for such an evaluation called value chain analysis (see Chapter 9). Value chain analysis can identify internal core competencies, which, in concert with an external industry structure, are seen as the critical elements of competitive advantage and profitability.

Internal environmental analysis can be done horizontally or vertically (Bates & Eldridge, 1984). Analysis under the horizontal approach looks at the strengths and weaknesses of each of the major functional areas of the firm and describes the strategies driving each. For the vertical approach, strengths and weaknesses are identified at each organizational level, such as senior management, middle management, lower management, and shift worker. Another cut at vertical internal analysis would look at the strategic, operational/managerial, and tactical levels of decision making. The horizontal approach is generally preferred by analysts.

STRATEGIC RATIONALE AND IMPLICATIONS

Environmental conditions affect the entire strategic management process. A key to effective strategic management is to make managerial decisions that shape actions by the organization that will correspond positively with the context within which those actions will ultimately take place. To some degree, this action context will be determined by an organization's internal conditions, in particular its strengths and weaknesses. On the other hand, the action context is often dictated to a major degree by conditions external to the organization in its environment. To some extent, the firm can shape the environment to its advantage, yet in another way, it also often has to adapt or react in ways that disadvantage it less than its competitors.

Hence, the most significant purpose underlying macroenvironmental analysis is to arm decision makers with accurate and objective forecasts of significant trends in environmental factors. It has the explicit task of leading executive thinking beyond current activities and short time horizons, although it must make frequent and sensible linkages to current and shorter-term activities to retain credibility. The constant maintenance of the delicate balance between the shorter term and the longer term remains a key challenge for the environmental analyst.

A second major rationale is the sheer overabundance of environmental information that is available to organizational analysts and decision makers. Millions of bits of external data bombard most organizations on a daily basis, especially so in economies driven by computer-mediated environments, information, and services. The organization's process of strategy formulation is weakened considerably unless the organization is able to develop a filtering process that allows it to establish the importance and relevance of external developments.

Another key rationale is to develop among the organization's decision makers a structured way of thinking about the identification and analysis of relevant trends, events, and stakeholder expectations in the STEEP environment. It also helps when the analysis process stresses the importance of systematic assessment of the impacts of environmental change on the businesses the organization is in and the action plans that it chooses to fulfill its mission. This can be accomplished at a broad, organizationwide policy role expressly for top decision makers or in a more narrow, functionally focused way that requires the analyst to translate environmental data and information into effective action for functional managers or decision makers (e.g., about new products for marketing managers or about lobbying strategies for government affairs managers).

Another vital and related task of environmental analysis is to provide assumptions for the organization's strategy development or planning system. Too many incorrect assumptions underlying strategy will lead to ineffective planning.

An organization's success or failure can substantially depend on how accurately its decision makers read the environment, and how effectively they respond to it. Accordingly, managers at various levels of the organization and in various functional departments spend a great deal of time and effort gathering and analyzing data related to what they see as important environmental factors. Large firms often rely on outside board members for advice and counsel on long-range political or macro-economic matters. The CEO, with help from internal functional experts from marketing, research, new product development, or production, must develop a solid grasp of the strategic issues at work in the competitive environment. Internal staffers, such as planners, financial analysts, personnel, and public affairs and stakeholder relations specialists, must always stay abreast of new techniques and methods that define the best practices in their respective professions in order to keep their input to the process valuable.

Clearly, many people, spread throughout an organization, contribute to environmental analysis. This can be important in and of itself as it can create an evergreen forum for sharing and debating divergent views on relevant STEEP changes. More individuals involved also provide for greater opportunities to identify opportunities or threats created in the environment. This fact underscores the importance of organizing effectively for environmental analysis. To assure themselves that they will have the information they need to make strategic decisions, top managers must think carefully about who should gather what information and how to structure the flow of information so that they can use it most effectively. Because the organization must gather and act on diverse information in a timely manner, cross-functional teams of internal specialists can often perform environmental analysis effectively.

To some degree, these varied rationales for environmental analysis will each exist in any organization at any given time, although the importance or precedence of a particular rationale or function may vary for many reasons. Given the differences in environments, environmental scope, organizational level, and constituencies, our experience would suggest that it is unlikely that any single rationale or set of rationales for environmental analysis will serve all organizational purposes. In any case, in order for it to fulfill these rationales, it must fit the organization's strategy, culture, planning processes, and decision makers and their unique styles.

STRENGTHS AND ADVANTAGES

Organizations perform environmental analysis to help them achieve their competitive goals. Naturally, some environmental analysis efforts are better than others, and research has demonstrated that companies in some environments can gain an advantage over their competition based on the quality of their environmental analysis (Miller & Friesen, 1977; Grinyer & Norburn, 1977/78).

Successful environmental analyses are linked conceptually and practically to current planning operations. If the environmental analysis system is not linked to planning, the results of the analysis will contribute little toward establishing the direction the organization will take in the long run. One method commonly used to achieve this vital integration is to involve key organizational planners in some facet of environmental analysis. To ensure a strong link between planning and environmental analysis at Atlantic Richfield, for example, the manager of environmental issues is directly responsible to the director of issues and planning (Arrington & Sawaya, 1984).

Like most effective competitive analytical techniques, successful environmental analysis is responsive to the information needs of decision makers. The client for whom environmental analysis is performed are the decision makers among the firm's top management team. Environmental analysis must thoroughly understand and meet the information needs of critical decision makers within their organizations. Effective analysts recognize that these information needs may change over time and adjust the environmental analysis in accordance with such changes.

To be successful, any organizational effort like environmental analysis needs the support and encouragement of top management. Environmental analysis activities are no exception. Organization members will perceive them as important only to the extent that such support is apparent.

Environmental analysts should focus on identifying existing and potential strengths, weaknesses, opportunities, and threats suggested by components of the firm's environment. Strategists must interpret the results of environmental analysis in light of their in-depth understanding of company operations. The analyst must share the strategist's skill to contribute to an effective strategy.

Effective environmental analysis will have positive competitive performance effects only if (1) proper actions are taken, (2) proper evaluations are made, and (3) timely actions yield good results over an extended time.

WEAKNESSES AND LIMITATIONS

Environmental analysis is not an easy analytical task. Several studies have shown that this form of analysis has proven to be difficult to do effectively over time (Stubbart, 1982). Different forms of environmental contexts (e.g., dynamic or placid, simple or complex, and continuous or discontinuous) also impact the perceptions and realities of the effectiveness of this analytical process (Diffenbach, 1983).

Problems in environmental analysis tend to fall within several categories, as detailed here (Diffenbach, 1983):

1. *Interpretation.* Organizational decision makers often have a great deal of difficulty in conceptualizing or defining what their environment is and in delimiting its domain. As such, it can be difficult to interpret the results of environmental analysis into the specific kinds of impacts the environmental variables will have and also in terms of the nature of effective responses that the organization may choose to pursue. Structuring meaningful studies, showing financial impact, synthesizing

short- and long-term implications, lack of senior management involvement in the analysis, difficulties in translating potential opportunities into action plans, and the time and resources required to do accurate analysis are all potential weaknesses of interpreting environmental factors.

2. *Inaccuracy and uncertainty.* Problems here include inaccuracies in the analytical output, the presence of too many uncertainties to put great faith in the results, or a combination of both. This can happen because it is difficult to effectively depict environmental events and trends, properly characterizing uncertainties in meaningful terms, discontinuities in forecasting, difficulties in forecasting the magnitude or level of impact of STEEP forces, and the troubles evidenced in trying to predict or forecast social or technological evolution and trends.

3. *Short-Term Orientation.* Many organizations preempt the environmental analysis process because they are overly occupied with short-term, quarterly decision making and actions. Many decision makers dislike spending "real" money today for speculative actions tomorrow, and organizational structures such as task forces and quarterly budgeting processes encourage concern with short-term matters. Many companies cut back their resourcing of the environmental analysis process during tough economic times, viewing it a luxury as opposed to a necessity. This is often the time that this analysis is needed most by organizations and it is instructive that this may be a counterintuitive view that could create advantages for those companies who can sustain the analytical effort through good times and bad. Last but not least, many of the variables in the STEEP sectors take many years to evolve, frequently far outlasting the analysts and decision makers in the organizations intent on impacting them.

4. *Lack of Acceptance.* Some companies do not accept the value of environmental analysis. This can be due to a lack of understanding of its value by top managers, difficulty in encouraging line managers to participate or utilize its outputs, resistance to change forecasting methods, and presumptions among many managers that they are already experts in the implementation or management of this process. Another related issue is the failure to link the STEEP analysis to competitive implications. STEEP should always have as a key goal the identification of competitive implications for the organization based on the environment analysis.

5. *Misperceptions.* Many decision makers hold narrow, limited, or invalid perceptions about the environment. For example, they think in country terms as opposed to global terms; they were not prepared during their education to deal with STEEP matters and therefore view it as being of lesser importance than those areas in which they received formal training or education.

6. *Diversified Businesses.* These create great complexity for environmental analysts, as they will have to grasp the implications of numerous environmental and organizational interactive dynamics. Human limitations, prior experience, and biases will affect environmental analysis. This is especially true in multinational environments where home-country biases and attitudes often lead organizations to superimpose their own experiences, views, and understandings on variables that do not act in ways supported by these factors.

PROCESS FOR APPLYING THE TECHNIQUE

Analyzing the environment usually begins with organizational decision makers defining environmental boundaries. These boundaries will bind the breadth, depth, and forecasting horizon of the analysis. Breadth refers to the topical coverage of the environmental data that are collected. Depth determined the degree of detail in the STEEP data being sought and analyzed. Forecasting horizons will usually span short, medium, and longer terms, as dictated within the relevant organization's specific environment.

Environmental boundaries can be typically established by examining the organization's strategic posture with respect to its geographic diversity (i.e., where it does and does not compete), its product or service market scope, its return horizon on its fixed resource commitments, technology and innovation, sources of its resources (capital, human, other financial, and raw materials), regulatory mandate, and flexibility. The process is also constrained by the amount of resources available to dedicate to the task along with the other FAROUT dimensions that need to be considered.

Once definition and delimitation have occurred, analyzing the five STEEP segments can be performed using the following five-step process (Fahey, 1984):

1. Understand the segment of the environment being analyzed.
2. Understand interrelationships between trends.
3. Relate trends to issues.
4. Forecast the future direction of issues.
5. Derive implications.

Step 1: Understand the Segment of the Environment Being Analyzed

What are the current key events and trends within the segment? This will tell you in broad terms what is happening and concerns the development of events and trends. Events are important occurrences in the different STEEP domains. Trends can be seen as the general tendency or course of events. For example, within the segment called lifestyles you would look to capture trends surrounding work and leisure, consumption and savings, education, travel, religious activities, and household work.

What is the evidence supporting the existence of these trends? It is important that data or evidence underlying the existence of trends is captured so as to facilitate continued monitoring and forecasting of the trend's direction and evolution.

How have the trends evolved historically? Like industries, products, and organizations, trends have life cycles with identifiable stages. Trends emerge, develop, peak, and decline. Analysts are well advised to identify where in its life cycle the important trends have evolved. An understanding of the cycle of trends is critical in identifying their subsequent evolution.

What is the nature and degree of change or turbulence within trends? Trends fluctuate according to the rate of evolution, magnitude, and fractionation. Rate of change in the trend requires the analyst to focus on whether the trend is accelerating, decelerating, or remaining neutral in its life cycle. Magnitude looks at the degree of spread associated with trend and whether it is affecting larger or smaller publics to lesser or greater degrees. Fractionation looks at the relationship of the trend with other trends to see whether the focal trend is impacting or being impacted by other trends.

What kind of impacts do the trends have for the organization? Conceptually, there are three different kinds of impacts that trends may have for the organization;

1. *Negative Impacts.* These are associated with threats to the organization's ability to achieve its goals. They may also prevent the organization from acting upon its current strategy, increase the risks associated with moving forward with the existing strategy, increase the level of resources required to operationalize the strategy, or suggest that a strategy is no longer appropriate at all.

2. *Positive Impacts.* These are associated with opportunities for the organization to achieve its goals. It may mean that the trends support or strengthen existing strategies, may increase the likelihood of the organization being able to implement its planned strategy, or suggest a new opportunity that can be exploited if one or more strategies were changed within the framework of the organization's existing mission.

3. *Neutral or Zero Impacts.* These may either be stabilizing or irrelevant forces. These may also increase the confidence decision makers have in their strategies.

Step 2: Understand Interrelationships Between Trends

What are the interrelationships between trends? This requires the analyst to use his or her creative capacity in identifying interrelationships between macroenvironmental subsegments. The analyst should be looking for areas where trends are suggesting redefinitions or changes from the expected evolutionary path or where trends are reinforcing one another.

What are the conflicts between trends? Trends often push in opposite directions. For example, people are becoming more committed to their work at the same time that they are seeking more family time outside of the workplace.

Step 3: Relate Trends to Issues

Not all trends are of equal importance to an organization or an industry. Some will impact an organization directly, while others may have only tangential impact depending on how the trend interacts with the organization's strategy. It is crucial that the analyst identify those trends and trend combinations that are likely to have the highest impact on the organization's goal pursuits. Those that are most critical are defined as "issues" for the organization.

Step 4: Forecast the Future Direction of Issues

Assessing the underlying forces. Forecasting the future evolution of the trend or set of trends within the issue requires analysis of the driving forces behind the issue. It is critical that the analyst is able to distinguish between symptoms and causes. This is very difficult, as often these driving forces work against one another and push simultaneously in multiple directions. Once the causes are accurately identified, the analyst can then develop alternative projections of the issue's evolution.

Make alternative projections of the issues. To avoid the limitations created by single forecasts, it is useful for the analyst to develop multiple projections or scenarios. Each of these scenarios will represent a differing view of the future that is carefully developed around clearly identified trends. For example, the analyst can identify a best case, worst case, and neutral case scenario for issue development. The analyst should then subject the scenario to a set of questions to test its veracity: What underlying forces are propelling the trends? What is the probability or likelihood that they will continue? How strong is the evidence that its component trends are accurate? Do the interrelationships among the trends make sense?

Step 5: Derive Implications

It is important that the macroenvironmental analysis actually makes a contribution and serves as an input to the organization's strategic planning. Implications should be focused on three levels in particular: (1) the structural forces surrounding your industry and any strategic groups within the industry; (2) how they affect your organization's strategy; and (3) how they are expected to affect competitors strategies. This assessment should provide the key inputs into determining what future strategies might be.

The following checklist presents a summary of questions to analyze strategic management problems that focus on environmental issues:

1. Does the strategic management problem raise environmental issues?
2. Are factors in the general environment being appropriately considered as part of the environmental analysis?
3. Are factors in the operating environment being appropriately considered as part of the environmental analysis?
4. Are factors in the internal environment being appropriately considered as part of the environmental analysis?
5. Does the organization spend enough time evaluating and improving its environmental analysis process?
6. Is environmental forecasting properly employed during the environmental analysis process?
7. Does the organization spend enough time evaluating and improving its environmental analysis process?

FAROUT SUMMARY

	1	2	3	4	5
F	■	■	■	■	
A	■	■			
R	■	■			
O	■	■			
U	■	■	■		
T	■	■			

Future orientation   Medium to high. Its focus on trends, and driving forces and their evolutionary development ensures that it is a highly anticipatory method. It is less useful when oriented toward the present.

Accuracy   Low to medium. The method requires sophisticated understanding and tracking of a wide variety of both qualitative and quantitative elements that often interact with one another.

Resource efficiency   Medium. Much information can be gleaned from secondary sources such as government agencies, specialist publications, consulting firms, and census data.

Objectivity   Low to medium. Understanding of trend interactions and driving forces requires a considerable amount of inventiveness and insight combined with useful and reliable data.

Usefulness   Medium. This is a valuable technique because few organizations do it explicitly or do it well; therefore, it provides opportunities to achieve strategic advantages if it can be effectively performed.

Timeliness   Low to medium. This method requires the organization to collect and track substantial data sources. In the absence of effective tracking systems, this method can require substantial developmental time.

RELATED TOOLS AND TECHNIQUES

- issue analysis
- S-curve analysis
- scenario analysis
- stakeholder analysis
- SWOT analysis
- technology forecasting

REFERENCES

Ackoff, R. (1981). *Creating the corporate future.* New York: John Wiley & Sons.

Aguilar, F. (1967). *Scanning the business environment.* New York: Macmillan.

Arrington, C., & Sawaya, R. (1984). "Issues management in an uncertain environment." *Long Range Planning,* 17(6), 17–24.

Bates, D., & Eldridge, D. (1984). *Strategy and policy: analysis, formulation, and implementation* (2nd ed.). Dubuque, IA: Brown.

Diffenbach, J. (1983). "Corporate environmental analysis in large U.S. corporations." *Long Range Planning,* 16(3), 107–116.

Dill, W. (1958). "Environment as an influence on managerial autonomy." *Administrative Science Quarterly,* 2(2), 409–443.

Fahey, L. (1989). "Understanding the macroenvironment: A framework for analysis." In L. Fahey, (ed.), *The Strategic Planning Management Reader,* Englewood Cliffs, NJ: Prentice Hall, pp. 38–43.

Fahey, L., King, W., & Narayanan, V. (1981). "Environmental scanning and forecasting in strategic planning—The state of the art." *Long Range Planning,* 14(1), pp. 32–39.

Grinyer, P. H., & Norburn, D. (1977/1978). "Planning for existing markets: An empirical study." *International Studies in Management and Organization.* Vol 7, pp. 99–122.

Lenz, R., & Engledow, J. (1986). "Environmental analysis: The applicability of current theory." *Strategic Management Journal, 7,* 329–346.

Miller, D., & Friesen, P. (1977). "Strategy making in context: Ten empirical archetypes." *Journal of Management Studies, 14*(3), 253–280.

Starbuck, W. (1976). "Organizations and their environments." In M. Dunnette (Ed.), *Handbook of industrial and organizational psychology.* Chicago: Rand McNally.

Stubbart, C. (1982). "Are environmenal scanning units effective?" *Long Range Planning, 15*(3), 139–145.

Thompson, J. (1967). *Organizations in action.* New York: McGraw-Hill.

Wilson, I. (1982). "Environmental scanning and strategic planning." In G. Steiner et al. (Eds.) *Management Policy ad Strategy* (Reading 7). New York: Macmillan.

Chapter 18

Scenario Analysis

SHORT DESCRIPTION

A scenario is a detailed, internally consistent description of what the future may look like and is based on a set of assumptions that are critical for the economy's, industry's, or technology's evolution. Scenario planning and analysis is a structured way of developing multiple scenarios that compensate for two common decision-making errors—under- and overprediction of change. The overall purpose of scenario planning and analysis is to build a shared baseline for strategic thinking.

Scenario analysis is a conjectural planning tool for environmental analysis in turbulent and rapidly changing conditions. Through a disciplined yet creative approach, scenario analysis is a combination of quantitative and qualitative analysis that imagines many possible futures of environmental change; reduces these many scenarios to a manageable number of possibilities; incorporates sensitivity analysis to determine dependent variable relationships; isolates trends and patterns to counteract blindspots in strategic decision making; and provides a framework to couch future decisions around strategic posture.

BACKGROUND

Environmental analysis has long been a fundamental component of strategy. By definition and necessity, long-range planning requires the analyst to look beyond the current situation and prepare the firm's resources and capabilities for competition in an uncertain future. For many years this was the purview of forecasting techniques such as trend extrapolation and econometric modeling. Forecasting, however, is fraught with conceptual flaws because it is based on the premise that the future can be extrapolated from past trends and patterns. This weakness has been manifested in the general failure of forecasting beyond short periods of time.

Many studies have challenged the validity of traditional forecasting methodologies and found their accuracy and hence, usefulness, lacking. In one comprehensive examination of U.S. quantitative econometric models built during the period 1970 to 1975, it was concluded that their accuracy could not be reliably extended beyond nine months (Spivey & Wrobleski, 1980). Similarly, they found virtually no difference in the accuracy of quantitative econometric models versus more qualitative approaches to forecasting. Another study sponsored by the United States in 1978 looked at energy price forecasting techniques. The conclusion was similar and suggested that, while all types of energy price forecasting techniques had dismal track records, the qualitative approaches had a tendency to outperform econometric models. Yet another large study found that forecasts were usually incorrect more as a result of incorrect assumptions rather than because of the specific methodology used (Ascher, 1978). Hence, the time was ripe for scenario planning and analysis to assume prominence because it explicitly focused on the assumptions that premise much long-range planning.

Studies like those discussed above, combined with general management despair over its inability to predict the future with forecasting, led to a general dismissal of traditional forecasting techniques. The limited value of forecasting as a strategic planning tool is perhaps best summed up by the thoughts of strategy guru Peter Drucker (1973) when he unequivocally asserted that strategic planning is necessary precisely because we cannot forecast.

In the 1970s, corporate planners adopted scenario analysis as a way to overcome the pitfalls of traditional forecasting technology. Given that the Greek root of strategy refers to planning a campaign of war, it is fitting that scenario analysis was first developed for military applications. In 1942, computer simulation models were first used by atomic physicists in the Manhattan Project to determine whether dropping a nuclear bomb would destroy the Earth in a huge fireball.

The next major development in the evolution of scenario analysis came from the RAND Corporation while consulting for the U.S. Air Defense Missile Command. Military strategists at RAND were the first to formally define scenarios as "hypothetical sequences of events constructed for the purposes of focusing attention on causal processes and decision points" (Kahn & Wiener, 1967). This definition of purpose signified a dramatic shift in thinking from established forecasting methods. Rather than attempt to accurately predict the future, scenario analysis was designed to assist the decision-making process by enhancing understanding of the mutual dependencies and implications of current and future trends.

This pioneering work at RAND was followed by the now-famous scenario analyses of sustainable global economic growth, *Limits to Growth* (Meadows et al., 1972) and *Mankind at the Turning Point* (Pestel & Mesarovic, 1974). The important contribution of these studies was the explicit recognition that mutual dependencies among the factors incorporated into scenario analysis often supercede the importance of the individual factors themselves. That is, scenario analysis should properly include the impact of "positive feedback loops" or interlinked chains of cause and effect relationships that serve to reimpact the initial dynamic factor(s) (Zentner, 1982). For example, if resource availability, one of the incorporated factors, were changed, it would set off a sequence of impacts in other factors (such as environmental pollution, food yield, population, and capital availability) that would, through positive feedback loops, impact resource availability.

Scenario analysis gained further credence through the 1982 study conducted by SRI International, *Seven Tomorrows* (Hawken, Ogilvy, & Schwartz, 1982). This scenario attempted to envision the future of the next two decades through analyzing trends in economic growth, energy availability, agricultural productivity, social value systems, and climactic change. By manipulating different variables driving each trend, they developed several very different future scenarios through positive feedback loops.

Despite the fact that most of these early scenario techniques were highly quantitative (i.e., some of them incorporated hundreds of thousands of mutually dependent relationships) more qualitative scenario analysis was also evolving during this time period as well. The most notable qualitative approach to scenario analysis was the Delphi method (developed by Olaf Helmer in 1960) and cross-impact analysis (developed in the early 1960s). Essentially, the Delphi method relies on the iterative inputs from expert panels rather than complex mathematical models.

By the mid- to late 1970s, when scenario analysis had developed a critical mass of intellectual credibility, it was formally adopted by many major corporations as an important part of the strategic planning process. The oil crisis of the 1970s served to underscore the importance of scenario analysis. Fittingly then, the most fervent adopters were major oil companies such as Royal Dutch Shell Company, who initiated formal scenario analysis into its analytical regimen in 1977. Some argue that scenario analysis was a major impact driving the improved global competitive position of Shell from number 6 in 1973 to number 2 by the late 1980s (Grayson & Clawson, 1996).

Scenario analysis became popular with oil companies because it is aptly suited to deal with vast changes in underlying economic, political, and social factors of which they were disproportionately vulnerable. As such, it was mostly used by large corporations in assessing the macro environment or in worldwide planning. By 1977, a survey of the Fortune Industrial 1000 indicated that 16 percent of the firms on the list were actively using multiple scenario planning (Linneman & Klein, 1979). By 1982, the same survey found that 32 percent of the Industrial 1000 were using this strategic management tool. Additionally, by 1982, scenario planning had also become well established in approximately the same percentage of nonindustrial U.S. firms and foreign firms of American parentage (Linneman & Klein, 1985).

Given the constant force of change wrought by globalization, trade liberation, and information technology, scenario analysis is now recognized as a fundamental tool for firms of all sizes to help them think strategically about the future.

STRATEGIC RATIONALE AND IMPLICATIONS

Contemporary organizations and industries face tremendous structural change, uncertainty, and decisions that include huge opportunities and risks. Anticipating the future in this volatile environment calls for more than just contingency planning, sensitivity analysis, or computer simulations: It also demands creativity, insight, and intuition. Scenario planning and analysis allows the analyst to structure these demands.

According to Schoemaker (1995), organizations facing the following conditions will especially benefit from scenario planning and analysis:

- Uncertainty is high relative to managers' ability to predict or adjust.
- Many costly surprises have occurred in the past.

- The company does not perceive or generate new opportunities.
- The quality of strategic thinking is low.
- The industry has experienced significant change or is about to.
- The company wants a common language and framework without stifling diversity.
- There are strong differences of opinion, with multiple opinions having merit.
- The company's competitors are using the technique.

Industries evolve and as they do, they change in their levels of attractiveness. Predicting how this evolution will unfold is an uncertain task at best. When uncertainty levels are very high, scenario analysis can be a helpful way to prepare for that future.

As previously mentioned, a scenario is a detailed, internally consistent description of what the future may look like and is based on a set of assumptions that are critical for the economy's, industry's, or technology's evolution. It is a story about a possible future, written or spoken, built upon carefully constructed plots. Stories can express multiple perspectives on complex events; scenarios give meaning to these events. Industry scenarios develop detailed, internally consistent descriptions of what the industry may look like in the future. They address what might be and what could be.

The output of a single scenario is one possible configuration for the industry, while a set of scenarios can be used to encompass a wide range of possible structures. The set can then be used to develop and assess competitive actions or movements.

Following are the four general types of approaches to scenario analysis.

Quantitative Methods

1. *Computer-Generated Econometric Model.* This model attempts to integrate a great number of identified interrelationships between trend factors. By changing one variable, the sequence of downstream impacts is analyzed along with positive feedback loop effects on the initial variable.

Qualitative Methods

2. *Intuitive Methods.* This method rejects the quantitative approach. Instead, it stresses the qualitative variables that are thought to disproportionately impact the future. Fundamental trends are identified and projected into the future to construct a surprise-free future. This is followed by changing some of the trend to explore other possible future issues. While this intuitive approach is appealingly simple, the high level of abstraction and lack of systematic application makes it difficult to operationalize.

3. *Delphi Method.* In this method, a panel of experts (both internal and external) is separately questioned (to reduce peer bias) through a series of interviews regarding current and possible future trends in their particular domain of expertise. After several iterations, the results are statistically manipulated to yield a description of both majority consensus as well as areas of different opinion. The Delphi approach focuses on determining the sequential causal paths of events and issues that will play out in the future.

4. *Cross-Impact Analysis.* This approach also employs the solicitation of expert opinion but adds a request for the experts' estimate of the probabilities and time of occurrence of future trends or events. The analytical product is a probability distribution of the likelihood and time frame of future events that can be manipulated to determine the impact of the removal of one trend or event on the remaining trends or events. Cross-impact analysis focuses on the interrelated dependencies between the various identified factors/events/issues that will impinge on the future.

Hybrid scenario analysis with a bias toward the qualitative approach seems to be the most effective method employed today. These generic approaches focus on a qualitative narrative that challenges key assumptions about the future. Initially, a large number of scenarios are developed that are subsequently reduced through either deductive or inductive processes. Deductive reduction of the number of factors first considers the general narrative themes of each scenario and then concentrates on the factors that will be dominant influences in each scenario. Alternately, inductive reduction requires the analyst to first reduce the number of factors to a manageable number and then project potential future values to multiple combinations of these factors to derive plausible scenarios.

Both deductive and inductive methods offer benefits but also carry risks (Schnaars, 1987). While deductive reduction allows the analyst to combine many factors into several narratives that describe the future, it may omit important combinations of factors. Hence, a critical scenario may be missed. Conversely, inductive reduction, by first reducing the number of factors, may omit an important variable. To protect against both of these blindspots, Schnaar recommends that both approaches be pursued. Once a manageable number of analytical inputs has been determined, the scenarios are subject to more rigorous analysis.

Regardless of which approach to scenario analysis is used, five specific purposes are usually pursued:

• *STEEP Scenario.* This focuses on events external to the firms. Less controllable factors—social, technological, economic, environmental, and political—are encompassed. The important distinction between a STEEP scenario and a traditional STEEP analysis is the characteristic of the former that incorporates factor dependencies to yield new competitive conditions not readily identified by the latter.

• *Sensitivity Scenario.* This is the opposite of a STEEP scenario in that internal factors tightly controllable by the firm are the subject of analysis. A common example of this type of scenario analysis is the spreadsheet approach used by the finance function.

• *Industry Scenario.* This focuses on industry-specific issues and trends relevant to the firm's established business model. The distinction from traditional industry analysis is an analysis of interrelated sequences of trends/events/issues over time.

• *Diversification Scenario.* This focuses on industry-specific issues and trends relevant to potential business models the firm may pursue in the future. It is essentially exploratory in nature and seeks to identify current and future trends in the firm's current industry. Additionally, this type of scenario analysis envisions the prospects for industry migration.

• *Public Issue Scenario*. Often, firms disproportionately exposed to specifically defined public issues will conduct a public issue scenario. For example, an oil company may choose to center the scenario analysis on energy economics by developing conceivable scenarios of the impact of cartel strength, discovery, taxes, and so on of their current and future business models.

Due to the importance of "soft" qualitative factors in scenario analysis, several organizational characteristics will have a dramatic impact on the success of any scenario-building program. The most important factor is the active involvement of top management. This will help to make the seemingly abstract intangibles of scenario analysis more concrete and tangible to various members of the management team charged with the responsibility of preparing the firm for future competition. Another important success factor is the involvement of analysts from diverse backgrounds. In this regard, analysts with strong backgrounds in liberal arts, humanities, and social sciences can really add value to the scenario-building process. They will be more attuned to the intangible qualitative factors that often have more bearing on future environments than their more technical or quantitatively oriented colleagues. They are also more likely to act as strategic challengers by holding contrarian viewpoints that do not take sacred cows for granted.

STRENGTHS AND ADVANTAGES

Testing Resource-Based View Strategy Options

Scenarios can be used to help determine the sources of competitive advantage or critical success factors as industries evolve. The consequences of the scenario for each competitor can be used to predict both offensive and defensive moves.

Organizational Flexibility

Another valuable aspect of scenario development is the sensitization of management to the importance of adapting to an industry's evolution. The condition of internal consistency that predominates scenario analysis forces the analyst to explicitly address the many interrelated sequences and causal paths that may result in conceivable future scenarios. The test of a good scenario is not whether it portrays the future accurately but whether it enables an organization to learn, adapt, and enrich the ongoing "strategic conversation." Through this process of understanding, the firm is much more able to grasp the nebulous importance of investing in strategic options as a risk contingency strategy. Scenario analysis is one of the best tools to mitigate the influence of corporate blindspots.

Scenario analysis is also extremely flexible in that the relative degree of quantification/qualification or formal/informal characteristics of the scenario approaches taken can be tailored to the individual firm's culture and capabilities.

Filling the Forecasting Void

Although, scenario analysis often incorporates forecasting techniques for raw analytical inputs, it goes one step further. Through narrative stories, scenario analysis starts where traditional forecasting ends. By including informal qualitative assessments of possible future environments, scenario analysis is able to embrace many more relevant variables that are beyond the quantitative purview of established forecasting techniques.

Information Overload Management Tool

Scenario planning is a very useful analysis tool because of its unique ability to reduce an overwhelming amount of data and information into actionable intelligence. By its very nature, scenario analysis is structured to help management understand future competitive environments. In this respect, it is very liberating from a procedural point of view because it is not necessary to capture all of the details.

WEAKNESSES/LIMITATIONS

Relegating Strategy Formulation Solely to Scenario Analysis

A potential downfall of scenario planning occurs when organizations use scenario planning to replace strategy formulation. Scenario planning allows a company to see the possible consequences of a predetermined strategy, whether this strategy is the company's current or possible future strategy. As such, scenario planning should be used for analysis. While it may support, decompose, and formalize a particular strategy, it does not create new strategies.

Inherent Bias

The tendency to select the scenario that best fits the firm's current strengths must be avoided. The analyst needs to divorce her- or himself from this natural tendency and remain objective to the very real possibility of each scenario materializing independent of the firm's current competitive position.

Group Consensus Difficulties

The need to get the group to agree on scenarios is critical but not always easy to manage. As scenarios often include both "soft" and "fuzzy" as well as quantitative and analytical aspects, getting people to agree on their labels can require much effort and time. There are always trade-offs to be made in developing simple versus complex scenarios.

Connecting Scenarios to Competitive and Financial Concerns

Scenarios are often appealing due to their conceptual simplicity. A difficult trade-off to make in scenario development is that between "accuracy" and "direction."

Part II   The Techniques of Strategic and Competitive Analysis

However, getting managers and decision makers to drill down from base scenarios to the level of competitive and financial implications can be difficult since most scenarios are constructed at a broad, macro level.

PROCESS FOR APPLYING THE TECHNIQUE

Despite its storylike qualities, scenario planning follows systematic and recognizable phases. The process is highly interactive, intense, and imaginative. It begins by isolating the decision to be made, rigorously challenging the mental maps that shape one's perceptions, and hunting and gathering information, often from unorthodox sources. While there is no one right way to conduct scenario analysis, several practical guidelines have been developed from collective experience with this approach. The process we describe here for developing scenarios is the one promoted by Schoemaker (1995).

1. *Define the Scope of the Analysis.* Set the time frame and the scope of the analysis in terms of products, markets, customer groups, technologies, or geographic areas. Time frame is dependent on several factors, including product life cycles, political elections, competitors' planning horizons, rate of technological change, economic cycles, and so on. Once the appropriate time frame has been determined, ask what knowledge would be of the highest value to your organization at that point in time.

2. *Identify the Major Stakeholders.* What parties will have an interest in the development of issues of importance in the future? Who will be affected or impacted by these parties and who will affect or impact them? Identify the stakeholders' current roles, interests, and power positions, and then assess how they have changed over time.

3. *Identify Basic Trends.* What industry and STEEP trends are likely to affect the issues you identified in the first step? Briefly explain each trend, including how (positively, negatively, neutrally) and why it influences your organization. Those trends in which there is disagreement over their likely continuation are dealt with in the following step.

4. *Identify Uncertainties.* Which outcomes and what events are uncertain or will significantly affect the issues you are concerned about? For each uncertainty, determine possible outcomes (i.e., legislation passed or defeated, technology developed or not developed). Also attempt to determine whether relationships exist among these uncertainties and rule out those combinations that are implausible (e.g., steadily increasing governmental and private debt and deficits with steadily declining interest rates).

5. *Construct Initial Scenario Themes.* Several approaches can be utilized, including (a) selecting the top two uncertainties and evaluating them; (b) clustering various strings of possible outcomes around high versus low continuity, degree of preparedness, turmoil, and so on; or (c) identifying extreme worlds by putting all positive elements in one scenario and all negative elements in another.

6. *Check for Consistency and Plausibility.* Assess the following: (a) Are the trends compatible within the chosen time frame? If not, remove those trends that do not fit. (b) Do the scenarios combine outcomes of uncertainties that indeed fit together? If not, eliminate that scenario. (c) Are the major stakeholders placed in positions they do not like and can change? If so, your scenario will evolve into another one.

7. *Develop Learning Scenarios.* Some general themes should have emerged from performing the previous steps. Your goal is to identify themes that are strategically relevant and then organize the possible trends and outcomes around these themes. Although the trends appear in each scenario, they should be given more or less weight or attention in different scenarios, as appropriate.

8. *Identify Research Needs.* You may need to delve more deeply into your blindspots and improve your understanding of uncertainties and trends. For example, consider if you really understand how stakeholders are likely to behave in a particular scenario.

9. *Develop Quantitative Models.* Reexamine the internal consistencies of the scenarios and assess whether certain interactions need to be formalized via a quantitative model. The models can help to quantify the consequences of various scenarios and keep managers from straying toward implausible scenarios.

10. *Evolve Toward Decision Scenarios.* Iteratively converge toward scenarios that you will eventually use to test your strategies and generate innovative ideas. Ask yourself whether the scenarios address the real issues facing your company and whether they will spur the creativity and appreciation of your organization's decision makers.

These steps should culminate in three or four carefully constructed scenario plots. If the scenarios are to function as learning tools, the lessons they teach must be based on issues critical to the success of the decision. Only a few scenarios can be fully developed and remembered, and each should represent a plausible alternative future, not a best case, worst case, and most likely continuum. Once the scenarios have been fleshed out and made into a narrative, the team identifies their implications and the leading indicators to be monitored on an ongoing basis.

Once the number of scenario "plots" has been decided upon, the strategic intent of the firm must be proactively determined. It is here that scenario analysis ends and strategic decision making begins. Courtney et al. (1997) suggest that essentially three options are open to the firm when dealing with future uncertainty:

1. *Shape the Future.* The most intense stance is for the firm to plan to be a shape-shifter by defining the competitive parameters of the future scenario(s) by betting on future trends such as technological discontinuities or the erosion of mobility barriers.
2. *Adapt to the Future.* Basically, this is the benchmarking approach that positions the firm in a position of operational excellence designed to capitalize on trends as soon as they develop.
3. *Strategic Options.* This is a more conservative, proactive strategy that invests the minimal amount necessary to purchase strategic options but avoids overt vulnerability.

The business environment surrounding the global defense industry in the early 1990s was extremely dynamic, incorporating many profound changes. Most notable were the end of the cold war between the USSR and the West and the increasing prominence of the Pacific Rim economies. Up until the early 1990s, global defense spending had been increasing at a rapid rate. When the Soviet threat had seemingly been significantly reduced, the total global defense market was poised to either stop growing or to actually start declining. Exacerbating the impact of the Cold War, newly industrialized Asian nations began to enter the global defense market, increasing global defense capacity.

These environmental trends presented management at U.S. defense firms with a great deal of uncertainty. Should they expand into foreign defense sales? Should they diversify into nondefense-related industries? Would the tentative Cold War peace last? Would regional conflict replace lost market demand derived from traditional bipolar conflict? Would increased terrorism increase the defense needs of all nations? To help frame these uncertainties, many defense firms actively engaged in scenario analysis. One firm, who will remain anonymous, employed the Futures Group to help develop a scenario analysis.

The key question around the scenario analysis was whether the U.S. government would continue to be a major client over the 1995–2005 planning horizon. This time frame was chosen because the average defense R&D cycle is between 10 to 15 years. The defense firm wanted to ensure that the scenario analysis extended beyond its current product cycle.

The first step was to identify key driving forces that would impact U.S. security and defense requirements. A long list was reduced to four key forces: (1) U.S. diplomatic, economic, and military involvement in the world's affairs; (2) character of countervailing military power; (3) vitality of the U.S. economy; and (4) level of global instability.

From these four key forces, a "scenario space" was created that incorporated them into 13 plausible alternative "worlds." Although 16 were possible (using a 4 × 4 matrix), three were rejected out of hand because they were illogical or implausible.

SCENARIO SPACE FOR FUTURE GLOBAL DEFENSE MARKET FROM 2005–2010

	NAME	PLAUSIBLE	LEVEL OF U.S. GLOBAL INVOLVEMENT		COUNTERVAILING MILITARY POWER		U.S. ECONOMIC VITALITY		LEVEL OF GLOBAL INSTABILITY	
			High	Low	Focused	Diffuse	Vibrant	Weak	High	Low
1	U.S.-Driven Market	Y	•		•		•		•	
2		Y	•		•		•			•
3	Dangerous Property	Y	•		•			•	•	
4		Y	•		•			•		•
5	Regional Markets	Y	•			•	•		•	
6	Peace and Prosperity	Y	•			•	•			•
7	Confused Priorities	Y	•			•		•	•	
8		N	•			•		•		•
9		Y		•	•		•		•	
10		N		•	•		•			•
11		N		•	•			•	•	
12		N		•	•			•		•
13		Y		•		•	•		•	
14	Isolationist's Dream	Y		•		•	•			•
15		Y		•		•		•	•	
16		Y		•		•		•		•

Plausible = Is the world plausible in the sense that the driver combinations make internally consistent and logical sense?
Level of U.S. Global Involvement includes military, economic, and diplomatic involvement.
Countervailing Military Power asks, "Is military power in the world focused on counteracting the "American preponderance" or is it more generally aimed at various local and regional threats?"

(Continued on following page)

The primary issue facing the defense firm was how each one of these scenarios would impinge on the competitive parameters of the industry if they materialize. Scenario analysis was able to help answer this question through the preparation of detailed forecasts for each scenario. These detailed analyses addressed such issues as future trends in various government defense spending, military hardware demand growth, and so on. Of the 13 remaining possible worlds, six of the more likely scenarios were selected for this type of analysis. Below are brief synopses of each scenario. In practice, each scenario would be elaborately described.

SCENARIO 1: U.S.-DRIVEN MARKET

- The United States remains the world's largest military buyer.

- Highly competitive trading blocs form in Europe, Asia, and North America that must contend with tensions and instability in developing nations as they compete for energy and resources.

- Rise of strong developing nations that control domestic arms industries.

- Regional conflicts in developing world and Western intervention ensure continued military spending.

SCENARIO 2: DANGEROUS POVERTY

- High global instability with much antagonism toward the United States.

- Huge economic problems prevent higher military spending (instability in eastern Europe, no unity in the EU, United States–Japan trade disputes, U.S. deficit, collapse of GATT trade talks).

- Global recession agitates political strife in the developing world and Middle East.

SCENARIO 3: REGIONAL MARKETS

- High global instability coupled with U.S. retrenchment creates regional defense markets.

- Western countries concentrate on economic recovery and only selectively involve themselves militarily in regional conflict to contain nationalist expansion.

SCENARIO 4: PEACE AND PROSPERITY

- Economic policy replaces defense as the primary tool of national U.S. policy.

- Global economies are thriving through free trade.

- Global defense industry stagnates.

SCENARIO 5: CONFUSED PRIORITIES

- Combination of global economic recession and little direction for defense policy.

- U.S. defense spending falls.

- Regional defense markets assume prominence.

SCENARIO 6: ISOLATIONIST'S DREAM

- Total withdrawal of the United States from aggressive military involvement.

- Strong economy, low instability, and pacifist political climate.

- Some defense industries may have to relocate internationally to survive.

The next step that the Futures Group undertook was to chart U.S. defense expenditures for each one of these six scenarios.

The figure exemplifies the vastly different strategic implications that each scenario has on the defense firm's long-range strategic planning. The next step

(Continued on following page)

Scenario Planning in the Post Cold War Global Defense Industry (Continued)

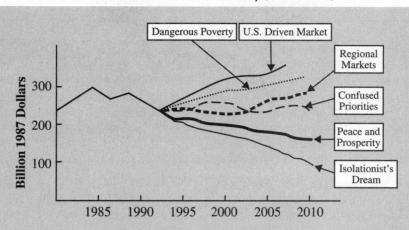

involved determining which strategies were required to successfully negotiate each scenario. Scenario analysis gave management the tools necessary to engage in strategic conversation about the future. The six scenarios developed by the Futures Group provided a framework to test the credibility of future strategy, develop strategic options, and beef up the required resources and capabilities required to ensure strategic success and competitive advantage in a radically altered future.

SOURCE: Adapted from "Alternative Scenarios for the Defense Industry After 1995," by M. A. Boroush and C. W. Thomas, 1992. *Planning Review,* 20(3) pp. 24–29.

These three strategic postures offer different levels of risk and hence different levels of potential reward from scenario materialization. Scenario analysis offers a framework in which to manage uncertainty to a level that allows the analyst to couch the selection of these various strategic intents.

Scenarios are powerful planning tools because the future is unpredictable. Unlike traditional forecasting or market research, scenarios present alternative images instead of extrapolating current trends from the present. Scenarios also embrace qualitative perspectives and the potential for sharp discontinuities that econometric and other stable-state quantitative models exclude. Consequently, creating scenarios requires managers to question their broadest assumptions about the way the world works, so that they can anticipate decisions that might be missed or denied. Within the organization, scenarios provide a common vocabulary and an effective basis for communicating complicated conditions and options.

Good scenarios are plausible, surprising, and have the power to break old stereotypes. Using scenarios is rehearsing the future, and by recognizing the warning signs and the drama that is unfolding, one can avoid surprises, adapt, and act effectively. Decisions that have been pretested against a range of possible futures are more likely to stand the test of time and produce robust and resilient plans of action. Ultimately, the end result of scenario planning is not a more accurate picture of tomorrow but better decisions today.

FAROUT Summary

	1	2	3	4	5
F	■	■	■	■	
A	■	■	■		
R	■	■			
O	■	■	■		
U	■	■	■	■	
T	■	■			

Future orientation   High. Scenarios are specifically developed to push the time boundary within which planning takes place out further into the future than most other methods.

Accuracy   Medium to high degree. Most scenario planning and analysis methods have several built-in checks for consistency and plausibility that help to produce more robust outcomes. Nonetheless, the assumptions of the input sources may slip through these screens. Further, the accuracy of these assumptions may change over time.

Resource efficiency   Low to medium. Scenario development can usually be done by a small number of individuals who must be supported by a moderate degree of research facts. Scenario analysis itself takes more time since it is usually done by larger groups of decision makers working collaboratively. The process can be accelerated through the use of one of the many available group decision support systems (GDSSs). However, such systems can be expensive. Scenario analysis that incorporates a higher degree of detail will be more costly. As such, the choice of technique will greatly impact total resource efficiency.

Objectivity   Medium degree. Depends heavily on the ability of the managerial team to arrive at a consensus view of the future and the most appropriate strategies for addressing it. Additionally, heavy emphasis on qualitative interpretation of trends and issues introduces much subjectivity into the analysis.

Usefulness   Medium to high degree. It can be very useful where conditions exist that have diminished the relevance of past strategic thinking. Usefulness is reduced in those industries or organizations not experiencing high complexity, uncertainty, or pace of change.

Timeliness   Low to medium. Developing robust scenarios and bringing together managerial teams to analyze them can be time-consuming.

RELATED TOOLS AND TECHNIQUES

- blindspot analysis
- functional capability and resource analysis
- industry analysis
- public issues analysis
- S-curve analysis
- stakeholder analysis
- STEEP analysis
- SWOT analysis

REFERENCES

Ascher, W. (1978). *Forecasting: An appraisal for policy-makers and planners.* Baltimore, MD: Johns Hopkins University Press.

Boroush, M. A., & Thomas, C. W. (1992). "Alternative scenarios for the defense industry after 1995." *Planning Review, 20*(3), 24–29.

Courtney, H., Kirkland, J., & Viguerie, P. (1997). "Strategy under uncertainty." *Harvard Business Review, 75*(6), 67–79.

Drucker, P. F. (1973). *Management: Tasks, responsibilities, practices.* New York, NY: Harper & Row.

Gilbert, L. G. (2000). "Using multiple scenario analysis to map the competitive landscape: A practice-based perspective." *Competitive Intelligence Review, 11*(2), 12–19.

Grayson, L. E., & Clawson, J. G. (1996). *Scenario building.* (UVA-BP-0338). Charlottesville, VA: University of Virginia Darden School Foundation.

Hawken, P., Ogilvy, J., & Schwartz, P. (1982). *Seven tomorrows.* New York, NY: Bantam Books.

Huss, W. R., & Honton, E. J. (1987). "Scenario planning: What style should you use?" *Long Range Planning, 20*(4) pp. 21–29.

Kahn, H., & Wiener, A. J. (1967). *The year 2000.* New York, NY: Macmillan.

Klein, H. E., & Linneman, R. E. (1981). "The use of scenario planning—Eight case histories." *Long Range Planning, 14*(5), 69–77.

Leemhuis, J. P. (1985). "Using scenarios to develop strategies." *Long Range Planning, 18*(2), 30–37.

Linneman, R. E., & Klein, H. E. (1979). "The use of multiple scenarios by U.S. industrial companies." *Long Range Planning, 12*(1), 83–90.

———. (1985). "Using scenarios in strategic decision making." *Business Horizons, 28*(1), 64–74.

Meadows, D., Randers, J., & Behrens III, W. (1972). *Limits to growth.* New York, NY: Universe Books.

Malaska, P., Malmivirta, M., & Hansen, T. (1984). "Scenarios in Europe—Who uses them and why." *Long Range Planning, 17*(5), 45–49.

Pestel, E., & Mesarovic, M. (1974). *Mankind at the turning point.* New York, NY: Readers Digest/Dutton.

Schnaars, S. P. (1987). "How to develop and use scenarios." *Long Range Planning, 20*(1), 105–114.

Schoemaker, P. J. H. (1992a). "How to link strategic vision to core capabilities. *Sloan Management Review, 34*(1), 67–81.

———. (1992b). "Multiple scenario development: Its conceptual and behavioral foundation." *Strategic Management Journal, 14*, 193–213.

———. (1995). "Scenario planning: A tool for strategic thinking." *Sloan Management Review, 36*(2), 25–39.

Schoemaker, P. J. H., & vanderHeijden, A. J. M. (1992). "Integrating scenarios into strategic planning at Royal Dutch/Shell." *Planning Review, 20*(3), 41–46.

Schwartz, P. (1991). *The art of the long view.* New York, NY: Doubleday Currency.

Simpson, D. G. (1992). "Key lessons for adopting scenario planning in diversified companies." *Planning Review,* May/June, 10–17, 47–48.

Spivey, W. A., & Wrobleski, W. J. (1980). *Surveying recent econometric forecasting performance* (Reprint No. 106). American Enterprise Institute, Washington, D.C.

von Reibnitz, U. (1987). *Scenario techniques.* Hamburg, Germany: McGraw-Hill.

Wack, P. (1985). "Scenarios: Uncharted waters ahead." *Harvard Business Review, 63*(6) 73–89.

Wack, P. (1985). "Scenarios: Shooting the rapids." *Harvard Business Review, 63*(5), 139–150.

Zentner, R. D. (1975). "Scenarios in forecasting." *Chemical and Engineering News, 53*, 6 October, 22–34.

———. (1982). "Scenarios, past, present and future." *Long Range Planning, 15*(3), 12–20.

Chapter 19

Stakeholder Analysis

SHORT DESCRIPTION

Stakeholder analysis systematically identifies important groups of people or individuals who can exert a significant amount of influence on the organization and its competitors. Stakeholder analysis can serve as a powerful technique in helping executives decide which stakeholders are important to a company's and competitor's activities and operations, what their interests are, when and how to initiate actions regarding them, and how to allocate organizational resources among critical stakeholders in order to maximize the likelihood of competitive success.

BACKGROUND

A central idea of business and society relationships, stakeholder analysis is a key component of the larger concept of stakeholder management. Growing out of and away from the popular idea of stockholders—the investors or owners in a business—stakeholder management became popular in the 1980s. Its arrival suggested that managers had come to the recognition that many groups in addition to the obvious category of the company's owners had to be relatively satisfied for companies to achieve their objectives. A key underlying philosophy of strategic stakeholder management is that decision makers need to gain knowledge about their stakeholders and use this information to predict and actively address their actions and behaviors.

It helps to understand what a stake is in order to better understand the idea of stakeholder. A stake is an interest, claim, right, or share in an undertaking. Stakes can range in the extremes from holding a simple interest in an undertaking right up to having a legal claim of ownership.

A key stakeholder is an individual or group that can materially affect or be affected by a company's actions, decision, goals, policies, or practices. It should be clear that the interaction between a focal organization and stakeholder can go two ways, and that the stakeholder can influence the organization and the organization can influence the stakeholder.

Although a premise of stakeholder analysis suggests that they change in their relationships with a focal organization over time, a few common stakeholders important to business and competitive analysis include:

- *Community groups* can stop plans to build sites, provide labor for a workforce, or develop an attractive environment in which to attract particular employees.
- *Customers* provide resources in exchange for products, shifting needs, and interests.
- *Employees* provide the "brain" or "sweat" capital for organizations, provide key skills, are a major source of resource utilization, and are the main link between organizations and customers.
- *Government* sets the rules of the game, affects returns through fiscal and monetary policies, can license or revoke licenses, and is a major purchaser of products.

There are several ways by which to categorize and classify stakeholders. Among the common forms of stakeholder categorization are the following:

1. *Production Versus Managerial Versus Stakeholder Views of the Firm (Freeman, 1984).* The traditional production view of the firm suggests that the key stakeholders will include those involved with the firm's value chain, and, in particular, its suppliers and customers. The managerial view of the firm suggests enlarging the production view by adding those individuals who provide capital (owners, lenders, investors, etc.) and those within the firm who actually generate its outputs for its customers (i.e., its employees). Last, the stakeholder view of the firm is the broadest and most multilateral view of stakeholders and includes nearly all individuals or groups in the STEEP environment that can impact or are impacted by a company's actions, decision, goals, policies, or practices.

2. *Primary Versus Secondary Stakeholders (Wheeler & Sillanpaa, 1997).* Primary stakeholders have a direct stake in the organization and its success and can therefore be very influential. Secondary stakeholders may also be influential, especially in impacting the organization's reputation or public perceptions, but their stake in the organization is more symbolic than direct in terms of its interactions.

3. *Core Versus Strategic Versus Environmental Stakeholders (Clarkson, 1994).* Core stakeholders are a specific subset of strategic stakeholders that are essential to the survival of the organization. Strategic stakeholders are those stakeholders that are vital to the organization and to the specific set of opportunities and threats that it faces at any specific point in time. Environmental stakeholders are all other stakeholders in the organization's environment.

STRATEGIC RATIONALE AND IMPLICATIONS

Stakeholder analysis is a tool that can be used to assist in decision-making situations where various stakeholders have competing interests, resources are limited, and stakeholder needs must be appropriately balanced. Managers use a stakeholder analysis for several critical reasons, to identify people, groups, and institutions that will positively or adversely influence the organization or its competitor's initiative; to anticipate the kind and degree or magnitude of influence, positive or negative, these stakeholders will have on planned market initiatives; and to develop strategies to get the most effective support possible for organizational initiatives and reduce any obstacles to successful strategy implementation.

Stakeholder analysis helps decision makers and managers to assess the market and nonmarket environments in which competition takes place, and to inform the organization's negotiating position in stakeholder discussions. More specifically, conducting a stakeholder analysis can do the following:

1. Draw out the interests of stakeholders in relation to the problems that the project is seeking to address (at the identification stage) or the purpose of the project (once it has started).
2. Identify conflicts of interests between stakeholders, which will influence the organization's assessment of a product or riskiness of an initiative before funds are allocated to it.
3. Help to identify relations between stakeholders that can be built upon, and may enable beneficial "coalitions" to enhance the likelihood of the project's or product's marketplace success.
4. Help to assess the appropriate type of participation by different stakeholders, at successive stages of the marketplace rollout of a new product, project, or service.

Surveys have demonstrated that stakeholder analysis is not used effectively or extensively in strategy development (Gib & Gooding, 1998). Its detractors suggest it does not provide enough specificity of action or direction and that it is difficult to address quantitative (i.e., economic or financial) aspects of the technique. In response, its supporters suggest that few organizations have the needed analytical skills to perform it properly or the appropriate culture and leadership that value its use in a stakeholder strategy–driven managerial approach.

Scholars in several academic areas, including business policy and competition and social issues in management, commonly include stakeholder analysis and management as part of the larger strategic management process. The view held by these scholars is that organizations that manage stakeholder relationships effectively over time should have advantages relative to market competitors that are not as effective. The reasoning suggested for this view includes the following:

1. Some stakeholders are in a position to influence the "rules of the game." For example, public policy makers often establish and enforce the conditions by which competition is played out in the marketplace. Those organizations that best understand these public policymakers and their needs should be in an advantageous position to benefit from the establishment of rules of competition. Indeed, a large number of industries and products have essentially been originated or decimated by public policy decisions (Fleisher & Baetz, 1994).

2. Studies have shown that companies that have superior investor relation functions receive better support from investment analysts and the investors they serve (Hoffman, 1996).

3. In a review of Collins and Porras's (1995) "Visionary Companies," Waddock and Graves (1997) concluded that the Collins and Porras study provided strong evidence that treating employees, community, environment, customers, and others is related to successful financial performance.

STRENGTHS AND ADVANTAGES

Stakeholder analysis has several advantages relative to other analytical tools and techniques:

1. It provides a different perspective from most other planning tools in that it looks at the individuals or groups that are most likely to support or resist marketplace initiatives. As such, it allows the organization to strategically plan who it will ally and partner with, and to take actions to minimize resistance. Of course, the same can be done relative to competitors, whereby the organization can work to maximize stakeholder resistance to a competitor's initiatives.

2. It is a way of systematizing what people naturally do in any case. Most planners tend to informally consider individual and group reactions to their initiatives and this is a way of formally building in these ideas to the plan.

3. Stakeholder analysis can be a powerful management technique in an age of international competition in that it provides companies with a way of proactively considering the proper individuals and groups they need to partner with as they consider international initiatives.

4. In today's competitive environment, alliances, networks, and partnerships are often the difference between marketplace success and failure. Stakeholder analysis is one of the few tools that explicitly considers both competitors and complementers, and can help firms both compete and cooperate, otherwise known as co-opetition (Brandenburger & Nalebuff, 1997).

5. Stakeholder analysis is also one of the few analytical tools that explicitly requires a consideration of the social and ethical aspects of business activity. In an age when these aspects have grown in prominence, this can be a powerful and differentiating competitive weapon for businesses that understand and can take advantage of this perspective.

WEAKNESSES AND LIMITATIONS

For the many unique dimensions stakeholder analysis can contribute to the strategist, there are several reasons why it is limited in the value that it brings to the planning and decision-making table:

1. Stakeholder perspectives are generally given lip service in the business education of most managers. Business majors are given much less access to it than many

other tools. As such, few of them would consider this approach as being as fundamental, as, say, financial analysis would be.

2. Stakeholders can be notoriously difficult to forecast and predict. They often follow the winds of public opinion and have been known to react emotionally, rather than logically, to developments affecting them. Quite frequently, stakeholders also wear different, and often contradictory, hats simultaneously (e.g., an employee of a power company considering expansion of a nuclear plant may also be an environmentalist and sit on local city planning boards). Trying to manage stakeholders may be far more difficult than trying to manage the organization's response to issues around which the stakeholders are organizing.

3. Analysts studying possible stakeholder reactions have to utilize a high degree of subjectivity in their analysis. Past behaviors are not always accurate predictors of future stakeholder behavior. Some stakeholders may also claim to believe one thing yet do another. In other words, their attitudes and opinions don't always translate into correlative actions.

4. Stakeholder prioritization relies heavily on the beliefs of the managers planning the decisions. As such, they often fall prey to the many blindspots (see Chapter 10) that impact business decisions of this nature. For example, some management decision makers always discount the adverse reactions of labor unions when those same labor unions may be supporters of some organizational marketplace initiatives that will simultaneously benefit their memberships.

5. To be valuable, stakeholder analysis needs to be practiced regularly over time. It requires constant environmental and issue scanning and monitoring. Few organizations have demonstrated the strategic perspective to put the necessary resources into place in order to generate the capacity to carry out these tasks effectively over extended periods of time.

PROCESS FOR APPLYING THE TECHNIQUE

Stakeholder analysis should always be done at the beginning or formulation stage of a new product, project, or service, even if it is just a brief list of stakeholders and their interests. It should also be done anytime the organization is considering a significant change in its marketplace product scope, posture, or goals. Frequently, and in any case, analysts do this on an informal basis. Such a list can be used to draw out the main assumptions that are needed if a product, project, or service is going to be viable, and to point out some of the key risks.

Stakeholder analysis is often done in a participatory fashion. Drawing up lists and diagrams in such a manner can share and clarify information quickly among groups. A team-based approach is likely to be more effective than a single person doing the analysis alone. However, stakeholder analysis often involves proprietary or sensitive data and information. Many interests are covert and agendas are deliberately camouflaged. In these situations there will be few benefits in trying to uncover such agendas in public.

The process of analyzing stakeholders for strategic and competitive analysis purposes requires the analyst to answer the following questions:

1. Who are the organization's stakeholders?
2. What are the stakeholders' stakes? This requires the analyst to understand the responsibilities the company has to its stakeholders, the importance of stakeholders to an initiative's success, and stakeholders' relative power and influence.
3. What challenges and risks do stakeholders present to the firm and competitors?
4. What strategies and actions should the company take to best deal with stakeholder challenges and opportunities?

Step 1: Who Are the Organization's Stakeholders?

This step requires the analyst to identify and list the organization's potential stakeholders relative to the initiative it is considering. In practice, answering the question of "who are the organization's stakeholders?" is a process that unfolds and evolves over time. It is part of the larger environmental scanning process and is usually known more specifically by the name *stakeholder identification*. This can provide an advantage to an organization, since many of its competitors may not be carefully (if at all) identifying stakeholders and how to address them.

The analyst must identify both the organization's *generic* and *specific* stakeholder groups. Generic stakeholders include such groups as consumers, employees, governments, interest groups, and shareholders. Specific stakeholders are subgroups within these categories who have material stakes associated with an issue or potential issue facing the company. The analyst would want to identify the specific government departments or agencies involved with a business or competitive issue as opposed to a generic group called "government." For example, a telecommunications issue in Canada might generally involve the Canadian Radio and Telecommunications Commission (CRTC), and particularly involve a designated commission hearing matters surrounding the competitive issue. More specifically, stakeholder analysis would require identifying specific individuals who are influential contact points for the specific stakeholders. A stakeholder table (see Table 19-1), can be a helpful starting point for this analysis.

It can also be helpful to do a stakeholder map that shows the linkages between the stakeholders themselves, because the interests of stakeholders often overlap. In these cases, they are likely to form coalitions or alliances with other groups that have similar objectives.

STAKEHOLDER	INTEREST(S) OR DEMANDS	IMPACT	IMPORTANCE OF STAKEHOLDER	STAKEHOLDER'S STRENGTHS	STAKEHOLDER'S WEAKNESSES
1.					
2.					
3.					
n.					

Table 19-1
Stakeholder Table

Step 2: What Are the Stakeholders' Stakes?

Once stakeholders have been identified, the next step is to determine the nature, some of which will be overt, some hidden, of their stakes in relation to the organization's planned market initiative. The challenge to the analyst is to identify the nature or legitimacy of a group's stakes and the group's power or ability to affect the organizations involved with an issue. What complicates this step is that each stakeholder may have multiple, and sometimes internally conflicting, interests.

For example, the generic group of stakeholders called corporate owners includes more specific groups such as institutional owners (foundations, trusts), large mutual fund organizations, board members who own shares, management and employees shareholders, and many small, individual shareholders holding blocks of shares. The nature of these groups' claims is legitimate as legal owners of the company. However, they are not equally powerful in influencing issue outcomes. Likely to be most influential in determining issue direction are the external groups such as the institutional owners and mutual funds, and the "internal" groups of board members and executives with their dual ownership and managerial roles.

It is important to consider why a stakeholder group might mobilize around an issue associated with your market initiative. Weiner and Brown (1986) suggest the following possibilities:

1. Your initiative may result in an economic loss to them.
2. They may view your initiative (e.g., using the application of a new technology) as a potential threat to their health and safety
3. Politicians may get involved as a way of showing their concern for their electors and the public in general (e.g., Not In My Back Yard or NIMBY).
4. Your initiative is critical to those most directly linked to it (e.g., you are considering resuscitating a mothballed factory that will provide the stakeholders some good new jobs).
5. Your initiative could reflect a change in values or lifestyles characteristic of the stakeholder group (e.g., a risqué new TV show that shows singles trying to lure away committed partners in relationships).
6. Your initiative is attractive to opportunists.
7. Your initiative could become a lightning rod for disaffected groups.
8. Your initiative can serve as currency for exchanging support among stakeholder groups (e.g., they help Group A against your initiative in order that Group A gives them help with one of their pet issues).

Wood (1994) suggests that stakes can be analyzed as falling into several useful analytical categories:

1. *Single- or Multiple-Issue Stakes.* Single-issue stakeholders are only concerned with one facet of a company's operations while multiple issue stakeholders care about many.
2. *Economic or Social Stakes.* Those with economic interests care about the distribution of financial or material resources (shareholders care about corporate profitability, employees about salary levels, etc.) while those with social interests

usually have beliefs or values concerns (corporate social responsibility, equal employment opportunity, wilderness protection, etc.).

3. *Concrete or Symbolic Stakes.* Concrete interests are related to the allocation of material resources, while symbolic interests are displayed in more difficult to define terms like demands for something to be done, reassurances, gestures, and goodwill.

4. *Local, National, or International Interests.* The boundaries of various stakeholders may vary from the local issue to the national agenda to an international or even global framework.

It can also be helpful at this point to determine what responsibilities the organization may have to stakeholders. Responsibilities the analyst must consider typically come in one of four forms (Carroll, 1991):

1. *Economic.* The firm's economic responsibility is to be profitable (e.g., the responsibility to generate an acceptable rate of return for shareholders).

2. *Legal.* The firm's legal responsibility is to obey relevant laws that are society's codification of right and wrong (e.g., the responsibility to file audited financial reports with governmental agencies).

3. *Ethical.* The firm's ethical responsibility is to do what is right, just, and fair and to avoid harm (e.g., the responsibility to choose wisely between several alternative investments of the firm's resources).

4. *Discretionary.* The firm's discretionary responsibility is to be a good corporate citizen by contributing its resources to improving stakeholders' quality of life (e.g., whether the company should devote some of its resources to a community in which it has a key plant).

Stakeholder interests may be drawn out by asking questions such as: What are the stakeholder's expectations of the organization's market initiative? What benefits are there likely to be for the stakeholders from this initiative? What resources will the stakeholder wish to commit (or avoid committing) to the initiative? What other interests does the stakeholder have that may conflict with the project? And finally, how does the stakeholder regard other stakeholders in the domain of the market initiative?

Step 3: What Opportunities and Challenges Do Stakeholders Present to This Firm and Its Market Competitors?

This step requires the analyst to briefly assess the likely impact of the market initiative on each of these interests (positive, negative, or unknown). Opportunities and challenges associated with stakeholders can represent the two opposite edges of the same sword. Opportunities include building harmonious, long-standing, positive, and productive relationships with stakeholders. Challenges usually take the form of varying degrees of expectations or demands and present themselves in a way that requires a company to manage its stakeholder interaction well so that it avoids being damaged or harmed in some fashion. Harm can be in the form of resource withdrawal (e.g., a mutual fund company sells its shares in a company due to its opinion that management was not making appropriate structural changes to the business) or reputational (e.g., a number of share-owning board members quit their positions and sell their ownership stakes due to longstanding disagreements with company direction). Opportunities and challenges may also be viewed in terms of potential for cooperation or confrontation.

Some of the best analytical categories for assessing opportunities or threats would include the following:

1. *Direction of effect* is the principal effect flowing from the company to the stakeholder (e.g., wafting fumes from a smokestack flowing over a residential area) or from the stakeholder group to the company (e.g., labor group demands not to move jobs to foreign countries).
2. *Importance of effect* is how seriously the stakeholders' interests and actions affect the company's performance.
3. *Immediacy of effect* means at what time period—short, medium, or long term—the company may be affected by stakeholder demands and actions.
4. *Probability of resolution* is whether the company has the capabilities and resources to deal with stakeholder demands.

Table 19-2 is a generic matrix for a company planning to open a new plant in a local community. It provides a simple illustration of how some of the categories described in this section may be employed in assessing the stakeholder environment.

Some companies choose to rate each of the above (or related categories of their own determination) on a quantitative scale (e.g., 1 to 5, with 1 being supportive/friendly and 5 being nonsupportive/adversarial) and then weigh the categories based on subjective managerial determinations. This can help executives decide which stakeholders require what type of attention and resources. Some analysts add an assessment of their confidence about their determinations. This can take the form of a scale ranging from 1 (high confidence/strong evidence supports this view) to 5 (low confidence/sheer speculation or guessing).

Key stakeholders are those who can significantly influence, or are important to the success of, the organization's market initiative. Influence refers to how powerful a stakeholder is; importance refers to those stakeholders whose problems, needs, and interests are the priority of the organization's initiative; if these important stakeholders are not benefited by the initiative, then it cannot be deemed a success. By combining influence and importance using a matrix diagram (see Figure 19-1), stakeholders can be classified into different groups, which will help identify assumptions and the risks that need to be managed through the market initiative's design. The list here is grouped by the letters in Figure 19-1.

A. Stakeholders of high importance to the initiative, but with low degrees of influence. This implies that they will require special initiatives if their interests are to be protected.

B. Stakeholders appearing to have a high degree of influence on the initiative, who are also of high importance for its success. This implies that the organization will need to construct good working relationships with these stakeholders to ensure their support. Key stakeholders with high levels of influence and importance to project success are likely to provide the basis of the initiative coalition of support, and are potential partners in planning and implementation.

C. Stakeholders with high influence, who can therefore affect the initiative's outcomes, but whose interests are not the target of the initiative. This group of stakeholders may be

Table 19-2

Generic Stakeholder Analysis Matrix for a Company Opening a New Plant

	COMMUNICATION FROM ORGANIZATION	COMMUNICATION FROM STAKEHOLDER	IMPORTANCE OF STAKEHOLDER	LIKELIHOOD OF STAKEHOLDER INVOLVEMENT	STAKEHOLDER GOALS	STRENGTHS OF STAKEHOLDER
Local Consumers	Full and accurate information about products and services	Needs, wants, purchases	Moderately high	Low, unless consumers are materially affected by an issue	Products and services that perform as advertised, pay the minimum for maximum product	Can affect public opinion and get media attention
Employees	Human resource management policies, supervision	Union demands, remain employed, attract recruits	High	Dependent on impact on existing and prospective employees	Better working conditions, enjoy work, higher pay, increased responsibilities, promotion, and recognition	Organization needs them to survive and prosper
Local government	Applications, permits, requests	Laws, public policies, regulations	High	Depends on state of economy and relative view about new plant's role in community	Receive taxes, increase employment, improve community infrastructure	Can impose strength of law to impact behavior
Investors	Annual report, analysts' meetings, investor relations	Buy/sell shares, motion at annual meetings	Moderate	Low unless new plant is viewed as high-risk endeavor	Make a profit, want plant to have positive ROI and future growth prospects	Can provide or withdraw funds needed for growth

Importance			
	High		Low
Low	A		D
Influence			
High	B		C

Figure 19-1
Stakeholder
Influence/
Importance Matrix

a source of significant risk and require careful monitoring and management. Key stakeholders in this category may be "managed" by being consulted or informed.

D. Stakeholders in this box, with low influence on or importance to the initiative's objectives, may require limited monitoring or evaluation, but are of low priority. They are unlikely to be the subject of managed activities or management.

Influence is the power that stakeholders have over a market initiative—to control what decisions are made, facilitate its implementation, or exert influence that negatively affects the planned action. Influence is perhaps best understood as the extent to which stakeholders are able to persuade or coerce others into making decisions and following certain courses of action. Power may derive from the nature of stakeholder's organization, or their position in relation to other stakeholders (for example, line ministries that control budgets and other departments). Other forms of influence may be more informal (for example, personal connections to public decision makers).

It may also be necessary to consider stakeholders whose power, and therefore influence, will increase because of resources introduced by the project. Assessing influence is often difficult and involves interpretation of a range of factors. By way of example, some of the variables that may be involved are illustrated in Table 19-3.

Another way for determining whether the stakeholder represents an opportunity or threat to an organization would be to understand the likelihood that the stakeholder will either cooperate (i.e., an opportunity) or resist the organization (i.e., a threat) vis-à-vis an initiative or an issue. Savage, et al., (1991) argued that this assessment of threat and cooperation is important for managers in order to identify strategies for dealing with stakeholders. In determining the potential for opportunities or threats, the analyst would need to consider the stakeholder's relative degree of power or influence to a particular issue confronting the organization. Savage et al. recommend assessing several variables such as whether:

1. The stakeholder controls important resources needed by the organization—if they do, the potential for threat increases as does their potential for cooperation. If they do not, their potential for threat declines.

Table 19-3

Variables Affecting Stakeholders' Relative Power and Influence

WITHIN AND BETWEEN FORMAL ORGANIZATIONS	FOR INFORMAL INTEREST GROUPS AND PRIMARY STAKEHOLDERS
Established hierarchy (command and control, those who allocate resources)	Socioeconomic and political status
Authority of leadership (examples; formal and informal, charisma, political, familial, or other connections)	Degree of organization, consensus, and leadership in the group
Control of strategic resources for the initiatives (e.g., ownership of land or permits to use a specific site)	Degree of control of strategic resources significant for the organization's market initiative
Possession of specialized know-how	Informal influence through connections with other stakeholders
Negotiating position derived from strength in relation to other stakeholders	Degree of dependence on other stakeholders

2. They are more powerful than the organization—if they are more powerful, the potential for threat increases, while the potential decreases if the stakeholder is less powerful than the focal organization but may also simultaneously increase their likelihood for actually cooperating with the focal organization.

3. They are likely to take action supportive of the focal organization—this decreases the stakeholders' potential for threat and increases their likelihood to cooperate, while stakeholders' likelihood to take nonsupportive action increases their potential for threat and decreases their potential for cooperation. Stakeholders unlikely to take any form of action would decrease their potential to threaten the focal organization along with decreasing their potential to cooperate.

4. The stakeholders are looking to ally and collaborate with other supportive or adversarial stakeholders—stakeholders likely to form coalitions with other stakeholders increases their potential for threat while may either increase or decrease their likelihood to cooperate with the focal organization, stakeholders that are likely to form a coalition with the focal organization have a decreased potential for threat and an increased potential for cooperation, while a stakeholder unlikely to form any coalitions would have both a decreased potential for threat and a decreased potential for cooperation.

The success of an organization's market initiative depends partly on the validity of the assumptions made about its various stakeholders, and the risks facing the initiative. Some of these risks will derive from conflicting interests. Visible initiatives are often particularly affected by stakeholder interactions and responses to project activities. Planners must therefore identify and assess the importance of the most plausible assumptions about each "key" stakeholder that is necessary if the initiative is to succeed.

By assessing the influence and importance of key stakeholders, some risks emerge from the matrix diagram. In general, risks will be evident from those stakeholders in box C of Figure 19-1 who have high influence but who have interests that are not in line with the initiative's objectives. These key stakeholders may be able to block or hinder the initiative in the marketplace, and if this is probable, the risk may constitute a "killer assumption." In summary, it is critical that the analyst understand which plausible assumptions about stakeholders support or threaten the project.

Some key questions to draw out these assumptions include, What is the role or response of the key stakeholder that must be assumed if the project is to be successful? Are these roles plausible and realistic? Are there negative responses that can be expected, given the interests of the stakeholder? If such responses occur, what impact would they have on the initiative? How probable are these negative responses, and are they major risks?

Step 4: What Strategies or Actions Should Management Take with Respect to Its Stakeholders?

In every issue situation, a multitude of alternative courses of action are available to the organization and its competitors. MacMillan and Jones (1986) suggest management should consider several basic approaches in dealing with stakeholders by answering the following: Do we deal *directly or indirectly* with stakeholders? Do we take the *offense or defense* with stakeholders? Do we *accommodate, negotiate, manipulate, or resist* stakeholder claims? Do we employ a *combination* of the above strategies *or pursue a singular course of action*?

Fleisher and Baetz (1994) have suggested that there are several tactical responses the organization can make based on its analysis of stakeholders. Their idea is framed under the rubric of implementing a stakeholder strategy. In implementing a stakeholder strategy, the four elements to be considered are: (1) timing, (2) techniques, (3) vehicles, and (4) style. There are several options associated with each of the four elements. In assessing these options, the following questions need to be considered: Which option(-s) will help us best accomplish our objective with respect to the resolution of the issue and why? Which of the option(-s) have worked historically with respect to the resolution of similar issues and why? and finally, what are the risks and opportunities, and costs (including resources required, harms/benefits), of selecting the option and why?

1. *Establish the Timing of the Organization's Response.* This establishes the sequence or chronology, including the rationale for these decisions, by which the organization intends to take the actions it has decided upon in the formulation stage. Timing is defined for our purposes to be the organization's response with respect to the stage of issue development (Buchholz, 1992).

The organization can establish its timing options along a couple of continuums, including the strategic timing of its response (i.e., Proactive–Interactive–Reactive–Inactive) and using a fixed time horizon (i.e., immediate–Short term–Medium term–Long term).

2. *Choose and Put into Action the Techniques Utilized in Accomplishing the Objectives.* We define techniques to be the form of the organization's response. The organization has several direct and indirect strategic implementation options available to it (Buchholz, 1992), including communication techniques speaking out on issues (advocacy/image ads, annual report, CEO speech, press releases, media presentations, etc.); participation

techniques (lobbying, general business associations, industry associations, constituency building, political contributions, etc.); and compliance techniques (cooperate with regulatory agencies, legal resistance, judicial proceedings, create new issue, noncompliance, etc.).

3. *Determine and utilize the vehicles that will carry out the formulated strategy.* We define vehicle to be those individuals or groups who actually carry out the chosen techniques and strategies. The firm has several options available to it, including organizational versus extraorganizational vehicles (carry out the strategy primarily by using internal organizational stakeholders or using stakeholders external to the organization, i.e., third party contractors); and individual versus coalitional vehicles (the organization may carry out the strategy through its own efforts or in collaboration with other organizations, i.e., its association, professional groups, activist/interest groups).

4. *Determine Style.* Refers to the tone or manner in which the organization will respond to its stakeholders with respect to the issue's resolution. For the purposes of this chapter, style is defined to be the manner in which the technique is carried out. There are several options available in implementing style, including whether it will be confrontational, neutral, or conciliatory.

Another model offered by Savage et al. (1991) suggests that whether the stakeholder has a high or low potential for cooperating or threatening an organization will determine the focal organization's response strategy. They argue that responses could take the form of:

1. Collaborating with the stakeholder (high potential for threat and for cooperation).
2. Involving the stakeholder in the issue (high potential for cooperation but low potential for threat).
3. Defending the corporation (i.e., stakeholder has a high potential for threat but low potential for cooperating).
4. Monitoring (i.e., the stakeholder has a low potential for threat and cooperation).

FAROUT Summary

	1	2	3	4	5
F	▓	▓			
A	▓	▓			
R	▓	▓	▓		
O	▓				
U	▓	▓	▓		
T	▓	▓	▓		

Future orientation Low to medium as is usually associated with emerging issues in practice, as opposed to longer-term issue forecasts.

Accuracy Low to medium degree. Requires sophisticated analytical skills in understanding sociopolitics that are generally not present in most companies. Stakeholders are dynamic and attach to different issues in different ways.

Resource efficiency   Medium degree. Much stakeholder information can be gleaned from previous experience and secondary data sources. Most important stakeholder intelligence, though, comes from human intelligence, raising the volume of resources needed to do it well.

Objectivity   Low. Generally requires high degree of subjectivity in knowing responsibilities of stakeholders. Influenced heavily by the analyst's and organization's beliefs, experiences, or values.

Usefulness   Medium. Stakeholder analysis is most valuable when used as part of a larger strategic stakeholder management approach. If few competitors take this approach, it can be potentially more valuable by providing a unique competitive perspective.

Timeliness   Medium. Can be done quickly if stakeholders are tracked on a regular basis, thus necessitating only the analyst's positioning of stakeholders vis-à-vis specific issues.

RELATED TOOLS AND TECHNIQUES

- customer segmentation analysis
- industry analysis
- issue analysis
- macroenvironmental (STEEP) analysis
- scenario analysis
- SWOT analysis.

REFERENCES

Brandenburger, A. & Nalebuff, B. (1997). *Co-opetition: 1. A revolutionary mindset that redefines competition and cooperation; 2. The game theory strategy that is changing the game of business.* New York: Doubleday.

Buchholz, R. (1992). *Public policy issues for management* (2nd ed.). Englewood Cliffs, NJ: Prentice-Hall.

Carroll, A. B. (1991). "The pyramid of corporate social responsibility: Toward the moral management of organizational stakeholders." *Business Horizons*, July-August, 42. Vol. 34. No. 4, pages 39–48.

Clarkson, M. B. E. (1994). *A risk based model of stakeholder theory.* Toronto: University of Toronto, The Center for Corporate Social Performance & Ethics.

Collins, J. C., & Porras, J. I. (1995). *Built to last: Successful habits of visionary companies.* New York: HarperBusiness.

Fleisher, C. S. & Baetz, M. (1994). "The strategic management of public affairs/government relations (PA/GR): A comprehensive framework." *Proceedings of the Fifth Annual Meeting of the International Association of Business and Society.* Hilton Head, SC.

Freeman, R. E. (1984). *Strategic management: A stakeholder approach.* Boston: Pitman.

Gib, A., & Gooding, R. (1998). "CI tool time: What's missing from your tool bag?" *Proceedings of the Annual Meeting of the Society of Competitive Intelligence Professionals:* 25–39.

Hoffman, A. J. (1996). "A strategic response to investor activism." *Sloan Management Review, 37*(2), 51–64.

MacMillan, I. C. & Jones, P. E. (1986). *Strategy formulation: Power and politics.* St. Paul, MN: West.

Savage, G., Nix, T. W., Whitehead, C. J., & Blair, D. (1991). "Strategies for assessing and managing organizational stakeholders." *Academy of Management Executive, 5*(2), 61–75.

Waddock, S., & Graves, S. (1997). "Quality of management and quality of stakeholder relations." *Business and Society, 36*(3), 250–279.

Weiner, E., & Brown, A. (1986). "Stakeholder analysis for effective issues management." *Planning Review, 14*(3), 27–31.

Wheeler, D., & Sillanpaa, M. (1997). *The stakeholder corporation: A blueprint for maximizing stakeholder value.* London: Pitman.

Wood, D. J. (1994). *Business & Society* (2nd ed.). New York: Harper Collins.

Chapter 20

Experience Curve Analysis

SHORT DESCRIPTION

Experience curve analysis is a conceptual framework premised on the fact that, in many industries, value-added costs often decline by a constant factor as cumulative production volume or experience is doubled. From this observed statistical law, wide-ranging strategic guidance is derived regarding competitive analysis; cost forecasting; market entry decisions and subsequent pricing strategy; budgeting, cost control, and benchmarking; and determining the strategic merits of choosing to compete on cost.

BACKGROUND

The antecedent theory of experience curve analysis was the learning curve, a phenomenon first observed during the U.S. manufacturing of World War II aircraft at the Wright-Patterson Air Base. Wright-Patterson management developed a production schedule graph that plotted labor hours on the vertical axis against output on the horizontal axis. This simple planning tool soon reflected a consistent trend of increasing labor productivity—each successive aircraft required fewer hours to complete. As the aircraft workers became more familiar with the repetitive production process, they were progressively more efficient. Writing in the February 1936 issue of *Journal of Aeronautical Sciences*, T. P. Wright observed that his production schedule graphs depicted a constant relationship between labor cost and the production volume of his plant. In other words, the average labor cost of his aircraft plant decreased by 20 percent with every doubling of plant production. On a logarithmic graph, this translates into an 80 percent learning curve. Then, in the mid-1940s, J. R. Crawford noticed a similar constant relationship between volume and marginal labor costs while working at Lockheed. Given the observed constancy of these factors, management could extrapolate with reasonable accuracy how many labor hours would be required to increase production output.

This theory then lay fairly dormant for several decades. The only refinements made were to include the concept of organizational learning—that is, as output

313

volume increased, management and technical support staff also became more adept at their interactions with the work processes. This refinement is generally attributed to a 1963 study performed at General Dynamics that indicated that only 25 percent of the cost reductions were solely attributable to labor learning economies. Much of the remaining cost reduction was associated with learning-related efficiencies in engineering (30 percent) and retooling (25 percent). This phenomenon, in addition to direct labor economies, contributed to the general acceptance that costs declined with volume-induced organizational learning, albeit primarily in industries characterized by repetitive and labor-intensive processes.

It wasn't until the mid- to late 1960s that Bruce Henderson, founder of the Boston Consulting Group (BCG), pushed the conceptual envelope with a radical new concept he called the experience curve. While sharing many similarities with the learning curve, the experience curve is separated from it by two key distinctions. First, the horizontal axis was replaced with *cumulative volume* as opposed to production rate (i.e., output per finite period). Second, the vertical axis was replaced with *total inflation-adjusted costs* (i.e., material inputs, distribution, marketing, overhead, and every other component of total unit costs) rather than just including labor costs. Thus, the experience curve was derived from plotting *total real cost* versus *cumulative volume*. In 1966, BCG explicitly used this new theory in a strategic recommendation to General Instrument Corporation to model and forecast the cost behavior of some of their nascent information systems technology. Then in 1968, Henderson and BCG formally published its experience curve logic in the book *Perspectives on Experience*.

The Conceptual Underpinnings of Experience Curve Logic

Theoretical

The theoretical rationale for the experience curve offered by BCG experience curve logic is best explained by its originator, Bruce Henderson:

> The experience curve is the rate of change in the cumulative cash input divided by the cumulative physical output. The denominator and the numerator are both cumulative. Because of that, the ratio between them is exponentially smoothed. If the experience curve rate of cost decline is constant, then the current unit cost will become the cumulative average cost when the total cumulative experience has doubled. This relationship between cumulative cash input and cumulative physical input is the central issue of the experience curve. It is the rate of change in that ratio which is the rate of cost decline of unit cost with each doubling of output. (Henderson, 1984a)

Graphical

Figure 20-1 depicts a stylized experience curve that shows the total costs of performing similar or repetitive activities declining by a constant ratio with each doubling of production volume. Assuming the experience curve depicted in Figure 20-1 has a 75 percent slope, this would indicate that the total cost of production would decline by 25 percent with each doubling of cumulative output (i.e., from $1,000 to $750 when doubling production from 500 units to 1,000 units, from $700 to $562.50 when doubling production from 1,000 units to 2,000 units, and so on).

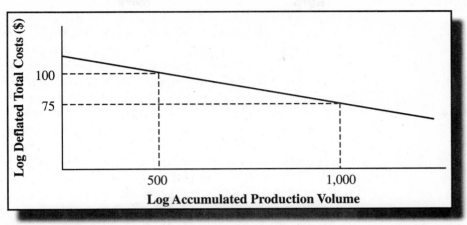

Figure 20-1
Logarithmic Learning Curve Example

Algebraic

Testament to the intuitive appeal of experience curve logic, the underlying algebraic representation is equally accessible. The generic equation for an experience curve is

$$C_t = C_0 \, (V_t/V_0)^{-E}$$

where

  C_t = real cash cost of the nth unit produced
  C_0 = real cash cost of the first unit produced
  V_t = accumulated volume at the time the nth unit is produced
  V_0 = accumulated volume at the beginning of the analysis
  E = constant elasticity coefficient of unit costs to accumulated production volume

The slope of the experience curve is given by the following derivation:

$$\text{Slope} = C_t/C_0$$

Therefore, whenever production volume is doubled (i.e., $V_t/V_0 = 2$), the equation describing the relationship between the slope and the elasticity coefficient is

$$C_t/C_0 = (V_t/V_0)^{-E} \text{ or}$$
$$\log \text{slope} = -E \log 2$$
$$E = -(\log \text{slope}/\log 2)$$

For example, in Figure 20-1, the constant elasticity coefficient, E, can be determined for the 75 percent experience curve depicted. Given that $(C_t/C_0) = 0.75$ and $(V_t/V_0) = 2$, then

$$C_t/C_0 = (V_t/V_0)^{-E}$$
$$.75 = 2^{-E}$$
$$E = -(\log \text{slope}/\log 2)$$
$$= -(\log 0.75/\log 2)$$
$$= 0.415$$

Empirical

Shortly after publication, BCG, and soon many other consulting firms and academics who recognized the powerful logic underlying this phenomenon, spearheaded approximately 2,000 experience curve analyses for a wide range of corporations in many different industries in order to determine a wide-ranging empirical basis for their experience curve doctrine. Table 20-1 shows the resulting variety of the empirical studies performed for U.S. industry. Numerous other international studies were also conducted, from the motorcycle industry in Britain to the steel industry in Japan. Typically, cost reductions with each doubling of accumulated output were found to be between 20 and 30 percent. Of particular note is the preponderance of heavy industry premised on competitive factors such as labor intensity, capital intensity, and repetitive manufacturing processes. In particular, the rapidly growing chemical, automotive, and electronics industries in the mid-1960s made heavy use of experience curve analysis.

Causal Factors Driving the Experience Curve

Experience curve effects don't just happen as a normal course of corporate existence. Rather, several factors must be explicitly managed in order for an organization to benefit from experience curve cost dynamics:

• *Learning.* The first and most intuitive reason for the existence of experience curves is the simple fact that humans become progressively more adept at performing repetitive activities. Experience acquired through volume generally results in increasing efficiency and productivity that, in turn, reduce both total and average unit costs of production.

• *Specialization.* Delineating production tasks into standardized processes and work flow allows individual workers to focus their learning on an optimal number of tasks to maximize productivity.

• *Product Design and Production Process Improvements.* As production volume increases, many operational enhancements are discovered and implemented, such as improved technology, more efficient plant layout, better maintenance, improved product engineering, and so on.

• *Scale Economies.* As volume increases, fixed costs can be spread over more volume, resulting in declining unit costs. Additionally, the acquisition of "lumpy" assets is justified by economies of scale furthering the relative unit cost of the acquiring firm.

• *Organizational Structure.* After a firm accumulates significant volume, many organizational improvements occur, such as developing optimal ways of employees' working together, systems efficiency, technology integration across departments, and so on.

• *Innovation.* Expensive to foster, innovation often requires significant investment in R&D technology, and customer intelligence that is only feasible at the critical financial mass, which is generated by higher unit volumes.

• *Reduced Cost of Funds.* Large firms, who have grown due to the generation of large production and sales volumes, have access to cheaper sources of debt and equity.

• *Reduced Cost of Inputs.* Larger firms can generally procure raw material inputs and supplies at lower average costs than that available to smaller firms.

Table 20-1
Examples of Experience Curves in U.S. Industry

EXAMPLE	IMPROVING PARAMETER	CUMULATIVE PARAMETER	LEARNING CURVE SLOPE (%)	TIME FRAME	NUMBER OF VOLUME DOUBLINGS
Ford Model T production	Price	Units produced	86	1910–1926	10
Aircraft assembly	Direct man-hours per unit	Units produced	80	1925–1957	3
Catalytic cracking units for petroleum	Days required per million barrels	Million barrels run	90	1946–1958	10
Cost of fluid cracking costs	Cost per barrel of capacity	Installed design capacity of plants	94 80[*]	1942–1958	5
Equipment maintenance in GE plant	Average time to replace a group of parts during shutdown	Number of replacements	76	Around 1957	4
Man-hours per barrel in the petroleum industry	Average direct man-hours per barrel refined	Millions of barrels of refined in the United States	84	1860–1962	15
Electrical power generation	Mils per kWh	Millions of kWh	95[*]	1910–1955	5
Steel production	Production worker man-hours per unit produced	Units produced	79	1920–1955	3
Integrated circuit prices	Average price per unit	Units produced	72[*]	1964–1972	10
MOS/LSI prices	Average price per unit	Units produced	80	1970–1976	10
Electronic digital watch prices	Average factory selling prices	Units produced	74	1975–1978	4
Hand-held calculator prices	Average factory selling prices	Units produced	74	1975–1978	2
Most dynamic RAM prices	Average factory selling price per bit	Number of bits	68	1973–1978	6
Disk memory drives	Average price per bit	Number of bits	76	1975–1978	3
Price of minimum active electronic function in semi-conductor products	Price of minimum semiconductor function	Number of functions produced by semiconductor industry	60	1960–1977	13

[*] Constant Dollars
Source: "Using the Learning Curve As a Management Tool," by J. A. Cunningham, 1980, *IEEE Spectrum*, June.

The preceding list reflects that the sources of the experience curve effect are a combination of scale economies, learning, and technology. The research on which general factor class is the most significant is, at best, industry and firm dependent and, at worst, inconclusive. However, as the following discussion on the strategic value of experience curve analysis shows, making this distinction is critical.

Underscoring the Importance of Market Share

The strategic implications offered by experience curve analysis are closely related to the concept of market share. The Boston Consulting Group was the earliest proponent of this critical connection. The fundamental proposition offered by BCG was a very intuitively appealing cause-and-effect relationship that commingled the concepts of experience curve with that of market share:

Perhaps the development that most firmly entrenched experience curve analysis into mainstream strategic analysis was the central role that this theory played in the now-famous portfolio matrix also developed by BCG in the late 1960s. The experience curve was used as the theoretical support for the horizontal axis of the growth/share matrix—relative market share. Essentially, market share was used as a proxy for the comparative cost advantages implied by the experience curve (see also Chapter 4). This linkage between the experience curve, the product life cycle, and BCG's portfolio matrix is graphically displayed in Figure 20-2.

This interlinked theory garnered even more credibility when professors at Harvard Business School conducted an extensive and statistically robust investigation through Harvard's affiliation with the Strategic Planning Institute. The Profit Impact of Market Strategies (PIMS) studied 57 corporations with 620 different businesses to determine the relationship between strategic planning and profit performance. Among the findings of PIMS was apparently credible support for BCG's proposition that a firm's profit performance was closely related to market share (see Schoeffler, Buzzell, & Heany, 1974; Buzzell, Gale, & Sultan, 1975).

If all of the firms in an industry are operating on the same experience curve, the strategic implications are self-evident. The firm with the highest market share will enjoy the lowest costs (by virtue of higher volumes and hence stronger experience curve effects), granting it a competitive advantage in the industry. Lower-volume firms will be at a steep competitive disadvantage because their higher costs (by virtue

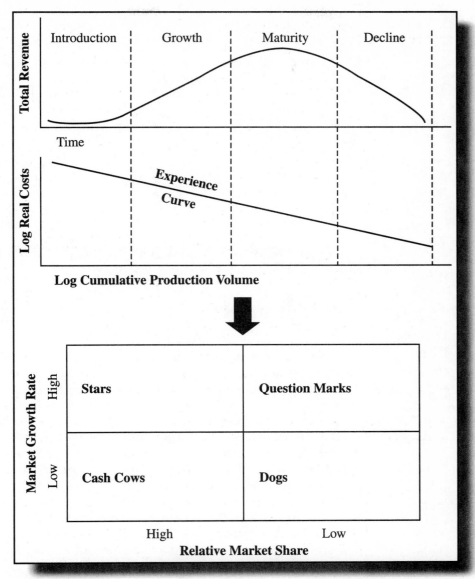

Figure 20-2
Relationship of the Experience Curve with Related Management Theory Constructs

of lower volumes and hence weaker experience curve effects) will make them less profitable. Figure 20-3 graphically demonstrates this industry structure scenario. The strategic recommendation for these low-share firms is to increase their competitive position by increasing market share. This is difficult to achieve, however, because firms with high market shares enjoy a virtually reinforcing position. High profitability firms can invest to establish an entrenched position of competitive superiority in the industry, thus further increasing their profits. So difficult is it for low volume/low

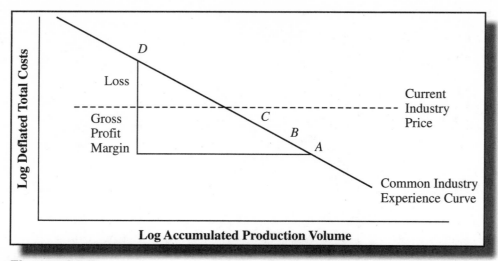

Figure 20-3
Industry Structure on a Common Experience Curve

Source: Adapted from "Competitive Cost Dynamics: The Experience Curve," by A. C. Hax and
N. C. Majluf, 1982, *Interfaces, 12*(5), pp. 50–61.

profit firms to increase market share that BCG suggested the "rule of three and four."
This rule asserts that a stable competitive industry or market rarely has more than
three main competing firms, with the smallest firm having no less than 25 percent the
market share of the largest firm. This is reflected in Figure 20-3 in that lower volume
firms (firm D) will be at a severe cost disadvantage to the three largest firms in the
industry (firms A, B, and C). The only recourse for a firm that finds itself outside of the
top three ranking in market share is to somehow increase its market share, continue to
operate at a loss, find a profitable niche strategy, or exit the industry in order to stem
the losses. Essentially, experience curve analysis suggests that the top three firms in an
industry pursue reinforcement strategies. For the unlucky firms out of the top three,
redeployment or exit strategies are most likely the only feasible alternatives. So pervasive was this theory that in the 1970s, GE incorporated a mandate into their strategic
mission to be first or second in market share or otherwise exit the industry or market.

Using the Experience Curve to Model and Analyze Industry Structure

The strategic implications offered by experience curve analysis are also closely
related to the concept of the product life cycle (see Chapter 23 for a detailed synopsis
of the product life cycle concept). Essentially, the strategic insight offered by the
experience curve is as follows for each phase of the product life cycle:

• *Introduction Phase.* The firm can either (1) set high prices and earn high profits, or
(2) lower their prices in line with decreasing costs to gain market share and to simultaneously inhibit potential competitors from gaining market share.

- *Growth Stage.* The profitability of the industry or market will eventually attract competition. Intense price competition will drive down prices faster than the experience curve can drive down costs. The resulting rationalization will eliminate many firms in the industry.

- *Maturity and Decline Stages.* Only the low-cost firms will be able to prevail from the growth stage. This will include those firms able to ramp down the common industry experience curve the farthest afforded by production volumes that in turn are accorded through market share.

Figure 20-4 shows the close relationship between experience curve cost analysis and the product life cycle. This linkage underscores the importance this model accords to securing dominant market share.

Market Entry Decisions

Armed with this knowledge of industry structure, the firm is better able to make market entry decisions. However, as we pointed out earlier, it is at this stage that a correct distinction between the root causes of the industry's experience curve is essential to successful application of experience curve analysis. The unrelenting pursuit of market share is not always the best strategy. Ghemawat (1985) suggests

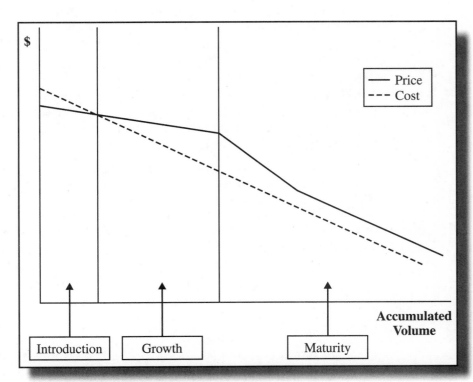

Figure 20-4
Strategic Implications of Linkage Between the Experience Curve and PLC

Source: Adapted from "Competitive Cost Dynamics: The Experience Curve," by A. C. Hax and N. S. Majluf, 1982, *Interfaces*, 12(5), pp. 50–61.

the following three distinctions between these causal factors and their requisite strategic responses:

- *Technological Progress.* The correct strategic response in this scenario is to focus on maximizing bargaining power with suppliers and buyers through prudent supplier and buyer selection, threats of vertical integration, and increasing upstream and downstream switching costs.

- *Scale Economies.* The correct strategic response in this scenario is to aggressively pursue market share, but only if rival firms cannot or will not match your investments in achieving scale. If this caveat is materialized, the firm risks entering a potential stalemate industry characterized by permanent excess capacity, price wars, and low profitability.

- *Learning Economies.* The correct strategic response in this scenario is to increase production volumes ahead of market demand to prevent rivals from achieving competitive cost levels.

Once the source of the experience effect is identified, environmental analysis is required to forecast the probability of strategic success in the prospective market. Ghemawat (1985) suggests three types of environmental analyses that are helpful at this stage of experience curve analysis:

- *Technological Risk.* This category of external analysis essentially boils down to a trade-off between (1) investing early/securing experience benefits but at the risk of being usurped by latent rivals employing better technology and competing on a lower experience curve or (2) waiting until the accepted technology is established but at the risk of missing the strategic window to achieve cost leadership and market dominance.

- *Analysis of Current and Potential Rival Firms in the Market.* Weak and maligned competitors will be undercapitalized, have high cost structures, and will not have incorporated experience curve analysis into their strategic planning arsenal. Strong and dangerous competitors, on the other hand, will be well capitalized, have low cost structures, and will show a willingness to perform tactics that allow it to effectively compete on the experience curve.

- *Government Intervention.* Two specific institutional constraints are relevant to experience curve analysis: government monetary and competition policy. Divergent monetary policies across national regimes will disadvantage firms competing in a high cost of capital countries vis-à-vis rival firms enjoying access to low-cost capital by virtue of interventionist industrial policies. Similarly, government competition policy may impinge on a firm's experience curve strategy if the firm is viewed by public policy makers in these nation states as being predatory or monopolistic.

Pricing Strategy

If the firm feels that it possesses the appropriate resources and capabilities to competitively manipulate these factors into a proprietary slide down the industry experience curve, market entry based on experience curve analysis is valid. Once

Part II   The Techniques of Strategic and Competitive Analysis

an affirmative market entry decision has been made, knowledge of the industry's experience curve is extremely helpful in determining a feasible introductory pricing strategy for new products. This logic combines the experience curve concept with the product life cycle concept described earlier. If the experience curve can be correctly estimated, a low-price strategy can initially be pursued in the interests of securing the level of market share necessary to achieve the experience effects. This will constrain rivals in achieving similar experience curve benefits and also discourage potential entrants from attempting the same. When costs eventually fall below price due to volume-induced experience effects, the firms with dominant market share will be able to competitively exploit their strong position in the industry or market.

Alternately, if the firm believes that the experience curve effects will not endure (e.g., will not be proprietary, will be easily copied by rivals, or that innovative technologies will usurp the competitive advantage by restructuring the industry on a lower experience curve) then the firm may decide to employ a price skimming strategy. In this scenario, high introductory prices would be pursued in order to maximize the economic rent associated with an ephemeral first mover advantage.

In either scenario, knowledge of the industry experience curve and the relative position of the competing firms on the curve are an essential part of this management tool in formulating insightful industry analysis and consequent business strategy.

Bidding on Contracts, Cost Control, and Benchmarking

Experience curve analysis often plays a pivotal role in securing and managing long-term contracts. Incorporated into the tendered bid are the lower costs that winning the bid would secure for the firm through increased volume and subsequent experience curve effects. These cost savings are passed along to the prospective client, making the tender more competitive. Once the contract is secured, the experience curve analysis then becomes a central component of cost control. Actual versus projected costs are used in variance analysis to determine and correct any deviation in order to realize projected profitability. In effect, the experience curve forms the basis of the firm's benchmark costing targets. Some government agencies use learning curve analysis to forecast the total costs of megaprojects that will be completed over extended periods of time. For example, The U.S. National Aeronautics and Space Administration (NASA) has made heavy use of experience curve analysis when projecting future project costs (see *www.jsc.nasa.gov/bu2/learn.html*).

STRENGTHS AND ADVANTAGES

As the previous discussion of the strategic value of experience curve analysis reflects, this management construct is extremely useful as a conceptual framework. Used properly, it is capable of shedding insight on the cost structure of an industry and how this might bear on the firm and its competition. It works best, however, when the following conditions exist:

- The analysis is used over a longer-term time span.
- Scale, technology and experience factors are significant.
- The most significant cost-reducing factors can be identified.
- There is low risk of technological innovation.
- There is low risk of external adoption of proprietary technology.
- There is low risk of government regulatory (e.g., antitrust) action.
- The product exhibits a high price elasticity of demand.
- Market customers are significantly cost conscious.
- The industry contains homogeneous, standardized products.
- Manufacturing comprises a large share of the value added component.
- All competitors are subject to a similar industry or market inflation rates.
- Fast-growing markets exist.
- The firm possesses the resources and capabilities to undergo dramatic growth.

The length of this list indicates that experience curve analysis is probably best treated as one tool in the competitive and strategic management tool kit. When some or all of the above conditions are not satisfied, systematic application of experience curve analysis is fraught with difficulties.

WEAKNESSES AND LIMITATIONS

While experience curve analysis has clearly made very valuable contributions to strategic management theory and practice, several weaknesses are also associated with this model.

Loss of Strategic Flexibility — Blindspots by Stealth

Perhaps the most critical flaw of experience curve analysis is the loss of strategic flexibility that commonly accompanies an unyielding preoccupation with cost control. If experience curve analysis becomes the sole focus of firm strategy, all of the efforts of the firm become centered on activities that will lower costs. The scale of the plant must be maximized, employees must become specialized, and the firm's organizational culture begins to foster an exclusive loyalty to the efficiency ethic imposed by experience curve discipline. While these developments may well give the firm a competitive cost advantage in some industries, there is a high probability of developing serious blindspots to evolving customer desires and/or competitive innovations (see Chapter 10 for more about this). Strict adherence to cost control by managing the established technology to ramp down the experience curve introduces rigidities that make the firm less responsive and flexible to changing market conditions. Instead of being customer and market focused, the firm becomes obsessively premised on the technology that they have harnessed to control costs.

Specifically, four types of blindspots can develop:

- *Technological Innovation by Rivals.* The introduction of superior technology by rivals can rapidly make the established experience curve obsolete. The new experience curve of a new technology will incorporate a full order of magnitude of change in the industry cost structure. This decline in costs then places costs for the rival firm on a lower experience curve, regardless of volume. The incumbent firm's competitive advantage subsequently suffers significant erosion. Figure 20-5 exemplifies this scenario.

- *Evolving Customer Preferences.* Strategy premised on an assumption that low costs are the primary driver of customer preferences can lead to a strategic window for competitors to offer a more-expensive rival product that incorporates a richer (i.e., deeper or broader) set of product attributes. For the customer, the marginal value of the new product offering may more than offset the marginal costs of the additional attributes. The ensuing customer migration may hold ruinous consequences for the established firm. For the established firm, the organizational capabilities and resources needed to compete on product differentiation have long been shed in the pursuit of a low-cost, low-volume strategy premised on a standardized product. Similarly, the high fixed costs necessary to establish the scale needed to extract experience curve benefits induce low-cost firms to focus on ensuring continued returns from this installed base of sunk costs. In many cases, they should instead be investing elsewhere. (See the box, "Experience Curve Analysis—Failures," which describes a case of this type of blindspot.)

- *Industry Migration by Rivals.* A sole focus on experience curve logic often blinds the firm to the very real threat of excess capacity in other industries that may have transferable technology, allowing them to invade the incumbent's market and pilfer customers.

Figure 20-5
Impact of Technological Innovation on Industry Cost Structure

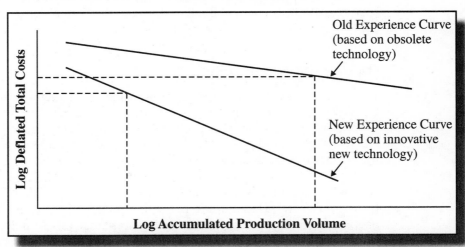

- *Ignorance About Broadening the Customer Base.* This is the converse of the previous type of blindspot. A sole focus on experience curve logic may also blind the firm to strategic opportunities to provide offerings to different customer sets currently being served by firms in other industries.

As Abernathy and Wayne (1974) observed, a firm using experience curve analysis must necessarily become more susceptible to competitive threats. The supporting logic given is that competition on volume-induced cost reduction requires an increasingly large market share to sustain itself. A natural outcome of this circumstance is that competitors will find it increasingly easier to segment the market with a differentiated product. At this point, the only recourse for the incumbent firm is to stop competing on scale or start increasing its product attributes to also differentiate. Regardless of the strategic choice, the flow of experience curve benefits declines and eventually ceases.

Selective Relevance

Experience curve analysis is not equally suitable for all industries and product markets. It is best suited for continuous processing, high-value-added industries that are labor and capital intensive, such as aerospace, electronics, shipbuilding, construction, defense contractors, petroleum refining, chemicals, and heavy equipment manufacturers. This model is less well suited for service industries, fragmented industries, or specialized industries where cost is a less-significant competitive parameter. The experience curve becomes increasingly irrelevant for differentiated products that share few commodity-like characteristics. The misapplication of experience curve analysis in this circumstance may result in incorrect strategies and poor market position.

Experience curve analysis is also not as relevant for industries in the maturity stage of the product life cycle. In this stage, slow market growth may infeasibly extend the time frame required to double accumulated volume. Experience curve theory implies that the cost reduction and volume sequence are infinite. In reality, the maturity phase presents the practical limit of cost reductions. Further growth will require a strategy change. Blindspots make the firm organized around experience curve logic hard-pressed to achieve this change in strategic orientation.

Dangerous Assumptions

Systematic application of experience curve analysis (Sallenave, 1985) requires at least three restrictive assumptions: (1) All rival firms make the same standardized product; (2) all rival firms use the same technology with the same factor costs; and (3) all rival firms are subject to the same inflation rate. Clearly, the full satisfaction of these assumptions is unrealistic. If the analysis doesn't incorporate this reality, the strategic recommendations may be faulty. Aaker and Day (1986) suggest several reasons why accumulated experience rarely reflects cost differentials between rival firms: (1) Followers can learn from the mistakes of incumbents through reverse engineering, hiring away key staff, and market research; (2) technological "leapfrogging" by entering an industry using the newer and superior technology; (3) in many industries, rivals also benefit from cost efficiencies delivered by suppliers; and (4) followers may have competitive cost advantages independent of experience curve effects, such as location, government largesse, or simply different cost structures.

Another dangerous assumption is in the implied expectation that the losses incurred in building market share will be more than offset by the profits after the firm ramps down the experience curve. This assumption is by no means set in stone.

Measurement and Implementation Problems

There are several practical challenges to effective implementation of experience curve analysis:

- *Definition of the Product Market.* As almost any analyst can tell you from experience, it is very difficult to accurately delineate the boundaries of the market, industry, or product to which the experience curve analysis is being applied. It is a rare occurrence where all competitors in an industry are pursuing the same customer base. Often, industry participants will target different customer segments within the industry. Logically, then, the whole concept of a common industry experience curve becomes a misnomer. Attributing strategic significance to market share as a proxy for accumulated experience lacks rigor when one of the critical analytical inputs, the definition of market share, is probably erroneous.

- *Disaggregating Cost.* Total product costs are a composite of many different cost drivers. Each cost driver will probably exist on a unique experience curve. Effective experience curve analysis must incorporate these differences. Additionally, it is difficult to define the separate experience curve for each cost component because of the existence of shared costs.

Simplistic Strategy Recommendations

The systematic application of experience curve analysis will result in simplistic generalizations that may have lesser relevance to market environment complexities. It is now generally recognized that there exists in most product markets a family of experience curves (Day & Montgomery, 1983). A more complete analysis incorporates three different experience curves: a firm-specific experience curve, the experience curve of competitors, and the industry price experience curve. Specific strategies cannot be generalized for each type of experience curve effect. Rather, differences and similarities among the different curves must be explicitly incorporated into the analysis and interpreted through several analytical techniques in addition to experience curve analysis.

Conclusion of Strengths and Weaknesses

Experience curve analysis should rightfully take its place as an important tool in the analyst's tool kit. The key to effective use of experience curve analysis, however, is to apply it in the right circumstances and to be aware of the caveats discussed earlier. Systematic application of this tool is akin to misapplication. Instead, the most appropriate use of experience curve logic is in defining the trade-offs between pursuing a low-cost strategy or a differentiation strategy through innovation.

More specifically, experience curve analysis can help to quantify and qualify one half of this trade-off—the relative merits of pursuing a low-cost strategy. If, indeed, the experience curve is chosen as the impetus for a low-cost strategy, care must be taken to ensure that the firm retains strategic flexibility. When competitive conditions (e.g., number and strength of rivals, evolving consumer tastes and preferences, innovative technology) change or the limits of the experience curve have been achieved, the firm that thrives will be the one that has retained strategic flexibility by keeping its options open. There are three ways to achieve this flexibility. For small firms, the most promise exists in dismissing a low-cost strategy and instead choose to target a segment of the market with a differentiated product or service offering that larger rivals, by virtue of their size, cannot or will not pursue. For larger firms, Abernathy and Wayne (1974) suggest two alternate courses of action. One, lead the market with intermittent product differentiation while continuing to pursue a low-cost/volume strategy between product changes. The second strategy for larger firms is to fund two different divisions in the same market, granting them each different strategic mandates—one premised on extracting the maximum benefits of the experience curve, the other premised on product differentiation through innovation.

PROCESS FOR APPLYING THE TECHNIQUE

Step 1: Determine If Your Product Market Is Amenable to Experience Curve Analysis

From the above (particularly the discussion of the strengths of experience curve analysis), a reasonably accurate assessment of whether a strategy based on the experience curve is appropriate needs to be determined for the product market under consideration.

Step 2: Define the Product Market

Day (1981) suggests that the choice of product market boundary might be based on segments that exhibit cost sharing between segments that are less significant than competitive cost differences that are dependent on the relative position inside of the segment. Several iterations based on different boundaries will probably be necessary before a satisfactory product market scope and boundaries are defined.

Step 3: Determine Your Firm's Experience Curve

Using internal cost and production data and the algebraic formula for the experience curve, determine the experience curve specific for your firm. This will require several substeps:

- *Decide Which Costs to Include.* The main focus should be on identifying the controllable value-added costs. Care should also be taken to incorporate shared joint costs into the analysis. Also remember to make adjustments for the fact that different cost drivers will have different experience curves, which when summed, total to the firm's experience curve. Additionally, the cost for taxes should be included as part of capital costs.

• *Adjust for Distorting Accounting Treatments.* The distorting impact of arbitrary cost allocations, deferrals, and changes in accounting procedures and policy over time should be eliminated by translating cost into cash inputs rather than the accrual accounting definition.

• *Decide on the Most Relevant Cost Object.* Preferably, the choice of your unit of analysis will be one broad enough to withstand changes in product mix without distorting the analysis.

• *Determine the Causal Factors Driving Your Firm's Experience Curve.* Distinguish between the relative impacts of scale economies, technology, and experience in the cost reduction process. This can be estimated through expert judgment or statistical regression analysis. This distinction will become important later in determining which strategy to pursue.

• *Translate Costs into Real Inflation Adjusted Figures.* Inflation usually impacts industries in a magnitude significantly different from the standard economywide inflation. For short-term analysis, an industry-specific cost deflator is required. For longer-term analysis, the standard GDP or GNP deflator is usually adequate.

Step 4: Determine the Experience Curves of Competing Firms

This curve is very useful because it will allow you to forecast the profitability of rival firms at various prices and volumes. Unfortunately, it is also the most difficult to determine because rival cost data are often proprietary and difficult to obtain. Therefore, this step generally requires estimation and extrapolation based on your firm's own experience curve. Take the slope of your own firm's experience curve and combine it with an estimation of your rival's accumulated experience based on their market share. Usually, this extrapolation will overestimate the slope of their experience curve, so an adjustment is necessary. The actual slope of your competitor's experience curve will be less steep than this estimate because of the opportunity of followers to learn from the mistakes of the incumbent, technological leapfrogging, access to cost reductions through factors other than those accorded through experience, and differences in overhead. In addition, the experience curve of competitors will very rarely be parallel to your firm's experience curve.

An important factor to consider in estimating competitive experience curves is to include an adjustment for joint costs. The best place to start is to acquire expert judgment from various specialists in your firm regarding the impact of joint costs on your firm's experience curve. Then, transpose these impacts onto any relevant joint costs applicable to rival firms to estimate a reasonable adjustment factor. It is also helpful to use computer modeling to support sensitivity analysis to determine the risk factor associated with unsure estimates.

Hax and Majluf (1982) warn analysts not to measure only at the end of the value chain. The reasons cited for this procedural prescription are twofold: different activities will exhibit different experience curve slopes, and different product mixes will be composed of activities comprising different learning curve slopes (e.g., marketing, R&D, assembly, and distribution).

For example: Assume Firm A has four times the market share of Firm B, Firm A has four times the distribution efficiency of Firm B, and Firm B has three times the manufacturing efficiency of Firm A. If the analyst measures only at the end of the value chain, then the market share calculations would peg Firm A as having quadruple the market share of Firm B. However, when the entire value chain is taken into account, radically different market shares are derived. Assuming for simplicity that each activity has the same slope experience curve and that each activity contributes the same value to the final product value:

$$\text{Firm A market share:} (4:1 \text{ or } \tfrac{4}{5})(0.5) + (1:3 \text{ or } \tfrac{1}{4})(0.5) = 0.525$$
$$\text{For Firm B, similar calculations derive a } 0.475 \text{ market share for Firm B}$$

The weighted average of Firm A's competitive cost advantage is $0.525/0.474 = 1.10$, far less than the quadruple advantage assumed by measuring only at the end of the value chain. This is why it is important to constantly monitor the cost impacts of evolving value chains of competitors.

Step 5: Determine the Industry Price Experience Curve

The industry price experience curve is even more difficult to determine than the competitive experience curves. Several factors are responsible for this difficulty: (1) Published list prices rarely reflect the many informal discounts that permeate many industries; (2) due to the variety of strategies in an industry (full service, attribute differentiation, sales mix, etc.) a single price is usually not realistic; and (3) estimating the industry volume is also very difficult because often these data are not readily available.

Despite these difficulties, the effort expended will offer valuable strategic insights into the industry structure.

Step 6: Determine the Price Elasticity of the Experience Curve

This particular step is also not an exact science. One way to estimate it is to use the algebraic formula. Next, as a check, estimate the elasticity coefficient by estimating the correlation between the changing industry volumes and prices. From this estimate the analyst may get a rough forecast of the product life cycle. Henderson (1984b) gives the following rationale for this link: "Any rate of cost decline on the experience curve requires a corresponding rate of increase in total experience. If that reduction in cost is translated into an equal percentage reduction in price, then the price elasticity should produce an increase in volume. That volume increase may be either more or less than that required to produce the cost decrease. If it is less, then the growth rate of volume and of experience will decrease. If it is more than the growth rate of volume will increase at a compound rate." Two caveats of this type of estimation are that price elasticity is notoriously fickle and can drastically shift with changing competitive parameters in the industry.

Experience Curve Analysis—Successes

BAUSCH & LOMB

In 1980, Bausch & Lomb ramped down the experience curve in the soft contact lens industry by a dual strategy of technology and capacity expansion. Computerized lens design allowed them to automate many manufacturing processes. At the same time, the capacity of its only soft lens plant was greatly expanded. Bausch & Lomb's market share correspondingly increased from 55 percent in 1980 to 65 percent in 1983, earning the company gross margins 20 to 30 percent higher than its rivals.

DU PONT

In the 1970s, Du Pont invested heavily in its proprietary ilmenite chloride process. Soon after this process was mastered, Du Pont invested to increase plant scale from pilot to commercialization. To foster this competitive advantage, Du Pont intermittently increased its scale and capacity ahead of market demand in order to prevent would-be rivals from achieving the same position on the industry experience curve.

SOURCE: Adapted from "Building Strategy on the Experience Curve," by P. Ghemawat, 1985, *Harvard Business Review, 63*(2), pp. 143–149.

Experience Curve Analysis—Failures

FORD MOTOR COMPANY

From 1908 to 1923, the Ford Motor Company operated exclusively on an experience curve strategy. Initially, this strategy was wildly successful, as the company achieved an 85 percent experience curve by building a huge production plant at River Rouge, Michigan, cutting management staff to 3 percent of all employees, vertical integration, and by building the moving assembly line. The price of the Model T was reduced from $850 in 1908 to $290 in 1924 while sales increased from 5,986 cars in 1908 to 777,694 cars in 1919. Ford's single-minded pursuit of low cost was perhaps best exemplified by the now-famous slogan, "I'll build any kind of car that you want as long as it is black."

In the early 1920s car buyers started demanding cars with a heavier chassis, a closed body, and a more comfortable ride. General Motors responded with new designs. Ford opted to continue down its experience curve and only dressed up the Model T to include more premium features. The costs of these product enhancements started increasing more rapidly than the decline in experience costs. Consistent with experience curve logic, Ford responded in kind by cutting list prices to secure more market share. Eventually, this combination started to severely erode Ford's margins. In addition, Ford's inability to innovate with totally new designs was rapidly making the Model T obsolete. Demand was drying up. In May 1927, Ford's entire operations shut down for almost a year to retool at a cost of $200 million. This belated recognition of changing consumer demand, combined with an innovative response from GM, finally deterred Ford from its obsession with the experience curve.

Ford's experience with the Model T offers a classic example of strategic blindspots that often follow the myopic pursuit of strategy based solely on the experience curve. High fixed costs, extensive vertical integration, and specialization blinded the company from capitalizing on changing customer tastes and preferences, competitive responses, and technological innovation. Perhaps even more damaging was the length of time it took Ford to change its strat-

(Continued on following page)

egy, resources, and capabilities to compete once again with GM on the automobile industry's new competitive premise. Many observers attribute

Ford's second-tier market share status below GM as the bitter harvest of seeds that were planted as far back as 1927.

SOURCE: "Limits of the Learning Curve," by W. J. Abernathy and K. Wayne, 1974, *Harvard Business Review, 52*(5), pp. 109–119.

Step 7: Reiterate Steps 1–6 Periodically

This step is especially necessary if new technology is introduced into the industry. If the new technology only reduces costs without offering new functions, then a new experience curve is generally not deemed necessary. However, if the new technology also offers new product functions, a new experience curve is probably a realistic alteration to the existing models.

Step 8: Develop Strategy

Using the discussion of the strategic value of experience curve analysis, determine the appropriate strategy. This decision should be tempered by the discussion of the weaknesses of experience analysis.

FAROUT SUMMARY

	1	2	3	4	5
F	■	■	■		
A	■				
R	■	■	■		
O	■	■	■		
U				■	
T	■	■	■		

Future orientation   Present to medium-term future. The theory is concerned with the strategic implications for market strategy as the product market cycle evolves in the future.

Accuracy   Low. The questionable conceptual validity coupled with many estimates and forecasts makes the accuracy of this tool very questionable. Accuracy is also limited by the fact that the predictions and forecasts are all based on projections of past trends, judgments, and extrapolations.

Resource efficiency   Medium. Time and effort are required to develop the first iteration of the analytical framework. Subsequent updates are recommended periodically or in response to competitive changes or technological innovation. This type of analysis is not expensive as the managerial skills are mainly of a technical diagnostic nature.

Objectivity   Medium. The critical role of product market definition may introduce some bias into the analysis.

Usefulness Medium to High. The systematic application of the model may be misleading. Nonetheless, when coupled with a firm understanding of the limitations of the analysis, the actual conceptual process forces management to explictly address the strategic trade-offs between low-cost and differentiation strategies. *Timeliness* Medium. Depending on the availability of information sources, experience curve analysis can be executed reasonably quickly.

RELATED TOOLS AND TECHNIQUES

- industry structure analysis
- strategic cost management
- product life cycle
- portfolio management
- competitor analysis
- environmental analysis

REFERENCES

Aaker, D. A., & Day, G. S. (1986). "The perils of high growth markets." *Strategic Management Journal, 7*(5), 409–421.

Abernathy, W. J., & Wayne, K. (1974). "Limits of the learning curve." *Harvard Business Review, 52*(4–5), 109–119.

Alberts, W. W. (1989). "The experience curve doctrine reconsidered." *Journal of Marketing, 53*(3), 36–49.

Boston Consulting Group. (1968; 1970; 1972). *Perspectives on experience.* Cambridge, MA: Boston Consulting Group.

Buzzell, R. D., Gale, B. T., & Sultan, R. G. M. (1975). "Market share—A key to profitability." *Harvard Business Review, 3*(1), 97–104.

Cowley, P. R. (1985). "The experience curve and history of the cellophane business." *Long Range Planning, 18*(6).

Day, G. S. (1981). "Strategic market identification and analysis: An integrated approach." *Strategic Management Journal, 2*(July–September), Vol 2, No. 3, 281–299.

Day, G. S., & Montgomery, D. B. (1983). "Diagnosing the experience curve." *Journal of Marketing, 47*(2), 44–58.

Fuller, C. B. (1983). "The implications of the 'learning curve' for firm strategy and public policy." *Applied Economics, 15*(4), 541–551.

Ghemawat, P. (1985). "Building strategy on the experience curve." *Harvard Business Review, 63*(2), 143–149.

Hall, G., & Howell, S. (1985). "The experience curve from the economist's perspective." *Strategic Management Journal, 6*(3), 197–212.

Hax, A. C., & Majluf, S. N. (1982). "Competitive cost dynamics: The experience curve." *Interfaces, 12*(5), 50–61.

Hedley, B. (1976). "A fundamental approach to strategy development." *Long Range Planning, 9*(6), 2–11.

Henderson, B. D. (1979). *Henderson on strategy.* Cambridge, MA: Abt Books.

———. (1984a). "The application and misapplication of the experience curve." *The Journal of Business Strategy, 4*(3), 3–9.

———. (1984b). *The Logic of Business Strategy.* Cambridge, MA: Ballinger.

Hirschmann, W. B. (1964). "Profit from the learning curve." *Harvard Business Review, 42*(1), 125–139.

Kiechel, W. III. (1979). "Playing by the rules of the corporate strategy game." *Fortune, 100*(6), 110–115.

———. (1981). "The decline of the experience curve." *Fortune, 104*(7), 139–146.

Pattison, D. D., & Teplitz, C. J. (1989). "Are learning curves still relevant?" *Management Accounting, 70*(1), 37–40.

Sallenave, J.-P. (1985). "The uses and abuses of experience curves." *Long Range Planning, 18*(1), 64–72.

Schoeffler, S., Buzzell, R. D., & Heany, D. F. (1974). "Impact of strategic planning on profit performance." *Harvard Business Review, 52*(2), 137–145.

Yelle, L. E. (1983). "Adding life cycles to learning curves." *Long Range Planning, 16*(6), 82–87.

Chapter 21

Growth Vector Analysis

SHORT DESCRIPTION

Strategy formulation requires that the analyst gain an understanding of the alternatives available to an organization, including identifying opportunities that are or are not being pursued by competitors. Growth vector analysis reviews the different product alternatives available to an organization in relation to its market options. By undertaking a systematic evaluation of the market, competitive conditions and market growth opportunities can be identified and understood.

BACKGROUND

H. Igor Ansoff was one of the early writers on corporate strategy and one of his major contributions was the development of the concept of growth vectors. He was concerned about the vague definitions of "strategy" that existed in his era, many of which apparently provided little guidance in selecting new product-market areas for firms to exploit.

Ansoff used four complementary characteristics for defining the common thread of strategy: product-market scope, growth vector, competitive advantage, and synergy.

1. The product-market scope specifies the particular industries to which an organization confines its product-market position.

2. The growth vector indicates the direction in which the organization is moving with respect to its current product-market posture and can be illustrated by use of the matrix in Figure 21-1.

a. Market penetration identifies the current direction for the present product markets through the increase of market share. In other words, the focal firm markets its existing products or services to its existing set of customers.

Figure 21-1
Ansoff's Original
Product-Market
Matrix

Source: Adapted and
reprinted by permission
of Harvard Business
Review (Ansoff's Original
Review—Market
Matrix). From "Strategies
for Diversification" by I.
Ansoff, Sept./Oct. 1957.
Copyright 1957 by the
President and Fellows of
Harvard College; all
rights reserved.

Market \ Product	Present	New
Present	Market Penetration	Product Development
New	Market Development	Diversification

b. Market development identifies new market opportunities being sought for products. The firm markets its existing range of products or services into a new market. The products or services are not altered, but the intended customer set is new to the firm. An example is when the organization exports or markets a product to a new geographic region.

c. Product development looks at the creation of new products to replace existing ones. In other words, the firm develops a new product or service that it plans to market to its existing base of customers. It accomplishes this through the development of innovative product or service offerings to replace outdated or stale ones. Automobile manufacturers are masters of this task as they bring out "new" (often slightly refined) models every year.

d. Diversification identifies new markets and new product opportunities available to the firm. The focal firm in this case markets completely new products or services to customers it had not previously served. There are two types of diversification: related and unrelated. Related diversification means that the focal firm remains in a product or service market with which it has some familiarity. For example, think about a retailer of shirts that diversifies into sales of pants and socks. Unrelated diversification is where the focal firm has no previous industry or market experience. For example, consider a shirt retailer that invests in the cola concentrate manufacturing business.

Another means for classifying diversification strategies is to break it down into horizontal, vertical, or conglomerate types. *Horizontal diversification* refers to the development of activities that are complementary to or competitive with the organization's existing activities. *Vertical integration* refers to the development of activities that involve the preceding or succeeding stages in the organization's value chain. Backward or upstream vertical integration takes place when the organization engages in an activity related to the proceeding stage in its production process. Forward or downstream vertical integration takes place when the organization engages in an activity related to a subsequent stage in its

Figure 21-2
3 × 3 Growth
Vector Matrix

Source: Adapted from
*Marketing Management:
Analysis, Planning and
Control* (6th ed.), by
P. Kotler, 1989, Upper
Saddle River, NJ:
Prentice Hall.

MARKET OPTIONS		Present Products	Improved Products	New Products
	Existing Market	Market Penetration	Product Extension (eg., variants/imitations)	Product Development (eg., line extension)
	Expanded Market	Market Extension	Market Segmentations/ Product Differentiation	Product Development/ Market Extension
	New Market	Market Development	Product/Service Extension & Market Development	Diversification

PRODUCT ALTERNATIVES

value chain. *Conglomerate diversification* refers to situations where the new activity of the organization bears little or no relationship to its existing products, services, or markets.

3. The third characteristic is competitive advantage, which Ansoff defined as particular properties of individual product markets, which will give the firm a strong competitive position.

4. The final characteristic is synergy (e.g., 2 + 2 = 5) where the combined effect on the firm's resources is greater than the sum of the individual parts. Synergy is a measure of the firm's ability to make good on a new product-market entry.

Since Ansoff's pioneering work, the model has been refined and expanded into a 3 × 3 matrix, as shown in Figure 21-2.

STRATEGIC RATIONALE AND IMPLICATIONS

The premise underlying the use of growth vector analysis is that corporate growth doesn't just happen by chance. Rather, management must explicitly attend to growth. Due to limited resources, the firm must necessarily make trade-offs between competing growth opportunities. Similarly, changing dynamic markets, shifting sources of competitive advantage, and ever-present competition from both current and potential rivals necessitate that the firm frequently revisit growth opportunities. A popular theme in strategic management is the necessity of pursuing profitable growth as opposed to growth for growth's sake.

Customer segmentation analysis can add another intrinsic dimension to this model as it demands an orientation toward customers by seeking to satisfy profitable customers and thereby profitable growth opportunities. By understanding where customer value lies, where different groups of customers exist in a market, and where there are economies of scope, analysts can develop valid growth and diversification strategies through a strong and differentiated competitive position.

Vector analysis is one of the first steps in the process of targeting profitable growth opportunities. This tool organizes the myriad of growth opportunities into a manageable framework. Hence, a platform is provided from which to further reduce the realm of opportunity to a subset composed of opportunities that are strategically consistent and show a high probability of profitability. Growth vector analysis explicitly forces the analyst to address the concept of strategic trade-offs in the pursuit of profitable and internally consistent growth.

STRENGTHS AND ADVANTAGES

One of the main benefits of growth vector analysis is the discipline that it imposes on the analyst in framing market strategies. While it is a relatively simple tool, it encourages the analyst to fully consider *all* of the various possibilities before deciding on a course of strategic action. This can be vastly superior to less systematic approaches that keep the analyst from considering new opportunities.

Another related strength of this model is its ability to hone in on several competing alternatives once a particular type of market or product strategy is chosen. For example, once a market option is chosen, the model allows for the relative comparison among several types of product alternatives. Similarly, once a particular product strategy is chosen, the model allows for the relative comparison among the types of market strategies that could be used to achieve the chosen strategy. In summary, once a market strategy is chosen, the analysis can be further delineated into the appropriate focus on present products, improved products, or new products. Or, the analysis can be further delineated into the appropriate focus on market development, promotion, or penetration.

In this way, growth vector analysis is a relatively flexible tool that allows for two levels of analysis. First, it assists in organizing and comparing the universe of options available for a particular market and product strategy. Second, once the general direction of the strategy is determined with regard to market versus product strategy, the analysis can be brought down to a more finely tuned comparison among alternatives within each broad category of market and product strategy. These two different types of analysis will help to ensure that the analyst adequately addresses all of the options facing the firm.

The growth vector also encourages the generation of multiple strategies. Of course, only a limited number of strategies would be selected in the current term. However, as markets continue to change, the generation of additional strategies allows the firm to adopt a proactive stance with regard to dynamic marketplaces.

When analyzing different directions for future growth, it is quite useful to use the model to try and determine competitors' options. This allows the analyst to consider their assumptions about growth, the business's competitive position, and positions for improvement, as well as to gain insight into where competitors may intend to evolve among specific product markets.

Finally, growth vector analysis can offer an effective method to simplify the analysis of many different market-growth strategies. By organizing all of these potential growth strategies into a nine-cell matrix, the analysis is clarified significantly, allowing the analyst to proceed by focusing on strategic comparisons between strategies.

WEAKNESSESS AND LIMITATIONS

The main weakness of this model is its apparent relative simplicity. That is, it limits the analysis to a consideration of only product and market strategies. Today, many growth strategies are premised on alliances and temporary networks made available through information and communication technologies over computer-mediated networks like the Internet. These strategies are not emphasized within the purview of the traditional growth vector model. Similarly, Daniels (1983) suggests that growth vector models fail to adequately consider other growth strategies such as joint ventures and horizontal integration. As such, when considering the array of growth options available, the analyst must consciously adjust for this weakness and take into account the firm's existing core competencies rather than remaining focused only on areas of fastest growth or greatest profitablity.

This model additionally is limited to the mind-set of the analyst and does not necessarily provide guidance to all the factors that may impinge on a firm's strategy. It does not necessarily take into account new product technology that may come from outside the industry being studied or stages in the product life cycle, nor does it address social trends that may influence a wider economic or political agenda. It is up to the analyst to include as many external factors as possible within the framework of their analysis.

The process of evaluating and selecting a specific growth vector can be more complex than it appears on the surface. To do it properly requires careful analysis of sales volumes, sales growth rates, and profit projections for existing products or services in existing markets. It is also useful to combine this previous set of factors with an assessment of the strengths and weaknesses (including vulnerabilities) of current products and services, along with gaining a similar understanding of competitors. Last but not least, it is helpful to identify whether any of the firms in the marketplace are leveraging their distinctive competencies.

Another related weakness is the lack of strategic recommendations offered by the model. While this tool offers a very useful organizing framework, it gives scant guidance as to which growth strategy to pursue once they have been generated and slotted into their relevant positions in the matrix.

The model is also premised on the assumption that firms must grow. Not all forms of growth are of equal profit potential, and, in some cases, retreat or cessation of product or service market activity may be warranted. The model does not compel the analyst to consider these tactics and therefore may be somewhat limiting in terms of the overall variety of strategic options available to the firm.

PROCESS FOR APPLYING THE TECHNIQUE

Using growth vector analysis, an analyst can establish a simple map forecasting a firm's possible growth potential in its particular market(s) with particular or potential products as well as anticipate possible gaps or missed opportunities early enough to allow management to take appropriate strategic action.

The objective is to identify and evaluate the company's current strategic position and its strategic alternatives in relation to its products and markets and ask where you can move your products or services and into which new markets. On the other hand, competitive intelligence (CI) analysts can also find out where competitors can move their products or services and into which new markets.

For organizations with a range of products or services, several differing marketing strategies will apply simultaneously. Each of these strategies will have advantages and disadvantages. (See Figures 21-3 and 21-4)

Varadarajan (1984) suggests the analyst conduct both quantitative and qualitative analysis in the process of choosing which growth vector to pursue.

Quantitative Considerations

• Growth vectors that offer the largest growth stand to yield the largest payoff in sales.

• Growth vectors that coincide with the "growth" phase of the product life cycle will meet the least competitive resistance. When markets are growing fast, marginal sales earned by the firm will be less likely to steal market share away from established incumbents. Instead, new sales will be generated by new market

Figure 21-3
Advantages and Disadvantages of Different Product Strategies in a Single Market

Source: Reprinted by permission of Alan J. Rowe.

	Present Product	Builds distinctive competence Economies of scale Clarity and unity of purpose Efficient utilization of resources	
Range of Product Strategies	Related Products	Broader product appeal Better use of salesforce and distribution network Motivation for doing something new Flexibility to respond to changing market conditions	
	New Products	Reduced competitive pressure Reduced risk of market saturation Smaller fluctuations in overall sales	

	Present Market	Maximum market penetration Possible market leadership Expertise in specific market or market segment Market visibility
Range of Market Strategies	Related Markets	Stable growth Stable cash flow requirements Increased plant utilization Extension of company's expertise and technology
	New Markets	Expansion of company's goodwill and reputation Reduced competitive pressure Diversification into more profitable markets Positive synergistic effects

Figure 21-4
Advantages and Disadvantages of Different Market Strategies for a Single Product

Source: Reprinted by permission of Alan J. Rowe.

growth and increases in underlying demand rather than a realignment of static market shares.

• When determining the optimal growth vector, the analyst should bear in mind the strategic benefits of integration with existing core competencies rather than remain blindly focused on the most profitable or fastest growth.

Qualitative Factors

- Company policy considerations
- Capacity/resourcing capabilities
- Technical and operational problems
- Marketing mix issues
- Threat of cannibalization
- Prevailing image/brand considerations
- Shifting competitive forces
- Cost–demand relationships
- STEEP aspects
- Changing lifestyles and shifting market preferences and tastes

One particularly useful application of growth vector analysis is in considering growth strategies in international markets. Given the pervasive impact of globalization on many of today's markets, using the growth vector provides a disciplined approach to framing new market strategies in an international context.

Given the often overwhelming array of growth options in international markets, growth vector analysis offers a useful method of organizing the analysis to ensure adequate scope of all possible alternatives. An examination of the way in which

Daniels (1983) applied the model to international growth considerations is helpful in gaining an appreciation of how the model works. In Figure 21-5, specific action alternatives, strategies, and examples of international implementation are given for each of the nine quadrants of the 3×3 growth vector matrix shown in Figure 21-2. This example also reinforces the need for the analyst to explicitly consider the options of diversification and joint venturing—options that are often ignored when considering growth options with the traditional growth vector matrix.

Figure 21-5
Alternatives, Strategies, and Examples

Quadrant 1: Existing Market/Present Products		
Action Alternatives	International Implementation	Example
a. Reduce costs to gain funds for price cutting or increased promotion.	a. Find cheaper source of product or component abroad by importing from another firm or from one's own production facility abroad; acquire foreign cost-saving process technology by importing equipment, imitating production methods, or licensing process technology.	Warnaco, a large global garment manufacturer, sourced out White Stag sportswear from Taiwan to lower prices.
b. Achieve better product or brand identification.	b. Acquire rights to use well-known or prestigious foreign brand names by licensing trademarks.	Warnaco also secured the rights to Christian Dior for its ties, allowing it to increase its brand equity in the United States.
Quadrant 2: Existing Market/Improved Products		
a. Introduce product variants.	a. Imitate or license product technology from abroad to differentiate present products.	
b. Differentiate through quality consistency.	b. Acquire foreign quality control (process) technology by importing equipment, imitating quality control methods, or licensing process technology.	In 1970, Chrysler established a joint venture with Mitsubishi in order to quickly and cheaply develop smaller and more fuel-efficient autos.
Quadrant 3: Existing Market/New Products		
a. Extend product line horizontally to existing customers.	a. Add complementary products by distributing for a foreign manufacturer; make product developed abroad by product imitation or license.	
b. Replace product line to existing customers.	b. Same as (a) except that products replace rather than complement an existing one.	American Home Products, a large pharmaceutical firm, pursues many cross-licensing deals with foreign firms granting reciprocal access to new products and sales channels.

Figure 21-5 (Continued)

Quadrant 4: Expanded Market/Present Products		
a. Promote aggressively, such as for new uses of the product or for availability by more distributors.	a. Find foreign markets with higher product usage rates and imitate those marketing methods, perhaps through assistance from firms in those markets.	Mitsubishi's agricultural division entered into a joint venture with Heublein's Kentucky Fried Chicken to sell whole chicken pieces. Mitsubishi's traditional market in Japan for primarily boneless chicken was regarded as a mature market.

Quadrant 5: Expanded Market/Improved Products		
a. Segment markets by developing more than one product variant.	a. Same as 2(a) and 2(b).	In order to quickly establish a position in the burgeoning electric shaver market, Gillette acquired the German firm Braun, primarily to acquire its superior electric shaving technology.
b. Extend product line vertically.	b. Same as 4(a).	

Quadrant 6: Expanded Market/New Products		
a. Extend product line horizontally.	a. Same as 3(a), except sales not necessarily to new customers.	Groupo Industrial Alfa, a large Mexican company, secured foreign licensing or joint venture agreements to diversify into televisions, electric motors, motorcycles, and artificial fibers. These products were sold to the same Mexican market as their traditional products of beer and steel.
b. Extend product line vertically.	b. Acquire foreign suppliers or foreign product technology to enable firm to integrate forward.	Internorth, a large American natural gas producer, licensed polypropylene technolgy from the German firm BASF. This allowed it to supplement its traditional product offering of products made from natural gas (i.e., propylene to chemical firms) with polypropylene products to the battery and luggage producers.

Quadrant 7: New Market/Present Products		
a. Expand into new geographical markets.	a. Same as 7(a), except that the product is differentiated through own R&D or through acquired product technology.	Source Perrier, the French bottled water firm, facing mature markets in France attempted a quadrant 3 strategy by producing soft drinks, milk, and chocolate, which ultimately failed. Subsequently, it began exporting to the United States, employing a different marketing strategy from the one used in France.

Figure 21–5 (Continued)

Quadrant 8: New Market/Improved Products		
a. Make product variant to appeal to new geographical markets.	a. Same as 7(a), except that the product is differentiated through own R&D or through acquired product technology.	NCR, a global leader in cash registers, developed crank-operated cash registers in order to expand markets in less-developed nations.
Quadrant 9: New Market/New Products		
a. Diversify to unrelated markets to sell in new geographical markets.	a. Add new products through own R&D, by acquiring domestic or foreign technolgy, or by acquiring a domestic or foreign firm in order to sell the output as in 8(a).	In an attempt to increase its relative proportion of North American sales, Nestle acquired Stouffers in the early 1970s. As a result; Nestle also became the owner of a chain of hotels.
		Seeking growth, Henkel, a German producer of detergents and cosmetics, acquired the chemical division of General Mills because it did not believe that it could compete effectively in the U.S. detergent and cosmetic market.

Source: Reprinted by permission of the Management International Review.

Although most of the discussion concerning growth vector analysis revolves around product strategy, the model is equally relevant to service firms. Consider the application of this model to potential growth strategies of banks.

BANKS

The massive deregulation of the American banking sector in the 1980s has presented significant challenges to smaller regional banks seeking growth in the smaller markets in which they typically operate.

- The market for large commercial loans has dried up as large companies often go directly to the capital markets for financing.

- Services such as payroll have similarly bypassed the small community banks, as many large companies now outsource to payroll specialists or perform these services in-house through corporate credit unions.

- Regulators take a dim view of small community banks getting involved in the merchant banking market.

- Small commercial loans to individual proprietors produce only low margins, often requiring just as much administrative expense as larger commercial loans.

- A heavy reliance on real estate loans is a very risky strategy regarding mismatches between long-term liabilities and short-term assets.

- The once-prosperous segment of auto loans has been captured effectively by automobile finance companies.

- The volume required to compete in the credit card market is beyond the scope of many smaller banks.

- Profitable and guaranteed student loans are often conducted in the same city in which universities and colleges are located.

As a result of these forces, small community banks appear to have limited avenues from which to pursue growth. Or do they? The use of growth vector analysis can highlight growth opportunities by ensuring that all avenues are properly considered. Most banks assumed that after deregulation, the strategic challenge would fall mainly on the liability side of the equation, that is, attracting deposits. Most of the challenge, however, was found to exist on the asset side, that is, finding attractive assets in which to invest the deposits. The following growth vector matrix shows how this tool can organize the analysis of growth potential:

Market Options	Service and Product Alternatives		
	Present	Improved	New
Existing	Cross-selling to induce current customers to use more existing services such as service packages, personal banker programs, financial planning seminars, reduced loan rates/fees for high-balance customers, interest rate "hotlines," trust packages Reduce loan rates below market rates to increase captured loans, drop deposit rates, and use aggressive marketing to increase matched deposits	Streamlined personal credit lines: attractive to upscale customers	New equity lines as a result of tax reform, allowing expanded portfolios Sweep accounts, variable rate mortgages, in-home banking, etc.

(Continued on following page)

Banking on Growth Vector Analysis (Continued)

| Expanded | Aggressively market traveler's checks, lockboxes, miscellaneous fee services
Credit cards: telemarketing outside branch market areas | | |
| New | Credit cards to preapproved segments out of state
Geographic expansion; increase branch locations
Financial counseling to affluent customers, newcomer programs, expansion of automatic teller machine (ATM) network, small business/professional packages | Streamlined personal credit lines: attractive to upscale customers | Turnkey solutions for business systems
Expansion into real estate services that would provide assistance into finding, buying, financing, selling, and maintaining homes |

As the table shows, not every cell in the matrix needs to be filled out. Some of these strategies may not make strategic sense and are left blank. Many banks that have used growth vector analysis have found that it broadened the scope of their analysis to consider strategies that might have been omitted under less-formalized approaches. Some banks have even made their vector analysis a permanent part of their "war room" wall. They have literally hung up a huge vector matrix on a wall covered in plastic to facilitate experimentation. This allows functional areas to analyze around their specific portion of the matrix while gaining a broad overview of the bank's growth marketing strategies. They claim it to be one of the most effective and efficient methods to strategize around market growth.

Adapted from the following sources: "The Service Marketing Planning Process: A Case for Accounting Firms and Banks," by J. H. Lindgren and W. K. Carter, 1986, *Journal of Professional Services Marketing*, 1(3), pp. 35–47; "Bank Marketing Strategist: Marketing Help via Vector Analysis," by R. O. Metzger, 1986, *Bankers Monthly*, 103(12), p. 8; "Vector Analysis II," by R. O. Metzger, 1987, *Bankers Monthly*, 104(1), p. 7.

FAROUT Summary

	1	2	3	4	5
F	■	■			
A	■	■			
R	■	■	■		
O	■	■	■		
U	■	■	■	■	
T	■	■			

Future orientation Medium. Needs to be reviewed regularly, as product and market issues change.
Accuracy Medium. Accuracy will be dependent upon biases held. The measurement of growth rates and sales volumes can be problematic depending on the nature of the industry. Cross-validation with outside experts will increase accuracy of the analysis.
Resource efficiency Medium. This can increase proportionately if the analyst performs rigorous quantitative analysis along the lines suggested by Varadarajan (1984).

Objectivity   Medium. This will vary depending on perspectives. Support from internal and external experts will increase objectivity.
Usefulness   Medium to high. Provides a quick picture of the opportunities available for a firm's products and services in existing or new markets.
Timeliness   Medium. Some time will be required to review market and product alternatives.

RELATED TOOLS AND TECHNIQUES

- competitor analysis
- product life cycle
- customer segmentation analysis
- customer value analysis
- functional capability and resource analysis
- strategic funds programming
- SWOT analysis

REFERENCES

Ansoff, I. (1957). "Strategies for diversification." *Harvard Business Review,* Vol. 35, No. 5, 113–24.

Daniels, J. D. (1983). "Combining strategic and international business approaches through growth vector analysis." *Management International Review, 23*(3), 4–15.

Kotler, P. (1989). *Marketing management: Analysis, planning and control* (6th ed.). Englewood Cliffs, NJ: Prentice Hall.

Lindgren, J. H., & Carter, W. K. (1986). "The service marketing planning process: A case for accounting firms and banks." *Journal of Professional Services Marketing, 1*(3), 35–47.

Metzger, R. O. (1986). "Bank marketing strategist: Marketing help via vector analysis." *Bankers Monthly, 103*(12), 8.

———. (1987). "Vector analysis II." *Bankers Monthly, 104*(1), 7.

Rowe, A. J., Mason, R. O., & Dickel, K. E. (1986). *Strategic management—A methodological approach.* Reading, MA: Addison-Wesley.

Varadarajan, P. (1984). "Product-market growth considerations: A microanalytic perspective." *Akron Business and Economic Review, 15*(1), 12–19.

Chapter 22

Patent Analysis

SHORT DESCRIPTION

Patent analysis is a unique management tool for addressing the strategic management of the firm's technology and product or service development process. Translating patent data into competitive intelligence allows the firm to gauge its current technical competitiveness, to forecast technological trends, and to plan for potential competition based on new technologies.

BACKGROUND

The U.S. Patent and Trademark Office defines a patent for an invention as the grant of a property right to the inventor. Standards for getting patents are not high, and incremental changes can be patentable just as easily as radical new advances. Patentable features may include (1) operating methods or processes; (2) physical structures; and (3) product features. A unique sequence of process steps may be patentable even if the individual steps are all commonly known; putting them together in a specific order may produce a unique result. Similarly, an old feature or structure may be patentable if it is used in a different or new context.

Patents have been developed as a sociopolitical mechanism to encourage innovation and progress. Lawmakers in governments worldwide have long recognized that innovators must be rewarded for their valuable discoveries and inventions. Protection from imitation and infringement was seen as an effective policy instrument to provide a robust innovative framework. Granting intellectual property (IP) rights in those nation-states where they are enshrined in public policy and legal frameworks, was commonly viewed as ultimately benefiting everyone in society by acting to keep the wheels of progress turning.

Since the earliest inception of the patent concept, those wheels of progress have been turning at an ever-increasing pace. One of the first patents was awarded in 1421 by the Italian state of Florence to Filippo

Brunelleschi for his invention of a gear for barge hoists. Soon after, in 1449, the English government awarded a 20-year patent to John of Utynam for his stained glass process (Ganguli & Blackman, 1995). Since these early beginnings, the issuance of patents gradually increased and experienced a dramatic increase after the onset of the Industrial Revolution. During the twentieth century, patents continued to dramatically increase as scientific exploration continued to advance. In 1993 it was estimated that 1,000 new patents were issued every business day (Narin et al., 1993). By 1997, this same statistic was presumed to have doubled to 2,000. By 1995, more than 32 million patents had been published cumulatively worldwide (Ganguli & Blackman, 1995).

This incredible growth rate of patents is testament to the value that the modern corporation ascribes to them as mobility barriers that foster competitive advantage. The business community, however, has only belatedly recognized the inherent value of competitive information embedded in this large global database of patent citation documentation. While many management tools and techniques have provided managers with much decision-making support around the essential marketing problem of satisfying customer value, far fewer tools have been developed to assist in formulating technology strategy. As the increasing pace of technological change began to create entirely new markets and destroy other markets, this policy vacuum in the field of strategy theory became ever more apparent. At least partially in response to this situation, patent analysis was developed as a tool to help firms anticipate technological change in order to meet the needs of the new markets that technical progress creates or facilitates.

Initially, this development was slow. Seidel was the first to formally articulate the concept of patent citation analysis shortly after the conclusion of World War II (Seidel, 1949). Patent citations refer to the reference on the first page of patent citations to previous patents based on similar scientific ideas. The underlying assumption of his proposal was that highly cited patents, that is, initial patents that are cited by a large number of subsequent patents, indicate the development of significant new technologies.

It wasn't until 1981, however, that this assumption was validated in a study that found that the patents for new products that embedded exceptionally innovative technology were highly cited in subsequent patent citations (Carpenter et al., 1981). This finding was reinforced by another study two years later, which found a high correlation between highly cited patents and expert opinion of the intrinsic value and significance of the technologies protected by those patents (Carpenter & Narin, 1983). The robustness of this analytical approach was also confirmed in a 1991 study that found a statistically significant relationship between the ranked opinions of 20 research experts at Eastman Kodak Laboratories regarding the technological importance of 77 silver halide patents and the number of times these patents were cited in subsequent patent citations (Albert et al., 1991).

Despite this theoretical validation and the recognized need to actively monitor the increasing pace of technological advance in the support of strategy, patent analysis was not widely used until recently due to feasibility constraints imposed by the manual searching of patents, limited access to databases, and disjointed, incomplete patent databases. Today, patent analysis is only starting to realize its full potential as an important management tool given the widespread availability of comprehensive patent databases on the Internet and the ability of information technology to efficiently analyze massive volumes of data. For example, as of 1997, approximately 6 million U.S. patent citations were available in computer databases, with proportionate availability of citations issued in many other nations (Sharpe, 2000).

STRATEGIC RATIONALE AND IMPLICATIONS

Even though technology is becoming a dominant competitive parameter in many markets, many managers and decision makers do not have enough information about the potential impacts of technological change on their firm's competitiveness. Where customer and market research can aid in marketing and financial data can assist the finance department, the explicit management of technology has been hampered by a lack of actionable data and information that can be converted into intelligence. As a result, firms are often blindsided by superior technology developed outside of the firm and, increasingly, from outside of the industry.

The main function of patent analysis is to provide this missing intelligence. The development of superior technology doesn't happen as quickly as it may appear from visible developments in the marketplace. Rather, innovative technical advances, from laboratory to store shelf, are often many years in the making. Unfortunately, much of the relevant information is kept proprietary and closely guarded during this incubation period. The value of patent analysis is its ability to indirectly uncover much of this information through the use of bibliometric techniques.

Bibliometrics applies the quantitative techniques of mathematics and statistics to analyze sources of information found in books, journals, and other bibliographic units. Patent analysis applies bibliometrics to the task of analyzing the wealth of data found in patent databases in order to identify leading indicators of technological change and discontinuity. The number of times a particular patent is cited offers strategic insights into which technologies are beginning to achieve critical mass. Further, patent analysis identifies which rivals and industries are actively pursuing these technologies.

Armed with this analysis, the firm can then integrate this intelligence to perform S-curve analysis (see Chapter 24) in mapping out its future technology strategy. Knowledge of impending discontinuities can give the firm ample lead time in preparing for competition in new and innovative technologies or in improvements in existing technologies.

Patent analysis offers a very efficient and effective method in this role. It is very efficient because 70 percent of patents are never cited (Karki, 1997) and of the remaining 30 percent, patents cited six or more times occupy the ninetieth percentile of most highly cited patents (Narin & Olivastro, 1988). Additionally, experts estimate that patent analysis can help reduce R&D duplication because approximately 30 percent of proposed R&D has already been completed (Ganguli & Blackman, 1995). Patent analysis is also very effective because the information contained in

80 percent of new patent citations is not available anywhere else (Ganguli & Blackman, 1995).

Clearly, patent analysis represents a preeminent source of competitive technical information. The value of this technique is manifested in its wide range of strategic applications (Campbell, 1983; Ashton & Sen, 1988; Pavitt, 1988; Mogee, 1991):

- *Technology Competition Analysis.* Determining the competitive strength of rivals by either analyzing all of the patents held by them or by focusing on a particular technology regardless of whether the holding firms are rivals. This latter method has the potential to reduce blindspots to migrating technology from other industries or markets. Additionally, the countries in which rivals file patents can often indicate their global market strategies.

- *New Venture Evaluation.* Supplementing expansion and diversification decisions by guiding the purchase of the appropriate technologies.

- *Patent Portfolio Management.* Providing decision support of issues regarding commercialization of the firm's technology such as selective new product introductions, licensing agreements, patent sales, alliance, and joint venture development.

- *R&D Management.* Optimizing the focus of R&D programs around considerations of incremental process/product improvement versus revolutionary technological change. Patent analysis frames this decision relative to competitive technologies.

- *Product Area or Market Surveillance.* Functioning as a fundamental component of the competitor profiling and environmental scanning aspects of the firm's competitive intelligence efforts.

- *Merger/Acquisition (M&A) Analysis.* More closely defining the elusive concept of synergy as the technological similarity between firms holding the original and subsequent patents premised on the same scientific idea or concept. Possible M&A strategies with identified candidates would simultaneously improve the firm's technology base as well as reduce technological threats.

- *Value Chain Analysis.* The patent activities of suppliers can be analyzed to ensure that they remain committed to upgrading technology used by the firm. Similarly, the threat of forward integration by suppliers can also be monitored by patent analysis. In addition, the threat of backward integration by the firm's customers can be monitored by patent analysis as well.

Figure 22-1 (Ashton & Sen, 1988) summarizes these strategic applications of patent analysis.

Patent analysis implicitly challenges the well-established precept of strategy theory that corporate planning should be premised upon customer value. Although it doesn't discredit the validity of this traditional approach, it suggests that it is incomplete given the furious pace of rapid technological change in many of today's markets. Rather, the suggestion we make is that technology planning should become an intrinsic component of market-based planning approaches. Patent analysis provides the methodology to fuse the demand and supply perspectives of corporate strategy.

Business Planning Application	User Benefits
Technology Competition Analysis	
Compare company portfolios and strategies	Improved product management strategies and decisions
Characterize high- and low-growth technologies for competitors	More focus on best long-term market gains
New Venture Evaluation	
Evaluate potential technology acquisitions	Better technology acquisitions
Analyze joint venture opportunities	Reduced investment risk
	Reduced planning uncertainty
Patent Portfolio Management	
Identify valuable patents, product areas, or spin-offs	Improved returns from patents (license, sell, develop)
Identify potential technical customers	Early identification of potential new spin-off business
R&D Management	
Evaluate process/product plans	Improved R&D allocation (pick winners, avoid losers)
Define pacing technologies	Better inventive idea awareness
Product Area Surveillance	
Review new patent content and ownership	Early warning of potential breakthroughs, development shifts and new market entrants
Check for infringements	Better protection of intellectual property

Figure 22-1
Patent Trend Analysis Applications

Source: Technology Management by B. Ashton and R. K. Sen. Copyright 1988 by Industrial Res. Inst. Inc. Reproduced with permission of Industrial Res. Inst. Inc. in the format Intranet via Copyright Clearance Center. The following conditions apply: on the first page copy should credit Research/Tech. MGT. and date.

STRENGTHS AND ADVANTAGES

The primary strength of patent analysis is its function as a leading indicator of technological change. This technique offers excellent analytical support to the strategic management of technological discontinuity. In addition, patent analysis provides several other valuable strategic insights from competitor analysis to mergers and acquisition analysis.

Effective patent analysis helps protect an organization against the many ways to blunder in protecting a firm's critical technologies. It is important because of the difficulty inherent in predicting a patent's impact on the firm's or its competitor's bottom line. Too many businesses and entrepreneurs postpone an investigation of patent potential until it is too late and they have been trumped in the marketplace by another entity. Also, many companies spend scarce funds on patent applications that provide for minimal competitive advantage.

Another strength of patent analysis is the availability of credible, external and objective technical information from which it draws its main source of analytical input. The global patent database is large, well structured, accessible, available in many languages and international in scope, is often the exclusive source of technical information, and is capable of allowing for cross-classification around a wide variety of analytical criteria. These characteristics make patent analysis a rich source of available technical information.

WEAKNESSES AND LIMITATIONS

The most common criticism of patent analysis is the fact that patent citations do not represent the entire realm of innovative activity. First, not every patent manifests into a commercial innovation. Second, many firms do not file patents, instead choosing to internally harbor closely held trade secrets. Third, the purview of patent analysis is strictly limited to commercial technology. Its applicability in analyzing basic research that often drives longer-term technological change is more problematic than when it is utilized to assess applied research.

Another weakness of patent analysis is the fact that it commonly assumes that all patent citations are of equal strategic significance. In reality, this is not the case. Some patents are merely incremental, technological improvements, while others incorporate a radical new technological paradigm. Blind analytical application of this tool treats the impact of both types of patents with equal import.

Similarly, more recent patents will often be more significant than older, potentially obsolete patents. In addition, researchers will cite differently, according to the tradition of their particular area of expertise. The point of this criticism is that the analyst must remain alert to the fact that neither all patents nor their citations are directly comparable; therefore, adjustments should be made before drawing conclusions of technical indication. Additionally, these adjustments should be supplemented with other types of information and strategic analysis.

Another issue concerns the time lag between the filing of a patent and its publication. In the United States this time lag can be up to two years, in Europe, lag time is up to 18 months. Thus, the strategic recommendations of patent analysis may not be as timely as would appear, depending on where the patents were filed and the quality and nature of the patent databases used.

PROCESS FOR APPLYING THE TECHNIQUE

There are many different ways to apply the process of patent analysis. Within each variant approach, however, lie several fundamental commonalties that are outlined here.

The first stage is to identify the scope of the technology area that will be the subject of the analysis. Depending on the purpose of the patent analysis, the patent search may include economy-wide trends; international, continental, and national trends; industry-wide trends; and industry segments.

There are two analytical approaches to a patent search (Ashton & Sen, 1988). The analyst may opt to focus on specific firms regardless of the specific technologies employed. Alternately, the analyst may choose to focus on a specific technology regardless of the companies employing that technology.

Next, the analytical framework that will guide the database search process must be determined. Six types of patent citation indicators are commonly used (Campbell, 1983; Karki, 1997):

- *Highly Cited Patents.* The absolute number of times a patent is cited in subsequent patents.

- *Technical Impact Index (TII).* In order to efficiently isolate those patents that are most significant, the top 10 percent of cited patents are usually the most impactful and will yield the most insightful analyses. The TII is often normalized to an expected value of 1, meaning that patents that score less than 1 are not as significant as those that score above 1.

- *Current Impact Index (CII).* This index essentially translates the absolute number of highly cited patents into a relative index to facilitate comparison across patents. The formula is

$$\text{CII} = \frac{\text{average citations per firm patent each year}}{\text{average number of citations for all patents in the database per year}}$$

A CII greater than 1 will indicate the percentage rate by which the firm's citation rates exceed the overall average.

- *Technology Cycle Time (TCT).* The median age of the earlier patents cited in the firm's most recent patents. Depending on the industry, the range could vary from 5 to 15 years. A lower TCT will indicate that the firm is a dominant competitor in the technological area under investigation by rapidly discovering incremental improvements of next generation technology. This is an important competitive variable, given the increasing importance of competing on time.

- *Technology Strength.* Indicates the robustness of the firm's technological competitiveness. The formula is

$$\text{Technological strength} = (\text{number of company patents}) \times \text{CII}$$

- *Dominance and Scope Indicators.* Refers to the observable patterns of citations between firms that reveal the competitive position of each firm's technology and strategic thrust.

This list of six indicators is far from exclusive, as most analysts will also devise their own particular criteria for analyzing the technological significance of the patents under investigation. Nevertheless, it can provide a helpful starting point to begin to decipher the strategic importance surrounding technologies.

Before initiating a database patent search, the analyst must be familiar with the structure of patent documents. Figure 22-2 summarizes the various components of this structure.

The next step is to determine which databases to search. The U.S. patent database is by far the most comprehensive and is usually the first place to start because as the world's largest market, it is a natural place for most of the world's patents to be registered. Nonetheless, patent searches in other countries may prove useful to

```
┌─────────────────────────────────────────────────────────────────────┐
│                           Title Page                                   │
│  Country of publication              Application number                │
│  National patent classification      Serial number of patent           │
│  International patent classification  Date of application               │
│  Title                               Priority date                     │
│  Abstract                            Priority number                   │
│  Inventor                            Priority country                  │
│  Applicant                           References cited by examiner       │
│  ─────────────────────────────────────────────────────────────────    │
│                              Text                                       │
│  Object of invention                                                   │
│  Prior association—references to previous patent citations that are based on similar scientific or tech-  │
│  nological concepts or ideas                                           │
│  Disclosure/description of invention, which may include diagrams and formulae if necessary   │
│  Examples with supporting data or other specific embodiments (apparatus, figures, flow sheets, etc.)  │
│  Claims defining the monopoly claimed (this helps in finding what constitutes infringement)  │
└─────────────────────────────────────────────────────────────────────┘
```

Figure 22-2
The Structure of Patent Documents

Source: Adapted from "Patent Documents: A Multi-edge Tool," by P. Ganguli and M. J. R. Blackman, 1995, *World Patent Information,* 17(4), pp. 245–256.

increase the comprehensiveness of results or to support specific analytical objectives. As Figure 22-3 reflects, many government patent offices have put their databases online, either individually or as part of a multigovernmental collaboration. Similarly, many other private organizations offer extensive patent databases. As the Internet is constantly evolving, the analyst is well advised to periodically search for any new or innovative patent databases or search services. A good place to start is by entering "patent database" in a search engine's keyword box. If extra credibility is desired, many universities with prominent law schools offer excellent patent information on their Web sites, including links to various patent databases.

Internet patent searches are generally composed of a six-step process as recommended by the United States Patent and Trademark Office (USPTO, see www.uspto.gov):

1. Identify the primary class using the Manual of Classification available on the USPTO Web site. This will require the formulation of a list of every possible keyword that describes the technology area under analysis. The keywords are then matched up with the corresponding Classification Code(s) listed in the 14-page Manual of Classification.
2. Identify the subclass using the United States Patent Classification System (USPCS), which is also available on the USPTO website. The subclass codes will allow for a more refined list of classification codes.
3. Examine the Classifications Definitions (statements of scope of each class and subclass) to ensure a correct correspondence between the keywords and classification and subclassification codes.
4. Search the USPTO database to locate all patents issued under the classification/subclassification code pairs. Return to step 1 if irrelevant results are returned.

International, Multigovernmental Databases

European Patent Office: www.european-patent-office.org/
European Union: oami.eu.int/en/default.htm
World International Patent Organization: www.wipo.int/

U.S. Database

U.S. Patent and Trademark Office: www.uspto.gov

Commercial Databases

Derwent: www.derwent.com
Dialog: www.dialog.com/
GetThePatent: www.getthepatent.com/
MicroPatent: www.micropatent.com/
Patent Miner: www.patentminer.com/LIVE/cgi-bin/pm.cgi
Questel Orbit: www.qpat.com/
SurfIP: www.surfip.com/

Patent Search Retrieval

Patent Gopher: www.patentgopher.com/

Selected Country Patent Office Web Sites (many with databases):

Andorra: www.ompa.ad/
Algeria: www.inapi.org/
Argentina: www.mecon.gov.ar/inpi/default1.htm
Australia: www.ipaustralia.gov.au/
Austria: www.patent.bmwa.gv.at/
Belgium: www.european-patent-office.org/patlib/country/belgium/
Benelux: www.bmb-bbm.org/
Brazil: www.bdt.org.br/
Canada: strategis.ic.gc.ca/sc_consu/trade-marks/engdoc/cover.html
China: www.cpo.cn.net/
Croatia: jagor.srce.hr/patent/
Cuba: www3.cuba.cu/OCPI/
Czech Republic: www.upv.cz/
Denmark: www.dkpto.dk/english/start.htm
Estonia: www.epa.ee/eng/index.htm
Eurasia: www.wipo.int/news/en/index.html?wipo_content_frame=/eng/newindex/links.htm
Finland: www.prh.fi/
France: www.inpi.fr/inpi/accueil.htm
Georgia: www.global-erty.net/saqpatenti/
Germany: www.dpma.de/
Greece: www.european-patent-office.org/patlib/country/greece/index.htm
Hong Kong: info.gov.hk/ipd/
Hungary: www.hpo.hu/
Iceland: www.els.stjr.is/vefur.nsf/pages/default.html
Indonesia: www.dgip.go.id/
Italy: www.european-patent-office.org/it/
Japan: www.jpo-miti.go.jp/
Lithuania: www.is.lt/vpb/engl/
Luxembourg: www.etat.lu/EC/
Macedonia: www.ippo.gov.mk/
Mexico: www.impi.gob.mx/Contador/index.html
Monaco: www.european-patent-office.org/patlib/country/monaco/
Mongolia: www.mongol.net/ipom/
Morocco: www.mcinet.gov.ma/mciweb/sipic/defaut.htm

Figure 22-3
Major Online Patent Databases

Netherlands: www.bie.minez.nl/
Malaysia: kpdnhq.gov.my/
New Zealand: www.iponz.govt.nz/search/cad/DBSSITEN.Main
Peru: www.indecopi.gob.pe/
Philippines: www.dti.gov.ph/ipo/
Poland: www.uprp.pl
Portugal: www.inpi.pt
Romania: www.osim.ro
Russia: www.rupto.ru
United Kingdom: www.patent.gov.uk/
Singapore: www.gov.sg/molaw/rtmp/
Slovakia: www.indprop.gov.sk
Slovenia: www.sipo.mzt.si/
Spain: www.oepm.es/
Sweden: www.prv.se
Switzerland: www.ige.ch/
Taiwan: nt1.moeaipo.gov.tw/eng/
Thailand: www.dbe.moc.go.th/DIP/index.html
Turkey: turkpatent.gov.tr
Ukraine: www.spou.kiev.ua:8101/eng/emenu1.html
Uzbekistan: www.patent.uz
Note: global updates and address information available at www.wipo.int/

Company-Specific Databases
IBM Patent Database: www.patents.ibm.com

Patent Portals
Yahoo: dir.yahoo.com/government/Law/Intellectual_Property/patents/

Industry Specific
Chemical: casweb.cas.org/chempatplus/
DNA: www.dnapatent.com/home.html
Biotechnology: www.nal.usda.gov/bic/Biotech_Patents/

Law School Portals
Law Guru List of U.S. Law School Internet Libraries:
www.lawguru.com/ilawlib/114.htm

Figure 22-3
(Continued)

5. Review the text portion of each identified patent to determine their relevance to the patent analysis. It is most efficient to read the Abstract portions as a first filter and then move to the full text.
6. Retrieve the full patent documentation (i.e., all supporting images, text) of the relevant patents for further manipulation.

Although these steps may seem rote, a significant amount of creativity, determination, and iteration is required to ensure accuracy, relevance, and comprehensiveness. Much process assistance is available on the USPTO Web site and through its offices. For a completely comprehensive analysis, the analyst may consider doing a "paper search" of older (i.e., pre-1971) patents issued that are not included in the database. The search portion of the patent analysis process is very tedious, time-consuming, and requires specialized expertise. As a result, many firms choose to hire the assistance of patent search consultants for this task.

Part II   The Techniques of Strategic and Competitive Analysis

BACKGROUND

A patent analysis of the global sodium-sulfur battery industry provides an excellent insight into the strategic value of this management tool. In 1966, the Ford Motor Company was the first to patent this technology. Subsequently, 284 patents were issued between the years 1966 and 1982. The competitive value of sodium-sulfur battery technology stemmed from its potential commercial applications in electrical vehicles and electric utility load leveling.

THE ANALYSIS

First, an international comparison of patent activity was conducted.

	Total	Issue Year					
	1965–1982	1965–1967	1968–1970	1971–1973	1974–1976	1977–1979	1980–1982
United States							
Patents	165	11	10	15	36	69	24
New assignees	29	3	1	4	9	9	3
Japan							
Patents	17	—	3	5	6	1	2
New assignees	7	—	2	2	1	1	1
United Kingdom							
Patents	55	—	—	4	23	16	12
New assignees	5	—	—	2	3	—	—
West Germany							
Patents	28	—	—	—	3	14	11
New assignees	5	—	—	—	2	2	1
France							
Patents	19	—	—	2	9	6	2
New assignees	4	—	—	1	1	2	—

Although domestic American firms were the first to innovate, Japanese rivals were close behind, filing for patents in the late 1960s. In the early 1970s, British and French firms moved in, followed by the West Germans several years later. While development activity remained high across the board as of 1982, in recent years the British and West Germans seem to be gaining ground.

The analysis started with a disaggregation of the 285 patents into four technical classifications of the technology:

1. electrodes
2. electrolytes
3. seals and containers
4. general design

(Continued on following page)

Using these categories, the international patent activity was further analyzed yielding these results:

United States (165 patents)

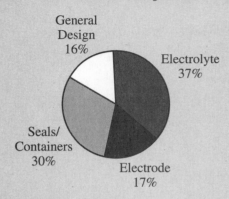

General Design 16%

Electrolyte 37%

Seals/ Containers 30%

Electrode 17%

Outside of United States (120 patents)

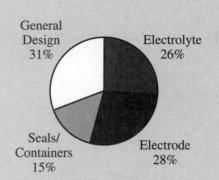

General Design 31%

Electrolyte 26%

Seals/ Containers 15%

Electrode 28%

From these graphs it became apparent that American R&D efforts were focused on electrolytes and seals and containers, whereas foreign R&D efforts were concentrated much more evenly on all of the categories. The relative foreign emphasis on general design indicates plans to commercialize soon, while the U.S. efforts seem to be premised on further research around unresolved technical issues.

Next, a patent analysis revealed the following characteristics of the significant competitors in the industry:

	Total Number of Patents	Number of Inventors	Number of Patents, 1974 to present	Number of Patents by Technology Type				Number of In-Set Citations	Number of Self-Citations	Cites/ Patent (Total)
				ED	EY	SC	DS			
Ford	45	23	33	11	6	16	12	223	57	5.0
U-Utah/Ceramatec	5	9	5	1	3	0	1	6	0	1.2
U.S D.O.E.	3	5	3	0	3	0	0	1	0	0.3
Dow	17	12	9	3	8	1	5	85	26	5.0
Dupont	5	3	5	0	5	0	0	4	0	0.8
Corning	5	2	5	0	1	2	2	0	0	0.0
General Electric	38	24	27	4	17	15	2	97	24	2.6
EPRI	22	10	22	7	0	12	3	36	14	1.6
Toyota	6	5	2	2	4	0	0	32	2	5.3
Agency Ind. Sci/Tech	4	3	3	2	0	0	2	16	1	4.0
Yuasa Battery	2	2	0	1	0	0	1	31	1	15.5
Chloride Silent Power	31	26	31	10	7	8	6	75	20	2.4
Electric Council	9	4	7	5	3	0	1	51	4	5.7
Sec./State Industry	8	10	8	4	1	0	3	35	2	4.4
British Railways	5	3	3	1	1	1	2	24	0	4.8
Brown Boveri & Cie	23	21	23	7	1	7	8	15	6	0.7
Generale d'Electricite	13	12	11	1	5	0	7	44	1	3.4
Others	44	—	38	4	27	5	8	80	—	1.8
Total	285	—	235	63	92	67	63	855	—	3.0

Key: ED = Electrodes; SC = Seals/Containers; EY = Electrolytes; DS = Design System

(Continued on following page)

The industry leaders were identified as four U.S. firms (Ford, GE, EPRI, and Dow Chemical), and three foreign firms (Chloride Silent Power from England, Germany's Brown Boveri & Cie, and Compagnie General d'Electicite of France). Since 1974, Ford has been the most active, followed by Chloride Silent Power, which recently surpassed GE. The Number of Inventors column, representing the R&D effort expended, shows that U.S. firms have invested less heavily per patent than have foreign rivals. The Number of Patents by Technology Type column indicates that GE, EPRI, Dow, and Dupont have focused on a few categories, while Ford, Chloride Silent Power, and Brown Boveri & Cie have focused on all of the technology categories. The Number of In-Set Citations column reflects the significance of the patents held by each firm. The rivals holding few patents (e.g., Yuasa Battery, Toyota, British Railways Board, the Electric Council, and the British Secretary of State of Industry) have generally developed the most significant innovations. The column Number of Self Citations indicates that Ford, Dow, and GE tend to focus on improving their own technologies while other firms tend to draw mainly from previous R&D of their rivals. Finally, the last column, Cites/Patent, indicates that several firms have not produced much groundbreaking R&D despite their high number of patents (e.g., Brown Boveri & Cie, GE, and Dow).

Although not illustrated here, the next phase of this patent analysis then sought to identify patent linkages between firms by examining cumulative patent citation patterns. To facilitate this, an intercitation matrix was constructed showing a cross-reference of which firms have cited which of their competitor's patents. The conclusions drawn from this matrix shed more insight into the relative importance of each firm's patents—an indirect proxy for the strength of rival technological competitiveness.

Next, a historical citation analysis was conducted to identify which individual patents had been cited more than 12 times:

Patent Number	Assignee	Filing Date	Number of Citations
340435	Ford Motor	10/22/65	28
3404036	Ford Motor	5/2/66	21
3476602	Dow Chemical	7/25/66	18
3413150	Ford Motor	9/28/69	31
3679480	Dow Chemical	5/8/69	23
3811943	Ford Motor	2/16/71	24
3758337	General d Electicite (France)	12/21/71	16
3770502	Yuasa Battery (Japan)	8/11/72	17
3841912	Yuasa Battery (Japan)	4/2/73	14
3993367	Toyota (Japan)	10/17/73	13
3982957	Electric Council (UK)	2/14/75	19
3946751	General Electric	2/18/75	15
3959013	General Electric	6/11/75	16
4048391	Chloride Silent Power	4/23/76	22

The general conclusions drawn from this table are that U.S. patents are the oldest, and so have had more time to be cited. Several significant Japanese patents follow indicating their further development of pioneering American R&D efforts. Rounding out the most recent technologically significant patents are several British firms.

(Continued on following page)

Still more detailed analysis was performed next by delineating the analysis to focus on only a handful of key competitors, Ford, Chloride Silent Power, and Brown Boveri & Cie.

Technology Category	Ford					Chloride Silent Power					Brown Boveri & Cie				
	T	ED	EY	SC	DS	T	ED	EY	SC	DS	T	ED	EY	SC	DS
Patents issued															
Total	45	11	6	16	12	31	10	7	8	6	23	7	1	7	8
Post-1974	33	10	2	15	6	31	10	7	8	6	23	7	1	7	8
Citations received															
Total	223	55	23	38	107	75	34	6	28	7	15	7	—	2	
Post-1974	70	31	3	28	8	75	34	6	28	7	15	7	—	2	6
Self	57	15	3	14	25	20	11	1	6	2	6	3	—	1	2
Citation rate															
Overall total	4.9	5.0	3.8	2.2	8.9	2.4	3.4	0.9	3.5	1.2	0.6	1.0	—	0.3	0.8
Post-1974	2.1	3.1	1.5	1.9	1.3	2.4	3.4	0.9	3.5	1.2	0.6	1.0	—	0.3	0.8

Key: ED = Electrodes; SC = Seals/Containers; EY = Electrolytes; DS = Design System

The patent activity data shows that the relative competitiveness of Ford's technology has decreased since 1974. Additionally, both Ford and Brown Boveri & Cie have little prominence in the electrolyte category, while Chloride Silent Power is equally represented in all four categories.

The citation rates analysis also yields valuable competitive intelligence. The patents owned by Ford and Chlorine Silent Power are much more highly cited than those of Brown Boveri & Cie. Citation rates for Ford are highest in electrode and design patents. In contrast, Chlorine Silent Power has had more citations on its electrodes and seals and containers. Additionally, Ford and Chlorine Silent Power focus more on developing from their own patents as opposed to Brown Boveri & Cie, which tends to develop more from the patents of rivals.

STRATEGIC INTEGRATION

Several strategic insights were gleaned from the above analysis:

Technology Competitive Analysis

The patent analysis provides a unique insight into the relative competitive position that various rivals occupy in the sulfur battery industry. Similarly, the relative technical strengths and weaknesses of each rival have been identified—an important strategic consideration regarding future competition and marketing penetration strategy. For example, Ford, GE, and Chloride Silent Power are market leaders in the electrolyte and design areas. Any potential rivals attempting to enter this market in the future would be well advised to consider this finding. Further examination of design patents will yield clues as to the commercialization intentions of various rivals, especially the Japanese.

New Venture Analysis

The identification of individual strengths and weaknesses of each firm within each technology category offers very useful information regarding licensing agreements, joint ventures, and so on. This intelligence can be used to identify complementary competencies. For example, firms that have achieved excellence in design technology might seek out another firm with a core competency in electrolyte technology. A case in point would be a potential collaboration between Ford and Chloride Silent Power.

(Continued on following page)

Another use of this analysis is to identify potential technology buyers in the event that a participating firm decides to divest or exit the industry. For instance, GE, which left the industry post-1982, might have used a similar analysis to locate potential buyers for its patents.

Business Area Surveillance
Continuous periodic monitoring of patent developments in this industry can help the firm maintain a current database of competitive technical intelligence regarding rival moves, technical developments, and competitive entry.

SOURCE: Adapted from "Using Patent Information in Technology Business Planning II," by W. B. Ashton and R. K. Sen, 1989, *Research Technology Management, 32*(1), pp. 36–42.

The next step requires a statistical manipulation of the large amount of data that will have been generated from the patent search. This is the process that translates data into information in the form of the leading indicators discussed earlier. Many firms employ the specialized services of patent search consultants for this process as well. One caveat of outsourcing these process components, however, is that the firm doesn't gain as intimate knowledge of the patent analysis as when this expertise is developed in-house.

Armed with this statistical information, the process turns to translating it into competitive intelligence. This requires analyzing the information within a strategic context:

- technology competition analysis
- integration with S-curve analysis
- new venture evaluation
- patent portfolio management
- R&D management
- product area or market surveillance
- M&A analysis
- value chain implications

The final step is to continue the patent analysis on a periodic basis in order to achieve the monitoring objectives of the firm's competitive technical intelligence scanning. This will function as an early warning system regarding future technological threats and opportunities. The box, "Strategic Assault and Battery with Patent Analysis," provides a helpful case study of this process as it was applied to the global sodium-sulfur battery industry.

FAROUT SUMMARY

	1	2	3	4	5
F	■	■	■	■	■
A	■	■	■	■	
R	■	■			
O	■	■	■	■	■
U	■	■	■	■	■
T	■				

Future-orientation   High. The identification of future technological threats and opportunities associated with discontinuity addresses future issues facing the firm.

Accuracy   Medium to high. Accuracy depends on correctly identifying the proper patents related to the technology under analysis. Patent analysis is probably the most accurate method available for technology forecasting.

Resource efficiency   Low to medium. Distilling massive amounts of data from disparate sources is time-consuming and requires specialized expertise. The availability of Internet databases and computerized analytical techniques mitigates these resource demands somewhat.

Objectivity   Medium to high. Much of the analytical input comes from external sources that are very credible by virtue of institutional credibility and the scientific method. The volume of different sources also reinforces the objectivity of the analysis.

Usefulness   High. Patent analysis can be leveraged into many different aspects of competitive and strategic analysis.

Timeliness   Low. A comprehensive patent analysis is time-consuming.

RELATED TOOLS AND TECHNIQUES

- blindspot analysis
- competitor profiling
- industry analysis
- S-curve analysis
- strategic group analysis
- value chain analysis

REFERENCES

Albert, M. B., Avery, D., Narin, F., & McAllister, P. (1991). "Direct validation of citation counts as indicators of industrially important patents." *Research Policy, 20*(3), 251–259.

Ashton, B., & Sen, R. K. (1988). "Using patent information in technology and business planning I." *Research Technology Management, 31*(6), 42–46.

———. (1989). "Using patent information in technology and business planning II." *Research Technology Management, 32*(1), 36–42.

Campbell, R. S. (1983). "Patenting the future: A new way to forecast changing technology." *The Futurist, 12*(6), 62–67.

Carpenter, M. P., & Narin, F. (1983). "Validation study: Patent citation as indicators of science and foreign dependence." *World Patent Information, 5,* 180–185.

Carpenter, M. P., Narin, F., & Woolf, P. (1981). "Citation rates to technologically important papers." *World Patent Information, 3,* 160–163.

Ganguli, P., & Blackman, M. J. R. (1995). "Patent documents: A multi-edge tool." *World Patent Information, 17*(4), 245–256.

Karki, M. M. S. (1997). "Patent citation analysis: A policy analysis tool." *World Patent Information, 19*(4), 269–272.

Minister of Supply and Services Canada. (1985). *Patents as indicators of invention,* (pp. 1–42) Ottawa, Canada.

Mogee, M. E. (1991). "Using patent data for technology analysis and planning." *Research Technology Management, 34*(4), 43–49.

Narin, F., & Olivastro, D. (1988). "Technology Indicators Based on Patents and Patent Citations." In A. F. J. Van Raan (Ed.), *Handbook of quantitative studies of science and technology.* Amsterdam: Elsevier Science Publishers.

Narin, F., Smith, V. M. Jr., & Albert, M. B. (1993). "What patents tell you about your competition." *Chemtech, 23*(2), 52–59.

Pavitt, K. (1988). "Uses and abuses of patent statistics." In A. F. J. Van Raan (Ed.) *Handbook of quantitative studies of science and technology.* Amsterdam: Elsevier Science Publishers.

Seidel, A. (1949). "A citation system for Patent Office." *Journal of the Patent Office Society, 31,* 554.

Sharpe, C. C. (2000). *Patent, trademark, and copyright searching on the Internet.* London: McFarland & Company Inc.

Van der Eerden, C., & Saelens, F. H. (1991). "The use of science and technology indicators in strategic planning." *Long Range Planning, 24*(3), 28–25.

Chapter 23

Product Life Cycle Analysis

Short Description

Product life cycle (PLC) analysis uses a biological analogy to describe the evolution of sales as a function of time. This model asserts that, similar to all living organisms, products pass through four stages during their life: introduction, growth, maturity, and decline. Taken together, these four stages represent the product life cycle that generally serves a dual function: a descriptive conceptual framework to aid management in understanding market dynamics and a normative product management framework that recommends specific marketing strategies for each PLC stage in order to maximize profitability over the product's life.

Background

The first formal treatment of PLC theory as a distinct conceptual model is generally attributed to the work of Joel Dean, who wrote about the concept in a 1950 article, "Pricing Policies for New Products," in the *Harvard Business Review*. Dean argued that throughout a product's life cycle, constant variation in promotional and price elasticity combined with continuing changes in production and distribution costs should be met with strategic pricing adjustments. In contradiction to the established practice of pricing products based on cost and guesswork, the concept of the PLC was offered as a strategic rationale for pricing products based on changing market dynamics. Since then, the full complement of marketing mix variables have been incorporated into PLC theory based in large part on Dean's pioneering work.

The PLC was embraced as a promising method of operationalizing the inclusion of external market analysis into marketing strategy. A large body of research was developed over the next few decades that sought to validate the existence of the product life cycle in the hopes of bolstering this model's usefulness with empirical support. Initially, the classical PLC consumed the energies of most academic researchers.

Schematically, this function manifests itself into a bell shaped logistic curve shown in Figure 23-1a and b.

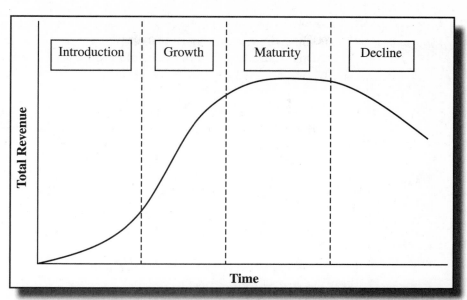

Figure 23-1a
The Classical Product Life Cycle

The underlying theoretical rationale for the classical PLC was strongly supported by the theory of diffusion and adoption of innovations developed by Everett Rogers (1962). Diffusion theory holds that there are four factors that influence the rate of diffusion in new product markets:

1. The real or perceived comparative advantage of the new product relative to competing offerings.
2. The real or perceived risk that adopting a new product poses to the consumer such as quality problems, technological obsolescence, financial risk, and so on.

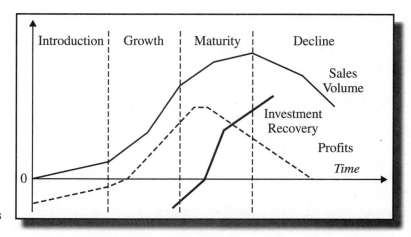

Figure 23-1b
The Product Life
Cycle Identifying
Sales, Profits and
Investment Factors

3. Barriers to adoption such as ideological incompatibility, psychological reasons, emotional attachment to the established status quo, concern for maximizing return on sunk costs spent on the old products, and so on.
4. The new product must be available for easy purchase and the consumer must be aware of the existence of the new product.

A significant portion of PLC theory is devoted to influencing the rate of diffusion during the introduction and growth stages by strategically and tactically manipulating the range of variables in the marketing mix.

The product life cycle provides an invaluable perspective on the development of both product and marketing strategies, as each phase of the life cycle has distinct characteristics that affect a firm's operation. Different strategies are often required through each stage as customer attitudes and needs, the number of competitors, and market forces change and evolve through the course of the product's life cycle.

Conceptual Description of PLC Stages

Stage 1: Introduction

Introduction refers to the development and market introduction of a new product. It is often accompanied by slow sales growth. Prior to introduction, the product may have undergone a long period of development and at introduction, the financial requirements to effectively roll it out can be extensive. When a product is first introduced into the market, it often meets initial consumer resistance because they are unaware of its existence or they are unsure of the nature and sum of its risks and benefits. Hence, only a small proportion of the potential market purchases the product.

Stage 2: Growth

Consumers become aware of the product and its benefits through heavy promotion by the pioneering firm(s). With increasing consumer acceptance, unit sales begin to grow at an increasing rate. This exponential growth characterizes the growth stage. During this stage, product and brand differentiation begin as firms start to jockey for competitive advantage. As demand outstrips supply, leading indicators at the wholesale and production levels provide an incentive for more growth than is warranted by retail demand. Typically, sales and profits rise, competitors are attracted, and improved products or imitations enter the market. Eventually, this increased competition leads some of the firms to consider competing on price. This signals the onset of the maturity stage.

Stage 3: Maturity

The profit associated by the growth stage attracts many more competitors to the product market. Market saturation soon ensues, resulting in a sales growth plateau as the majority of potential consumers have already purchased the product. Replacement purchases become the major factor driving subsequent sales. Signaling the end of the growth stage, the maturity stage starts at the point of inflection in the PLC graph shown in Figure 23-1. As the maturity stage unfolds, price competition intensifies, ever-finer distinctions between competitive product attributes are made, and promotion and advertising to niche segments within the product market rapidly develops.

Stage 4: Decline

In stage 4, the industry structure becomes radically altered. Sales begin to rapidly drop from the plateau of the maturity stage as consumers start to buy newer and more innovative products. Overcapacity results in an industry shakeout. Industry concentration is precipitated by severe price competition, mergers and acquisitions, and bankruptcies. Sales continue to decline. The few remaining firms may then decide to take the product off the market. Alternately, sales may plateau at a lower level or even experience a minor rejuvenation, indicating what some researchers have suggested is a fifth stage—the petrification stage (Michael, 1971).

STRATEGIC RATIONALE AND IMPLICATIONS

These theoretical explanations for the shape and stages of the classic PLC curve were concurrently embellished with various strategic prescriptions designed to optimally guide product managers making decisions through the various stages. In effect, the theory evolved from a descriptive framework into a predictive and normative strategic management system. Several generalized strategic prescriptions became routinely associated for each stage of the PLC. They are described below and summarized in Tables 23-1 and 23-2.

Stage 1: Introduction

Product life cycle theory prescribes a strategy of aggressive promotion during the introduction stage. Heavy investment is required to establish a market by educating consumers about the existence of the product and the relative benefits from using the product. The main message of marketing efforts should be directed toward convincing potential early adopters of the merits of the product as compared to the status quo of existing products. Typically, PLC theory advocates a selective distribution strategy premised on securing channels used by early adopters. Retail prices are usually set fairly high in order to recover costs of product investment and development. A generalized manufacturing strategy is employed in order to defer heavy fixed-cost investments until a feasible market demand is justified.

Potential strategies available to the organization at this stage of the PLC:

- *Rapid Skimming.* Launching the new product at a high price and with heavy promotion. This strategy attempts to accelerate the rate of market penetration, for example, the introduction of the Lexus automobile.
- *Slow Skimming.* Launching the product at a high price, but using low promotional activity (e.g., Bang & Olufsen products). Using this strategy opens the firm to greater potential competition.
- *Rapid Penetration.* Launching the product at a low price with heavy promotion. This is a common strategy used for household consumer products.
- *Slow Penetration.* Launching the product at a low price with little promotion. This is characteristic of introductions of products by small businesses.

Table 23-1

Normative PLC Strategies

STRATEGY	INTRODUCTION	GROWTH	MATURITY	DECLINE
PRICING	Two options: High to offset costs of product launch Low to induce adopters	Two options: High—Skimming Low—Penetration	Market bearing price Low enough to avoid price war or entry of private label competition	Low to reduce risk of unsold inventory
TRADE PROMOTION	High intensity Heavy discounts	Low intensity	Heavy promotion to protect shelf space	Low intensity Close unprofitable distribution channels
CONSUMER PROMOTION	High intensity and focus on early adopters through samples, coupons, etc.	Low to medium intensity as resources shifted to advertising	High intensity to induce brand switching form substitutes	None
ADVERTISING	Focus on product attributes and early adopters	Medium intensity focus on mass market and brand attributes	Medium intensity to support brand differentiation from substitutes	Minimum intensity needed to move inventory
MANUFACTURING	Job process	Batch process	Assembly line	Continuous flow

Source: Adapted from *Strategic Management,* (p. 156), by A. Rowe, R. Mason, and K. Dickel, 1986, Reading, MA: Addison-Wesley.

Stage 2: Growth

During the growth stage, the emphasis switches from a focus on early adopters to the entire market, as more customers acquire the product. The marketing strategy now focuses on the firm's proprietary branding attributes. Generally, advertising emphasis will be of medium intensity, as sales growth will normally challenge production capacity even in the absence of intensive advertising. Additionally, during the growth stage, the firm may consider switching its manufacturing strategy to a batch process to support the growing demand. With the increase in demand, most distribution channels will no longer need to be convinced to carry the product.

One of the most important strategic decisions to make in the growth stage regards pricing strategy. Essentially, the firm can pursue a skimming or penetration pricing policy. A skimming strategy involves setting an initially high price in order to capture the economic rents associated with first mover advantage. The rationale for such pricing policy is elegantly captured by the pioneer of PLC theory (Dean, 1950, 1976):

- This pricing strategy is warranted if consumer demand in stage 2 is price inelastic and cross-elasticity of demand is low due to the paucity of rival products. Conversely, promotional elasticity that may be high in the growth stage because the

Table 23-2

Strategies for PLC Stages

	INTRODUCTION	GROWTH	MATURITY	DECLINE
CONCENTRATION OF COMPETITORS	High; few pioneers, monopoly	Declining as more competition enters	Increasing industry shakeout	High; few players
PRODUCT	One	Variety, brand building	Battle of the brands	Drop out
PRODUCT DIFFERENTIATION	Low, if any	Increasing; imitations and variations	High; increasing market segmentation	Decreasing as competitors leave market
BARRIERS TO ENTRY	High, if product can be protected	Decreasing; growth technology transfer	Increasing as capital intensity increases	High capital intensity, low returns
BARRIERS TO EXIT	Low; little investment	Low, but increasing	High for large company	Decreasing; endgame
PRICE	Skimming or penetration	Meet competition; Price dealing/ price cutting	Meet competition; Price dealing/ price cutting	Meet competition; Price dealing/ price cutting
PRICE ELASTICITY OF DEMAND	Inelastic; few customers	Increasingly elastic	Inelastic only in segments	Very elastic; bargaining power of buyers high
RATIO OF FIXED TO VARIABLE COST	Generally low	Increasing	High	Decreasing
ECONOMIES OF SCALE	Few; unimportant	Increasing capital intensity	High	High
EXPERIENCE CURVE EFFECTS	Large early gains	Very high; large production volume	Decreasing magnitude	Few
VERTICAL INTEGRATION OF COMPETITORS	Low	Increasing	High	High
RISK INVOLVED IN BUSINESS	Low	Increasing	Increasing	Declining exit barriers

Source: Adapted from *Strategic Management*, (p. 156), by A. Rowe, R. Mason, and K. Dickel, 1986, Reading, MA: Addison-Wesley.

newness of the product usually precludes the consumer making price comparisons as a rational basis of value judgments.

• Price skimming allows effective market segmentation by leveraging the cascade of price elasticity of demand. This strategy maximizes return on limited production capacity by first satisfying the consumers with lower demand elasticity. When capacity expands, consumers with higher price elasticity of demand are then offered an amenable price. Over the PLC's course, this strategy is more profitable than initially pricing to satisfy the lowest common denominator of price elasticity of demand across the entire market.

• In light of the uncertainties associated with new markets, a skimming strategy will ensure a higher probability of mitigating the loss of introducing a product into a market that fails to expand and flourish.

- A skimming pricing policy can be viewed as a helpful method of financing the aggressive and intensive marketing strategies required of the growth stage.

- If total market volume is expected to be or actually is relatively low, the threat of competitive entry will be low. The attendant forecasts of low volume will not entice a battle for market share given the low prospects for a successful strategy based on experience effects.

Alternately, the firm may choose to implement a penetration pricing policy. The rationale for pursuing such a pricing policy is to underprice the competition in order to secure a larger market share in the long run as the PLC progresses. Concomitant experience curve benefits secured through higher production volumes (earned through supplying a high market share) will allow the firm to eventually establish a competitive cost structure. Penetration pricing strategy essentially defers profits until the maturity stage, when having the lowest cost structure in the market assures high profitability. A penetration strategy assumes that the losses incurred during share building in the growth stage will be more than offset by profits in the maturity stage. Some of the strategic rationale for a penetration pricing strategy include the following (Dean, 1950, 1976):

- The short-term price elasticity of demand may be high, inferring that penetration pricing will be successful in securing market share.

- Securing early market share will give the firm access to production volumes necessary to be the first to ramp down the experience curve and to enjoy a competitive cost structure.

- Penetration pricing may be a sound strategy if the risk of competitive entry is high. If the market potential is high, competitors banking on eventual experience curve cost effects will be lured to the industry. Alternately, if the product technology is not proprietary or the product attributes can be easily mimicked or surpassed, penetration pricing may be the best strategic option. In each of these market scenarios, the advantages of skimming would be temporary. In contrast, the advantages of penetration pricing to secure market share are more likely to secure longer-term competitive advantage.

In summary, following acceptance by early innovators, conventional consumers will start following their lead. New competitors are now likely to enter the market attracted by the opportunities for large-scale production and profit. New product features may appear as the market expands. Prices will remain steady or fall only slightly. Profit margins will peak as expenses are spread over a larger volume.

Strategies include improving quality and adding new features or models, sourcing new market segments, sourcing new distribution channels, shifting marketing strategy focus to increase demand, and lowering prices to attract price sensitive buyers.

Stage 3: Maturity

During this stage, generalized PLC strategy reverts to holding market share as opposed to expansion. Pricing strategy is limited to setting prices in sync with the market's willingness to pay. An important dimension of this stage is the avoidance of initiating a price war in which none of the participants emerge victorious. Price wars will effectively transfer any available producer surplus over to consumer surplus— an outcome that benefits none of the firms involved. It is equally important for the firm to recognize the onset of maturity so as to delay the entry of private label competition into the product market with deterring price reductions. The ultimate pricing strategy in stage 3 hinges on the selection of a broad strategy for the product market. During the maturity stage, the primary strategic choice is whether to pursue a low cost-based or differentiation strategy.

Promotional strategy focuses on the distribution channel offering heavy trade discounts to established retailers in order to protect valuable shelf space rather than to attempting to expand distribution channels. Advertising expenditures are moderate and developed to support brand differentiation. More intense during this stage are promotional strategies targeted to consumers to encourage rivals' customers to switch brands. To support low costs and consequent margins, manufacturing strategy often switches to assembly line processes to maximize experience effects associated with higher volumes.

Many firms today operate in a mature market that in itself has three stages: growth maturity (sales start to decline due to distribution saturation), stable maturity (sales remain level as market saturates), and decaying maturity (sales decline as consumers move to new products and services.)

As mentioned previously, a key feature of this stage is that of overcapacity due to the intensifying competition.

There are three main strategies available to be used here:

- *Market Modification.* Looking for new markets and market segments to stimulate increased usage. This strategy may include repositioning the brand.
- *Product Modification.* Addressing issues of product relaunch, quality improvement, product feature and style enhancements.
- *Marketing Mix Modification.* Reviewing several elements of the marketing mix such as pricing, advertising and distribution channels. The danger here is that any step would be quickly imitated by the competition.

Stage 4: Decline

The PLC theory essentially offers two strategic choices for managing a product in the decline stage. The first is to exit the product market in order to stem financial losses in a rapidly declining market. The second is to extract as much cash flow as possible with minimal promotional investment. This involves a low pricing strategy in order to ensure no unsold inventory. Unprofitable distribution channels are systematically closed. Advertising, consumer incentive programs, and trade discounts are phased out. Some firms may choose to extend feasible production volumes by acquiring rival firms wishing to exit the market. A common supporting manufacturing strategy in this scenario may be to switch to a continuous flow process in order to achieve minimum cost structures. Eventually, the product sales decline, resulting in eventual removal from the market. (See Tables 23-1 and 23-2.)

The key problem in this stage is the lack of systematic policies to manage declining products. Management's attention has often shifted to new or mature products.

The key actions to be reviewed in the decline stage are identifying weak products; determining whether there are marketing strategies and opportunities still available (milking strategy) and deciding whether to abandon the product.

It is the last action that creates a great deal of angst and reluctance. Logic and good analysis play key roles here as the premature acceptance of product decline often predisposes managers to focus more intently on new products much to the detriment of older established brands. This fixation is fraught with at least two dangers. First, the introduction of new products is extremely resource intensive. Second, the premature neglect of established brands essentially orphans the large investment and valuable consumer goodwill generated from previous brand-establishing campaigns.

STRENGTHS AND ADVANTAGES

Many studies have attempted to validate the existence of the product life cycle. Their success has been decidedly mixed. While the classic bell-shaped PLC discussed earlier has been validated in some industries, it is only one of many different types of product life cycles. Some researchers have identified as many as a dozen distinct types of cycles. In the absence of robust quantitative evidence of causal factors, these studies reverted to qualitative assessments of possible determinants such as generalized market dynamics. Most of the research done on PLC theory has been limited to consumer products that are frequently purchased, low-priced, widely distributed, and relatively isolated from supply side effects (Rink & Swan, 1979).

A natural development from the normative prescriptions of the classic PLC curve is the strategic value of forecasting the transition from one PLC stage to another. Again, research regarding the predictive power of this model has been limited to mixed results from short-term forecasting around the PLC stages.

Despite this lack of empirical support, the PLC continues to make a deep impact on management thought. General acceptance of PLC theory reached its zenith with its intrinsic inclusion in portfolio matrix theory in the 1970s. Most notable was the use of the PLC combined with experience curve analysis (see Chapter 20) as the basis of the BCG growth/share matrix (see Chapter 4)—the BCG to justify the selection of product market growth rate as the vertical axis; the experience curve to justify the horizontal axis of market share. Thus, the dogma of PLC theory became an integral component of management thought for many decades. In fact, even today, most new marketing textbooks still devote several pages to a discussion of the PLC. In terms of the strategic choice between low-cost and differentiation strategy, when combined with the experience curve in portfolio models, the PLC has a deterministic bias toward low-cost strategy. Perhaps the greatest contribution of the product life cycle to strategy theory was as a contributing basis to evolutionary S-curve analysis—a promising theoretical development (see Chapter 24) that deals with shortening product life cycles and the pervasive impact of proliferating innovation in technology.

Ironically, the main weakness of PLC theory may turn out to be its most significant contribution to management thought. By applying diffusion theory to market analysis, the PLC has shed much insight into the demand-side issues of strategy. It appears that research into the PLC has pointed the way forward to exploring supply-side issues through continuing exploration of the biological analogy by leveraging evolutionary theory to explain the other side of the market dynamic equation—the supply dimension.

WEAKNESSES AND LIMITATIONS

By defining markets too narrowly as a result of a product focus rather than customer orientation, management often instigates market decline of its own accord (Levitt, 1960).

The PLC is impacted heavily by marketing effort. The strongest cases in point in support of this are products that rejuvenate after a long period of stability, or the persistence of products that have been in the maturity stage for an inordinate period of time without showing any signs of decline. The continued existence and sales acceptance of product brands such as Jell-O desserts, Listerine antiseptic mouthwash, Tide detergent, 7-Up soda, Anacin pain reliever, Colgate toothpaste, Budweiser beer, Dristan cold medicine, Kleenex tissue, Maxwell House coffee, and Planter's peanuts challenge the assumptions of the PLC. Similarly, product classes such as nylon, Scotch whiskey, Italian vermouth, French champagne and perfume, and cold breakfast cereal also defy the conventional logic of PLC theory. The distinguishing features of all of these products is the fact that they satisfy a basic human need and have unique product attributes supported by creative promotion and marketing communications.

Many of the underlying premises of PLC theory are flawed (Lambkin & Day, 1989) if the analyst does not take them into consideration:

• The deterministic bias of the PLC invites firms to view eventual decline of their markets as a certainty. This leads to a self-fulfilling prophecy as the acceptance of maturity and decline fosters generalized strategies that reduce investment and often cause the market decline.

• The generalized strategies do not adequately incorporate competitive market dynamics (e.g., differences between large and small firms, established vs. new firms, original entry vs. market entry through acquisition, licensing, joint venture, or by firms employing different strategies from the firm central to the PLC analysis).

• The PLC theory does not address the implications of supply-side shakeouts and fails to offer strategies for firms to survive these periods of restructuring due to competitive overcrowding and overcapacity.

Many successful and profitable firms are competing in low-growth mature markets. Strategy based on PLC theory has a decided bias against competing in low-growth mature markets. The continuing success of many firms in these types of product markets serves as an important caveat.

PROCESS FOR APPLYING THE TECHNIQUE

Step 1: Estimate Potential Demand

The first step in applying PLC theory is to understand market demand. Market research is required to identify the consumer segment(s), estimate total demand, understand tastes and preferences, identify unmet needs, and gauge the strength of potential and incumbent substitutes. All of the standard tenets of market research apply to this first step and must be analyzed to determine whether and where the market exists to support a reasonable probability of success.

Step 2: Determine Price Range

There are several methods to approximate a competitive price point:

• *Expert Consultation.* Ask internal and external sources to suggest a reasonable price. Engineers, operations managers, and other technical staff can offer insights into the technical feasibility of producing the item at a specified price range. Established distribution channels often offer a rich source of information as to the relative value the proposed new product would offer the consumer compared to competitive offerings.

• *Consumer Research.* Many of the standard techniques of consumer research can be used to determine a reasonable price range such as barter-equivalent analysis and in-depth interview techniques. These techniques will also give the analyst a rough approximation of price elasticity.

Step 3: Forecast Sales for a Range of Possible Prices

Use the concept of customer value analysis (see Chapter 13) to determine the total value of ownership of the proposed product that includes a breakdown of all of the costs and all of the benefits that the product bestows over its life span. This customer value analysis should then be repeated for competing products. Next, use this analysis as a backdrop to compare the relative competitiveness of the new product as compared to potential and incumbent products at the various price points.

Step 4: Consider the Risk Associated with Competitive Price Cuts

If a product will not compete directly with any substitutes or will only encroach on a small portion of the incumbent's established market, the probability of a competitive price decline will be lower. If, however, the new product is presumed to displace a significant portion of the incumbent's market share, a competitive price cut can be expected and must be incorporated into any pricing and costing decisions to ensure future product profitability.

Step 5: Determine the Fundamental Market Strategy for the Growth Stage

A fundamental decision must be made at this point in the analysis about the selection of the targeted market segment. Incorporating the analysis from the previous four steps, the firm must decide to pursue a skimming or market penetration strategy. The analyst should use the earlier discussion on normative PLC strategies to weigh the relative trade-offs associated with each strategy. Although a generalized analysis can never hope to capture all of the potential idiosyncrasies of specific markets, the PLC curve offers these general guidelines for deciding on a skimming or a penetration strategy:

SKIMMING STRATEGY

- New product is truly unique
- Total market demand is forecasted to be small
- Demand is price inelastic
- Cross-elasticity of demand is low
- Promotional elasticity is high

PENETRATION STRATEGY

- New product shares many qualities with established products so that attribute superiority is small
- High price elasticity of demand
- Experience curve effects will probably be realized
- Total market demand is expected to be large
- Steep experience curve
- High risk of competition

This selection of a fundamental marketing strategy will determine the pricing strategy over the growth stage.

Step 6: Define the Level of Aggregation

The level of aggregation between product class, form, or brand is vital to PLC analysis. While each level of aggregation will offer the analyst unique insights, practical application criteria usually override theoretical concerns. Product life cycle research has shown a tendency to favor product form as the best level of aggregation. Product class usually does not reveal any trends because it includes too many different product markets. In addition, product class shows trends only over a very long time period. Conversely, aggregating around product brands will not reveal trends because their volatility makes them difficult to model properly. Abell (1980) offers a helpful definition of product that may help the analyst negotiate this problem: A product is the application of a particular technology to satisfy a specific need or desire of a customer segment. In the final analysis, the final selection of product definition depends in large part on the analyst's judgment.

Step 7: Forecast Turning Points

At this stage PLC analysis starts to distinguish itself as separate from traditional marketing strategy. In PLC theory, each cycle stage requires radically different strategies.

Thus, implementing the normative strategies offered by PLC analysis hinges on the correct identification of turning points when the product moves from one stage to another. While there are many business and economic forecasting techniques (e.g., regression analysis, exponential smoothing, leading indicators, and market research), all of these techniques extrapolate from past data. Hence, they are useful only for short-term forecasting, and then only as long as the independent variable assumptions do not radically change. Further, they are most useful for predicting turning points in the economywide business cycle. For PLC analysis, however, these techniques are not applicable at the micro level.

What is required are several turning-point forecasting techniques. Unfortunately, this is the most difficult part of PLC analysis. Nonetheless, several helpful methods of forecasting these turning points are readily available (Dean, 1950, 1976; Moyer, 1981):

• *Declining Prices.* This indicator of weakening prices will manifest itself in several ways, such as reduced retail prices or the increasing prevalence of discounting, which are often informally negotiated. The important distinction for turning-point analysis is to detect when the magnitude of discounts changes substantially.

• *Increasing Sales Resistance.* A weakening market will require increasing sales effort such as more salespeople, higher frequency of calls, more attention addressed to individual consumer needs, and increased time that products spend on market floors or shelves.

• *Increasing Inventories.* Declining market demand usually precedes excessive inventory accumulation. While macroeconomic measures of inventory buildup will indicate a general slowing of economic growth, the analyst needs to focus on inventory buildup in the relevant product market. Sources of information to aid detection include market-specific inventory data published by the government or available through subscription from private sources. When composing the subsequent time series, the use of a moving average will help prevent misleading temporary aberrations.

• *Decreasing Order Backlogs.* Sources of information include company announcements, financial reports, government statistics, and trade association data. Again, current data are the most relevant to performing turning point analysis.

• *Analysis of Internal Sales Data.* Changes in the rate of growth of product sales may indicate the point of inflection on the PLC between the growth and maturity stages. It is recommended to employ a moving average to remove any distorting temporary aberration from the analysis.

• *Media Analysis.* Turning points are often predicated by negative press and editorial commentary regarding the product.

• *Bubble Syndrome.* Ironically, turning points often occur when market participants unanimously assert that the sky is the limit. Such unbridled optimism often indicates that the market is close to saturation.

• *Declining Brand Preferences.* Weakening markets are often preceded by escalating cross-elasticity of demand.

- *Increasing Product Standardization.* Decreasing attribute differentiation may signal a turning point into the maturity stage, as commoditization initiates.

- *Market Entry by Private Labels.*

- *Market Saturation.* Sated market demand is often indicated by an increasing ratio of replacement sales to initial sales.

- *Common Production Processes.* One sign of a maturing market may be the uniform adoption of a particular production process, indicating an increasing focus on benefiting from experience effects across the industry.

Step 8: Modification of Strategy for Each Stage

The normative strategies for each stage in the PLC are then implemented in a staged process with the identification of the turning points for each stage of the PLC. Guidance for managing the variables of the market mix in each PLC stage is given in the earlier discussion of normative PLC strategies and is summarized in Tables 23-1 and 23-2.

Step 9: Remain Watchful for a New PLC

The introduction of innovative technology or any other disruptive competitive parameter may precipitate the evolution of a new PLC. In this case, a new PLC analysis will have to be conducted that incorporates these altered assumptions driving the independent analytical variables.

DU PONT AND NYLON

The initial nylon market was for military applications during the 1940s and 1950s. After product sales began to fall, Du Pont, the inventor of nylon, boldly targeted the consumer market. Sales soon rejuvenated, as promotional efforts were successful in displacing the incumbent substitute, silk stockings. Sales grew even faster when Du Pont's brilliant marketing strategies transformed nylon into an indispensable fashion item. This is a classic example of marketing creativity and effort forming the PLC and not vice versa.

IPANA TOOTHPASTE

In 1968, the Ipana toothpaste brand was labeled as a declining product by its developers who became more focused on newer brands in development. Consequently, the Ipana brand was sold in 1969 to two Minnesota businessmen who proceeded to change only the formula. The original packaging was kept and very little promotion was pursued by the new owners. Contrary to PLC theory, sales for the first seven months were a surprising $250,000. Sales continued to increase, as indicated by a major consumer survey in 1973 that found Ipana was still being used by 1,520,000 consumers.

KELLOGG'S COLD CEREAL

As the traditional children's market for cold cereal began to decline as baby boomers matured, traditional PLC theory would suggest considering exiting the market or at least favoring newer products in the Kellogg stable. Instead, they intensely promoted ready-to-eat cold cereal as a viable breakfast alternative for adults. The results were astounding—the market increased from $3.7 billion in 1983 to $5.4 billion in 1988 when the age group 25 to 49 was consuming 26 percent more cereal than at the start of the promotional campaign developed by Kellogg's imaginative marketing strategy.

SOURCE: Adapted from "Forget the Product Life Cycle," by N. K. Dhalla and S. Yuspeh, 1976, *Harvard Business Review, 54*(1), pp. 102–111; "Controlling the Uncontrollable: Managing Your Market Environment," by P. R. Varadarajan, T. P. Clark, and W. Pride, 1992, *Slaon Management Review, 33*(2), pp. 39–50.

FAROUT SUMMARY

	1	2	3	4	5
F	■	■			
A	■	■	■		
R	■	■	■		
O	■	■	■		
U	■	■	■		
T	■	■	■	■	

Future orientation Low to medium. PLC analysis requires the analyst to consider future impacts, although admittedly it is typically focused on the near-term (i.e., the subsequent life cycle product phase). The inability to handle the dimensions of technological innovation and supply-side market dynamics renders the technique less capable of long-term predictions.

Accuracy Low to medium. Theoretically, reasonable accuracy can be supported only by confining the analysis to a tightly defined set of parameters. Many of the parameters are a matter of judgment by the analyst.

Resource efficiency Medium. The PLC concept requires both qualitative and quantitative skills. Resource efficiency depends on the breadth and depth of analysis and the prior establishment of a functioning market research department.

Objectivity   Medium. Important assumptions about the model (e.g., product definition) are extremely ambiguous and subject to judgment and bias.

Usefulness   Medium. The PLC is a useful tool in developing an understanding of product markets and competitor strategies.

Timeliness   Medium to high. Can be done more quickly if the organization has a well-developed marketing infrastructure already in place.

RELATED TOOLS AND TECHNIQUES

- experience curve analysis
- BCG growth/share portfolio matrix
- S-curve analysis
- customer value analysis
- competitor analysis

REFERENCES

Aaker, D. A., & Day, G. S. (1986). "The perils of high growth markets." *Strategic Management Journal, 7*(5), 409–421.

Abell, D. F., (1980). *Defining the business: The starting point of strategic planning.* Englewood Cliffs, NJ: Prentice-Hall.

Ayres, R. U., & Steger, W. A. (1985). "Rejuvenating the life cycle concept." *The Journal of Business Strategy, 6*(1), 66–76.

Cox, W. E. Jr. (1967). "Product life cycles as marketing models." *The Journal of Business, 40*(4), 375–384.

Day, G. S. (1981). "The product life cycle: Analysis and applications issues." *Journal of Marketing, 45*(4), 60–67.

Dean, J. (1950; 1976). "Pricing policies for new products." *Harvard Business Review, 29,* 45–53. (Reprinted with retrospective commentary in *54*(6), 141–153.)

Dhalla, N. K., & Yuspeh, S. (1976). "Forget the life cycle concept!" *Harvard Business Review, 54*(1), 102–111.

Field, G. (1971). "DO products really have life cycles." *California Management Review, 14*(1), 92–95.

Fruhan, W. E. Jr. (1972). "Pyrrhic victories in the fights for market share." *Harvard Business Review, 50*(5), 100–106.

Hayes, R. H., & Wheelwright, S. G. (1979). "The dynamics of process-product life cycles." *Harvard Business Review, 57*(2), 127–136.

Hamermesh, R. G., & Silk, S. B. (1979). *"How to compete in stagnant industries." Harvard Business Review, 57*(5), 161–168.

Hunt, S. D. (1976). *Marketing theory: Conceptual foundations of research in marketing.* Columbus, OH: Grid Inc.

Lambkin, M. & Day, G. S. (1989). "Evolutionary processes in competitive markets: Beyond the product life cycle." *Journal of Marketing, 53,* 4–20.

Levitt, T. (1960). "Marketing myopia." *Harvard Business Review, 38*(4), 45–56.

———. (1965). "Exploit the product life cycle." *Harvard Business Review, 43*(6), 81–94.

Michael, G. C. (1971). "Product petrification: A new stage in the life cycle theory." *California Management Review, 14*(1), 88–91.

Moyer, R. (1981). "Forecasting turning points." *Business Horizons, 24*(4), 57–61.

Polli, R., & Cook, V. (1969). "Validity of the product life cycle." *The Journal of Business, 42*(4), 385–400.

Rink, D. R., & Swan, J. E. (1979). "Product life cycle research: A literature review." *Journal of Business Research, 7*(3), 219–242.

Rogers, E. (1962). *The diffusion of innovations.* Glencoe, Ill.: Free Press.

Rowe, A., Mason, R., & Dickel, K. *Strategic Management* (p. 156). Reading, MA: Addison-Wesley.

Swan, J. E., & Rink, D. R. (1982). "Fitting market strategy to varying product life cycles." *Business Horizons, 25*(1), 72–76.

Tellis, G. J., & Crawford, M. (1981). "An evolutionary approach to product growth theory." *Journal of Marketing*, 45(4), 125–132.

Varadarajan, P., Clark, T. & Pride, W. M. (1992). "Controlling the uncontrollable: Managing your market environment." *Sloan Management Review*, 33(2), 39–50.

Yelle, L. E. (1983). "Adding life cycles to learning curves." *Long Range Planning*, 16(6), 82–87.

Chapter 24

S-Curve (Technology Life Cycle) Analysis

SHORT DESCRIPTION

S-curve analysis integrates technological change into strategic planning. This tool for managing technological change allows the analyst to compare the limits of the firm's current technologies to that of competing and potential technologies in order to decide upon which technologies to base its future strategy as well as when to deploy this new technology.

BACKGROUND

The concept of logistical functions, or S-curves, has been applied to studying technological change since the 1930s (e.g., Kuznets, 1930). Initially, these diffusion models attempted to explain the speed at which a new technology is substituted for an existing technology. The underlying premise was simple enough: The speed of technological diffusion in an industry depends on the number of firms that have adopted it and the number of firms still employing the "old" technology. Hence, diffusion models have three distinct phases that manifest themselves graphically into the classical S-curve shown in Figure 24-1(a).

During the 1960s and 1970s, numerous studies confirmed the theory of technological diffusion in a range of industries, including agricultural machinery, household appliances and color televisions, industrial robots, telecommunications technologies, oxygen steel technology, and hybrid corn seeds (Nieto et al., 1998). In general, diffusion theory is useful for macroeconomic or industry-level analysis, but its applicability to strategic management of technology at the firm level has been more limited to date. The main reason for this is the theory's focus on time as the dependent variable and on speed of diffusion as the independent variable. Time is not easily manipulated by strategic action and speed of diffusion is more relevant for industry-level analysis.

In an attempt to make diffusion theory more relevant for decision making at the firm level, Levitt (1965) introduced the product life cycle (PLC). Instead of

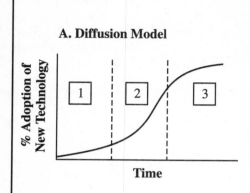

A. Diffusion Model

% Adoption of New Technology (vertical axis)

[1] [2] [3]

Time

1. *Embryonic*: The new technology has not been proven and so very few firms adopt it. As a result, the rate of learning about the new technology is slow, causing performance improvement to increase at a marginal rate.
2. *Growth*: Eventually, the performance of the new technology improves, inducing many more firms to substitute the old technology for the innovative new technology. The fast pace of adoption reinforces organizational learning about the new technology, resulting in further performance improvements.
3. *Maturity*: As the number of firms that have adopted the new technology exceeds those that have not, the speed of technological diffusion slows. Performance improvements approach natural limits; inducing a marginal decline in innovation around the new technology.

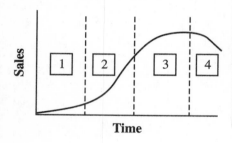

B. Product Life Cycle Model

Sales (vertical axis)

[1] [2] [3] [4]

Time

1. *Introduction*: Introduction of new product or service into the market. First mover customers begin to purchase.
2. *Growth*: Mainstream consumers begin to purchase the new product. Sales explode.
3. *Maturity*: As the majority of consumers have adopted the product, repeat sales dominate. Sales growth reaches its maximum and begins to decline.
4. *Decline*: For whatever reason, sales begin to decline and eventually taper off to zero or a much lower level.

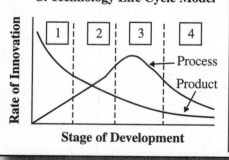

C. Technology Life Cycle Model

Rate of Innovation (vertical axis)

[1] [2] [3] [4]

Process

Product

Stage of Development

1. *Fluid*: Consumer needs are not fully defined so the focus is on product innovation by very entrepreneurial and flexible firms.
2. *Transition*: Innovations begin to become standardized, resulting in the transition to a focus on process improvements by increasingly structured firms. Competition becomes premised on price and low costs.
3. *Specific*: The predominance of process over product innovation becomes rigidly entrenched. Firms become even more structured.
4. *Mature*: Product innovation ceases as the industry becomes commoditized.

Figure 24-1a,b,c
Three Precedent Models of S-Curve Analysis

Source: (a) Adapted from Kuznets, 1930; (b) Adapted from Levitt, 1965; (c) Adapted from Utterback and Abernathy, 1975.

focusing on the speed of diffusion over time, the PLC concept attempted to explain sales over time by using the biological analogy embodied by the S-curve (see Figure 24-1b). Hence, four stages were identified in the typical product life cycle: (1) introduction, (2) growth, (3) maturity, and (4) decline (see Chapter 23 for a more detailed treatment of the PLC). While this development greatly expanded strategy theory, the PLC model failed to adequately delineate which factors actually influence the PLC given its continuing reliance on time as the dependent variable. Time does not provide many useful insights into what action levers management may manipulate in order to drive strategy. Additionally, knowledge of sales over time does not confer any strategic insights as to the explicit management of technology as one of the drivers of future sales. In the PLC model, technology is not explicitly addressed but is instead embedded as one of the derivative factors driving sales.

The next major development in the related field was the concept of technology life cycles proposed by Utterback and Abernathy (1975). This model plotted the rate of innovation against the stage of development of the technology under analysis (see Figure 24-1c). In these types of models, product and process are examined over each stage of technological development. While these models attempt to explicitly address the strategic management of technology, the choice of independent variable—rate of innovation—proved to be difficult to operationalize in terms of management tactics. Similarly, the stage of technological development is difficult to define at the tactical level of implementation.

In many ways, the lack of adequate analytical tools to address the strategic management of technological change was a manifestation of an inappropriate philosophical approach to technology and innovation. For many years, technology lay outside of the traditional purview of strategy, despite the fact that technology was rapidly becoming one of the preeminent competitive parameters in most industries. Many firms chose by default to allow themselves to be driven and managed by technological discontinuities as opposed to managing it explicitly.

This strategic myopia caused intense fallout. Business history contains many examples of the devastating impact of technological discontinuity. Foster (1986a) and others have cited several examples that encapsulate the pervasive impact of technology and what happens to incumbents when technology is not an explicit consideration in their strategy:

Mechanical Versus Electronic Cash Registers. As Figure 24-2 depicts, in 1972, 90 percent of the market belonged to firms producing mechanical registers. By 1976, that market share had declined precipitously to 10 percent, having been displaced by the electronic models offered by DTS, IBM, and Burroughs. National Cash Register (NCR), one of the major manufacturers of mechanical models, continued to pursue the "old" technology. They were devastated. Subsequently, NCR wrote off $140 million, lost $60 million the next year, demoted 28 of 35 executive officers, fired the chairman, and laid off 20,000 workers.

Bias-Ply Tires Versus Radial Tires. In the mid-1970s, bias-ply tire manufacturers relinquished a 50 percent market share to radial tire producers inside of 18 months. Today, the market for bias-ply tires has been virtually eliminated.

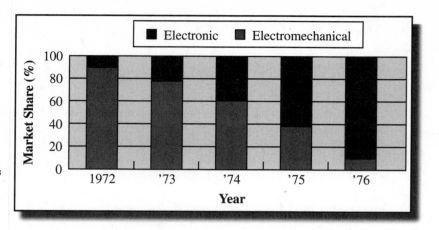

Figure 24-2
Deliveries of New Cash Registers in the United States

Source: Adapted from *Innovation: The Attacker's Advantage,* by R. N. Foster, 1986, New York: Summit Books

Orthoxylene Versus Naphthalene. In the early 1970s, orthoxylene increased its market share of the phthalic anhydride market from 30 percent to 80 percent in four years at the expense of the incumbent naphthalene technology.

Germanium Transistors Versus Silicon Integrated Circuits. In the span of six years, producers of integrated circuits stole a 60 percent market share from germanium transistor manufacturers. Similarly, developments in the silicon integrated circuit market have seen the progressive invention of PMOS to NMOS to CMOS with each new platform securing a 10 to 15 percent market share per year after adoption.

LP Records Versus 8-Tracks Versus Cassettes Versus CDs Versus DAT Versus MP3s. In the span of less than two decades, the favored mode of transmitting audio has shifted dramatically approximately every four to five years to a new mode. The most recent introduction of Web-based formats and delivery mechanisms suggests a continuation of this trend.

S-curve analysis was developed to specifically address the challenges associated with these types of technological discontinuities. The concept of S-curve analysis as a management tool explicitly geared toward integrating technology into strategy at the firm level was formally articulated in the early 1980s by Richard Foster (1982(a), (b), 1986(a), (b)), a principal with McKinsey & Co. While consulting for organizations such as Union Carbide, NASA, and Exxon, Foster wondered why there was no clear connection being drawn between technological development and corporate success. Most organizations, he asserted, did not adequately integrate the R&D function into strategic planning. Innovation was regarded as the result of creativity and genius, with the result that many R&D programs were premised on the thin foundation of "hoping for the best." The strategic management of innovation was often passive, in that the economics of innovation were thought to be exogenous to the firm, something to be reacted to instead of actively pursuing.

While the idea that innovation was the result of creativity and genius was well accepted, many firms did not internalize the premise that innovation processes can and should be strategically managed as well. This was due to both a lack of adequate analytical tools for technology assessment as discussed above *as well as* this strongly held and increasingly outdated philosophical approach to innovation and the strategic management of technological discontinuity. S-curve analysis provides both of these requirements needed to integrate technology into strategy.

STRATEGIC RATIONALE AND IMPLICATIONS

The S-curve concept explicitly addresses the need to incorporate technology into strategic planning. It accomplishes this by plotting the effort expended into a product or process technology and the resulting return. Operationally, this translates into a plot of R&D investment or man-hours versus some proxy for technological product or process.

The essential strategic rationale of S-curve analysis is that every technology has a natural limit to the benefits it can generate. At some point, increased R&D effort will reach the point of inflection resulting in a decreasing rate of growth in productivity. This is shown in the lower graph of Figure 24-3 that represents the first derivative, or slope, of the S-curve. At this point, the firm may consider reducing investment in the current technology as the payoff will be low, or switching to another S-curve, which will potentially offer a higher R&D payoff.

Empirically, Foster demonstrated the S-curve phenomenon in technologies such as orthoxylene, naphthalene, rayon, cotton, nylon, and polyester, among others (Foster, 1982(a), 1986(a)). Similarly, other researchers produced S-curves in their investigations of many other technologies, including agricultural insecticides (Becker & Speltz, 1986); rubber and latex foam technologies (Roussel, 1984), energy technologies of wood, coal, natural gas, oil, and nuclear (Lee & Nakicenovic, 1988); and air and rail transportation technologies (Lee & Nakicenovic, 1988), among others that confirmed presence of the S-curve phenomenon.

At the heart of the S-curve graph in Figure 24-3 is the relationship between R&D productivity, yield, and the firm's return on R&D investments. Algebraically, Foster derives the return on R&D by the following equation:

$$\frac{\text{Technical progress}}{\text{R\&D investment}} \times \frac{\text{Net present value of R\&D investment}}{\text{Technical progress}}$$

The first term represents the firm's R&D productivity and is also the slope of the S-curve. The last term represents R&D yield. This formula reflects the integration of technology with strategy in that R&D productivity represents the technical aspect of dealing with discontinuity, whereas R&D yield embraces the business aspects of managing technological change. Multiplied, these two elements represent a holistic approach to technology strategy encompassed by S-curve analysis. It is this integrated formula that frames the strategic decisions surrounding the strategic management of technological discontinuity, such as what technology to premise business strategy upon and when to deploy it.

The existence of more effective or more efficient technologies frequently results in multiple S-curves. This common situation directly challenges the current technology strategy of the firm in two primary ways:

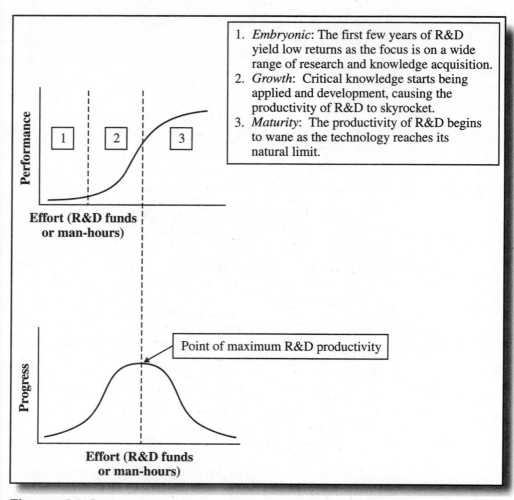

Figure 24-3
The S-Curve Model

Source: Adapted from Foster, 1982, 1986a.

1. Rivals operating on S-curves above and to the left of the firm's current S-curve will almost always be competitively superior in the form of lower costs, higher quality, or increased differentiation. The result is a superior delivery of customer value.

2. Even if rivals are not operating on another S-curve, the firm is well advised to make a jump if it results in increased return on R&D, the fulfillment of a higher order of customer value, and increased competitive superiority over rival firms.

Thus, the strategic challenge facing the firm is not *whether* to move to another S-curve but rather *when* to make a move. New technologies, however, are often discontinuous. That is, they are not associated or related to the incumbent technology in any way. Effectively competing in a new technology means entirely new processes, skills, and strategies. Achieving this transition is very difficult for most firms. Achieving this transition before it is too late to make a difference in the marketplace can be even more difficult.

The main problem that occurs is that technology leaders often unwittingly become technology followers. This ultimately results in strategic failure. The roots of this dangerous reality lie in an inappropriate philosophical managerial approach to technology.

Many firms have internalized that an evolutionary or incremental approach to managing technological change is adequate for strategic success. Innovation is perceived as too risky and customers are assumed to be adequately served with incremental improvements in the *efficiency* of existing technology. In many instances, consumers can't accurately articulate their needs because their perspective is also limited by the constraints of existing technology. The faults of these assumptions are only recognized after customers have permanently left for superior offerings of rivals. These same rivals often arrive, seemingly by stealth, from entirely different industries and are viewed by customers to be employing more *effective* technology. For example, electronic watches were not invented in the Swiss watch industry, polyurethane foam was not invented by the rubber industry, and the glass bottle industry did not develop bottles (Roussel, 1984).

While rivals are busy investing in innovative technologies, many firms continue to invest in traditional technologies. Another facet to the problem is the pragmatic reality that initial investments in new technologies often yield disappointing results. That is, return on R&D is initially low because the firm is operating on the flat, lower portion of the new S-curve. The long-term benefits become apparent when this position is compared with operating on the flat, upper portion of an inferior S-curve. Such knowledge will solidify the "stick-to-it-ive-ness" of the innovative R&D programs because it gives the firm strategic vision.

Another source of complacency rests in the fact that financial indicators of economic health function only as a lagging indicator. As such, the bottom line impacts of technological discontinuities materialize well after the damage has been done. Similarly, firms often enjoy their best financial results just as they are ramping up against the top flat portion of their S-curve. At this point, the firm has enjoyed very steep R&D productivity as a result of climbing up the steep portion of their S-curve. As a result, the current technologies receive the lion's share of investment just when the firm ought to be considering moving to another S-curve. Continued investment in the incumbent technology at this position in a mature S-curve is much less productive than investing in another S-curve. The latter strategy will yield a much higher R&D yield. Relying on financial performance indicators without the benefit of S-curve analysis will blind the firm to this dangerous reality.

For example, consider the situation in the recorded music industry. Currently, record companies are premised on leveraging compact disc (CD) technology. Royalties aside, they have refined this technological platform to such an extent that it literally costs pennies to physically record and press a CD. This is the result of having ramped up the steep portion of their existing S-curve associated with CD technology. In fact, in the third quarter of 2000, the recording industry enjoyed one of its most profitable periods of CD sales ever.

However, despite this rosy financial scenario, the business model of the recording industry is under direct threat from the technological discontinuity of online

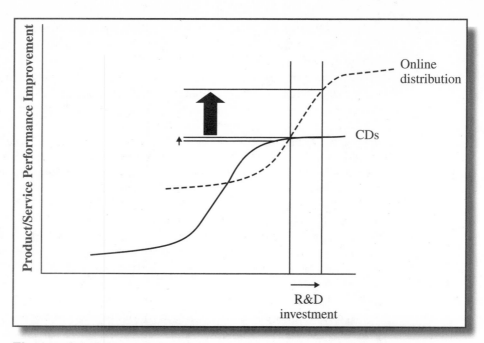

Figure 24-4
Strategic Implications of Online Distribution vs. CD Technology in the
Recording Industry

Source: Adapted from "Boosting the Payoff from R&D," by R. N. Foster, 1982, *Research Management,* 15(1), pp. 22–27.

delivery of music over the Internet from peer-to-peer sharing services such as Gnutella and Napster. Figure 24-4 compares the relative R&D productivity for a company such as Napster versus a traditional recording company. Despite the logic that S-curve analysis provides, the record companies are concentrating their efforts to protect their traditional model through legal means instead of investing in the new technology or forming alliances to benefit from it.

This example reflects two common symptoms of strategic myopia around managing technological discontinuity. First, firms often experience maximum profitability just as they are reaching the top flat portion of their S-curve. Second, the response of record companies reflects the difficulty that entrenched corporate mind-sets have in wrapping their collective heads around a new technology.

Compare this to the pharmaceutical industry, traditionally premised on drugs discovered through the application of complex chemistry. Realizing the threat presented by the technological discontinuity of gene therapy and other types of biotechnology, they have proactively invested in the new S-curve by acquiring many young biotech start-ups or by forming alliances with them. S-curve analysis can help other firms avoid the myopia of the recording industry and emulate the strategic foresight shown by pharmaceutical firms.

Obviously, the most important strategic issue in technology is choosing the correct technology at the right time. Thus, it is absolutely vital for firms to both increase investment in R&D while simultaneously employing S-curve analysis for two reasons:

- to identify the firm's current position on the S-curve to isolate R&D opportunities for efficiency improvements in product and service performance
- to turn the threat of discontinuity into R&D opportunities for effective improvements by identifying potentially superior S-curves represented by new technologies

Another strategic rationale that underlies S-curve analysis is associated with the nature of customer changes in line with innovations (Rogers, 1995). As technologies mature, the nature of customers evolves as well. When a new product technology is introduced, innovators and technology enthusiasts, who represent a very small portion of the total potential customer market, are the first to acquire it. Early adopters and visionaries pick it up next and continue to drive the technology and its benefits forward. These customers appreciate the newness of the technology and the performance gains it entails. Between the early adopters and early majority (the third customer category) sits the chasm (Moore, 1991), that point in a technology's evolution when sales could potentially take off at their greatest pace if marketing changes are effectively put into play. The fourth category is the late majority (or conservatives). The third and fourth categories of customers are the largest part of the potential customer market. The last category is composed of the laggards or skeptics—when they appear, the original technology has likely reached the limit of the S-curve.

These strategic imperatives encourage the firm to adopt a change in philosophy regarding the strategic management of technology. In today's fast-paced markets fueled by rapid and radical change, technology must be fully integrated into the firm's strategy. This means that R&D and related functions must become equal members of the strategic team. It also implies that firms must be prepared to constantly reinvent themselves. Congruent with these implications is the heightened need for specialized competitive intelligence techniques such as technology scouting and patent analysis. S-curve analysis sensitizes the firm to these new competitive realities.

STRENGTHS AND ADVANTAGES

The primary strength of S-curve analysis is in its integrative capacity for blending considerations of technology within the broader purview of strategy development. Not only does this model encourage an enlightened philosophical approach to technology strategy, it equips the analyst with a robust methodology for manifesting this philosophy into tangible results. S-curve analysis provides valuable insights into many facets of technology strategy including:

- natural limits of the firm's current technology
- firm's current position on the S-curve
- amount of effort required to increase technical performance
- existence of threatening S-curves

- best technology upon which to build strategy
- timing of switching to another S-curve

S-curve analysis is one of the few analytical models that explicitly addresses the vital issue of technological discontinuity. It forces strategic integration by meshing the concept of opportunity costs with R&D costs.

Another benefit of S-curve analysis is the degree of confidence that it instills within management. Rather than backing away from technological change and viewing it as a threat, S-curve analysis encourages the firm to view discontinuity as a constant source of opportunity and challenge. It replaces evolutionary complacency with revolutionary vision.

Technology planning is perhaps one of the areas of strategy that suffers from the highest degree of uncertainty. S-curve analysis provides the analyst with a structured and disciplined approach to decision making under this type of uncertainty. Despite the fact that it may not produce extremely accurate results, S-curve analysis is very valuable in developing appropriate technology strategy.

S-curve analysis can also function as a tool to improve organizational performance. Incorporating R&D and related functions in the strategy process will do much to bolster the morale of personnel in these functional areas. It will also increase the cross-pollination of ideas between the various functions by reducing communication barriers that often exist between the scientific and business realms of the firm.

WEAKNESSES AND LIMITATIONS

Critics of S-curve analysis caution that it is too simplistic in its strategic prescriptions. Specifically, the recommendation to consider leaving strategies premised on mature technologies may, in fact, be premature in some cases. Sometimes, investing in technologies approaching their natural limit is profitable if the industry experiences high sales turnover. Similarly, some industries and technologies can experience a revival.

Applying S-curve analysis overzealously may desensitize the analyst to the inherent risks in reducing R&D in one technology to support an increase in a new technology. First, even though the new technology may create customer value, the firm may not be able to capture this value due to changing customer values, industry competition, environmental changes, and so on. Second, reducing support too early in still-profitable mature technologies may reduce the financial flexibility the firm needs to move on to the new S-curve where R&D returns are often deferred until the firm can ramp up the steep portion of the new S-curve. Third, first-mover advantages often are eroded by followers who can often improve upon the innovative technology at lower cost. For these reasons, many recommend taking a balanced approach instead of "betting the firm." The analyst must remain aware, however, of the cruel irony that "not betting the firm" may actually be tantamount to "betting the firm." That is, the perceived safe strategy of a hedge biased toward the status quo may be much riskier than hedging biased toward innovation. This caveat is especially pertinent in the case of technical continuities where the points of inflection of multiple S-curves are symmetrical.

From an operational perspective, estimating the parameter of product performance is very difficult. Similarly, the methodology is rife with subjective estimation on the analytical inputs, many of which are difficult to predict with any degree of precision. Additionally, when analyzing multiple S-curves, the points of inflection may not be symmetrical. This makes any switch more risky, as the R&D returns will be deferred even further into the future.

From an organizational perspective, not all firms are well equipped for all of the stages of technological innovation. Unstructured firms, for example, may excel at inventing and creating new ideas but may lack the resources, organization, and control to commercialize these innovations. Conversely, large firms may have the latter but lack the former. Ideally, the firm should embrace all of these capabilities, but the analyst is well advised to consider whether her firm is missing crucial organizational capabilities along the innovation value chain.

PROCESS FOR APPLYING THE TECHNIQUE

Foster (1982, 1986(a), (b)) suggests that the process of S-curve analysis can be divided into two main phases:

1. Assessing the technological threat facing the firm
2. Developing a timely strategic response to any identified technological threats

Phase 1: Assessing the Technological Threat Facing the Firm

Knowledge of any technological threats facing the firm is a necessary precursor to developing technology strategy. Four different analytical approaches make up this first phase of S-curve analysis.

1. *List Current and Potential Alternatives to the Firm's Technology.* It is important to resist the temptation to immediately start analyzing and evaluating potential technologies at the onset. Instead, just list the various alternatives both from within *and outside of* the firm's industry. Brainstorming among a number of colleagues from different functional and experiential backgrounds can be helpful.

2. *Identify the Current and Future Technical Drivers of Customer Value.* Find out which specific technological product and process factors drive customer value. To make the analysis manageable, focus on only the main critical technical success factors responsible for delivering key attributes that are attractive to customers. Next, estimate the likelihood of change in customer value. Sources of change can come from the evolving tastes and preferences of customers, needs, usage contexts, and motivations. Often, however, sources of change are induced by competitive innovation offering an enhanced set of attributes, the possibility of which current customers aren't even yet aware. Another potential source of change may also come from changes in the evolving STEEP environment (see Chapter 17 for more on this technique).

Once these sources of potential change are identified, make a prediction about the future technical factors, or performance parameters, that will impinge on the delivery of future definitions of customer value. Then, refine the analysis to a forecast of the rate of change and eventual timing of technological change.

3. *Establish the Limits of the Firm's Existing Technological Platform.* For each identified performance parameter, establish the natural physical limits of the firm's existing technology. This requires close interaction between the firm's technical personnel and strategic challengers from other functional areas. Encourage and expect iteration composed of several different creative loops attacking the same problem differently. Once the natural limit of the technology is determined, assign the technical personnel to establish a quantitative value to this limit. Next, compare this natural limit to the level that the firm is currently operating at. Is there room to increase the efficiency of the firm's current use of the technology? If there is, then increasing the productivity of the R&D function may offer a way forward. The generation of alternative application of technological processes either alone or in sequence with other established technologies will offer solutions to increase the efficiency of the R&D function. More often than not, however, the perceived "inefficiency" of the R&D function is mistaken for actually "hitting the wall" of the natural limits of the firm's current technology.

4. *Plot the S-Curve.* The analysis of the firm's past experience with developing technology is the first step in drawing the S-curve. Data to support plotting both axes of the S-curve are required. Some type of performance parameter for each new product developed on the technology under analysis in the past decade or some other appropriate time frame is plotted against the y-axis. Next, the cost of bringing that product to market is plotted against the x-axis. Often, this cost is translated into man-years of effort and incorporates consistent treatment of ancillary costs associated with marketing, prototypes, and so on.

The natural limit of the firm's existing technology that was determined in step 3 is plotted as a horizontal line across the top of the graph in the same terms of reference as the performance of each of the firm's products. Essentially, this line represents the upper flat portion of the S-curve.

The final step involved in developing the S-curve is to predict how the firm's product or process performance around an existing technology will likely evolve in the future. There are three increasingly complex, time-consuming, and costly methods to do this with each one delivering increasingly more insight:

- *Simple.* Draw the bottom portion of the S-curve symmetrical to the top portion and overlay a straight line that connects the points between the two portions.
- *Intermediate.* Use the mathematical theory underlying logistic curves. It posits that once any three points on a curve are known, the rest of the curve can be drawn. Two of these points can be derived from previous product innovations in the current technology that the firm has introduced to the market. The third point is supplied by the natural limit of the technology determined in step 3 and how much effort it will take the firm to reach it from its current position on the S-curve.
- *Complex.* Use the Putnam formula on the following page to determine project cost associated with each performance improvement.

$$\text{Project cost} = \text{Projected performance}/[(\text{Efficiency}) \times (\text{Time})]$$
where projected performance and time are constants unique to each R&D laboratory.

Phase 2: Developing a Timely Strategic Response to Any Identified Technological Threats

The first aspect of phase 2 is to visualize the realm of possible competitive technologies that could impinge on the firm. Take the simplest alternative generated by the marketing and R&D personnel as the base point of reference. Determining the upper limit will require considerable creativity. Next, analyze the total costs associated with each alternative which includes a full costing analysis of opportunity costs, entry and exit costs, switching costs, sociopolitical compliance costs, costs of vertical or horizontal integration, and so on. An appreciation of all of these costs will help to determine how long the firm's current technology will remain economically viable and how soon alternative technologies will become feasible and possibly supplant it. Essentially, this analysis attempts to mentally map out the possible existence of other S-curves currently impacting or likely to impact the firm's market in the future.

The next step involves determining the strategic validity of staying on the current S-curve or, alternately, jumping to another S-curve by embracing or developing a new technology. A helpful tool to use in timing the move to another S-curve is to plot a projection of future costs associated with the existing technology strategy or moving to another S-curve. Figure 24-5 depicts such an analysis.

Plot forecasted variable costs associated with products and services produced with existing technology (i.e., the incumbent product). Next, plot the forecasted full costs (i.e., depreciation, interest, and capital charges) for the defending product. Repeat these two steps for the costs forecasted with the strategy of moving to another S-curve on "new" technology (i.e., the innovative product). The resulting graph will isolate four points where the cost lines overlap and where the contribution margins of the incumbent and innovative products collide. Each point has strategic implications for the firm's technology strategy:

- *Point 1.* The earliest time when the firm can expect a threat from rivals operating on the competing technology. The economic viability of the innovating product is equal to that of the defending product because the contribution margins of each are close to equal.
- *Point 2.* The latest time when the firm can expect a threat from rivals operating on the competing technology. Any position to the left of this point on line N_c would make even a variable cost pricing strategy infeasible for an innovative product.
- *Point 3.* The earliest time when the firm can expect the threat of the attacking product to cease. At this position, the variable costs of the innovative product equal the variable costs of the incumbent product.
- *Point 4.* The latest time when the firm can expect the threat of the innovative product to cease. At this position, the full costs of the incumbent product equal the variable costs of the innovative product.

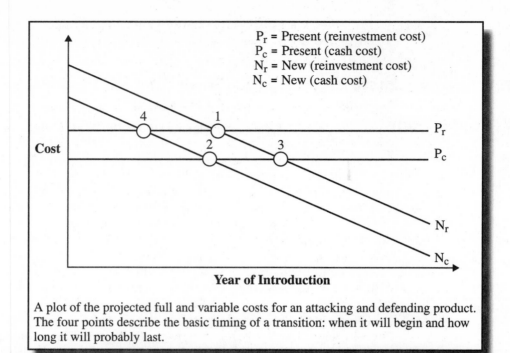

A plot of the projected full and variable costs for an attacking and defending product. The four points describe the basic timing of a transition: when it will begin and how long it will probably last.

Figure 24-5
Transition Prices

Source: Reprinted with permission of Simon & Schuster from *Innovation* by Richard N. Foster.

By comparing the predicted relative contribution margins associated with incumbent and innovative products over time, the incumbent firm can isolate time frames where jumping onto another S-curve will be economically feasible. To estimate the profitability over each time period, microeconomic theory is applied to forecast the price during the time periods between each of the four points:

- *Before point 1.* Prices will track the incumbent's full cost.
- *Between points 1 and 2, between points 2 and 3, between points 3 and 4.* Under conditions of industry overcapacity, prices may fall as low as the incumbent's variable costs.
- *After point 4.* Prices will fully track the innovator's full cost.

The incumbent's market share will soon become totally displaced after the total contribution margins of both the incumbent and the innovative product are equal. In order to survive the technological discontinuity, the incumbent firm must act before this situation materializes.

Through this analysis, the incumbent firm can achieve several important strategic insights. First, the timing of the economic impacts of the technological discontinuity can be predicted. Second, the competitive position of the incumbent firm can be forecasted at each stage of the discontinuity. Finally, the financial profitability of the incumbent can be estimated at each point of the transition. Armed with this

Part II   The Techniques of Strategic and Competitive Analysis

knowledge, the incumbent firm will be better able to manage the decision of when to start competing on the innovative technology.

Although this discussion has focused on the incumbent firm, S-curve analysis can be employed by the innovative firm in determining the competitiveness of its technology strategy at different points in time. This analysis can then be used to guide the timing of attack from a strictly offensive orientation.

The possibility exists that the predicted discontinuity lies well into the future. In this circumstance, S-curve analysis is equally adept at helping the incumbent firm to manage its current technology before it jumps onto another S-curve. Knowledge of the natural limits of the firm's current technology can function as an appropriate goal for the firm until the new S-curve becomes a dominant theme of the firm's strategy. Similarly, this knowledge can function as an appropriate basis for control and performance measurement of the R&D function during this time. Instead of basing performance goals on marginal improvements of the last period's technical performance, S-curve analysis allows performance to be recast relative to the natural limit of the firm's existing technology. Where the above analysis focused on the effectiveness of the R&D function with regard to technological discontinuity, S-curve analysis can also be used to guide the efficiency of the firm's R&D function on its current S-curve.

As S-curve analysis is expensive, costly, and complex, the final consideration of the analysis is to determine when to repeat the methodology. Rather than rigidly schedule, say, an annual or biannual iteration, Foster (1982) suggests 10 key signals through which the analyst may infer that the firm is reaching the natural limits of its current technology or that rivals have started operating on a superior S-curve:

1. A gut feeling that R&D productivity is on the wane
2. Increasing tendency of the R&D department to miss deadlines
3. A disproportionate focus on process rather than on product performance improvement
4. A gut feeling that the R&D function isn't as creative or innovative as it used to be
5. Petty infighting in the R&D department
6. No discernable performance improvements even after firing and replacing key R&D staff
7. Profitability becomes increasingly dependent on more sharply defined customer segments
8. The displacement of market share by rivals premised on niche strategies
9. No discernable performance improvements even after increasing R&D investment
10. Rivals are perceived to be pursuing illogical strategies that "are bound to fail".

An analysis of the technological advances in aircraft engine technology underscores the importance of considering multiple S-curves. The figure here depicts the two S-curves representing a distinct technological discontinuity in the aircraft engine industry:

1. the increase in take-off thrust (Kp) of jet engines
2. the increase in horsepower (hp) of piston aircraft engines

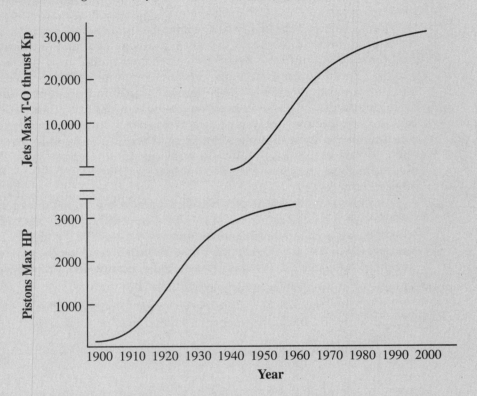

An analyst in 1930 might have concluded that the natural limit of piston engine hp was approximately 3800 hp. During the 1940s, however, the aviation market was enjoying rapid growth. As experience curve theory was beginning to gain credence during this era (in fact, it was initially developed in an aviation plant), the same analyst might be tempted to recommend a considerable expansion in piston engine production capacity to exploit experience curve effects.

Given the imminent approach of jet technology, this strategy would have been potentially devastating for the analyst's firm.

The fact that the natural limit of piston technology seemed to begin during a period of robust market growth would have pointed the analyst to an investigation of potential competing technologies. Further investigation through S-curve analysis would have reduced the probability of pursuing the wrong technology.

SOURCE: Adapted from "Technology Life Cycles and Business Decisions," by T. H. Lee and N. Nakicenovic, 1988. *International Journal of Technology Management, 3*(4), pp. 411–426.

In 1983, the Agricultural Research Division of the Cyanamid Company conducted a retrospective S-curve analysis of its organophosphate insecticide technology. A distinctive S-curve was produced, as shown in the graph.

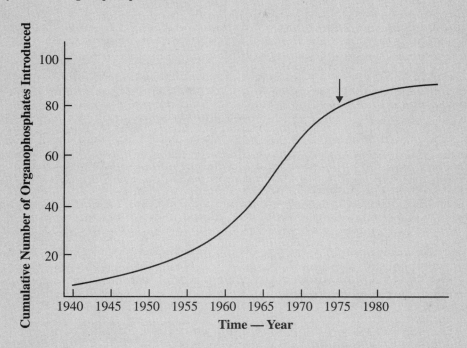

The arrow corresponds to the year 1974 when Cyanamid stopped investing in discovery research of organophosphate insecticides. Had they had access to S-curve analysis during the time span, the researchers concluded that the optimal time to have discontinued discovery research would have been 1968—the point of inflection. That would have saved millions of research dollars.

In an effort to explain this apparently illogical decision, the researchers surmised that the reason was that business is usually at its best in the "management comfort zone" shown in the figure on p. 398. At this point, management has little incentive to assume the risk associated with investing in a new technology because technology matures before sales and profits.

In actuality, Cyanamid was unwittingly assuming a greater risk in 1968 by continuing to invest in the mature technology instead of moving to another S-curve by investing in a new technology. The perceived risk of investing in a new technology is explained by the "management discomfort zone" also indicated in the figure. In this area on the S-curve, technical progress is hard to portray for two reasons:

1. The area on the new S-curve is relatively flat.
2. It is difficult to show tangible results of the R&D.

Nonetheless, it is important for management to recognize these perceptual barriers to R&D success. S-curve analysis can lift the blinders.

(Continued on following page)

S-Curve Analysis at Cynamid (Continued)

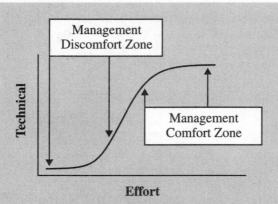

FAROUT SUMMARY

	1	2	3	4	5
F	███	███	███	███	███
A	███	███	███		
R	███				
O	███	███			
U	███	███	███	███	███
T	███				

Future orientation High. Addressing technological discontinuity explicitly predicates this model on a solid future orientation.

Accuracy Medium. The methodology is heavily reliant on subjective estimates of future technology and product usage contexts. In addition to this "crystal ball gazing," S-curve analysis requires the analyst to consider innovation from any and all sectors in the economy, a difficult task to achieve within any degree of accuracy given the wide array of potential sources of discontinuity. S-curve analysis, however, should not be used as a forecasting tool but rather as a tool for assessing different contingency strategies.

Resource efficiency Low. Requires extensive time and expense to conduct properly.

Objectivity Medium to low. The methodological approach is vulnerable to the personal biases of the analyst. Many of the estimates and forecasts are contingent on subjective inputs, such as estimates of the contribution margins associated with future technologies.

Usefulness High. Operating on the correct S-curve is directly related to the competitiveness of the firm.

Timeliness Low. S-curve analysis requires an extended amount of time to conduct.

RELATED TOOLS AND TECHNIQUES

- blindspot analysis
- competitor profiling
- experience curve analysis
- industry analysis
- product life cycle analysis

REFERENCES

Becker, R. H., & Speltz, L. M. (1983). "Putting the S-curve concept to work." *Research Management, 16*(5), 31–33.

———. (1986). "Making more explicit forecasts." *Research Management, 19*(4), 21–23.

Foster, R. N. (1982a). "Boosting the payoff from R&D." *Research Management, 15*(1), 22–27.

———. (1982, May 24). "A call for vision in managing technology." *McKinsey Quarterly,* Summer 1982(b), pp. 26–36.

———. (1986a). *Innovation: The attacker's advantage.* New York: Summit Books.

———. (1986b). "Assessing technological threats." *Research Management, 19*(4), 17–20.

Kuznets, S. (1930). *Secular movements in production and prices.* Boston: Houghton Mifflin.

Lee, T. H., & Nakicenovic, N. (1988). "Technology life cycles and business decisions." *International Journal of Technology Management, 3*(4), 411–426.

Levitt, T. (1965). "Exploit the product life cycle." *Harvard Business Review,* November/December, 81–94.

Moore, G. A. (1991). *Crossing the chasm: Marketing and selling high-tech goods to mainstream customers.* New York: Harper Business.

Nieto, M., Lopez, F. & Cruz, F. (1998). "Performance analysis of technology using the S-curve model: The case of digital signal processing (DSP) technologies." *Technovation, 18*(6,7), 439–457.

Pogany, G. A. (1986). "Cautions about using S-curves." *Research Management, 19*(4), 24–25.

Rogers, E. M. (1995). *Diffusion of innovations* (4th ed.). New York: Free Press.

Roussel, P. A. (1984). "Technological maturity proves a valid and important concept." *Research Management, 17*(1), 29–34.

Utterback, J. M., & Abernathy, W. J. (1975). "A dynamic model of process and product innovation." *Omega, 3,* 639–656.

Chapter 25

Financial Ratio and Statement Analysis

SHORT DESCRIPTION

A company's published report and accounts will contain a bewildering array of figures. How do analysts know if their company or competitors are operating in an effective or efficient manner? One way of determining this is through the use of financial ratio and statement analysis (FRSA). FRSA provides the manager with an understanding of the firm's competitive performance.

BACKGROUND

The relationship between sales revenue and expenses, and between assets and liabilities is measured by ratios. A ratio is calculated by dividing one number by another. There are many different kinds of ratios, but they are traditionally classed to reflect five main aspects of businesses: liquidity, leverage, asset turnover, profitability, and market value.

Financial ratio and statement analysis (FRSA) is an excellent tool for providing critical insight about a company's financial condition and future competitive prospects. Ratios allow analysts to assess current performance, examine business trends, evaluate business strategies, and monitor progress.

1. *Assess Performance.* Ratios serve as an analytical tool for measuring the performance of the enterprise in terms of margin, asset use, and cost control. Ratio analysis also allows analysts to analyze the financial liquidity and stability of the enterprise by reference to the mix of assets and liabilities in place.
2. *Examine Business Trends.* When ratios are applied to the results of a number of years, ratio analysis allows analysts to examine trend performance in the context of their existing business strategy.

3. *Evaluate Business Strategies.* When ratios are applied to a business plan, ratio analysis allows analysts to examine performance in relation to alternative business strategies.
4. *Monitor Progress.* Having selected their optimal business strategy, managers can monitor the progress of their enterprise by continuing to examine selected key ratios.

Ratio analysis is the art of analyzing the relationships between two or more amounts in a company's financial statements. The actual ratio results are even more meaningful when compared with a company's historical results or industry averages. Analysts employ financial ratios because numbers in isolation have little value. The true meaning of figures from the financial statements emerges only when they are compared to other figures. Such comparisons are the essence of why business and financial ratios have been developed. Financial ratios are particularly useful for analyzing a company's performance relative to its industry. The influence of industrywide conditions of the companies within the industry is almost always strong (see Chapter 6 for more on industry analysis and industry effects on competition).

Ratios are typically generated from a company's financial statements. Financial statements are necessary sources of information about companies for a wide variety of users. Besides analysts, those who use financial statement information include company management teams, investors, creditors, and governmental oversight agencies. Users of financial statement information do not necessarily need to know everything about accounting to use the information in basic statements. However, to effectively use financial statement information, it is helpful to know a few simple concepts and to be familiar with some of the fundamental characteristics of basic financial statements. The following section will provide some of these basics.

Basic Concepts Underlying Financial Ratio and Statement Analysis

The accounting equation is an essential notion for analyzing financial ratios and statements. It derives from assets and claims on assets. Assets are what a company owns, such as accounts receivables, buildings, cash, equipment, and inventory. Claims on assets include liabilities and owner's equity. Liabilities are what a company owes to others, such as accounts payable, bonds, notes, and taxes payable. Owners' equity represents the claims of owners against the business and takes the form of common and preferred stock, capital surplus, and retained earnings. The basic equation that expresses the relationship of assets and claims on assets is called the accounting equation

$$\text{Assets} = \text{Liabilities} + \text{Owners' equity}$$

Assets are generally classified into three categories:

1. Current assets include cash and other assets expected to be converted into cash within one year, such as marketable securities, accounts receivable, notes receivable, inventories, and prepaid expenses.

2. Property, plant, and equipment (fixed assets) includes business assets that have relatively long lives. These assets are typically not for resale and are used in the production or sale of other goods and services. Examples are equipment, machinery, furniture and fixtures, land, and plant.
3. Non-current assets include the company's investments in securities, such as stocks and bonds, and intangible assets such as patents, franchise costs, and copyrights.

Liabilities are generally divided into two classes:

1. Current liabilities include the amounts owed to creditors that are due within one year, such as accounts payable, accrued liabilities, and notes payable.
2. Long-term liabilities are claims of creditors that do not come due within one year. Included in this category are bonded indebtedness, long-term bank loans, and mortgages.

Owners' equity is the claims of owners against the business. This is a residual amount computed by subtracting liabilities from assets. Its balance is increased by any profit and reduced by any losses incurred by the business.

In studying financial statements, it is helpful to remember that they are only tools to be used by different entities. For the purposes of this chapter, the perspective is that of the analyst. Think about the kinds of information managers need to have in order to make effective decisions and how that information might be used. Statements commonly used by analysts include the income statement, balance sheet, statement of changes in financial position, and statement of changes in owners' equity.

The income statement, also referred to as a profit and loss statement, statement of incomes and losses, or report of earnings, summarizes the results of a company's operations, in terms of revenues and expenses, for a period of time, called the accounting period. Net income is derived from the accrual measurement of revenues and expenses. It is generally perceived as the most important financial statement for several reasons. Not least among these is that it reveals whether the stockholders' interests in the organization have increased or decreased for the period after adjusting for dividends or other transactions with owners. The income statement also helps users assess the amount, timing, and uncertainty of future cash flows.

The balance sheet and income statement are both basic statements common to most businesses. The balance sheet is a statement detailing what a company owns (assets) and claims against the company (liabilities and owners' equity) on a particular date. Some analysts liken the balance sheet to a photograph or snapshot illustrating a company's financial health at a particular point in time. Balance sheets may be quite detailed, depending on the nature and complexity of a business.

Another group of statements is based on the concept of how funds flow through a business. The position statement, also known as the statement of changes in financial position or sources and uses of cash, helps to explain how a company acquired its money and how it was spent. The statement of changes in owner's equity is used to bridge the gap between the amount of owners' equity at the beginning of the period and the amount of their equity at the end of the period.

STRATEGIC RATIONALE

The main competitive analytical purpose of financial ratio and statement analysis is to gain an insight into the company's financial decision making and its operating performance. It therefore reduces the analyst's reliance on guesses, hunches, and intuition, which minimizes uncertainty in decision making. Comprehensive analysis requires detailed calculations involving financial ratios, historical financials, and future growth estimates, combined with industry and economic analysis. The more analysis you do on a company, the more you will learn about it and its products.

Although financial statements provide much useful information, the large numbers and varying sizes and accounting practices of companies, especially in multinational contexts, make it quite difficult to compare performance from company to company and from year to year within one company. Ratio analysis is a useful technique for evaluating a company's various financial characteristics.

Applying ratio analysis to financial statements enables the analyst to make judgments about the competitive success, failure, and evolution of a company over time and to evaluate how a company is performing compared with similar companies in the same industry. Ratio analysis can also help internal management of an organization gain an awareness of their company's strengths and weaknesses (see Chapter 8). And, if the analyst finds weaknesses, the analyst can recommend actions to correct them before irreparable damage is done. If the analyst finds weaknesses in a competitor's performance, the company can take measures to exploit these in the marketplace!

The analyst can assess the appropriateness of ratios on the basis of some benchmark or basis for comparison. There are three principal benchmarks. The first is the firm's own performance history. It is always useful to review the ratios for the firm this year, as compared to what they were in several prior years. This enables the analyst to discover favorable or unfavorable trends that are developing gradually over time, as well as pointing out any numbers that have changed dramatically in a defined space of time.

The second type of analytical benchmark is to compare the firm to specific competitors. If the competitors are publicly held companies, it is easy to obtain copies of their annual reports and compare each of the focal company's ratios with each of the competitors. This approach is especially valuable for helping to pinpoint why the focal firm is doing particularly better or worse than a specific competitor. By identifying where ratios differ, it is possible to determine what the focal company is doing better or worse than the competition.

The third type of benchmark is an industrywide comparison. Most industry and trade associations publish industry-average ratios based on data compiled by the association from member reports. Considerable data regarding industry averages are available from a wide variety of producers, many of which can be readily acquired for free via the Internet and government sources. Dun & Bradstreet and Robert Morris Associates are two examples of commercial sources that collect financial data, compute ratios by industry, and publish the results. Not only are industry averages available, but the information is often broken down both by size of firm and in a way that allows determination of relatively how far away from the norm any firm is.

Strengths and Advantages

Financial ratio and statement analysis has many fundamental benefits, some of which are detailed in entire books dedicated to the topic such as the ones we suggest in the References section of this chapter. The analysis of financial statements is a common practice for creditors and investors, but their purposes differ from those of the strategic and competitive analyst who is seeking to interpret and assess an organization's strategy and performance. A careful analysis of a company's financial condition immensely improves the entire competitive and strategic analysis process. Financial data represent the actual and concrete results of the company's strategy, structure, and systems and can be beneficial in understanding the implications for a firm's strategic options. We cannot imagine a comprehensive competitive and strategic analysis being done in the absence of any FRSA!

FRSA is also an extremely helpful information overload tool. One of the main challenges of competitive intelligence is how to find patterns in mountains of disjointed data. FRSA achieves this in two ways: It transforms reams of financial data into a manageable handful of meaningful outputs and it connects the dynamic income statement with the static balance sheet into one integrated analysis.

Another fundamental benefit of financial ratio analysis is its versatility. It is easily amenable to both internal firm analysis and competitive analysis of both rivals and industry structure. Generally, analytical rigor can be achieved by calculating two or three key ratios in each category.

FRSA also allows the analyst to determine a company's ability to succeed through its application of a generic strategy such as low-cost producer, niche pursuer, or differentiator. By combining the FRSA with other related techniques described in this book, the analyst gains the most complete picture of a firm's likelihood of strategic and competitive success.

Weaknesses and Limitations

Financial ratios have some limitations that must be considered when the analyst uses them in analyzing a company.

Financial ratios are based on historical accrual-based accounting information. As such, financial ratios do not offer the analyst any direct insights into cash flow, an important component of value-based management. This can be even more important with embryonic, entrepreneurial firms that have proportionately greater burn rates and needs for cash in their earlier years.

A single ratio will not give you enough information to make a judgment about the firm. You must have additional data to make these judgments. The source of these data might be from comparing the ratios to the industry average or past company performance. Intracompany trends over time can also be enlightening to the analyst. The meaningfulness of an individual ratio also tends to be inversely related to the size of the initial base (i.e., denominator). Therefore, huge percentage changes on ratios with a small starting base are of limited analytical value. Similarly, ratios derived from negative denominators should be carefully interpreted.

Accountants do not include as assets certain items that are critical to the growth and well-being of a company. The quality of its employees is probably the most significant asset for many businesses, yet this vital asset is not reflected in the balance sheet. Financial statements virtually ignore these increasingly important intangible assets—a key source of competitive advantage in an information- or knowledge-driven economy. FRSA is inherently limited as an analytical tool for firms with valuable brand names or corporate reputations, intellectually skilled workforces, or other intellectual capital.

Not all financial statements are of equal quality. It is best to use audited financial statements whenever they are available. Audited statements provide you with a far higher probability of using accurate financial information. Bear in mind, however, that published ratios are not subject to public audits, with the exception of the EPS ratio.

Even though it is important to use industry norms to evaluate your financial performance against your industry peers, caution should be applied in interpreting the results. Analysts who overly rely on industry comparisons risk leading their firms to the netherworld of what Michael Porter aptly describes as being "Stuck in the Middle" on the industry's parabolic profit curve (Porter, 1980). To see how this may occur, consider an industry in which half of the rivals are pursuing a low-cost strategy while the other half are pursuing a differentiated strategy. Comparing your firm's ratios to the industry norms will, by definition target the average performance. Success in meeting these average targets will necessarily relegate the firm to the lowest point on the industry profit curve. At one end, the average firm's cost structure will be higher than that of the low-cost specialists. At the other end, premium firms will surpass the average firm's level of differentiation. Overreliance on industry norms is akin to benchmarking for mediocrity instead of best practice.

When using industry norms, the analyst must also remain aware of the issue of comparing dissimilar industry groups. Direct financial comparisons to rivals outside of your industry group may have low short-term utility. Even comparisons within industry groups are fraught with difficulty when rival firms are operating on a different portion of the industry profit curve by virtue of the chosen low cost, differentiation, or focus strategies. Additionally, since most industry norms are calculated from aggregated financial statements, rating your firm's financial performance to a diversified firm will cause a critical comparability problem if the lines of business are radically different.

A fixation on internal comparisons to past firm performance is also risky. Several manifestations of this risk are complacency from seemingly adequate improvements while, in reality, the firm is slipping relative to even better performance of rivals. This problem is especially prevalent in fast-growth markets when differences in relative competitive performance may not be painful in the short-term but will nonetheless have serious repercussions on long-term competitive positioning.

In closely held businesses, it is not uncommon for the financial statements to reflect discretionary choices of the business owner as opposed to being limited to stating ordinary and necessary business expenses. The analyst should carefully consider the effects of management choices on the results of operations as reported in the financial statements. Sometimes, significant adjustments can be required to restate the financial statements to accurately portray the operations of the business.

Another problem that one must consider is whether the financial information was developed using the same accounting methods. The choice of an accounting method may have a significant impact on the income reported in the income statement and the value of the asset reported in the balance sheet. This is especially pertinent when doing international competitor comparisons and when competitors have multinational operations that potentially utilize different accounting standard schemes. Some other technical considerations are to keep a sharp eye for differences in accounting policies (different depreciation schedules, inventory valuation, capitalization), account classification, or year-ends across firms that could distort the validity of the comparison.

Even when a firm's financial ratios appear to conform to industry averages, this does not mean that the firm has no financial or other strategic management problems. For example, perhaps the firm is neglecting to exploit a clear differential advantage by which it could far outstrip average industry performance. Alternatively, perhaps the firm's finances look good at the moment, but a serious competitive threat could wipe it out in the near future. In short, financial ratio analysis is a very useful tool for analyzing strategic management, but it cannot replace different considerations that can only come by the application of a variety of analysis tools.

PROCESS FOR APPLYING THE TECHNIQUE

Performing a financial ratio analysis can be divided into several steps. First, the analyst must choose the appropriate ratios to analyze. Next, the appropriate sources must be located in order to provide the raw data in which to calculate the ratios, a topic better covered in one of the many books available on the larger competitive intelligence data collection process. Following this, the analyst makes comparisons of the ratios. Last, a check is performed for opportunities and problems.

Key Ratio Types

Let's begin by identifying the key ratio types:

1. Activity or efficiency ratios
2. Leverage or solvency analysis ratios
3. Liquidity analysis
4. Profitability
5. Other (shareholder return or capital markets) ratios

Activity or Efficiency Ratios
Activity or efficiency ratios include inventory ratios, accounts receivables ratios, fixed and total asset turnover.

There are several common ratios used to perform inventory analysis. Inventory is the amount of merchandise, parts, supplies, or other goods your business keeps on hand to meet the demands of your customers. Depending on the nature of your business (i.e., retail, wholesale, service, manufacturing), the efficiency of your inventory management may have a significant impact on your cash flow and, ultimately, your business's success or failure.

Average Inventory Investment Period.   The average inventory investment period is calculated by dividing your present inventory balance by your average daily cost of goods sold:

Average inventory investment period = Current inventory balance/Average
daily cost of goods sold (COGS)

The average daily cost of goods sold is computed by dividing your annual COGS by 360.

The average inventory investment period measures the amount of time it takes to convert a dollar of cash outflow, used to purchase inventory, to a dollar of sales or accounts receivable from the sale of the inventory. The average investment period for inventory is much like the average collection period for accounts receivable. A longer average inventory investment period requires a higher investment in inventory. A higher investment in inventory means less cash is available for other cash outflows, such as paying bills.

Inventory to Sales Ratio.   The inventory to sales ratio is calculated by dividing your inventory balance at the end of any month by your total sales for the same month. It is seen as follows:

Inventory to sales ratio = Inventory/Sales for the month

The inventory to sales ratio looks at the company's investment in inventory in relation to its monthly sales amount. The inventory to sales ratio helps the analyst identify recent increases in inventory. In contrast, the average inventory investment period reports only inventory information from the previous year, if that was the only information available to calculate the period.

The inventory to sales ratio can serve as a quick and easy way to look at recent changes in inventory levels, since it uses monthly sales and inventory information. This ratio will help predict early cash flow problems related to a business's inventory.

Turnover Analysis.   Turnover analysis is the most basic and fundamental tool for assessing the organization's investment in inventory. Turnover analysis looks at a business's investment in individual items or groups of items making up its entire inventory. Turnover analysis then helps the analyst to decide if the organization's investment in an inventory item, or groups of items, is excessive, too low, or just right. From a cash flow perspective, performing turnover analysis is particularly useful for finding inventory items that are overstocked. Remember, an excessive investment in inventory results in less cash available for other cash outflow purposes, such as paying bills. The formula for inventory turnover is

Inventory turnover = Sales/Inventory of finished goods

Turnover analysis goes beyond the average assumptions made by the average inventory investment period. It does this by requiring the analyst to look at each product or line individually, taking into account the number currently on hand, the number sold, and the number on hand in relation to the rate at which each item sells. So, turnover analysis can be used to pinpoint the specific inventory items that are creating an excess investment in inventory, thus creating cash flow problems.

Accounts Receivable. Represents sales for which payment has not yet been collected. If the business normally extends credit to its customers, the payment of accounts receivable is likely to be its single most important source of cash inflows.

The following analysis tools can be used to help determine the effect the company's business's accounts receivable is having on its cash flow:

Average collection period measures the length of time it takes to convert average sales into cash. This measurement defines the relationship between accounts receivable and the company's cash flow. A longer average collection period requires a higher investment in accounts receivable. A higher investment in accounts receivable means less cash is available to cover cash outflows, such as paying bills.

The average collection period is calculated by dividing the present accounts receivables balance by average daily sales. It is calculated as

Average collection period = Current accounts receivables balance/Average daily sales.
Average daily sales = Annual sales/360.

Accounts receivable to sales ratio is calculated by dividing your accounts receivable balance by your total sales. Its formula is

Accounts receivables to sales ratio = Accounts receivables/Sales

The accounts receivable to sales ratio looks at the company's investment in accounts receivable in relation to the sales amount. The accounts receivable to sales ratio helps the analyst identify recent increases in accounts receivable. In contrast, the average collection period may only report accounts receivable information from the previous year, if that was the only information available to calculate it. The accounts receivable to sales ratio can serve as a quick and easy way to examine any recent changes in accounts receivable. The more recent information of the accounts receivable to sales ratio will quickly point out cash flow problems related to the business's accounts receivables.

Another form of the accounts receivables to sales ratio is called *accounts receivable turnover.* This is a measure of the average length of time it takes the firm to collect the sales made on credit. It is calculated by the formula

Accounts receivable turnover = Accounts receivable/Average daily sales

Asset Rurnover. This is the ratio of sales (on the income statement) to the value of the company's assets (on its balance sheet). It indicates how well a business is using its assets to generate sales. Generally speaking, the higher the ratio, the better, because a high ratio indicates the business has less money tied up in assets for each dollar of sales revenue. A declining ratio may indicate that it has overinvested in plant, equipment, or other fixed assets. Companies with low profit margins tend to have high asset turnover, those with high profit margins have lower asset turnover— this indicates pricing strategy.

$$\text{Asset turnover} = \text{Revenue/Assets}$$

The ratio of total sales (on the income statement) to total assets (on the balance sheet) indicates how well a company is using all of its business assets rather than just its inventories or fixed assets to generate revenue. A high asset turnover ratio means a higher return on assets, which can compensate for a low profit margin. In computing the ratio, it may be helpful to compute total assets by averaging the total assets at the beginning and end of the accounting period.

Leverage or Solvency Analysis Ratios

This group of ratios is designed to help the analyst assess the degree of financial risk that a business faces. *Financial risk,* in this context, means the extent to which the company has debt obligations that must be met, regardless of its cash flow. By looking at these ratios, the analyst can assess the firm's level of debt and decide whether this level is appropriate or not. Commonly used solvency ratios are debt to equity, debt to assets, coverage of fixed costs, and interest coverage.

Debt to Equity Ratio. The ratio of debt-to-owner's equity or net worth indicates the degree of financial leverage that the firm is using to enhance its return. It provides a measure of the fund provided by creditors versus the funds provided by owners.

$$\text{Debt to equity} = \text{Total debt/Total stockholder's equity}$$

A rising debt to equity ratio may signal that further increases in debt caused by purchases of inventory or fixed assets should be curtailed.

Improving this ratio involves either paying off debt or increasing the amount of earnings retained in the business until after the balance sheet date. For instance, can expenses be deferred beyond the balance sheet date to increase retained earnings? What about bonuses? Delaying any planned bonus expense can effectively increase retained earnings. As another example, the company might think about repaying revolving debt (such as a line of credit) before the balance sheet date and borrowing again after the balance sheet date.

Debt to Assets Ratio. The debt to assets ratio measures the percentage of assets financed by creditors, compared to the percentage that have been financed by the business owners. Historically, a debt to asset ratio of no more than 50 percent has been considered prudent. A higher ratio indicates a possible overuse of leverage, and it may indicate potential problems meeting the debt payments. The debt to assets ratio is calculated as

$$\text{Debt to assets} = \text{Total debt/Total assets}$$

Improving this ratio means taking steps either to increase the value of the firm's assets, or to pay off debt. For example, the analyst might explore whether inventory or other assets can be given a higher value. If it goes the route of paying off debt, it will also concurrently improve its current ratio and debt to equity ratio.

Fixed Charge Coverage. This is also sometimes called times fixed charges earned. The resulting number shows the firm's ability to meet its fixed obligations of all types—the higher the number, the better.

$$\text{Fixed charge coverage} = \text{Profits before taxes and interest} + \text{Lease obligations/Total interest charges} + \text{Lease obligations}$$

Obviously, an inability to meet any fixed obligation of the business threatens the business's well-being. Many working capital loan agreements will specify that a company must maintain this ratio at a specified level, so that the lender has some assurance that it will continue to be able to make its payments.

Interest Coverage Ratio. This is also sometimes known as the times interest earned ratio. It is very similar to the times fixed charges earned ratio but focuses more narrowly on the interest portion of your debt payments.

$$\text{Interest coverage ratio} = \text{Operating income/Interest expense}$$

By comparing the ratio of operating income to interest expense, the analyst measures how many times the firm's interest obligations are covered by earnings from its operations. The higher the ratio, the bigger the firm's cushion and the more able the business is to meet interest payments. If this ratio is declining over time, it's a keen indication that its financial risk is increasing.

Liquidity Analysis Ratios

These ratios indicate the ease of turning assets into cash. They include the current ratio and quick ratio. Liquidity ratios are sometimes called working capital (the difference between current assets and current liabilities) ratios because that, in essence, is what they measure. A general observation about these three liquidity ratios is that the higher they are, the better, especially if the company is relying to any significant extent on creditor money to finance its assets.

Current Ratio. The current ratio is one of the most popular measures of financial strength. It is a good indicator of a company's ability to pay its short-term obligations.

$$\text{Current ratio} = \text{Total current assets/Total current liabilities}$$

The main question this ratio addresses is: "Does the company have enough current assets to meet the payment schedule of its current debts with a margin of safety for possible losses in current assets, such as inventory shrinkage or collectable accounts?" The higher the ratio is will tell you how much more liquidity the company has. A generally acceptable rule of thumb for a current ratio is 2:1. But whether a specific ratio is satisfactory depends on the nature of the business and the characteristics of its current assets and liabilities. The minimum acceptable current ratio is 1:1, but that relationship is usually suggestive of potential risks or problems.

Quick Ratio. The quick ratio is sometimes called the acid-test ratio and is one of the best measures of liquidity. It describes how quickly a company can turn its assets into cash,

$$\text{Quick ratio} = \text{Cash} + \text{Government securities} + \text{Receivables/Total current liabilities}$$

The quick ratio is a much more exacting measure than the current ratio. By excluding inventories, it concentrates on highly liquid assets, with value that is fairly certain.

It helps answer the question: "If all sales revenues should disappear, could my business meet its current obligations with the readily convertible 'quick' funds on hand?"

An acid test of 1:1 is considered satisfactory unless the majority of your "quick assets" are in accounts receivable, and the pattern of accounts receivable collection lags behind the schedule for paying current liabilities.

Working Capital. Working capital is basically an expression of how much in liquid assets a company currently has to build its business, fund its growth, and produce shareholder value.

The best way to look at current assets and current liabilities is by combining them into something called working capital. Working capital can be positive or negative. If a company has ample positive working capital, then it is in good shape with plenty of cash on hand to pay for the items it needs to buy. If a company has negative working capital, then its current liabilities are greater than its current assets and it lacks the ability to spend as aggressively as a company with positive working capital. *Ceteris paribus,* a competitor with positive working capital will always outperform a company with negative working capital.

$$\text{Working capital} = \text{Current assets} - \text{Current liabilities}$$

Profitability Analysis Ratios

You can use another set of ratios to assess the profitability of a business and changes in its profit performance. These ratios are probably the most important indicators of a business's financial success. These ratios demonstrate the performance and growth potential of the business. The most common of these include return on assets (ROA), return on equity (ROE), profit margin (which can be in either gross or net form), and asset turnover and are all used to assess how profitable the target company is.

Return on Assets. This is the ratio of net income to total assets. It is basically a measure of how well a business is using its assets to produce more income. It can be viewed as a combination of two other ratios, net profit margin (ratio of net income to sales) and asset turnover (ratio of sales to total assets). A high return on assets can be attributable to a high profit margin, a rapid turnover of assets, or a combination of both.

$$\text{Return on assets (ROA)} = \text{Net income/Assets}$$

The ratio of net income (from the income statement) to net worth or stockholders' equity (from the balance sheet) shows what the company earned on its investment in the business during the accounting period. This ratio is often referred to as return on investment (ROI).

Return on Equity. You can compare a business's return on equity to what it might have earned on the stock market during the same accounting period. Over time, a business should be generating at least the same return that it could earn in more passive investments like bank CDs. A high return on equity may be a result of a high return on assets, extensive use of debt financing, or a combination of the two.

$$\text{Return on equity (ROE)} = \text{Net income/Shareholders' equity}$$

In analyzing both ROE and ROA, don't forget to consider the effects of inflation on the book value of the assets. While financial statements show all assets at their book value (i.e., original cost minus depreciation), the replacement value of many older assets may be substantially higher than their book value. A business with older assets, generally, should show higher return percentages than a business that is using newer assets.

Gross Profit Margin.   Recall that gross profit is the amount of sales dollars remaining after the cost of goods sold has been deducted. If a company's gross profit margin is declining over time, it may mean that its inventory management needs to be improved, or that its selling prices are not rising as fast as the costs of the goods it sells. If the firm is a manufacturer, it may mean that its costs of production are rising faster than its prices, and adjustments on either side (or both) are necessary.

$$\text{Gross profit margin} = \text{Gross profits/Sales}$$

The net profit margin shows the analyst the company's bottom line: how much of each sales dollar is ultimately available for its owners to draw out of the business or to receive as dividends. It's probably the figure that people are most accustomed to looking at. This ratio takes into account all the company's expenses, including income taxes and interest.

The astute analyst should have some idea of the range within which to expect the company's profit margin to be, which will be determined in large part by historical industry standards. If a company fails to meet its targets, it could mean that it has set unrealistic goals, or it could mean that it is not managing as efficiently and effectively as possible. However, the ratio itself will not point to *what* a company may be doing wrong. Looking at the gross margin or operating margin is a better way to get a fix on that problem.

Even if a company meets its goal, the analyst should always keep an eye on its profit margin. If it should decline, for example, it may indicate that the company needs to take a look at whether its costs are getting too high.

The absolute level of profit may provide an indication of the size of the business, but on its own it says very little about company performance. In order to evaluate the level of profit, profit must be compared and related to other aspects of the business. Profit must also be compared with the amount of capital invested in the business, and to sales revenue.

Profitability ratios will inevitably reflect the business environment of the time. So, the business, political, and economic climate must also be considered when looking at the trend of profitability for one company over time. Comparisons with other businesses in the same industry segment give an indication of how well management is performing compared to other firms in the same business environment.

Other (Capital Market or Shareholder Returns) Analysis Ratios

The use of capital market or shareholder returns analysis ratios probably has a higher level of importance for investors than it would for the purposes of strategic or competitive analysis. These are more commonly thought of as investment, as opposed to performance, measures.

Earnings per Share (EPS).   This is the single most popular variable in dictating a share's price: It indicates the profitability of a company.

$$\text{EPS} = \text{Net income} - \text{Dividends on preferred stock/Average outstanding shares}$$

Company earnings are the sum of income from sales or investment after paying expenses. The way in which a business conducts its operations is an important element to understand when evaluating a company's earnings. Companies that are devoting significant resources to creating a new product may have relatively weak earnings now. But, if that new product catches on with customers, profits could quickly rise and the earnings may begin to rapidly rise. Meanwhile, companies that now have strong earnings, but are not investing any money to ensure that their business success will continue, may have significant problems in the future.

Price/Earnings (P/E) Ratio. This is often referred to as "the multiple."

P/E ratio = Current market value per share/Earnings per share

The earnings per share figure is usually from the last four quarters (the trailing P/E ratio), but sometimes from the estimates of the earnings expected in the next four quarters (the projected P/E ratio), or from the sum of the last two actual quarters and the estimates of the next two quarters.

For the most part, a high P/E means high projected earnings in the future. But actually the P/E ratio on its own doesn't really tell all that much, but it's useful to compare the P/E ratios of other companies in the same industry, or to the market in general, or against the company's own historical P/E ratios.

Methods of Ratio or Measure Comparison

We cannot overemphasize the statement that no single ratio has meaning by itself. In other words, comparing ratios is critical for effective financial ratio analysis. A helpful solution to combat sources of analytical myopia is to strike an appropriate balance between the industry norm, historical analysis/internal benchmarking, and competitive external benchmarking approaches.

There are two basic methods for using financial ratios. The first is by comparing the firm's ratios with those of other companies in the industry. The second method is to compare the firm's present ratios with their own past performance ratios, in other words, across time.

Industrial Comparison

In industrial comparison we look at the company's performance in relationship to it competitors. By comparing the company to others; any differences in their operating efficiency will show up. Once the problem is found then the company can take action to correct the problem. These industry averages can be found in publications like Dun & Bradstreet's Key Business Ratios.

To compare an organization's ratios with those of similar firms in the industry or with industry averages, the analyst must look up the industry information. Common sources of industry information include:

- *Annual Statement Studies.* Published by Robert Morris Associates, this work includes 16 financial ratios computed annually for over 150 lines of business. Each line of business is divided into four size categories.
- Dun & Bradstreet provides 14 ratios calculated annually for over 100 lines of business.

- *The Almanac of Business and Industrial Financial Ratios.* This work, published by Prentice-Hall, lists industry averages for 22 financial ratios. Approximately 170 businesses and industries are listed.
- *The Quarterly Financial Report for Manufacturing Corporations.* This work, published jointly by the Federal Trade Commission and the Securities and Exchange Commission, contains balance sheet and income statement information by industry groupings and by asset-size categories.
- Trade associations and individual companies often compute ratios for their industries and make them available to analysts.
- Standard & Poor's Industry Surveys and Corporation Records.
- Value Line Investment Surveys
- Published financial statements on the Internet offer a source of raw material for firms not covered by the above sources.

In order to deal with corporations of significantly different sizes in a particular industry, it can often be helpful to create what are called common-size financial statements. The common size usually utilized is 100. This procedure can help the analyst to identify when a competitor departs from the industry norms. It will allow the analyst to ask a more refined set of questions in order to gain an understanding of what causes are driving this phenomenon.

Across Time Performance

The analyst can also spot problems by comparing a company's present performance to how well it did in the past few years. This will give an indication of how well they are progressing in correcting any problems. By looking at the past trend, a company can determine how effective it is in accomplishing the company's goals. You should use the same time frame in making any comparison. If you don't use the same time frame, effects caused by recessions or seasonal fluctuations could result in erroneous conclusions or judgments.

Another helpful approach at this point in the analyst's process is to bring the FRSA information together with other non–FRSA analytical method types.

All the ratio types discussed above are related because they relate to the fundamental components of the accounting identity:

$$\text{Assets} = \text{Liabilities plus owner's equity}$$

This constant can be leveraged through the Du Pont formula to diagnose the profitability of the firm. The Du Pont formula disaggregates the return on equity ratio into its constituent parts:

$$
\begin{aligned}
\text{ROE} &= \text{Return on assets} \times \text{Leverage} \\
&= \text{Profit margin} \times \text{Asset turnover} \times \text{Leverage} \\
&= \frac{\text{Net income}}{\text{Sales}} \times \frac{\text{Sales}}{\text{Assets}} \times \frac{\text{Assets}}{\text{Equity}} \\
&= \frac{\text{Net income}}{\text{Equity}}
\end{aligned}
$$

This formula offers the analyst a way to determine the intermediate reasons for the performance of the return on equity ratio over time. Increasing values for the numerators will positively impact ROE, while decreasing values will negatively impact ROE. The converse relationship holds for the denominators of the Du Pont formula. The net offset determines the ultimate ROE. This will provide clues about where to further investigate the primary business forces driving the components of the firm's ROE :

- Deteriorating profit margins point toward deteriorating market position, demand, or poor cost control.
- Deteriorating asset turnover points toward deteriorating operational management of working capital, declining sales, or capital asset intensity.
- Changes in leverage are negative only if it assumes a suboptimal risk profile. Otherwise, increases in leverage will safely increase ROE.

The Du Pont formula also offers an integrated approach to the financial analysis of competitors. Specifically, it offers a very concise method of capturing the morass of competitive financial information confronting the analyst. By integrating the Du Pont formula with the concept of strategic groups, the analyst can map financial performance as it relates to industry structure (Sammon et al, 1984). Further, this type of analysis can be refined to analyze firms *within* each strategic group. Figure 25-1 shows a typical strategic group—Du Pont profitability matrix.

By mapping out the various strategic groups along the parameters of the ROA equation, asset turnover versus profit margin, the analyst gains insight into how

Figure 25-1
Strategic Group—Du Pont Profitability Matrix

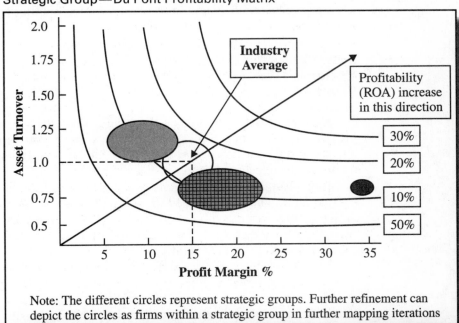

Note: The different circles represent strategic groups. Further refinement can depict the circles as firms within a strategic group in further mapping iterations

Source: Adapted from *Business Competitor Intelligence: Methods for Collecting, Organizing and Using Information,* by W. L. Sammon, M. A. Kurland, R. Spitalnic, 1984, New York: John Wiley & Sons.

strategic groups are competing on resources. (see Figure 25-1.) A similar map is then constructed to compare firms *within* each strategic group. These maps will provide a strong foundation for first reducing the analysis to a manageable number of variables and then pointing the way forward for more detailed competitive intelligence. Financial ratio strategic group maps provide a cogent visual analysis of the important financial ratios that describe one aspect of industry structure.

Consolidation and Segmented Analysis

Financial statements of public companies are legally mandated to provide segmented reporting in addition to consolidated operations. Most countries require public firms to provide enough information to explain about three-quarters of the firm's revenue. However, due to the competitive sensitivity of segmented information, public firms generally follow the letter of the law rather than the spirit of the law. That is, proprietary concerns outweigh the need for public accessibility to information. Therefore, segmented reporting only includes the bare minimum of information regarding the revenues, net income, and total assets of each segment. The only supplement to this meager reporting is information about the industry and geographic dispersion of its facilities and customers.

While segmented reporting is certainly more valuable than consolidated information when comparing a company to distinctly diversified rivals, it should not be relied upon. The accuracy and comparability will be minimal because segmented revenues will be derived from internal transfer prices, and the basis for allocating costs will be unknown to the external analyst.

Despite the requirement to reconcile or integrate the segment information back into the consolidated statements, segmented data will not provide enough information to calculate many ratios. Further, even when ratios can be calculated, the analyst must remain aware of the above limitations when performing ratio analysis on segmented data in an attempt to compare similar divisions or operations of diversified companies.

Keep in mind that a company's financial statements are only a starting point for analysis. For instance, if a statement shows that accounts receivable have experienced a significant downward trend over the last few years, it could mean that the company is collecting the accounts more aggressively (which is good), or it could possibly mean that it is writing off accounts as uncollectible too soon (which is bad). Individual numbers aren't good or bad in themselves. As an analyst, you may have to dig for the reason behind any numbers that seem out of whack. The key is to use financial ratio and statement analyses to spot trends and anomalies, and then follow these up with further investigation.

To complete the picture, you must acquire more information about the company's products, people, technology, and other resources that may give it a competitive advantage in the marketplace. One of the best sources of supplemental information is the nonfinancial section of the annual report. This section, usually found at the beginning of the document, often provides an outline of top management's views on the company's future and ability to compete.

FRSA is a critical part of a larger, integrated financial statement analysis plan. This plan should include the following key steps:

1. Determine the objectives of the financial statement analysis.
2. Review the current and predicted economic conditions in the industry in which the company operates.
3. Consult the annual report and other regulatory filings to glean information about management and the company's accounting methods.
4. Analyze the financial statements using the means described in this chapter.
5. Draw relevant conclusions based on the initial objectives.

FAROUT SUMMARY

	1	2	3	4	5
F	██				
A	██	██	██		
R	██	██	██	██	██
O	██	██	██	██	██
U	██	██		██	██
T	██	██	██	██	██

Future orientation   Low. Financial ratio analysis is based on historical information and analysis of past trends.

Accuracy   Medium. Depends on the comparability of inputs vis à vis correctly identified strategic groups, accounting policies, national GAAP regimes, and time frame. Accuracy also depends on the analyst's understanding of these caveats. Further, agency problems such as earnings management and "window dressing" may result in an analysis in which inputs do not measure what they purport to measure.

Resource efficiency   High. Financial ratio analysis requires a relatively low investment to perform, as the methodology is well established and systematic and the input variables are freely available.

Objectivity   High. Highly quantitative analysis based on publicly audited input variables.

Usefulness   Low to Medium. Financial ratio analysis only identifies symptoms based on historical information. As such, it functions as a lagging indicator pointing the analyst to problems or opportunities that are already established or developing. It does not offer strategic guidance.

Timeliness   High. Financial analysis can be performed more quickly than most other methods using readily available data for most public companies. It can take longer when dealing with private companies that are not required to disclose the same amount of financial data as public companies.

RELATED TOOLS AND TECHNIQUES

- functional capability and resource analysis
- industry analysis
- strategic group analysis
- strategic funds programming
- sustainable growth rate analysis
- SWOT analysis
- value-chain analysis

REFERENCES

AICPA Web site at www.aicpa.org/cefm/index.htm

Atrill, P., & McLaney, E. (1997). *Accounting and finance for non-specialists* (2nd ed.). Englewood Cliffs, NJ: Prentice-Hall.

Beechy, T. H., & Conrod, J. E. D. (2000). *Intermediate accounting.* New York: McGraw-Hill Ryerson Limited.

Foster, G. (1986). *Financial statement analysis* (2nd ed.). Englewood Cliffs, NJ: Prentice-Hall.

Fraser, L. M., & Ormiston, A. (2001). *Understanding financial statements* (6th ed.). Upper Saddle River, NJ: Prentice-Hall.

Internet Finance Resources Web site at www.lib.lsu.edu/bus/finance.html

Porter, M. (1980). *Competitive strategy.* New York, NY: Free Press.

Revsine, L., Collins, D. W., & Johnson, W. B. (1999). *Financial reporting and analysis.* Upper Saddle River, NJ: Prentice-Hall.

Sammon, W. L., Kurland, M. A., & Spitalnic, R. (1984). *Business competitor intelligence: Methods for collecting, organizing and using information.* New York, NY: John Wiley & Sons.

Schoenebeck, K. (2001). *Interpreting and analyzing financial statements* (2nd ed.). Upper Sadle River, NJ: Prentice-Hall.

The Financial Data Finder, Ohio State University, Web site at www.cob.ohio-state.edu/dept/fin/overview.htm

The Syndicate Finance Web site at www.moneypages.com/syndicate/finance/

Van Horne, J., & Wachowicz, J. (1998). *Fundamentals of financial management* (10th ed.). Englewood Cliffs, NJ: Prentice-Hall.

Chapter 26

Strategic Funds Programming

SHORT DESCRIPTION

Strategic funds programming is a formal strategic planning process that provides the linkage between strategy formulation and implementation by defining company objectives, strategies, and priorities; defining the realm of potential strategies consistent with corporate objectives; deciding on which strategic programs to pursue; and implementing chosen programs by allocating resources and responsibility through formal capital budgeting and control mechanisms.

BACKGROUND

It is vitally important for firms to pursue new strategies while simultaneously maintaining existing strategies. As environmental conditions change or as demand changes, the effectiveness of old strategies will eventually erode. In order to ensure the future prosperity, or even survival, of the firm, new strategies must be proactively developed before the demise of established strategies. While a myriad of strategy theories offers the analyst advice on formulation, a relative paucity of implementation guidance exists as to how to allocate resources among competing strategies.

Implementation has long been the weak link in competitive and strategy theory. A common complaint offered by managers and decision makers is its high level of abstraction. Often, the best-laid corporate strategies turn to naught for lack of an effective implementation methodology. The high level of generalization offered in many strategy theories makes them impractical to implement. The sources of this dissatisfaction are many and varied:

• *Business Strategy as Essentially a Social Science.* Unlike the pure and applied sciences, the study of business strategy does not offer practitioners many universal laws of application. The introduction of noncontrollable factors such as human nature and turbulent environments makes the study of business strategy more akin to an art rather than a science.

419

- *Lack of Future Orientation.* The pervasive influence of established, historically oriented accounting systems upon which most managers are judged leads to a fixation with short-term results and the next quarter's financial results. Further, the pressures of attending to the daily challenges of managing their responsibility often leads managers to give short shrift to long-range or strategic planning.

- *No Prioritization Criteria.* For the minority of firms who have successfully rebuffed the natural tendency to fixate on short-term issues, the lack of a robust framework to gauge the relative importance of various components of the strategic plan often obscures the optimal course of action.

- *Lack of Organizational Structure.* Many firms are extremely rich in human resources but still fail in implementing strategic planning. The fault usually can be traced to poor organizational structure and systems. Once strategy has been formulated, the job is only half done. The firm is absolutely dependent on leveraging its most valuable asset, human talent, to turn the dreams into reality. Without providing managers with the appropriate tools to do this, strategy is often halted in its tracks.

There is a very logical explanation for why good, long-range planning often suffers from poor implementation. In order to manage an objective, managers require a decision-making framework to frame their perspective. Consider the parameter of managing operational decisions. Many firms have excelled at efficiently managing operational variables. This is not surprising, given the robust decision-making framework provided them in this regard: budgets, operations management, and control all tied explicitly into a performance measurement and compensation system. All of these mechanisms provide explicit links between possible actions and impacts on highly specified financial and operational goals. Hence, managers are given the raw material needed to make trade-offs among competing resource allocation opportunities.

In stark contrast, strategic planning often does not offer managers the robust decision-making framework that they need to implement long-range planning initiatives. Rather, strategic planning commonly becomes a "fuzzy" exercise that offers no basis for managers to make trade-offs between competing resource allocation opportunities.

Strategic funds programming is designed to fill this vacuum by providing the essential link between strategy formulation and implementation. By implementing strategic funds programming, managers are given the tools necessary to make effective long-range decisions. Armed with a systematic decision-making framework to manage around longer-term objectives, managers will be much more attuned to correctly identifying strategic trade-offs around the long-term resource allocation decisions so necessary for ongoing strategic success.

STRATEGIC RATIONALE AND IMPLICATIONS

A generic way to map out the planning cycle is shown in Figure 26-1. The first stage is strategy development, followed by strategic funds programming, and finally budgeting. The narrowing of the throughput in the diagram reflects

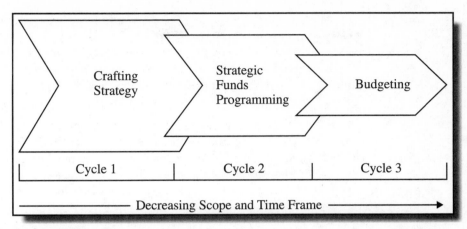

Figure 26-1
The Three Cycles of the Planning Process

the narrowing of scope within each successive cycle from the general to the specific. Often, firms formulate strategy very early in the planning cycle but specific implementation guidance is only given for the final stage. That is, each year the annual budgeting process draws up specific objectives, goals, resource allocations, and organizational tools only for the next year. Thus, the first stage, formal planning, and the third stage, budgeting, are given the majority of the focus. Somewhere in the process, strategic funds programming often gets lost or overlooked in the shuffle.

Three interrelated factors cause this all too common scenario. (1) There is often a perceived lack of urgency associated with strategic funds programming because, while the associated expenses are incurred in the current year, the benefits of strategic funds accrue to the firm in later years. (2) Many managers are predisposed to working within sharply defined plans associated with numerical budgets rather than vague, qualitative, and uncertain long-range decisions that is the purview of strategic funds programming. (3) Most performance evaluation and compensation systems provide a perverse, but entirely rational, incentive for "short-termism." Small wonder, then, that strategic funds programming loses the battle for "share of mind" to the budgeting cycle. This is a damaging omission because strategic funds programming serves several critical purposes:

- Allows for a variety of managers to come together to analyze strategic options available to the firm.
- Builds a realistic decision-making framework to guide strategic choice by explicitly incorporating the trade-offs involved in allocating resources to one strategy over another.
- Develops implementation methodology that "makes strategy work" through the use of measurable and, hence, controllable long-range decision criteria for resource allocation.
- Provides managers with the organizational tools required to turn corporate plans into action.

The purpose of strategic funds is to simultaneously provide resources for growing existing strategies, building cash stocks for new strategies, or actually funding new strategies. They are distinct from investments that fund current strategies, existing productive capacity, operational expenses, or current working capital. Rather, strategic funds look further afield in that there is an element of strategic change or growth associated with strategic funds. There are three different sources of strategic funds:

1. *Additional Working Capital.* This is investment in current assets to increase the scope of the firm's existing product or service attribute offering. For example, a large industrial equipment manufacturer may decide to offer a leasing service in order to capture market share. Similarly, a firm might decide to extend the receivables period in order to offer a more attractive payment structure.

2. *Capital Investments.* These are investments in fixed tangible assets such as plant and equipment to support a major expansion of existing strategies or forays into new competitive arenas. Capital investments often propel the firm into a new product or service market or result in an expansion of scale or scope in the existing strategy that is of a higher order of magnitude.

3. *Investments Innovation.* These are investments in developmental initiatives such as R&D, advertising, technological processes, management information systems, distribution channels, consulting fees, and so on. Often, these investments are intangible and are designed to build the infrastructure for a major expansion of existing strategy or an entirely new strategy.

Without clearly distinguishing between strategic funds and shorter-term budgetary expenditures, the analyst is at risk of sharing a myopic view of investment that often plagues the traditional accounting perspective. This limited view treats tangible costs as increases in assets to be depreciated in annual chunks over time through depreciation. Alternately, accountants are often required to write off intangible, unrecoverable costs in the year they are incurred. This methodology, while necessary for public reporting, is focused on annual periods and so often overlooks the implications current investments have on future profits. Conversely, the strategic funds approach explicitly recognizes the impact of investments on future periods. That is, strategic funds programming incorporates the concept of the net present value of cash inflows and outflows over an expanded time horizon.

The practical manifestation of the accounting approach to investment is the lumping of overhead as an annual expense with little or no regard for the important distinction between current and future impacts. The current impact relates to annual budgetary concerns and the satisfaction of annual operational goals. The future impacts, however, relate to the strategic positioning of the firm several years hence. In order to effectively implement strategic planning, these investments must be explicitly planned and managed well before they become recognized as expenses on the accountant's ledger.

Strategic funds programming is very forward looking in this regard. Its purpose is to ensure that the firm properly analyzes future investments and returns of long-term investment opportunities. In doing so, it prevents critical information from becoming lumped anonymously in the overhead accounts or as an innocuous budget line item. Rather, strategic funds programming provides a systematic and formal

Table 26-1

Example of Traditional Income Statement Versus the Strategic Funds
Programming Approach

TRADITIONAL APPROACH		STRATEGIC FUNDS PROGRAMMING APPROACH	
Sales	$12,000	Sales	$12,000
Cost of goods sold	7,000	Cost of goods sold	7,000
Gross margin	5,000	Gross margin	5,000
Selling, general and administration Expenses (including all overhead)	2,500	Selling, general and administration expenses (only including operational overhead)	2,000
Operating income	2,500	Operating income	3,000
		Strategic investment income	0
		Strategic funds investment	1,000
		Strategic funds income (or relevant performance measure if returns are expected in the medium to long term)	(1,000) • Completed market research study • Technology installation 25 percent complete

analytical approach to building the firm's business model. Highlighting long-term costs and benefits of various strategies provides a robust decision-making framework from which to make important resource allocation decisions and to exercise subsequent control after the decisions are made.

In essence, strategic funds programming provides the critical link between strategy development and budgeting, the vacuum that often exists between the first and third cycle of the strategic planning process. Table 26-1 compares a traditional income statement with the segregated approach related to strategic funds programming. When managers are evaluated on both operating return as well as the return from strategic funds, they are encouraged to balance short-term concerns with a longer-term focus. In this way, strategic funds programming provides an important framework that allows managers to manage using two important strategic imperatives: current operational performance *and* the performance of strategic investments designed to build a platform for competition in the future.

STRENGTHS AND ADVANTAGES

Integration.   One of the primary strengths of strategic funds programming is the functionality of this model in filling the so-called implementation gap in strategic management. By linking strategic formulation and development to the budgeting cycle, strategic funds programming provides a strong integration that helps to operationalize strategy. Additionally, strategic funds programming will highlight strategies that may rest on their own merits but are not cohesive with existing projects, competing projects, overall corporate strategy, or feasibility constraints.

Optimal Resource Allocation.   The continual comparison of current strategic investments with projected performance targets and against new opportunities ensures optimal resource allocation. As Figure 26-2 indicates, a firm that doesn't utilize strategic funds programming is liable to experience many counterproductive effects such as information fatigue, incomplete analysis, or even outright neglect of some valid strategic options. In contrast, the firm with a strategic funds programming approach is able to narrow the universe of strategic options to only those that are consistent with broader corporate strategy objectives and feasibility constraints. As such, each strategic investment that the firm makes will get the attention that it requires.

Inclusive.   Strategic funds programming is an excellent vehicle through which to foster organizational learning. Its inclusive approach offers many levels of rich management insights into firm strategy and their own particular role in contributing to possible synergies.

Figure 26-2
Strategic Budgeting with and without Strategic Funds Programming

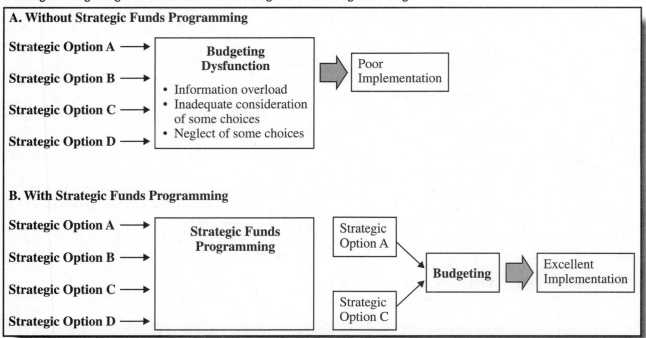

Source: Adapted from *Management Control Systems,* (9th ed.), by R. N. Anthony and V. Govindarajan, 1998, New York: Irwin/McGraw Hill.

Encourages Forward Thinking.   Strategic funds programming makes explicit the resources invested in growth and the subsequent performance of those investments. Managing a corporation in the absence of this approach is akin to a ship's captain navigating with a compass but no ship's rudder. Strategic funds programming offers management a strong link from strategic conception to reality. By separating strategic costs from operational costs, managers are encouraged to optimally manage current operations while also strategically managing the firm's future competitive position.

Strategic Challenger.   Each cycle of the strategic funds programming process will both challenge the underlying strategic assumptions of existing programs and give birth to new ideas. These are conditions necessary to encourage innovation.

Management Training Tool.   Strategic funds programming affords an excellent opportunity for the firm to train promising executives in the strategic planning process. A manager who has risen through the ranks will commonly be a more effective executive after having been steeped in the strategic funds programming process.

Performance Measurement.   The insistence on continuous performance measurement introduces strong discipline into the strategic management system to ensure that it is delivering what it purports to deliver. This introduces much-needed standards of accountability into what has traditionally been a gray area in many companies.

Ancillary Benefits.   The separation of developmental investment from operational costs often reveals opportunities to save costs or to increase operational productivity.

WEAKNESSES AND LIMITATIONS

Difficult to Implement.   The tight integration of strategic funds programming is also a source of potential weakness. The importance of simultaneously managing the accompanying organizational change necessarily will present managerial challenges. If strategic funds programming is not integrated properly with the management information system, performance measurement system, or compensation structure, it will remain at higher risk of failure.

Tendency Toward Bureaucratization.   The model's formal and systematic approach predisposes it to inherent dangers of becoming a sterile exercise in form and not substance. Important defenses against this potentially damaging bias are to include as many different managers as possible in the formal process. When selecting input, management should seek individuals who exhibit lateral "out of the box" thinking and complement them with linear analytic types to foster an optimal combination of creativity and realism. The management team should also solicit ideas from staff—often a source of great insight born from being closest to the customer.

Time-Consuming and Costly.   Strategic funds programming is time-consuming and expensive and so may not be as worthwhile for smaller firms to implement. Rather, these firms might integrate strategic planning informally with the budget process. The conditions where strategic funds programming will be worthwhile are the following (Anthony & Govindarajan, 1998): There is full commitment from top management; the firm is large and complex; and the firm is operating in a relatively unstable environment but forecasting can still be done with reasonable accuracy. If the environment is stable, contingency plans will suffice. If the environment is so unstable that it makes reasonable accurate predictions impossible, strategic funds programming is likely to be pointless.

PROCESS FOR APPLYING THE TECHNIQUE

The process of strategic funds programming will in practice vary from company to company depending on organizational culture. Strategic funds programming is more of a tactical planning tool rather than an explicit strategic planning method. As such, it is only part of a larger cohesive framework that encompasses performance measurement, management control, executive compensation, and operational budget methodology.

Before the strategic funds programming approach can begin, however, the analytical boundaries defining strategic business units (SBUs) as well as strategies for each of the firm's SBUs must be developed. This does not preclude the development of new or modified strategies during the strategic funding process. Rather, each business's strategy is usually crafted during the strategy development process that is outside of this chapter's scope. Nonetheless, firm performance is often enhanced if a permeable membrane is fostered between the three cycles of the strategic planning process.

Step 1: Determine the Existing Financial Capacity of the Firm

The amount of cash that the different SBUs generate must be netted against the cash requirements of existing SBUs to determine the net funds position of the firm. This will determine the base level of funds available for strategic programming.

A helpful methodology to use in this stage is the Du Pont formula that disaggregates the return on equity (ROE) formula:

$$\text{ROE} = \text{Leverage} \times \text{Asset turnover} \times \text{Profit margin}$$

$$\text{ROE} = \frac{\text{Total assets (year } t-1)}{\text{Equity (year } t-1)} \times \frac{\text{Sales (year } t)}{\text{Total assets (year } t-1)} \times \frac{\text{Net income (year } t)}{\text{Sales (year } t)}$$

where

$$\text{Year } t = \text{Current year}$$
$$\text{Year } t - 1 = \text{Last year}$$

Aside from its traditional use as an analytical tool to dissect financial performance, the Du Pont formula can also be used to estimate next year's financial results of each SBU.

Next year's sales = Asset turnover × Total assets (year *t*)
Next year's net income: Profit margin (year *t*) × Sales (year *t*)
Next year's incremental equity: Retention ratio × Net income (year *t*)
Next year's assets: Leverage × Equity (year *t*)
Next year's total debt: Total assets (year *t* + 1) − Total debt (year *t* + 1)

Of course, these estimates are rough first approximations, but they provide a good foundation for the analyst to start defining the base level of funds produced by existing SBUs. Implicit in the Du Pont approach is the maintenance of the status quo in terms of market demand, the relative competitive position of the SBU, and stable financial policy. Environmental shocks or significant changes in financial policy or capital structure would severely impact these estimates.

A more direct form of this same methodology would be to calculate directly the sustainable growth rate to determine the maximum rate of growth that the SBU can internally finance given the existing financial policy, operational productivity, capital intensity, and capital structure (see Chapter 27 for a more detailed treatment of sustainable growth rate analysis). If the estimated growth rate of the SBU is expected to exceed the sustainable growth rate, then the SBU will be cash insufficient and require additional funding. On the other hand, if the SBU is expected to grow at a rate below its sustainable limit, then the SBU will throw off cash that acts, in effect, as an internal source of strategic funds. These estimates will give a fairly reasonable approximation of the amount of each SBU's relative cash sufficiency. The analyst should note that these estimates are made under the qualifying condition of *ceterus paribus*. Significant changes in any of the assumed constants will change the cash sufficiency of the SBU.

Step 2: Separate Strategic Programs from Operational Maintenance

Often, the criteria used to determine the internal funding balance of current operation is called the *baseline* (Stonich & Zaragoza, 1980). At one extreme, a full activity-based costing (ABC) analysis of all of the activities in the firm's SBUs could be conducted to give a full classification of each activity as operational or developmental or a combination of both. The other important distinction in this stage is to separate strategic costs (e.g., developmental costs, working capital increases over and above the rate of inflation, capital investments) from operational costs. Often, the analyst will be surprised at the proportion of regular overhead charges that should be rightfully classified as strategic rather than operational. Another positive benefit is the identification of undefined areas of overhead that haven't been producing any beneficial results. However, this breadth of analysis is expensive and time-consuming. Strategic funds programming can be adequately conducted with a less robust ABC analysis, but accuracy will suffer.

Instead of a full-blown ABC analysis, the analyst may use several other criteria to define the baseline. Other possible definitional criteria include (Stonich & Zaragoza, 1980):

- Firms in commodity industries may decide to use the maintenance of a production throughput variable as the baseline.
- Firms producing consumer goods may decide to use the maintenance of market share as the baseline variable.
- Fast-growing firms may decide to use a broad definition of *baseline*, choosing to use strategic funds programming only for radical innovations.
- Capital intensive firms may decide to use a continuous production as the baseline.

Once activities have been defined as baseline, a separation of operational costs from strategic costs can be made. Operational costs are included in the budget stage, while strategic costs are included in the strategic funds programming stage. By netting out the forecasted cash sources and uses from all of the SBUs, the analyst will have a fairly robust indication of how cash sufficient the current operations of the firm are and their capacity to internally fund strategic programs. The use of strategic growth rate analysis will help the analyst identify potential levers to increase fund availability from current operations. Once all options to maximize internal fund generation have been exhausted, the estimated internal fund availability is then added to external fund availability to determine the maximum amount of strategic funding available.

Step 3: Analyze Competing Strategic Investment Opportunities

In step 2, the level of aggregation is further delineated by dividing the SBUs into various investment opportunities that represent funding proposals. If step 1 has been done correctly, each funding proposal will regard future-oriented proposals based on substantial increases in working capital, capital investments, developmental investment in innovation, or a combination of all three types of strategic funds. Additionally, each proposal will require the firm to incur significant expenses in the short term to secure benefits that will accrue to the firm in the medium to long term.

Each funding recommendation is formally introduced through a written proposal describing the relative merits of investing in it. At a minimum, each proposal should contain the following elements:

- Cost/benefit analysis
- Metrics to measure future success
- Future performance targets
- Sensitivity analysis under various scenarios and assumptions. A common one is the pessimistic, status quo/neutral, or optimistic framework
- Integration with overall firm strategy and existing projects

Step 4: Rank Competing Strategic Investment Opportunities

A set of criteria from which to judge the relative merits of each proposal is then composed. While there is no universal set of ranking criteria, it should be analytically rigorous and impartially applied. Some common criteria that should be included as a minimum are:

- The performance of past strategic funds investments
- The forecasted cost/benefits of new proposals compared to the current and predicted performance of existing projects and strategies
- The tightness of the strategic fit of the new proposals against the backdrop of the firm's strategy and past investments
- The risk profile of each proposal as well as the impact it would have on the firm's total risk profile
- A consideration of the benefits associated with financial leverage if the proposals require external debt financing
- Practical considerations of the funding pattern of the proposal over the short, medium, and long term and the impact on the firm's total cash flow balance.

Step 5: Selection of Strategic Funding Proposal

After each proposal has been screened through these filters, the optimal proposals are selected for investment. This step will often require significant iteration to change or refine the proposals. Additionally, it is helpful to seek the advice of many different types of managers in this process. This is one of the great strengths of strategic funds programming. The more internal consulting that is done, the more robust the proposals will become. The process soon becomes self-reinforcing as managers gain an intimate knowledge of the firm's strategy and the synergy between functional areas and businesses of the firm. As a result, the firm becomes more adept at implementing strategy as the strategic funds programming approach becomes entrenched in the corporate culture.

Step 6: Initiate Formal Release of Strategic Funds

Once the proposals have been selected for funding, the amount, timing, and procedures for implementing strategic funds programming are required. This is the threshold of the third cycle, budgeting. The first year of strategic funding must now be integrated into the annual budget and the management information system.

Step 7: Performance Evaluation and Control

A myriad of established techniques, such as variance analysis, financial analysis, and balanced scorecard measures, can be used to monitor the progress of each chosen strategic funding proposal. The knowledge gained in this step can be used to fine-tune the selection criteria for future rounds of strategic funds programming.

At this stage, the organizational culture will dictate the type and intensity of performance evaluation and control. Different cultures and industries will have a large impact on how step 7 is implemented. Some examples of the extreme differences are suggested:

- Formal versus informal
- Centralized versus decentralized
- Hierarchical versus lateral
- Production/process oriented versus market oriented versus financially oriented

An important consideration of strategic funds programming is to recognize that the organization may require significant structural or systemic changes to be made in adopting a future-oriented perspective. For example, the optimal result could be subverted by inappropriate compensation systems. As such, executive, managerial, and, quite possibly, staff compensation should be altered to encourage and reward forward-looking behavior. Similarly, from a process viewpoint, strategic funds programming must be incorporated into the management information system.

An illustrated summary of the strategic funds programming process is depicted in Figure 26-3. Also see the box, "Case Excerpt: Strategic Funds Programming at Merck & Co." for a real-world sense of the application of this method.

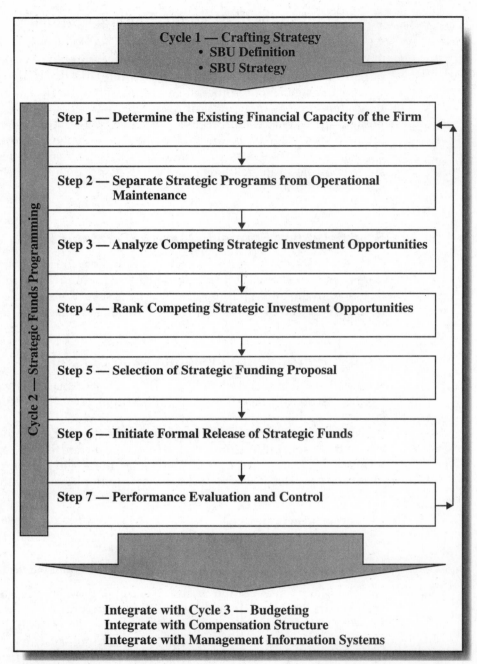

Figure 26-3
The Strategic Funds Programming Cycle

The pharmaceutical industry is rife with risk. Huge unrecoverable investments in R&D must be made in the face of great uncertainty. Adding to this risk are the constantly increasing costs of pure and applied research. Consider the manifestations of these risks:

- One drug discovery requires the intense scrutiny of thousands of chemical compounds.

- There is a one in eight chance that promising drugs will pass the seven-year development phase.

- Only one in three commercial drugs recover their full costs of development.

- Each new drug costs an average of $230 million.

Given these risks, Merck closely monitors R&D to ensure that it exceeds the costs of capital. Their highly complex quantitative planning model tightly integrates strategic funds programming with discounted cash flow analysis and probabilistic risk analysis. Attesting to the complexity of their planning model, consider the following features of the model:

Time Horizon	20 years
Monetary Factors	Unit volume forecasts
	Pricing projections
	Manufacturing costs
	Manufacturing capital
	Exchange rate projections
	Inflation rate projections
	Patent life
	Competitive products
	Size of market
	Optimistic/most likely/pessimistic scenarios
	Annual nominal dollar sales projections
	Cash flows
	Return on investment
	Net present value
Nonmonetary Factors	Therapeutic and diagnostic profiles
	Dosage
	Launch date
	Probability of technical success
Statistical Analysis	Frequency distribution inputs rather than single point data
	Financial analysis of expected returns and project risk

Individual product managers present an optimistic/most likely/pessimistic scenario analysis of sales levels to the senior marketing manager for approval. Before approval, the potential drug is subjected to a battery of financial statistical analyses that includes hundreds of iterations for each product. These tests include plotting the probability distribution of several critical variables such as net present value, cash flow, and return on investment and sales projections in order to develop a risk profile and determine expected returns. An example of one of these plots is shown here.

(Continued on following page)

Case Excerpt: Strategic Funds Programming at Merck & Co. (Continued)

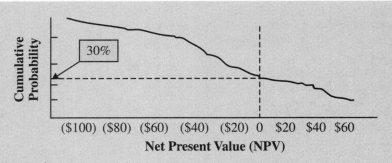

In the figure, NPV for a certain drug shows a 30 percent chance of exceeding the cost of capital. This type of sensitivity analysis allows Merck to quantify risk across a number of NPV targets.

Often, approved drugs are subjected to performance measures to test the validity and accuracy of the model as well as to test the assumptions driving the input variables.

Merck uses this model in three important ways:

1. Evaluating Business Opportunities
   a. Evaluating proposed product licensing candidates
   b. Capital expenditures
   c. Existing businesses
   d. Acquisition candidates

2. Managing R&D
   a. Go–no go investment decisions for product development
   b. Optimizing portfolio of product development
   c. Performance measurement of the R&D function

3. Long-Range Planning
   a. Extending five-year operating plan to 10 to 15–year time horizons
   b. Issue analysis
   c. Impact of potential alliances on long-term growth prospects

SOURCE: Adapted from *Management Control Systems,* (9th ed.) by R. N. Anthony and V. Govindarajan, New York: Irwin/McGraw Hill.

FAROUT SUMMARY

	1	2	3	4	5
F	■	■	■	■	■
A	■	■	■		
R	■	■			
O	■	■			
U	■	■	■	■	
T	■	■			

Future orientation   High. Often, strategic funds programs cover a time period of five years or more.

Accuracy   Medium. Strategic funds programming depends on quantitative skills and the subjective inputs of area managers.

Resource efficiency Medium. Cost depends on the comprehensiveness and extent of programming and how widely baselines are defined.

Objectivity Medium. Highly dependent on forecasting and scenario analysis.

Usefulness Medium to high. Useful for large, complex firms or firms operating in stable or extremely unstable environments operating in uncertain environments. Limited usefulness for smaller firms.

Timeliness Low to medium. Because of the number of people involved, strategic funds programming can become a protracted, time-consuming process.

RELATED TOOLS AND TECHNIQUES

- BCG growth share matrix
- comparative cost analysis
- functional capability and resource analysis
- GE business screen
- scenario analysis
- sustainable growth rate analysis
- value chain analysis

REFERENCES

Anthony, R. N., & Govindarajan, V. (1998). *Management control systems* (9th ed.). New York, NY: Irwin/McGraw Hill.

Salter, M. S. (1973). "Tailor incentive compensation to strategy." *Harvard Business Review, 51*(2), 94–102.

Stonich, P. J. (1980). "How to use strategic funds programming." *The Journal of Business Strategy, 1*(2), 35–40.

———. (1981). "Using rewards in implementing strategy." *Strategic Management Journal, 2*(4), 345–352.

———. (1984). "The performance measurement and reward system." *Organizational Dynamics, 12*(2), 45–57.

Stonich, P. J., & Zaragoza, C. E. (1980). "Strategic funds programming: The missing link in corporate planning." *Managerial Planning, 29*(2), 3–11.

Vancil, R. F. (1972). "Better management of corporate development." *Harvard Business Review, 50*(5), 53–62.

Vancil, R. F., & Lorange, P. (1975). "Strategic planning in diversified companies." *Harvard Business Review, 53*(1), 81–90.

Chapter 27

Sustainable Growth Rate Analysis

SHORT DESCRIPTION

Sustainable growth rate analysis is a dynamic analytical framework that combines financial analysis with strategic management to explain critical relationships between strategic planning and financial/operational variables; test whether corporate growth objectives are compatible with financial policy; determine the firm's existing capacity to finance growth; determine how existing financial policies will impact future growth; and analyze the strengths and weaknesses of competitive strategies.

BACKGROUND

Classical economic theory asserted that growth is the driving force behind our ever-increasing standard of living and hence exalted it as a societal goal. An implicit but strongly connected conviction expects the corporation to deliver this growth. In fact, growth became a central tenet in the unwritten social charter that allowed corporate existence in many countries. The majority consensus was that corporate growth and its presumed consequent, higher profits, would translate into larger social benefits that would accrue through full employment, high incomes, and, ultimately, a higher quality of life for everyone. Growth was seen as the fuel to keep this cycle of perpetual human advancement forging ahead.

Many early strategy theories were developed to support this goal of corporate growth. The supporting philosophy underlying these strategies maintained that, like biological systems, corporations require growth for survival. Growth secures excess resources (often termed *slack*) needed to adapt to evolving environmental conditions. Often in times of change, this slack is tapped to successfully support the evolutionary process. Once environmental change stabilizes, growth serves to sustain the firm in its newly occupied niche while simultaneously preparing for the next round of evolution.

A key risk of rapid growth is the ability to efficiently convert sales to cash. A company that has dealt effectively with this risk and converted it to a competitive edge is

Dell Computers. Dell is well-known for using the cash conversion cycle (CCC) as a key performance measure. By focusing on metrics such as days sales outstanding, days sales in inventory, and days of payables outstanding, Dell has been accelerating inventory turns, collection activities and slowing down supplier payments. By keeping its CCC lower than its competitors, Dell gains a powerful market advantage.

Early strategy theory revolved around this concept of growth as a necessary condition for survival and prosperity of the firm. Most notably, the portfolio models embraced this concept and used the experience curve and product life cycle as adaptive tools to support current growth to ensure future survival. In many ways, these tools extended the Darwinian analogy to business models. The experience curve can be considered as the adaptive methodology during periods of environmental stability in the occupied niche(s). The product life cycle can be viewed as the niche that the firm currently occupies. During stability, competition is eliminated or marginalized, thus securing the resources needed to fatten the corporate beast to support the inevitable transition to another niche. When the current niche's environment grows increasingly hostile to the corporate life form in its existing manifestation (i.e., the decline stage of the PLC), these surplus resources can then be applied to the evolutionary process of adaptive selection of another niche (i.e., finding another experience curve in the current industry or moving to another industry)—hence, an underlying rationale for portfolio theory.

Huge diversified firms, encouraged and sustained by the adaptive methodology of portfolio models, required increasing amounts of surplus resources to make the evolutionary jump to other niches (i.e., product markets or different bases of competition). Portfolio strategies designed to grow, maintain, or harvest market share in high growth markets carried with them different cash flow and profitability impacts, requiring an explicit recognition of the need for cash balance across corporate strategy. Similarly, the high inflation and resulting high interest rates of the 1970s exacerbated this cash deficiency by rendering the infusion of external debt or equity infeasible. So much so, that many of the portfolio models (especially the BCG growth/share matrix) incorporated an explicit assumption of internal resource allocation. It became clear that another adaptive mechanism was required to ensure that diversified conglomerates didn't suffer the fate of the dinosaur. This is where sustainable growth rate analysis entered the picture.

The earliest explicit development of the concept was first coined "supportable growth" by Manown Kisor Jr. (1964). He combined the established Du Pont formula with contemporary finance theory into a financial model designed to predict the maximum amount of growth that a firm could experience before having to secure external debt or equity financing. Thus, a firm's financial policies could be seen as having a direct impact on the firm's ability to grow. Given the assumption of internal financing inherent in the portfolio approaches, this model was quickly adopted into the portfolio methodology. Often, multiproduct and multimarket firms faced investment opportunities exceeding their resource capability. Sustainable growth analysis provided a robust technique for determining the threshold at which to control growth within the internal financing constraint.

Prior to this development, it was assumed that increasing sales would be accompanied by increasing cash flow and profitability. Portfolio models optimistically assumed that market share would provide sufficient cash requirements and that market growth would correctly predict cash requirements. The counterintuitive observation that many high-growth firms were failing refuted this central premise of portfolio theory. Kisor's model essentially gave theoretical support to these anecdotal realities and gave firms an operational financial model to manage portfolio strategy in the absence of low capital intensity or strong mobility barriers.

Even though portfolio theory has been supplanted by more robust forms of strategy theory, sustainable growth rate analysis continues to be a valuable analytical technique. The development of efficient capital markets has lifted the internal financing constraint. Firms now regularly use sustainable growth rate analysis to test the feasibility of their corporate strategies by determining if further growth will be constrained by the firm's current financial policies. It can then be used to examine how growth will affect financial leverage and what variables the firm can manipulate in order to restore balance between financial policy and the growth objectives of corporate strategy. Additionally, sustainable growth rate analysis has seen increasing use as a competitive intelligence tool for assessing the strengths and weaknesses of rival strategies.

STRATEGIC RATIONALE AND IMPLICATIONS

Investing in growth-oriented corporate strategies poses liquidity risk as a result of long-term financial policies. Capital investments to support the operating cycle must necessarily be made before the ultimate payback is received. Rapid growth will require investment in new capital resources that often overwhelm the financing capacity of existing operating cycles generated from previous capital investments.

The need for sustainable growth analysis also finds its roots in short-term financial policies associated with working capital. The cash conversion cycle (CCC) is the period of time between the purchase of material inputs and the collection of accounts receivable from the ultimate sale. The CCC explains the amount of time between the initial cash expenditure the firm incurs to secure resources and the associated recovery of that cash. The components of the CCC are

$$CCC = \text{Operating cycle} - \text{Payment cycle}$$

whereby

Operating cycle = Inventory conversion period + Receivables conversion period
Payment cycle = Accounts payable period

From these equations, it can be seen that growth often stresses the cash liquidity of the firm. The cash inflow of investing in growth-oriented corporate strategies often precedes the ultimate realization of the associated cash inflows. This can leave the firm in an unsustainable cash flow position that can only be remedied either by scaling back growth or by securing external financing, assuming that all efficiency measures to tighten up the CCC have been pursued.

A poignant case in point of the importance of the sustainability concept was the 1975 bankruptcy of the American specialty retailer W.T. Grant Company. From

1966 to 1974, Grant enjoyed positive income and working capital and paid regular dividends. By 1973, Grant shares were trading at a P/E ratio of 20. Additionally, Grant's financial health was seemingly strong during this period, as evidenced by a favorable return on equity, turnover, current, and debt to equity ratios. Grant experienced extremely rapid growth, and by 1973 was the largest specialty store chain in the United States. This growth proved unsustainable, however, since Grant's cash flow from operations had taken a nosedive since 1966, hitting its trough at $100 million in the year before its bankruptcy (Largay & Stickney, 1980).

The W.T. Grant bankruptcy highlights the importance of sustainable growth rate analysis. The growth rate of a firm is sustainable when cash inflow equals or exceeds cash outflow. That is, can the realized returns generated from past and current investments provide the required investment funds to support future corporate strategy? If not, financial policy will have to be changed in order to avert serious and potentially fatal ramifications. Sustainable growth rate analysis is an effective tool to find feasible methods to accomplish this objective. An in-depth understanding of the factors impacting cash inflow and cash outflow are prerequisites to understanding sustainable growth rate analysis. Other examples of the application of SGRA on strategic decision can be found in the box, "Contrarian Strategy and Sustainable Growth Rate Analysis (see page 448)."

Cash Inflow

Cash inflow is essentially created from three sources:

1. Internal generation, that is internal operational cash flow from current operations and/or disposal of assets or divestment
2. Debt
3. Equity

Cash Outflow

Cash outflow is created by six uses of funds:

1. Investments in working capital (cash, payables, inventory, receivables, etc.) to finance the CCC related to increasing sales from existing or new strategies
2. Reinvestment to maintain exiting capital assets such as plant and equipment
3. New capital investment to support increasing sales from existing or new strategies
4. Taxes
5. Debt servicing costs
6. Dividend payouts

For a firm to achieve sustainable growth, cash inflow must at least equal cash outflow. Numerical formulas that capture each of the six factors listed above provide a quantitative equality function between the sources and uses of funds. Figures 27-1a and 27-1b depict this equality function and process that provides the sustainable growth rate formula.

By keeping external cash inflows constant (i.e., assuming no additional debt or equity), the analyst can determine the maximum increase in sales that a firm can

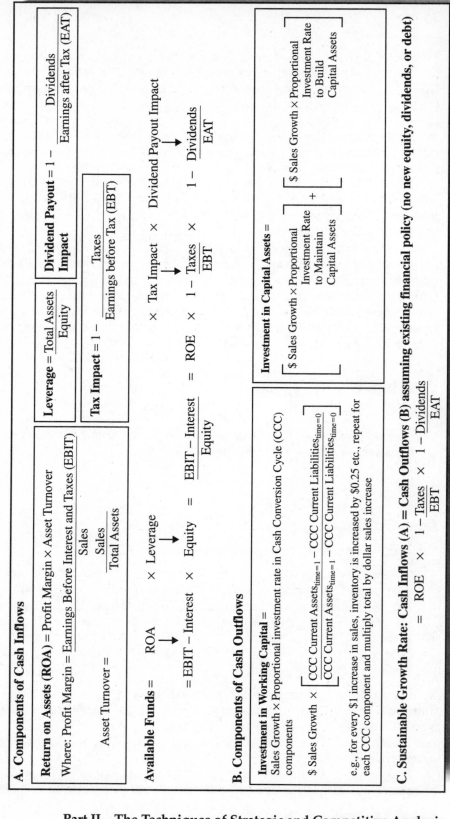

Figure 27-1a
Derivation of the Sustainable Growth Rate Formula

A. Components of Cash Inflows

Return on Assets (ROA) = Profit Margin × Asset Turnover

Where: Profit Margin = $\dfrac{\text{Earnings Before Interest and Taxes (EBIT)}}{\text{Sales}}$

Asset Turnover = $\dfrac{\text{Sales}}{\text{Total Assets}}$

Leverage = $\dfrac{\text{Total Assets}}{\text{Equity}}$

Tax Impact = $1 - \dfrac{\text{Taxes}}{\text{Earnings before Tax (EBT)}}$

Dividend Payout Impact = $1 - \dfrac{\text{Dividends}}{\text{Earnings after Tax (EAT)}}$

Available Funds = ROA × Leverage × Tax Impact × Dividend Payout Impact

= $\dfrac{\text{EBIT} - \text{Interest}}{\text{Equity}}$ = ROE × $\left(1 - \dfrac{\text{Taxes}}{\text{EBT}}\right)$ × $\left(1 - \dfrac{\text{Dividends}}{\text{EAT}}\right)$

= EBIT – Interest × Equity

B. Components of Cash Outflows

Investment in Working Capital =
Sales Growth × Proportional investment rate in Cash Conversion Cycle (CCC) components

\$ Sales Growth × $\left[\dfrac{\text{CCC Current Assets}_{time=1} - \text{CCC Current Liabilities}_{time=0}}{\text{CCC Current Assets}_{time=1} - \text{CCC Current Liabilities}_{time=0}}\right]$

e.g., for every \$1 increase in sales, inventory is increased by \$0.25 etc., repeat for each CCC component and multiply total by dollar sales increase

Investment in Capital Assets =

\$ Sales Growth × $\left[\begin{array}{c}\text{Proportional}\\\text{Investment Rate}\\\text{to Maintain}\\\text{Capital Assets}\end{array}\right]$ + $\left[\begin{array}{c}\text{\$ Sales Growth × Proportional}\\\text{Investment Rate}\\\text{to Build}\\\text{Capital Assets}\end{array}\right]$

C. Sustainable Growth Rate: Cash Inflows (A) = Cash Outflows (B) assuming existing financial policy (no new equity, dividends, or debt)

= ROE × $\left(1 - \dfrac{\text{Taxes}}{\text{EBT}}\right)$ × $\left(1 - \dfrac{\text{Dividends}}{\text{EAT}}\right)$

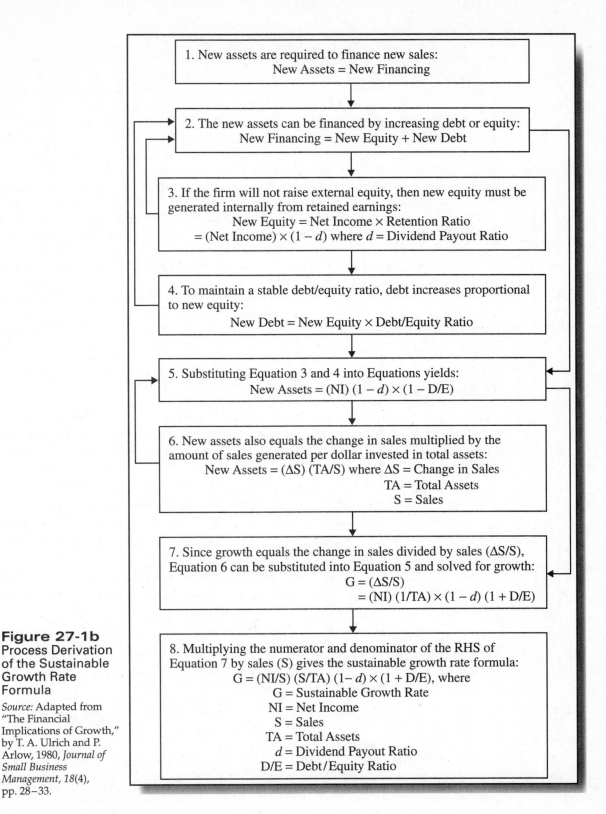

Figure 27-1b
Process Derivation of the Sustainable Growth Rate Formula

Source: Adapted from "The Financial Implications of Growth," by T. A. Ulrich and P. Arlow, 1980, *Journal of Small Business Management, 18*(4), pp. 28–33.

The content of the flowchart:

1. New assets are required to finance new sales:
New Assets = New Financing

2. The new assets can be financed by increasing debt or equity:
New Financing = New Equity + New Debt

3. If the firm will not raise external equity, then new equity must be generated internally from retained earnings:
New Equity = Net Income × Retention Ratio
= (Net Income) × $(1 - d)$ where d = Dividend Payout Ratio

4. To maintain a stable debt/equity ratio, debt increases proportional to new equity:
New Debt = New Equity × Debt/Equity Ratio

5. Substituting Equation 3 and 4 into Equations yields:
New Assets = (NI) $(1 - d)$ × $(1 - D/E)$

6. New assets also equals the change in sales multiplied by the amount of sales generated per dollar invested in total assets:
New Assets = (ΔS) (TA/S) where ΔS = Change in Sales
TA = Total Assets
S = Sales

7. Since growth equals the change in sales divided by sales $(\Delta S/S)$, Equation 6 can be substituted into Equation 5 and solved for growth:
G = $(\Delta S/S)$
= (NI) (1/TA) × $(1 - d)$ $(1 + D/E)$

8. Multiplying the numerator and denominator of the RHS of Equation 7 by sales (S) gives the sustainable growth rate formula:
G = (NI/S) (S/TA) $(1 - d)$ × $(1 + D/E)$, where
G = Sustainable Growth Rate
NI = Net Income
S = Sales
TA = Total Assets
d = Dividend Payout Ratio
D/E = Debt/Equity Ratio

sustain. At this rate of growth, internal funds generated by operations plus debt are just enough to finance the firm's working capital requirements, capital asset maintenance, and capital asset expansion necessary to support this rate of sales. Cash flow is in equilibrium. Hence, the sustainable growth rate has been reached.

Any growth above this rate will necessarily introduce disequilibrium into the balance of fund sources and uses. Since some of the firm's business strategies will throw off cash while others will absorb cash, one of the goals of corporate-level strategy is to maintain balance between sources and uses of funds. Most firms are regularly presented with the very real prospect of achieving a firm-wide growth rate above the sustainable growth rate. That is, the number of projects promising returns above the firm's cost of capital exceeds the firm's present financial capacity. This leaves the analyst with two options to manage this scenario: (1) reduce growth by not investing in some projects even though they may offer a positive net present value, or (2) manipulate one or a combination of the components of cash inflows or cash outflows introduced in Figure 27-1a and 27-1b.

Once the analyst has determined that sales growth would be profitable or strategically valuable, various manipulations of the financial policy variables under the second option can be explored in order to increase the sustainable growth rate.

Cash Inflow Levers

1. *Earnings Before Interest and Taxes (EBIT).* Increase EBIT through more productive operations (cost cutting, business process reengineering, etc.) or more effective operations by analyzing the cost–volume–price–profit relationship that drives EBIT.

2. *Tighten Up the CCC Components.* Decreasing the CCC will free up cash resources. This can be accomplished by decreasing the inventory conversion period; increasing the payable period (bearing in mind the potentially negative impacts on credit relations); and decreasing the receivables period (bearing in mind the potentially negative effects on customer loyalty).

3. *Servicing Costs on Existing Debt.* Reduce interest expense as a proportion of total sales through more favorable financing terms or by transferring debt interest for lease payments.

4. *Tax Planning.* Implement financial policies that reduce actual taxes paid below the mandated statutory rate.

5. *Dividend Policy.* This is a lower dividend payout or frequency, bearing in mind potentially negative market-signaling effects.

6. *Leverage.* Increasing debt has several positive impacts, bearing in mind the increased risk:
   a. Increased cash flow to support growth
   b. Higher financial leverage to allow the firm to earn higher ROE with the existing pricing policy

c. Higher financial leverage relative to rivals to allow the firm to undercut competitive prices, increase quality, or the richness of product or service attributes, while still earning the same ROE

d. Higher market shares earned through aggressive pricing to ultimately result in higher total assets (i.e., reinvested profits) providing further room to expand debt to fund growth

7. *Issue New Equity.* This option generally has a lower attraction on the analytical action list. Modern corporate finance theory, most notably the work of Modigliani and Miller (1958), holds that shareholder wealth effects of lower dividends are less damaging than those imposed by equity dilution through additional equity issues.

Cash Outflow Levers

1. *Reduce Investment in Working Capital.* Decreasing the investment and increasing the cash velocity in working capital can involve doing such things as reducing inventory across the value chain, leveraging the company's market power to delay payables, and reducing receivables by understanding the "cost" to customers and to recognize that every customer needs to show a positive return on investment (ROI) to the firm.

2. *Reduce Investment in Capital Maintenance.* To free up cash for new strategies, investments designed to preserve the firm's existing capacity could be curtailed. The analyst must remain aware of the potential danger of inadvertently postponing expenses. For example, reducing maintenance may just defer an even higher realized cost through higher downtime, missed orders, lower quality, and customer defection. Activity-based costing (ABC) will be helpful in finding the optimal balance.

3. *Reduce Investment in Expanding Capital Assets.* The capital intensity of new strategies or expansions of existing strategies may be reduced to decrease outflow. Again, an associated caveat is the potential damaging impact this action will have on the efficacy of the associated strategies. Downgraded capital intensity may leave the firm vulnerable to rivals who are actively pursuing technological innovation in the hopes of being able to reduce prices and/or increase differentiation in the future. Thus, this lever may reduce the firm's strategic position in the industry.

Many of the variables are mutually dependent. Since the sustainable growth formula incorporates all of these variables, it is an ideal tool to quantify these trade-offs. A sensitivity analysis of these levers can shed important insights into the options at the firm's disposal. Govindarajan and Shank (1986) suggest that a particularly valuable application of this type of sensitivity analysis of sustainable growth rate is to hold all of the levers in the formula constant except for one key policy lever. By solving for the one key variable, the analyst can determine the impact of sales growth on either the sources or uses of funds. Table 27-1 depicts the output of such a sensitivity analysis.

As Table 27-1 shows, the sustainable growth rate formula offers rich insights into the architecture of the firm's business model. It is the feasibility filter that all strategies must be passed through in order to assess the impact of the future sales

Table 27-1

Simple Sensitivity Analysis Example

Specified Lever	Impact on Sources and Uses of Funds of a 15 percent Change in the Unspecified Lever (holding other levers constant)	
Cash Outflow Lever	Cash Sources (%)	Cash Uses (%)
Tighten up CCC		7.2
Capital maintenance		3.6
Capital expansion		2.1
Cash Inflow Lever		
EBIT	3.2	
Debt interest	7.2	
Tax planning	1.2	
Dividend payout ratio	0.85	
New debt	2.1	
New equity	1.5	
Strategic Implications	The greatest impact for freeing up cash sources would be to focus on renegotiating debt financing arrangements, or possibly transferring high debt expenses with lower lease payments. Conversely, decreasing the dividend payout by a full 15 percent will only raise available funds by 0.85 percent—a most unfavorable trade-off given the potentially negative market reaction from such a dividend cut. The most effective area of focus to reduce cash uses would be on short-term financial management by tightening up the components of the cash conversion cycle.	

growth on the firm's financial liquidity. As with all sensitivity analyses, it is important for the analyst to remember that these mutual dependencies may hold only over a relevant range. Nonetheless, if the firm's growth projections show a high possibility of surpassing the sustainable growth rate, sensitivity analysis can pinpoint where the analytical focus should rest. Armed with this information, the analyst can delve deeper into the most effective levers of financial policy to support future strategy. In the absence of broader strategic trade-offs, these isolated variables are often chosen as the ones that are ultimately acted on by the firm to support growth.

Another valuable aspect of sustainable growth rate analysis is its application to competitive intelligence. Estimating the sustainable growth rate of rivals will reveal both threats and opportunities. If competitors are at or near their sustainable growth rates, they may not have the financial capacity to launch an effective threat to the firm's established competitive advantage. Similarly, a rival's limited financial capacity may offer strategic windows for the analyst's firm to make strategic inroads.

Part II   The Techniques of Strategic and Competitive Analysis

Conversely, if rivals are deemed to have significant room to grow, the firm's radar screen can be more finely tuned to that potential source of competition. Further, the array of options available to rival firms may be analyzed by looking at potential levers available for them to fund growth. This often points toward future competitor strategies. One of the strongest benefits of sustainable growth rate analysis is that it is a relatively easy and quick way to bolster competitive intelligence. Much of the required raw material is freely available from publicly accessible financial statements.

STRENGTHS AND ADVANTAGES

Reality Check. Sustainable growth analysis provides a comprehensive link between broad strategy and financial policy. It serves as an effective reality check to determine if strategic growth objectives are financially feasible under existing financial policy. In this way, this model partially fills the implementation vacuum that other strategic analysis models often leave wide open.

Future Oriented. Most descriptive strategic models stop at identifying the strategic problem. In addition to determining if future strategy is feasible, sustainable growth rate analysis, while still a descriptive model, goes a valuable step further. By allowing the analyst to determine the areas that offer the most impact, this model points toward the most effective way forward. Even though it doesn't offer any advice on how to manipulate the levers, it does aid greatly in helping the analyst decide which ones to pull.

Efficient. Sustainable growth rate analysis is extremely resource efficient; the methodology is not complex and the information requirements are freely available in the firm's accounting data. Further, a wide variety of different accounting reporting methods are amenable to this type of analysis. The analytical inputs are of a high enough level of abstraction that access to competitors' internal financial information is not necessary. This model is also very timely, as it can be conducted very quickly.

Versatile. The sustainable growth rate model is extremely versatile as indicated with its multifunctional application. It can analyze current strategy, test the feasibility of future strategy, pinpoint action levers to financial barrier to growth, and is a useful competitive intelligence tool.

WEAKNESSES AND LIMITATIONS

Strategic Myopia. Heavy reliance on sustainable growth rate analysis may lure the analyst into assuming that financial considerations present the highest barrier to growth. Care must be taken to include issues concerning technology, human capabilities, risk aversion, and management preferences as potentially equal or greater barriers to growth. In this regard, funds availability is only one necessary but insufficient prerequisite for successful strategy.

Profitless Growth. An extreme reliance on sustainable growth rate analysis can blind the analyst to the prospect of profitless growth. Even though the model has the rare combination of intuitive appeal and ease of application, it is no substitute for robust strategic analysis. Even if funds are available to invest in new strategies, liquidity-driven growth must not supplant value creation as the ultimate strategic criterion. The analyst must remain alert to the temptation to build empires on growth and prestige rather than on profitability. The possibility always exists that returning wealth to shareholders is the optimal strategy.

Limited Scope. Sustainable growth rate analysis only isolates financial variables with the highest action payoff. The creativity of the analyst is a critical ingredient to move the analysis forward from where sustainable growth analysis stops. Sustainable growth analysis is not strategy—it is only a tactical financial analysis tool, albeit a very valuable one, from which to test the feasibility of strategy.

Unintended Consequences. When examining the various financial levers with sensitivity analysis, it is important for the analyst to be sensitive as well. The quantitative and rather formulaic approach of this model may lull the analyst into believing that there are no trade-offs between financial variables that have crossover effects on the firm's broader strategy. Rather, negative second-order effects of sustainable growth analysis may unwittingly wring first-order damage to the firm's strategy. Customers or suppliers may be alienated by a seemingly innocuous attempt to tighten up the cash conversion cycle. Quality and safety may be compromised by reductions in capital maintenance. Long-term technological supremacy may be eroded by short-term concerns about saving funds through reductions in capital intensity. The point of these examples of unintended consequences is that acting on the various levers offered by sustainable growth rate analysis often carries wider strategic ramifications.

Potentially Dangerous Assumptions. The sustainable growth rate model assumes a constant market growth rate during the forecast period. This may not necessarily be a correct assumption as the competitive structure may drastically change during the planning period, causing an uneven or different rate of market growth during the planning period. For example, intensified marketing and the entry or exit of dominant firms in the industry may radically affect the rate of market growth by stimulating, stunting, or decreasing primary demand. (Varadarajan, 1983). The analyst must remain wary of these impacts and the conceivable need to revisit sustainable growth analysis earlier than expected.

PROCESS FOR APPLYING THE TECHNIQUE

Step 1: Gather Information from the Firm's Accounts

These materials can be collected from the individuals and systems responsible, generally found within the accounting and control functions, for keeping track of the firm's critical financial measures and performance status.

Step 2: Calculate the Firm's Existing Sustainable Growth Rate

Calculating a separate sustainable growth rate for each SBU will give the analyst the ability to desegregate and fine-tune the analysis by netting the growth rates of each SBU in managing total growth across the firm. Depending on the information secured by the analyst, alternate variations of the formula may be used to determine the firm's existing sustainable growth rate:

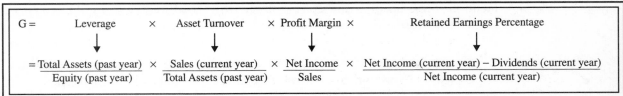

$$G = \text{Leverage} \times \text{Asset Turnover} \times \text{Profit Margin} \times \text{Retained Earnings Percentage}$$

$$= \frac{\text{Total Assets (past year)}}{\text{Equity (past year)}} \times \frac{\text{Sales (current year)}}{\text{Total Assets (past year)}} \times \frac{\text{Net Income}}{\text{Sales}} \times \frac{\text{Net Income (current year)} - \text{Dividends (current year)}}{\text{Net Income (current year)}}$$

$$G = \text{Before tax ROE} \times \left(1 - \frac{\text{Taxes}}{\text{EBT}}\right) \times \left(1 - \frac{\text{Dividends}}{\text{EAT}}\right)$$

where
G = Sustainable growth rate
ROE = Return on equity
EBT = Earnings before tax
EAT = Earnings after tax

$G = \text{ROE} \times \text{Retention Ratio}$
where
ROE = Net Income/Equity
$\text{Retention ratio} = \dfrac{\text{Net Income} - \text{Dividends}}{\text{Net Income}}$

---

1. First, estimate
   - The marginal investment in working capital for every marginal \$1 in sales
   - The marginal investment in maintaining existing capital assets for every marginal \$1 in sales
   - The marginal investment in new capital assets for every marginal \$1 in sales
   - Profit margin
   - Interest rate on debt
   - Depreciation % of sales
   - Tax rate
   - Dividend payout rate
   - The marginal increase in debt for every marginal dollar in retained earnings

2. Next, determine funds generated from operations =
   (Profit margin rate − interest %) × (1 − tax rate) × (1 − dividend payout rate) + depreciation % of sales

3. Determine Total Available Funding and Funding Requirements
   - Total Available Funding formula =
     Funds generated by operations × (1 + sales growth %) × (1 + % increase in debt for every marginal \$ in retained earnings)
   - Funding Requirements formula =
     (Sales growth % × marginal working capital investment rate) + (Sales growth % × new capital asset investment rate) + ([1 + Sales growth %] × investment rate in maintaining existing capital assets)

4. Equate Total Available Funding formula to Funding Requirements formula and solve for the sales growth percentage that equalizes the two formulas to each other. This number is the sustainable growth rate.

While the analyst will be able to secure as much internal data as needed for any of the formulas in the figure, the alternate versions of the same formula are helpful when using sustainable growth rate analysis to conduct competitive intelligence.

Step 3: Integrate with Strategic Funds Programming

The strategic funds programming process (see Chapter 26 for a detailed treatment of strategic funds programming) will project the amount of new investment proposed over the forecast period. If this growth rate is above the sustainable growth rate, one component of the formula or a combination of them must be altered to restore balance. If this balance cannot be restored, the growth will exert severe financial stress on the firm.

Essentially, the analyst has three options in this scenario:

1. By using the Du Pont formula to expand the ROE component of the sustainable growth rate formula, the analyst can analyze the options available to increase the sustainable growth rate:

$$G = \frac{\text{Total assets}}{\text{Equity}} \times \frac{\text{Sales}}{\text{Total assets}} \times \frac{\text{Net income}}{\text{Sales}} \times \text{Retention ratio}$$

- Increase the leverage ratio by increasing debt.
- Increase the asset turnover ratio by increasing sales from existing assets through operational productivity or by reducing assets.
- Increase the profit margin ratio by reducing costs.
- Increase the retention ratio by decreasing dividends.

2. Raise equity.
3. Constrain growth by changing the strategic funds programming.

These three options are not mutually exclusive. Indeed, the optimal solution will often combine all three options. The sensitivity analysis discussed earlier and depicted in Table 27-1 is a helpful tool to frame the decision. An algebraic version of these three options provides the analyst with a helpful analytical tool that captures all of the variables in one dynamic equation (Higgins, 1977). Essentially it is a quantification of the sensitivity analysis:

$$\frac{\Delta S}{S} = G = \frac{p_1(1 - d)(1 + L) - t_1(k_1 - n_1) + \Delta t_1}{t_2(1 + k_2 - n_2) - p_2) - p_2(1 - d)(1 - L)}$$

where
p_1 = Profit margin on sales after tax in current period
p_2 = Profit margin on new sales after tax in forecast period
t_1 = Ratio of assets to sales in the current period
t_2 = Ratio of assets to sales in the forecast period
Δt_1 = The change in t_1 over the forecast period
k_1 = The investment required per dollar of assets to maintain the value of existing assets in the current period
k_2 = The investment required per dollar of assets to maintain the value of existing assets in the forecast period

Part II   The Techniques of Strategic and Competitive Analysis

n_1 = Depreciation per dollar of total assets in the current period
n_2 = Depreciation per dollar of total assets in the forecast period
d = Target dividend payout ratio
L = Target debt to equity ratio
S = Sales at the beginning of the period
ΔS = Increase in sales during the period

This formula suggests that the three options described earlier can be concisely quantified as follows:

1. Adjust d, L, p, and t until the sustainable growth rate meets the growth rate dictated by strategic funds programming.
2. Raise new equity.
3. Change the strategic funds programming to reduce the expected growth rate.

The analyst must remain aware of the potentially negative impact on broader strategic implications associated with each type of option. Often, the choice of the optimal variable from a financial perspective (i.e., the variable that increases sustainable growth rate the most) is not chosen in light of its potentially harmful wider effects.

In the early 1970s, many case examples refute the conventional logic of portfolio theory. The application of sustainable growth rate analysis most certainly had a bearing on the decisions here.

RCA

In the 1970s, RCA divested its computer business, despite its position of low market share in an attractive industry. Rather than investing to build market share, RCA decided to exit in light of the heavy fund requirements needed to strengthen its market-share position in the extremely capital-intensive computer industry.

B.F. GOODRICH

In 1978, B.F. Goodrich began to invest heavily in strengthening its already large market share in the polyvinyl chloride (PVC) industry. Despite the fact that the "mature" PVC industry was slow growing, B.F. Goodrich embarked on this initiative because it offered an excellent way to generate cash flow with very low capital intensity.

GENERAL ELECTRIC

Opting not to divest or harvest its strong position in the low growth lightbulb industry, GE instead chose to hold its market share. The low capital intensity, coupled with GE's dominant market share, provided the company with a steady supply of operational funds to fund growth opportunities elsewhere.

BOWMAR

Despite earning excellent profit margins in the calculator industry in the early 1970s, Bowmar eventually was forced to divest because of financial strain induced with the exceptionally rapid growth of both its own calculator business and the product market in general.

CONTROL DATA CORPORATION

Acquiring Commercial Credit Corporation (CCC) in 1970 seemed nonsensical given its low market share in the low-growth consumer finance industry. Nonetheless, the strategy provided a nice fit in terms of providing funds from its low-capital-intensity cost structure.

SOURCE: Adapted from "Cash Sufficiency: The Missing Link in Strategic Planning," by V. Govindarajan and J. K. Shank, 1986, *The Journal of Business Strategy,* 7(1), pp. 88–95.

FAROUT SUMMARY

	1	2	3	4	5
F	▓	▓	▓	▓	
A	▓	▓	▓	▓	
R	▓	▓	▓	▓	▓
O	▓	▓	▓		
U	▓	▓	▓	▓	
T	▓	▓	▓	▓	

Future orientation   Medium to high. By definition, this tool is future oriented.

Accuracy   Medium to high. The quantitative accuracy depends on input variables controlled by relative strategic success or failure from the forecast.

Resource efficiency   High. Sustainable growth rate analysis can be calculated from existing firm data and forecasts from the strategic funds programming process. Also, it requires very little staffing resources.

Objectivity Medium to high. Calculating the firm's existing sustainable growth rate is very objective. Projecting future sustainable growth requires subjective estimates of sales growth and the effectiveness of the various cash inflow and cash outflow levers.

Usefulness Medium to High. A useful tool for identifying the existing upper limits of the firm's growth and how to best increase that ceiling for future growth. It is also a useful tool for competitive intelligence.

Timeliness High. This methodology can be done very quickly by one or two analysts.

RELATED TOOLS AND TECHNIQUES

- competitor profiling
- experience curve analysis
- industry analysis
- portfolio approaches
- product life cycle analysis
- strategic funds programming

REFERENCES

Babcock, G. C. (1970). "The concept of sustainable growth." *Financial Analysts Journal*, 26(3), 108–114.

Clark, J. J., Clark, M. T., & Versilli, A. G. (1985). "Strategic planning and sustainable growth." *Columbia Journal of World Business*, 20(3), 47–51.

Emery, G. W. (2000). "Sustainable Growth for Credit Analysis." *Business Credit*, 102(2), 35–39.

Govindarajan, V., & Shank, J. K. (1986). "Cash sufficiency: The missing link in strategic planning." *The Journal of Business Strategy*, 7(1), 88–95.

Higgins, R. C. (1977). "How much growth can a firm afford?" *Financial Management*, 6(3), 7–16.

Kisor, M. K. (1964). "The Financial Aspects of Growth." *Financial Analysts Journal*, 20(2), 46–51.

Largay, J., & Stickney, C. (1980). "Cash flow, ratio analysis and the W.T. Grant Company bankruptcy." *Financial Analysts Journal*, July/August, 54.

Modigliani, F., & Miller, M. (1958). "The cost of capital, corporation finance, and the theory of investments." *American Economic Review*, No. 48 June, pp. 261–296.

Moore, D. M. (1988). "Credit technique: Growing broke." *Business Credit*, 90(8), 49–51.

Robinson, S. J. Q. (1979). "What growth rate can you achieve." *Long Range Planning*, 12(4), 7–12.

Ulrich, T. A., & Arlow, P. (1980). "The financial implications of growth." *Journal of Small Business Management*, 18(4), 28–33.

Varandarajan, P. (1983). "The sustainable growth model: A tool for evaluating the financial feasibility of market share strategies." *Strategic Management Journal*, October/December, 353–367.

INDEX

intensity, 69, 76, 86, 326, 427, 441, 449
investment, 85, 422, 428, 437
maintenance, 441, 443
markets, 47
requirements, 69
structure, 427
working, 428, 436–437, 440–441
Capitalization, 31
Cash
cows, 34–35, 37, 41–44
flow, 33, 41, 148
Cash conversion cycle (CCC), 435–436, 440, 443, 446
Cash registers
electronic, 383
mechanical, 383
Causal ambiguity, 210, 212
Cause-and-effect, 37, 318
Certainty effect, 126
Chamberlain, Edward, 162
Channel management, 114
Channel selection, 84
Chemical industry, 316
Chief executive officer (CEO), 243
Chief knowledge officer (CKO), 135
China breaker, 135, 138
Chinese walls, 139
Chloride Silent Power, 359
Christian Dior, 341
Chrysler Corporation, 341
Classical economic theory, 162
Coalitions, 309
Coca Cola, 210
Cognitive
dissonance, 124
psychology, 11, 122, 141
simplification, 128
Colgate toothpaste, 373
Columbia Studios, 220
Commodity, 63, 377
Communication processes, 212
Communication techniques
advocacy ads, 310
annual report, 310
CEO speech, 310
image ads, 310
media presentations, 310
press release, 310
Community relations, 253
Companie General d'Electricite, 359
Compaq Computer, 124
Comparison grids, 156
Competencies, 2, 7, 17, 97, 164, 186, 209, 216, 218
Compensation, 425
structure, 430
Competition
imperfect, 60
perfect, 163
Competitive
advantage, 51, 60, 64, 66, 71–72, 79, 96, 99, 101, 107–114, 117, 122, 127, 139, 148–149, 159, 163, 165–166, 171, 179, 182, 186, 189, 197, 203, 205–207, 210, 212, 215–223, 276, 323, 325, 334, 336, 366, 405
analysis, 16, 112
forces, 64
position, 33
preemption, 131
reaction, 123
strength, 40
technology, 360
Competitor
analysis, 11, 107, 144–161, 203
intelligence system, 11
profiling, 350
response profile, 146, 148
strength grid, 156–157

Compliance techniques
cooperate with regulatory agencies, 311
create new issue, 311
judicial proceedings, 311
non-compliance, 311
Computer-aided design (CAD), 169
Computer-aided manufacturing (CAM), 169
Computer simulations, 286
Concentration, 62–63
Conglomerates, 31, 47, 49, 51, 57, 109
Consumer research, 374
Contingency, 123, 130, 398
plans, 52, 128, 286, 426
Contingent competitive reaction, 131–132
Contextual evaluation, 18
Consumer surveys, 174
Consumption patterns, 173
Continuous improvement, 181
Control Data Corporation, 448
Control systems, 86
Co-opetition, 81, 301
Copyrights, 8, 62, 147, 210
Core competencies, 66, 77, 97, 104, 115, 117, 139, 147–151, 200, 202, 206–208, 215, 217, 338
Corporate
control, 125
myth, 124
reputation, 207
taboo, 124
Cost
advantages, 62, 104, 114, 327
analysis, 114
compliance, 393
deflator, 329
drivers, 108, 112, 117
life cycle, 185–186
model, 188
of entry, 77, 79, 87–88, 393
of exit, 393
of ownership, 185, 192
servicing, 440
sociopolitical compliance, 393
structure, 35, 63
switching, 393
transaction, 185–186
Cost/value analysis, 110
Cost/volume/profit (CVP), 110
Counter-argumentation, 137
Cradle-to-grave, 273
Creative destruction, 64, 76
Credit card companies, 120
Credit union, 158–159, 344
Critical intelligence needs (CINs), 14, 20, 24
Critical success factor (CSFs), 205, 207, 216–219, 391
Cross elasticity, 39
of demand, 75, 368, 375–376
Cross-functional teams, 277
Cultural profile, 246
Cultures, 17, 99
Custom Foot, 170
Customer
conversation, 190
defection, 184
intimacy, 190–192
loyalty, 62, 166, 183
preferences, 163
research, 112, 114
retention, 182–184, 228
sacrifice gaps, 170
satisfaction, 96, 181, 184, 188
segment, 87, 164
segmentation analysis, 162–179
self-service, 118
service, 147

surveys, 190
value, 105–107, 109, 116, 118, 147–151, 165–166, 168, 171, 175, 178–179, 180–204, 206–207, 209, 348, 350, 386, 391
value hierarchy model, 188
value maps, 190–196
Cyanamid Company, 397
Cycle time, 8, 147

D

Databases, 153, 348, 354–356
Data collectors, 22
Dean, Joel, 364
Decentralization, 48
Decision
makers, 23, 151, 157, 225, 278, 349
making, 24, 284–285
operational, 420
optimal, 122,
Decline stage, 40
Deduction/deductive methods, 16, 288
Dell Computers, 435
Delphi panels, 257, 286–287
Demand curves, 163
Demand functions, 163
Demand perspective, 166
Demand side, 81, 373
Demographic, 173, 272
Demography, 262
Deregulation, 69
Differentiation, 37, 62–63, 66, 68, 72, 78–79, 105, 106, 108, 114–117, 153, 163, 167, 169, 173, 326, 366, 369, 372, 386
Diffusion theory, 372, 381
Digital, 70
Disaggregated ratio analysis, 148
Disaggregation, 15, 113, 202, 327
Discontinuities, 349
Disequilibrium, 2, 440
Disinformation, 15
Distinctive competencies, 2, 338–339
Distribution channels, 212, 371, 374
Distribution system, 139
Diversification, 30, 57, 62, 83, 86, 165, 168, 215, 219, 222, 337, 341
conglomerate, 336
horizontal, 76
vertical, 76
Diversified, 85, 279
Diversity, 64
Divested, 34
Divestiture, 51
Divestment, 108, 443
Dividend policy, 440
Dogs, 34–35, 38, 41–43
Dow Chemical, 359
DRAM, 70
Dristan cold medicine, 373
DTS Company, 383
Dun & Bradstreet, 403
Du Pont, 331, 358, 378, 427
formula, 414–415, 426, 435, 445
profitability matrix, 415
Durability, 209–210, 214
Dynamics model, 243

E

E-commerce, 111–112
Early warning, 9, 132, 141, 171
Earnings
before interest and taxes (EBIT), 440
per share (EPS), 48, 412
Eastman Kodak, 348